European Clocks and Watches IN THE METROPOLITAN MUSEUM OF ART

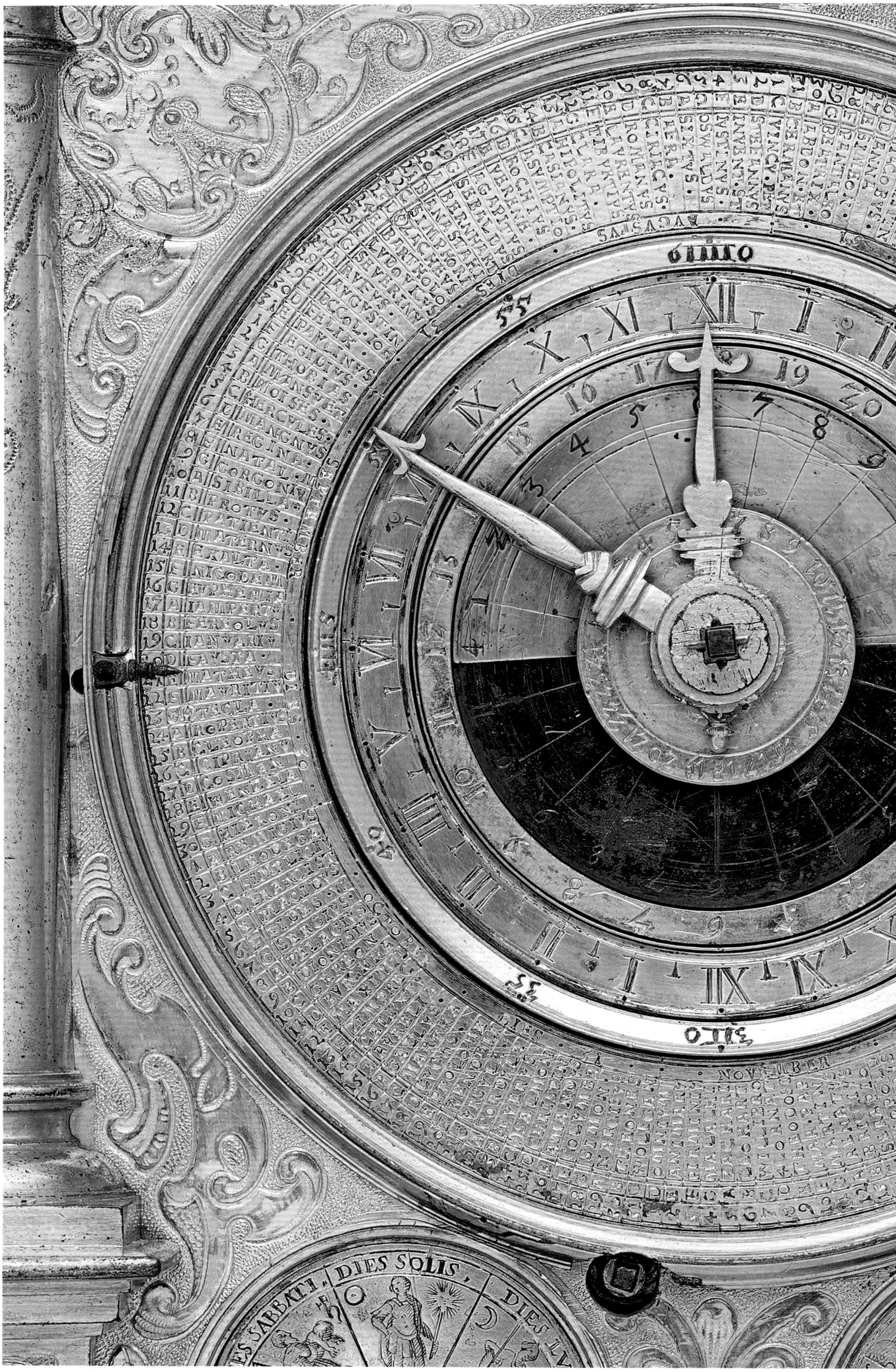
DIES SOLIS
NOVEMBER

HIGHLIGHTS of the COLLECTION

European Clocks and Watches

IN THE METROPOLITAN MUSEUM OF ART

Clare Vincent and
Jan Hendrik Leopold

with Elizabeth Sullivan

The Metropolitan Museum of Art, New York

DISTRIBUTED BY YALE UNIVERSITY PRESS
NEW HAVEN AND LONDON

This publication is made possible
by Marica and Jan Vilcek.

PUBLISHED BY
THE METROPOLITAN MUSEUM OF ART, NEW YORK
Mark Polizzotti, Publisher and Editor in Chief
Gwen Roginsky, Associate Publisher and
General Manager of Publications
Peter Antony, Chief Production Manager
Michael Sittenfeld, Senior Managing Editor
Robert Weisberg, Senior Project Manager

Edited by Elizabeth Franzen
Designed by Lucinda Hitchcock
Production by Paul Booth
Bibliography edited by Jayne Kuchna
Image acquisitions and permissions by Jane S. Tai

Photographs of works in the Metropolitan Museum's collection are by Juan Trujillo, The Photograph Studio, The Metropolitan Museum of Art, unless otherwise noted.

PHOTOGRAPH CREDITS
© Trustees of the British Museum, London: fig. 32
Courtesy Performing Arts Collections, Rare Book & Manuscripts Library, Butler Library, Columbia University, New York: fig. 21
© MAK: figs. 19, 30
© Mauritshuis, The Hague: fig. 28
© Victoria and Albert Museum, London: figs. 17, 23

All diagrams are by David Penney, unless otherwise noted.

Typeset in Kievet and Whitman
by Carol Liebowitz
Printed on 130 gsm Creator Silk
Separations by Professional Graphics, Inc.,
Rockford, Illinois
Printed and bound by Verona Libri,
Verona, Italy

Jacket illustrations: front, Mirror Clock, German (Nürnberg), ca. 1565–70 (entry 2, detail); back, Mantel Clock, French, ca. 1750 (entry 38, detail)
Frontispiece: Astronomical Table Clock, German (Augsburg), second quarter of the seventeenth century (entry 11, detail)
Page vi: Wall Clock (Cartel), French (Paris), probably ca. 1740–45 (entry 36, detail)
Page x: left to right, top to bottom, details of entries 5, 23, 20, 51, 39, fig. 58, 45, 44, fig. 43, 44, 44, 52, 50, 29, 22, 4, 1, 3, 11, 19, 9, 38, 40, 47
Page 2: Celestial Globe with Clockwork, Austrian (Vienna), 1579 (entry 4, detail)
Page 8: Mirror Clock, German (Nürnberg), ca. 1565–70 (entry 2, detail)

First printing

The Metropolitan Museum of Art
1000 Fifth Avenue
New York, New York 10028
metmuseum.org

Distributed by
Yale University Press, New Haven and London
yalebooks.com/art
yalebooks.co.uk

Cataloguing-in-Publication Data is available from the Library of Congress.
ISBN 978-1-58839-579-5

CONTENTS

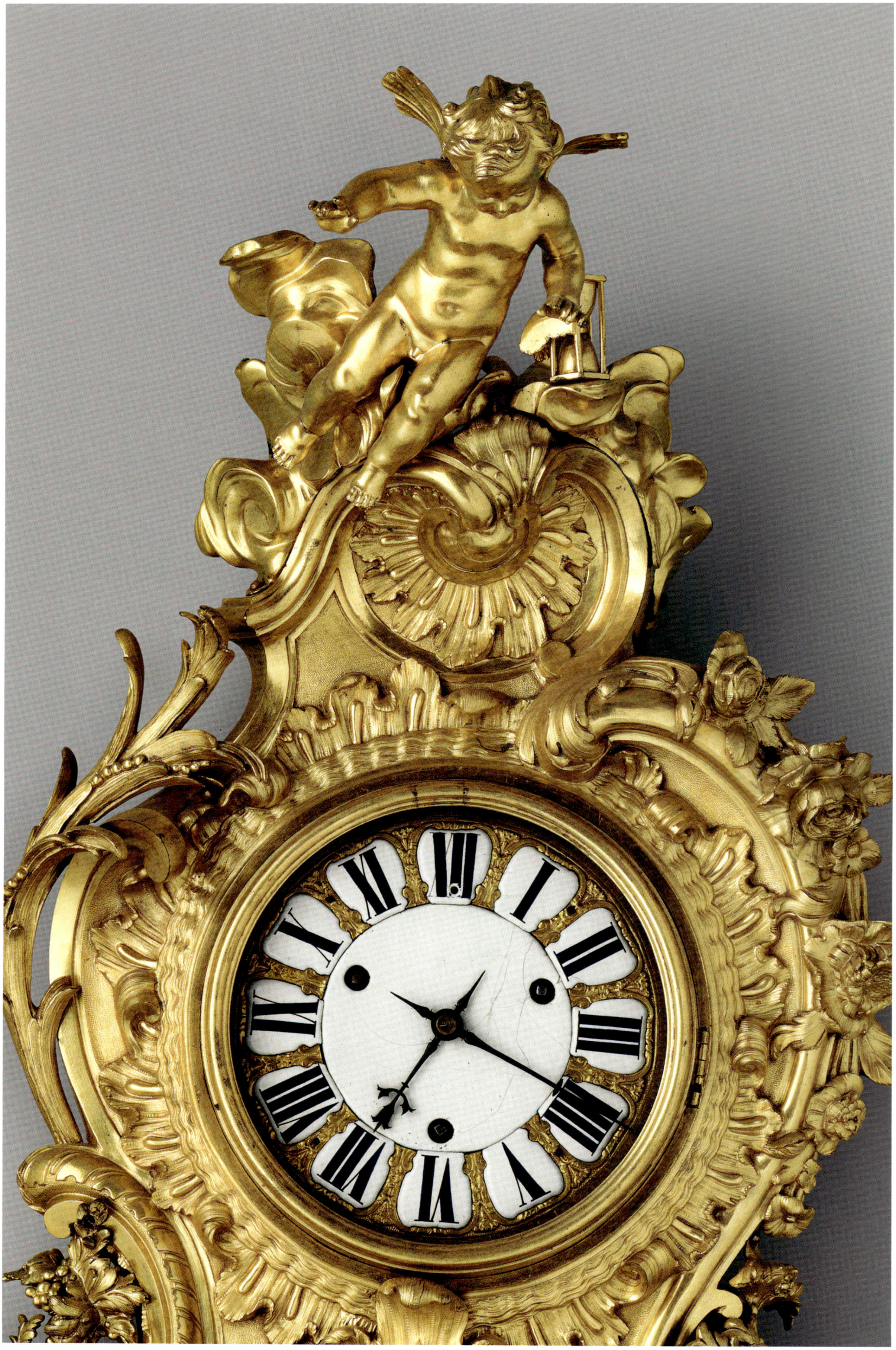

Director's Foreword

For centuries, writers, philosophers, and scientists have felt compelled to account for the elusive nature of time, and artists and craftsmen have found ingenious ways to make beautiful timepieces. The Metropolitan Museum of Art has been at the forefront of collecting such pieces, particularly from Europe, and is proud to possess over six hundred works from Austria, England, Flanders, France, Germany, Italy, the Netherlands and Switzerland.

The fifty-four examples presented in this volume, which showcases some of the highlights of the Met's collection, attest to both the exquisite artistry and the technical skill of their makers. Spanning the late Renaissance to the nineteenth century, these timepieces include a sixteenth-century celestial globe with clockwork, a seventeenth-century automaton clock in the form of an eagle, an eighteenth-century musical longcase clock, and watches of every conceivable kind.

The principal author of this volume, Clare Vincent, Associate Curator in the Department of European Sculpture and Decorative Arts, has devoted a large part of her career to clocks and watches. Her prodigious knowledge of the timepieces gathered here, as well as hundreds of others housed at the Metropolitan Museum, reflects her research as well as the groundbreaking work of her late husband, Jan Hendrik Leopold, former Assistant Keeper in the Department of Medieval and Modern Europe at the British Museum, London. This book is the culmination of decades of dedicated effort, and it is a pleasure to publish it. The realization of this catalogue was made possible with the support of the Museum's close friends, Met Trustee Marica Vilcek and her husband, Jan Vilcek. We are deeply grateful for their vision and long-standing commitment toward the Met's scholarly work.

Thomas P. Campbell, Director
THE METROPOLITAN MUSEUM OF ART

Acknowledgments

I would never have begun writing this book if not for the generosity with which my late husband, Jan Hendrik Leopold, former Assistant Keeper in the Department of Medieval and Modern Europe at the British Museum, London, shared his time and knowledge of European clocks and watches in the Metropolitan Museum's collection.

I would never have finished the book without the critical advice and encouragement of my longtime friend and sometime coauthor Bruce Chandler, Professor Emeritus, the College of Staten Island of the City University of New York. My warmest thanks to Marica and Jan Vilcek, whose support of the publication is deeply appreciated, especially as they have been friends of long-standing.

Many thanks are due to Elizabeth Sullivan, Associate Research Curator, and Rose Whitehill, former Research Associate, for their invaluable assistance, as well as to other colleagues in the Department of European Sculpture and Decorative Arts: Ellenor M. Alcorn; James David Draper, former Henry R. Kravis Curator; Daniëlle O. Kisluk-Grosheide; Wolfram Koeppe, Marina Kellen French Curator; Jeffrey Munger; and Melinda Watt; all of whom shared knowledge of their various specialties with me. Denny Stone, Senior Collections Manager, and current and former departmental technicians Jacob D. Goble, Juan Stacey, Bedel Tiscareño, and Sam Winks were instrumental in preparing and moving both the clocks and watches for conservation and photography. I would like to extend my thanks to Kenneth Soehner, Arthur K. Watson Chief Librarian, and the staff of the Thomas J. Watson Library for their consistent helpfulness, as well as to Stuart W. Pyhrr, Distinguished Research Curator in the Department of Arms and Armor.

The objects would not have looked their best without the skills of the Museum's conservators Mechthild Baumeister, Linda Borsch, Marijn Manuels, and Wendy Walker, and the talents of the Photograph Studio, especially Juan Trujillo, Senior Photographer, Wilson Santiago, Imaging Specialist, and Joseph Coscia Jr., Chief Photographer.

I am equally grateful to Elizabeth Franzen, Editor, and Jayne Kuchna, Bibliographic Editor, for their work with the text, and to Luke Syson, Iris and B. Gerald Cantor Chairman of the Department of European Sculpture and Decorative Arts, and his predecessor, Ian Wardropper, for allotting me the time to write.

Mark Polizzotti, Publisher and Editor in Chief, was supportive and helpful at every turn, and I wish to thank him as well as his colleagues Associate Publisher Gwen Roginsky, Chief Production Manager Peter Antony, and Senior Managing Editor Michael Sittenfeld. I am grateful to Production Manager Paul Booth, who made countless contributions to the beauty of this book, poring over color proofs and coordinating his work with Lucinda Hitchcock, who created the elegant design of this volume. Anne Rebecca Blood, Assistant Managing Editor, played a key role in this book's completion, as did Jane S. Tai, Acquisitions Manager.

Anne L. Poulet, Director Emerita of the Frick Collection, New York, shared thoughts about one of her specialties, the sculptor Jean-Antoine Houdon, and Eugene J. Kisluk, Independent Researcher, translated relevant publications from Russian and Polish. Other colleagues who have been particularly helpful are former Curator David Thompson and former Curator Jeremy L. Evans, both of the Horological Collections in the Department of Britain, Europe and Prehistory of the British

Museum, and Jonathan Betts, Curator of Horology at the National Maritime Museum, Greenwich, England.

In France, my thanks to Daniel Alcouffe, retired Curator of the Département des Objets d'Art, Musée du Louvre, Paris; Maxime Préaud, retired from the Cabinet des Estampes, Bibliothèque Nationale de France, Paris, as well as to horologists Anthony J. Turner and Adolphe Chapiro. In Switzerland, my gratitude to Ludwig Oechslin, Director of the Musée International d'Horlogerie, La Chaux-de-Fonds; Fabienne Xavière Sturm, Curator, Musée d'Art et d'Histoire, Geneva; Arnaud Tellier, Director, Patek Philippe Museum, Geneva; and to Jérôme Meier, Collections Manager for Vacheron Constantin, Geneva. In Italy, I am grateful to the late horologist Giuseppe Brusa; Cristina Piacenti Aschengreen, former director of the Museo degli Argenti, Palazzo Pitti, Florence; and to the collector Giancarlo Del Vecchio. In Sweden, I wish to thank Barbro Hovstadius, retired from the Nationalmuseum, Stockholm, and to horologist Gunnar Pipping. In Denmark, my gratitude to Jørgen Hein, Curator, Kongernes Samling, Rosenborg Castle, Copenhagen. In the Netherlands, my appreciation to Reinier Baarsen, Curator of Furniture, the Rijksmuseum, Amsterdam, and Professor Johan Koppenol, Vrije Universiteit, Amsterdam. In Germany, my thanks most particularly to Klaus Maurice, former Curator of Horology at the Bayerisches Nationalmuseum and at the Deutsches Museum, both in Munich; and to Klaus Schillinger, former Director, and the late Joachim Schardin, Conservator, both of the Mathematisch-Physikalischer Salon, Dresden, and to Joachim Menzhausen, former Director of the Grünes Gewölbe, Staatliche Kunstsammlungen, Dresden. In Austria, I am indebted to the late Rudolf Distelberger, former Director of the Kunstkammer, the Kunsthistorisches Museum, Vienna; and finally, but not least, to Erwin Neumann, Director of the Sammlung für Plastik und Kunstgewerbe at the Kunsthistorisches Museum, Vienna, who died much before his time, eternal thanks for his enthusiastic encouragement of our study of Renaissance clocks.

CLARE VINCENT

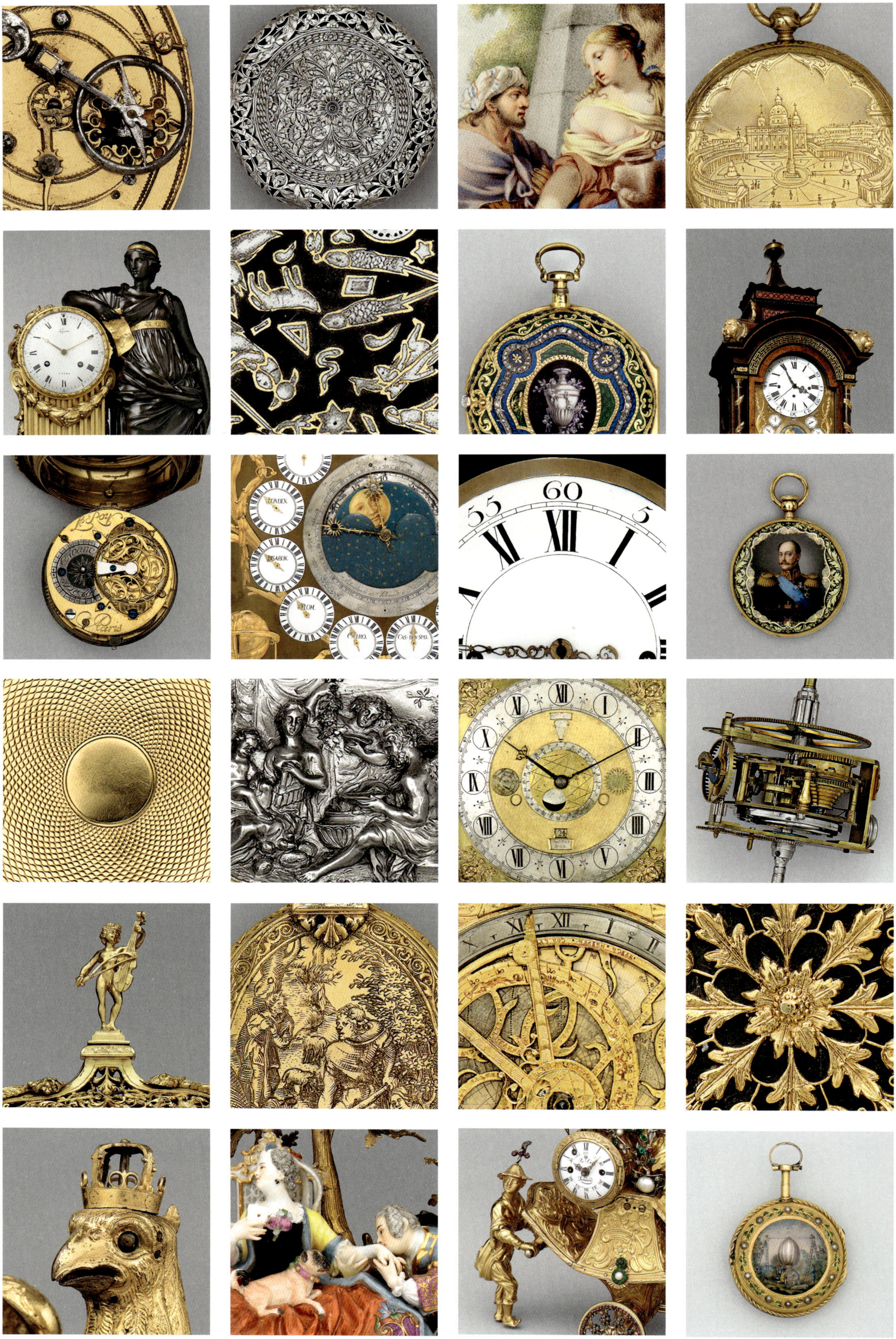

European Clocks and Watches IN THE METROPOLITAN MUSEUM OF ART

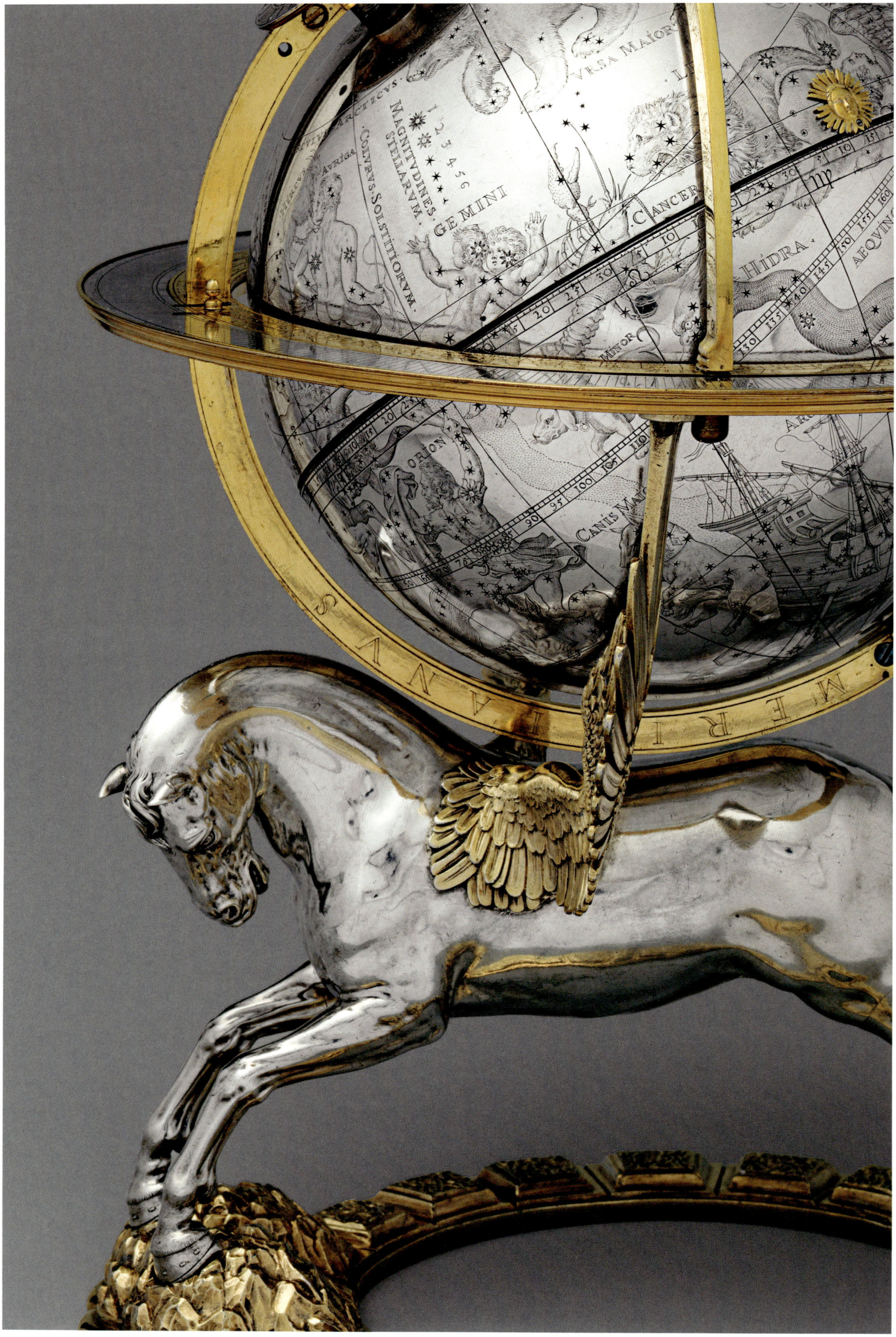
VRSA MAIOR
MAGNITVDINES STELLARVM
GEMINI
CANCER
HIDRA
ORION
CANIS MAIOR
MERIDIANVS

A Brief History of the Collection

ELIZABETH SULLIVAN

There are around six hundred timepieces in The Metropolitan Museum of Art's collection of European clocks and watches. Though the stewardship of Museum curators and scholars has been crucial, the collection is testimony to the knowledge and taste, as well as the generosity, of a noteworthy handful of donors and collectors. Historically, there have been two types of collectors: one who collects clocks and watches specifically, and one who collects other works of art, among which clocks and watches might feature as harmonious elements within the larger group. Furthermore, clocks and watches straddle traditional boundaries of collecting by encompassing the territories of furniture, decorative arts, and jewelry, as well as technology; clocks and watches are acquired both for their technical and mechanical qualities and for the beauty of their cases.

From the beginning, timekeepers were as much objects of status and desire as they were about telling time. During the sixteenth century, the inclusion of clocks within a scientific collection of a royal *Kunstkammer* would illustrate not only the owner's wealth but also his broad humanist education. Not until the mid-nineteenth century, however, were antique timepieces seriously collected as part of a burgeoning antiquarian effort. Early collectors, primarily in Britain, acquired pieces both for their decorative qualities and, perhaps especially, for their place in the history of technology as "industrial art." The proto-academic approach of nineteenth-century collectors, such as Octavius Morgan (1803–1888) and Augustus Wollaston Franks (1826–1897), was instrumental to the establishment and growth of some of the most comprehensive collections of horology, chief among them found in the British Museum, London. Though two early antiquarian watch collections ultimately ended up in the Metropolitan Museum after they were purchased and then donated by the financier John Pierpont Morgan (1837–1913), the Museum's horological collection reflects a different vein in the history of collecting: the rise of twentieth-century American collectors of European decorative arts. At the turn of the century, wealthy American collectors acquired art on a grand scale, whereby clocks were of interest primarily as furnishings for an integrated interior of luxurious eighteenth-century decorative arts. Watches, on the other hand, were often collected as ornamental items, equivalent to jewels or precious trinkets.

The maturation of the Metropolitan Museum's horological collection can be traced to the gift of about 250 watches and clocks from the Morgan collection in 1917. One of the most powerful men of his time, Morgan was a voracious collector who spent lavishly on art—an astonishing $60 million, or about $90 million today, during the last two decades of his life. His extensive collection of art spanned a wide range of materials, including rare books, drawings, paintings, furniture, tapestries, ceramics, armor, and ancient artifacts. He was also an early supporter of the Metropolitan Museum, becoming a trustee in 1888, and its president in 1904. His gift of French eighteenth-century decorative arts that he had acquired from the French collector and decorator Georges Hoentschel (1855–1915) in 1907 led to the establishment of the Department of Decorative Arts at the Museum and the construction of a new Decorative Arts Wing in March 1910. In total, the Museum would receive about 7,000 works of art from Morgan's collection.

The Morgan watch collection was largely comprised of two celebrated private collections: those of Carl Heinrich Marfels (1854–1929) and Frederick George Hilton Price (1842–1909). A British banker and amateur historian and archaeologist, Hilton Price collected watches in addition to Egyptian antiquities, fossils, and English silver spoons. Chiefly interested in early English timepieces, Hilton Price lent his watch collection to the Victoria and Albert Museum, London, in 1906, but following his death in 1909, the collection was purchased by Morgan. A German watch dealer and collector, Marfels was a prominent figure in the

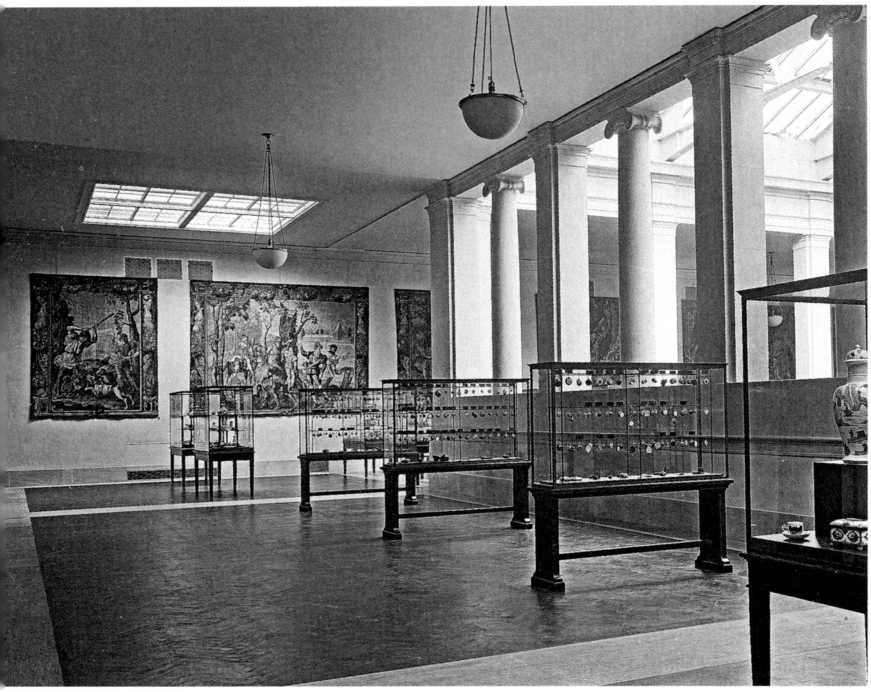

fig. 1 *Gallery of watches shown in the loan exhibition of the J. Pierpont Morgan Collection, The Metropolitan Museum of Art, New York, 1914*

fig. 2 *View of Irwin Untermyer's apartment at 960 Fifth Avenue, New York, ca. 1964, showing longcase clock by Daniel Delander*

fig. 3 *The sitting room of the Sheafer residence at 45 East 66th Street, New York, ca. 1963, showing Gudin mantel clock with Meissen porcelain figure group*

field of horology, known for his rare collection and scholarly expertise. In addition, he was the founder in 1897 of the Deutscher Uhrmacher-Bund (German Clockmakers' Alliance), Berlin, and editor of the *Deutsche Uhrmacher-Zeitung* (German Watchmakers' Review, published in Berlin). Through the Paris art dealer Jacques Seligmann (1858–1923), Morgan purchased about forty timepieces from the Marfels collection, also in 1909. The following year, Marfels exhibited his remaining watches in Neuchâtel, the Swiss watchmaking city, where Morgan purchased the balance of the collection, despite efforts by local syndicates to keep the Marfels collection in Switzerland. In total, Morgan purchased about eighty pieces from the Marfels collection, for a total of $360,000.[1] By acquiring the Marfels and the Hilton Price collections, Morgan assembled one of the greatest collections of watches, one that illustrated the history of watchmaking in Europe from the sixteenth century through the early nineteenth century. With a large concentration on Renaissance timepieces, the collection was representative of the work of some of the best craftsmen in Austria, England, Flanders, France, Germany, Italy, the Netherlands, and Switzerland. As he had with other areas of his collections, Morgan commissioned a catalogue for his watch collection, which was published in 1912 and written by art historian George C. Williamson. At the time, it was proclaimed, "Mr. Morgan's collection of early watches, with which this volume is wholly occupied, is the most important in private hands; it is, in fact, one of the most complete and instructive in the world, and has been gathered not only for its artistic value, but for its educational value as well. . . ."[2]

In the early 1900s, Morgan housed the majority of his collection in the United Kingdom; however, he began transferring his artwork to New York in 1912 for the eventual exhibition in The Metropolitan Museum of Art. On March 31, 1913, while these plans were well under way, Morgan died suddenly in Rome, never seeing his vast collection assembled in one place. The Morgan loan exhibition featuring approximately 4,100 works proceeded, nonetheless, opening in February 1914 to record crowds. It remained on view for more than two years and closed in May 1916. As part of the show, the watch collection was displayed in a small traverse between galleries for French and German porcelain (fig. 1). Perhaps unsurprising for the era, the watches, like the porcelains, received little attention in comparison to the galleries of Gothic, Renaissance, and Ancient art. Nevertheless, the guidebook reads, "This collection gives the student a complete illustration not only of the gradual and steady progress of horological art, but also of the beauty of some of the finest examples of it in existence."[3]

In 1917, Morgan's son Jack officially donated the watches, with much of the rest of his father's art collection, to the Museum. At that point the watches went on display in the new Decorative Arts Wing, which was renamed the John Pierpont Morgan Wing in 1918. Though the Morgan collection was dispersed throughout the Museum after 1943, the Morgan watches have remained the core of the Museum's horological collection. Of the fifty-four clocks and watches discussed in the present volume, nearly half bear the Morgan credit line. Among the masterpieces, there are important examples of early timekeeping, such as the richly decorated astronomical table clock by Caspar Behaim (see entry 1) and the celestial globe with clockwork supported by Pegasus by the imperial clockmaker Gerhard Emmoser (see entry 4).

The same year as the Morgan gift, the Museum received another addition to the collection when it was bequeathed eighty-seven watches from Laura Frances Hearn (died 1917), the widow of George A. Hearn (1835–1913). A dry goods merchant and collector of American paintings, Chinese porcelain, and ivories, Hearn gave much of his collection to the Museum, as well as endowing the Hearn Fund. Of interest primarily for eighteenth- and early nineteenth-century enamel cases, the collection of watches seems, however, to have

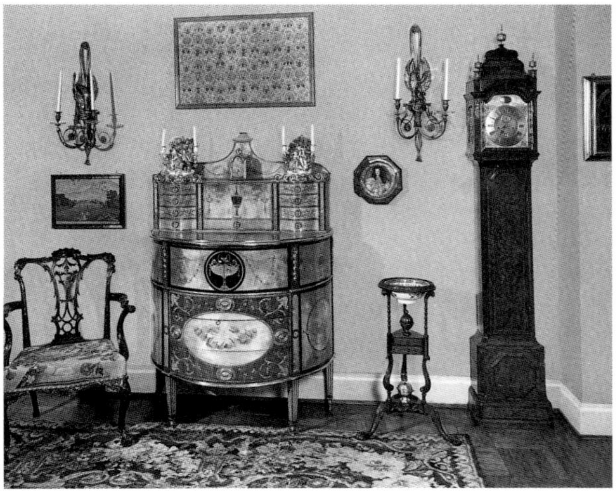

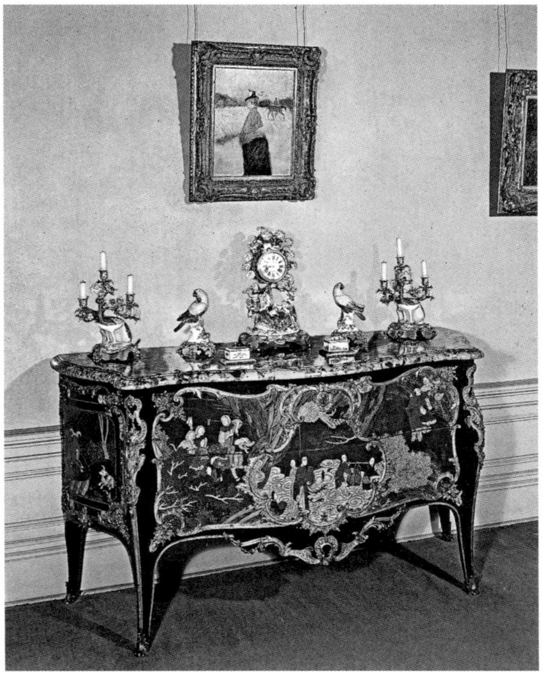

been entirely Laura Hearn's. Perhaps due to their scale and kinship with jewelry, watches and small clocks were of particular interest to women collectors. In her bequest, Laura Hearn also left a collection of European lace to the Museum. Ten years earlier, in 1907, she had presented her watches as a loan exhibition to the Museum, for which she funded the publication of an accompanying catalogue. Art historian Wendell Stanton Howard writes in that catalogue's introduction, "Since men must collect, how fortunate are they when the objects of their search show the change and development of an artistic handicraft through a course of centuries." Howard goes on to explain that, "No attempt has been made in this collection to cover the field of watch-making; on the one hand the desire was to acquire certain examples of pocket time-keepers, which were interesting because of the artistry which had been lavished upon them, and on the other to add contrasting examples of early craftsmanship."[4]

By the mid-1920s, the Morgan watch collection was on view on the second floor galleries of the Morgan Wing in "two tall thin cases and two low flat cases," where one could expect to find "compressed the whole history of watchmaking from the sixteenth to the early nineteenth century."[5] The Hearn Collection, somewhat overshadowed, was housed in an additional gallery as the central component of a "supplementary collection."[6] Nevertheless, the Museum received another welcome gift in 1926, which included over one hundred early nineteenth-century watches that were donated anonymously in memory of Lady May Fletcher-Moulton (née Mary May Davis, died 1909). This gift came at a time when the nineteenth century was an area of increasing focus for the Museum, and as a group, the watches were shown to illustrate the stylistic developments of that century when watchcases became slimmer and flatter. Seventy-five of these watches were of Swiss manufacture, including examples by Vacheron and Constantin, a firm that remains in operation (see entry 30 and 51). The 1920s came to a close with two more important gifts in 1929. The Museum received a small, but exceptional group of clocks (see Eagle automaton, entry 9) donated by Mrs. Simon Guggenheim (née Olga Hirsch, 1877–1970), who would go on to become a supporter of the Museum of Modern Art, New York. The focused nature of the Guggenheim collection suggests that it was formed by an antiquarian with a clearly defined interest in clocks. It is unclear whether the collection was assembled by Mrs. Guggenheim or whether she inherited it from someone else. During the same year, the Museum also received several French eighteenth-century clocks bequeathed by Ogden Mills (1856–1929), a collector of decorative arts who, in addition, donated his French furniture (entry 39) to the Museum.

The Museum's collection of English clocks was formed above all through gifts and by a large bequest from Irwin Untermyer (1886–1973), whose vast collection included European bronzes and English furniture, silver, textiles, and porcelain, with a particular focus in early English pendulum clocks. The elegant ebony and walnut cases of English clocks were in keeping with Untermyer's taste in unadorned wood furniture, which once decorated his spacious Fifth Avenue apartment (fig. 2). Over two thousand objects came to the Museum from the Untermyer collection, including an important early wall clock by Ahasuerus I Fromanteel (entry 17) and longcase clocks by and Thomas Tompion Daniel Delander (entry 28 and 31).

Lesley G. Sheafer (died 1956) and Emma A. Sheafer (1891–1973) were collectors of Impressionist and Post-Impressionist paintings, but they also collected eighteenth-century French and German furniture, ceramics, silver, and other decorative arts. Following her husband's death, Emma Sheafer continued to build the collection, and when she died in 1973, the Museum became the recipient of her bequest of approximately 620 objects. The gift included furniture and decorative arts that once decorated the Sheafers' residence on East 66th Street in New York, including an important suite of German rococo furniture and a clock by Gudin le Jeune with a

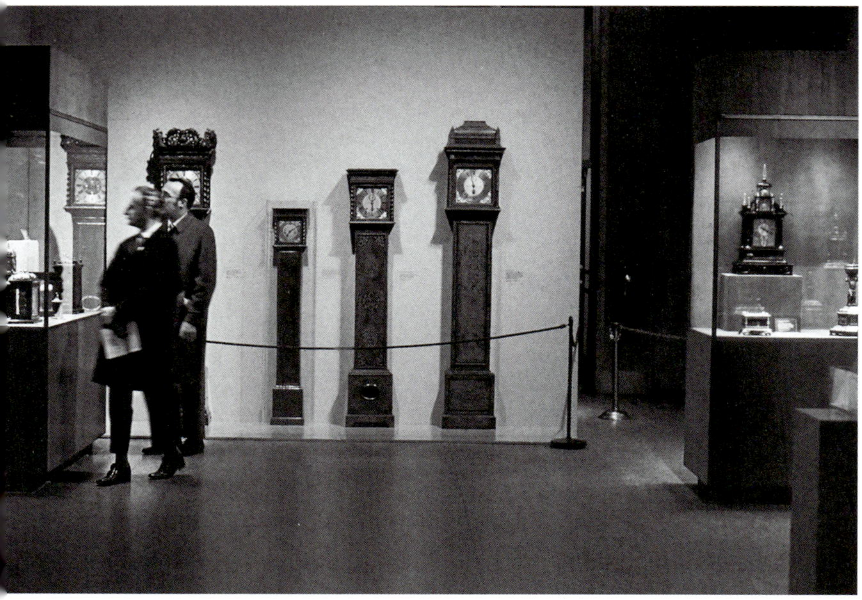

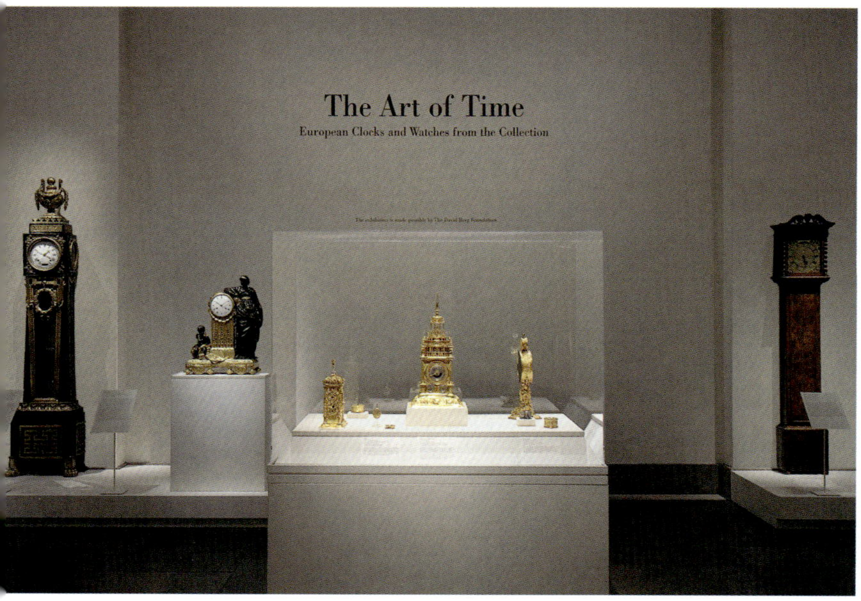

fig. 4 *"Northern European Clocks in New York Collections," special exhibition, The Metropolitan Museum of Art, New York, 1972*

fig. 5 *"The Art of Time," special exhibition, The Metropolitan Museum of Art, New York, 2007–8*

Meissen porcelain figure group (fig. 3; entry 38). Another large collection that included a number of important clocks came from Jack (1897–1980) and Belle Linsky (1904–1987). In 1982, two years after the death of her husband Belle Linsky gave the Museum their collection of over 380 works of art, including Old Master paintings, French furniture, porcelain, Renaissance bronzes, and jewelry. Several French clocks, including a longcase clock by Ferdinand Berthoud (entry 42) and a rare Le Noir cartel clock with a Chantilly porcelain case (entry 35), were part of the Linsky gift. These gifts from the Linsky collection have continued and bolstered the tradition of collecting timepieces as furnishings and decorative arts.

The most important benefactors of French decorative arts to the Metropolitan Museum, Mr. and Mrs. Charles Wrightsman, have also contributed to the development of the horological collection in much the same spirit. The Wrightsmans presented gifts of clocks that had been in their private collection (fig. 6; entries 36 and 54), as well as purchasing new acquisitions for the Museum through the Wrightsman Fund. Following the death of her husband in 1986, Mrs. Wrightsman, a trustee of the Museum, has continued to support the growth of the collection, giving or funding the acquisition of additional clocks to the present-day. Like all works of art bearing the Wrightsman credit line, the clocks are of exceptional quality, beauty, and importance.

One of the few Italian clocks to enter the Museum's collection, a rarity by Mario Gambelli (entry 41), was donated by Lilliana Teruzzi (1899–1987), a former opera singer, whose gifts in the late 1960s and early 1970s included important examples of Italian Baroque and rococo furniture. Other individual gifts and acquisitions have further strengthened the collection. The bequest of Giulia P. Morosini in 1932 from the collection formed by her father, Giovanni P. Morosini, consists of arms and armor and additional objects that include four eighteenth-century watches. A gift made by Mrs. Edgar Worch in 1975 provided the Museum with an important eighteenth-century German clock by Hermann Achenbach and case by the cabinetmaker David Roentgen (entry 44). In 1999, Marilyn Preston Graves bequeathed a highly important Thomas Tompion longcase clock, known as the Graves Tompion, after its former owner, her grandfather, Henry Graves Jr. (entry 22). Curators have made their contributions as well. The Rogers Fund and the Samuel H. Kress Foundation have made it possible to acquire notable clocks, such as the Augsburg clock by Franz Xavier Gegenreiner with a silver case by Johann Andreas Thelot (entry 29), and a French mantel clock by Jean-Baptiste-André Furet (entry 46). More recently, using the Anna-Maria and Stephen Kellen Acquisitions Fund, the Museum was able to purchase an important Nürnberg automaton clock (entry 8) from the collection of John Abbott (born 1925) and Peter D. Guggenheim (1927–2012).

After that first display of watches loaned by Laura Hearn in 1907, and the inclusion of watches as part of the larger Morgan loan exhibition in 1914, the Met had to wait until 1972 for its next exhibition of timepieces. "Northern European Clocks in New York Collections" (fig. 4), which was accompanied by a descriptive catalogue, featured important loans from the Abbott-Guggenheim Collection, and from Winthrop Kellogg Edey (1938–1999), who later gave his clock col-

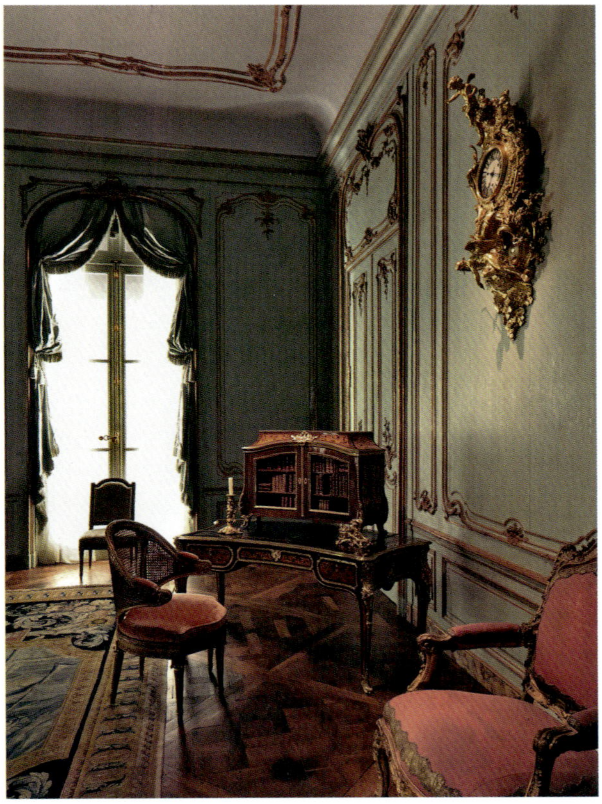

lection to the Frick Collection, New York.[7] The 1972 exhibition was organized by Clare Vincent, curator of the Museum's timekeepers for over forty years and principal author of the present volume, who would go on to mount additional exhibitions, including "The Art of Time" (2007–8) (fig. 5) and "The Luxury of Time" (2015–16). Vincent worked for many years with her late husband, Jan Hendrick Leopold, former Assistant Keeper in the Department of Medieval and Modern Europe at the British Museum, London. This book, the first dedicated study of European clocks and watches in the Metropolitan Museum's collection, is the product of their hard work and profound passion, together with the enthusiasm of all the collectors who built the Metropolitan's collection.

1 "Watches Bought by J. P. Morgan" 1910.
2 "Morgan's Watches" 1912.
3 Bruce M. Donaldson in *Morgan Collection* 1914, p. 127.
4 Wendell Stanton Howard in *Collection of Watches* 1907, p. 3.
5 Avery 1927, p. 46.
6 Ibid.
7 Vincent 1972.

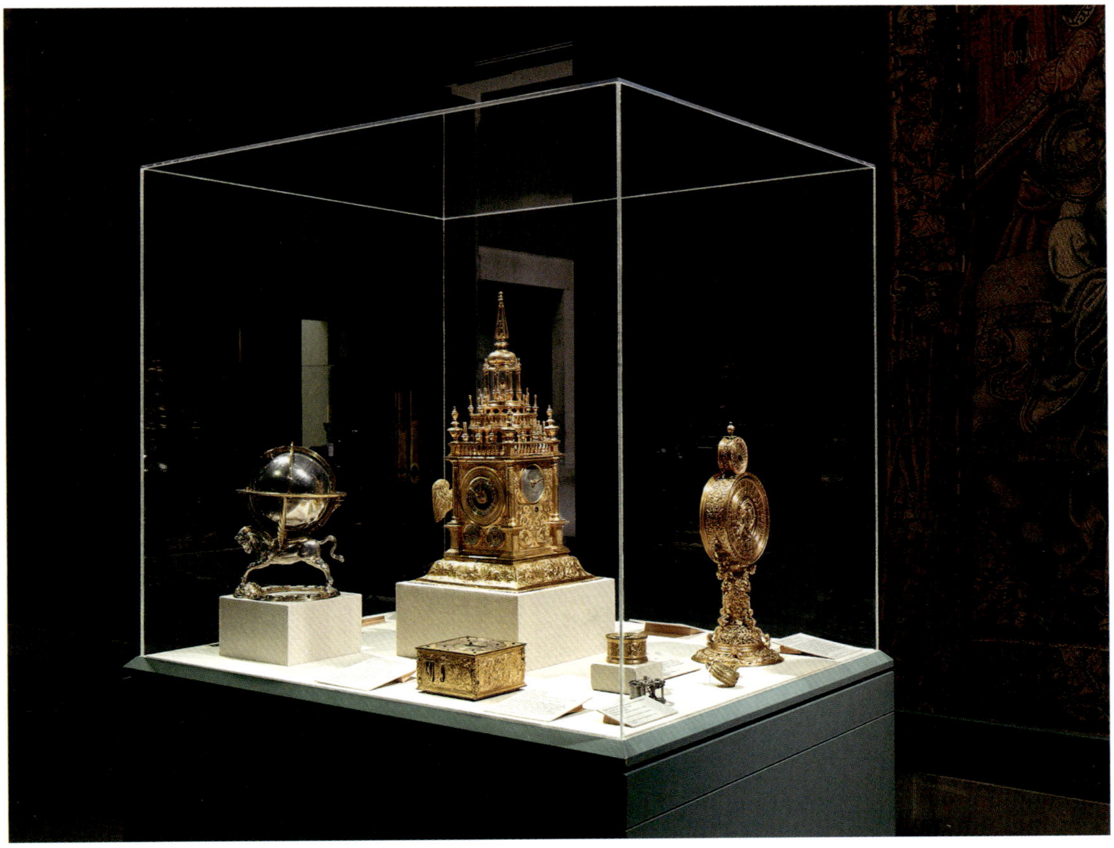

fig. 6 *Wall clock with case by Charles Cressent and movement by Jean Godde l'aîné in the Paar Room in the Wrightsman Galleries for French Decorative Arts, The Metropolitan Museum of Art, New York, in 2008*

fig. 7 *A case of early clocks in the collection on display in the Northern Renaissance Gallery in The Metropolitan Museum of Art, New York, in 2015, featuring the Celestial Globe with clockwork, Augsburg table clock, and Nürnberg mirror clock*

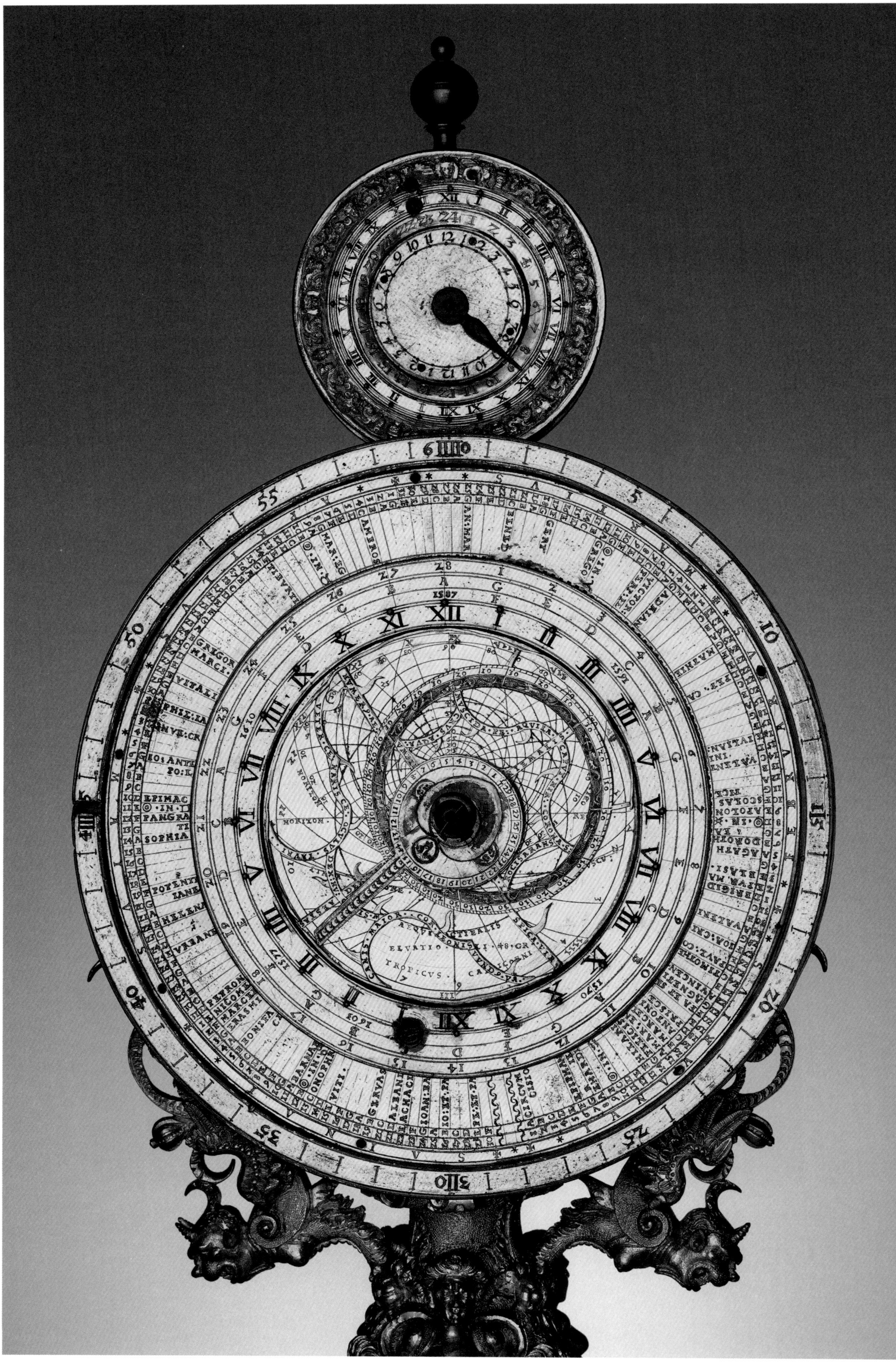
1587

Time and Time Again: A Selection of European Clocks and Watches in The Metropolitan Museum of Art

CLARE VINCENT AND JAN HENDRIK LEOPOLD

Before the application of electricity to a clock's movement, the mechanical clock needed two components to function. The first was a source of power; the second was the ability to control that release of power. A power source was nearly always a falling weight or a coiled spring, and the release of power was controlled by an escapement, a device that divides the delivery into small intervals for recording the passage of time. With the notable exceptions of sundials, sandglasses, and the occasional water clock, improvements to these two components of mechanical timekeepers constitute the main history of horology from the Middle Ages to the nineteenth century. The European clocks and watches in The Metropolitan Museum of Art do not constitute a complete representation of the history of mechanical timekeepers, but the collection does provide a fascinating portrait of some of the major historical developments during this period.

The first mechanical clocks probably appeared sometime in the latter part of the thirteenth century, but it is difficult to identify the early examples. Some of the best evidence of these clocks is found in England, where one is known to have existed in the Dunstable Priory in 1283. It appears that from the advent the function of the mechanical clock remained the same: a wheel with teeth, or a train of wheels, called a going train, is set in motion by a falling weight. This motion is slowed by an escapement. The oldest form of escapement is a device with an arbor, named a balance staff, which contains two pallets placed across the last wheel in the going train. Together, the balance staff and pallets are termed a verge. The verge is attached in such a way that when the wheel revolves in a particular direction, its teeth engage a pallet, which in turn releases the going train in short measured intervals. The escapement is regulated by either a crossbar, called a foliot, or by a weighted wheel. By the application of a foliot and verge, the speed of the falling weight that drives the wheels of a clock is greatly reduced. Their motion produces the familiar ticking of a clock.

Evidence of large time-telling dials driven by clockwork during the thirteenth century is slight, but they begin to be discussed after about 1300. For instance, a large astronomical dial, accompanied by moving figures, or automata, was commissioned for Norwich Cathedral in East Anglia in 1322. The best-known example, however, is the very complicated clock that was designed and built from 1327 to 1336 (or 1337) by Richard of Wallingford (ca. 1292–1336) for the Abbey of Saint Albans, located a few miles north of London. Around this same time, a device for striking the hours, known as a counting striking train, was invented and became a very useful addition to the mechanical clock. Earlier clocks may have signaled the hours by a single blow or a series of blows on a bell, but in 1336, we find the first report of a clock that sounded one stroke at one o'clock, two strokes at two o'clock, and so on. This clock had recently been installed in the church of San Gottardo in Milan. By the middle of the fourteenth century, public clocks were found in northern Italy and France, and soon after in the Netherlands; sometime before 1400, they spread through Germany and reached Poland.

Meanwhile, there is ample evidence that domestic clocks were also made during this period, but few details are known. One domestic clock, however, became famous. Built by the clockmaker Giovanni de' Dondi (1318–1388) of Padua in northern Italy, the astrarium was finished about 1375. This remarkable clock had seven main dials showing the positions of the planets, sun, and moon, as well as a complicated calendar. The clock disappeared in the course of the sixteenth century, but a description by the maker survives in many manuscript copies. Smaller clocks, made for personal use by the privileged, had their own development. The most important improvement was the introduction of a mainspring to replace the weight as the driving force of the clock. The spring allowed a clock to be portable. The action of a coiled

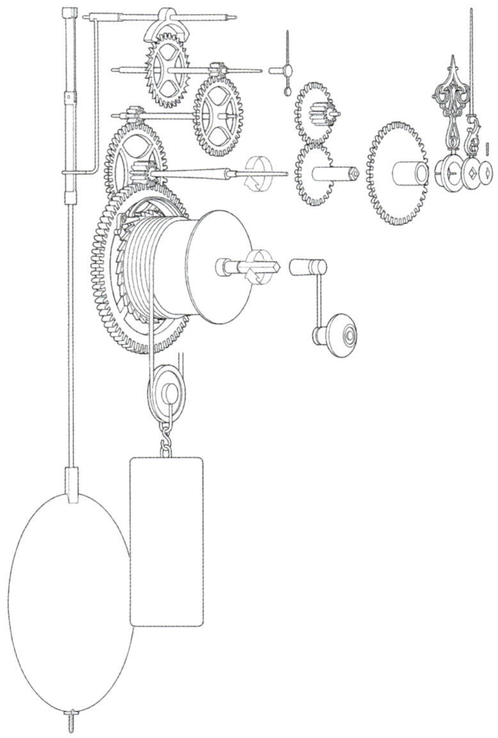

fig. 8 *Diagram of the going train and motion work of a weight-driven clock with an anchor escapement and long pendulum, shown with abbreviated rod*

spring is, however, more complicated than the motion of a falling weight. The weight exerts a constant force during its fall, whereas a fully wound spring when released produces a gradually decreasing force. Therefore, a construction had to be found to even out the spring's decreasing force as it unwound. An ingenious device, called a fusee, possibly originating about 1400 along with the technology of crossbows,[1] was inserted between the spring and the going train that drives the hands of the clock. The fusee is a cone, usually made of metal or sometimes of wood, with a spiral groove in its surface to accommodate a cord or chain, which is attached at one end to a barrel containing the coiled spring and at the other end to the fusee. As the power of the spring decreases, the cord unwinds, engaging the fusee at points of increasingly greater diameter, thus balancing the force transmitted. Early clocks were made with the wheels in pivoted vertical bars held in a constructed frame. This type of construction is designated a posted frame movement. From about the middle of the fifteenth century, however, there appears an alternative construction in which the wheels are pivoted in plates held together by pillars: these are known as plated movements. The first record of a plated movement dates from about 1450. Once the plated movement was perfected, the next step was to make the clock movement smaller. These small, portable clocks with plated movements may be regarded as forerunners of the watch.

The primary purpose of clocks is to measure time, but during much of the early period of mechanical timekeeping (ca. 1280–1656), there was little improvement in their timekeeping properties. For the reason that clockmakers could do little to improve these timekeeping properties, a good clock became synonymous with a complicated clock. It is not surprising, therefore, that until the middle of the seventeenth century clockmakers of high quality delighted in producing complex movements with complicated striking trains and a proliferation of astronomical and calendrical information that was furnished by multiple dials. Moving figures, or automata, were often added. The masters of this sort of complications were the German clockmakers of the sixteenth and early seventeenth centuries, and their clocks were often housed in sumptuously ornamented cases.

During the entire early period, clocks continued to be regulated by devices for controlling the release of the power source that were little better than simple breaks. Consequently, clocks tended to tick in an uneven fashion, and for that reason, they gave poor results. All of this changed dramatically in the second half of the seventeenth century as the result of the work of the Dutch mathematician Christiaan Huygens (1629–1695). Huygens replaced earlier methods of regulating

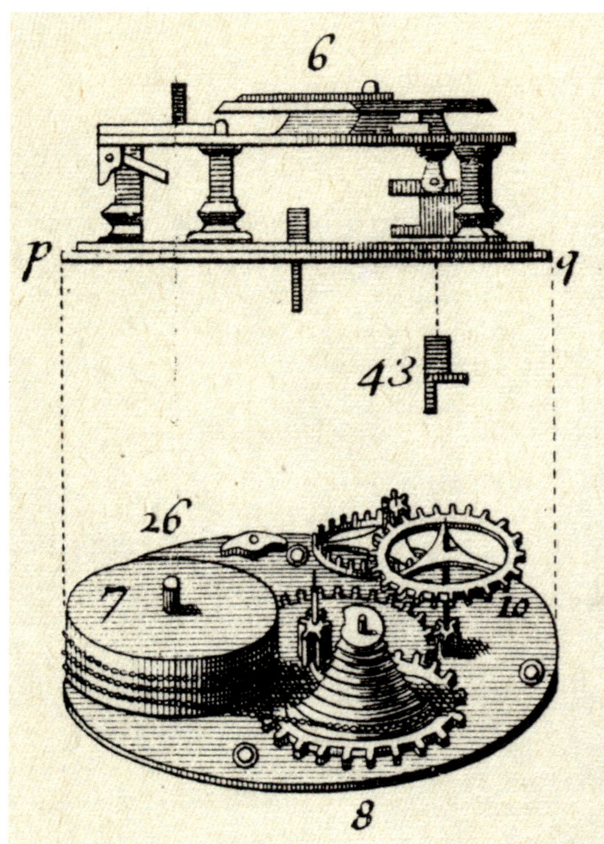

fig. 9 *The principal parts of a watch with a plated movement. Detail of an engraving from Antoine Thiout l'aîné's* Traité de l'horlogerie méchanique et pratique *(Paris, 1741), vol. 2, pl. 34. 9½ × 15 in. (24.1 × 38.1 cm). Thomas J. Watson Library, The Metropolitan Museum of Art, New York*

fig. 10 *Christiaan Huygens's application of a pendulum to a clock movement, shown with his rope-and-pulley device for maintaining power. Originally published by Huygens in his* Horologium *(1658), reproduced from his* Opera Varia *(Leiden, 1724), vol. 1, pl. 1, opp. p. 14. 11⅛ × 4⅞ in. (28.3 × 12.3 cm). Private collection*

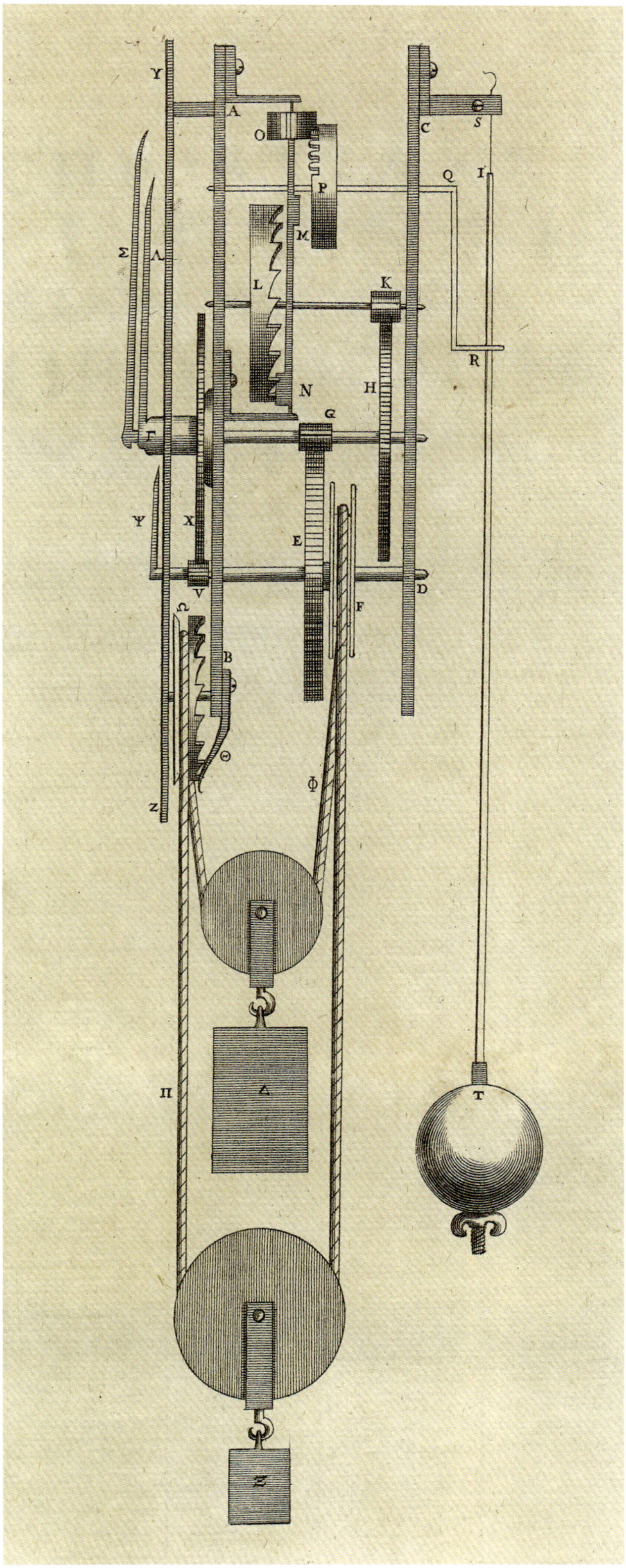

power with the pendulum. The great advantage of the pendulum for controlling the escapement of power was that unlike earlier mechanisms the freely swinging pendulum had a definite duration.

The claims for the invention of the pendulum for the purpose of timekeeping have long been in dispute. The concept was discovered in Italy by Galileo Galilei (1564–1642), but he never successfully applied a pendulum to a clock. Huygens described his first version of the pendulum clock toward the end of 1656. The illustration shown here (fig. 10) reproduces Huygens's idea for the application of a pendulum to the movement of a clock that accompanied his description of the clock published in The Hague in a small edition titled the *Horologium* (1658). The principle was immediately adopted by clockmakers, but Huygens continued his work on a pendulum clock in an attempt to remove a small error to which a pendulum is subject. The clockmakers, nonetheless, found that it was sufficient to use a pendulum with a small arc to obtain good results.

In 1666 Huygens was invited to join the Académie Royale des Sciences in Paris. This was a signal honor, and it was customary to thank the French King Louis XIV (1638–1715) by dedicating an important study to him. Huygens decided to offer a survey of his work on the pendulum. Huygens's *Horologium Oscillatorium: sive, De motu Pendulorum ad Horologia Aptato Demonstrationes Geometricae* was published in Paris in 1673 and is considered one of the most important mathematical treatises of the seventeenth century. For clockmaking, of course, it was even more important, because it led Huygens to the insight that produced his second great horological invention, in late 1674: the spiral balance spring. During the remainder of his life, Huygens would often turn to problems of timekeeping, but he never improved on these two great inventions. After the introduction of his inventions to the clockmakers, all attention was focused on the timekeeping aspect of the clock; most clocks now had large, easily read dials that registered the time.

In 1657, Salomon Coster (died 1659) obtained exclusive patent rights for making Huygens's pendulum clocks in the Netherlands. The Fromanteels, a prominent

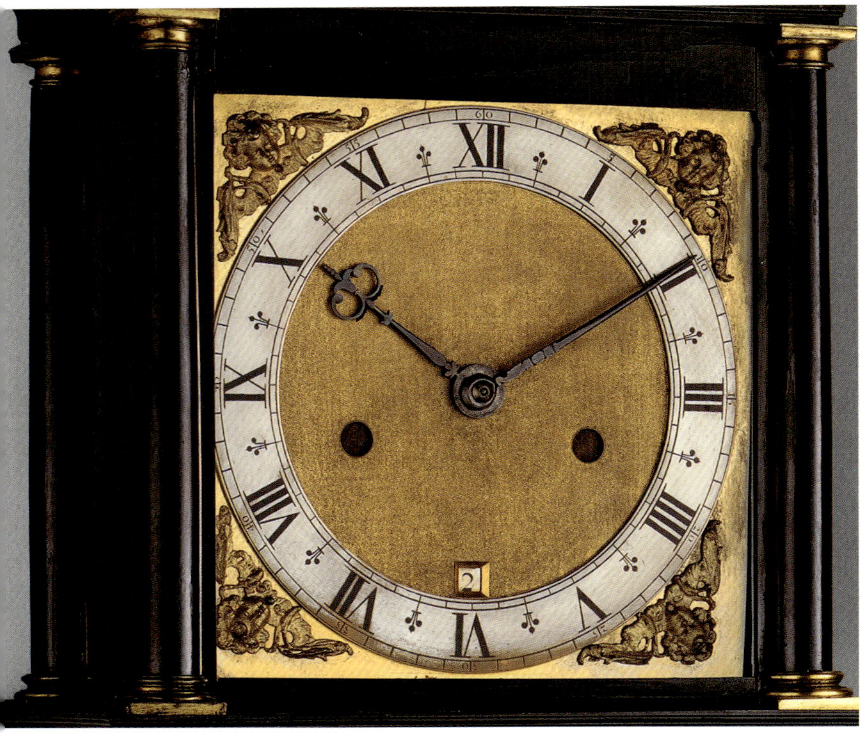

fig. 11 *Detail, showing the dial of a hooded wall clock. Dial: gilded brass with a silvered brass chapter ring, signed "A. Fromanteel Londini" (Ahasuerus I Fromanteel, 1607–1693). British (London), ca. 1660–65. Width of dial plate: 8¼ in. (21 cm). The Metropolitan Museum of Art, New York, Bequest of Irwin Untermyer, 1973 (1974.28.93)*

family of London clockmakers, sent a family member, John Fromanteel (1638–1692), to become a journeyman in Coster's workshop, and by October 1658, the Fromanteels were able to advertise their pendulum clocks in London (fig. 11). About 1670, Isaac II Thuret (1630–1706), clockmaker to King Louis XIV, made a very accurate variety of pendulum clock, known as a regulator, which included a dial that indicated not only hours and minutes but also seconds. The clock is said to have been the personal possession of Huygens, and it is the oldest preserved regulator to have been used for astronomical observation.

There were a number of challenges in making a pendulum clock before it would become a remarkably accurate timekeeper during the course of the eighteenth century. The pendulum had to be lengthened and the arc of the swing reduced. A new escapement had to be found to help shorten the arc while keeping the clock reliable. Next, the problem of friction caused by air resistance had to be lessened as much as possible. Finally, the effects of changes in temperature on the expansion and contraction of the pendulum had to be overcome. A weight at the bottom of the pendulum in the form of a vertically attached, double-sided convex disk, called a bob, was found to offer the least resistance to air. During the latter part of the seventeenth century, many constructions were attempted to solve the first three problems. The standard solution to the escapement problem, probably achieved in 1670 by the British clockmaker Joseph Knibb (1640–1711), proved to be the anchor escapement, so called because of its resemblance to a sea anchor. A pendulum of slightly more than thirty-nine inches in length, known as the Royal Pendulum, was attached to the anchor escapement and provided a beat of one second, allowing a seconds dial to be added to the clock without the use of complicated gearing. The resulting mechanism (fig. 8) was soon routinely housed in a wooden longcase, which came to be known as a grandfather clock.

Technical advances and excellent workmanship by such masters as Thomas Tompion (1639–1713), Daniel Quare (1647/49–1724), and Daniel Delander (1678–1733) continued to place England in the forefront of clockmaking during the latter part of the seventeenth century. In the next century, George Graham (1673–1751) and John Harrison (1693–1776), together with his brother James, and John Ellicott (1706–1792) individually offered solutions to the problem of temperature compensation. Graham is credited with improving the anchor escapement by inventing a recoilless version, called the dead-beat escapement. In the late seventeenth and eighteenth centuries many French clockmakers, however, preferred to make clock movements regulated by short pendulums, often suspended from silk threads, to be used in ornamental cases made of gilded brass; gilded, silvered, lacquered, or patinated bronze; marble; porcelain; including all materials that were abundantly available thanks to the presence of the luxury trades that flourished in Paris at the time (fig. 12). Eighteenth-century French clockmakers also produced precision clocks (*regulateurs*).

By the end of the seventeenth century clocks were accurate enough to be used for serious astronomical observations. Tompion had, in fact, made two remarkable clocks with thirteen-foot pendulums that were finished in 1676 for the Royal Observatory in Greenwich, England. Harrison invented marine clocks and a chronometer, familiarly known as H.4, and with them proved that it was possible to solve the age-old problem of finding the longitude at sea using an accurate timekeeper that compensated for weather conditions and a ship's motion. Pierre Le Roy (1717–1785) and Ferdinand Berthoud (1727–1807) competed for the lucrative honor of making chronometers and sea clocks for the French navy. But French chronometers were expensive and time-consuming to construct, and it remained for John Arnold (1735–1799) and Thomas Earnshaw (1749–1829) to make chronometers in England with sufficient quantities and at moderate prices so that by the early

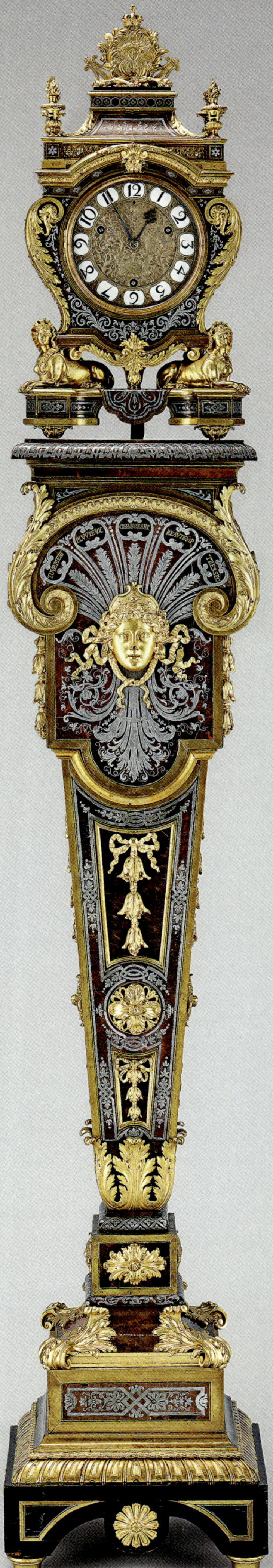

fig. 12 *Clock with pedestal. Case of tortoiseshell and brass veneer and gilded brass mounts attributed to André-Charles Boulle (French, 1642–1732) after designs by Jean Berain (French, 1640–1711). Movement probably by Isaac II Thuret (French, 1630–1706). French (Paris), ca. 1690. 7 ft. 3¼ × 13¾ in. (222 × 34.9 × 28.9 cm). The Metropolitan Museum of Art, New York, Rogers Fund, 1958 (58.53a–c)*

nineteenth century, the chronometer could become a standard instrument of navigation.

About 1500, or a few years earlier, the watch evolved from the small, portable, spring-driven clock, and it began to be carried or worn on the person. Although its origin has been disputed, it seems to have been invented in northern Italy. Most watch movements made before 1780 consist of two circular or oval plates, which are held apart by pillars of various shapes, ranging from simple, square-sectioned posts to circular or square-sectioned balusters (fig. 9). The pillars were customarily riveted to one plate and pinned to the other, and the operative parts of the movement were installed between the two plates. In their simplest form, these watch movements consisted of a coiled spring, a train of wheels, and an escapement. It also became customary to augment some of the movements with a device for striking the hours on a bell that was incorporated in the watchcase. Some early watches sounded each hour with a single blow (striking in passing), others with a blow for each hour individually (one through twelve, or one through twenty-four). These watches are, in fact, miniature versions of portable clocks, and they are traditionally called clock watches. Alarms were added features of some clock watches.

Two varieties of watches were well established by 1600. The first type was primarily a source of information about the time of day, and it often included a calendar and even the phases of the moon. Cases for such watches were usually made of metal, sometimes skillfully engraved and gilded. The second type was primarily intended as jewelry. Reports and records of this type of watch include one that was incorporated into the handle of an eyeglass that belonged to Pope Leo X (1475–1521).[2] A design for a watch that was embedded in a finger ring appears in an engraving by Pierre II Woeiriot (1532–1596/99) published in Lyon, France, in 1561 (fig. 13).[3] Agates and quartz crystals quarried in southern Germany and Switzerland provided raw material for watchcases, including some made of transparent rock crystal that were known to exist in late sixteenth-century London

fig. 13 (below) *Engraving by Pierre II Woeiriot (French, 1532–1596/99). Design for a ring watch. Plate 32 for his* Livre d'aneaux d'orfevrerie *(Lyon, 1561). 3¼ × 2½ in. (7.9 × 5.6 cm). The Metropolitan Museum of Art, New York, Harris Brisbane Dick Fund, 1926 (26.57.50)*

fig. 14 (right) *Peter Paul Rubens (Flemish, 1577–1640). Portrait of a Man, Possibly an Architect or Geographer, 1597. Oil on copper, 8½ × 5¾ in. (21.6 × 14.6 cm). The Metropolitan Museum of Art, New York, The Jack and Belle Linsky Collection, 1982 (1982.60.24)*

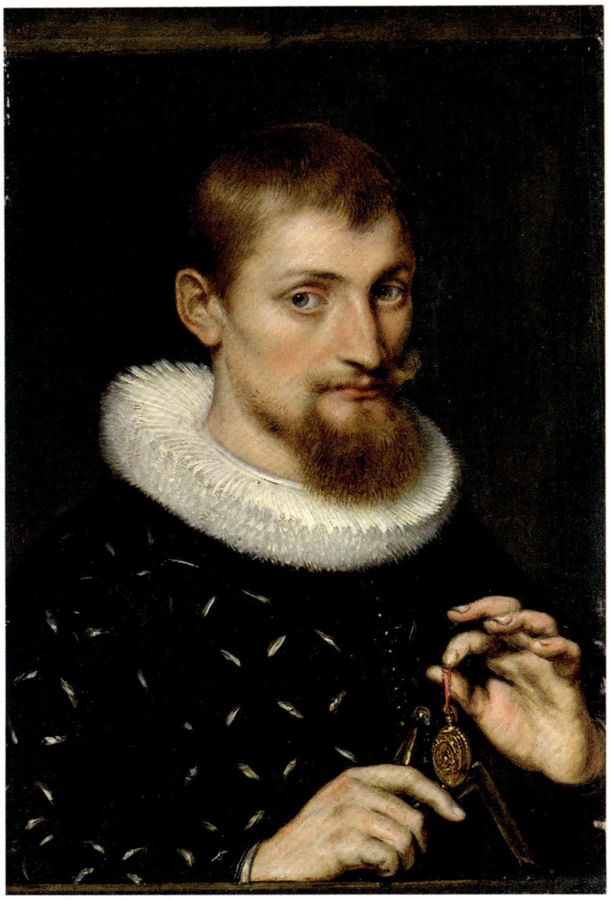

and fifty years later in the Low Countries, although it is uncertain where they originated (fig. 14). In the seventeenth century, watchmakers in Dresden, Geneva, Leeuwarden, Lyon, Paris, Prague, Rouen, and Strasbourg were fitting rock crystal cases of varying quality with movements of their own making. Agates and other polished hardstones were also in demand for casemaking. Even more opulent cases were set with gemstones. Some of the most beautiful and highly treasured cases, however, were the painted enamels on gold (fig. 15). The best enameled cases were made in Blois, France, beginning about 1640 and later in Paris, and some were signed by Henri Toutin (1614–1684). In the last part of the century, the Huaud family of Geneva supplied enamels for use by foreign watchmakers, while masters such as Georg Cameel, recorded in Strasbourg between 1650 and 1660, or Nicolaus II Rugendas (1619–1694/95) in Augsburg, enriched their watches with painted enamels either imported or of local origin.

Neither the watch as time-telling device nor the watch as personal adornment was a very accurate timekeeper, as indicated by the absence of a minute hand in all but the most exceptional watches made before 1675. The technology of watchmaking remained, with several exceptions, nearly standard throughout the first three quarters of the seventeenth century. This changed in 1675 as the result of another of Huygens's inventions, the isochronos spiral spring balance. First published in the February 25, 1675, issue of *Le journal des sçavans*, the official publication of the French Académie Royale des Sciences, the invention was almost immediately adopted by watchmakers throughout Europe. In one stroke, watches became serious timekeepers. They were now routinely supplied with two hands, and their dials were calibrated to register minutes.

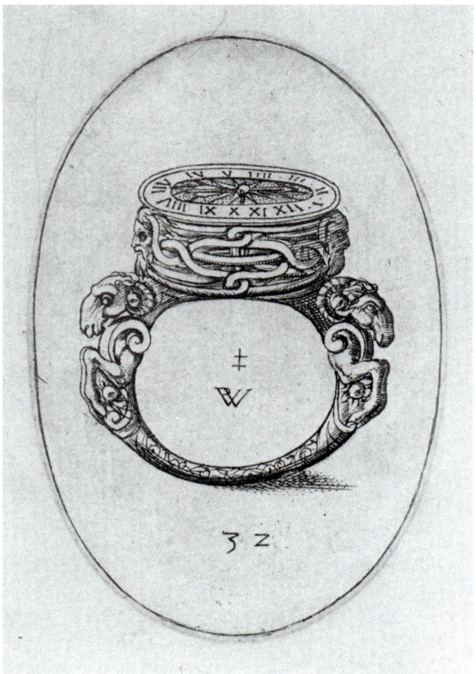

In the course of the eighteenth century, new escapements were invented. The older verge, to a large extent, was replaced by the cylinder, which was in turn more or less superseded by the lever. Using an invention of the late seventeenth century, watches could repeat the last hour and the last quarter hour on a bell, and they could be activated at will, a useful improvement for telling time in darkness. By the last quarter of the eighteenth century, their accuracy was still further improved by inventions connected with the chronometer, made by the Swiss-born horological genius Abraham Breguet (1747–1823) working in Paris. The innovations in the layouts of watch movements begun in 1780 (fig. 16) by the Frenchman Jean-Antoine Lépine (1720–1814) became the models for those used in the elegantly thin watches produced in nineteenth-century France and Switzerland.

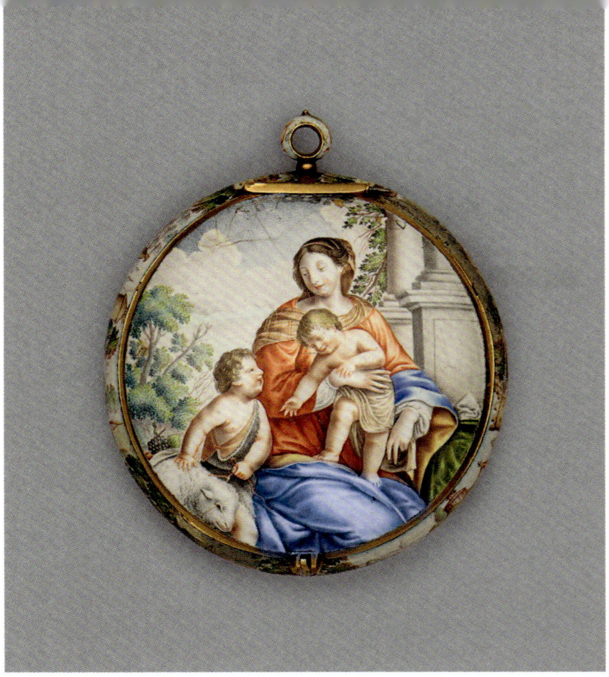

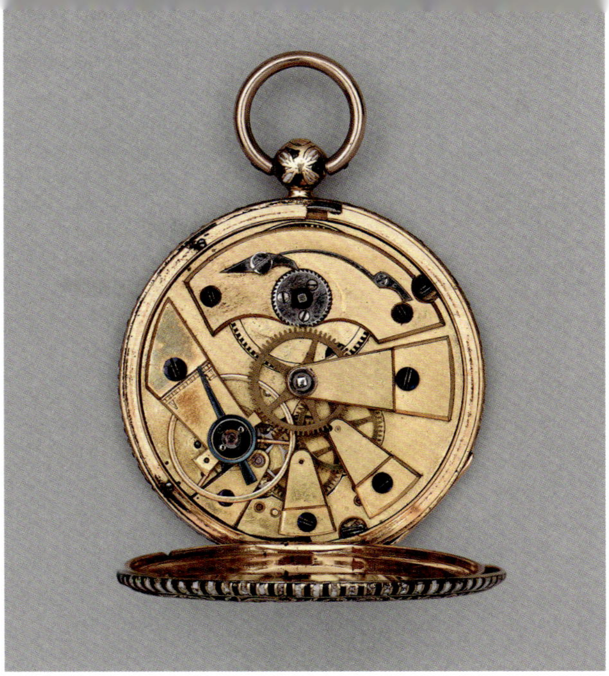

Like Switzerland, England produced far more watches than domestic consumption could support. In the eighteenth century, England had been the preeminent exporter, but by the early nineteenth century, English-made watches were beginning to be eclipsed by watches made both in Geneva and elsewhere in Switzerland. Reliable figures for the output of individual firms are difficult to find, but by 1844, in Neuchâtel in the Swiss Jura district, it has been reported that 280,000 finished watches were produced per year.[4] The production of unfinished watch movements (*ébauches*), which were supplied to individual watchmakers, who assembled the wheels of the train, added an escapement and a balance, and adjusted the parts until they ran accurately, was a much earlier practice in both England and Switzerland. Nevertheless, Frenchman Frédéric Japy (1749–1812) established a factory in Beaucourt in eastern France for the manufacture and export of *ébauches* on a scale previously unknown. Japy is reported to have had fifty employees producing 40,000 unfinished movements per year in 1795, and 300 employees producing 100,000 per year by 1805.[5]

Improved tools and toolmaking documented in Lancashire, England, during the late eighteenth century were matched by improvements such as those invented in the 1840s for Vacheron and Constantin, a firm in Geneva. More is still to be learned about the coming of fully developed industrialization in watchmaking even before the advent of the American Watch Company in the early 1850s and successive American competitors. Even with the continued growth of the American factory system, however, Swiss watches dominated the export market in the second half of the nineteenth century.[6]

With the application of electricity to an oscillating quartz crystal, Warren A. Marrison (1896–1980), working for Bell Telephone Laboratories in 1927, created a timekeeping device that was based on the regular vibrations of the crystal. Later, in 1955, a similar application was developed by Louis Essen (1908–1997) and J. V. L. Parry (1923–1995) with a resonating element, known as caesium, and resulted in the practical atomic clock for the National Physical Laboratory in Teddington, England, which, for ordinary purposes, made even the most accurate mechanical timekeeper superfluous.

While the best mechanical clock is not quite able to obtain the precision of atomic timekeepers, mechanical clocks and especially mechanical watches are still capable of enchantment. Many clocks and watches—whether through the varied information that they convey on multiple dials, through the self-propelled motion of visible skeletonized movements, or through the beauty of their cases, which are sometimes set with extravagant quantities of gemstones—are, finally, objects of conspicuous consumption. These are the characteristics that were so highly prized in pre-pendulum clocks and pre–balance spring watches.

1. Vincent and Leopold 2009.
2. Giraldi 1541; see also Leopold 1990.
3. At least one of these tiny ring watches is extant. It is today in the Schatzkammer der Residenz in Munich; see Leopold and Vincent 2000, pp. 137, 147, n. 3, and p. 138, fig. 2.
4. Landes 1983, p. 289.
5. Girod 1975, p. 42; Landes 1983, pp. 261–62, 449, n. 11.
6. Landes 1983, pp. 290–320.

fig. 15 *Watch with a painted enamel scene depicting the Virgin and Child with the Infant Saint John the Baptist from an engraving by Gilles Rousselet (French, 1610–1685) recording a painting by Jacques Stella (French, 1596–1657). French (Paris or Blois), ca. 1645–50. Diameter 2¼ in. (5.8 cm). The Metropolitan Museum of Art, New York, Gift of J. Pierpont Morgan, 1917 (17.190.1627)*

fig. 16 *Watch with back cover open to show a single plate movement and bridges for securing the wheels of a train, signed: "Lépine Paris" (Maison Lépine, 1766–1919). French, probably ca. 1830–40. Diameter 1⅜ in. (3.5 cm). The Metropolitan Museum of Art, New York, Bequest of Laura Frances Hearn, 1917 (17.101.6)*

1. Astronomical Table Clock

GERMAN (AUGSBURG), 1568
14¼ × 8½ × 5¾ in. (36.2 × 21.6 × 14.6 cm)
Gift of J. Pierpont Morgan, 1917
17.190.634a–d

CASE AND DIALS: gilded brass, signed (on left side of case): MEFECIT • CHAS / PARVS • BOHEMVS / INVIÆNNA • AVS / TRIA ANNO / 1568

MOVEMENT: iron-posted frame, signed with maker's marks (punched, in cameo): CB and moon and stars within a shield

TO A LARGE EXTENT, COLLECTIONS IN SIXTEENTH-CENTURY Europe reflected the interests of those who were powerful or wealthy enough to form them. In German-speaking areas, in particular, many collectors were greatly influenced by the theoretical concept of the *Kunstkammer* as an assemblage of objects organized to display the owner's cognizance of both the natural world and the products of human artifice. Many *Kunstkammern*, but by no means all, contained at least a few mathematical instruments, globes, and clocks. The clocks prized for inclusion in a *Kunstkammer* customarily displayed not only the time in several different systems for counting the hours, but also as much calendrical and astronomical information as the clockmaker could devise.[1]

The Behaim clock, because of its astronomical and calendrical dials, would have been an ideal addition to any *Kunstkammer*. It belongs to a series of clocks made from a comparable construction known as Metzger-type clocks, because some of them are signed by the clockmaker Jeremias Metzger, or Metzker (ca. 1525–ca. 1597). Like other clocks in this series, the clock has a spring-driven movement, consisting of two rectangular plates that are held in place at the four corners by iron pillars, a structure that supports three trains of wheels. The train in the center drives the dial for time telling, or length of day, on one long side of the clock, as well as an astrolabe dial on the other long side. The principle arbor of this train is perpendicular to the dials on the exterior of the long sides of the clock and projects through the dials to carry the hands (now missing). The central train is flanked by two trains set at right angles. These trains primarily operate the hammers that strike two bells on stands that are attached to a plate at the top of the clock, one for hours and one for quarters. With a few exceptions, this construction is the essence of a Metzger-type clock. Although the product of more than one clockmaker, this group of clocks was first identified by historian Erwin Neumann, who chose as his prototype a clock in the collection of the Kunsthistorisches Museum, Vienna, signed: "Jeremias 1564 Metzker Vrmacher, Vrmacher in Augspur." The movement also bears his punchmark, consisting of his monogram, "I M," within a shield, as well as the pinecone, or *pyr*, the town mark of Augsburg, Germany.[2]

Like the case of the clock in Vienna, the case of the Museum's clock is rectangular, with applied colonettes at the corners, which are set upon a base ornamented with cast reliefs depicting triumphal processions and supporting an openwork dome with interlaced foliage inhabited by figures variously engaged in hunting bear and ducks. Partial figures of winged horses spring from the four corners where the dome joins the main body of the clock. The astrolabe dial was probably intended as the front of the clock, because the winding square for the

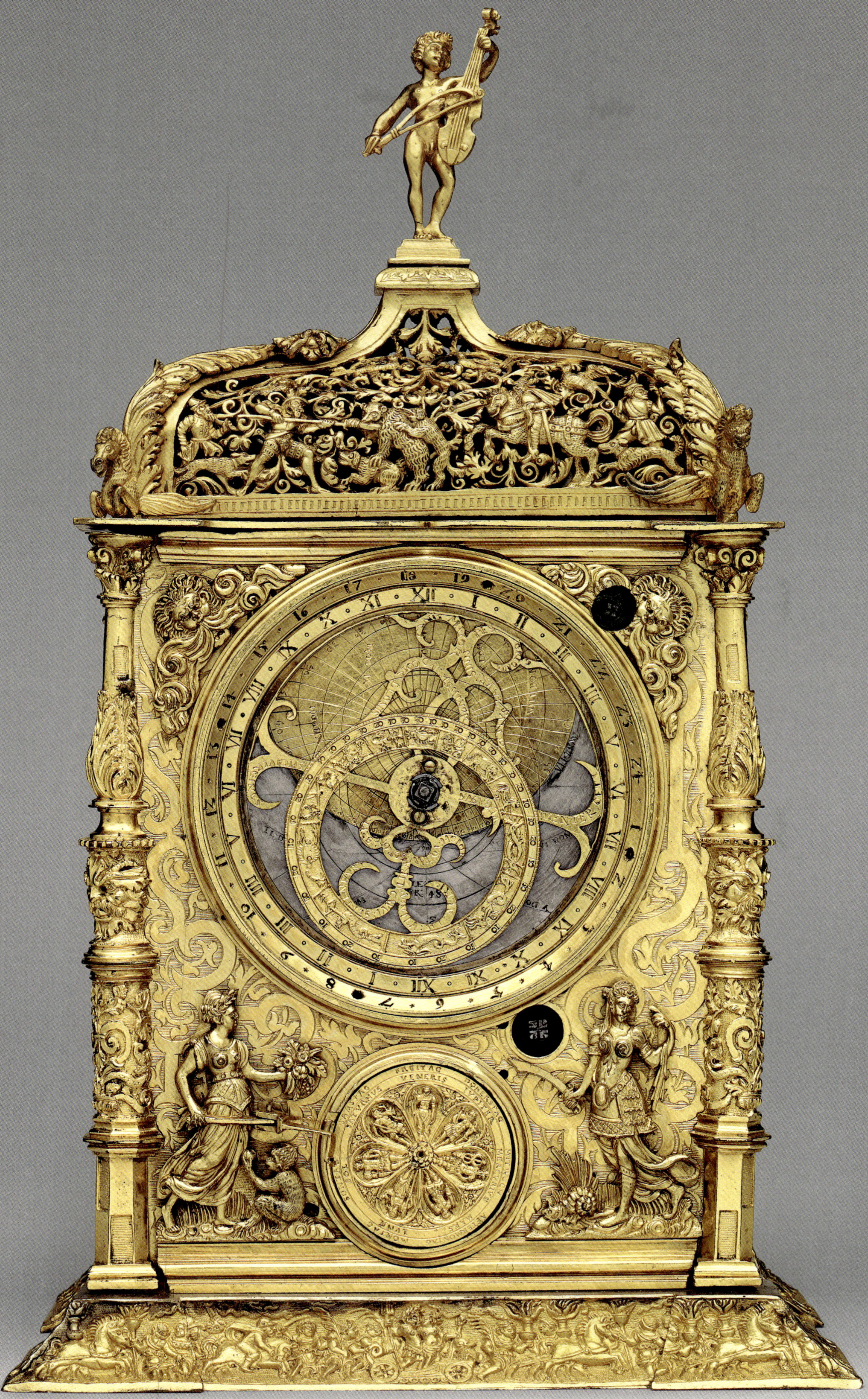

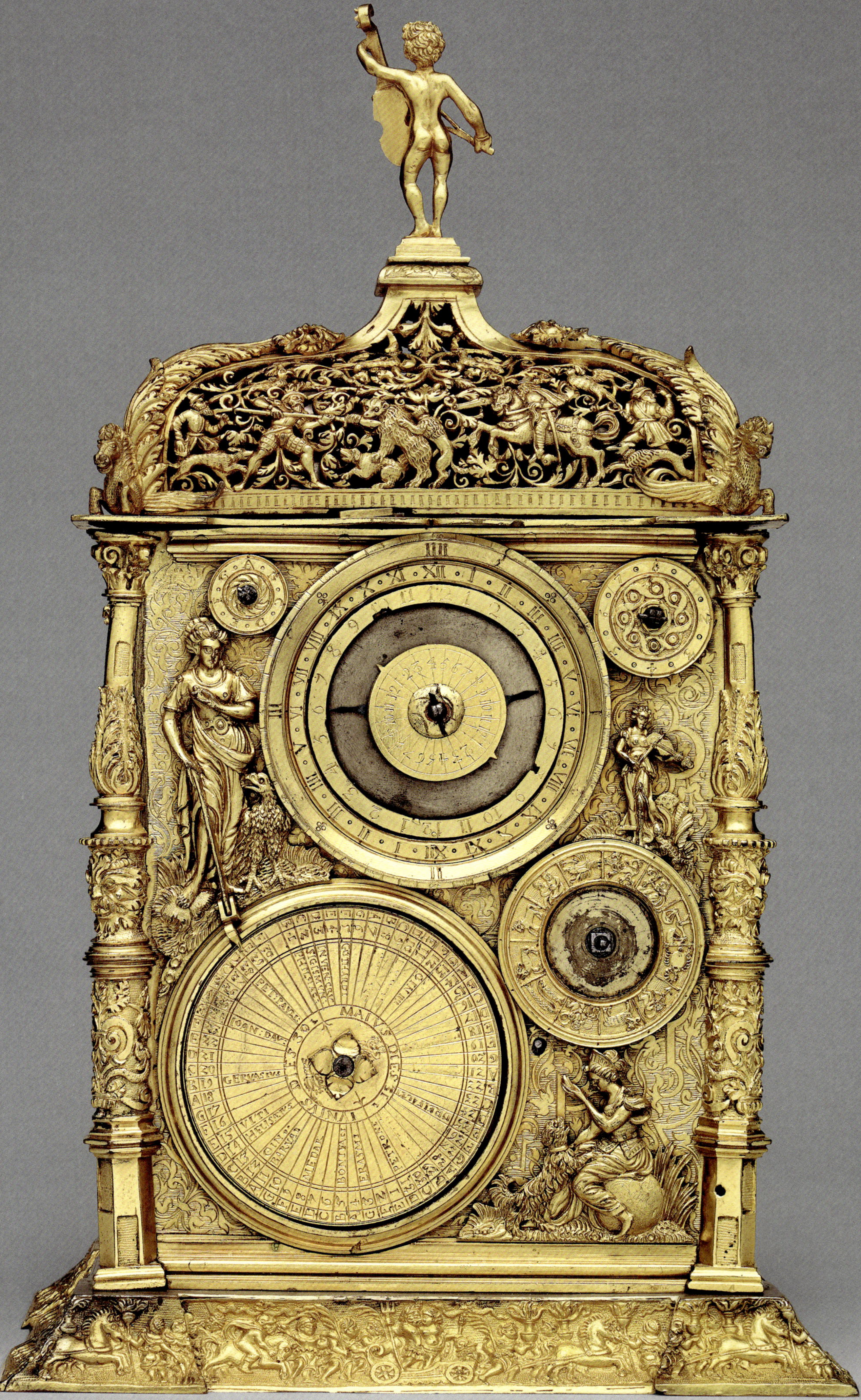

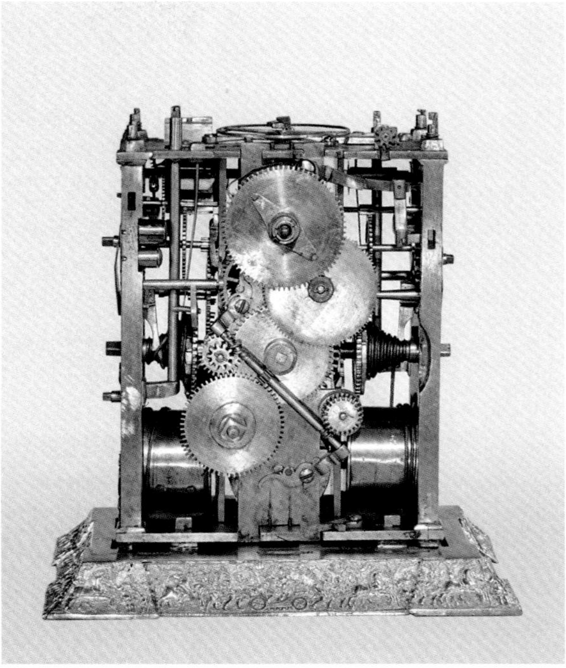

Movement with motion work for time-telling dial

mainspring of the time train projects through a hole in the case just below the astrolabe, therefore facilitating the insertion of the key. The revolving rete of the astrolabe on this clock shows the positions of fourteen stars, and it has two reversible tympans (or plates) for use in latitudes of 45, 48, 51, and 54 degrees. A subsidiary dial, which is driven by the astrolabe, revolves to show the days of the week with their planetary rulers. This dial is flanked by two female figures cast in relief: one figure is accompanied by a monkey that wields a pointer to mark the days, and the other figure is holding a nautilus shell. At the top of the same side are personifications of two of the Four Winds.

The other long side has two large circular dials, including a chapter ring that shows the time (I–XII, twice), an inner ring that now shows the time in Arabic numerals (1–12, twice), and an outer ring that shows the quarter hours (I–IIII) and is also marked for minutes (the latter markings probably not original to the clock). In the center, there is a disk for setting the clock's alarm, and between this disk and the three chapter rings is a large open space that once contained movable shutters, one for the number of daylight hours and one for the night hours (Nürnberg hours). At the lower right is a subsidiary dial (hand now missing) showing the months with their associated zodiacal signs that functioned as an adjustment for the shutters according to the time of the year. The other large dial (lower left) is equipped with three revolving circular plates, which are engraved with the days of the year and indicate holidays and Saints' Days. A draped female figure holds a staff that points to the day. Beside her is an eagle and above her a subsidiary dial with the Dominical Letters (hand manipulated). A somewhat larger subsidiary dial (a later addition), at the top right, regulates the spring balance. Two other female figures in relief complete the side, one seated with a dog, and the other playing a viol.

The short side to the left of the astrolabe registers the quarter-hour striking, and the short side to the right registers the hour striking. The dial below the latter allows for adjusting the mechanism to strike twelve or twenty-four times as desired. The twenty-four-hour striking (now inoperative) has a subsidiary count wheel (sometimes erroneously called Canonical striking), in addition to the usual count wheel that serves to make the twenty-four-hour striking more reliable.[3]

Close comparison of the Museum's clock with the clock in Vienna makes it evident, as clock historian Klaus Maurice has proposed, that in spite of the inscription on the case and the punchmarks on the movement, the Museum's clock must have been made by the same clockmaker and probably the same casemaker as the Vienna clock.[4] Other clocks belonging to this group and signed by Metzger are now known to be in the collection of the Nicolae Simache Clock Museum, Ploieşti, Romania

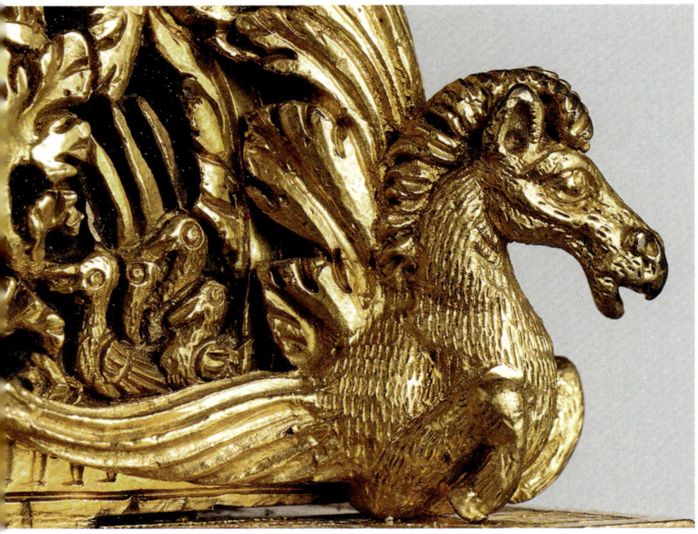

Detail of dome with partial figure of Pegasus

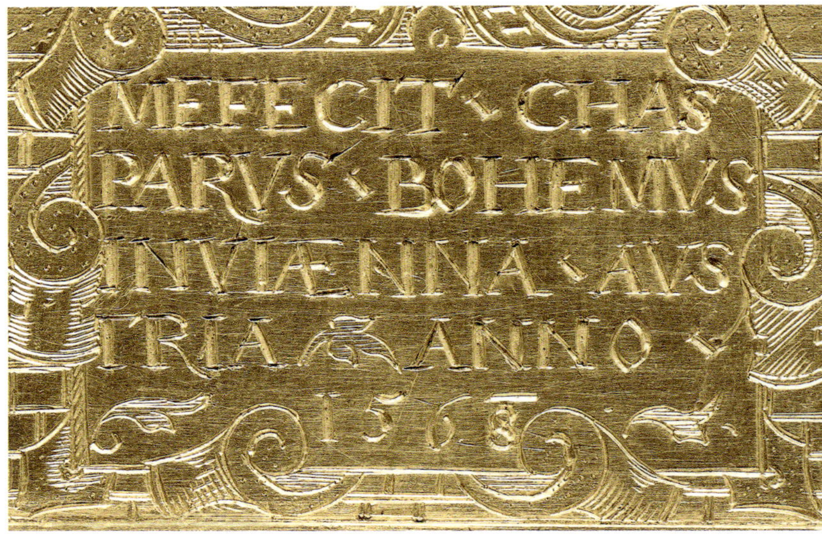

Signature and date on side of the case

(dated 1562),[5] and the James A. de Rothschild Collection at Waddesdon Manor near Aylesbury, Buckinghamshire, England (dated 1563).[6] Still, other clocks with similarly constructed movements also exist.

While there is no documentary evidence that the Museum's clock was actually made by Jeremias Metzger, or in his workshop, the supposition can be supported by some of what is known about Metzger and about Behaim. Metzger, born in Augsburg about 1525, was a highly successful maker of small clocks and seemingly an influential member of the newly created Augsburg guild of clockmakers owing to the fact that he is recorded as an inspection master for the guild (*Geschaumeister*) in 1564. Nevertheless, he apparently ran afoul of the rules that governed the activities of journeymen in Augsburg, probably because the demand for his clocks outstripped the traditional supply of skilled labor.[7] Caspar Behaim (or Behaimb, or Beham, or Chasparus Bohemus; active 1568–84), whose latinized name appears conspicuously on the case of the Museum's clock, is recorded as a clockmaker working in Vienna between 1573 and 1584 and paid for work on the Viennese city hall (*Rathaus*) clock in 1578.[8] The city hall clock would undoubtedly have been a large, wrought-iron framed turret clock requiring very different skills than those of a maker of small clocks who would have used different tools. It seems reasonable, therefore, to suppose that Behaim must have had an Austrian patron for whom he obtained the clock from a well-established maker of small clocks in Augsburg, the most important center of German clockmaking. The connection between the two clockmakers remains unknown.

Clockmakers in Nürnberg, Augsburg's chief competitor in the second half of the sixteenth century, seem to have owned some of the models for the cases of their clocks.[9] Ownership of models is less certain in Augsburg, but at least some clockmakers are known to have produced their own cases. Historian Eva Groiss cites records in the Stadtarchiv Augsburg that show five goldsmiths were permitted to specialize in making clock cases by 1567. Metzger was, in fact, one of the clockmakers for whom the goldsmith and embosser Hans Helmbrecht (active 16th century) is known to have worked.[10] But the Metropolitan Museum's clock case is made of brass, in large part cast brass, and thus fell at least partly under the jurisdiction of the brass founders, who were even more restricted than the goldsmiths of Augsburg. Surviving evidence, nevertheless, indicates that these shops were capable of serial production of the cast-brass components of clock-cases.[11] For that reason, the case of the Museum's clock was probably the work of several skilled craftsmen, one of whom may, indeed, have been Metzger.

The applied figures on the cases of the Metzger clocks in the Kunsthistorisches Museum and Waddesdon Manor, as well as the Behaim clock, are prime examples of serial casting from the same models. It has been suggested that the figures represent personifications of the Five Senses.[12] The source of the processions on the front and back of the base of the clock has long been known as a print by Hans Sebald Beham (1500–1550), dated 1549, which has had various titles but appears in a publication by a recognized authority on German prints and is titled *The Triumphal Procession of the Noble Glorious Women*.[13] Noted historian of decorative arts Geoffrey de Bellaigue identified the figures in the dome in three engravings by Virgil Solis (1514–1562) of Nürnberg,[14] the long sides from the right side of a bear hunt (*Bärenjagd*)[15] and the short sides from the centers of two engraved duck hunts (*Entenjagd*).[16]

The plates that form the sides of the case are particularly felicitous examples of a variety of ornament usually identified as moresque, which Italian artists adapted from Islamic sources and spread throughout Europe through the medium of prints. No exact model for the ornament of the plates of the Behaim and Metzger clocks has been found, but somewhat comparable designs appear in prints signed with the initial "f," an anonymous Italian who probably worked in Venice, and whose ornament was republished about 1550 by the printmaker Hieronymus Cock (1518–1570) in Antwerp.[17] This variety of ornament found its way into the prints of the Dutch-born Balthazar Sylvius (Balthasar van den Bos/Bosch, 1518–1580), also working in Antwerp, whose designs of the 1550s and 1560s combined pure moresques with patterns of interlaced strapwork[18] in a style that is beautifully employed on the sides of the case of the Behaim clock.

Unlike many late-Renaissance clocks, this one was not converted to a pendulum. Instead, the original circular balance was fitted with a balance spring, probably not long after the invention by the Dutch mathematician Christiaan Huygens (1629–1695) was published in 1675. At the same time the chapter ring for Italian hours (1–24, starting at sundown) of the time-telling dial was replaced by a chapter ring (reading 1–12, twice), and the outermost ring was marked for minutes, now practical given the greater accuracy of the newly invented spring balance. Two new plates for the calendar were added, one given the names of saints favored by the Dutch, and the other now displaying the Dutch word for Christmas (Kerstmis), suggesting that the conversion was made in the Netherlands.

The clock is now missing most of its hands and the movable shutters adjusting the length of the days and nights. A new finial for the dome was supplied in Paris by Alfred André (1839–1919) at some time between 1886 and 1893.[19] In addition, an ebony base of uncertain age was supplied for the clock before it entered the collection of the Museum's donor J. Pierpont Morgan. The clock had earlier belonged to Frédéric Spitzer in Paris (1893),[20] who may have added the André finial. Before Spitzer the clock belonged to Charles Stein, who sold it in Paris in 1886.[21]

At some point in the nineteenth century at least one copy of the case of the Museum's clock was made probably as an electrotype.[22] The copy is not to be confused with the much larger edition of electrotype made by the Viennese firm of C. Haas and Company in 1864 or 1865 from the Metzger clockcase in the Kunsthistorisches Museum,[23] examples of which can still be found throughout the world. CV / JHL

1 Leopold 1995. See also Daston and Park 1998.
2 Kunsthistorisches Museum, Vienna (inv. no. 852). See Neumann 1961, pp. 91–101, 110–11.
3 See Leopold 1971, pp. 52–53, for an explanation of this mechanism.
4 Maurice 1976, vol. 1, p. 105, and vol. 2, pp. 29–30, nos. 158, 159, and figs. 158a–d, 159a–e.
5 The authors are grateful to Paulus Rainer of the Kunsthistorisches Museum and to the staff of the Nicolae Simache Clock Museum for this information.
6 See de Bellaigue 1974, vol. 1, pp. 146–53, no. 29.
7 See *Clockwork Universe* 1980, p. 189, no. 26.
8 Uhlirz 1897, p. XCVII, no. 15809, fol. 110 (1573), and p. CXI, no. 15833, fol. 68 (1584).
9 Leopold 2002, pp. 522, 524–25.
10 Groiss 1980, pp. 70–71 and n. 82.
11 Maurice 1976, vol. 1, pp. 99–107; Groiss 1980, pp. 70–71 and n. 82.
12 De Bellaigue 1974, vol. 1, p. 152.
13 Hollstein, *German*, 1954–2014, vol. 3 (1954), p. 145.
14 De Bellaigue 1974, vol. 1, pp. 151–52.
15 O'Dell-Franke 1977, p. 134, no. g 1, and pl. 71.
16 Ibid., p. 139, nos. g 39 and g 40, and pl. 77.
17 Byrne 1981, pp. 32–33, nos. 13, 14.
18 Ibid., p. 36, no. 20.
19 The authors are indebted to the late Rudolf Distelberger, formerly of the Kunsthistorisches Museum, for the evidence of the origin of the finial figure.
20 *Collection Spitzer* 1891–93, vol. 5 (1892; plate vol.), "Horloges," pl. IV; Palustre 1892, p. 37, no. 7.
21 Galerie Georges Petit 1886, p. 56, no. 215.
22 Hôtel Drouot 1981, no. 47.
23 Neumann 1961, p. 121.

2. Mirror Clock

GERMAN (NÜRNBERG), CA. 1565–70
16 × 6¼ × 1¼ in. (40.6 × 15.9 × 3.2 cm)
Gift of J. Pierpont Morgan, 1917
17.190.639

CASE: gilded brass and gilded copper; stem and foot probably cast from designs by Matthias Zündt (German, probably ca. 1498–1572); band of case from design by Cornelis Bos (Dutch, ca. 1510–1556)
DIAL: gilded brass
MOVEMENT: plated frame of iron, iron wheels; attributed to Master CR (probably active before 1565)

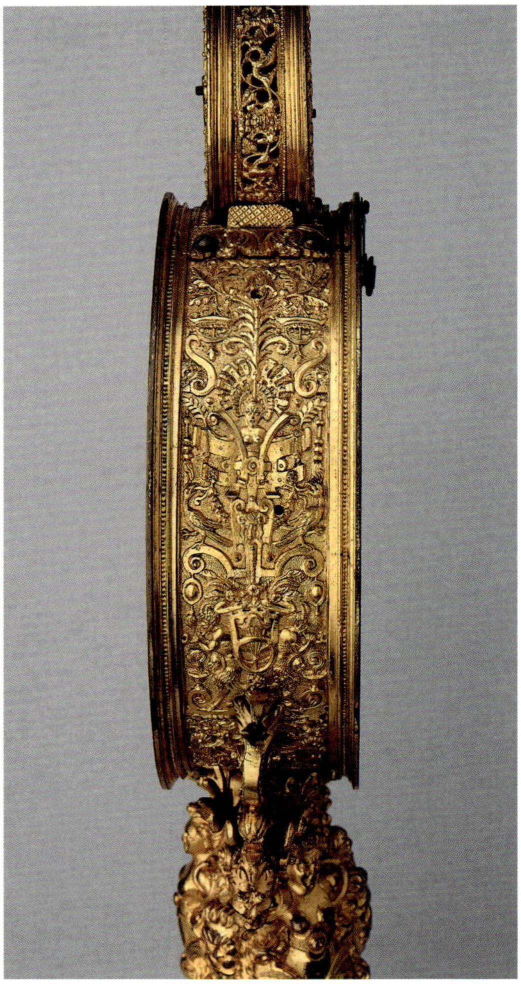

Detail showing side, or band, of the case

TIMEKEEPING HAS BEEN ASSOCIATED WITH ASTRONOMICAL events from the earliest civilizations. Horologists and historians of science have long debated the question of whether the mechanical clock is a direct descendant of the late-medieval instruments that were invented to demonstrate the apparent motions of the heavens, or whether the invention of the mechanical escapement for use in a clock subsequently permitted the construction of a mechanically driven astronomical device.[1] It has not been satisfactorily resolved even as yet.

The large circular dial of the Metropolitan Museum's clock exemplifies the close connection between timekeeping and astronomy during late-Renaissance Germany. Incorporated into Renaissance clocks, as it appears in the center of the dial of this clock, the astrolabe represents the stellar sky. The device employs one or more tympans (or circular plates) that are engraved with flat projections of terrestrial latitudes and longitudes, which form the grid for a map of the stars from the horizon to the zenith as seen from a given latitude on earth. The revolving rete is mounted on top of the tympan, and its components consist of the circle of the zodiac and an openwork design that incorporates flame-like pointers, which represent the relative positions of the brightest stars.

This variety of astrolabe exists as two types. One type is the ordinary, manually adjustable instrument that is used for locating the positions of the brightest stars at any moment in time: past, present, and future. The second type is driven by clockwork and, when incorporated into a clock and properly adjusted, demonstrates the positions and the apparent motion of stars to be seen at a specific time from the latitude for which the clock was intended to be used. Unlike the manually adjusted instruments, the mechanically driven astrolabes were usually furnished with two concentric hands: one for the sun, which tells the time of day, and the other for the moon; together, they show the place of the sun and the moon in the zodiac circle. The hand for the moon is missing on the Museum's clock, but the hand for the sun still exists, and the images of the moon's phases are visible and would have been seen through an aperture in the moon's hand. Visible, too, is the ring marked 1–29+ along the edge of the hand for the sun, which served to indicate the age of the moon in its monthly cycle. The tympan for the Museum's clock is reversible and can be used for 40 degrees latitude on one side and 50 degrees latitude on the other, and there are twenty-three stars that appear on the rete with their names and pointers.

The second most visible feature of the dial is the revolving calendar ring that indicates the months, each day of the month, the Dominical Letters, and the Saints' Days with six months to a side and beginning with Aries marked on the eleventh of March. The calendar ring and the

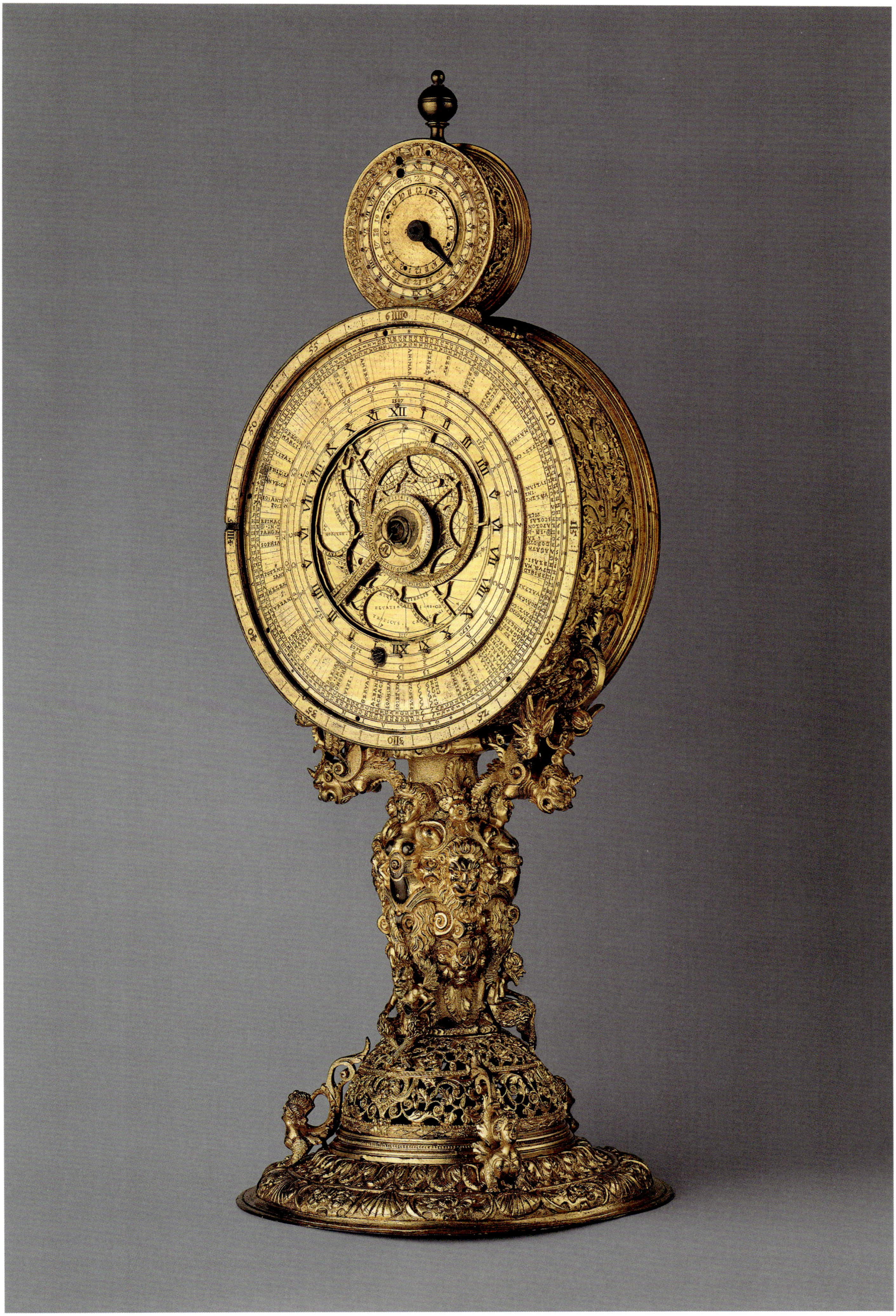

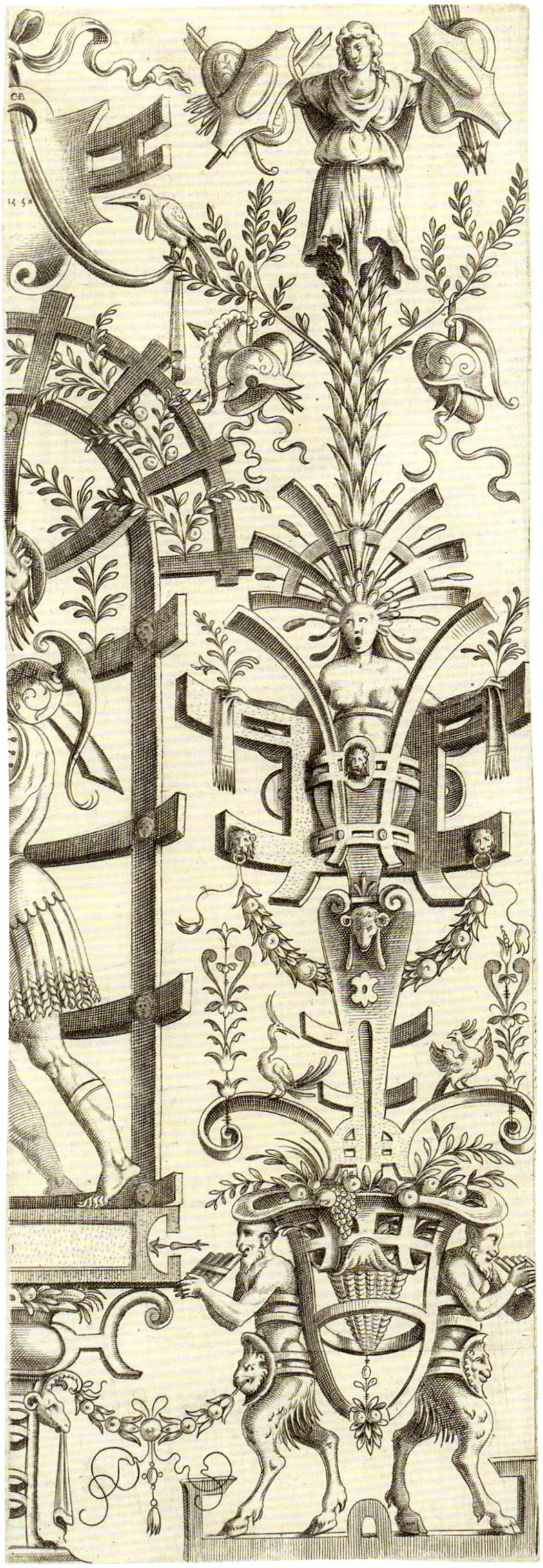

fig. 17 *Cornelis Bos (Dutch, ca. 1510–1556). Panel of grotesque ornament with strapwork, 1550. Engraving, 11⅞ × 4 in. (30.3 × 10.3 cm). Victoria and Albert Museum, London*

astrolabe are held in place by a ring with bayonet fittings that are spring held on the reverse, which serves as the chapter ring for the hours (I–XII, twice), as well as rings that are marked with the numerals of the twenty-eight-year solar cycle, including the Dominical Letters for the years beginning in 1570 and ending in 1610.[2] These concentric rings are framed by a thin band at the outer rim of the ring that now registers minutes and quarter hours. Most likely, the ring originally registered only five-minute intervals and quarters, for which it is marked 5–60 and I–IIII. The numerals on the hour chapter are augmented by touch pins for using the clock in darkness.

Here, the Museum's clock functions as a drum clock, but it is turned on its side and supported by an elaborately decorated stem and an openwork foot. The foot originally contained a bell upon which a hammer in the clock would have struck the hours. A second drum-shaped unit is attached to the top of the clock, and it contains an alarm mechanism with a second bell (now missing), which also served as the bell for the quarter striking of the clock. The movement consists of two circular iron plates that are held apart by four cylindrical iron pillars. The movement contains a going train and two striking trains of iron wheels, originally laid out for twelve- and twenty-four-hour striking. The trains are driven by open springs, and parts of the original stackfreed regulation remain.

This type of clock was once called a monstrance clock because its form resembled that of the container for displaying the Consecrated Host. It is certain from the references in the Augsburg guild specifications for masterpiece clocks, however, that as early as the first clocks of this description were being made in Germany, they were called mirror clocks (*Spiegeluhren*), presumably as a result of their likeness to a lady's mirror. Soon after, a "clocke made lookinge glassewise," presumably referring to a similar type of clock, was listed in the will of the clockmaker Nicholas Vallin from London (active ca. 1565–1603),[3] whose exquisite watch in the form of a Lesser George made for a member of the Order of the Garter (the highest order of the English knighthood) appears elsewhere in this survey (see entry 6 in this volume).

It is not the form of the Museum's clock but the ornament that places its maker in late-Renaissance Germany, and Nürnberg, in particular. The hollow stem of the case is covered with a distinctive variety of ornament called grotesque, because of its origins in antique Roman wall decorations discovered in Italy during the late fifteenth century and buried underground or in grottos: hence grotesque. Here, the elements of grotesque ornament (hybrid human and animal figures, satyrs, fruits, and masks) are piled one next to another in a sort of high relief (horror vacui). The same kind of overloading of ornament can be found in a group of designs for jewelry and weaponry published in Nürnberg in 1553 by the goldsmith and etcher Matthias Zündt (ca. 1498–1572).[4]

Zündt is recognized as a journeyman in the workshop of his father-in-law Wenzel Jamnitzer (1508–1585), who was probably the most famous goldsmith in sixteenth-century Nürnberg. By 1560 Zündt had also become a master goldsmith in Nürnberg,[5] and records show he was a stone carver at the same time. According to John Hayward, there are four carved models for casting the sides of cases for table clocks that have been attributed to Zündt,[6] but these models are of pear wood and not stone. Hayward also found evidence that Zündt referred to himself as a wood-carver (*Bildenschnitzer*) in 1559, when he was working for the Habsburg Ferdinand II, Archduke of Austria (1529–1595), perhaps a more likely occupation than stone carver for a future goldsmith.

The Zündt-derived clockcase found in the Museum's collection has added supports for the heavy clock movement, which seem to have been directly borrowed from the gargoyles that inhabit a great deal of late-medieval architecture. The openwork base of the clock is made from a somewhat less florid design, but one is still less than eager to pick up the clock either by the stem or the base. The design of the base bears close comparison with those of earlier designs for drinking vessels attributed to Zündt and published in 1551 with the title *Insigne ac Planè Novum Opus Cratero Graphicum*.[7] Several of these vessels are embellished with freestanding figures of satyrs or partially human figures that are comparable to the ones found on the bottom of the stem and on the base of the Museum's clock. The ornament that appears on the side (or band) of the clock, while adhering to the grotesque vocabulary, is somewhat less crowded and more restrained in the depth of its cast relief. This ornamentation is derived directly from an engraving believed to have appeared in 1550 by Cornelis Bos (ca. 1510–1556), the Dutch designer of grotesque ornament[8] and part of a series of prints combining such ornaments with three-dimensional strapwork (fig. 17).

From evidence provided by the regulations recorded in 1563, when clockmaking in Nürnberg ceased to be a free trade, candidates for admission to the newly created company of clockmakers were required not only to make the movement of the clock but also to design the case. These case-design patterns would then be carved in wood by a wood-carving specialist, thereby facilitating the models for eventual casting in metal. It is not certain that a master clockmaker was always expected to provide an original design for his clockcases. The regulations from 1563 show that the clockmaker and the wood-carver were separate individuals, and the former, not the latter, might expect to retain the wooden patterns as his property.

In addition, the Museum's clock has been identified as one in a group of clocks made in Nürnberg during this time. Most of these clocks are signed by an as-yet-unidentified clockmaker with the initials "C.R."[9] This group includes a so-called Metzger-type table clock now in the Museo Galileo/ Istituto e Museo di Storia della Scienza, Florence,[10] and a mirror clock now in the Landesmuseum Württemberg, Stuttgart.[11] The Museum's clock is not signed, which is probably due to the fact that the cover for the back of the movement is a replacement of the original. Nürnberg clockmakers often signed their drum-shaped clocks on the bottom of the case in a location comparable to that of the missing cover for the back of the Museum's clock, which may explain its lack of a punchmark or signature.

The clock has had an eventful, if not entirely happy, existence. A short pendulum with an anchor-shaped weight has been substituted for the original balance. Probably around the same time as this substitution, the clock was turned into a simple timepiece—all of the underdial motion work for the astrolabe and the calendar is now missing, as are the bells for both the hour- and quarter-striking mechanisms. The hand for the sun has been shortened, and the hand for the moon is missing, as is a pointer to mark the day on the revolving calendar and probably one for the solar cycle. The clock is likely to have had a later minute hand too. The disk for setting the alarm is a late replacement, and it has been immobilized with solder; the finial above the alarm is most likely even later in date. Finally, a large crack near the base of the stem has been repaired with little effort to disguise the work.

Nothing is known of the clock's provenance before J. Pierpont Morgan acquired it. Yet it remains one of the earliest survivors of a type of clock that was in vogue in Germany for nearly a hundred years, and its case is a particularly exuberant example of a distinctive type of metalwork produced in Nürnberg in the second half of the sixteenth century. CV / JHL

1 See Price 1955, pp. 810, 814; Landes 1983, pp. 53–58, 402–3, nn. 4–8. See also North 1975, pp. 383, 385; Turner 1985, pp. 1–10; J. Evans 1998, pp. 141–55.
2 Leopold 1974, pp. 101–3. See also Vincent and Chandler 1969, pp. 381–82.
3 Lloyd and Drover 1955, p. 111.
4 See Warncke 1979, vol. 2, pp. 64–65, nos. 423–31.
5 Martin Angerer in *Wenzel Jamnitzer* 1985, p. 372. See also J. C. Smith 1983, p. 270; O'Dell-Franke 1996.
6 Hayward 1975, p. 67. The title of Hayward's article is somewhat misleading as the models are without doubt intended for the sides of more than one clock. See also Leopold 2002, p. 524, n. 39.
7 See Angerer in *Wenzel Jamnitzer* 1985, pp. 372 and 373, no. 372, with a discussion of the attribution to Zündt. See also Warncke 1979, vol. 2, p. 61, no. 388.
8 Berliner and Egger 1981, vol. 1, p. 67, no. 636, and vol. 2, ill. no. 636.
9 Leopold 2002, pp. 522, 524–25 and n. 38.
10 Ibid., p. 522, and p. 521, fig. 21.
11 Ibid., p. 525 and n. 41, and p. 523, fig. 23.

3. Watch

FLEMISH (ANTWERP OR POSSIBLY GHENT), 1571
1⅞ × 1¼ × ⅞ in. (4.8 × 3.2 × 2.2 cm)
Height of back plate: 1⅝ in. (4.1 cm)
Gift of J. Pierpont Morgan, 1917
17.190.1548

CASE AND DIAL: gilded brass
MOVEMENT: gilded brass and polished steel, signed WA conjoined (unidentified maker)
ARMS: three martlets, 2 and 1 between L and S (unidentified owner)

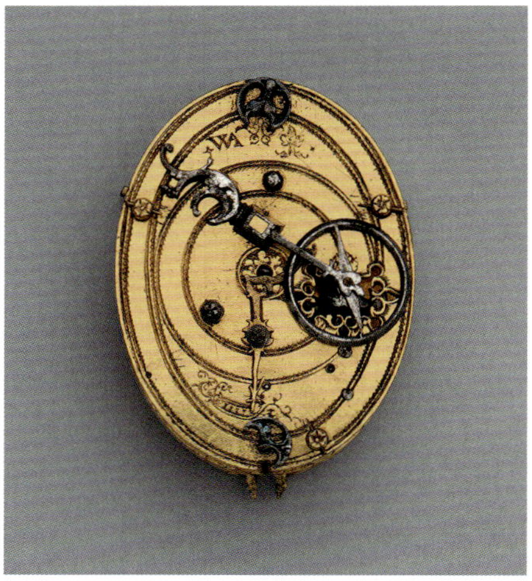

Back plate of the movement with initials of the watchmaker

left: *View of the back cover of the case*
right: *View of the dial and the movement*

DURING THE LATE MIDDLE AGES AND THE PERIOD THAT immediately followed, the Low Countries were a patchwork of independent territories. As early as the fourteenth century, turret clocks, or large, iron-framed structures created for use in churches and public buildings, are recorded to have existed in the southern parts of the Low Countries (modern Belgium and the southern Netherlands).[1] Small clocks for domestic use were also made there, but relatively little is known about watchmaking in this region before the late sixteenth century. During the sixteenth century, as part of the Habsburg Empire, the region enjoyed great prosperity under the regencies of two successive Habsburg archduchesses: Margaret of Austria, Duchess of Savoy and regent of the Netherlands (1480–1530), whose court, famed for its luxury, was centered at Mechelen (Malines), a town halfway between Brussels and Antwerp; and Mary of Hungary, regent of the Netherlands (1505–1558), whose palace was in Binche, the ancient fortified town that was located south of Brussels but later destroyed by the French. Under the rule of these two archduchesses, the city of Antwerp, located on the Schelde River and easily navigable to the North Sea and to the Atlantic beyond, permitted a thriving maritime trade with the New World, as well as with the traditional ports of the Old World. Trade required adequate provisions for credit and for other financial arrangements,[2] and while Antwerp's Nieuwe Beurs (new exchange) opened in 1531, the Fuggers of Augsburg had already set up a branch of their banking system in Antwerp in 1510, helping to finance the city as a major center of commerce and the arts. Brugge and Ghent, prosperous throughout the late Middle Ages, continued to flourish as well. Ghent, especially, is believed to have rivaled Antwerp in its remarkable number of resident clockmakers, followed at some distance by Brussels and Louvain (Leuven).[3]

The increasing spread of Protestantism and Catholic reaction was followed by the Protestant revolt against the Spanish Habsburg King Philip II (1527–1598) and the so-called Iconoclastic Fury. Fernando Álvarez de Toledo, the Third Duke of Alba (1507–1582) and King Philip's representative in the Low Countries after 1566, instituted a veritable reign of terror, and the Flemish region was not wholly pacified until the appointment of Alexander Farnese, the Duke of Parma (1545–1592) in 1578, who took control of Ghent and later Antwerp in 1585. As a result, many Protestants fled to England, the Dutch United Provinces, and Germany during this period. Among those who immigrated to England were John and Nicholas Vallin, makers of some of the more remarkable clocks and watches of the late sixteenth century (see entry 6 in this volume).[4] By the early seventeenth century, the Low Countries again became a battleground, pitting the Spanish Habsburgs against the French, the English, and the Dutch United Provinces.

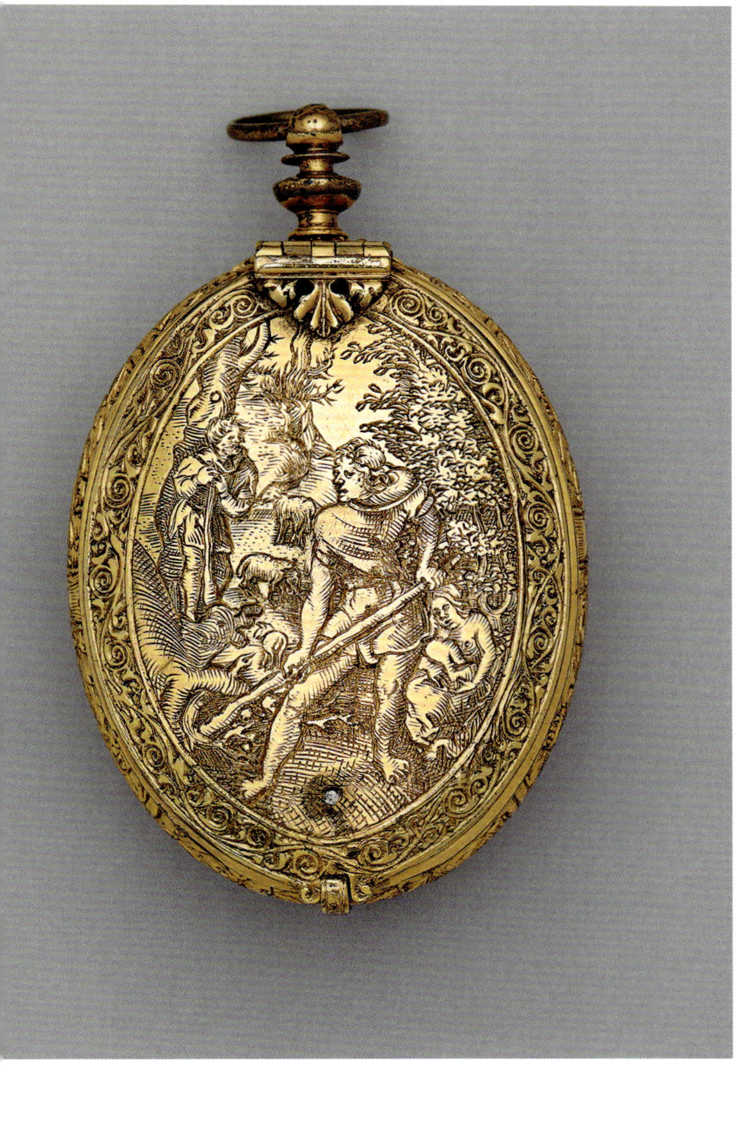

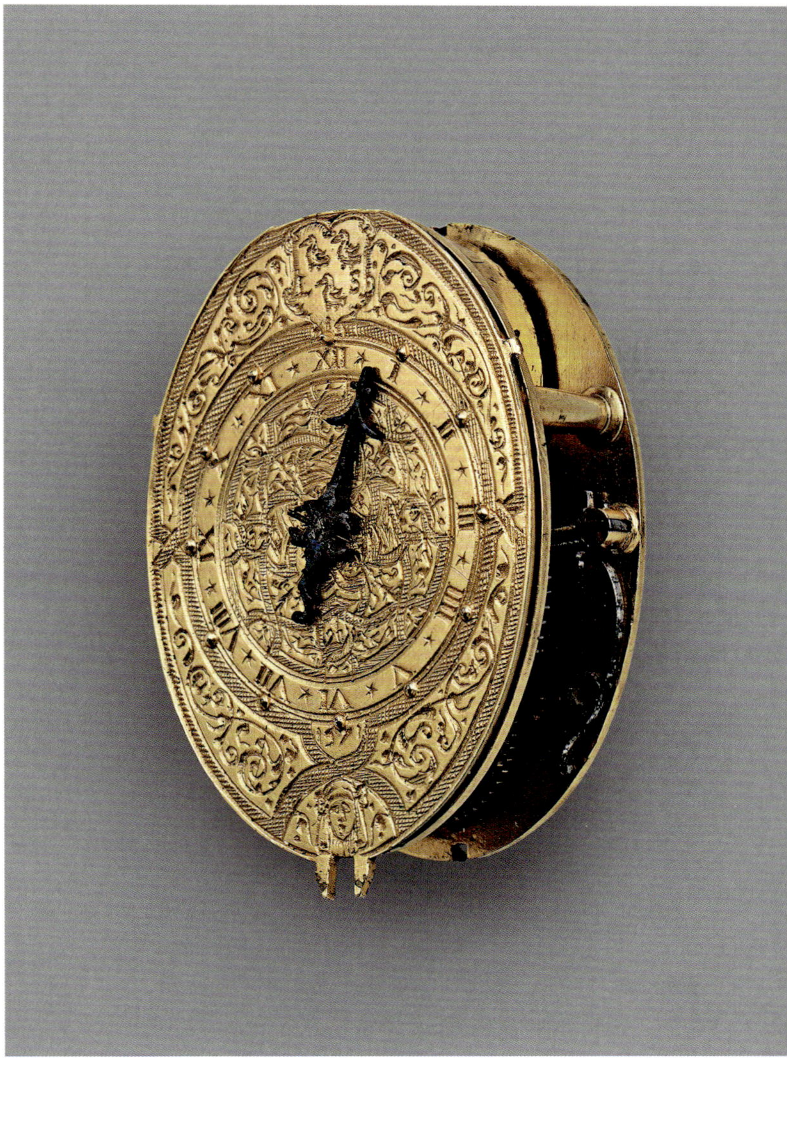

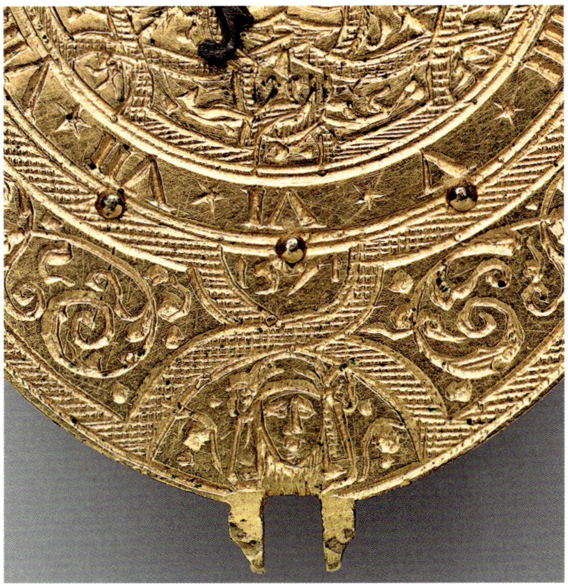

Detail of the dial showing the date

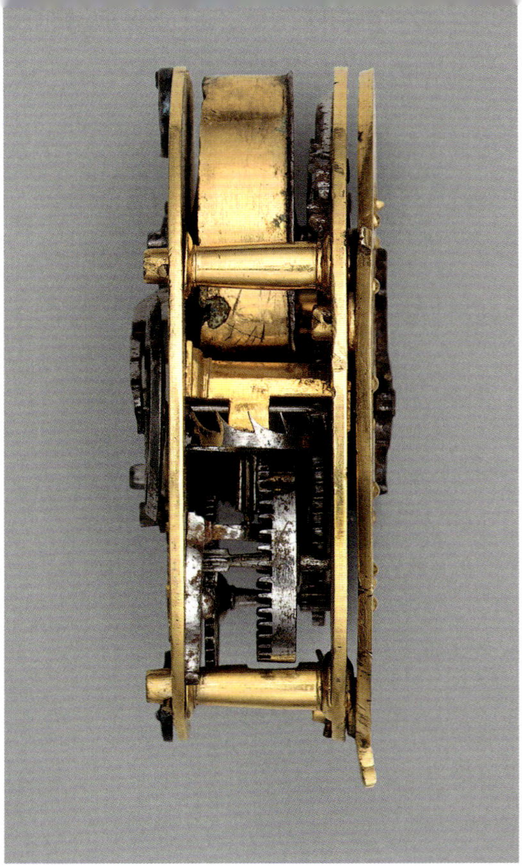

Side view of the movement

The devastation left by the revolt, war, and the periodic destruction of the Flemish economy probably accounts for the fact that so little sixteenth-century Flemish horology has survived. Records of clockmakers and watchmakers, too, have vanished,[5] but something of their reputation can be recovered from remarks by contemporaneous authors. For example, the Englishman William Cunningham recommended in 1559 the usefulness for navigation of "watches such as are brought from Flanders" that could be bought in London outside the Temple Bar;[6] and the Italian Lodovico Guicciardini authored a guide to the Low Countries in 1581 that cited the Flemish region as famed for the production of sea compasses and horological items.[7]

Little is known about the maker whose mark was "WA," except what is inferred from the surviving timepieces he produced, which are limited to two: a weight-driven chamber clock with an alarm mechanism that was formerly in the Time Museum in Rockford, Illinois (fig. 18),[8] and the spring-driven watch that appears in this entry. Both lack town marks and are signed with only the maker's initials. The case of the chamber clock does, however, bear a number of inscriptions in Flemish, as well as engravings of the biblical scenes of David with the Head of Goliath and Judith with the Head of Holofernes on its sides. The dial of the watch is engraved with the year 1571.

In a Sotheby's sale of 2002, the chamber clock was described as "probably Flemish."[9] Two of the most recent publications by historians of Belgian and Flemish horology have accepted Antwerp as the probable place of its origin.[10] Neither author apparently knew of the existence of the Metropolitan Museum's watch, which, after all, had been published in the 1912 catalogue of J. Pierpont Morgan's watches as the work of the English clockmaker William Anthony, who was active about 1525.[11] One of these publications included a list of names of clockmakers and scientific instrument makers, but the only entry in the list that could reasonably refer to a "WA" was one for Walter (Gualterus) Arsenius (recorded 1554–80),[12] a member of a prominent family of astrolabe makers working in Antwerp in the mid-sixteenth century. Arsenius is a most improbable maker of the Museum's watch,

fig. 18 *Clockmaker with the initials WA (unidentified). Weight-Driven Chamber Clock with Alarm, Flemish (Antwerp or possibly Ghent), ca. 1571. Formerly Time Museum, Rockford, Illinois*

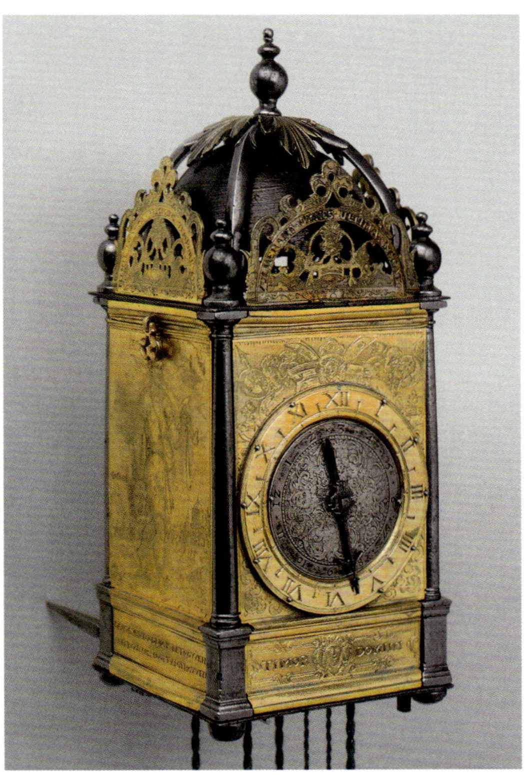

but the attribution of the clock, and by extension the watch, to Antwerp seems likely to be correct.

The watch is oval, as are most of the surviving watches of this period made either in the Low Countries or by Flemish émigrés working elsewhere. Despite several features that tie it to sixteenth-century watchmaking practices, however, it is remarkably more forward looking than the iron-plated, drum-shaped watches and the spherical-cased watches made by the Germans and French about the middle of the century.[13] It is, in fact, quite early for an oval watch to have been made anywhere.[14]

The movement consists of two oval plates of gilded brass that are held apart by three cylindrical pillars decorated with tiny floral designs at the ends, which are pinned to the back plate. It contains three polished-steel wheels that end in a verge escapement with a polished-steel escape wheel and a balance wheel regulated by a hog's-bristle device with a decorative pointer for adjustments to the regulation. The large mainspring is encased in a brass barrel with steel caps and set up by a steel bow-and-arrow ratchet system located on the interior side of the top plate of the watch. The mainspring is connected by a gut line (now missing) to a fusee made of ten turns, which gives a duration of around twelve hours before needing to be rewound.

The back plate is chased with double circles within double ovals and with a central rosette. Openwork tripartite designs decorate the opening for the balance staff. The cock of the balance is a primitive shaft that is pinned to a stud on the back plate at one end. At the other end, a blued-steel fleur-de-lis secures the end of the balance staff. The tail of the cock ends in a flourish of scrolls made of chiseled steel, and at the top and bottom of the plate, revolving latches of chiseled and blued steel secure the movement inside the case. Like the Vallin watch also in the Museum's collection (see entry 6 in this volume), the winding square of the mainspring of this watch is finished on the end by a tiny ornamental cross. The initials "WA" appear below and to the right of the top latch, and ornamental scrolls accompany both the maker's initials and the scale for adjusting the hog's bristle.

The dial, a separate plate of cast and gilded brass, is attached to the top plate of the watch by means of three pinned-on feet. It has a central chapter of hours (I–XII) with star markings for the half hours and touch pins for telling the time in darkness. An armorial shield representing that of the original owner appears above the chapter, and the year 1571 and a decorative human head appear below. All these elements are framed by strapwork that also encloses areas of arabesque ornament. Inside the chapter of hours, additional strapwork completes a design that employs an ornamental vocabulary comparable, for example, to that found a few years earlier in the borders of illustrations for several editions of Ovid's *Metamorphoses*, designed by Bernard Salomon (1505/10–ca. 1568) and published in Lyon in 1557 by Jean de Tournes (1504–1564).[15] The single hand made of elaborately sculptured and blued steel contrasts sharply with the bright gold of the dial.

The case, into which the movement fits snugly, consists of a cast oval with decorated moldings and two hinged covers. Both covers have decorative borders that frame the high-quality engravings, unusual for

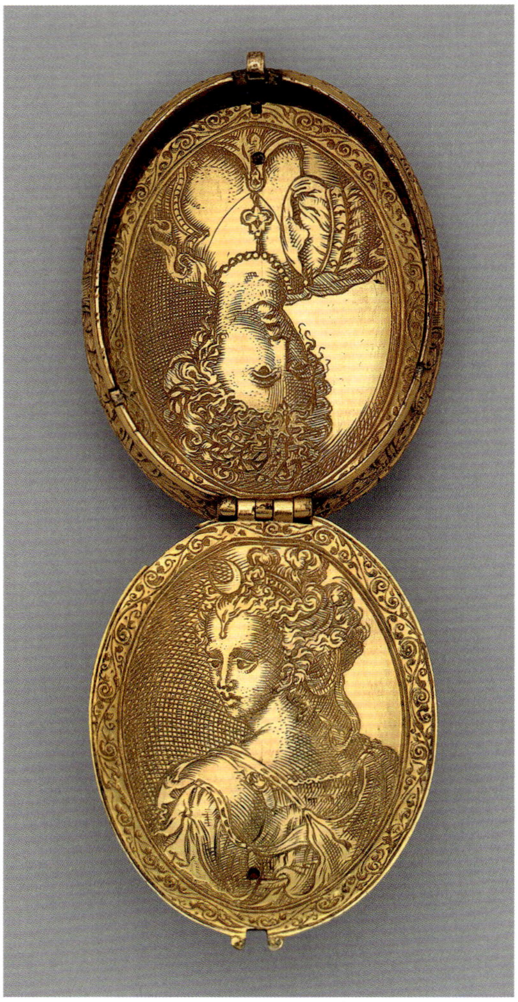

The case open to show the interiors of the front and back covers

watchcases, but not so surprising if the origin of the watch is accepted as Antwerp, well known for its publishers of prints and book illustrations. The subjects of the engravings on the Museum's watchcase do not immediately present a coherent narrative in the same manner as the engravings on the clock. The scene on the exterior side of the cover for the dial of the watch is a close copy of a print by the German-born painter and engraver Jacob Binck (ca. 1494/1500–1569), who is known to have been working in Antwerp in 1549 and 1552. The print was later given the descriptive title by F. W. H. Hollstein of *A Roman Soldier Presenting Grapes to a Nude Woman*,[16] but it may have had an allegorical meaning as well. The exterior side of the cover for the back of the movement depicts Adam in a forest digging the earth with a spade. Eve is seated beside him, and in the distance, a shepherd tends sheep. No precise printed model for the image has been found, but a scene of comparable activity titled *Adam at Work After the Fall* appears in an engraving dated 1583 and published by Johannes Sadeler I (1550–ca. 1600), which is based on a design by the prolific sixteenth-century Antwerp painter and draftsman Maarten de Vos the Elder (1532–1603),[17] therefore permitting identification of the subject on the watchcase.

The reverse side of each of the two covers presents bust-length engravings of handsome ladies. The woman who appears on the interior of the back cover has an elaborate coiffure and wears a jewel hanging from a chain around her neck, which calls attention to her plump bosom exposed by a low-cut bodice; the woman who appears on the interior image of the cover for the dial wears a more modest costume but has a more elaborate coiffure with a small crescent moon on her forehead. The moon, ordinarily associated with the Roman goddess Diana, may be associated here instead with the woman in an allegory of the spiritual marriage by Benito Arias Montano (1527–1598), titled the *Divinarum Nuptiarum Conventa et Acta* (1573), in which she is instructed in the virtues befitting the bride of Christ. An edition of the

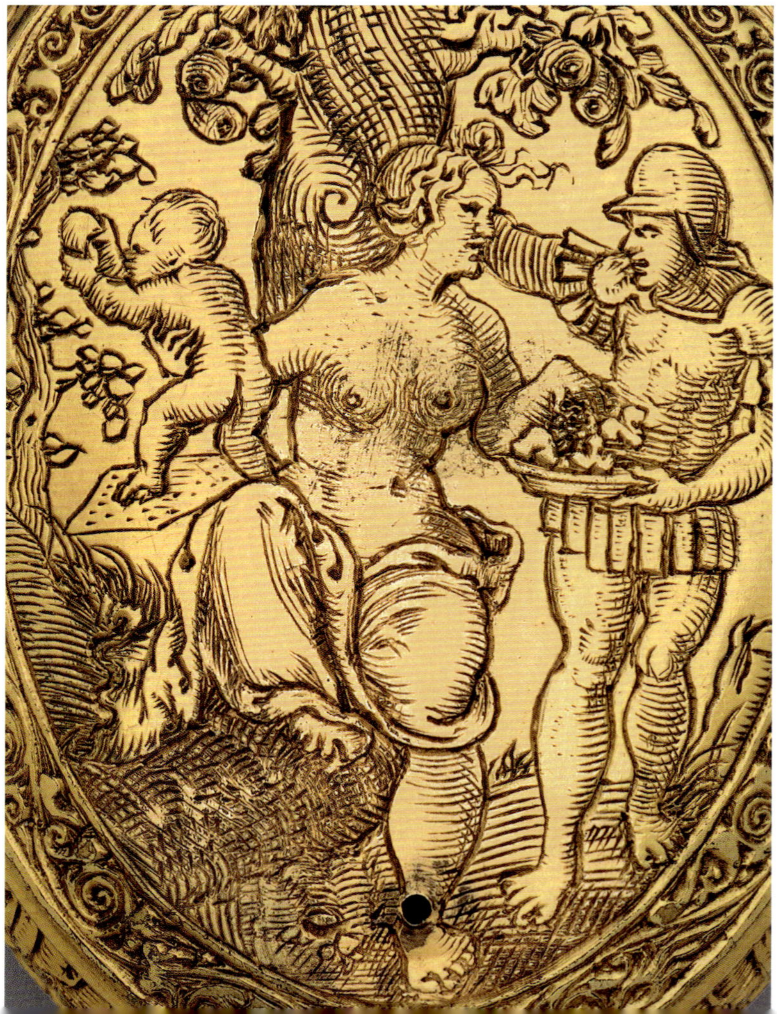

Detail of front cover

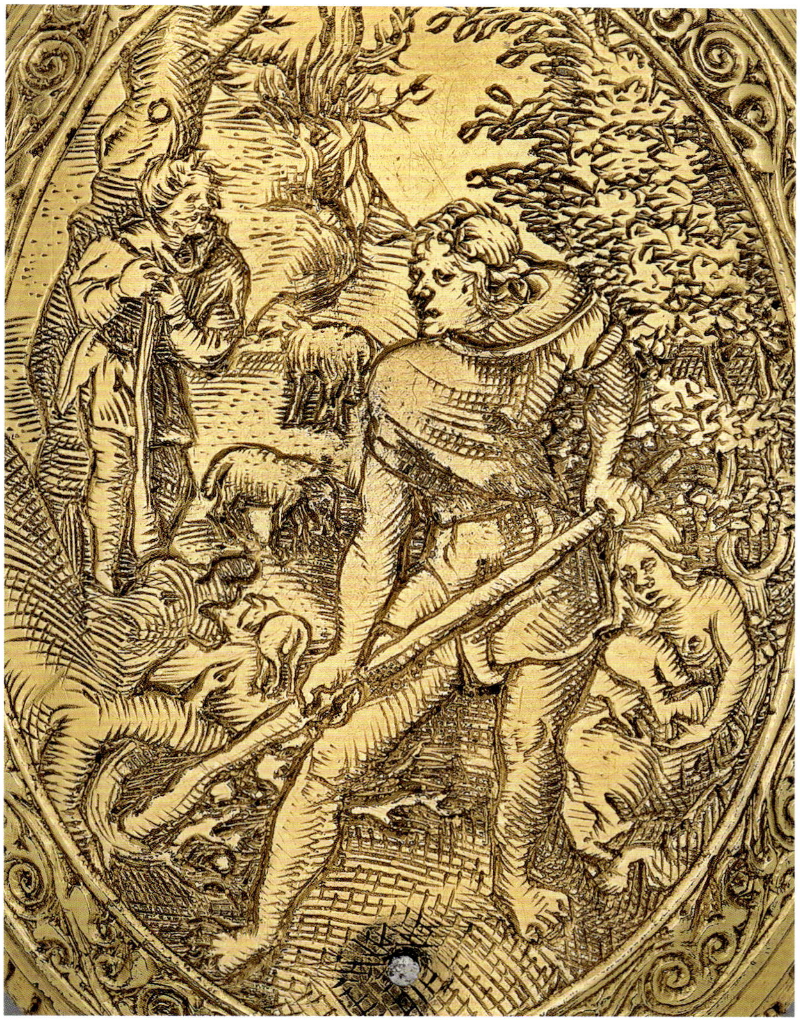

Detail of back cover

allegory, published in Antwerp about the same time by Philips Galle (1537–1612) with illustrations by Gerard van Groeningen (active in Antwerp 1561–76) and Jan (Johannes) Wierix (ca. 1549–ca. 1618), shows the prospective spouse as a young woman with a small crescent moon on her forehead.[18] The meaning of the woman wearing the jewel in her décolletage is not immediately apparent, but it seems to have nothing to do with spirituality. Perhaps one of them was truly meant to portray the moon goddess, or perhaps they are simply two attractive women, but the choice of the subjects on the watchcase cries out for deeper interpretation.

Some of the steel parts of the movement have areas of rust that are not now active, and some of the bluing on others has been lost. The latch on the lower end of the back plate is now incomplete. The balance wheel and verge are possible replacements, but both movement and case are in remarkably good condition. Nothing is known of the provenance of the watch before J. Pierpont Morgan acquired it from Carl H. Marfels of Frankfurt am Main and Berlin.[19] CV / JHL

1 For the list of fourteenth-century turret clocks in cities that are now in Belgium, see Fraiture 2009, pp. 16, 338.
2 Voet 1993, pp. 15–17.
3 Fraiture 2002, p. 158.
4 For the carillon clock in the British Museum, London (inv. no. CAI-2139), see Thompson 2004, pp. 56–57.
5 See de Caluwé 2008, pp. 68–70.
6 Cunningham 1559, quoted in Waters 1958, p. 58.
7 Guicciardini 1581.
8 *Time: The Greatest Innovator* 1986, p. 94; Sotheby's 2002, pp. 120–21, no. 90, ill.
9 Sotheby's 2002, p. 120.
10 See de Caluwé 2008, p. 66, and p. 63, ill. no. 4; Fraiture 2002, p. 281.
11 Williamson 1912, pp. 121–22, no. 125. Williamson seems to have ignored the date on the watch, to say nothing of its style.
12 Fraiture 2002, p. 169.
13 For examples of the two forms, see Maurice 1976, vol. 2, pp. 59–60, nos. 59, 60, and figs. 59, 60, and pp. 60–61, nos. 429–36, and figs. 429–36; Cardinal 1989, pp. 111–14.
14 Maurice illustrated an oval watch hanging from a chain around the neck of a man in a portrait said to date from 1567 and now in the Germanisches Nationalmuseum Nürnberg. See Maurice 1976, vol. 2, p. 60, no. 427, and fig. 427.
15 Mortimer 1964, pp. 505, 506, nos. 403, 404.
16 Hollstein, *German*, 1954–2014, vol. 4 (1957), p. 67, no. 138.
17 Hollstein, *Dutch and Flemish*, 1949–2010, vol. 44 (1996), p. 14, no. 28/II, and vol. 45 (1995), p. 14, pl. 28/II.
18 Schuckman and Luijten 1997, pt. 2, pp. 69–73, and p. 76, pls. 290/I, 291/I, p. 81, pl. 301/I, p. 82, pls. 302/I and 303/I, and p. 83, pl. 304/I.
19 Williamson 1912, p. 121.

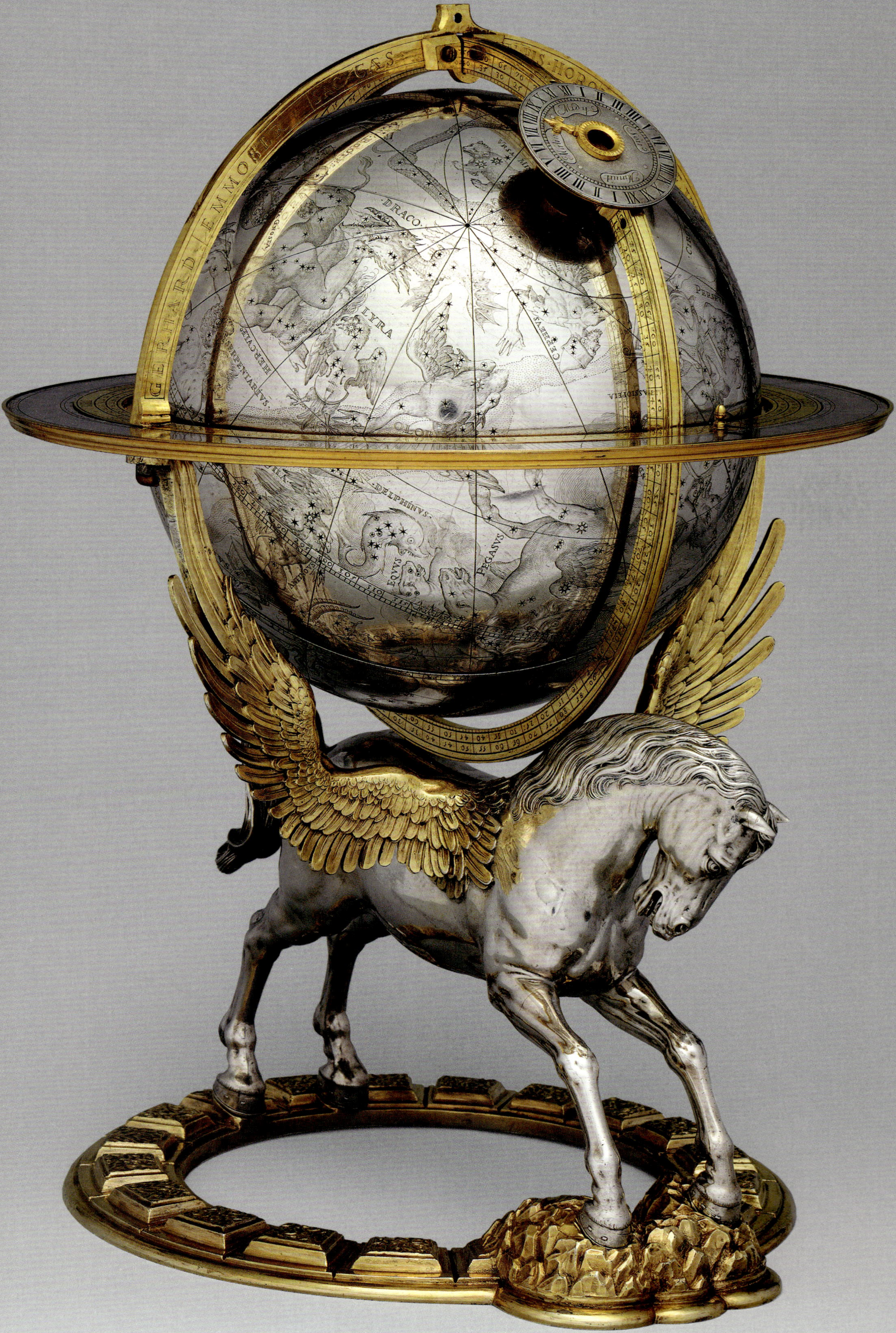
DRACO
LYRA
DELPHINUS
PEGASUS

4. Celestial Globe with Clockwork

AUSTRIAN (VIENNA), 1579

10¾ × 8 × 7½ in. (27.3 × 20.3 × 19.1 cm)
Diam. of globe: 5⁷⁄₁₆ in. (13.9 cm)
Gift of J. Pierpont Morgan, 1917
17.190.636

CASE: silver, partly gilded, and gilded brass, signed (on semicircle mounted at right angles to meridian ring): GERHARD / EMMOSER • / SAC • CÆS • MEIS • HOROLOGIARIUS • F • VIENNÆ• A • 1579 (Gerhard Emmoser Sacrae Caesareae Maiestatis Horologiarius Fecit Viennae Anno 1579) [Gerhard Emmoser, German, active 1556–84]
MOVEMENT: brass and steel

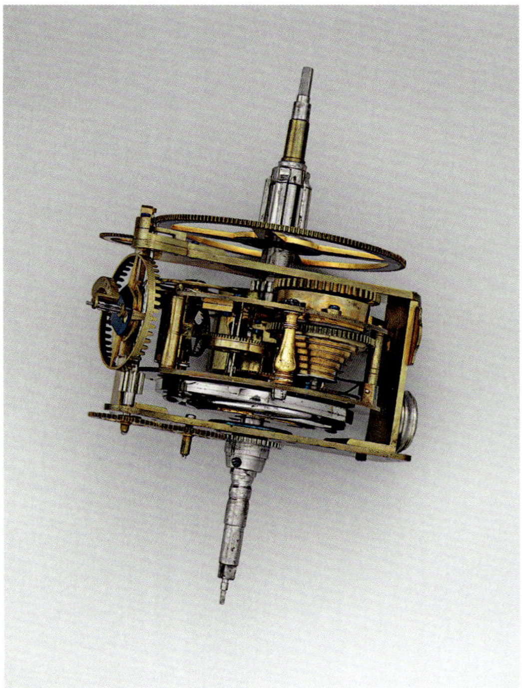

Movement

OF THE TWO TYPES OF GLOBES, THE TERRESTRIAL AND THE celestial, the celestial globe, which demonstrates the apparent motion of the heavens, is by far the more complex and challenging to produce. This richly ornamented clock is immediately recognizable as a *Kunstkammer* piece, an object that has become practically a symbol of itself. We know, in fact, that this globe supported by a figure of Pegasus formed part of the fabulous collection of the Holy Roman Emperor Rudolf II (1552–1612),[1] and it may have held a deeply personal meaning for him.

The silver globe is engraved with fifty-two constellations, including their names and their stars from the first through the sixth magnitudes. (The forms of the stars are differentiated according to their sizes or magnitudes.) The constellations consist of the forty-eight that are listed by the leading classical astronomer Claudius Ptolemy in his *Almagest* (ca. 150), plus Antinous and Cincinnus in the northern hemisphere and Arsinoë in the southern hemisphere.[2] The meridian ring is calibrated in one-degree divisions, and they are numbered (5–90 degrees) from both the equator to the poles and from the poles to the equator; the quadrants of the horizon ring are similarly divided and numbered. The semicircular ring is attached at right angles to the meridian ring and divided and numbered (7–12) for determining the astrological houses.

The sphere divides along the ecliptic line and encloses a circular-plated brass movement that rotates the sphere once every sidereal day, while moving a sun image along its yearly path through the ecliptic. The hour, expressed in mean solar time, is indicated on a dial attached to the meridian ring at the top of the polar axis of the sphere, and the day of the year is indicated on a calendar that rotates within the instrument's horizon ring. The spring-driven movement is fixed on the plane of the polar axis but has been extensively repaired and renewed. The movement drove a revolving cage with attached gearing that originally propelled both the sphere and the sun. (The connection between the cage and the sphere with its sun is now missing.) The revolving cage seems to have been the original contribution of clockmaker Gerhard Emmoser (active 1556–84) to the technology of clockwork-driven globes.[3]

In 1566 Emmoser was appointed clockmaker to the Holy Roman Emperor Maximilian II (1527–1576), and subsequently reappointed by Maximilian's son and successor Rudolf II, thereby keeping the title until his death in 1584. Nothing definite is known of Emmoser before 1556, at which time Prince Ottheinrich of Pfalz-Neuburg (1502–1559) sent him to Tübingen, Germany, to help carry out the ambitious ideas that mathematician Philip Imser (active 1531–62, died probably 1570) had proposed in regard to the construction of a planetary clock

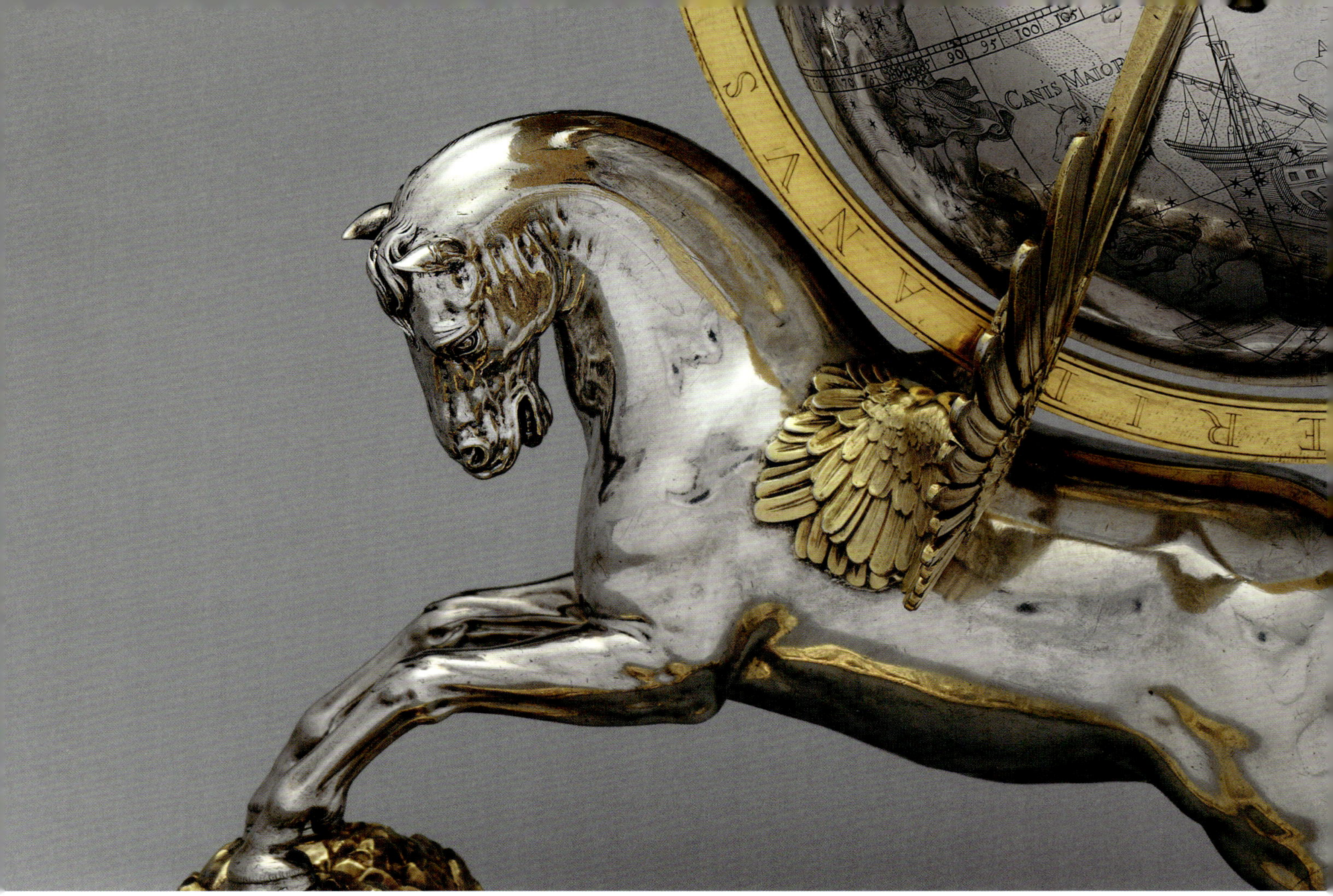

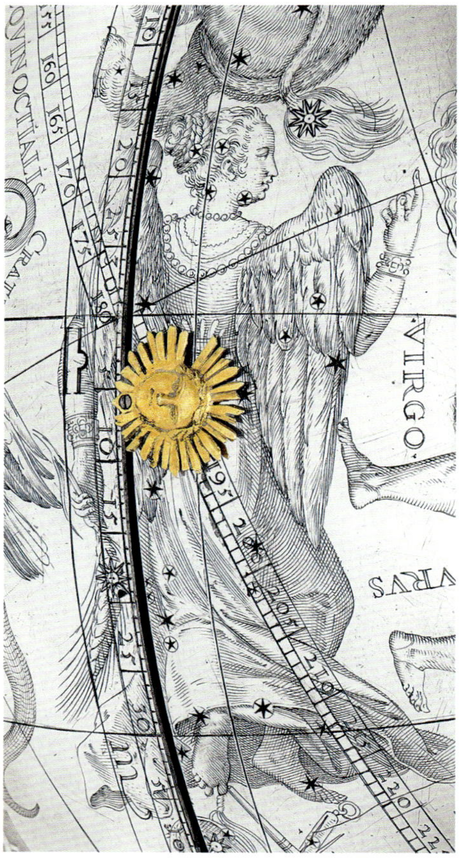

Detail of the engraved sphere, showing the constellation Virgo and the image of the sun

surmounted by a clockwork-driven celestial sphere.[4] This remarkable clock survives in the collection of the Technisches Museum für Industrie und Gewerbe, Vienna. Unfortunately, Prince Ottheinrich died before the clock was completed, and it was ultimately sold to Emperor Ferdinand I (1503–1564), who installed Emmoser the clockmaker in the imperial city of Augsburg in 1563, then a major center for European clockmaking. Before Emmoser could finish the masterpiece clock, which was one of the requirements for admission to the Augsburg guild, Emperor Ferdinand died, and his successor, Maximilian II, called the clockmaker back to Vienna.[5]

Emmoser was thus imperial clockmaker when Landgraf Wilhelm IV of Hessen-Kassel (1532–1592) sent his clockmaker, Hans Bucher, to the imperial court with a gift for the emperor of a clockwork-driven celestial globe, which was designed by Eberhard Baldewein (ca. 1525–1593) and completed by Bucher in 1574. This globe has been identified with another globe, now greatly altered, formerly in the Kunsthistorisches Museum, Vienna, and it has been convincingly demonstrated that Emmoser's globe, although made in the imperial workshop, is, in fact, similar in so many ways that it must be considered part of the line of clockwork-driven globes that were developed at Kassel in conjunction with the astronomical activities at the Landgraf's observatory.[6]

No record of the commission for the globe has been found, but it has been identified from a description recorded in the inventory of the Prague Kunstkammer of Emperor Rudolf II from 1607 to 1611.[7] By 1652, the globe was in the collection of Queen Christina of Sweden.[8] More than a century later, on April 20, 1770, it reappeared in Paris for the sale of the collection of Avocat Fortier, *conseiller du Roi*.[9] An inscription inside the globe dated May 15, 1781, states that a clockmaker, Gautrin (probably Pierre-Laurent Gautrin [died 1823]), repaired the globe in 1767 for a Monsieur Delacronière, *conseiller en la cour des aydes de Paris*. It was probably Gautrin who made most of the changes to the movement and to the exterior of the globe.

Both the goldsmith who made the extraordinary figure of the winged horse and the engraver of the constellations, whose difficult and exacting work was so precisely executed, remain anonymous. Here it is Pegasus, the winged horse of of classical mythology, who supports the celestial sphere rather than the usual demigod Atlas. After many years of speculation, it is now possible to trace the symbolism of the globe to Renaissance Neoplatonism, specifically to the preface to *Arithmetic* (1536) by the German reformer Philip Melanchthon (1497–1560). A key figure in the Lutheran Reformation and rector for the University of Wittenberg, Germany, Melanchthon proposed that "Those who busy themselves with studies and strive for complete knowledge should see clearly that there is no access to the science of celestial things except through arithmetic and geometry."[10] Based on a metaphor in Plato's *Phaedrus* (360 B.C.), Melanchthon's text elaborated on the idea that

> the wings of the human mind are arithmetic and geometry. . . . Carried up to heaven by their help, you will be able to traverse with your eyes the entire nature of things, discern the intervals and boundaries of the greatest bodies, see the fateful meetings of the stars, and then understand the causes of the greatest things that happen in the life of man. . . . For I know that you are certainly convinced that the science of celestial things has great dignity and usefulness.[11]

The idea that celestial things (i.e., the science of astronomy) must be supported on the wings of arithmetic and geometry was current at the imperial court, as documented by surviving comments of two court mathematicians, both appointed by Rudolf II: Nicolaus Raimarus Ursus (1551–1600) and Johannes Kepler (1571–1630).[12] Thus, the use of Pegasus, a creature from classical mythology, to render an abstraction concrete suggests that the globe was intended as a beautiful, perhaps even poetic, way of representing the metaphor.[13] CV / JHL

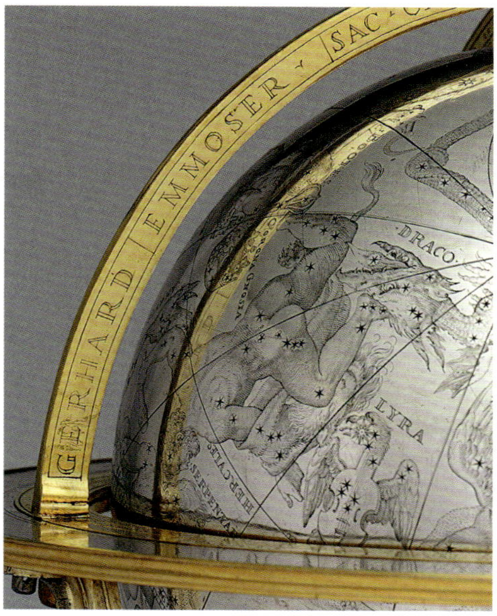

Detail of the semicircular mount for the globe with signature of the clockmaker

1 See *Prag um 1600* 1988; *Rudolf II and Prague* 1997.
2 Rosenfeld 1980, pp. 181–89.
3 See Leopold 1986, pp. 107–11, for an extended analysis of the movement.
4 See Chandler and Vincent 1980.
5 For a more extensive account of what is known about Emmoser, see ibid., pp. 111–13.
6 Leopold 1986, pp. 88–92; see also Vincent and Chandler 1989–90, p. 181, and p. 178, fig. 141.
7 Neumann 1966, pp. 264–65, n. 12; see also Bauer and Haupt 1976, p. 111, fol. 339v, no. 2158.
8 *Christina* 1966, p. 495, no. 1225, and pl. 85.
9 The authors are indebted to the late Jean-Nérée Ronfort for this information as well as for the identification of the globe in the sale of the collection of a Monsieur Daugny at the Hôtel des Commissaires-Priseurs, Paris, on Mar. 8, 1858. See Hôtel Drouot 1858, p. 17, no. 62.
10 Melanchthon 1999, p. 92. For the discovery by Volker R. Remmert of the preface to Melanchthon's *Arithmetic* as read at the University of Wittenberg in 1536 by Georg Joachim Rheticus (1514–1574), see Remmert 2009.
11 Melanchthon 1999, pp. 93–94.
12 Rosen 1986, pp. 30–44.
13 For further discussion of the globe and its meaning, see Vincent and Chandler 2011–12.

5. Table Clock with Traveling Case

BRITISH (LONDON), 1580–85

Clock: H. 3 in. (7.62 cm), Diam. 3½ in. (8.9 cm), Diam. of back plate 3¹⁄₁₆ in. (7.8 cm)

Traveling case: 4 × 10 in. (10.2 × 25.4 cm), H. of dial: 1¾ in. (4.4 cm), Diam. of back plate: 3½ in. (8.9 cm)

Gift of J. Pierpont Morgan, 1917

17.190.1514a, b

CASE: engraved, chased, and gilded brass

DIAL: silver

MOVEMENT: brass and steel, signed: BARTHOLMEW NVSAM [Bartholomew Newsam, recorded 1565, died 1587]

TRAVELING CASE: leather and brass, partly gilded

SOME OF THE EARLIEST MECHANICAL CLOCKS IN EUROPE WERE produced by English clockmakers. Church records document the existence of *horologia* in the late thirteenth century, which may or may not refer to mechanical clocks, but by 1322, it is known that Norwich Cathedral Priory had a new astronomical clock with accompanying automata that consisted of fifty-nine figures and a procession of (mechanical) monks.[1] In his *Tractatus Horologii Astronomici* (A Treatise on the Astronomical Clock) (1327–36), Richard of Wallingford (ca. 1292–1336) described an ambitious clock with a mechanically driven astrolabe, containing a moving sun, moon, and planets, made for the Abbey of Saint Albans, and which was reconstructed in the twentieth century using Wallingford's treatise.[2] The turret clock in Salisbury Cathedral (probably ca. 1386, although extensively rebuilt) and the clock from Wells Cathedral (1392–93) in the Science Museum, London, both large, iron-framed, weight-driven striking clocks, are fourteenth-century survivals, now believed to be the work of Flemish clockmakers.[3]

The introduction of the spring to fifteenth-century horological technology and the attendant changes to clockmaking do not seem to have interested English clockmakers, and as late as the turn of the seventeenth century, most small, spring-driven clocks and watches were made by émigrés. Many of the clockmakers were refugees from the Low Countries,[4] including Andrewe Noway (or Nawe) and Michael Nouen (or Noewen), the latter represented by a watch in the Metropolitan Museum's collection,[5] John Vallin and Nicholas Vallin, the latter the maker of an extraordinary enameled gold watch in the form of the ensign of the English Order of the Garter (see entry 6 in this volume).[6]

The earliest-known native-born English maker of small domestic clocks was Bartholomew Newsam (Nusam or Newsham). It is not certain where or when he was born, but John Newsam, probably a brother, who was also a clockmaker, lived in York. At the time of his death, Bartholomew owned lands and dwellings in the same area.[7] Records show that Bartholomew married Parnell Younge at the church of Saint Mary-le-Strand in London in September 1565.[8] Records from April of the same year show that he obtained from the Crown a thirty-year lease on

fig. 19 *Virgil Solis (German, 1514–1562). Frieze with Medallion with Bust of a Warrior and Arabesque Ornament, German, mid-16th century. Copperplate engraving and etching, 11⅜ × 65¾ in. (29 × 167 cm). MAK—Austrian Museum of Applied Arts/Contemporary Art, Vienna*

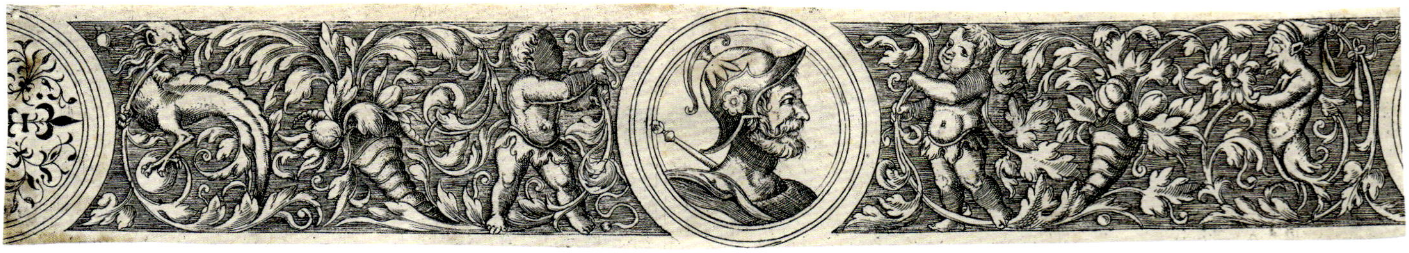

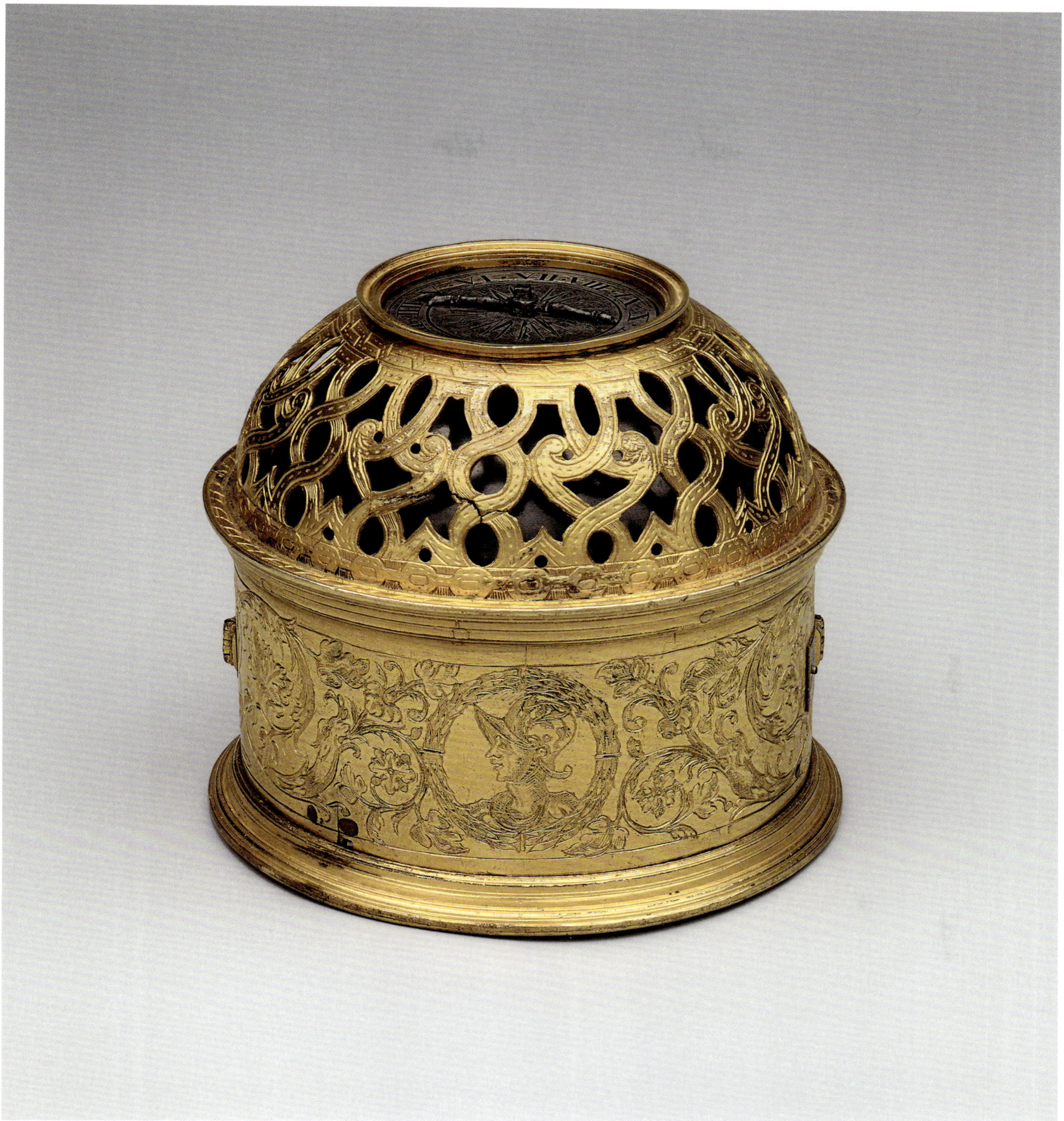

premises in the Strand,[9] which is presumably where he was living with his wife and four of their children when he made his will.[10] To judge from his bequests, he died a wealthy man.

As clockkeeper to Queen Elizabeth I (1533–1603) for at least part of the time during his residence in London, he was paid 32 shillings and 8 pence by the Queen's Privy Seal in 1583 for "mending of clockes' during the previous year."[11] A document from 1572 provides evidence that Newsam was to be granted the post of Clockmaker to Queen Elizabeth when it should become vacant.[12] The then-current office holder was the long-lived Nicholas Urseau (died 1590), and if we accept Adrian Finch's discovery of the date of Newsam's death as January 17, 1587, and burial on February 9 in Saint Mary-le-Strand, Urseau outlived Newsam.[13]

The cylindrical case of the Metropolitan Museum's table clock is made from engraved, chased and gilded brass with a profile molding that supports a gilded, pierced, and chased strapwork dome. On opposite sides of the case, there are hinged doors that open for viewing the position of the gut on the fusees of both the going and the striking train of the clock. A small silver dial with a chapter of hours marked I–XII and a single, sculptured, iron hand (neither original to the clock) are attached to the top of the dome and framed by another profile molding. The bottom of the case is friction fitted and framed by a third profile molding. The molding is pierced by two holes to permit winding and marked "S" and "M" (for "striking" and "movement"). It is signed on the exterior side, "BARTHOLMEW NVSAM," within a stylish strapwork-ornamented frame that hangs from a ribbon with tasseled ends. The side of the cylinder is ornamented with two roundels that depict, respectively, a helmeted warrior in profile and a longhaired female figure wearing a topknot. Both figures are encircled by wreaths of laurel leaves and flanked by plump foliate scrolls, which incorporate berries, flowers, and half-human, half-goat grotesques.

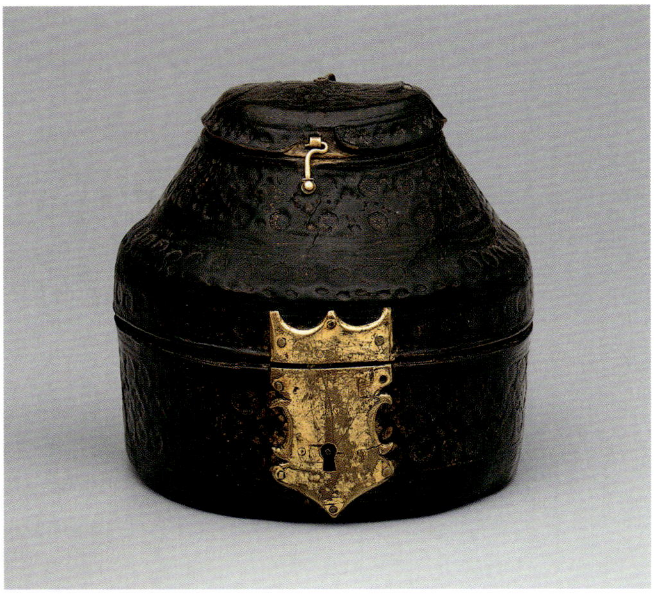

Leather traveling case

The spring-driven movement, with fusees cut to accommodate gut, consists of two circular-brass plates held apart by four turned-brass pillars pinned to the top plate, which extend through the bottom plate and end in ball feet. It has a going train made up of three wheels with a verge escapement regulated by a balance, and a striking train of four wheels that ends in a fly. The present count wheel permits the striking of the hours, one through twelve, by activating a hammer mounted inside the bell. It has a fusee of eighteen turns and a duration of not quite twenty-four hours. The going train has a going fusee of sixteen and one-half turns and a duration of slightly more than twenty-four hours.

At some point in its past the steel parts of the movement apparently rusted, and perhaps as early as the eighteenth century, a serious attempt to remedy the damage was undertaken. The arbors have been replaced, and they now have pinions of six leaves, but the clock is geared for pinions of five leaves. With the exception of the escape wheel, the contrate wheel in the going train, and the fly in the striking train, the remaining wheels, all of them brass, are apparently original to the clock. The steel verge, the balance, and also probably the balance cock have been replaced. The mainspring in the going train is old and slightly too big for its barrel, which indicates that it, too, is a replacement. The bell has been broken and repaired. The silver dial, now calibrated for twelve hours, replaces one that probably indicated the days of the week as well as the hours, and there is a new hour-wheel assembly. At one point the movement was attached to the case by two screws instead of the steel latches secured by *S*-shaped springs that are now employed to create a very French-like construction. Plugged holes in the side of the case indicate the former position of the screws.

The overall form of the case is also comparable to a series of French clocks believed to have been made during the last quarter of the sixteenth century.[14] Various details of the construction of the movement of the Museum's clock also suggest that Newsam may have been trained by a French clockmaker. A second table clock now in the British Museum, London,[15] one of the few clocks by Newsam known to survive, supports this supposition. Its movement is closely allied to a sixteenth-century French variety of clock in which the going and striking trains are laid out one above the other with the going train at the top just below the bell.

Unlike the French-influenced ornament engraved on the sides of the British Museum's clock, the band of ornament that encircles the Metropolitan Museum's clock bears a strong resemblance to ornament prints (fig. 19) by the Nürnberg goldsmith and engraver Virgil Solis (1514–1562).[16] The band of crisply engraved and chased ornament of the Museum's clock may, in fact, have been the product of a South German craftsman working in London. There is no name or signature to support the speculation, but it is known that foreign craftsmen, especially émigrés from the Low

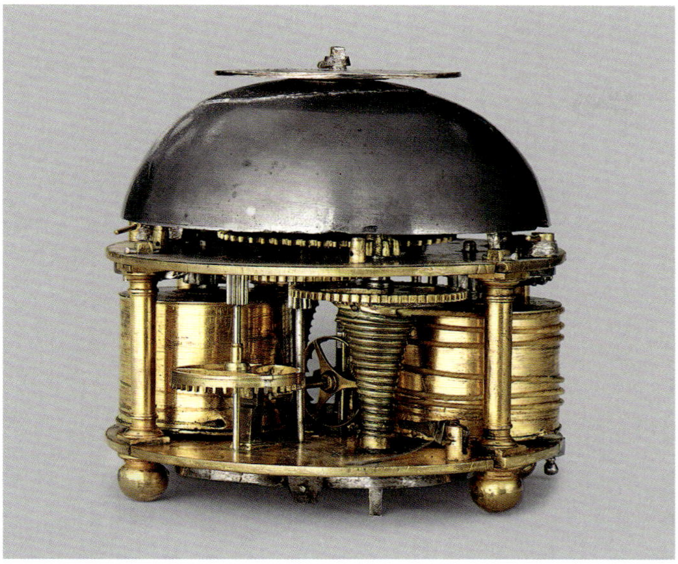

The movement with the bell and dial

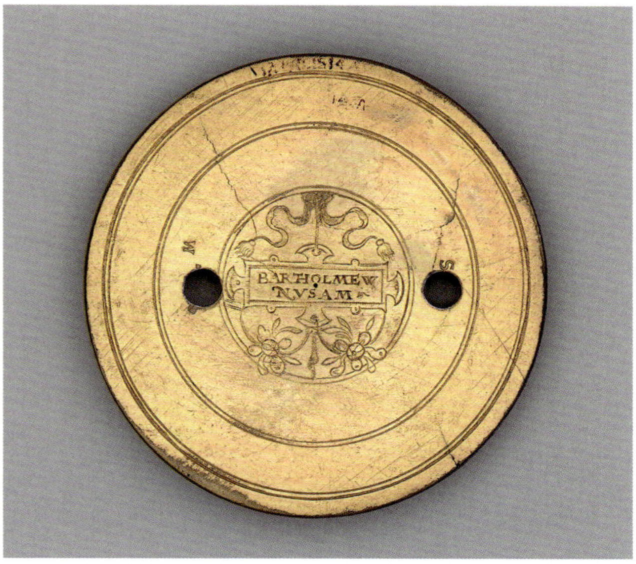

The bottom of the case with the signature of the clockmaker

Countries, as well as from France and Germany, found a ready reception for their talents among sixteenth-century London goldsmiths.[17] The design of plump foliate arabesques punctuated by portrait roundels was certainly not new to the English in any case, and the German artist Hans Holbein the Younger, who died in London in 1543, left a drawing for a gold cup and cover made for the marriage of King Henry VIII to Jane Seymour in 1536 in which a band of ornament around the waist of the cup prefigures the Solis designs.[18] Holbein's designs must also have had a lasting effect on English taste.

The strapwork of the dome of the Metropolitan Museum's clock is an unusual example of another older variety of ornament, one originating in the Low Countries in the 1540s, for example, in ornamental engravings by the Dutch artist Cornelis Bos (ca. 1510–1556). The style eventually lost its connection to the conceit of depicting and curling strips of leather (hence the designation "strapwork") to become the linear, almost abstract patterns found in the designs of printmakers and also on the dome of this clock.

The cylindrical case of boiled and molded leather (*cuir-bouilli*) with stamped ornament is most likely original to the clock and suggests that the timepiece was intended from the beginning to be used for traveling. The case opens at two levels, one about an inch and one half from the bottom and the second near the top. Both pieces are hinged. The bottom one, intended to be locked, has a gilded brass, shield-shaped keyhole escutcheon; the top one is secured at the front by a brass hook-and-eye that opens for easy access to the dial of the clock.

A printed label on the underside of the leather case identifies the object as number 141 in the Hilton Price Collection. Frederick George Hilton Price was the British banker who probably sold the table clock to J. Pierpont Morgan about the same time Morgan acquired Hilton Price's watch collection sometime before 1911. The clock and case are believed to have been owned earlier by W. Jerdone Braikenridge in Somerset, England. CV / JHL

1 Beeson 1971, pp. 15–17.
2 For a translation from the Latin, with commentary, see Richard of Wallingford 1976, vol. 1, pp. 441–526.
3 See Cipolla 1967, p. 51, who suggested that the makers of both clocks might have been foreign. For their probable Flemish origin, see Fraiture and Van Rompay 2011, p. 29.
4 For a succinct summary of a lecture by David Thompson on watchmakers working in sixteenth-century England, see Hutchinson 2011.
5 Acc. no. 17.190.1549. See Vincent and Leopold 2009.
6 See Leopold and Vincent 2000.
7 Portions of his will are cited in Britten 1982, p. 316; Jagger 1983, p. 13; Thompson 2004, p. 38.
8 Finch 2004, p. 677.
9 Jagger 1983, p. 13.
10 There is some disagreement about the date of the will. Finch has stated that Newsam's will is dated Jan. 7, 1587, but the will itself is dated Jan. 7, 1585, in the 29th year of the reign of Queen Elizabeth I (new style 1586, but not 1587). See Finch 2004, p. 678. Newsam's will, probated on Dec. 18, 1593, Neville Quire Numbers 48–96, Public Record Office, National Archives.
11 Finch 2004, p. 677; see also Britten 1982, p. 316.
12 Jagger 1983, p. 13.
13 Finch 2004, p. 678. Confusion may have arisen about the date because it took until 1593 for Newsam's will to be probated. See Ponsford 2008, p. 810.
14 For examples of the type, see Tardy 1981a, pp. 75–83.
15 Inv. no. 188812-1.126. See Thompson 2004, pp. 38–39.
16 O'Dell-Franke 1977, p. 160, nos. h 79, h 80, and pl. 99.
17 Glanville 1990, pp. 185–96.
18 Now in the collection of the Ashmolean Museum, Oxford, inv. no. WA1863.424. See ibid., p. 92, and p. 93, fig. 36; Schroder 2009, vol. 1, p. 62, and p. 63, fig. 20.

6. Watch in the Form of a Lesser George

BRITISH (LONDON), CA. 1600
1 7/16 × 15/16 in. (3.7 × 2.9 cm)
Gift of J. Pierpont Morgan, 1917
17.190.1475

CASE AND DIAL: gold, partly enameled
MOVEMENT: gilded brass and steel, signed: *N. Vallin* [Nicholas Vallin, Flemish, active in London ca. 1565–1603, recorded ca. 1590–1603]

MADE IN THE SHAPE OF THE ENSIGN OF THE ORDER OF THE GARTER and named after Saint George, this watch was the epitome of prestigious watches when it was made. Founded in the fourteenth century by the English King Edward III (1312–1377), the Order of the Garter still exists. Its knights are installed according to custom in the magnificent fifteenth-century chapel of Saint George at Windsor Castle, and the ceremony is presided over by Queen Elizabeth II. In his history of the order, court historian Elias Ashmole (1617–1692) lists as part of its insignia the Greater George, an elaborate pendant image of Saint George fighting a dragon, which is worn on a collar as part of full ceremonial dress; and the Lesser George, a simpler pendant that the knights were obliged to wear in daily dress. Ashmole describes the Lesser George as being

> for the most part made of pure Gold, curiously wrought by the hand of the Goldsmith, but we have seen divers of them exquisitely cut in Onix's, as also in Agats. . . . In this Jewel is St. George represented in a riding posture, encount[e]ring the Dragon with his drawn Sword. . . . This George is allowed to be enriched and garnished at the pleasure of him that wears it.[1]

Two historical references of a George incorporating a watch have so far come to light. The first watch appears in the inventory from 1587 of the jewels of Queen Elizabeth I,[2] and the second watch is found in an inventory from 1614 of the possessions of Henry Howard, Earl of Northampton (1540–1614).[3] The George watch in the Metropolitan Museum's collection is apparently the sole surviving example of this kind of watch.

The Museum's watchcase, made of gold and decorated with variously colored enamels, consists of an oval band with a pendant and two hinged covers. The front cover has a hinged gold bezel set with an oval plaque of rock crystal. The exterior side of the band has a representation of the garter (or symbol of the order) located between its two beaded borders, and includes the motto: "HONI.SOIT.QVI / MAL.Y.PENSE" (Evil be to him who thinks of it). The beaded borders carry traces of opaque blue enamel *en ronde-bosse*, or applied to a raised metal surface, as does the sculpted fleur-de-lis-like pendant. The remainder of the band is decorated with champlevé enamel, a technique achieved by cutting away, or excavating, the underlying gold ground so that colored enamels can be applied to the hollowed-out area, fired in a kiln, and subsequently polished down to the level of the gold ground, a process that creates a design in which each color is separated by a gold border that is actually part of the metal band. The colors of the band are translucent blue for the garter, opaque white for the

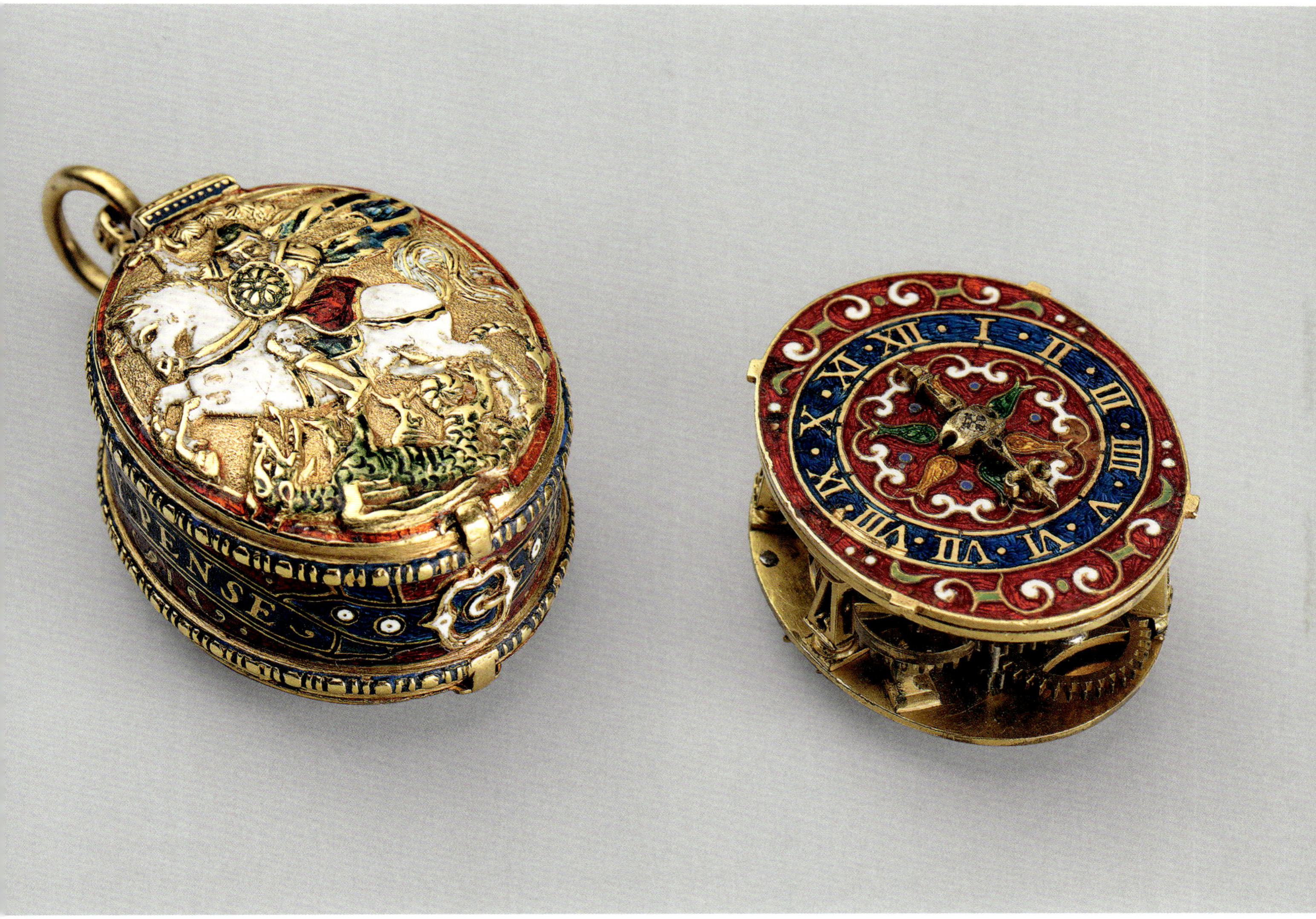
PENSE

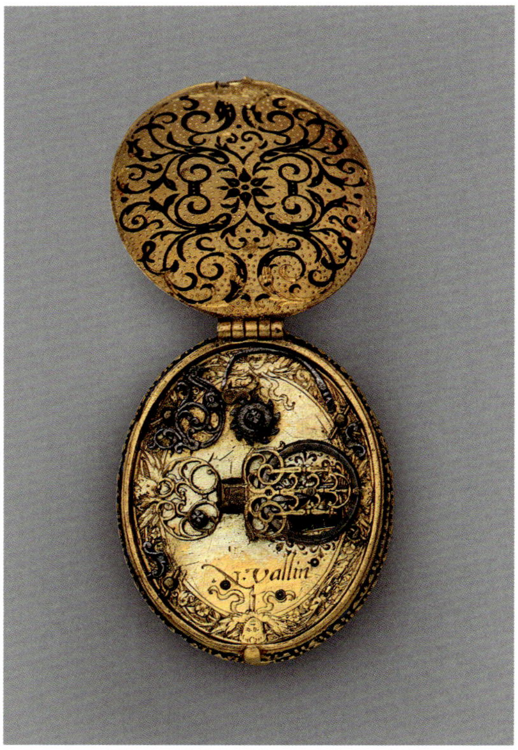

The back cover of the case open to display the back plate of the movement and the signature of the watchmaker

buckle and holes of the garter, and translucent red for the background. The hinged back cover is cast, and its exterior bears an image in relief of Saint George slaying the dragon. These figures are enameled *en ronde-bosse* on a matte gold ground in white, green, blue, and red. The interior of the cover is decorated with scroll ornament in opaque black champlevé enamel on a stippled gold ground.

The dial is attached to the movement, which can be made to slide into the band of the case, where it is held by two latches that are attached to the back plate of the movement. These latches engage two holes in the band of the case. The dial has four lugs that fit into slots in the band of the case and three feet by which it is pinned to the movement. The back plate of the movement carries the signature of the watchmaker, "N. Vallin." The decoration of the dial is executed in champlevé enamel with the numerals and half-hour marks in gold on the translucent blue chapter ring. The remainder of the dial is ornamented with scrolls on a background of translucent red. The single sculptured hand is made of gilded brass with traces of black filling.

The maker of the case and dial is unknown, but the George watches found in late sixteenth-century or early seventeenth-century records have been in English possession, hardly surprising since the order is English. It would, therefore, seem likely that the Metropolitan Museum's watchcase was made in England.[4] A traditional theory holds that this watch is of Continental European origin, which is not implausible.[5] It was not unheard of for English and Scottish watchmakers to make movements for French cases,[6] and until comparatively recent scholarship established the identity of the watchmaker who signed the movement "N. Vallin," the name could easily have been understood as French.[7] Thanks to the research of H. Alan Lloyd and Charles B. Drover, we have a great deal more information about the maker of the watch than we had before the middle of the twentieth century. Nicholas Vallin (active ca. 1565–1603), the son of Johannes (or John) Vallin (ca. 1535–1603), was born in the town of Ryssel, Flanders, which is now Lille, France. By 1567, John was in Brussels working as a clockmaker, a move undoubtedly precipitated by the political troubles in the Netherlands, and subsequently he and Nicholas immigrated to London, probably before 1590. Soon thereafter Nicholas became the leading clock- and watchmaker in London, his Flemish training probably responsible for the sophistication of his clocks and watches.[8] Records indicate both he and his father died in the plague epidemic of 1603.

The technological importance of the Metropolitan Museum's watch lies in its diminutive size.[9] The movement consists of a single train of four wheels, which is driven by a coiled spring regulated by a cone-shaped fusee, and the fusee is connected to the spring barrel by a length of gut. These elements are contained within two oval brass plates that are held apart by four early Egyptian-style pillars, which are riveted to the front plate and pinned to the back plate. When fully wound, the watch has a duration of around fifteen and one-half hours.

The outside of the back plate is engraved with the signature "N. Vallin" with a border of floral scrolls, and includes the head of a putto made in a fashion characteristic of English watches of the late sixteenth century and first quarter of the seventeenth century.[10] The back plate also carries a gilded-brass cock that supports a circular steel balance, a steel click wheel, a brass-nosed steel click, and a click spring for setting up the mainspring (adjusting its initial force). The click wheel, click, and click spring are mounted above the balance, and there are two steel latches for securing the mechanism within the case, one on the left below the foot of the cock, and one on the right above the balance. The cock, click, and latches are richly decorated with pierced work, and the cock is pinned over a stud, or post, which is riveted to the back plate. The steel parts, including the rim of the circular balance, carry traces of gilding.

One of the metal tags that hold the rock crystal cover for the dial is now broken off, and one side of the catch on the back cover of the watch is missing. There are losses of *en ronde-bosse* enamels on numerous areas of low relief in the scene of Saint George, and the surface of some of the champlevé enamels shows decomposition, especially the areas with blue. Otherwise, the watch is in remarkably good condition. It is not known for whom the watch was originally intended. The inventory that lists a George watch in Queen Elizabeth's possession is dated 1587, or two years before evidence indicates that Nicholas Vallin was in London. In any case, the description of the queen's watch does not match that of the watch in the Metropolitan Museum's collection. The description of the one that belonged to the Earl of Northampton in 1614 is too concise to warrant any conclusion. Furthermore, the earl was not created a Knight of the Garter until 1605, or two years after Vallin's death. Although two beguiling, though mutually contradictory, theories have been propounded,[11] very little is known of the watch's provenance before 1857, when it was both illustrated and described as part of the collection of the Englishman Albert Conyngham (1805–1860), who was created first Baron Londesborough in 1850.[12] The watch subsequently came into the hands of Paris antique dealer and collector Frédéric Spitzer (1815–1890), and it is described and illustrated in a volume of his collection catalogue published in 1892.[13] After the auction of his collection in Paris the following year, the watch passed into the collection of Carl H. Marfels, the German watch dealer and collector.[14] Marfels exhibited his collection in Neuchâtel, the Swiss watchmaking city, in 1910, and on that occasion the collection was sold to J. Pierpont Morgan, despite a concerted attempt by local businessmen to keep it in Switzerland.[15] The watch finally entered the Metropolitan Museum's collection in 1917, as one of Morgan's many gifts. CV / JHL

1 Ashmole 1672, sect. IX, p. 226.
2 "A book of soche Jewells . . . delivered to the charge and custodie of Mistress Mary Radclyffe," Ms. Royal Append. 68, British Library, London. Quoted in Britten 1894, p. 61, and Hayward 1969, pp. 2–4, among others.
3 Shirley 1869; for the watch, see p. 350.
4 For a discussion of the probable origin of the case, see Leopold and Vincent 2000, pp. 141–43.
5 Ibid., pp. 145–46.
6 Ibid., p. 148, n. 12; Vincent 2007, pp. 317–21.
7 Lloyd and Drover 1955.
8 For Vallin's musical clock in the British Museum, London (inv. no. CAI-2139), see Thompson 2004, pp. 56–57.
9 For further discussion of the effect of size on the technology of the watch, see Leopold and Vincent 2000, pp. 144–45.
10 Hayward 1969, p. 6, and pls. 1, 2, 5, 7, 9.
11 See Leopold and Vincent 2000, pp. 145–46.
12 Fairholt and Wright 1857, p. 80, and pl. XXVI, figs. 6, 6a.
13 *Collection Spitzer* 1891–93, vol. 5 (1892; plate vol.), "Horloges et montres," pl. VII, no. 3; Palustre 1892, p. 53, no. 3.
14 Speckhart 1904, pl. II, nos. 1–3. For Marfels, see Marfels 1921; Otto 1929; von Osterhausen 2003. See also Williamson 1912, pp. 136–37, no. 143, and pl. LXIV.
15 "Morgan's Collection of Watches" 1913; "Collection of Watches" 1914.

7. Clock Watch with Astronomical Dial and Sundial

DUTCH (HAARLEM), CA. 1605–10
3½ × 2⁷⁄₁₆ × 2⁵⁄₁₆ in. (8.9 × 6.2 × 5.9 cm)
Width of back plate: 2⅛ in. (5.4 cm)
Gift of J. Pierpont Morgan, 1917
17.190.1603

CASE: gilded brass, signed (on cover): IAN•IANSEN BOCKELS•INVE / ET SCVLP. [Jan Janssen Bockelts the Elder, Dutch, active ca. 1590–1626]
DIAL: gilded brass, silver, and copper
MOVEMENT: gilded brass, partly blued steel, and silver, signed (on back plate): *Ian•Ianssen•Bockeltz / Van Aec ken* (see above)

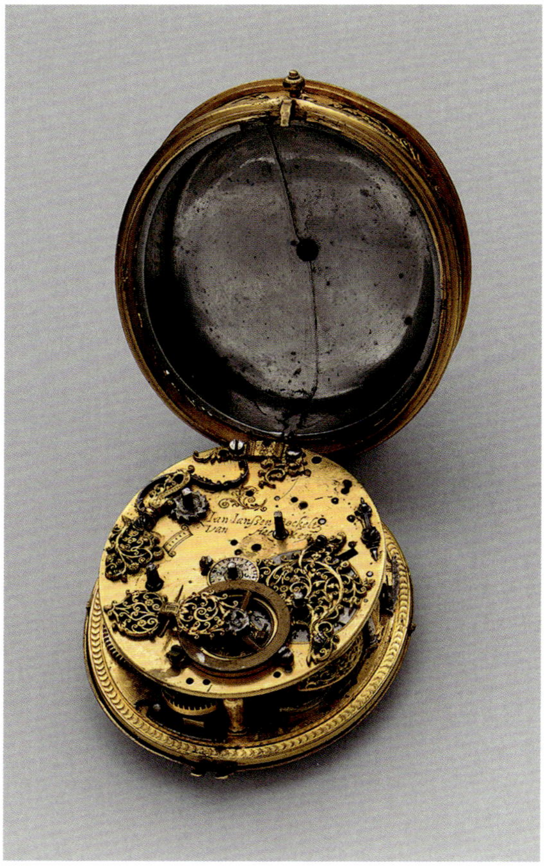

The case open to show the back plate of the movement

THE DUTCH REPUBLIC, OR THE REPUBLIC OF THE UNITED Provinces, as it was officially recognized, became an independent state in 1581 when King Philip II of Spain (1527–1598) abjured his right to rule over the Netherlands. Nonetheless, the civil war that had started in 1560 continued after the declaration of independence, and by the early seventeenth century the Dutch Revolt gradually turned into a stalemate.[1] By 1609, a truce was agreed upon, which lasted until 1621. When the Peace of Munster finally ended all hostilities in 1648, the Netherlands was halfway through a period of prosperity now regarded as the Golden Age. Many successful merchants had settled in the new Dutch Republic, and the early voyages of the newly formed Dutch East India Company (1602–1799) brought unprecedented wealth. Amsterdam was rapidly becoming the richest city in Europe. With independence and wealth came a taste for luxury goods and the need for skilled craftsmen, and among these craftsmen were the earliest Dutch watchmakers.

Two of these watchmakers were Jan Janssen Bockelts (or Bockeltz) the Elder (active ca. 1590–1626), who settled in Haarlem before 1607, and Wijbe Wijbrandts (or Vibrandi, a latinized form of the family name), who was a maker of both watches and astronomical instruments. Wijbrandts was born in Sneek, and about 1600 or 1601 he settled in Leeuwarden, the capital of the province of Friesland and another Dutch city made remarkably prosperous by commerce during the seventeenth century.[2] Within forty years, his son Jacob Wijbrandts (active 1635–78)[3] would make a movement for a rock crystal case that would rival those made in France or Switzerland (fig. 20).[4]

It is not certain where Bockelts was born, but it is known that he was an Anabaptist. Anabaptist families are hard to trace because of their reluctance to baptize their children, thus making it difficult to prove family relationships. His birthplace may have been the Flemish city of Ghent, but, as attested by his signature on the back plate of the Metropolitan Museum's watch, he had spent some time in Aachen, Germany. The signature could be understood as "Bockelts from Aachen," rather than "Bockelts in Aachen," as has sometimes been proposed.[5] It seems probable that he was not born in Aachen, however, and was more likely to have been among the large number of Protestants, many of them Anabaptists, who took refuge in Aachen during the conflict with King Philip II in the 1580s. Many of these émigrés were known to be skilled craftsmen.[6] In 1598, a Spanish-backed coup restored a Catholic regime in Aachen,[7] and the increasing prosperity of the Dutch Republic resulted in the return of many of the Dutch and Flemish émigrés.

It is not known where Bockelts acquired his considerable skills in watchmaking, but certain technical practices evident in his watches

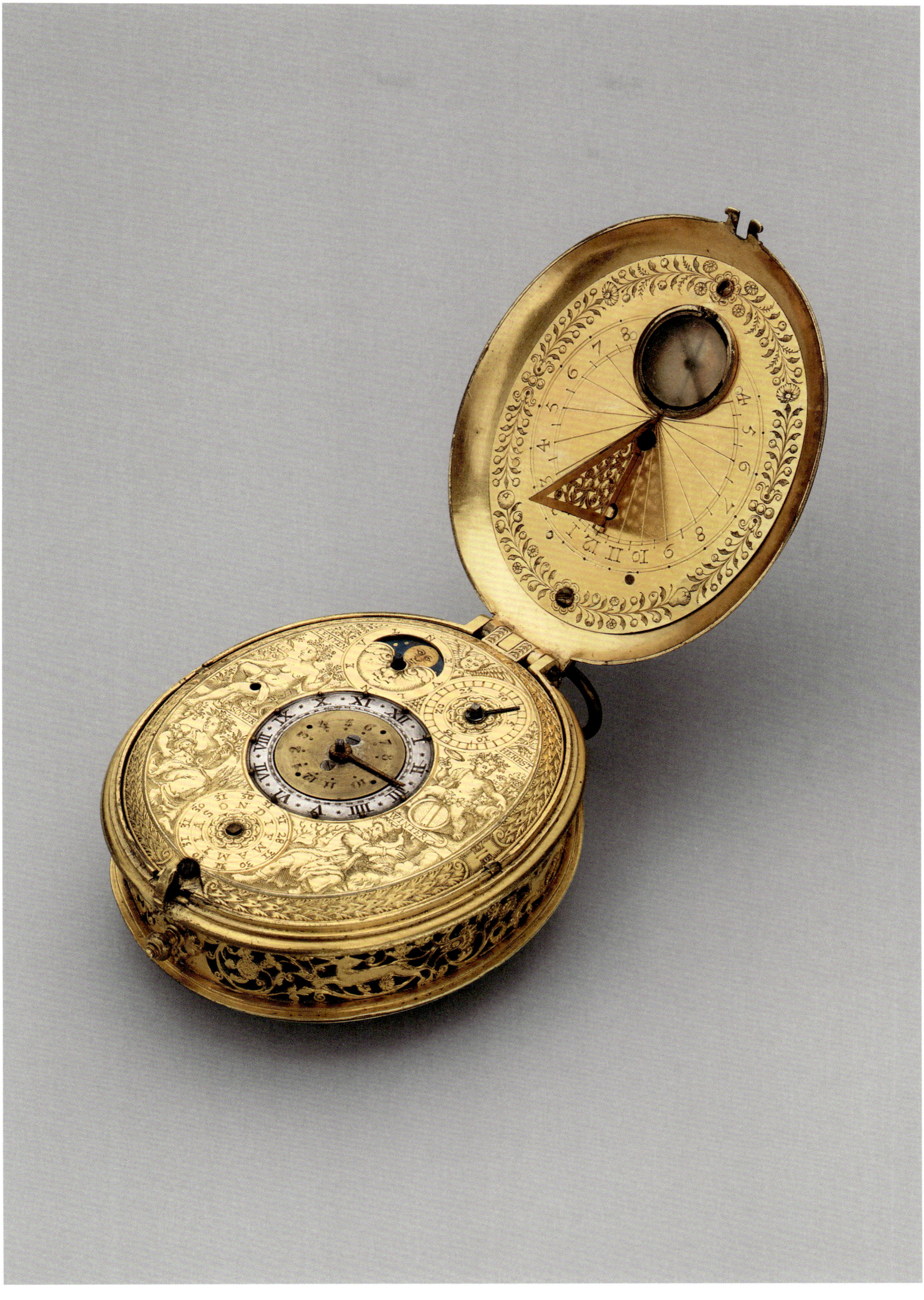

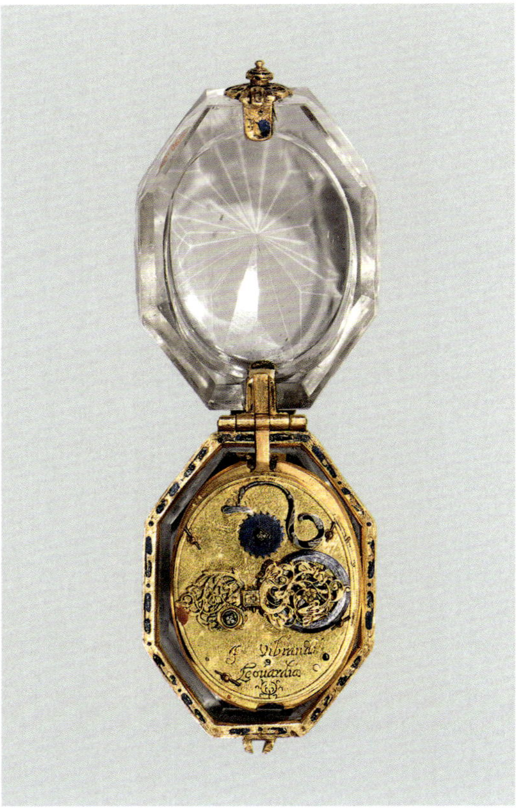

fig. 20 *Jacob Wijbrandts (J. Vibrandi; Dutch, active 1635–78). Watch Movement, Dutch (Leeuwarden), ca. 1640. Case: rock crystal and partly enameled gold; movement: gilded brass and partly blued steel, 1½ × 1⅛ in. (3.8 × 2.9 cm). The Metropolitan Museum of Art, New York, Gift of J. Pierpont Morgan, 1917 (17.190.1019)*

would suggest that he was trained in Germany.[8] By 1607, however, he was in Haarlem, near the North Sea coast. A watch signed "Jan Janss Bockelts" and inscribed with its owner's name and the date, "Abraham Ampe anno 1607," is in the collection of the Ashmolean Museum, Oxford.[9] As David Thompson has pointed out, Ampe is known to have been a merchant in Haarlem and a friend of the watchmaker's family.[10] A third watch, or clock watch (a watch that strikes the hours), signed "Jan Janssen Bockeltz/Fes" is in the collection of the British Museum, London,[11] and constitutes, along with the Metropolitan Museum's clock watch, the surviving unquestioned evidence of Bockelts's production of watches.[12] An inventory found in the city records of Haarlem and drawn up in 1626 for the estate of the clockmaker refers to him as Jan Janssen the Elder. Two sons—Jan Janssen the Younger (active 1625–35), whose work has sometimes been confused with that of his father,[13] and Matthijs—were also watchmakers.

The movement of the Metropolitan's watch is hinged to an oval case and cover at the twelve o'clock position. It consists of two gilded-brass plates, which are held apart by four elongated, vase-shaped pillars that are pinned to the front plate. The movement also contains a going train of three wheels that end in a verge escapement, now with a steel balance wheel, balance spring, and regulator. The mainspring is encased in a brass barrel with flanges at top and at bottom. The fusee, which was originally cut to accommodate a gut line, has twelve turns that provide a duration of two days before rewinding becomes necessary.

The striking train has five wheels and a fly, which strikes the hours on a bell that is screwed to the interior of the back case. It is driven by an iron spring encased in a gilded and engraved, openwork brass barrel and is regulated by a steel count wheel with interior-cut teeth mounted on the exterior of the back plate. Also mounted on the back plate is a lever that permits the silencing of the striking mechanism. The alarm train has three steel wheels, and it is powered by an open spring. The back plate supports a ratchet and an ornamented click, which are held in place by an S-shaped, blued-steel spring for regulating the setup of the mainspring (top left) and, continuing in counterclockwise order, the engraved scale for a hog's-bristle regulator of the balance (now superseded); an openwork scrolled cock for the balance pinned to the back plate; a figure plate for regulating the present balance spring; the count wheel for the striking train, protected by an openwork bridge; and the strike/silent lever. The watchmaker's name, "Ian•Ianssen•Bockeltz/Van Aec ken," is engraved in the center of the upper half of the back plate. (The winding square for the spring to the alarm projects through the back plate

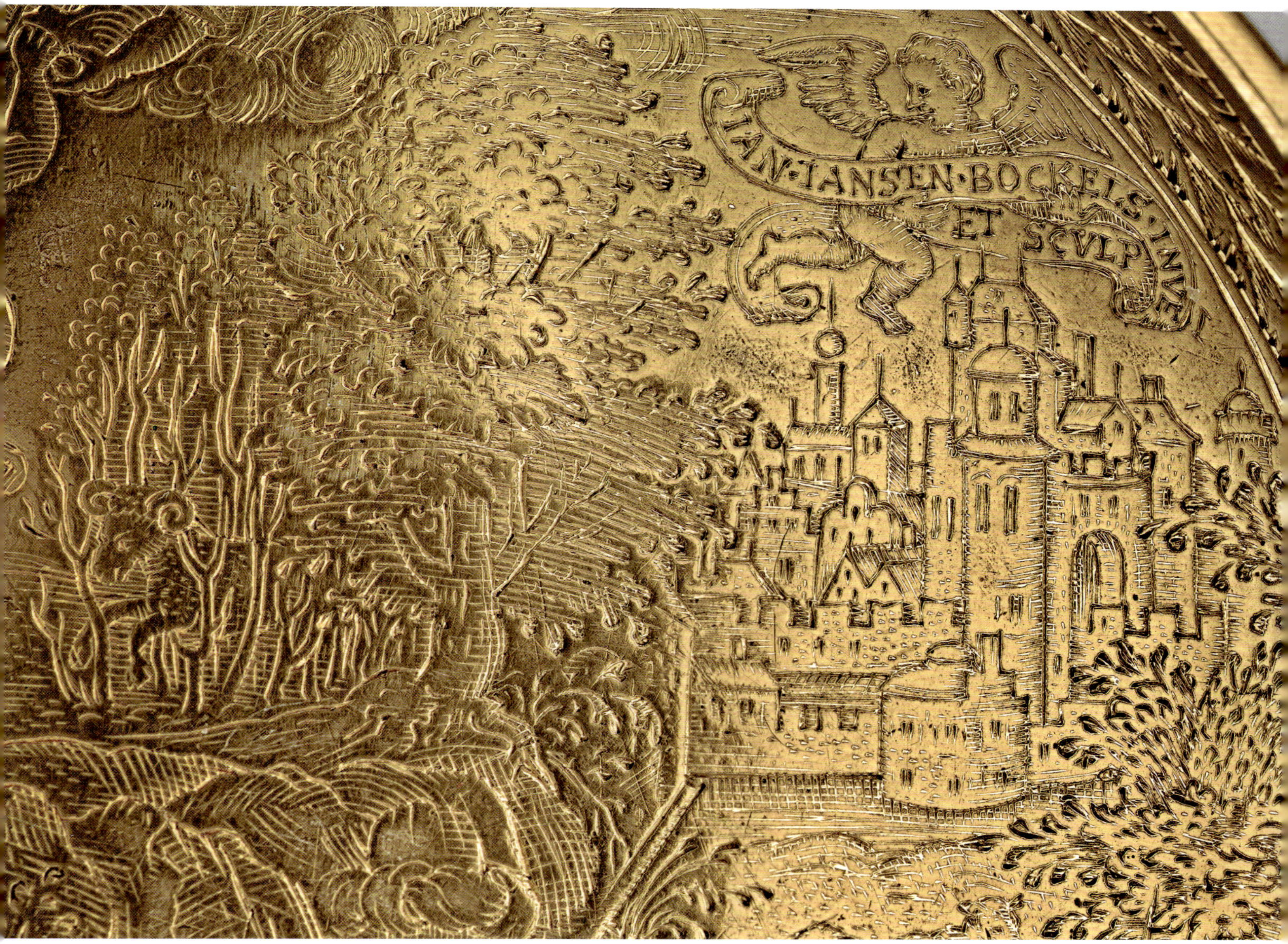

Detail of the exterior of the cover for the dial, showing the watchmaker's signature

and interrupts the lettering of the place name in the signature, and traces of its cross-shaped ornament are still visible on the end.)

The front plate of the movement is attached with steel latches to the dial plate by three feet. The dial plate carries a silver chapter of hours (I–XII), with stars marking the half hours and touch pins. The central disk for setting the alarm is a replacement that may date to as late as the nineteenth century. There are subsidiary dials for demonstrating the phase of the moon (upper left), the day of the month (upper right), and the month with the number of days in the month (below the center.)

The remaining areas of the dial plate are filled by engraved figures that personify the Four Seasons. Starting from the top left and proceeding counterclockwise, these are a seated nude female figure with a bouquet of flowers in her upraised hand, labeled "LENTEN" [spring]; a seated female figure with a cornucopia in one hand and a sickle in the other, labeled "SOMER" [summer]; a bearded old man warming his hands at an open fire, labeled "WINTER"; and a youth seated on a barrel, holding a wine cup and pouring out the contents of a jug, labeled "HERBST" [autumn]. All Four Seasons are adapted from

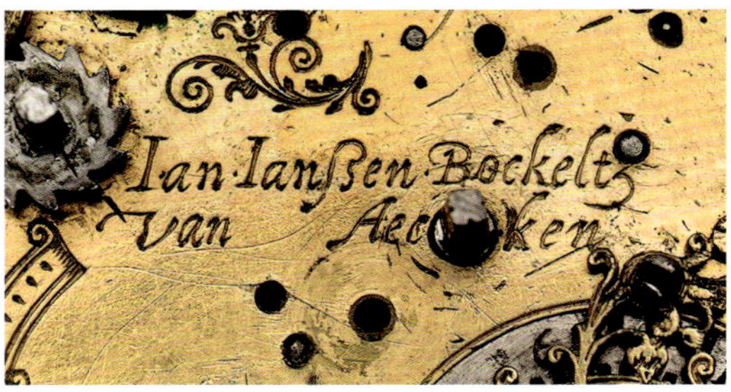

Detail of the back plate of the movement with the signature of the watchmaker

engravings by Crispijn Van de Passe the Elder (1564–1637) from designs by the Flemish artist Maarten de Vos the Elder (1532–1603), who supplied numerous images for both narrative purposes and personifications.[14] The engravings are not dated and are identified in Latin. As the labels on the watch dial could be in either Dutch or German, they are not particularly helpful in determining whether the watch was made in Germany or in the Dutch Republic.

The back of the oval case is made of pierced and gilded brass and chased on the exterior surface with leafy foliage inhabited by a seated youth under a canopy, who is playing a pipe and holding another pipe. He is flanked by two birds with wings spread. A squirrel hoarding a nut and a monkey reaching for fruit are depicted on either side of a central landscape with a stork and below, a Roman soldier, with a shield and spear, is seated beneath an arch and flanked by a horse and a unicorn, both prancing. All of these figures display an engaging spiritedness. The same qualities hold true for animals on the band or side of the case: a hound chasing a stag on one long side, and a hound chasing a hare on the other.

The exterior of the case cover is a shadow of its original appearance, owing, no doubt, to wear resulting from prolonged use of the watch. A remarkably ambitious scene based on the biblical story of the sacrifice of Isaac by Abraham (the angel staying Abraham's hand), still remains. To the scene in the foreground Bockelts added two men beside a donkey that is helping itself to a tuft of grass. As the donkey is saddled and one of the men is seated, they are apparently resting during a journey. Flying in on the right side of the sky, above a walled city, a winged putto holds a scroll proclaiming the identity of the engraver as well as the provider of the design: "IAN•IANSEN•BOCKELS• INVE/ET SCVLP." Both the case and the cover are framed by neatly engraved borders of ears of wheat, and on the cover a small grotesque mask appears at the hinge. These elements also exist on the other two known watches with movements signed by Bockelts, suggesting that he probably made those cases as well.

A portable horizontal sundial with a folding-style compass that is usable at 42-degree latitude is screwed to the interior of the cover. The openwork scrolling on the style repeats that of the click, the cock for the balance, and the bridge for the count wheel on the back plate of the watch. The sundial would have been a useful addition for setting and correcting the watch, which in spite of its multiple functions, could not have been a very good timekeeper until the application of the balance spring.

While it is unwise to draw many conclusions from comparisons with the engraved cases of the other two Bockelts watches, it does seem possible that the Metropolitan Museum's watchcase is not too distant in date and place of origin from the Ashmolean Museum's. The Metropolitan's clock watch is not only one of the earliest known Dutch watches still in existence but also a rare example of a watchcase and watch movement that can be reliably assigned to the same maker.

Due to the extensive amount of wear on the exterior of the case, it is probable that the watch was in use throughout most of the seventeenth century, and at some point after 1675, it was thought worth adding a balance spring. The motion work for the moon dial has been largely repaired, and the gearing for the month is missing entirely. The original hog's-bristle regulation for the balance has been removed, and the installation of the balance spring probably accounts for the replacement of the original verge and balance. In addition, the table of the balance cock has been awkwardly strengthened. A chain for the fusee has replaced the gut line. The fly (a roller pinion) in the striking train is a replacement, and the bell is cracked. The disk for setting the alarm is a replacement, and neither of the hands are original to the watch. On the side of the clasp, there is a repair to the border at the bottom of the dial plate, and on the other side, the repair is now missing. The bezel for the compass on the sundial has deteriorated.

J. Pierpont Morgan purchased the watch from the British banker Frederick George Hilton Price,[15] and it appears in the Morgan collection in 1911, when it was illustrated in a publication by F. J. Britten.[16] CV / JHL

1 The authors would like to thank Professor Johan Koppenol of Vrije Universiteit, Amsterdam, for his assistance in summarizing the events of this complicated period in Dutch history.
2 See Ottema 1923, pp. 10–11, and figs. 2–4; Morpurgo 1970, p. 144. His watches, usually dated about 1600 to 1610, are in the Stichting Museum en Archief van Tijdmeetkunde, Schoonhoven (Beringen 2012, p. 28, no. 1; Peeters 2012, pp. 20–21); the Rijksmuseum, Amsterdam (Spierdijk 1973, p. 207, no. 36, and fig. 36; Peeters 2012, pp. 16–19); and the Museum Willet-Holthuysen, Amsterdam (*Hoe laat was het?* 1956, no. 4a).
3 Ottema 1923, p. 11, and figs. 5, 6.
4 The Metropolitan Museum of Art, New York (acc. no. 17.190.1019). See also entry 10 in this volume.
5 See Williamson 1912, p. 91.
6 Israel 1995, p. 348.
7 Ibid., p. 366.
8 See Thompson 2008, p. 22.
9 Inv. no. WA1947.191.13. See Thompson 2007, pp. 14–15, no. 6.
10 Ibid., p. 14.
11 Inv. no. 1888,1201.170. See Thompson 2008, pp. 22–23.
12 A fourth watch in the British Museum (inv. no. CAI-2225), signed with the monogram "14B," has been attributed to the elder Bockelts. See Tait 1987, pp. 58–59, no. 41, and pl. 22, f, and pl. 23, a, b.
13 For an account of the scandal that caused Jan Janssen the Younger to move from Haarlem to The Hague, see Leopold 1989, p. 156; Peeters 2012, p. 303.
14 See Hollstein, *Dutch and Flemish*, 1949–2010, vol. 44 (1996), pp. 282–83, nos. 1420–23, and vol. 46 (1995), pt. 2, pp. 210–11, pls. 1420–23.
15 Williamson 1912, p. 90.
16 Britten 1911, pp. 143–44, and p. 141, fig. 145, and p. 142, fig. 146.

8. Automaton Clock in the Form of Urania, Muse of Astronomy

GERMAN (NÜRNBERG), CA. 1620–30

8½ × 10 × 6¾ in. (21.6 × 25.4 × 17.1 cm)

Purchase, Anna-Maria and Stephen Kellen Acquisitions Fund, 2015

2015.76

CASE: partly gilded and partly silvered brass, copper with traces of silver, ebony, and ebony veneer

MOVEMENT: gilded brass and partly blued steel, signed (on back plate): *Paullus Schiller* [German, 1583–1634]

IN 1471 THE GERMAN ASTRONOMER JOHANN MÜLLER (1436–1476), better known by his latinized name, Regiomontanus,[1] left Vienna, where he had been a pupil of and later an assistant to the astronomer Georg Peuerbach (1423–1461).[2] Regiomontanus settled in Nürnberg, and soon became the central figure in a circle of amateurs and aristocrats who were interested in cosmology and astronomy. One member of the circle, Bernard Walther (ca. 1430–1504), set up an astronomical observatory in his house, as well as the press that published Peuerbach's highly influential treatise *Theoricae Novae Planetarum* (New Theory of Planets) about 1474.[3] Regiomontanus is credited with the construction of the astronomical instruments that he and Walther used in the observatory,[4] and he probably provided the calculations for an ambitious astronomical clock that registered not only the time but also the positions of the sun, moon, and planets. The clock no longer exists, but it was mentioned in a broadsheet Regiomontanus printed in 1475, and it is likely that it was the same clock sold in 1529 to the Archbishop of Mainz, Cardinal Albrecht IV of Brandenburg (died 1545).[5]

Sixteenth-century Nürnberg craftsmen inherited these skills, and their grounding in astronomy and mathematics combined with the tradition of working in brass that flourished in the city produced some of the most celebrated mathematical instruments and domestic or small clocks (*Kleinuhren*) of the century. These included, for example, the classic astrolabes of Georg Hartmann (1489–1564)[6] and the ingeniously nesting clockwork-driven globes of Christian Heiden (1526–1576).[7] Clocks with movements by Hans Gruber (died 1597) of Nürnberg are often housed in cases made of cast, chased, and gilded brass; one such clock includes plaquettes depicting scenes from the biblical parable of the Prodigal Son by the sculptor Leonhard Danner (1507–1587),[8] and another, initialed "MZ," has been identified as the design of the Nürnberg goldsmith Matthias Zündt (ca. 1498–1572).[9]

In spite of the fame of their timepieces, however, sixteenth-century records of Nürnberg craftsmen reveal remarkably few identified as clockmakers, even if some of them are known to have joined other companies of craftsmen.[10] Their relatively few numbers probably account for the rarity of surviving Nürnberg clocks.

Conditions in the early seventeenth century were not materially different. By then, the clockmakers of Nürnberg's chief rival, Augsburg, were making mechanized miniature figures of human beings, birds, animals both real and fantastic,[11] and ships that moved along a tabletop, spitting fire from tiny cannons[12] while marking the hours. At first, the figures for these clocks were made of gilded repoussé copper and were supported on circular or oval bases of richly embossed metal housing the springs that drove the motions of the figures as well as the hands of

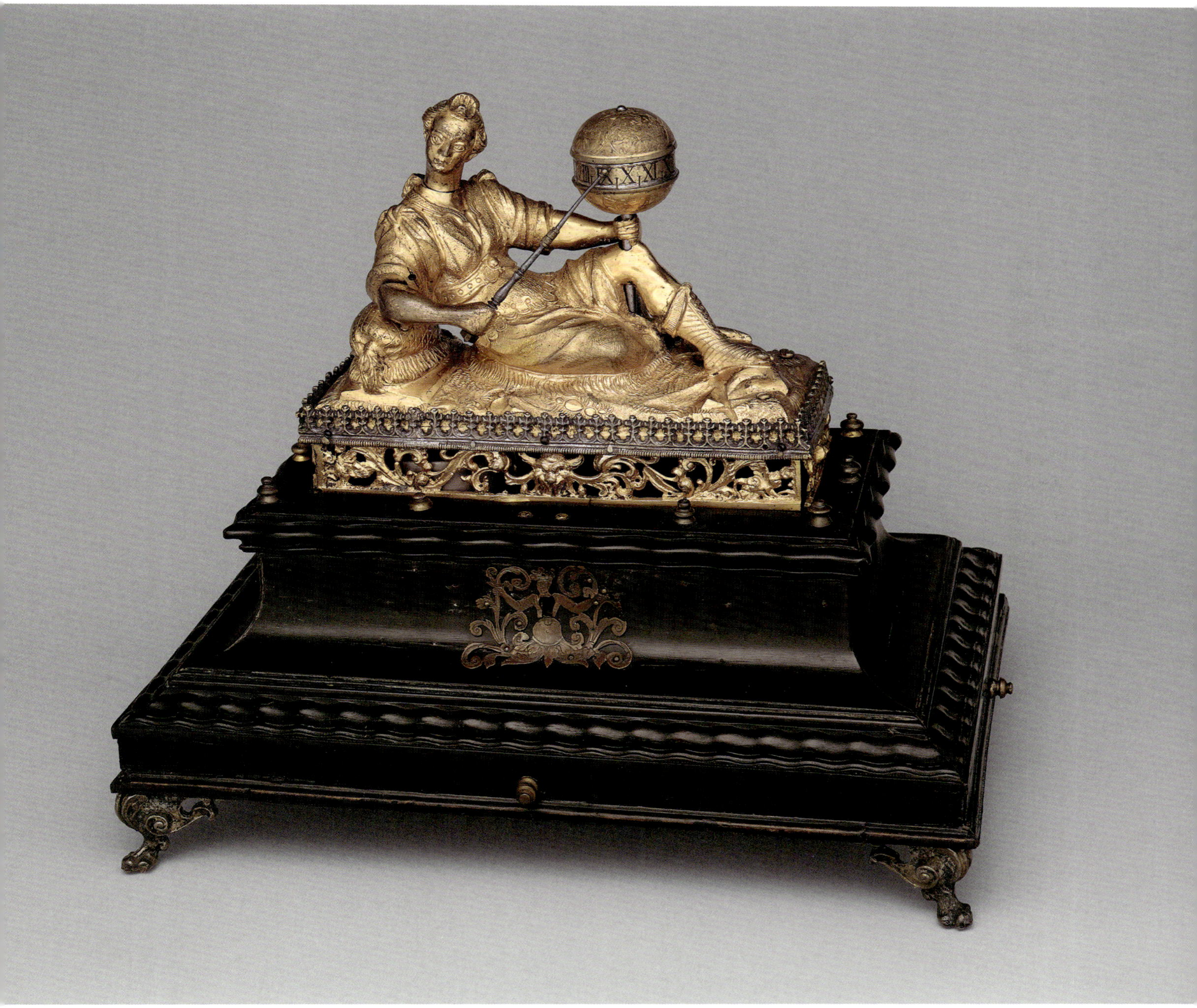

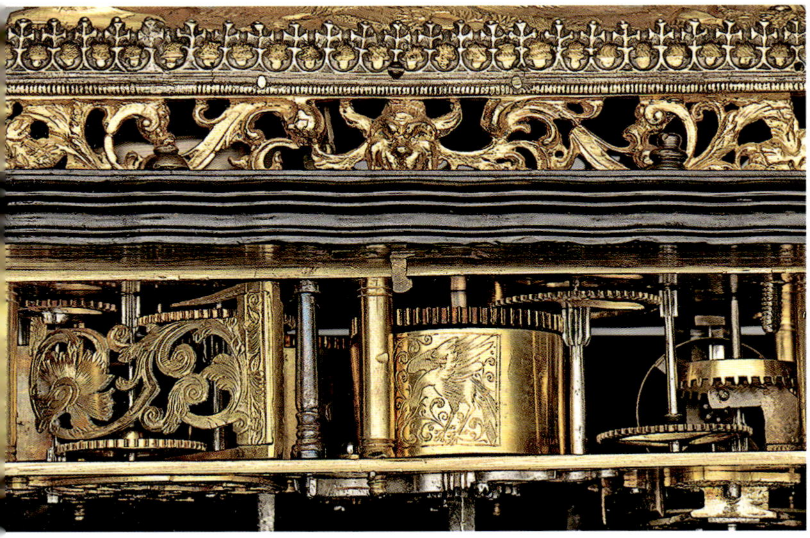

The case open to show the movement

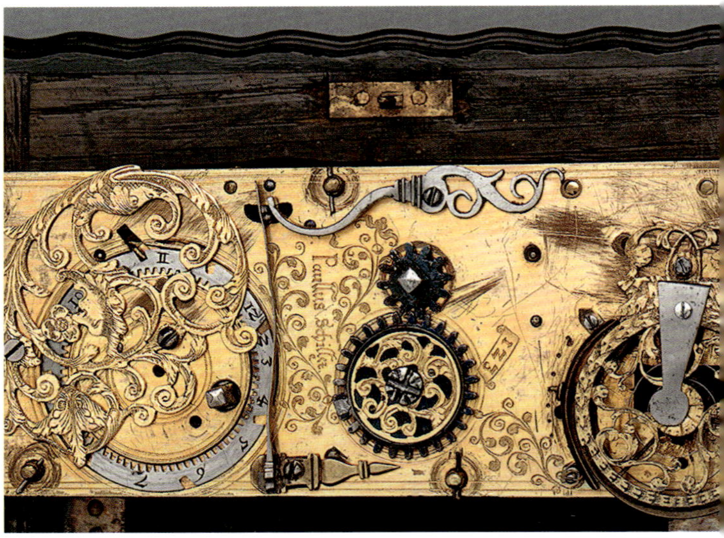

The case open to show the back plate of the movement

the clocks they incorporated. About the end of the sixteenth century metal bases began to be superseded by wooden bases made of ebony, ebony veneer, and sometimes fruitwood darkened to look like ebony.[13]

With the coming of the wooden base, cast figures of gilded brass, such as the lion,[14] which must have been a popular model, or the rarely encountered Imperial Eagle,[15] among many other small statuettes, quickly replaced figures largely made of embossed and gilded copper. Nürnberg's tradition of casting figures in bronze was comparable to Augsburg's, and the technology for casting in brass was well understood in both cities. Thus the makers of Urania, the Muse of Astronomy, were easily able to produce a line of serially cast brass automaton figures. At least seven of these still exist; four of them are illustrated by Klaus Maurice.[16] All were activated by movements provided by the Nürnberg clockmaker Paullus Schiller. Born in Nürnberg on October 11, 1583, Schiller is now known primarily for the Urania automata. He married on May 11, 1614, became a master clockmaker in 1617, and died in Nürnberg on April 13, 1634.[17]

On the clock, Urania reclines on a grassy hillock; each hour she turns her head to watch the revolving sphere mounted beside her while lifting her arm to move her pointer to the correct hour displayed on a chapter of hours (I–XII) mounted on the circumference of the sphere. Not only is she an appropriate representative of the city of the astronomical observatory, but also, as Maurice has observed,[18] her reclining form alludes to a figure atop a writing chest, the product of another proud tradition in Nürnberg, that of the goldsmith, and in particular one of Nürnberg's best: Wenzel Jamnitzer (1508–1585).[19]

The miniature muse of the clock is supported above a gallery of foliate scrolls and animal masks in an openwork pattern designed to allow the sound of the bell mounted inside it to be heard. The gallery, in turn, rests on a rectangular platform of ebony with ebony ripple moldings on all four sides, and it supports a decorative frieze of brass trefoils that bears traces of silvering. Attached to the bottom of the structure is the rectangular brass plate that serves as the top plate of the movement of the clock. The entire assembly is hinged to the rest of the wooden base so that the movement can be lifted and its springs wound from the underside without upending the entire clock. The remaining portion of the base consists of a concave molding above a second band of ripple molding and a base with a shallow drawer that opens on the proper left side of the base. One of the small brass studs that dot the wooden base serves as a knob for the drawer that was intended to hold both a key for the case and one for winding the movement. The center of the front portion is now ornamented by an openwork escutcheon of the keyhole for the lock of the case. The entire clock is now supported on four feet that are replacements for an earlier type of foot. To judge from circular holes that remain in the wood on the underside, these were originally the bun-shaped variety still found on the Metropolitan Museum's Eagle Automaton.[20]

The movement contained within the wooden base consists of two rectangular, gilded-brass plates held apart by six cylindrical pillars riveted to the top plate and pinned to the back plate. The striking train (on the proper right side) consists of a going barrel, three brass wheels, and a fly. It strikes the hours (1–12) on a bell mounted on the outside of the top plate, and it is governed by a large, floridly ornamented indexing arm and a steel count wheel with interior cut teeth. The count wheel is held in place by an ornamented openwork cock that is screwed to the exterior side of the back plate (see illustration above). A shaft transmits motion from the train through the back of the figure of the muse to her head and right arm.

The going train (on the proper left side of the movement) has an engraved brass going barrel and three brass wheels ending in a verge escapement. A balance with a spiral hair spring and a new cock has been added, probably not long after the invention of the balance spring in late 1674 by the Dutch mathematician Christiaan Huygens (1629–1695).[21] The Arabic numbers 1, 2, 3 engraved directly on the back plate are now without purpose; they are all that remain of the hog's bristle regulation for the original balance. As in the striking train, a shaft transmits motion to the revolving sphere on which the hours (I–XII) are inscribed. In addition to the count-wheel assembly and the balance, the back plate carries two toothed wheels, one with the winding square for the going train in its center, whose purpose is to prevent overwinding the mainspring. The signature of the clockmaker "Paullus Schiller" is accompanied by impressive foliate flourishes.

There is no fusee in either the striking train or in the going train, where it might be more reasonably expected. In this particular as in others, this clock is quite unlike the large majority of automata made in Augsburg where the spring and fusee device was employed. The timekeeping properties of this clock originally must have been fairly poor. The dial of the clock, in fact, registers hours and half hours only, but the application of the balance spring would have made a significant difference in the accuracy of the clock. In fact, for a few years after Huygens's invention, several well-known clockmakers, including Thomas Tompion (1639–1713) in London[22] and Nicolas Gribelin (1637–1719) in Paris,[23] made watches without fusees that relied on their balance springs alone for accurate timekeeping. These experiments were, however, soon abandoned.

As might be expected of a clock that was active for a long period, there are repairs to both the movement and the case. A keyhole-shaped steel coqueret now attached to the table of the balance cock, and one or two wheels replaced in the going train attest to a long history of use. The ornament that now serves as an escutcheon for the keyhole in the middle of the front of the case has been removed from the concave molding on one side of the case, and it has been modified in an attempt to fit the keyhole. The keyhole is now unusable. Traces of the mounting of a similarly shaped ornament on the opposite side of the case and a third that was originally on the front are visible. Other replacements include the four baroque feet, some of the brass knobs attached to various parts of the wooden base, and a few areas of ripple molding that are made of stained fruitwood instead of ebony. The two ends of the trefoil frieze on the back of the clock are missing, as is one of the trefoils on the remaining frieze. The gilding of the figure is worn and lightly abraded, but not in a way that is inconsistent with normal use. The clock is in running condition.

A part of the distinguished New York collection of Peter D. Guggenheim for more than forty-five years, the clock was purchased at auction by the Museum with funds provided by the Anna-Maria and Stephen Kellen Acquisitions Fund.[24] CV / JHL

1 For more about Regiomontanus, see Zinner 1968.
2 Hellman and Swerdlow 1978.
3 Ibid., p. 474.
4 Zinner 1956, pp. 482–83; Pannekoek 1961, pp. 181–82.
5 A drawing of the clock is preserved in the Bayerisches Nationalmuseum, Munich. See Maurice 1975; Maurice 1976, vol. 1, pp. 56–58, vol. 2, p. 36, no. 211, and fig. 211; Leopold 2002, p. 505, n. 1.
6 See, for example, R. Webster and M. Webster 1998, pp. 53–57.
7 Leopold 1986, pp. 72–86; Leopold 2002, pp. 518–19 and figs. 18, 19.
8 Formerly in the collection of Ruth and Leopold Blumka in New York. See Maurice 1976, vol. 2, p. 70, no. 530, and fig. 530.
9 Ibid., pp. 24–25, no. 112, and fig. 112.
10 Maurice 1976, vol. 1, pp. 142–43. An addendum (pp. 299–300) lists the records of clockmakers found in the Staatsarchiv Nürnberg, among them only six who specialized in domestic clocks in the sixteenth century. Only a few more were recorded in the seventeenth century.
11 See entry 9 in this volume for two examples in the Metropolitan Museum's collection.
12 See de Conihout et al. 2001.
13 For a further discussion of ebony bases as they were made in Augsburg, see Himmelheber 1980.
14 For the Metropolitan Museum's example (acc. no. 29.52.15), see p. 56, fig. 22, in this volume. Many others exist.
15 See entry 9 in this volume for the Metropolitan Museum's example.
16 Maurice 1976, vol. 2, p. 55, nos. 378–81, and figs. 378–81; no. 380 is the Urania automaton clock now in the Metropolitan Museum. An additional example was included as no. 354 in a sale held at Auktionen Dr. Crott in Mannheim, Germany, on Nov. 13, 2004. Another was formerly in the collection of Yves Saint Laurent and Pierre Bergé; see Christie's 2009, vol. 5, no. 721. See also Artcurial 2012, pp. 30–35, no. 34, ill., for another example in a recent sale.
17 See Grieb 2007, vol. 3, p. 1329, in which he is identified as a *Kleinuhrmacher*. See also Maurice 1976, vol. 1, pp. 141, 300.
18 Maurice 1976, vol. 2, p. 55, no. 374, and fig. 374.
19 The chest, known to have been the property of the Saxon Electress Sophia in 1623, is now in the collection of the Grünes Gewölbe in Dresden (inv. no. V 599). See Sponsel 1925, p. 48; see also Martin Angerer in *Wenzel Jamnitzer* 1985, pp. 225–26, no. 20 (with bibliography).
20 See entry 9 in this volume.
21 See entry 20 in this volume.
22 See entry 23 in this volume.
23 Acc. no. 17.190.1559 is an example in the Museum's collection. See *Sun King* 1984, p. 223, no. 76.
24 Christie's 2015, no. 30, ill.

9. Automaton Clock in the Form of an Eagle

GERMAN (AUGSBURG), CA. 1630

13¼ × 9⅛ × 7⅝ in. (33.7 × 23.2 × 19.4 cm)

Width of back plate: 5⅛ in. (13 cm)

Gift of Mrs. Simon Guggenheim, 1929

29.52.14

CASE: gilded brass on base of ebony and ebony veneered on fruitwood, stamped (on base): *pyr* (or pinecone) mark for Augsburg and MS conjoined with a shield (unidentified cabinetmaker's mark)

MOVEMENT: brass and iron

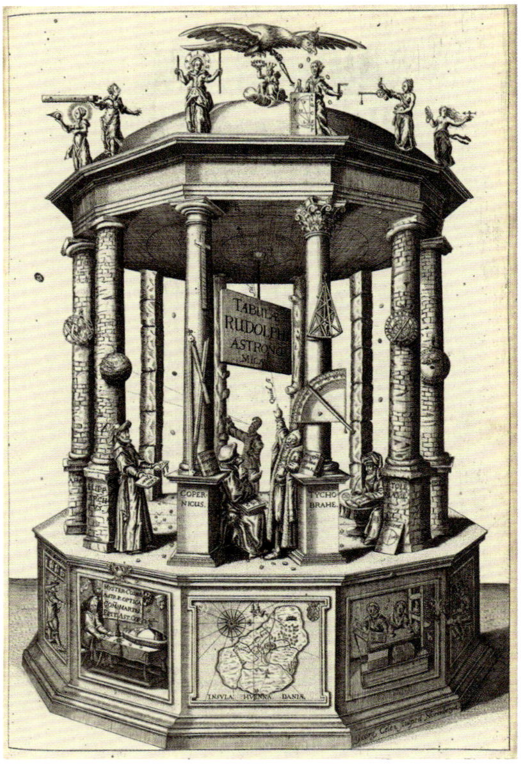

fig. 21 *Georg Celer (German [Nürnberg], baptized 1599, died 1638).* Frontispiece *from Johannes Kepler,* Tabulae Rudolphinae *(Ulm: Typis Jonae Saurii, 1627). Engraving, Height of page 13⅝ in. (34.5 cm). Butler Library, Columbia University, New York*

MECHANICAL AUTOMATA, OR SELF-MOVING FIGURES, HAVE BEEN associated with European mechanical clocks from their earliest development. Unlike the clocks, which have the practical purpose of telling the time, automata were often made with the deliberate aim of inspiring awe in the beholder. Whether religious or secular in nature, there is something magical in the most domesticated of automata. By the early sixteenth century the artist Leonardo da Vinci would be engaged to design a clockwork-driven lion that reportedly greeted King Louis XII (1462–1515) of France during his triumphal entry into Milan in 1509 by lying down and opening its chest with its paw to release a shower of golden lilies, which were symbolic of both Florence and France.[1] The reputation of this lion was apparently such that when Louis XII's successor, François I (1494–1547), made his formal visit as king to the banking city of Lyon in 1515, the colony of Florentine bankers commissioned a second automaton from Leonardo. This one greeted the king by walking and strewing the golden lilies.[2]

With the rise of Augsburg as the German clockmaking center during the sixteenth century, another series of automata paid tribute to the power of the Habsburg Holy Roman Emperors. These automata were nefs in the form of warships that propelled themselves along a tabletop while shooting miniature cannons as tiny trumpeters and kettle drummers played a fanfare for a figure of the emperor. When in action they were doubtlessly calculated to promote a somewhat uncomfortable shiver in the spectator. Three of these vessels survive, one presided over by Holy Roman Emperor Charles V (1500–1558) and two presided over by his grandson Holy Roman Emperor Rudolf II (1552–1612). Two of the automata incidentally incorporate a clock; all are attributed to the Augsburg clockmaker and maker of automata Hans Schlottheim (master in 1576), with contributions by the various anonymous craftsmen who made the cases and provided the sound.[3]

In the late sixteenth century a number of other clockmakers in Augsburg produced automata in combination with clocks. They were largely made with gilded-copper cases, often supporting automata in the form of a single animal or bird, or a human figure riding an animal. By the second decade of the seventeenth century, these figure clocks (lions, elephants, ostriches, dogs, and birds) were being made in quantity, their animated components of cast and gilded brass supported on wooden bases, sometimes darkened to look like ebony and sometimes made of the precious black wood. The names of the cabinetmakers who made the wooden bases are not known, but by the early seventeenth century those who worked in ebony had adopted special "EBEN" and Augsburg pinecone stamps,[4] as well as maker's marks. Unfortunately, most of these maker's marks have never been identified. The individual

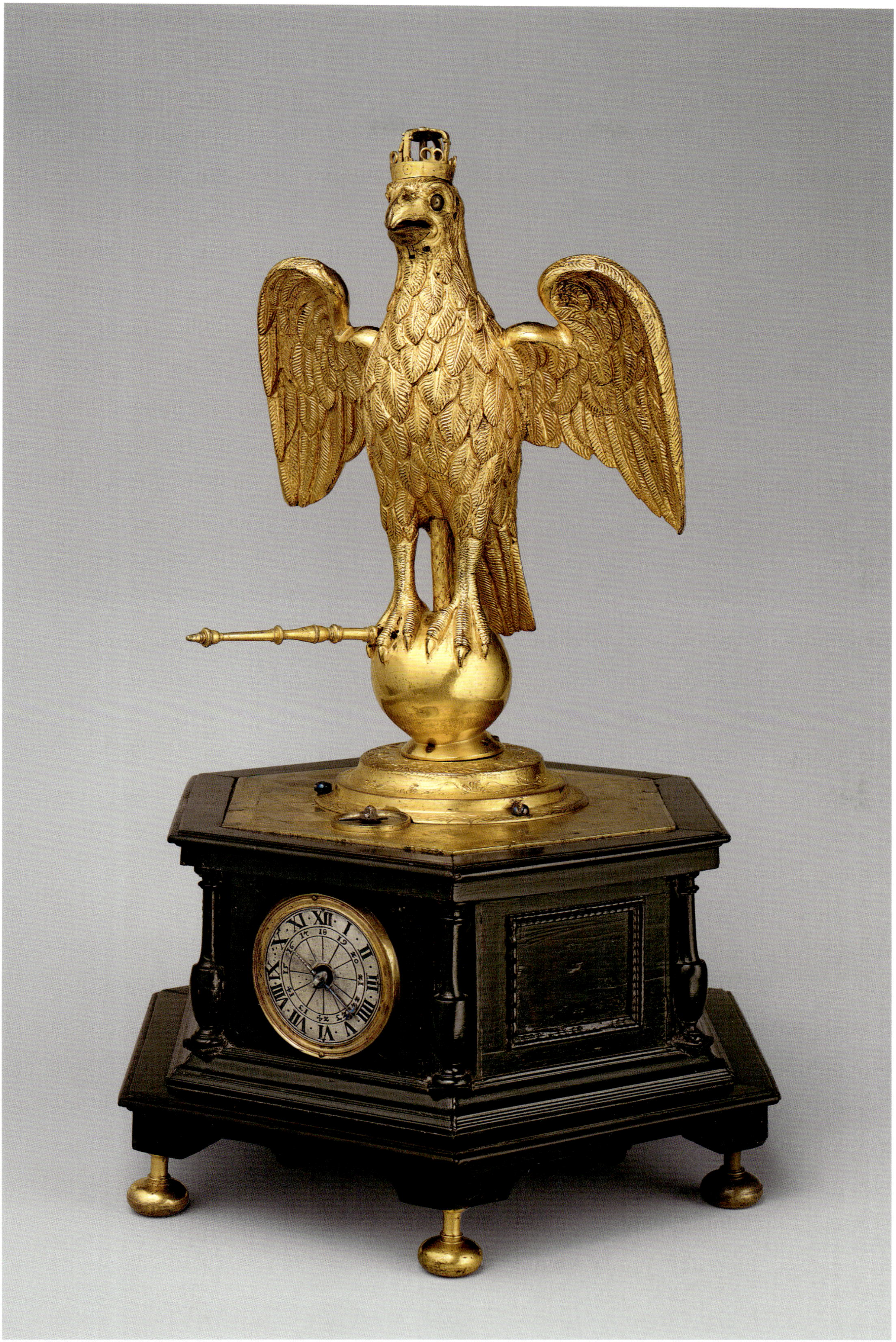

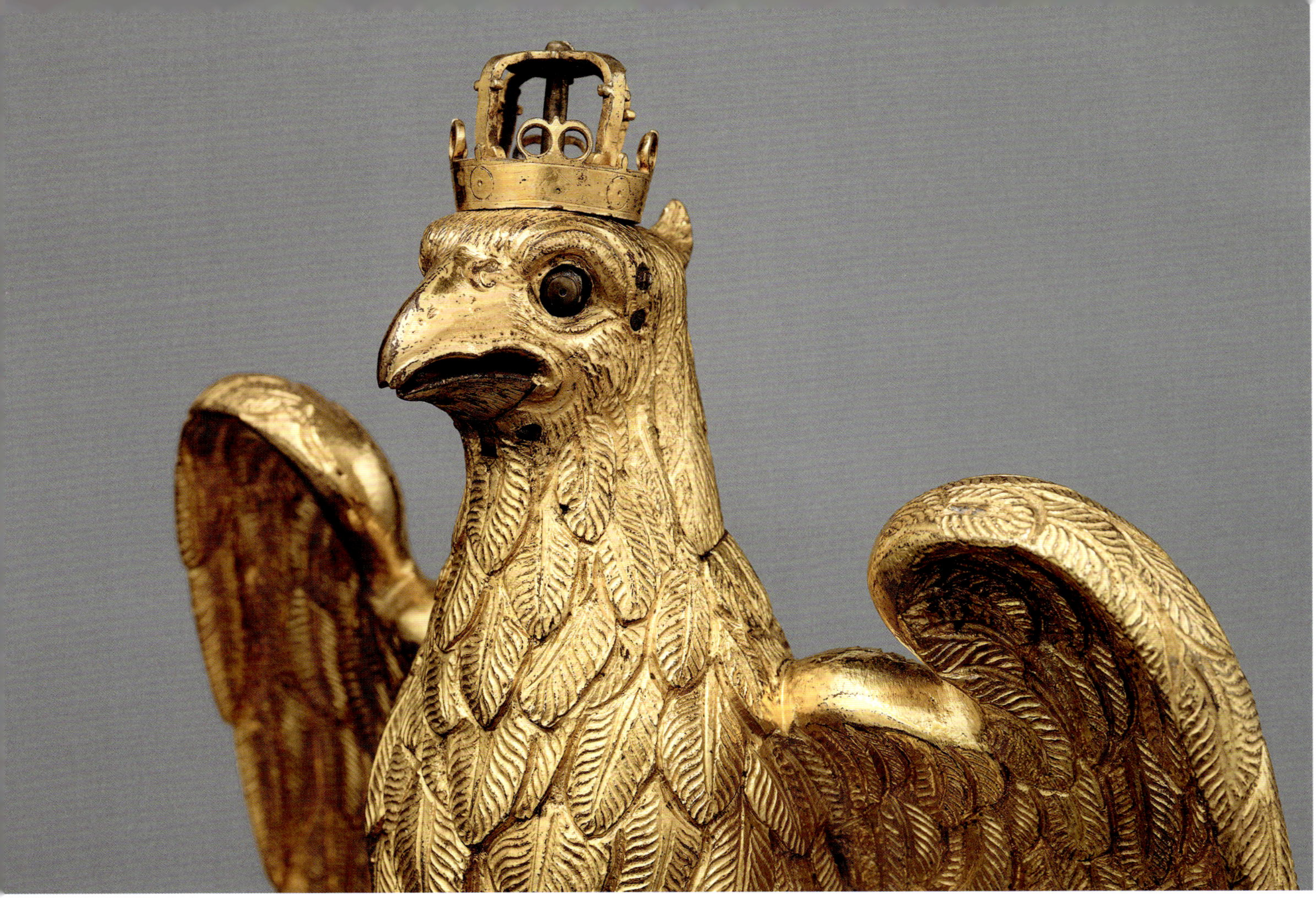

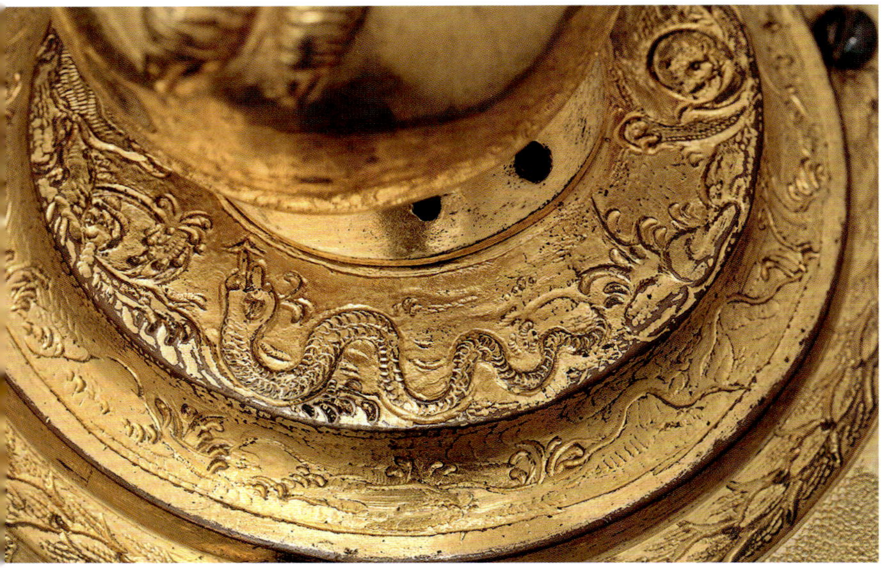

top: *Detail of the eagle's head with moving eye and beak*
above: *Detail of plinth on which the eagle stands*

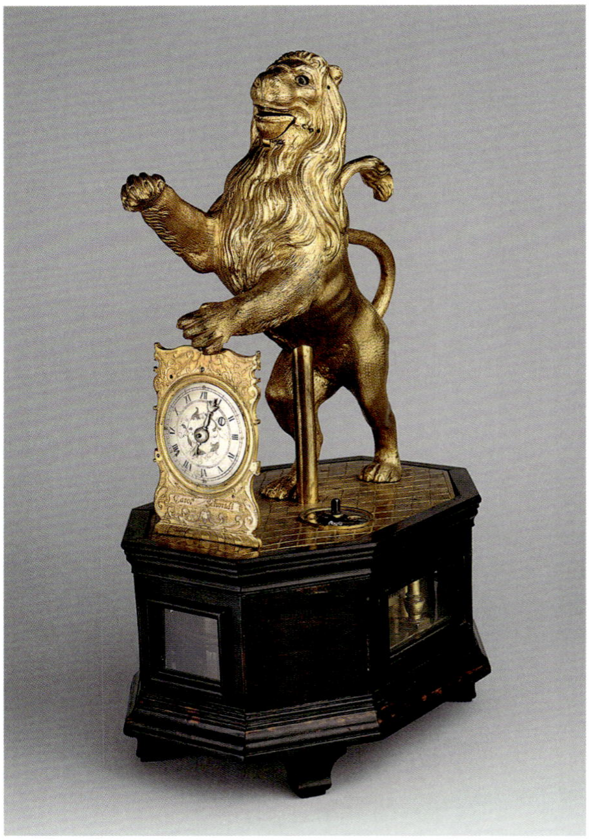

fig. 22 *Carol Schmidt (German, ca. 1590–1635/36). Automaton Clock in the Form of a Lion, German (Augsburg), ca. 1620–35. Case: gilded brass and gilded silver on base of ebony and fruitwood veneered with ebony; dial: silvered brass; movement: iron and brass, 13½ × 8 × 5½ in. (34.3 × 20.3 × 14 cm). The Metropolitan Museum of Art, New York, Gift of Mrs. Simon Guggenheim, 1929 (29.52.15)*

brass founders, too, remain anonymous, but a surviving record from 1588 indicates that only seven independent founders were permitted to work for clockmakers.[5] Nevertheless, by about 1600, these founders, whatever their number, had the capacity for serial production of the brass figures. Some, but not all, of the clockmakers who participated in this production signed their movements. Thus, we can identify, for example, the automaton clockwork by Nicholas Schmidt the Elder (master in 1576) and Carol (or Karl) Schmidt (master in 1614), both represented in the Metropolitan Museum's collection, the latter by one of the popular rampant lion automata (fig. 22).[6]

The figure of the eagle on the Museum's clock, with its wings spread in heraldic fashion, wears an imperial crown, grasps a scepter in its talons, and stands on a gilded ball supported by a circular plinth. The plinth is stepped and ornamented by a natural landscape that is inhabited by tiny figures, including a snail, a snake, and a lizard. The plinth that forms the top of the base for the clock, in turn, rests on a hexagonal brass plate that is engraved with lozenges, alternately plain and matte. The remainder of the base is veneered with ebony and has ebony moldings at the top and bottom of its six sides, five ornamented by rectangular ripple moldings, with turned ebony balusters applied to all six corners. The structure is supported on six brass feet. The sixth side of the case displays a circular silver dial with a single, sculptured-iron hand. The hours on the outer chapter ring are marked one–twelve, and the half hours are indicated by dots. The hours on the inner chapter ring (thirteen–twenty-four) begin at the seven o'clock position instead of the one o'clock—probably a way of using the clock to register Italian hours, which begin at sundown. A small dial on the top of the base and in front of the eagle registers the last quarter hour struck (one–four).

The spring-driven movement consists of three trains made of iron wheels that are mounted between two hexagonal brass plates, which are held apart by six pillars. The movement is wound from the underside of the base, and it strikes hours and quarters on two bells mounted on the back plate. The eagle's scepter moves up and down when the clock strikes the hours; the bird originally opened and shut its beak and probably rolled its eyes when the clock struck the quarter hours.

As a free city of the Holy Roman Empire, Augsburg owed allegiance directly to the Habsburg Holy Roman Emperors. The eagle, an emblem of the Habsburgs, thus had special meaning for the city. The stiff heraldic pose of the bird with the crown and scepter was doubtlessly intended as a felicitous reminder of imperial patronage, a patronage that supported, among others, two of the best mathematicians/astronomers of the age: Tycho Brahe (1546–1601) and Johannes Kepler (1571–1630). This eagle may plausibly be considered a close relative of the magnanimous imperial bird that showers coins upon the scientists of the court of Rudolf II, as depicted on the title page of the *Tabulae Rudolphinae*, the astronomical tables published in Ulm, Germany, in 1627 by Kepler (fig. 21). It may also be regarded as an evocative survivor of an era that has been described as the transitional period in which the quasi-magical worldview of the sixteenth century began to give way to the mechanical universe of the seventeenth.[7]

The connection between the clockwork movement and the automaton's eyes is now missing, but it is possible that the eyes originally moved from side to side with the ticking of the clock. Probably in the second half of the seventeenth century, the original verge escapement and balance of the clock were replaced with a short and shoddily constructed pendulum. The suspension for the pendulum required a sizeable slot to be cut in one side of the case. In 1978, both the pendulum and the suspension were removed, and the slot was filled. At the same time, two trapezoidal brass plaques of relatively modern origin that were attached to the sides of the hour dial were removed and replaced with wooden panels to allow the mounting of the dial to more closely resemble the mounting of dials on other wooden bases in Augsburg figural clocks of the first half of the seventeenth century. In addition, the left rear foot was replaced by a cast of one of the originals.

It is not known when or where Mrs. Guggenheim acquired this clock. In contrast to the many lion and dog automata still in existence,[8] only one other eagle automaton is known, which is in the collection of the Mathematisch-Physikalischer Salon, Dresden.[9] The Dresden eagle is identical to the Museum's piece but lacks the scepter. The base is ebony but differently shaped. In addition, the Dresden movement strikes only the hours and activates only the beak and eyes. Like the Museum's automaton, it is unsigned. CV / JHL

1 For a more complete description, see Burke 2006.
2 Garai 2007, pp. 11–23.
3 The automata are now in the British Museum, London; the Musée National de la Renaissance, Ecouen; and the Kunsthistorisches Museum, Vienna (the last most beautifully finished with painted sails and supplied with both musical and nautical sounds). See de Conihout et al. 2001.
4 Himmelheber 1980.
5 Groiss 1980, p. 71. For a discussion of the brass-founders' models, see Maurice 1976, vol. 1, pp. 111–18.
6 Acc. nos. 29.52.13 and 29.52.15.
7 See, for example, Yates 1984, pp. 219–20.
8 See, for examples, Maurice 1976, vol. 2, p. 51, nos. 318–27, and figs. 318–27, and p. 52, nos. 332–36, and figs. 332–36.
9 Ibid., p. 50, no. 308, and fig. 308.

10. Watch

FRENCH (AGEN), CA. 1630–40
1¼ × 1¹⁄₁₆ × 1 in. (3.2 × 2.7 × 2.5 cm)
Gift of J. Pierpont Morgan, 1917
17.190.1579

CASE: rock crystal and enameled gold mounts
DIAL: gold, champlevé, enamel, and painted enamel
MOVEMENT: gilded brass and partly blued steel, signed (on back plate): *P / Vernede / Agen* [Pierre Vernède, probably French, active ca. 1630]

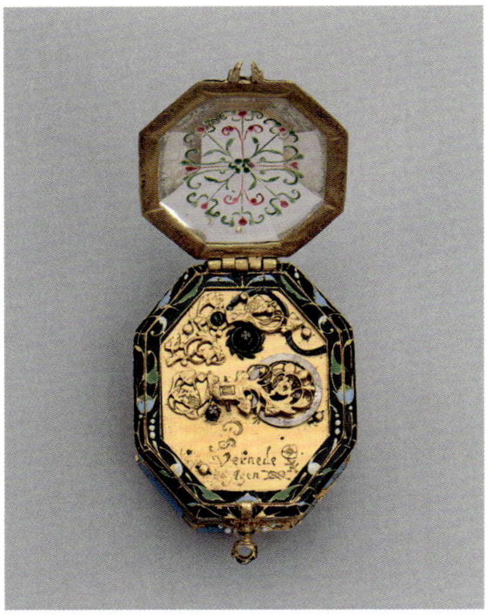

Case open to show movement

DURING THE REIGN OF KING LOUIS XIII (1601–1643), A SINGULAR variety of ornament now known as *cosses de pois* (or peapod) became fashionable largely for the embellishment of jewelry but also for the enameled gold mounts of precious objects,[1] watchcases, and horse gear.[2] The origins of the style, as traced by art historians Peter Fuhring and Michèle Bimbenet-Privat, lie in the ornamental use of depictions of peapods split open to reveal rows of peas.[3] Found, for example, in a sixteenth-century German print by Hans Leinberger (active 1510–30), these rows were created in a somewhat analogous way to the bunches of grapes used by the better-known Albrecht Dürer as framing elements for some of his woodcuts.[4] Fuhring and Bimbenet-Privat also pointed out the similarities of certain leaf motifs found in the peapod style to those in the moresque ornament that was in vogue in the sixteenth and early seventeenth centuries throughout Western Europe.[5] By compiling numerous examples of ornament prints, for the most part by French and German artists, including some designs for black-and-white ornament, Fuhring and Bimbenet-Privat were able to document the increasing stylization of the pea and leaf motifs over the course of the first forty years of the seventeenth century.

It is among these prints that the sources of the three Metropolitan Museum watches with enameled gold and rock crystal cases can be established. All three watches have signed movements, but it is not certain who the casemakers were or where they might have been working. The dial plate for the Vernède watch displays the chains of graduated spheres, or "peas," and the trifid-shaped leaf motifs that are characteristically found in the ornament prints, for example, in the two series of engravings published between 1618 and 1619 in Châteaudun, France, by Jean I Toutin (1578–1644). The medallion from the Toutin series supported by a lion above two human figures—one singing and the other inexplicably playing a gridiron with a pair of tongs as though it were a musical instrument—reveals a decorative vocabulary that is closest to that of the Vernède watch dial. An eight-sided watchcase depicted in Toutin's Plate 4 compares closely in shape to the Museum's watch (fig. 23).

The second watch in the Museum's collection (fig. 24),[6] also in a rock crystal case, exhibits a far more abstract version of the peapod style. It has a movement signed "Noel Hubert à Gros Horloge a Rouen." Noël Hubert (1612–1650), founder of a dynasty of watch- and clockmakers, was keeper of the fourteenth-century public clock in the city of Rouen, France. The dial of Hubert's watch and the mounts of the case and cover display enameled gold designs that are abstract versions of peapod ornament leaves. They are comparable in type to the abstraction found in a number of anonymous prints dated to the 1620s,[7] but a few of these motifs can still be found in prints from designs by the Parisian

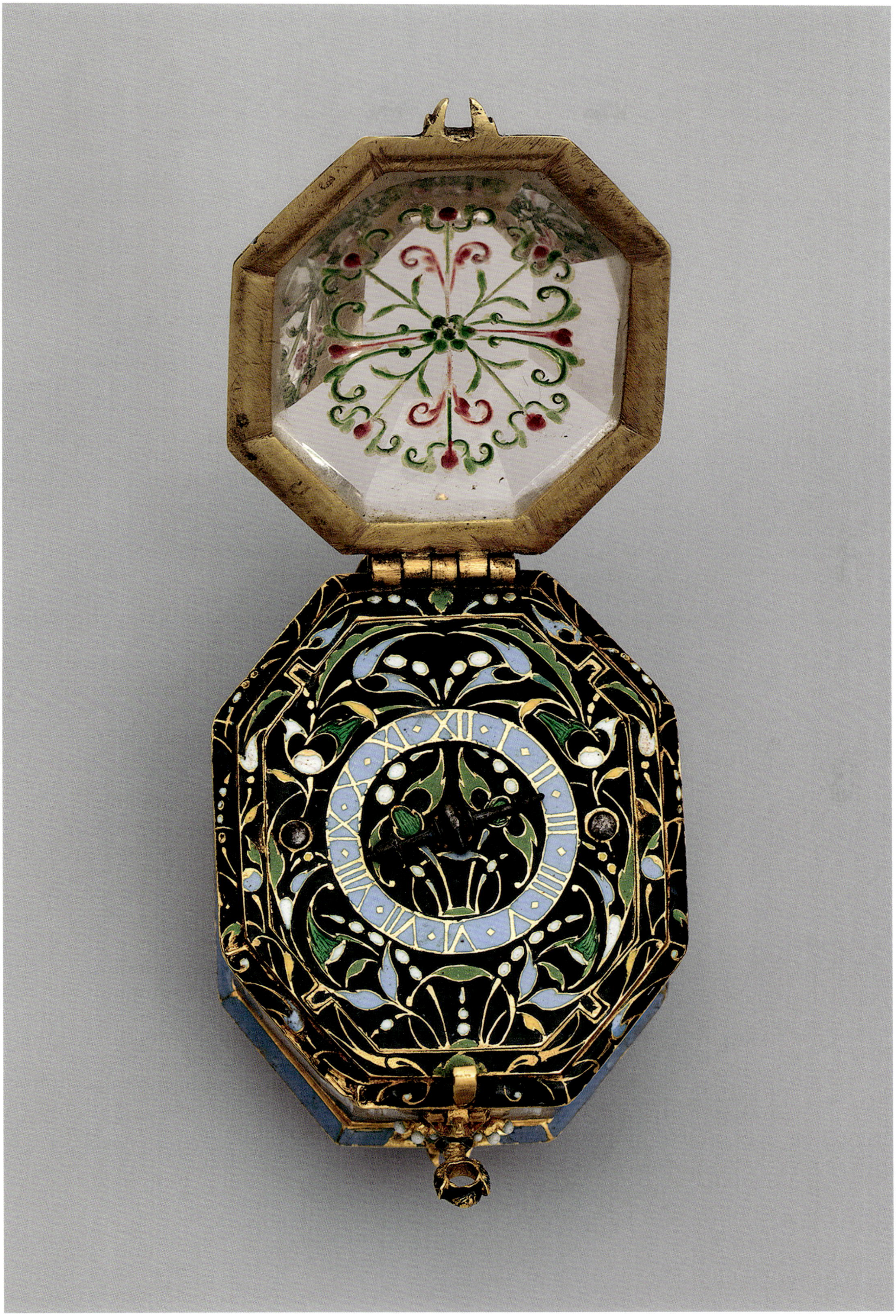

fig. 23 *Jean I Toutin (French, 1578–1644). Plate with Incidental Figures Engraved from Suite of Blackwork Designs for Jewelry, 1619. Engraving, 4¼ × 3⅛ in. (10.7 × 7.9 cm). Victoria and Albert Museum, London*

fig. 24 *Noël Hubert (French, 1612–1650). Watch, French (Rouen), ca. 1612–50. Case: rock crystal, gold, and enamel; movement: 1¼ × 1⅛ in. (3.2 × 2.9 cm). The Metropolitan Museum of Art, New York, Gift of J. Pierpont Morgan, 1917 (17.190.1594)*

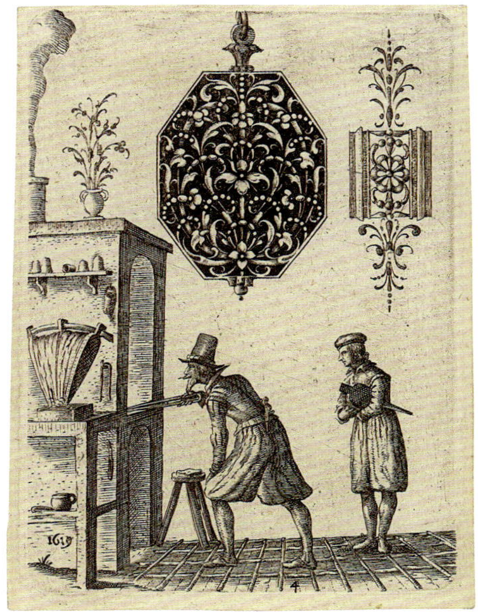

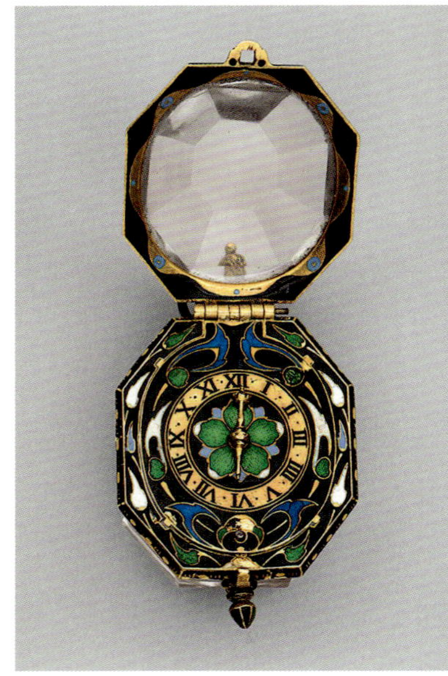

goldsmith Gédéon Légaré (1611–1676), especially some of those published by François Langlois, dit Ciartes (1588–1647), probably about 1635–40, but certainly before 1647.[8] The design of the Hubert watch dial was not, in fact, recognized as a variety of peapod design by some scholars, but considered instead to be the product of a nineteenth-century goldsmith.[9]

Further abstraction of the style appears on the enameled gold dial of a third watch with a rock crystal case in the Museum's collection, this one signed only with the initials of the watchmaker, "M I," on the back plate of the movement.[10] The movement is so small that the mainspring has been left open instead of being encased in a protective barrel, and a fusee has been omitted altogether. As might be expected, all of these watches are more clearly understood as jewelry that incidentally tells time rather than as serious timekeepers.

Rock crystal, a clear, transparent quartz that was in abundant supply in sixteenth- and seventeenth-century Europe from deposits in the Alps, was an ideal medium for the display of increasingly decorative movements of watches. The embellishment of the movement's pillars, set-up regulator, fusee stopwork, and balance cock made by skilled watchmakers; the moving wheels of the train, many with finely cut teeth; and above all the back-and-forth movement of the verge and balance could be observed through a transparent rock crystal case. The cutting, polishing, and engraving of rock crystal need both human skill and special equipment. Lapidary craftsmen concentrated in centers such as Paris, Venice, Milan, Florence, and Prague turned this craft into high art. But there were other, lesser-known centers; for example, lapidaries working in Freiberg im Breisgau, Germany, specialized in making necklaces and bracelets of rock crystal beads as well as other small objects for use by jewelers.[11] Very little is known, however, about the craftsmen who may have specialized in making rock crystal watchcases or about where they worked. Some were undoubtedly from Geneva, but surely they were not exclusively based there.

A few contemporary references found to either the watches with rock crystal cases or to other cases provide some evidence that these cases were used by watchmakers in widely divergent locations. For example, the will of the London clockmaker Bartholomew Newsam, dated in early 1585, states that he owned a "cristall Jewell with a watch in it,"[12] but we cannot be sure that the movement was made by Newsam or where he might have acquired it. In 1623 the Augsburg connoisseur and art agent Philipp Hainhofer (1578–1647) wrote to his German patron Prince August dem Junger of Braunschweig-Lüneburg (1579–1664) about a crystal watch in the possession of the English ambassador to Venice,[13] adding in another letter[14] that a similar one could be made in the town of Kempten in Bavaria, presumably by the master clockmaker Georg Hipp.[15] By 1648, the estate of the Dutch goldsmith Minne Sikkes (active 1618, died 1648), who worked in the Friesian city of Leeuwarden, is known to have contained one large crystal watchcase and four smaller ones. We do not know where he obtained them.

Agen, a small city on the Garonne River about halfway between Bordeaux and Toulouse, would have been an unlikely place for fashioning rock crystal into watchcases. Further, the exquisite case of the Museum's Vernède watch suggests that it must have been made in a center of skilled jewelers, which seventeenth-century Agen is not known to have possessed. The case consists of an elongated, octagonal band of rock crystal. The exterior surface of each of the eight sides is cut with a rectangle bordered by four trapezoids. A second border frames the first with rectangles alternating with trapezoids. On the interior surface of each facet of the cover is an engraved design of scroll embellishment, which is colored red and green and radiates from a central rosette. The crystal elements are all mounted in enamel and gold, each with a design drawn from the peapod vocabulary on a ground of black.

The dial expands on the peapod theme with symmetrical designs of leaves in opaque light blue, translucent green, opaque green, mustard, and white champlevé and painted enamels on a black ground. The chapter ring is created from a light-blue champlevé enamel that encompasses the numerals I–XII in gold for the hours and gold dots for the half hours. A single blued-steel hand completes the functional portion of the design. The enameled gold pendant at the top of the watchcase band continues the theme with three-dimensional peapods and peas covered with *en ronde-bosse* enamel and flanking a central floral bud that serves as the support for a loop for hanging the watch. A finial at the bottom of the band repeats the pea- and bud-shaped loop motifs. The plated movement fits snugly into the case held by four lugs and two spring catches that are manipulated by tiny knobs at the three and nine o'clock positions on the dial plate.

The movement, as exquisite as the case, consists of two elongated octagonal plates of gilded brass, which are held apart by four baluster-shaped pillars. The movement contains a train of three wheels with a verge escapement, a steel balance, and a tall, French-style fusee with fine grooves to accommodate a thin gut line. The back plate carries elaborately pierced and engraved ornament of gilded brass for the ratchet and click set-up regulator of the mainspring. A similarly elaborate ornamented cock for securing the top pivot of the verge staff is pinned to a post attached to the plate, and through a hole in the plate below the foot of the cock projects the winding square (the end of the steel shaft for winding the mainspring), its tiny tip embellished by shaped grooves in a Greek cross design. Below the cock the signature of the watchmaker is engraved, "P / Vernede / Agen." Almost nothing is known of this maker except that he was apparently the first in a family of resident clockmakers in Agen who are recorded throughout the remainder of the seventeenth century and the first half of the eighteenth century.[16]

The Noël Hubert watch in the Museum's collection is encased in a single piece of hollowed-out rock crystal with a central trapezoid faceted on the exterior and surrounded by alternating triangles and trapezoids, including a second frame of trapezoids that forms the transition to the eight square and trapezoidal facets on the side of the case (fig. 24). A similar pattern of facets shapes the convex cover for the dial of the watch. Like the Vernède watch dial, the gold dial of this watch is embellished with champlevé and painted enamel on a black-enamel ground, but with a gold chapter of hours, the numerals (I–XII) in black enamel and the half hours marked by dots. A single, sculptural gold hand completes the face of the watch.

The movement, like the cover for the dial, is hinged to the mounting of the case and consists of two oval plates of gilded brass, which are held apart by four baluster-shaped pillars. It has three wheels and a verge escapement with a steel balance, a decorative set-up regulator for the mainspring, and a pinned on, openwork cock for securing the staff of the verge. The signature on the back plate now reads "Noel Huber (t) / A gros Hor / (lo)ge ARouen," the partial effacement indicating that the arbors for the second and third wheels of the movement have been disturbed, either for repair or more likely replacement, and the back plate has been regilded. The Vernède watch movement is in good condition, but the finial at the bottom of the case is bent and most of its enamel lost. The pendant, too, has lost much of its enamel, and there are small losses to the enamel on both cases, especially in the areas around the catches for closing the covers and on the Vernède for securing the movement within the case.

It is not known where J. Pierpont Morgan acquired the Varnède watch, but the third one, signed with the initials "M I," belonged to Carl H. Marfels of Frankfurt am Main and Berlin.[17] CV / JHL

1 See, for example, Alcouffe 2001, pp. 379–98, including mounts by Pierre Delabarre and Jean Vangrol.
2 For the trappings for the horse ridden by the Danish king Christian IV (1577–1648) at the wedding of his son in 1634, see Hein 2009, vol. 3, pp. 242–50, nos. 1010–18.
3 Fuhring and Bimbenet-Privat 2002, pp. 5–7.
4 For example, see the Carthusian Madonna with St. John the Baptist and St. Bruno spandrel decoration or the Conrad Celtes Presenting the *Quattuor Libri Amorum* to Maximilian I, Nürnberg, Apr. 13, 1502; Knappe 1965, figs. 324 and 210, respectively.
5 Fuhring and Bimbenet-Privat 2002, pp. 9–10.
6 Acc. no. 17.190.1594.
7 Fuhring and Bimbenet-Privat 2002, pp. 51–63.
8 Ibid., pp. 112–14.
9 Recent analyses by Mark T. Wypyski, Research Scientist in the Metropolitan Museum's Department of Scientific Research, have confirmed the composition of the enamel to be compatible with that of seventeenth-century enamel, rather than that in use during the second half of the nineteenth century.
10 Acc. no. 17.190.1551. The watchmaker M. I. has not been identified, but he was probably German. He was not Matthew Ive, as proposed in Williamson 1912, pp. 128–29.
11 Irmscher 1997, p. 34.
12 The will of Bartholomew Newsam, Clock Maker of Saint Mary in the Strand, Middlesex, probated on Dec. 18, 1593, Neville Quire Numbers 48–96, Public Record Office, National Archives. See also entry 5 in this volume for more about Newsam.
13 Gobiet 1984, p. 374.
14 Ibid., p. 378.
15 See Maurice 1976, vol. 1, p. 175. Hipp was listed among notable citizens of Kempten in Zorn 1820, p. 67.
16 Tardy 1971–72, vol. 2, p. 639. See also Hayard 2004, p. 135. Williamson 1912, pp. 1 and 2, confused Jean Vernède, one of the eighteenth-century Vernèdes, with Pierre Vernède.
17 Williamson 1912, pp. 128–29, no. 130.

11. Astronomical Table Clock

GERMAN (AUGSBURG), SECOND QUARTER OF THE SEVENTEENTH CENTURY

25 × 10 × 10 in. (63.5 × 25.4 × 25.4 cm)
Gift of J. Pierpont Morgan, 1917
17.190.747

CASE: gilded brass and gilded copper, marked (on interior of each side panel, in cameo): *pyr* (or pinecone) for Augsburg within a shield-shaped reserve
DIALS: gilded brass and silver
MOVEMENT: brass, gilded brass, and steel

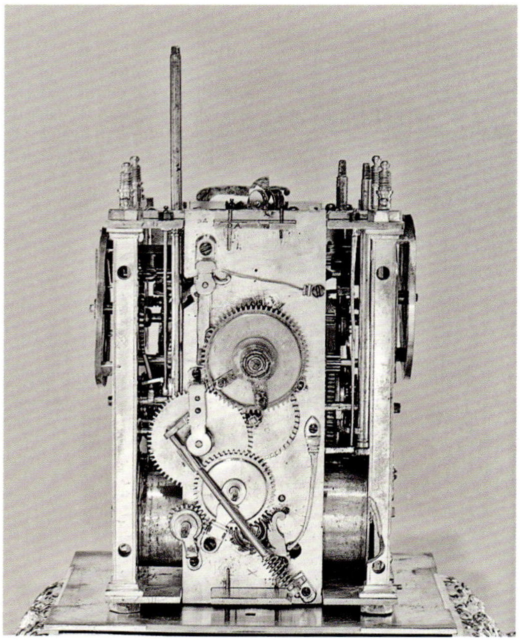

Posted frame movement with the motion work for the time-telling side of the clock

CLOCKMAKING WAS AN ESTABLISHED CRAFT IN THE FREE IMPERIAL city of Augsburg as early as the end of the fourteenth century. Two centuries later, the increasing prosperity of the city, led by the Fugger and the Welser families of merchants and bankers, supported a flourishing trade in clockmaking, and by the second half of the century the city had become the most important center of European clockmaking.[1] In fact, the talented Gerhard Emmoser, later clockmaker in Vienna to two Holy Roman Emperors, was sent by Emperor Ferdinand I (1503–1564) to Augsburg in 1563, specifically to improve his clockmaking skills.[2]

Originally Augsburg clockmakers belonged to the city's guild of blacksmiths due to the similarity of material with which they worked.[3] In 1558, no doubt at least in part as the result of increasing success, the requirements for membership in the guild included prescribed demonstrations of the clockmaker's skill in the form of a masterpiece, or admission piece.[4] One of the requirements at this time consisted of making a spring-driven, quarter-striking movement with a mechanically driven astrolabe dial. Within a few years, however, this requirement was deemed inadequate, and by December 1577, a new set of requirements were agreed upon. An aspiring clockmaker would make one clock chosen by the guild officials from a list of five. One of the clocks on the list of five was a spring-driven, quarter-striking clock movement with an alarm, a mechanically driven astrolabe, and mechanisms showing the length of the days (Nürnberg hours), the days of the year (calendar), and the days of the week (the planets with their signs). All these dials were to be interconnected and to move together with the motion of the hand on the main time-telling dial, and the clock was to strike the hours, one through twelve or alternatively one through twenty-four, according to the desire of the user.[5] These rules remained in force until 1650.

These specifications for an Augsburg masterpiece account for the form of the Metropolitan Museum's astronomical table clock and explain its peculiarly old-fashioned character. Shaped like a miniature tower with two bells and a cupola at the top with a finial in the form of an openwork obelisk, the clock has a movement constructed of four brass pillars that separate two square, horizontal brass plates. Four brass bars are pinned to the top and bottom plates, and these bars support the arbors of the going train and the two striking trains. In addition, they support the motion work for the multiple dials found on two of the four sides of the tower, one principally devoted to time-telling, the other to astronomical information. The large dial on the time-telling side consists of a calendar ring with Saints Days, which frames the concentric chapter rings for various methods of dividing the day. These rings are calibrated respectively Arabic numerals 1–60 by 5s;

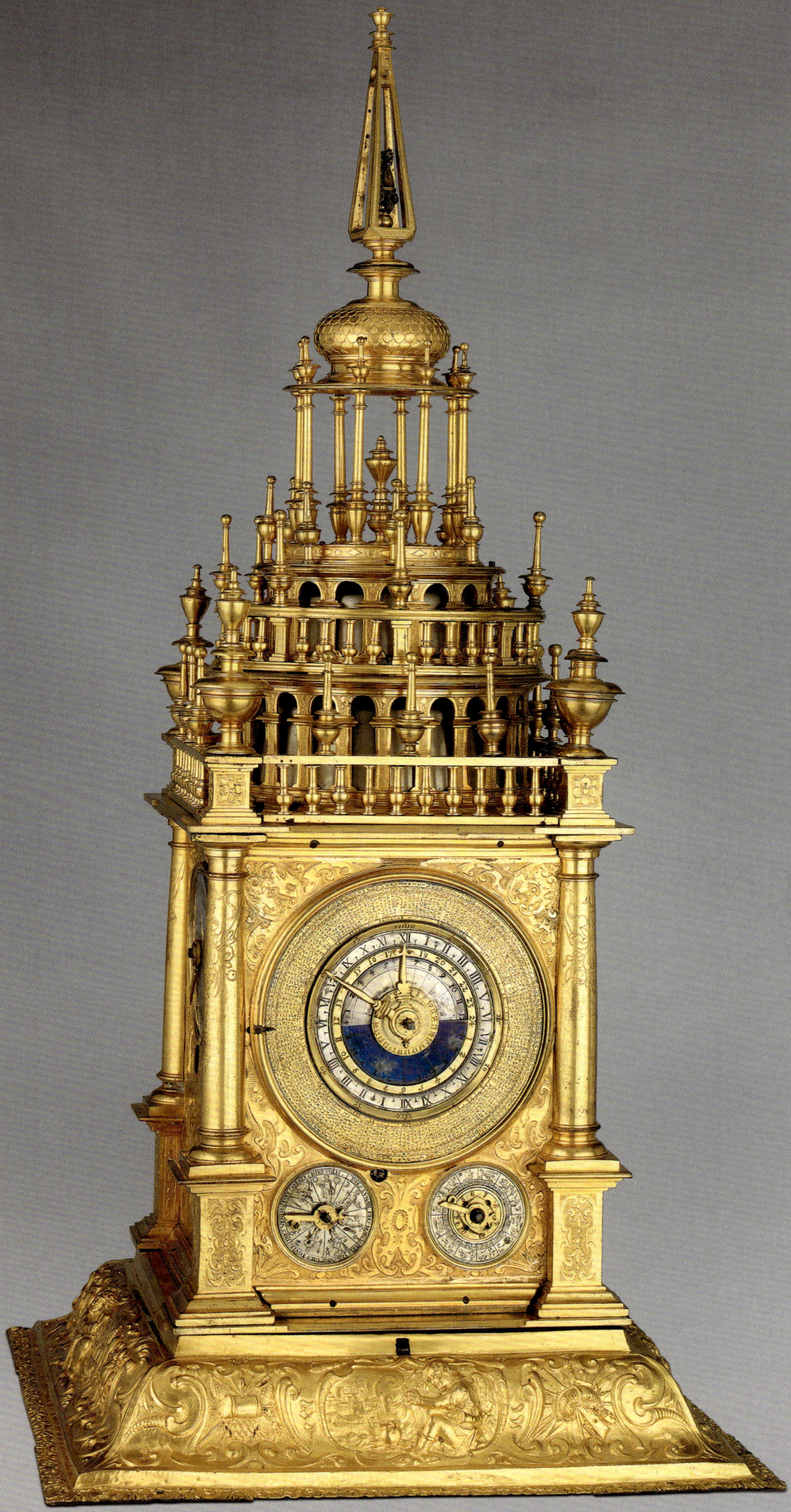

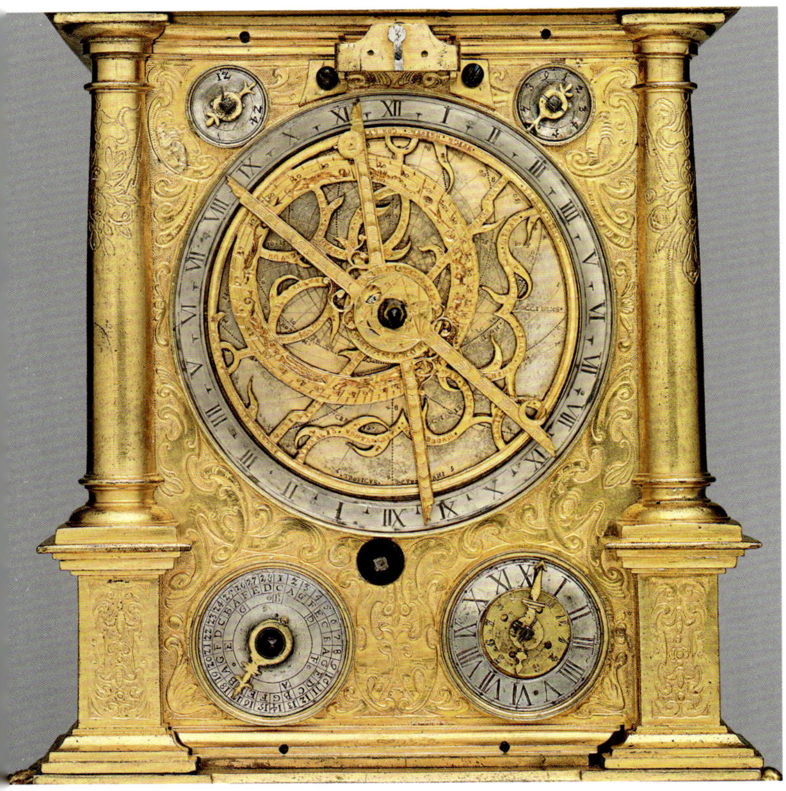

Detail of the case showing the astrolabe

roman numerals I–XII twice, with half hours marked; and Arabic numerals 1–24 beginning at sundown (Italian hours). The center of the dial consists of sliding shutters, one made of silver (day), the other of blued steel (night), which are mechanically adjusted for dividing daylight and nighttime hours. These are of equal length but vary in number according to the season of the year. The dial at the lower right governs the movement of the shutters according to the length of the day, and the hand in the center of this dial can be adjusted for the latitude in which the clock is to be used. The dial on the lower left indicates the days of the week, each with a representation of its planetary god or goddess.

The large dial on the opposite side of the tower is a mechanically driven astrolabe showing the apparent motions of nearly twenty stars in the sky as seen on earth from latitude 40 degrees in the northern hemisphere. Two hands show the positions of the sun and the moon in the zodiac, and the phases and age of the moon in its monthly cycle, as well as mean solar time. The central disk also includes an aspectarium, primarily for use by astrologers. At the upper left is a small dial for adjusting the striking of the clock for twelve or twenty-four hours and on the upper right is an adjustment for the going train of the clock. The small dial at the lower left is an epact that can be manually adjusted for a system called Dominical Letters, by which the date for Easter, as well as of each Sunday in the year, can be determined.[6] The small dial on the lower right, marked I–XII, is the setting for the alarm that is powered by its own separate spring, which is wound by the square in the center of the dial for the Dominical Letters.

Two major trains, each placed perpendicular to the going train, power the striking of the hours and quarters on the two bells that are installed at the top of the clock. The bars securing the striking trains are ornamented with elaborately pierced and engraved scrolls, which serve as covers for the clicks of the ratchet wheels that control the setups of their springs. On the sides of the clock, there are two engraved silver dials that register the quarter striking of the clock (1–4, each hour) on one side, and an alternative Italian system for striking the hours (1–6, four times a day) on the other.

It is evident that this clock displays all of the elements required for an admission piece to the Augsburg guild in 1577: it is spring-driven and quarter striking with an alarm; it has a mechanically driven astrolabe and a dial for the length of the day; it has a dial for the days of the week and a calendar for the days of the year; and it was made to strike the hours on both the one–twelve and one–twenty-four systems. If the aspiring clockmaker had to construct a movement that met the requirements of the guild, there were no corresponding rules for making the case, and the clockmaker was free to take advantage of the variety and skill of the metalworkers who were available in Augsburg at the time. Thus the tower-like form, developed during the course of the late sixteenth century, could be covered with ornament that was in fashion about three-quarters of a century later.

The entire body of the clock can be turned on its base to allow for easy viewing of all sides. The repoussé copper base depicts infant personifications of the Four Seasons, each framed by a baroque cartouche and flanked by appropriate trophy designs: Winter, a tiny figure warming his hands over a steaming pot; Spring, an infant with a spade and potted plant, seated in a landscape; Summer, holding a sickle and grain sheaf in his left hand and a scythe in his right hand, with peasants in the background harvesting sorghum; and Autumn, seated on a wine cask and holding a very large drinking cup. The cartouches, lighthearted versions of a style favored by Augsburg metalworkers, were originally introduced in the more sober baroque designs published by the Augsburg engraver and printmaker Lucas Kilian (1579–1637), whose *Nevves Schildtbyhlin Gstochen* appeared in 1610.[7] The gilded-brass sides of the clock are covered with foliate scrolls that display traces of the auricular style invented by Dutch silversmiths in the early seventeenth century. The spiky exuberance of the scrollwork owes a great deal, however, to Kilian's later designs, such as those that appeared in the *Newes A B C Büechlein* (1627)[8] and the *Newes Schild Büchlein* (1633).[9]

It is the ornament that places this clock firmly in the second quarter of the seventeenth century, probably only a few years before the application of the pendulum to clockwork permitted routine production of really accurate timekeepers. As it was fitted with a short pendulum at some point, perhaps not long after the publication of the invention by the Dutch mathematician Christiaan Huygens (1629–1695),[10] the museum's clock was presumably made before 1658. In any case, Huygens's invention so changed the timekeeping properties of the mechanical clock as to render obsolete clocks such as this one and its many complications, but less-than-precise timekeeping.

The clock bears only the town marks of Augsburg. This appears to be an incomplete method of signing, because the complete signature during this period usually consists of the town mark and the maker's mark. It has become quite certain that as a general rule, clockmakers did not use a maker's mark unless authorized by guild authorities. In many important centers, however, it was customary for a young master to put his name or his mark on his masterpiece after being admitted to the guild. As a result of this practice, signatures do sometimes appear on masterpiece clocks, but since there is neither a signature nor a maker's mark on the Museum's clock, it may best be considered an unsigned masterpiece.

The short pendulum that was substituted for the original balance has been removed and stored. Keys for the striking trains, the alarm, and for setting the various subsidiary dials are missing, but the openwork obelisk of the top of the clock is removable and doubles as the key for winding and setting the going train. A tiny key with a bow in the shape of a horse's head fits nicely within the obelisk, but it has nothing to do with the functioning of the clock. Associated with the clock by 1917, it is likely a nineteenth-century watch key. A square wooden base supported by four gilded-brass, split-tailed lions, the latter of distinctly inferior quality, had become attached to the clock by 1917. It is not known when or by whom the wooden base was made, or where or from whom the donor, J. Pierpont Morgan, acquired the clock. CV / JHL

1 Maurice 1976, vol. 1, p. 167. See also Groiss 1980, pp. 57–60.
2 Chandler and Vincent 1980, p. 112. See also entry 4 in this volume.
3 Maurice 1976, vol. 1, p. 293.
4 Bobinger 1969, p. 16.
5 Akt Uhrmacher, 1544–1602, Stadtarchiv, Augsburg; see ibid., p. 17 and pl. 2.
6 For a fuller explanation of the Dominical Letters, see Vincent and Chandler 1969, p. 382.
7 Berliner and Egger 1981, vol. 1, p. 78, nos. 864, 865, and vol. 2, ill. nos. 864, 865. See also Hollstein, *German*, 1954–2014, vol. 17 (1976), pp. 156–57, nos. 674–97.
8 Hollstein, *German*, 1954–2014, vol. 17 (1976), p. 151, nos. 572–96.
9 Berliner and Egger 1981, vol. 1, p. 79, no. 869, and vol. 2, ill. no. 869. See also Hollstein, *German*, 1954–2014, vol. 17 (1976), pp. 156–57, nos. 674–97.
10 Huygens (Christiaan) 1658.

12. Watch

FRENCH (PROBABLY PARIS), CA. 1645–50
Diam. of case: 2 5/16 in. (5.9 cm)
Diam. of back plate: 1 15/16 in. (4.9 cm)
Gift of J. Pierpont Morgan, 1917
17.190.1557

CASE AND DIAL: painted enamel on gold with brass hand
MOVEMENT: gilded brass and partly blued steel, signed (on the back plate): *Goullons Æparis* [Jacques Goullons or Coullons, French, recorded 1626; active in Paris ca. 1640–60, died 1671]

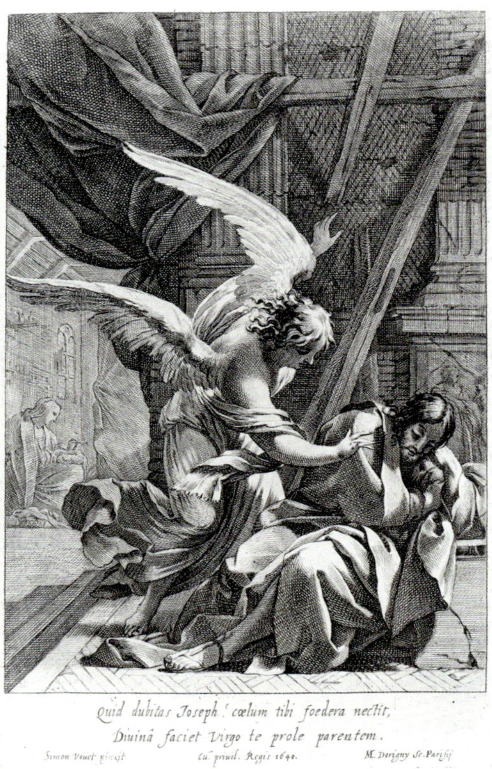

fig. 25 *Michel Dorigny (French, 1617–1665), after Simon Vouet (French, 1590–1649).* Joseph Awakened by the Angel, *1640. Engraving, 12¼ × 8 in. (31.1 × 20.2 cm). The Metropolitan Museum of Art, New York, Harris Brisbane Dick Fund, 1945 (45.97[16])*

top: *Joseph Awakened by the Angel on the exterior of the cover of the watchcase*
bottom: *The Virgin and Child with an Angel on the back of the watchcase*

DURING THE SEVENTEENTH CENTURY, WATCHCASES MADE BY French enamelers include some of the most magnificent examples ever produced. The enameled scenes on this watchcase are beautiful demonstrations of the variety of enameling on a pure white ground, which at its best rivaled miniature painting on paper or parchment. Developed in France about 1630, the technique is generally ascribed to Jean I Toutin (1578–1644). The earliest watchcases enameled in this technique probably originated in Blois, a French city known for both its enameling and its watchmaking,[1] where the enamelers were under the special protection of Gaston, duc d'Orléans (1608–1660), who was also the brother of the the king of France. Paris was an early and important center of enamel production as well, and Toutin's son Henri (1614–1684) settled there in 1636, as we know from an inscription on the reverse of an enameled portrait of King Charles I (1600–1649) of England, which is now in the Mauritshuis Royal Art Gallery in The Hague.[2] Henri signed a gold watchcase with painted enamel scenes alluding to the marriage in 1641 of the Stadtholder of the United Provinces, William II, Prince of Orange (1626–1650) to Mary Stuart (1631–1660). Now in the Rijksmuseum in Amsterdam,[3] the watchcase is an extraordinary work of art, and its design was perhaps originally conceived by Henri Toutin.

Most enamelers, however, were not creative artists. As an increasing number of sources have been identified from which the painters of enameled watchcases took their designs, it now seems safe to say that most, if not all, of these painters were content to reproduce in miniature the work of other artists. Most of the enamelers remain anonymous, and usually the style of their enamels reflects the style of the artist whose work they reproduced.[4]

The scenes on the exteriors, both front and back, of this watch provide an excellent example of the propensity to reproduce not only the design but also the style of their prototypes, and both were inspired by the paintings of Simon Vouet (1590–1649), First Painter to King Louis XIII. With certain modifications made chiefly to fit the circular shape of the watch, the biblical scene of the Virgin and Child with an Angel on the back of the case is the reproduction of an engraving by Pierre Daret (1605–1678), based on a Vouet painting. As the watchcase figures are oriented in the same direction as the figures in the print, it seems reliable to conclude that the enameler was, in fact, working from the print, because in the original painting, now in the Musée des Beaux-Arts de Caen, the composition is reversed. The scene on the front cover of the watch depicts Joseph Awakened by the Angel and retains the orientation of the two figures found in another engraving based on a Vouet painting, this one made by Michel Dorigny (1617–1665) (fig. 25). Like the scene of the Virgin and Child with an Angel, this

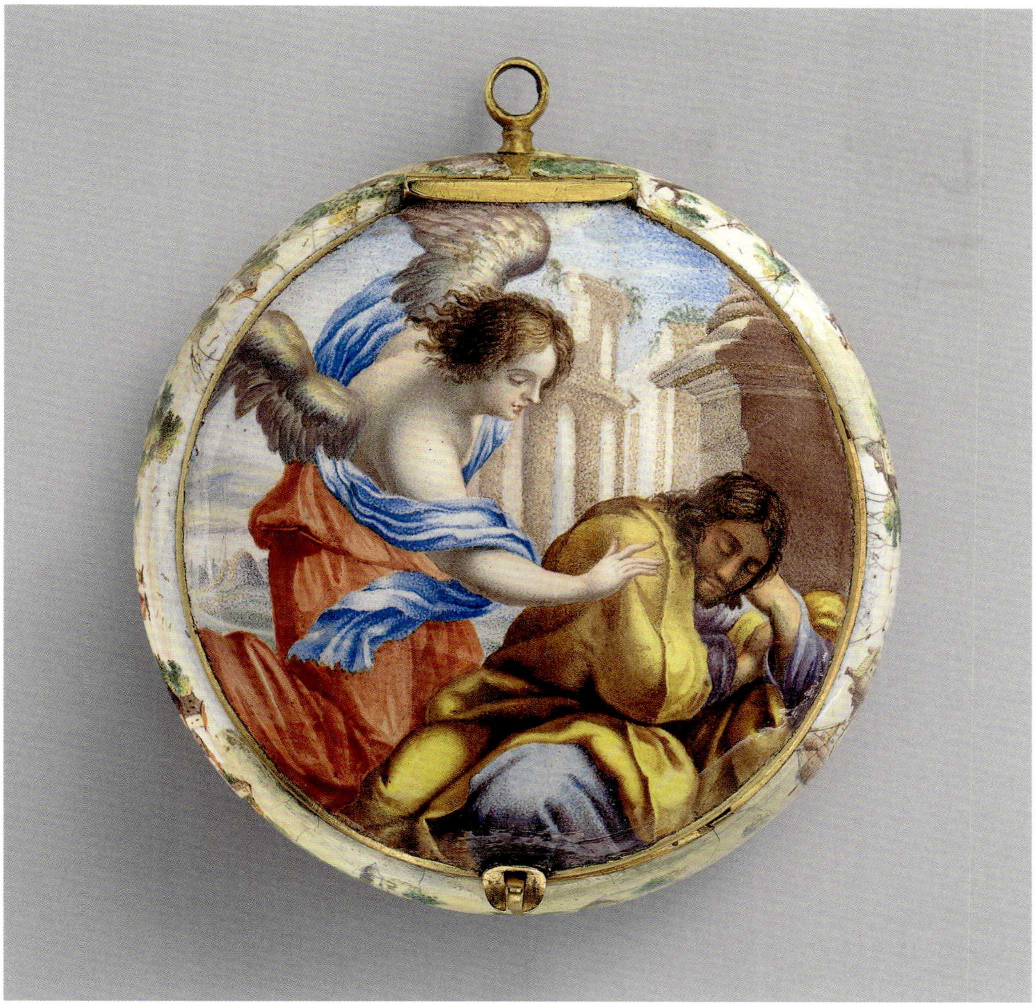

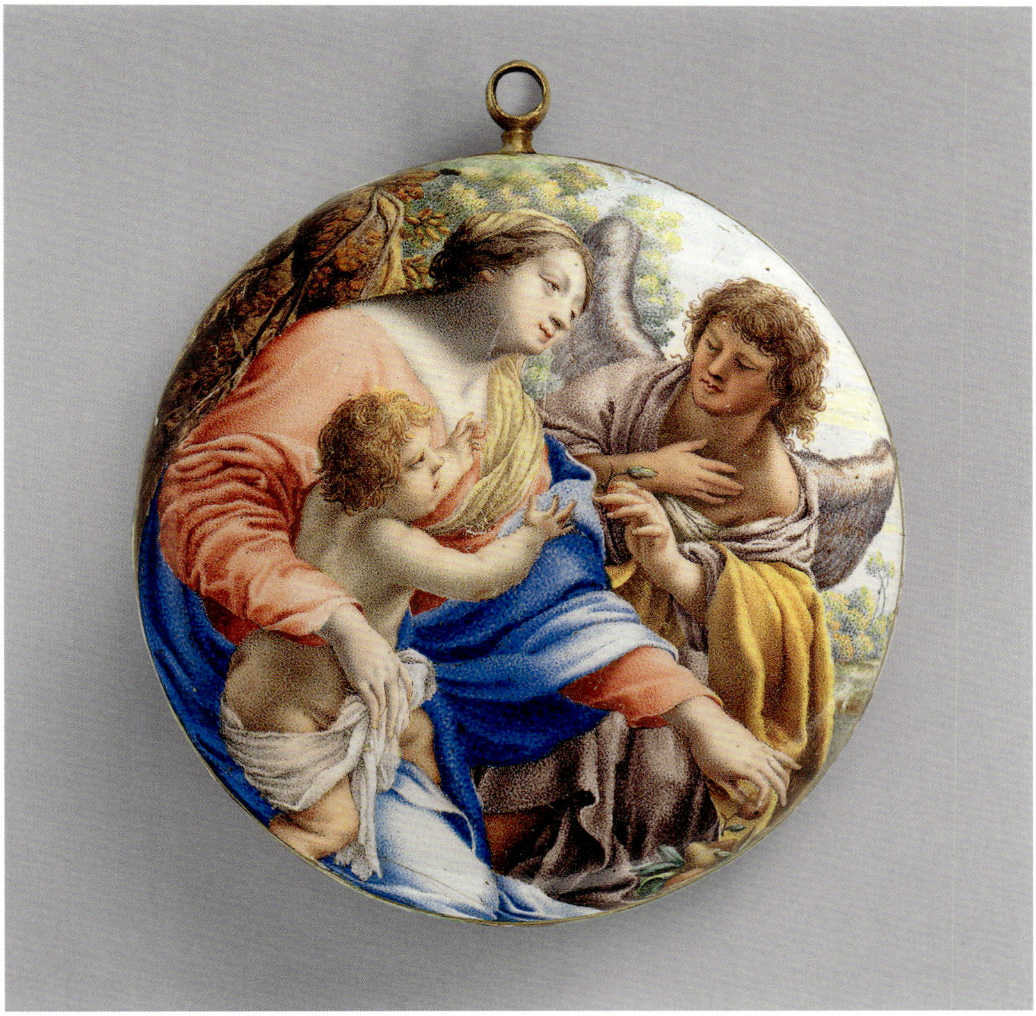

scene preserves the style and immediacy of Vouet's vision, although in this case, the original painting is lost.[5]

Two other religious scenes, the Rest on the Flight into Egypt and the Virgin and Child with the Infant Saint John the Baptist, are represented on the interior of the case and on the cover of the watch, respectively. The origin of the former so far remains unidentified, but the latter has been recognized as an adaptation of an engraving by Gilles Rousselet (1610–1685), which depicts the Holy Family with the Infant Saint John the Baptist and in turn records a painting by Jacques Stella (1596–1657), another French artist from the generation of Vouet (fig. 15).[6] Stella's delightfully domestic vignette depicts the Christ Child astride a lamb that is enticed by a handful of flax proffered by the infant Saint John and at the same time urged on with a twig wielded by the Child, who is steadied by the Virgin's protective hand. The sweetness of Stella's vision as reflected in the watchcase enamel is far removed from Vouet's robust imagery, but there is no reason to suppose that the scene on the interior of the watchcase is the product of a different enameler than that of the two scenes on the exterior of the watch.

The single hand of this watch indicates the hours (I–XII) and half hours only. At some point, probably later in the seventeenth century, the balance for its verge escapement was fitted with a spring, and a silver figure plate used to regulate the balance spring was attached to the back plate covering part of the watchmaker's signature. The addition of the spring, an invention in late 1674 by the Dutch mathematician Christiaan Huygens (1629–1695), would have greatly increased the accuracy of the watch, making it not only a treasured ornament but also a useful timekeeper.

The watch entered the collection of J. Pierpont Morgan before 1912.[7] Nothing is known of its previous owners. CV / JHL

1 Develle 1913, pp. 26–27. See also Fourrier 2004, pp. 100–101, 123–25.
2 Schaffers-Bodenhausen and Tiethoff-Spliethoff 1993, pp. 19–20, and fig. 12.
3 Brusa 1978, p. 105, nos. XVII/XX and color ill. nos. XVII/XX; Cardinal 1989, pp. 138–39, and figs. 104a, 104b.
4 See Vincent 2002, pp. 89–95.
5 Ibid., p. 90, figs. 3, 4, and p. 91, figs. 5–7.
6 Ibid., p. 93, fig. 12, and p. 97, fig. 21.
7 Williamson 1912, pp. 47–48, no. 45.

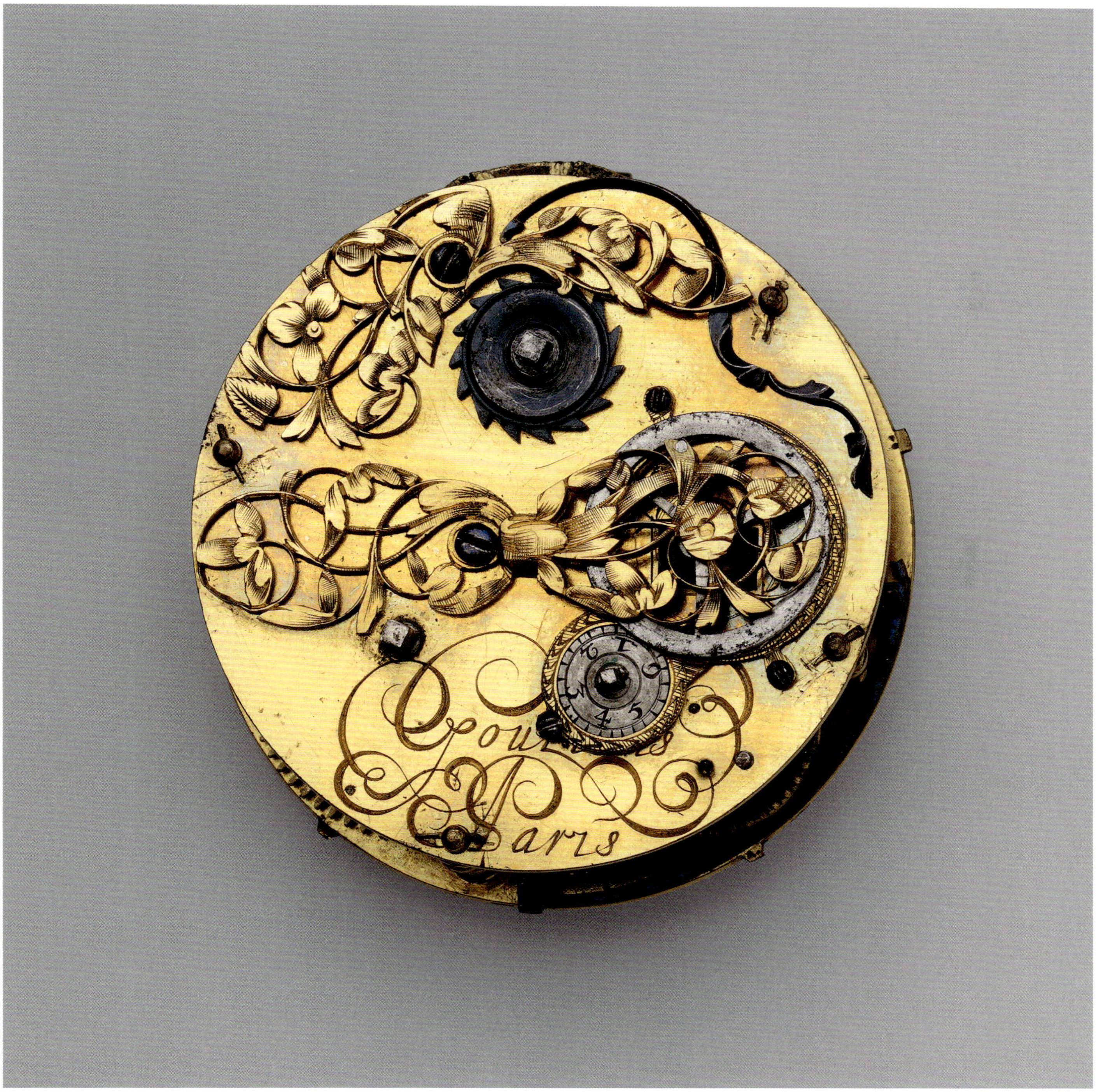

The back plate of the movement of the watch with the partially covered signature of the watchmaker

13. Watch

SWISS (GENEVA), CA. 1650–60
Diam. of case: 1⅝ in. (4.1 cm)
Diam. of back plate: 1⁵⁄₁₆ in. (3.3 cm)
Gift of J. Pierpont Morgan, 1917
17.190.1014

CASE: rock crystal mounted in gilded brass
DIAL: silver and black enamel with gilded-brass hand
MOVEMENT: gilded brass and partly blued steel, signed (on back plate): *Jean Rousseau* [probably Jean Rousseau the Younger, Swiss (Geneva), 1606–1684]

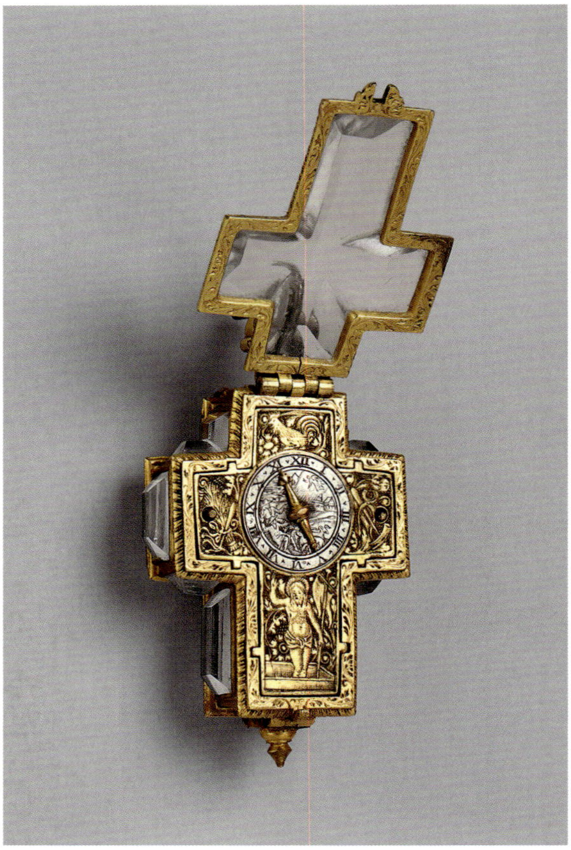

fig. 26 *Anthoine (Antoine) Arlaud (French, 1590–after 1641). Watch, Swiss (Geneva), ca. 1620–30. Case: rock crystal with gilded-silver mounts; dial: partly gilded silver; movement: gilded brass and steel, 1⅞ × 1¼ in. (4.8 × 3.2 cm). The Metropolitan Museum of Art, New York, Gift of J. Pierpont Morgan, 1917 (17.190.1610)*

IT HAS BEEN SAID THAT FRENCH PROTESTANTS WHO WERE FLEEING religious intolerance in their native country brought the craft of watchmaking to Geneva in the seventeenth century. Some of them had already settled in the city by the sixteenth century, especially in the years following the Saint Bartholomew's Day Massacre in Paris in 1572.[1] It is certain that by 1564 watches were being made and sold in Geneva,[2] whether by French émigrés or native-born Genevans. French goldsmiths and lapidaries had fled to Geneva as well. Although seemingly related skills were needed for the creation of small precious objects, goldsmiths and lapidaries were considered separate occupations from watchmakers until 1625, when a city ordinance expressly permitted cooperation between the crafts to make watchcases. In addition, Geneva watchmakers were permitted to make their own watchcases if they chose to do so.[3]

Thus, Geneva, which had had a strict code of sumptuary laws forbidding the wearing of jewelry since the establishment of theocracy in 1541 by John Calvin (1509–1564), found itself in the seventeenth century as the prime source of jewel-like timepieces made of precious and semiprecious materials. Small mechanisms in cases shaped like crosses, human skulls, fleurs-de-lis, stars, hearts, seashells, tulip buds, dogs, doves, hares, and lions became a specialty; these pieces have become known as form watches. The Metropolitan Museum has a tulip bud–shaped watch with a movement by the well-regarded watchmaker Jaques Sermand (1595–1651),[4] and a number of shell-shaped and cross-shaped watches in rock crystal cases. One of the earliest cross watches (fig. 26) contains a movement by Anthoine (Antoine) Arlaud (1590–after 1641).[5] Arlaud, born in Maringues in the Auvergne region of central France, became a burgher in Geneva in 1617[6] and the founder of a dynasty of watchmakers. From a contract signed in 1631, Arlaud is known to have been the supplier of watches to the merchant and clockmaker Pierre II Cuper (1604–active in Constantinople 1634), in Blois, France, for further shipment and sale in Constantinople.[7] Although these watches were not form watches—they were to be oval and made of silver—the contract nevertheless implies the existence of an extensive export trade. Cuper would later join his uncle Michel Cuper (died 1633) in Constantinople.[8]

The Museum's Arlaud watch is housed in a gilded-brass case that is set with eleven separate pieces of faceted rock crystal. A twelfth piece made of cross-shaped glass appears to be a skillful replacement for the original back cover of the case. There is no casemaker's signature or mark, and his identity will probably never be known, but the small pieces of rock crystal and their separation by the metal frame of the case might suggest an early date of about 1620–30 for the object.

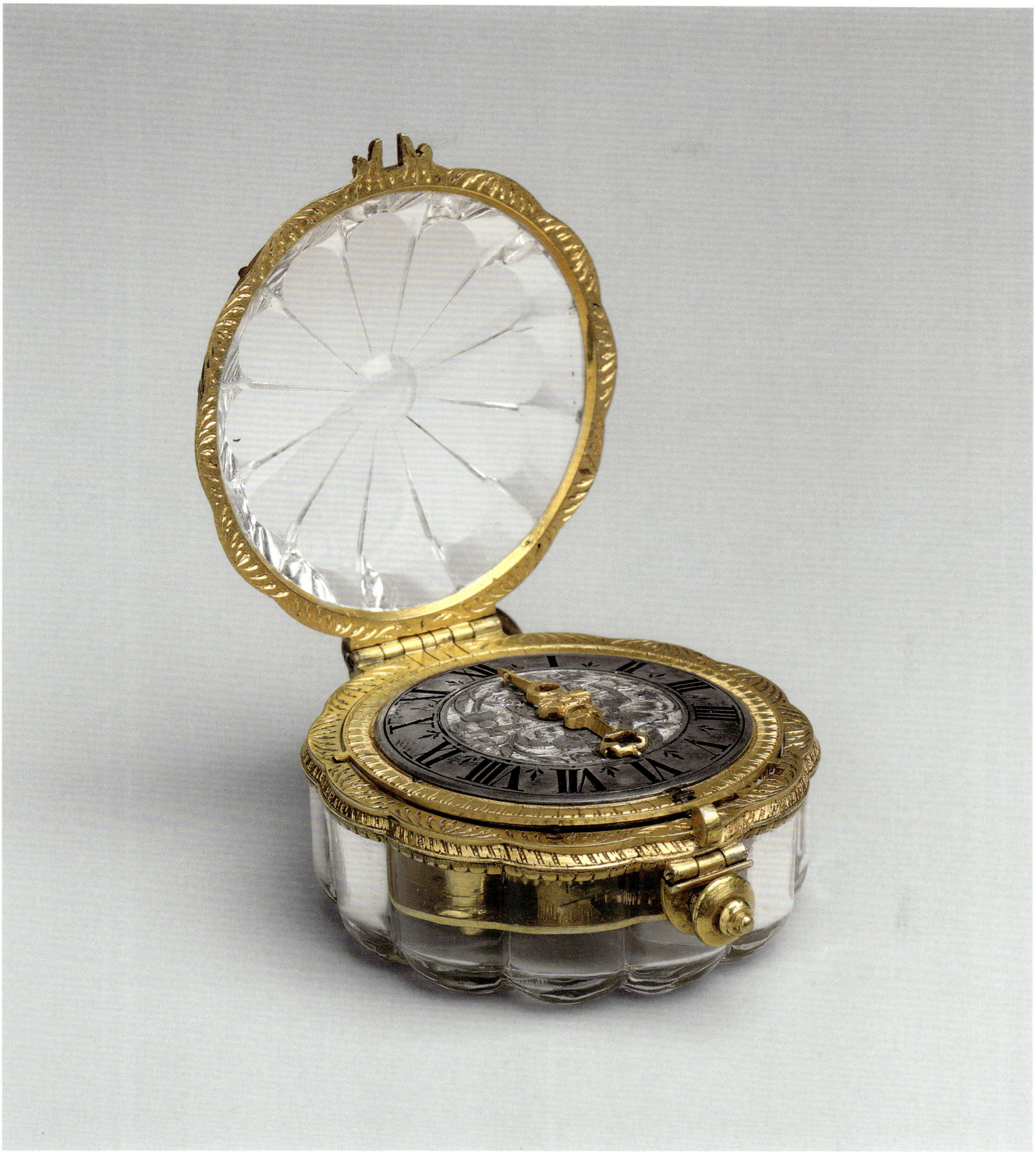

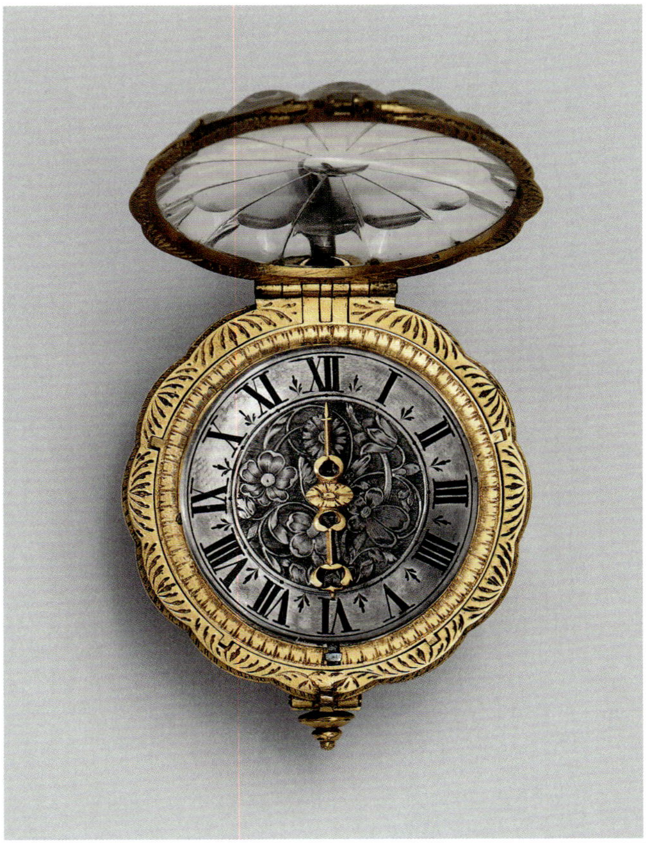

Watchcase open to show the dial

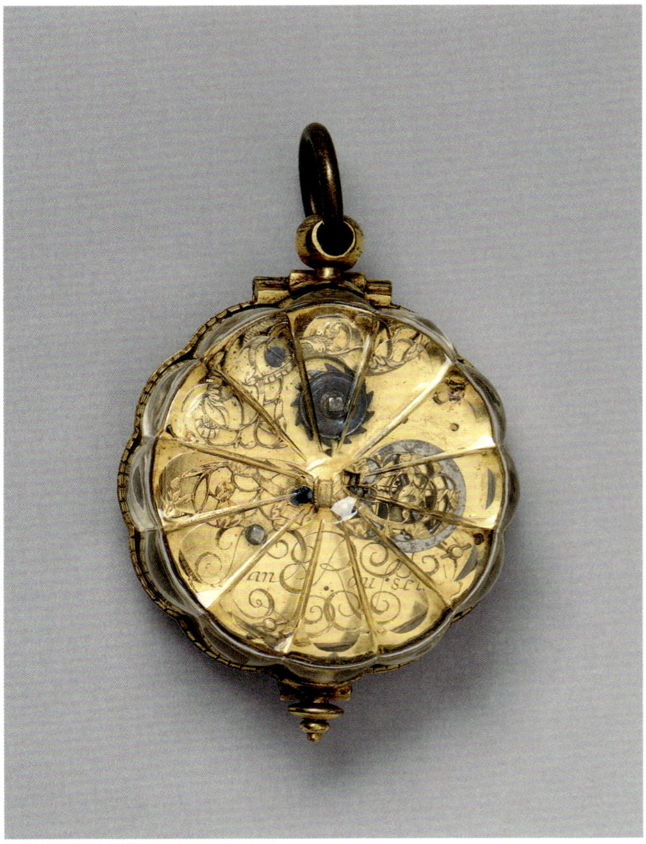

View of watchcase from the back

Rock crystal, a form of colorless, transparent quartz, was readily available in the seventeenth century from sources in the Swiss Alps. In 1650, at the height of its popularity as a medium for watchcases, Constantijn II Huygens (1628–1697) wrote from Geneva to his brother, the Dutch mathematician Christiaan, to report that he had just bought a watch "à la mode" with a case made from rock crystal that permitted a view of the movement such as one would see if the case were made of ice.[9] In any event, by 1650, such watches had become, along with form watches, another Genevan specialty. Huygens bought his watch at its place of origin, but such watches were exported both as complete pieces with movements signed by Genevan watchmakers and as empty cases for use by foreign watchmakers. Records for this trade include three crystal cases for "clock watches" ordered in 1623 by Pierre Lourteau (or Louteau; active 1603–28), a watchmaker in Lyon, France, from the Genevan lapidary Paul Tillier.[10]

The trade can be further inferred from an example provided by a watch in the Museum's collection with a movement signed "Jean Rousseau" (probably Jean Rousseau the Younger, 1606–1684), and the great-grandfather of the philosopher Jean-Jacques Rousseau (1742–1778). Part of a series that has both circular and oval cases, this watch consists of a single piece of hollowed-out rock crystal with a second piece set in the hinged cover. Both case and cover are cut in a lobed pattern that radiates from a central lens. The twelve lobes of the cover are carefully spaced so that the numerals on the dial of the watch can easily be read through the crystal. The pattern on the back of the case is sufficiently reticent so that the back-and-forth movement of the balance, as well as the finely pierced and engraved ornament of the balance cock, can be admired without opening the case. The dial plate, with a decoratively chased border, carries a large, pinned-on, silver dial with robust flowers in the style of the French engraver Jacques Vauquez (1621–1686), framed by a chapter of hours with the roman numerals I–XII for the hours and sprigs for the half hours clearly marked in black.

The pre–balance spring movement of the Rousseau watch consists of two circular, gilded-brass plates that are held apart by four baluster pillars and contains a train of three gilded-brass wheels ending in a verge escapement with a steel balance. Its fusee is cut for thirteen turns of gut line, which provide approximately twenty-six hours before the mainspring needs rewinding. The back plate carries a ratchet and click set-up regulator for the mainspring. The cock for the verge, with its pierced and gilded strawberry-leaf ornament, is screwed to the plate. The winding square projects through the plate below the tail of the cock and just above the name "Jean" in the floridly engraved signature of the watchmaker. Details such as the ratchet wheel of the setup, the ornamental screw for the spring of the case bolt, and the bolt are constructed from blued steel. All are visible through the crystal.

A nearly identical watch, also signed "Jean Rousseau," is in the collection of the Musée du Louvre,[11] and closely comparable watchcases by Joost Silleman of Leeuwarden in the Netherlands[12] and J. B. Gebhart (or Gebhardt; active 1661) of Strasbourg[13] (then part of Germany), one by the native Genevan Denis Bordier (1629–1708),[14] and an oval version used by J. Hediger of Zug in Switzerland,[15] are also in the Louvre's collection; there must have been quite a few of these watches. The fact that they were considered treasures can be inferred from the presence of one of them that is displayed on a golden stand in a painting of an imagined *Kunstkammer*, a cabinet with shelves full of examples of the wondrous products of nature, as well as the ingenious creations of man. The painting, dated 1666 by the artist Johann Georg Haintz (or Hainz or Hinz; 1630–1688), working in Altona and Hamburg in North Germany, records a twelve-lobed Swiss watch that must have belonged to the artist or, more likely, to a member of the Danish royal family for whom the canvas was painted.[16]

The Rousseau watch in the Museum's collection is in excellent condition, missing only a spring for the set-up regulation. It is probably the watch that was sold in Paris in 1891 from the collection of Georges-Louis-Claude Lebeuf, comte de Montgermont.[17] This sale also included the Jacques Goullons (or Coullons; recorded in 1626; active in Paris ca. 1640–60, died 1671) watch with a portrait of the young King Louis XIV that is now in the Robert Lehman Collection in the Metropolitan Museum,[18] and a cross-shaped rock crystal watch by Pierre-Martin Scheult of Paris (active 1654–57), later given to the Museum by J. Pierpont Morgan.[19] Along with the Arlaud watch, the Rousseau watch was purchased by Morgan from the Frankfurt am Main and Berlin collector and dealer Carl H. Marfels. CV / JHL

1 Patrizzi 1998, pp. 17–18.
2 Jaquet and Chapuis 1970, p. 18.
3 Patrizzi 1998, pp. 36, 45.
4 Acc. no. 17.190.1015. See Jaquet 1938; Jaquet and Chapuis 1970, pl. 5.
5 Acc. no. 17.190.1610.
6 Patrizzi 1998, p. 75.
7 Jaquet and Chapuis 1970, p. 27.
8 Fourrier 2000, pp. 18–19.
9 Constantijn Huygens to Christiaan Huygens, Jan. 5, 1650, Municipal Archives, Amsterdam, quoted in Huygens (Christiaan) 1889, suppl., p. 570, no. 69.
10 Quoted in Jaquet and Chapuis 1970, p. 22.
11 Inv. no. OA 7065. See Cardinal 2000, p. 86, no. 56.
12 Musée du Louvre, inv. no. OA 7073. Ibid., p. 146, no. 131.
13 Musée du Louvre, inv. no. OA 7051. Ibid., p. 86, no. 57.
14 Musée du Louvre, inv. no. OA 7064. Ibid., p. 85, no. 54.
15 Musée du Louvre, inv. no. OA 7067. Ibid., p. 88, no. 61.
16 Now in the collection of the Kunsthalle, Hamburg (inv. no. 435), and said to be signed "Georg Hainz Altona fecit Ao 1666." See Hans Werner Schmidt in Hamburger Kunsthalle 1995, p. 131, no. 227; Koeppe 2008, pp. 62–63, and p. 65, fig. 66. See also Raulet 1999, p. 143, for a detail of the painting showing the watch.
17 Galerie Georges Petit 1891, p. 56, no. 174, ill.
18 Acc. no. 1975.1.1244. See Vincent 2012, pp. 78–83, no. 21.
19 Acc. no. 17.190.1621.

14. Watch

SWISS (GENEVA), PROBABLY CA. 1655–60
Diam. of case: 1 5/16 in. (3.3 cm)
Diam. of back plate: 1 1/16 in. (2.7 cm)
Gift of J. Pierpont Morgan, 1917
17.190.1617

CASE: agate with enameled gold mounts
DIAL: white enamel with gold hand
MOVEMENT: gilded brass and partly blued steel, signed (on back plate): *Charles Bobinet* [1610–1678]

IN GENEVA DURING THE SEVENTEENTH CENTURY, WATCHMAKERS were permitted to make their own watchcases and to employ specialists who did not belong to the guild of goldsmiths. While in 1625 goldsmiths and lapidaries were expressly allowed to cooperate in the making of watchcases, it was not until 1698 that the making of watchcases became a separate trade with its own set of regulations. Forty-three masters were listed in the guild.[1] Their cases were often of sufficiently high quality to be mistaken for products from Paris or Blois. One such example is this watch in the Museum's collection with a movement by Charles Bobinet (1610–1678), housed in a case and cover of agate that is mounted in enameled gold. The identity of the casemaker is unknown, but the watchmaker has been repeatedly identified as French not only by the author of the catalogue of watches belonging to J. Pierpont Morgan[2] but also by the compiler of what has become the standard dictionary of French clock- and watchmakers.[3] As recently as 2004 the author of the catalogue for the notable Edouard Gelis Collection in the Musée Paul Dupuy, Toulouse, has repeated a theory that Bobinet was a Frenchman from the Poitou region who worked in Paris from about the middle of the seventeenth century.[4] The author was apparently unaware of the 1949 publication by Eugène Jaquet that cited Bobinet's birth and death records from the Geneva Archives de l'Etat.[5]

Bobinet was noted for supplying movements for cases that were made from various kinds of hardstone. The Museum's watchcase is hollowed out from a single piece of partly translucent rose-colored agate. The cover, made from similarly colored agate, exploits the decorative effects in the mineral, which features lighter and darker rose-colored bands. A floral design in mustard-colored enamel in relief with dark-red highlights and a dark-blue ground ornaments the gold mount on the case. The design repeats in dark-blue and dark-red painted enamel on the gold bezel of the cover and at the base of the pendant. The pendant is plain gold and has a loop to which a gold chain is attached. The relatively large and easily read white-enamel dial is marked by roman numerals (I–XII) painted in black to designate the hours; three graduated dots for the half hours; and short lines in the inner edge of the hour chapter for the quarter hours. A small circle surrounds the end of the arbor for the single, sculptured, gold hand, and the motif of the bezel repeats for the cover.

The movement, like the cover, is hinged to the case at the twelve o'clock position. It consists of two circular, gilded-brass plates held apart by four turned pillars and contains three wheels ending in a verge escapement with a steel balance. The fusee is fitted with gut, and there are sculptured and blued-steel springs for the fusee stopwork

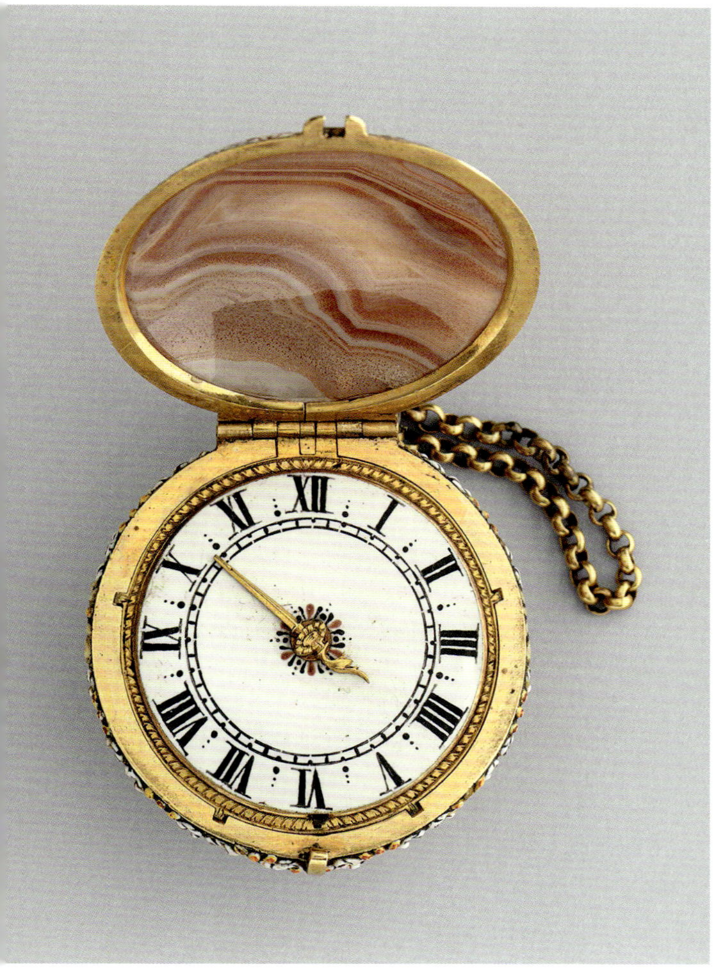

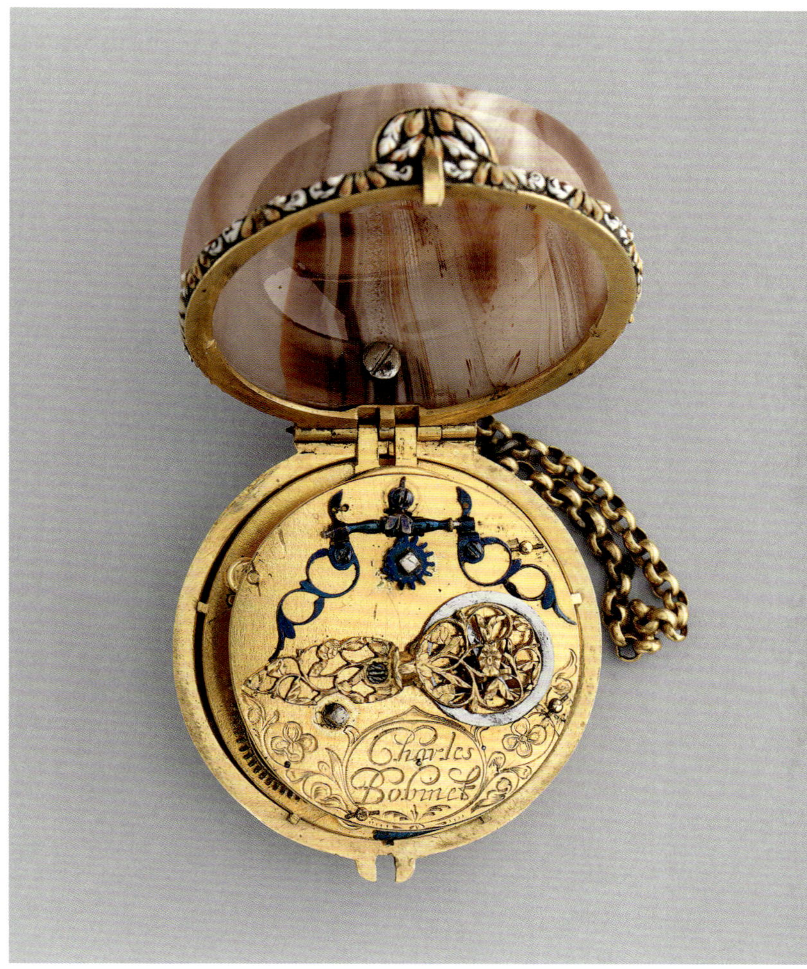
Charles
Bobinet

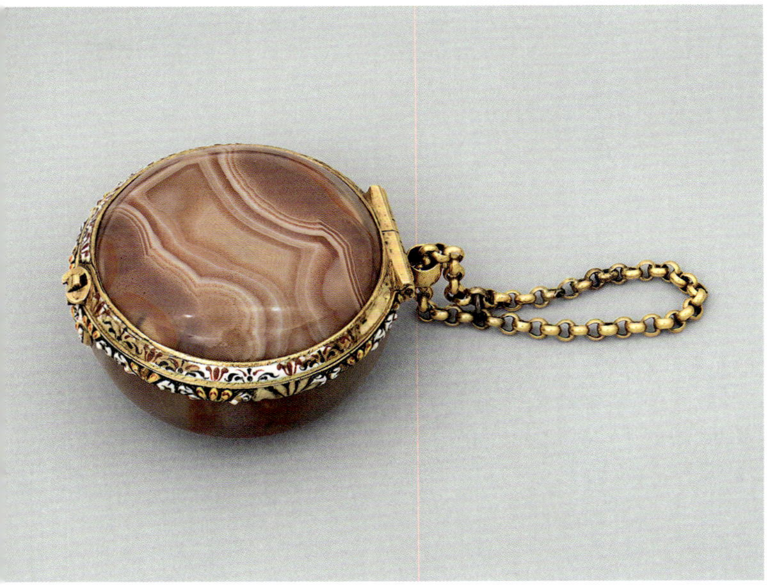

Agate case of Bobinet watch

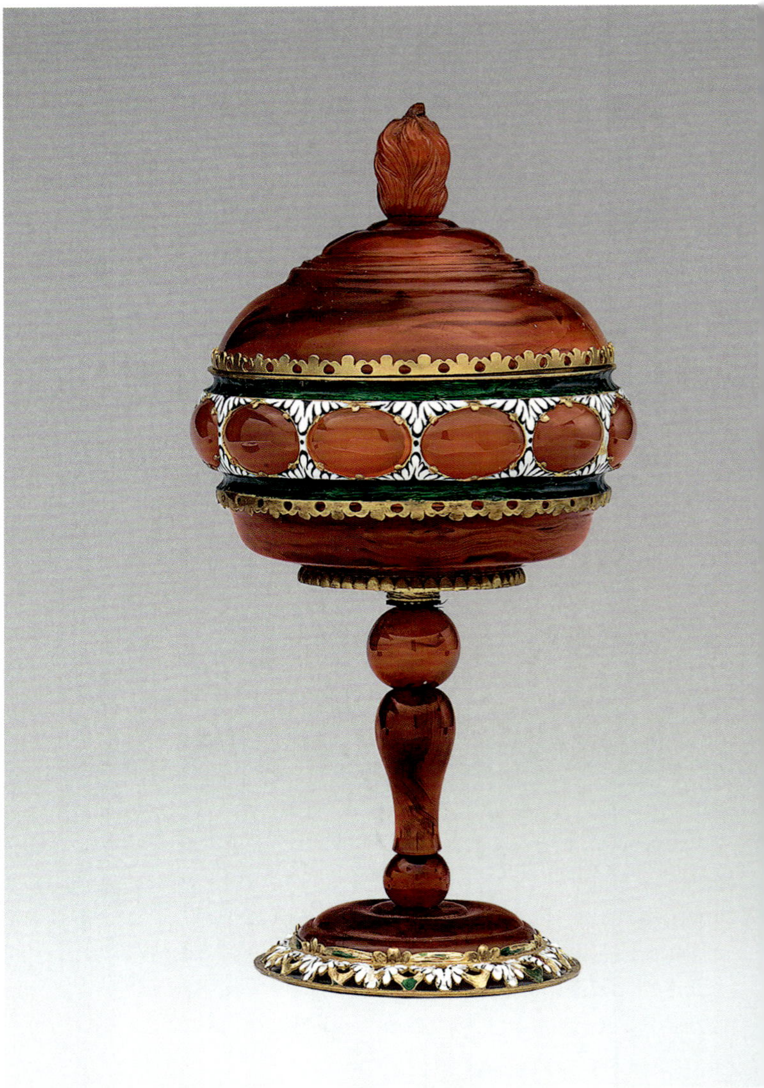

fig. 27 *Cup with Cover, French, ca. 1650–60. Carnelian with enameled gold mounts, Height 4⅞ in. (12.4 cm). The Metropolitan Museum of Art, New York, The Jack and Belle Linsky Collection, 1982 (1982.60.134a, b)*

and for the case bolt. The back plate carries an ornamental openwork balance cock that is screwed to the plate below a worm-and-wheel set-up regulator for the mainspring. The assembly of the set-up regulator is made of blued steel with extra scrolled flourishes attached to the mounting. The signature "Charles/Bobinet" is engraved within an ornamental cartouche situated below the balance cock.

The case and cover of this watch could, in fact, be mistaken for the work of a French goldsmith and lapidary. The Museum has a carnelian and enameled gold standing cup and cover produced in mid-seventeenth-century France and known to have belonged to King Louis XIV (1638–1715) (fig. 27).[6] While the cup and cover are the product of craftsmen with admittedly greater skills, a comparison with the Bobinet watchcase and cover does not make the attribution of the latter to French craftsmen implausible.

While it has been shown that the watchmaker Bobinet was born in Geneva, other watchmakers who were born in France provided movements for similar agate cases. One watchcase with a movement by Barthélemy Soret (1633–1717), who settled in Geneva in 1654, appeared on the auction market in 1996.[7] Another watch with similar enameled gold mounts, a comparable dial, a case of similar shape but made of serpentine, and a movement signed by Estienne Ester, a master in Geneva in 1652, is now in the Ashmolean Museum, Oxford.[8] The existence of these two watches, with movements by masters who are known to have been working in Geneva, lends further support for the attribution of the Museum's watchcase to Geneva, in spite of the fact that both Soret and Ester are believed to have been born in France. Another watch with a similar agate case mounted in enameled gold and a movement signed "Gedeon de Combes" exists in La Chaux-de-Fonds, Switzerland,[9] but Osvaldo Patrizzi's *Dictionnaire des horlogers genevois* lists de Combes (or Decombes) as a master clockmaker in Geneva during the second half of the seventeenth century.[10] Given the existence of these watches, all with movements presumably made in Geneva, it seems safe to suggest that the anonymous maker of their cases (known to be rarities) may have been a French émigré.

The Metropolitan Museum's watch is for the most part in excellent condition with the exception that much of the original enamel on the bezel of the cover has been lost, and the repairs are deteriorating. There are also imperfections in the agate of both the case and the cover. The left mount for the worm-and-wheel set-up regulator of the mainspring is bent.

J. Pierpont Morgan purchased the watch from the Frankfurt am Main and Berlin collector and dealer Carl H. Marfels sometime after 1904.[11] CV / JHL

1 Patrizzi 1998, pp. 45–49. See also entry 13 in this volume.
2 Williamson 1912, p. 36.
3 Tardy 1971–72, vol. 1, p. 61.
4 Hayard 2004, pp. 120–21.
5 See Jaquet 1949 for the place and dates that are accepted in Gibertini 1964, p. 220, and Patrizzi 1998, pp. 107–8.
6 Acc. no. 1982.60.134a, b. See Clare Vincent in Metropolitan Museum of Art 1984, p. 178, no. 94.
7 Antiquorum 1996, p. 498, no. 637, ill. p. 499.
8 Inv. no. WA1974.186. See Thompson 2007, pp. 36–37, no. 16.
9 Inv. no. I-487. See Cardinal and Piguet 2002, pp. 118–19, no. 114.
10 Patrizzi 1998, p. 152. No trace of de Combes can be found in Tardy 1971–72 or Augarde 1996.
11 Speckhart 1904, pl. x, no. 3.

15. Watch in the Form of a Skull

CASE: SWISS (GENEVA), CA. 1810–20; MOVEMENT: SWISS (GENEVA), CA. 1650
2 × 1⅜ × 1⁹⁄₁₆ in. (5.1 × 3.5 × 4 cm)
Gift of J. Pierpont Morgan, 1917
17.190.1575

CASE: silver, probably by Moulinié, Bautte & Moynier (1808–21)
DIAL: silver, partly nielloed
MOVEMENT: gilded brass and steel, signed (on back plate): *Isaac Penard* [Swiss, 1619–1676]

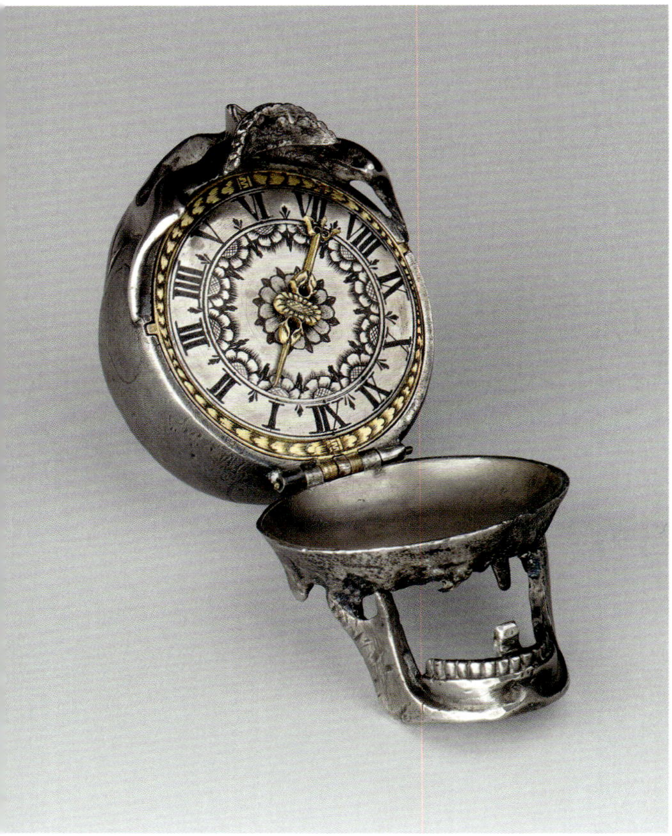
The case open to show the dial

A SUNDIAL MOTTO, "OH REMEMBER HOW SHORT MY TIME IS," from a verse in the Old Testament (Psalms 89:47) explains the form of this watch. Reminders of the imminence of death were appropriate to an age when wars and plagues carried off great numbers of people. Numerous *vanitas* can be found in the seventeenth century; a painting from 1630 in the collection of the Mauritshuis in The Hague (fig. 28) by the Dutch artist Pieter Claesz (1596/97–1660), for example, depicts both a skull and a watch, as well as other symbolic reminders of the shortness of human life.

Among those who subscribed to the Calvinist form of Protestantism there was an inherent focus on time, and watches counted the hours. The skull-shaped watch was one of the products of this tradition, and while some of these watches were made in southern Germany,[1] more of them seem to have been made in seventeenth-century Blois, a center of Calvinist, or Huguenot, watchmakers in France.[2] But the theocracy established in 1541 by John Calvin (1509–1564) became the prime source of watches with cases in the shape of human skulls in seventeenth-century Geneva.[3] The earliest of these watches is thought to have been made by Martin Duboule (1583–1639) and is now in the collection of the Musée du Louvre.[4] A watch in the Metropolitan Museum's collection (fig. 29) made by Pierre Landré of Blois (born 1610–active 1637)[5] is not unlike the Duboule watch, and both are believed to be from about 1630. Skull watches continued to be made throughout the eighteenth century in Geneva, and the local firm of Moulinié, Bautte and Moynier (partnership recorded 1808–21) was still making them in the early years of the nineteenth century.[6]

Isaac Penard (1619–1676), once thought to have been a watchmaker in Blois,[7] is now known to have been born in Geneva and apprenticed in 1632 to Jaques Sermand (1595–1651), a noted maker of so-called form watches, or watches in fanciful-shaped cases. Penard married in 1644,[8] and while the actual date when he became a master in Geneva is not known, it was usual for a craftsman to marry only after becoming a master and establishing a workshop. The misattribution to Blois was easily made because Genevan masters were required to engrave only their names on their watch movements and not their place of origin.

The Museum's Penard watchcase consists of a hand-raised silver cranium with a riveted loop and ring at the top to which a cast-silver front plate and facial structure has been brazed. The lower skull and jaw, a separate piece of cast silver that displays the naturalistic details of a human skull, is hinged to the back of the cranium and can be opened to reveal the dial of the watch inside. The catch is a separate piece that is brazed to the back of the teeth in the lower jaw. The dial

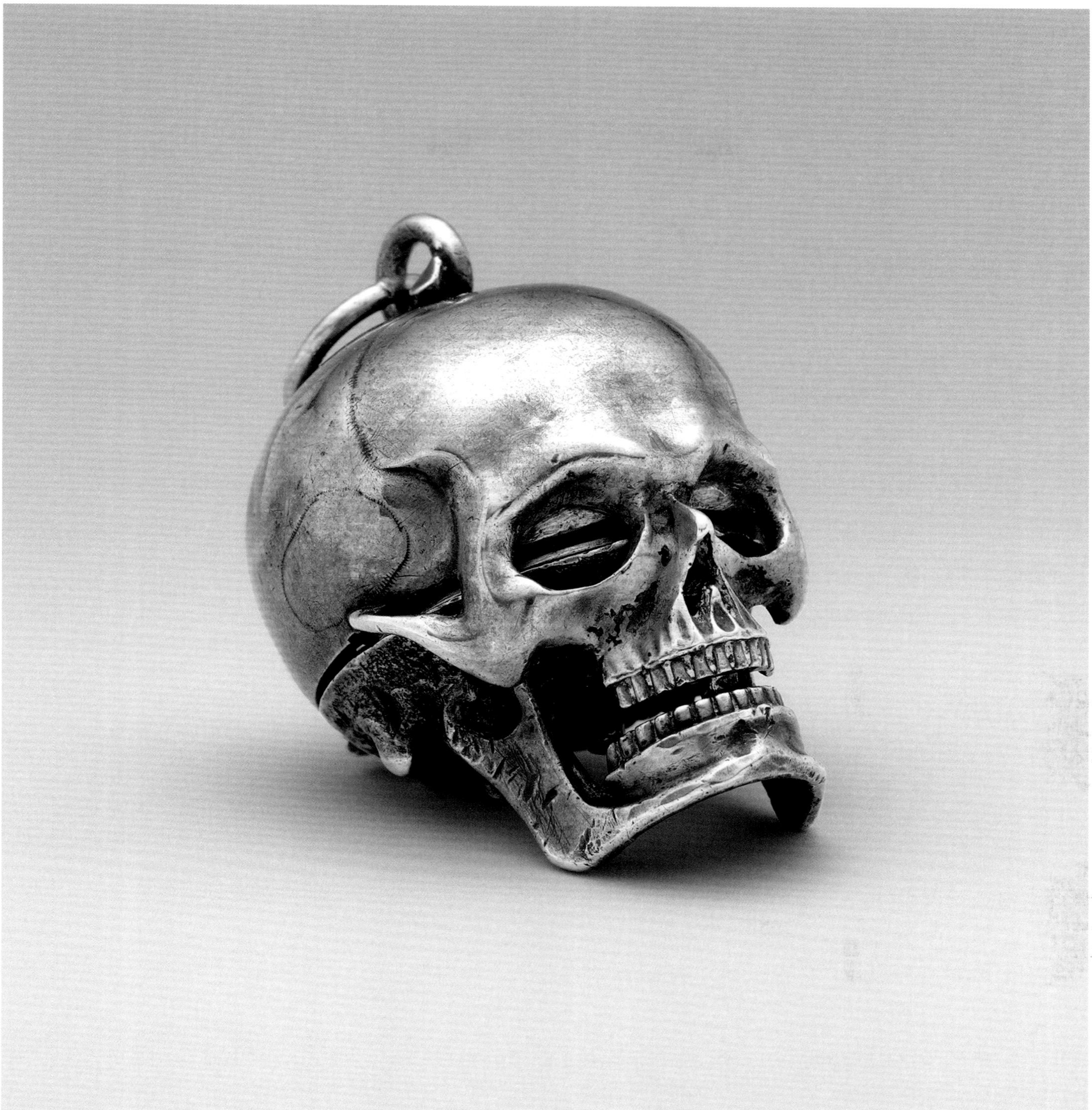

plate is brass and has a repeating leaf design that encircles a silver chapter of hours (I–XII), with the half hours marked by sprigs. A ring of floral ornament and a single brass hand issuing from a central flower-like ornament completes the design.

The movement is also hinged to the back of the cranium. It consists of two oval brass plates held apart by four baluster pillars; three pillars are pinned to the back plate of the watch. The movement is spring driven with a gut fusee, and it has three wheels ending in a verge escapement. The back plate was originally fitted with a ratchet and click regulator for the setup of the mainspring. Only the openwork click and the ratchet wheel remain. The screwed-on balance cock is ornamented with openwork floral scrolling, and the engraved signature "Isaac Penard" appears below the cock.

The movement of this watch has had a difficult existence. The spring for the click of the setup of the mainspring is missing, and the ratchet wheel has bent and broken teeth. The contrate wheel in the going train is probably a replacement, and the escape wheel, verge, and balance of the escapement are particularly clumsy replacements. The present balance wheel is a solid disk that makes the watch useless as a timekeeper. In addition, the end of one of the pillars has been cut off to accommodate the disk. The case for the watch movement is a replacement for one that may or may not have been skull-shaped. It closely resembles the case of a skull watch with a movement by Moulinié, Bautte and Moynier in the collection of the Musée International d'Horlogerie in La Chaux-de-Fonds, Switzerland,[9] and it was probably made about the same time. The La Chaux-de-Fonds watch is the product of a partnership between Jacques-Dauphin Moulinié (active 1793–1828), Jean François Bautte (1772–1837), and Jean-Gabriel Moynier (1772–1840).[10] As Moulinié and Bautte began as watchcase makers, it is probable that the case and the movement of that watch was their work. The dial is quite different from that of the Metropolitan Museum's watch, and the niello-ornamented dial of the latter may be the product of an even later period, when it was made to fit the Penard movement and evidently to create a watch to be sold to a nineteenth-century collector. Nonetheless, the case remains a fine example of the period.

According to George C. Williamson, the historian and author of the Morgan collection catalogue, the watch was part of the collection of the British banker Frederick George Hilton Price, who had acquired it from the British collector J. Dunn Gardner.[11] CV / JHL

1 For German examples, see one in the British Museum, London (inv. no. 1874,0718.41, signed "J C Vuolf"); this was probably Johann Conrad Wolf, who was recorded in Donauwörth in 1638. See Thompson 2008, pp. 46–47. Another with an automaton jaw is in the Kunsthistorisches Museum, Vienna; see Maurice 1976, vol. 2, pp. 61–62, no. 447, and figs. 447a, b.
2 Fourrier 2001, pp. 38–46.
3 Jaquet 1948c; Jaquet and Chapuis 1970, pp. 23–24.
4 Inv. no. OA 7036. See Cardinal 2000, p. 80, no. 51.
5 Acc. no. 17.190.1574. For Landré, see Tardy 1971–72, vol. 2, p. 348; Fourrier 2000, p. 39.
6 Meis 1980, pp. 138–39.
7 Williamson 1912, p. 13, no. 8.
8 Jaquet 1948a; Gibertini 1964, p. 239.
9 Inv. no. I-2. See Musée International d'Horlogerie 1974, p. 39; Cardinal and Piguet 2002, pp. 230–31, no. 276.
10 Pritchard 1997, vol. 2, p. M-108. See also Patrizzi 1998, pp. 285, 96, 286, respectively.
11 Williamson 1912, p. 13, no. 8.

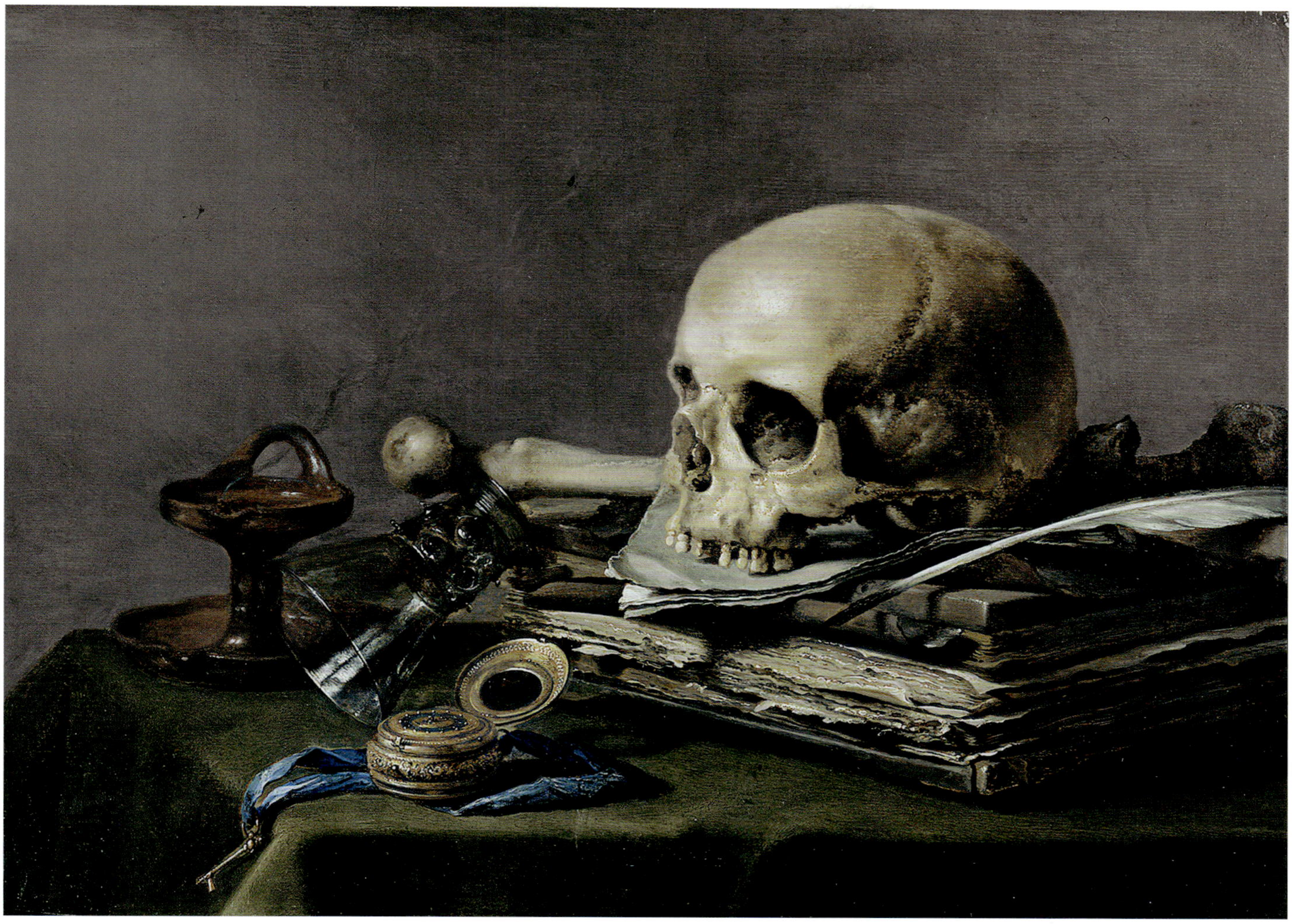

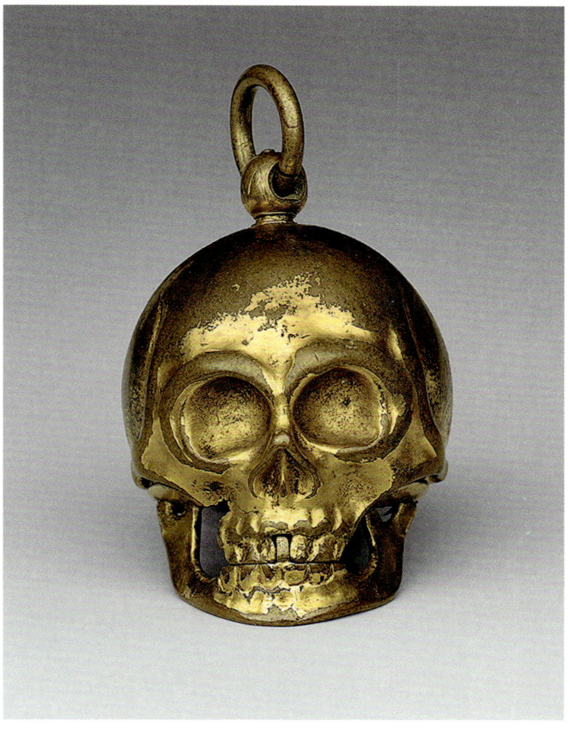

fig. 28 *Pieter Claesz (Dutch, 1596/97–1660). Vanitas Still Life, 1630. Oil on panel, 15½ × 22 in. (39.5 × 56 cm). Royal Picture Gallery Mauritshuis, The Hague*

fig. 29 *Pierre Landré (French [Blois], born 1610, active 1637). Watch, French (Blois), ca. 1630–40. Case: gilded brass; movement: brass and steel, 1⅝ × 1⅛ × 1⅜ in. (4.1 × 2.9 × 3.5 cm), diam. of back plate: 13/16 in. (2 cm). The Metropolitan Museum of Art, New York, Gift of J. Pierpont Morgan, 1917 (17.190.1574)*

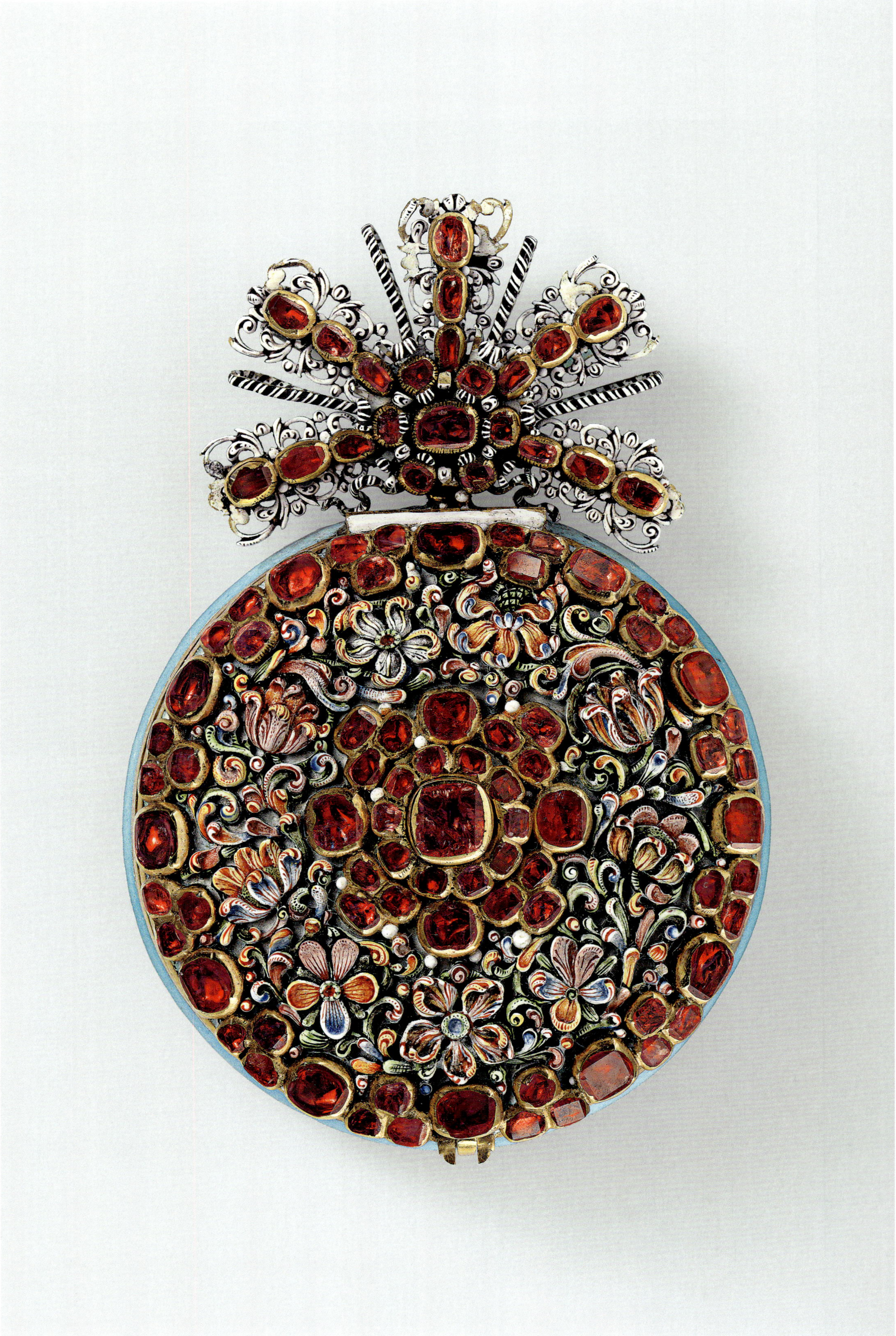

16. Watch

GERMAN (AUGSBURG), CA. 1670
3⅛ × 2⅛ × ⅞ in. (7.9 × 5.4 × 2.2 cm)
Diam. of back plate: 1¾ in. (4.5 cm)
Gift of J. Pierpont Morgan, 1917
17.190.1520

CASE AND DIAL: painted and raised enamel on gold, set with gemstones, with a single hand
MOVEMENT: gilded brass and partly blued steel, signed (on back plate): *Nicolaus Rugendas / Aug* [Nicolaus II Rugendas, German (Augsburg), 1619–1694/95, master 1662]

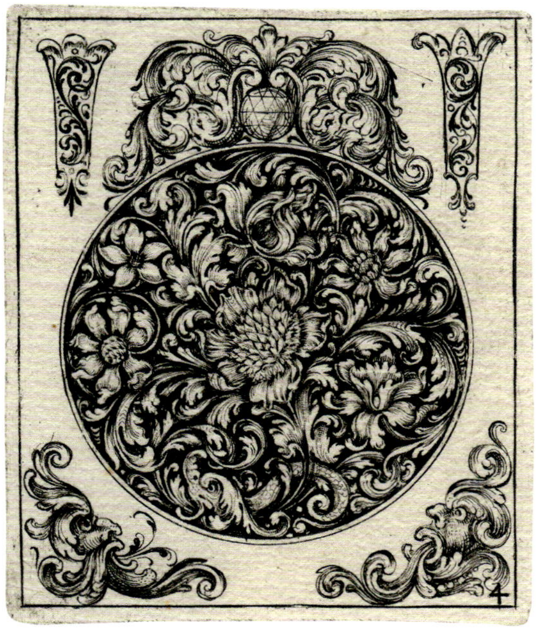

fig. 30 *Johann Wilhelm Heel (German, 1637–1709). Plate from* Schneid-Büchlein (Series of Ornaments)*, German, after 1664. Copperplate engraving, 3 × 2⅜ in. (7.5 × 6 cm). MAK—Austrian Museum of Applied Arts/Contemporary Art, Vienna*

UNTIL 1702 THE AUGSBURG MAKERS OF SMALL GOLD OBJECTS ornamented with enamel and often set with gemstones were craftsmen who belonged to the same guild as the makers of silverware.[1] As in most European centers of metalworking, objects of gold and silver were usually required to bear the punchmark of the town where they were made and the maker's mark. Enameled gold objects, such as this watchcase, were usually exempt from the requirement owing to the danger of cracking the enamel. The maker of this watchcase thus remains anonymous. The cover of the case, however, displays a floral design that is typical of products made by South German goldsmiths from about 1660 to 1680.

This variety of dense ornament, which is arranged without an easily detected axis, has its sources in earlier printed designs for jewelry and watchcases as, for example, prints by the Swiss Claude Rivard (active 1623–70),[2] or the Frenchman Jacques Vauquer (1621–1686),[3] brother of the watchcase-enameler Robert Vauquer (1625–1670) who is acknowledged to have been one of the best in Blois. Jacques worked for a time as an engraver for Jean-Baptiste Monnoyer (1636–1699), a flower painter and favorite of the French royal court. On his own, Jacques published designs for watchcases and for watch cocks, some not unlike the openwork cock of the Museum's Rugendas watch. The enameled pendant of the watch, shaped like a twice-tied bow, is only a little less extravagant than designs by another Frenchman and court jeweler, Gilles Légaré (1617–1663), whose *Livre des ouvrages d'orfevrerie fait par Gilles Légaré orfevre du Roy* appeared in 1663 and in four subsequent editions.[4] As the title page for the series of prints indicates, Légaré was goldsmith to King Louis XIV (1638–1715) and therefore played a major role in setting fashion in French jewelry.

But closer to Augsburg, a comparable style of dense floral ornament appeared in prints made by Johann Wilhelm Heel (1637–1709). Born in Augsburg, Heel settled in Nürnberg, where he produced several series of engraved designs beginning in 1664, including six series titled *Schneid-Büchlein*, published by David Fünck (1642–1705) in Nürnberg.[5] One of these, probably intended as a design for a watchcase, displays a large flower in the center of a dense, circular floral design (fig. 30). The Museum's watchcase has a similar floral design, except that a splashy cluster of twenty-six rubies instead of a flower occupies the center. Heel's design includes an elaborate foliate pendant that is set with a jewel in the center,[6] but the bowknot-shaped pendant on the Museum's watchcase relates more closely to Légaré's designs.

The maker enameled the cover of the Museum's watchcase with an openwork design over a gold ground in low relief, adding a circular border of forty-seven rubies that are organized in a repeating pattern of one large stone, three small stones. The pendant is set with another

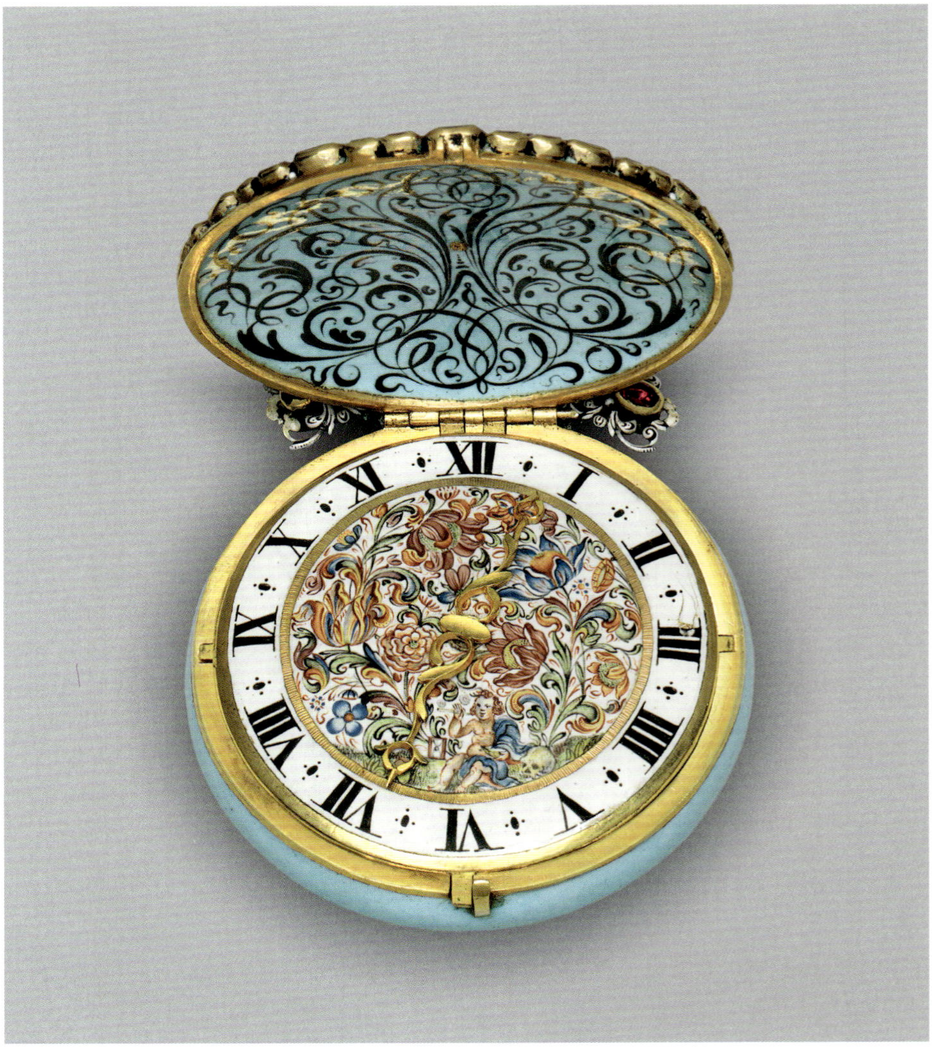

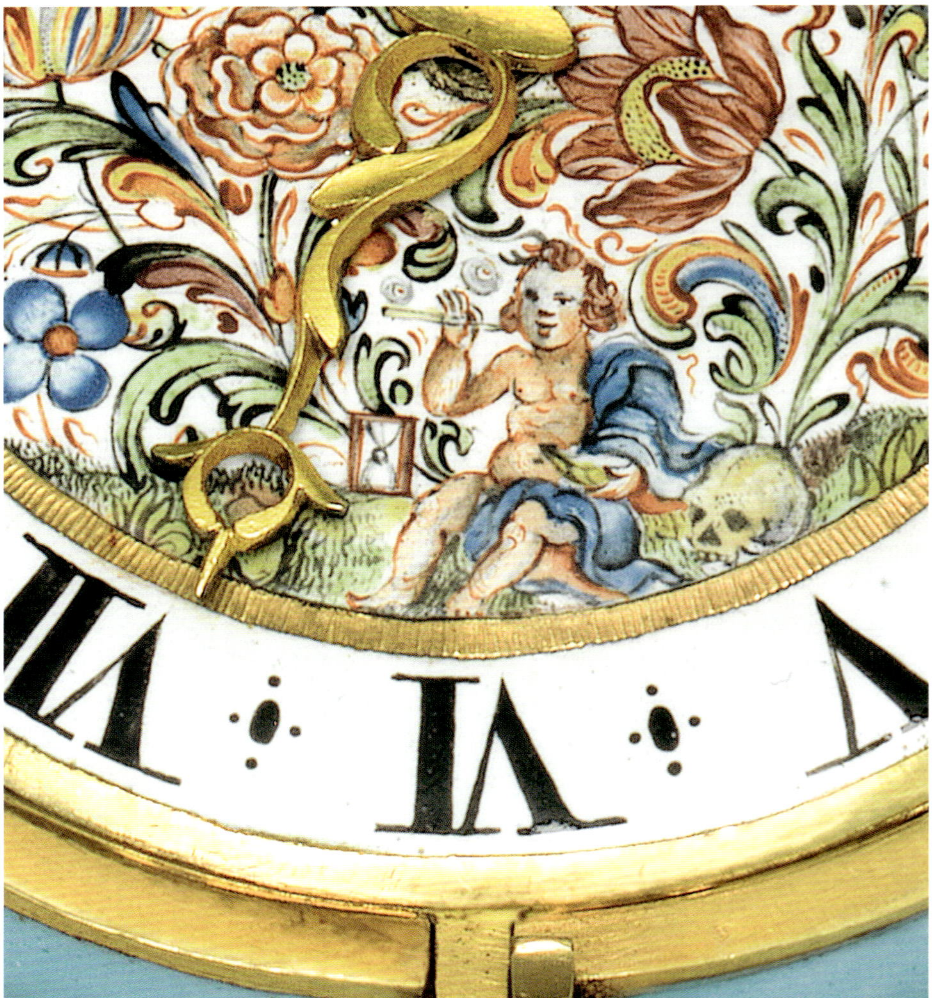

twenty-two gems completing the design. The case is enameled, inside and out, in a shade of pale blue that was much favored by seventeenth-century Augsburg enamelers. When open, the inside of the cover reveals more of the same shade of blue but overlaid with a playful design of scrolls painted in black.

The dial of the watch contains yet another enamel with the center painted in natural colors in an allover floral design. At the bottom, in the six o'clock position, an infant personification of Time sits between a sandglass and a human skull as a reminder that life is fleeting. A single ornamented hand indicates the time. The pure-white enamel chapter ring registers only hours (I–XII) and half hours. Quarter hours may be estimated, but in sum, the watch was intended to be as much a piece of jewelry as a serious timekeeper.

The pre–balance spring movement is a finely finished but otherwise unremarkable product from a member of a prominent family of clockmakers, three of whom were named Nicolaus (or Nikolaus) Rugendas. The first Nicolaus (1585–1658) came from the Hessian town of Melsungen, worked for a time in Regensburg, and moved to Augsburg in 1608.[7] His son, Nicolaus II (1619–1694/95), was born in Augsburg and became a master clockmaker there by inheritance in 1662.[8] His status as the son of a master clockmaker would have carried with it advantages that would not otherwise be granted to aspiring clockmakers in the city. Nicolaus III (1665–1745), the son of Nicolaus II, became a master clockmaker by inheritance in 1669, but he is best known not for clocks or watches but for portable sundials.[9]

Not many timepieces that were housed in cases made of precious metals and set with gemstones have survived, subject as they are to destruction owing to the intrinsic value of their materials, as well as to changes in fashion. It is, therefore, difficult to know whether Nicolaus II Rugendas may have specialized in supplying movements for opulent cases, but a clock with a movement signed "Nicolaus Rugendas Aug" in a gilded-silver case and enriched with garnets, amethysts, hyacinths, peridots, and turquoises can be found in the collection of the Wittelsbach Electors of Bavaria preserved in the Schatzkammer der Residenz in Munich.[10]

Like most seventeenth-century watches in the Metropolitan Museum's collection, this watch was the gift of J. Pierpont Morgan. In Morgan's collection catalogue published in 1912, it is called the "Great Ruby Watch" and documented as coming from the collection of Baroness Alphonse de Rothschild (Leonora von Rothschild, 1837–1911).[11] Previously, the watch had been in the possession of Charles Mannheim.[12] CV / JHL

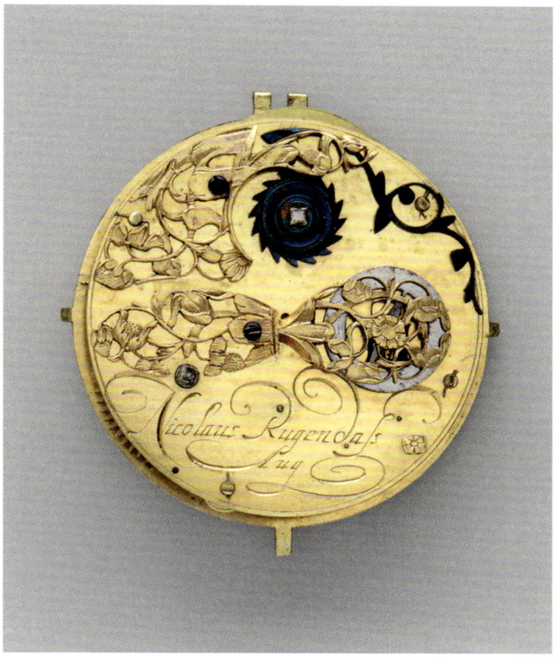

Back plate of the movement with the signature of the watchmaker

1 Weinhold 2000, p. 44 and n. 6.
2 See Fuhring and Bimbenet-Privat 2002, pp. 144–58, especially the medallion, or watchcase, in no. 382.
3 For a selection of Vauquer's engravings, see Tardy 1971–72, vol. 2, pp. 634–36.
4 Bimbenet-Privat 2002, vol. 1, p. 396, and vol. 2, p. 467.
5 Hollstein, *German*, 1954–2014, vol. 13 (1984), pp. 88–89, no. 25.
6 Ibid., p. 90, no. 28.
7 Bobinger 1966, pp. 156–59, 291; Maurice 1976, vol. 1, p. 295, no. 167b.
8 Bobinger 1966, pp. 159 and 291, where the author's description of the Museum's watch is not accurate. See also Maurice 1976, vol. 1, p. 296, no. 215a.
9 Bobinger 1966, pp. 158–62, 292–98. See also Maurice 1976, vol. 1, p. 297, no. 259a.
10 Thoma and Brunner 1964, p. 286, no. 723, where it is dated about 1660 and cited as the clock in an inventory of the collection made in 1730.
11 Williamson 1912, p. 102, no. 95, and pl. XLV.
12 Galerie Georges Petit 1910, p. 42, no. 114, ill.

17. Hooded Wall Clock with Calendar

BRITISH (LONDON), CA. 1660–65
19½ × 12 × 7¼ in. (49.5 × 30.5 × 18.4 cm)
Width of dial plate: 8¼ in. (21 cm)
Bequest of Irwin Untermyer, 1973
1974.28.93

CASE: ebony and oak veneered with ebony, ebonized wood, and gilded brass
DIAL: gilded brass with silvered-brass chapter ring, signed: *A. Fromanteel Londini* [Ahasuerus I Fromanteel, British (Norwich), 1607–1693]
MOVEMENT: brass and steel

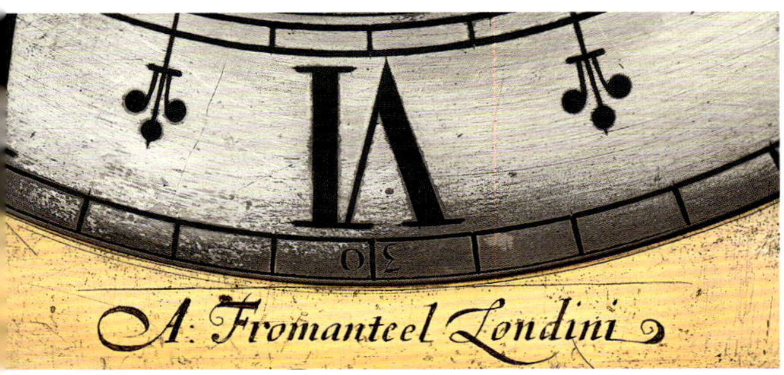

Detail of the dial with the signature of the clockmaker

THE MOST RELIABLE EVIDENCE SURROUNDING THE INTRODUCTION of the pendulum clock to England remains an advertisement found in the London *Mercurius Politicus* and posted by Ahasuerus I Fromanteel (1607–1693) dated October 21–28, 1658. In the announcement he states that

> there is lately a way found out for making of Clocks that go exact and keep equaller time than any now made without this Regulater. . . . Made by Ahasuerus Fromanteel, who made the first that were in England: You may have them at his house on the Bank-side in Mosses Alley, Southwark, and at the sign of the Maremaid in Loathbury, near Bartholomew Lane end London.[1]

There has been considerable speculation about whether it is possible that English clockmakers, and Fromanteel in particular, had experimented with applications of the pendulum to clockwork before the end of 1656, when the Dutch mathematician Christiaan Huygens (1629–1695) announced the invention that would revolutionize clockmaking. The invention was published in Latin in a small book titled *Horologium* (1658),[2] but Huygens was a scientist, not a clockmaker. Therefore, it was the Dutch clockmaker Salomon Coster (died 1659), working in The Hague, who was granted the patent on June 16, 1657, by the States General of the Netherlands to make the newly invented pendulum clocks. The right to make clocks incorporating Huygens's invention and to sell them in the Dutch Provinces of Holland, West-Friesland, and Zeeland was to be exclusively Coster's. Thus, it was to the workshop of Coster and not to the aristocratic Huygens that Fromanteel sent his son John to learn the technology of pendulum clocks.[3]

Fromanteel was born in Norwich, England, to a family of Flemish extraction. He was apprenticed to Jacques van Barton, a clockmaker in Norwich, but moved to London, where he was made free of the Blacksmiths' Company in 1630, and subsequently became a brother in the newly chartered Clockmakers' Company in 1632.[4] In 1646 Fromanteel left the Dutch Church, Austin Friars, in London, to become an Anabaptist. His religious conversion, together with evidence that he was bilingual in English and Dutch, may partly explain why Fromanteel was quickly able to form a productive relationship with Coster, who was also an Anabaptist.[5] Eventually Coster employed Fromanteel's son as a journeyman in his workshop from September 1657 until May 1658, and at this time, John Fromanteel learned to make the pendulum clocks that would become a great success in England.[6] Perhaps Ahasuerus I Fromanteel found Restoration England a less-than-comfortable society

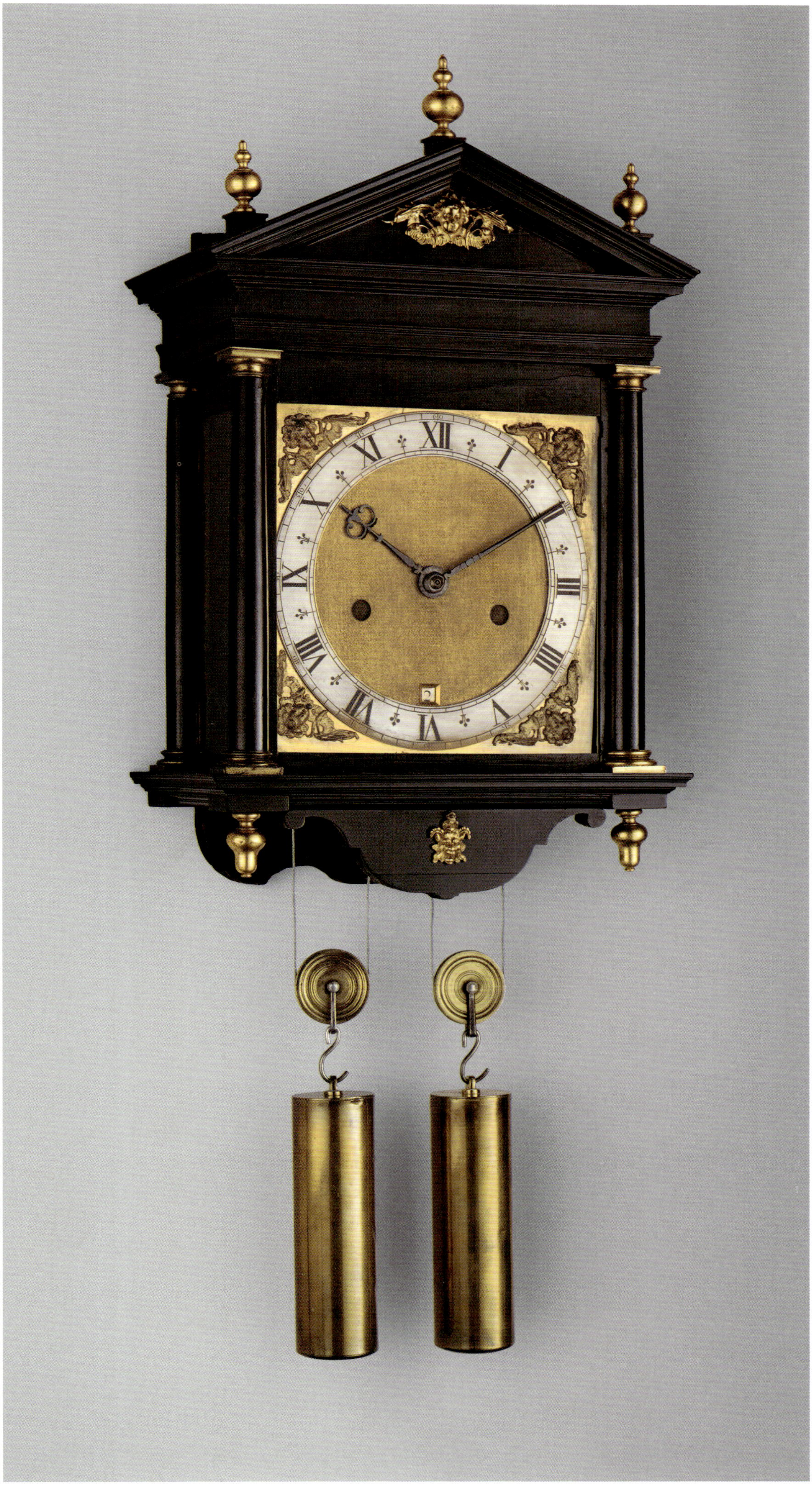

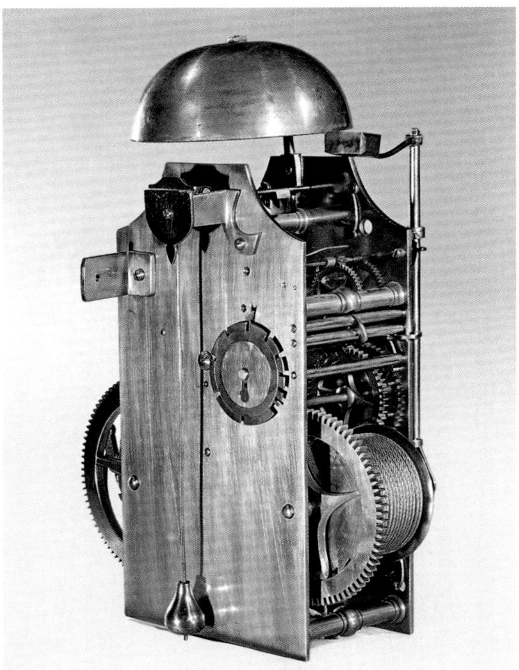

Movement of the clock, showing the back plate and short pendulum

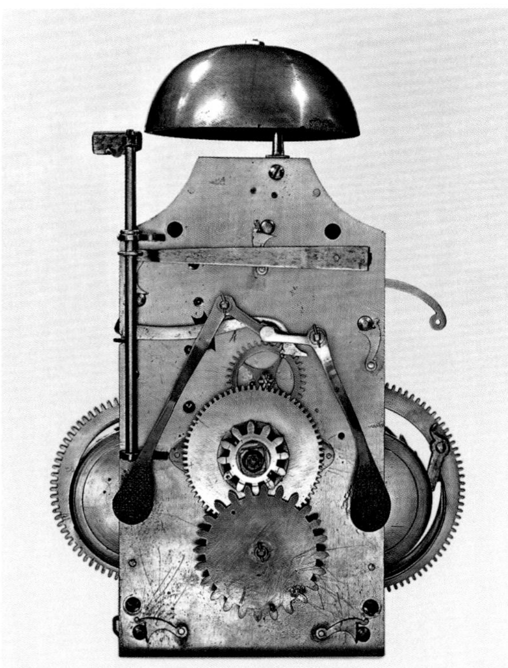

Movement of the clock, showing the motion work and the shutters for maintaining power in the closed position

for Anabaptists, but for whatever reason, in 1667, he left England for the Netherlands, where he remained for the next ten years, spending part of this time in The Hague.[7] Fromanteel returned to England in 1677, and died in 1693. Meanwhile, John Fromanteel (1638–1692), who had been made free of the Clockmakers' Company in 1663, continued the London business during his father's absence.

The eight-day, weight-driven movement of the Museum's clock is a type more often used by the Fromanteels in longcase clocks in the 1660s. It has two narrow brass plates shaped at the top and held apart by five turned pillars that are latched to the front plate. It contains a going train of four wheels with a verge escapement that is regulated by a short pendulum attached directly to a verge staff. The striking train has four wheels and a fly. A count wheel for hour striking is mounted on the back plate, its indexing arm slotted through the plate. The hours are struck on a bell that is mounted on the front plate, where the hammer is also mounted. A bolt-and-shutter device provides continuity of power while the clock is being wound.

The dial is classic Fromanteel, consisting of a gilded square plate to which a narrow chapter ring of silvered brass is attached. The spandrels are filled with applied winged cherub-head reliefs.[8] The chapter ring registers hours (I–XII) and minutes (5–60, each minute marked by a line and every fifth minute by a number). Half hours are indicated by fleurs-de-lis. An aperture at the six o'clock position reveals the day of the month. Two holes for winding (closed between windings) are the only other interruptions on the finely matted surface of the center of the dial; this design provides an uncluttered view of the steel hour and minute hands that is typical of early Fromanteel pendulum clocks. The signature "A. Fromanteel Londini" appears at the lower edge of the dial.

The movement is mounted on a bracket attached to a backboard of oak. Grooves in the sides of the hood allow it to slide down the edges of the backboard to the closed position, where it can be secured by a lock behind the apron at the bottom. Access to the keyhole is hidden by a gilded-brass satyr's head. The hood, with its four subtly curved Doric columns with gilded-brass capitals that support the perfectly proportioned architrave, cornice, and pediment, exemplifies the restrained architectural character of the cases of some of the best English pendulum clocks of the period. The historian Larry Fabian has proposed that the design of these cases might be traced to the mathematician and architect Christopher Wren (1632–1723), whose Italianate buildings played a large part in the rebuilding of London after the Great Fire of 1666. Fabian has offered, in evidence, two engravings that reproduce drawings for weather clocks by Wren.[9] The clocks in Wren's drawings have hoods that are of a style comparable to the hoods of surviving pendulum clocks, but the drawings cannot be dated before about 1663 with any certainty. In the absence of documentary evidence of connections between Wren and either the clockmakers or the clock casemakers in this period, it remains uncertain whether Wren's designs simply reflect the forms of existing clocks, or his original ideas for clockcases.

With the removal of the winged cherub's head (a later addition) from the pediment of the Metropolitan Museum's clock, it is evident that the remarkable sobriety of the design must have been in keeping with Fromanteel's religious sympathies. The restrained style was not, however, confined to Fromanteel's clocks: the clocks of Edward East (1602–1697), John Hilderson (ca. 1630–ca. 1665), and Samuel Knibb (1625–1690), among others, were housed in similar cases made in England during the decade of the 1660s.[10] We know the names of Joseph Clifton (working 1663), John Gutch (admitted Clockmakers Company, 1673), and Robert Player (admitted Clockmakers Company, 1700), as makers of the clockcases during this period,[11] but their individual work has remained unidentified.

The present verge and crown-wheel escapement is probably a reconversion from an anchor escapement. The cock for the pendulum assembly and possibly the pendulum are modern replacements. The weights and pulleys are also of modern origin. The ornament in the pediment of the case, based on the design of ornaments for the spandrels of early pendulum clock dials, is a modern addition, as are probably the acorn-shaped ornaments at the bottom of the case. The lock for the hood of the case is now lost.

In 1952, the clock with its present escapement was included in the "British Clockmaker's Heritage Exhibition" organized by the Antiquarian Section of the British Horological Institute and held in the London Science Museum. Lionel H. Moore was listed as the lender in the catalogue.[12] Moore sold the clock in London in 1960,[13] and subsequently it was purchased, probably from the London dealer Ronald A. Lee, by Irwin Untermyer, who bequeathed it to the Metropolitan Museum. CV / JHL

1 With concessions to modern spelling and capitalization, the advertisement has been quoted in its entirety in recent times by, among others, Ronald A. Lee in the introduction to *English Pendulum Clock* 1969; Thompson 2004, p. 74; Vehmeyer 2004, vol. 2, pp. 497–98. A photograph of the page of the Oct. 21–28 advertisement appeared in the appendix to Penney 2009, p. 620.

2 Huygens (Christiaan) 1658.

3 The attempts to discredit this narrative are without merit. For a reasoned summary of the evidence, see Whitestone 2012.

4 Loomes 1981, pp. 236–37.

5 Aghib and Leopold 1974, p. 892.

6 Leopold 1989, pp. 158–59; Leopold 2005c.

7 Aghib and Leopold 1974, pp. 891–93; Leopold 1989, pp. 158–60.

8 See Robinson 1981, pp. 26–28, and fig. 2/3, for the design, said by the author to be one of the earliest used on longcase clock dials.

9 L. Fabian 1977.

10 *English Pendulum Clock* 1969.

11 Vehmeyer 2004, vol. 2, p. 526.

12 *British Clockmaker's Heritage Exhibition* 1952, p. 39, no. 84, and cover ill.

13 Sotheby's 1960, p. 36, no. 117, ill.

18. Table Clock

BRITISH (LONDON), CA. 1665

14 9/16 × 11 11/16 × 6¼ in. (37 × 29.7 × 15.9 cm)

Height and width of dial plate: 8⅝ × 8 in. (21.9 × 20.3 cm)

Bequest of Irwin Untermyer, 1964

64.101.860

CASE: ebonized fruitwood and rosewood with ebony moldings

DIAL: gilded brass and silver

MOVEMENT: brass and steel, signed (on back plate): *Edwardus East Londini* [Edward East, British (Southill), 1602–1697]

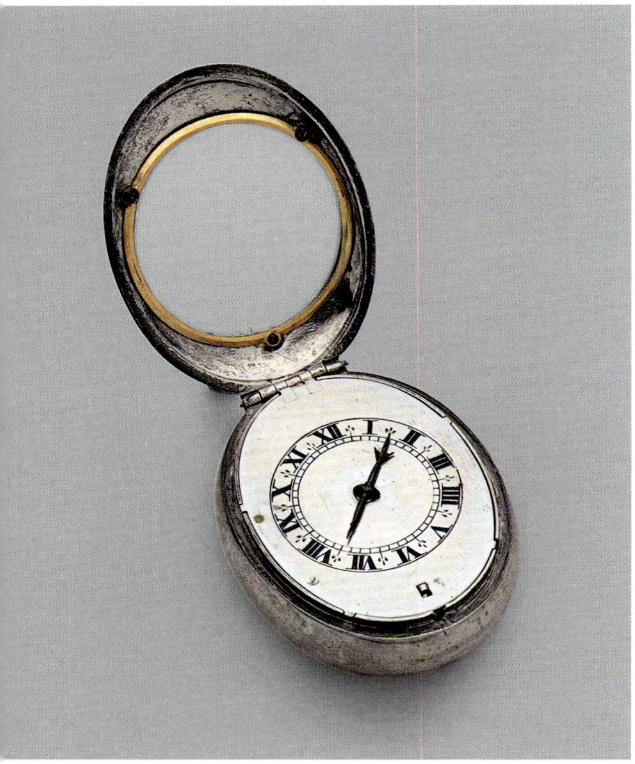

fig. 31 *Edward East (British [Southill], 1602–1697). Watch, British (London), ca. 1640. Outer and inner cases: silver with plain silver dial; movement: gilded brass, silver, and partly blued steel, 1¾ × 1½ in. (4.5 × 3.8 cm). The Metropolitan Museum of Art, New York, Gift of J. Pierpont Morgan, 1917 (17.190.1468a, b)*

EDWARD EAST (1602–1697) LIVED SUCH A LONG LIFE THAT IT WAS once thought that there were two clockmakers by the same name who worked in seventeenth-century London.[1] A large portion of his early timepieces were watches, and the Metropolitan Museum has two: one of which is a silver-cased Puritan watch from about 1640 (fig. 31), so called because its plain, almost egg-shaped case is commonly thought to have been developed in England in reaction to the elaborately decorated cases of the earlier seventeenth century.[2] Watches of the same variety, however, are known to have been made in the Dutch cities of Haarlem and The Hague from about 1625.

Born in Southill, Bedfordshire, East was a royalist and a watchmaker during the reign of King Charles I, and in 1631, he was a founding member of the Clockmakers' Company. After the Restoration in 1660 he was immediately appointed clockmaker to the new king, Charles II (1630–1685).[3] Like the Fromanteels, he quickly recognized the importance of the Huygens pendulum to timekeeping. East's pendulum clocks from the 1660s were sometimes housed in plain wooden cases similar to the example in the Metropolitan Museum and owe much to the design of the first Dutch pendulum clocks. East's clocks, however, more often share the design of the architectural models favored by the Fromanteels.[4]

The spring-driven movement of the Metropolitan's table clock consists of two unusually thick rectangular brass plates held apart by seven baluster-shaped pillars that are pinned to the back plate. The movement contains two trains. The going train consists of three wheels with a verge and crown-wheel escapement, and it is regulated by a short pendulum. The striking train consists of four wheels and a fly, and strikes the hours on a bell (now missing but originally mounted on the front plate). The count wheel, engraved with a characteristic East rosette, is mounted on the upper right side of the exterior of the back plate. East's latinized signature engraved in script, "Edwardus East Londini," curves across the otherwise unadorned back plate. The two spring barrels are unusually wide in diameter, and the fusees are cut for gut. There is no center arbor; instead, the motion of the minute hand is driven indirectly from the second wheel of the going train, giving the hands of the clock a characteristic loose feel.

The gilded-brass dial has a matte surface with a thin polished border and a rosette engraved in the center. The narrow chapter ring is made of silver with black wax-filled numerals (I–XII) for the hours. Minutes are indicated by lines and numbered at five-minute intervals (five–sixty). Two-and-one-half-minute intervals are marked by trident-shaped symbols. The sculptured steel hands, with traces of bluing, are friction fitted. The case now consists of a rectangular, boxlike structure with a

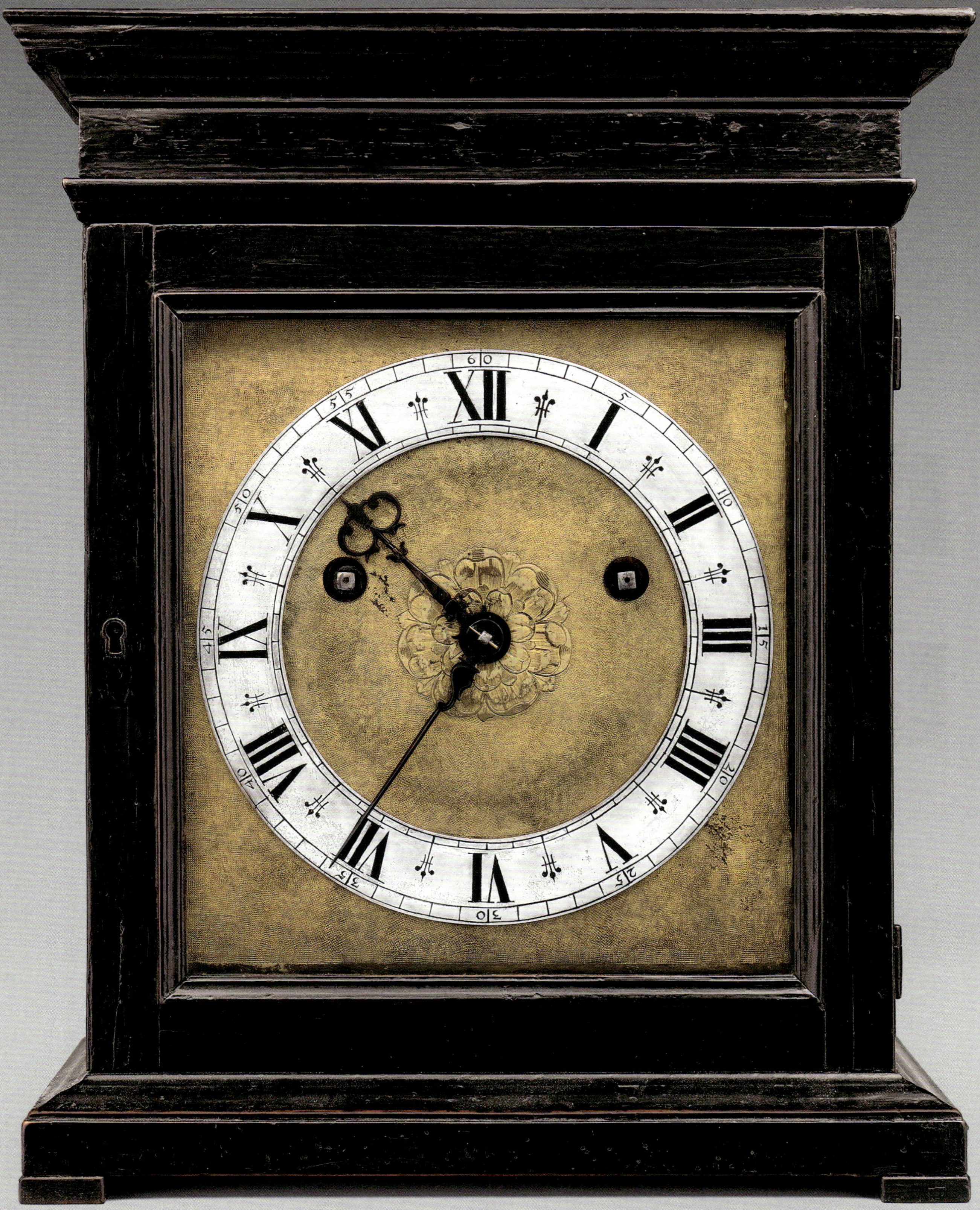

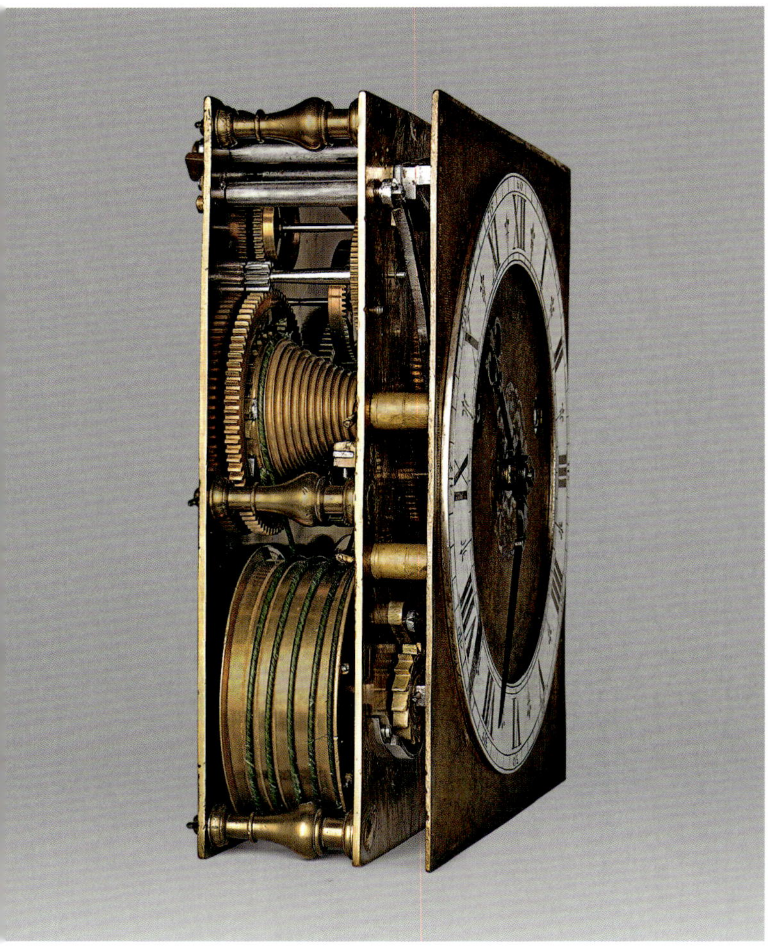

The movement with the view of the striking train

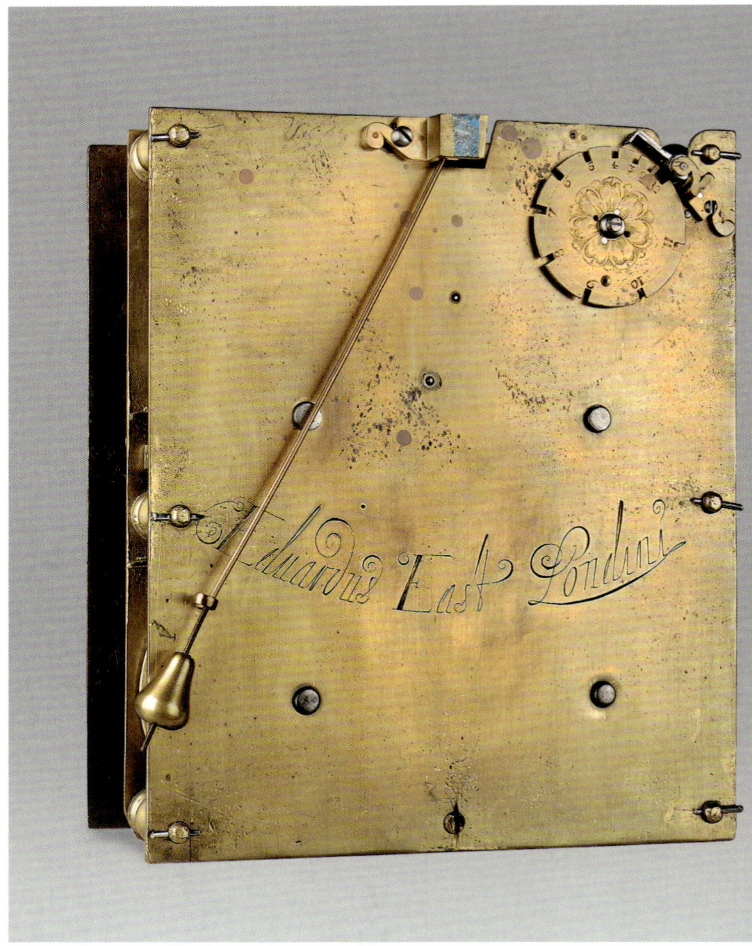

Back plate of the movement with a short pendulum, count wheel, and the signature of the clockmaker

wooden-framed glass door that locks in the front, glass panels in the sides, and a wooden door in the back. It rests on a simple molded plinth, and is surmounted by an architrave and cornice.

This clock had undergone at least two serious modifications before it entered the Museum's collection. At some point, probably early in its history, it was likely given a more up-to-date anchor escapement. At a later time, a simple verge with crown-wheel escapement was reinstated in keeping with what was known to have been the type used by East in these clocks. All the wheels of the going train were replaced, as were the fusee and spring barrel with its spring. A new bell and bell stand were added, but traces remained of the position of the older stand for a horizontally mounted bell. The original hammer remained, but it was severely bent to accommodate a vertically mounted bell, now missing.

The case, too, underwent considerable change at least once. It was given an inverted bell top and bail handle that would have been fashionable about fifty years after the clock was made. Probably from this period the ubiquitous winged cherubs' heads (later removed) were added to the dial. Traces of their former application can still be seen on the dial plate. Gilded-brass ornaments on the top and the keyhole escutcheon, probably products of the rococo revival in the nineteenth century, were added, together with a gilded-metal frieze in Neoclassical style on the architrave and pinecone finials at the corners of the cornice. The quality of the frieze, finial, and front feet, even poorer than that of the rococo-style ornaments, would argue that these were still later additions, probably products of the late nineteenth or early twentieth century. The above modifications to the case can be seen in the illustration of the clock in the catalogue of the Metropolitan Museum's Irwin Untermyer Collection.[5] All of them were made before Untermyer acquired the clock from the New York sale of Frank Garrett's collection in 1926.[6]

Using a table clock from the same period with a movement by the same clockmaker in the British Museum, London, as a guide,[7] the case has been newly returned to something approaching its original simplicity in order to restore the look of a now rather rare variety of East clock. The metal ornament was removed; the feet were replaced by wooden blocks; and the inverted bell top was replaced by a simple flat wooden top. The movement, like that of the Fromanteel wall clock (see entry 17 in this volume), had already been reconverted to a historically correct verge escapement. No attempt was made to mount a new bell. The movement was cleaned, given new gut for the fusees, and otherwise left as it had been when it entered the Museum's collection. CV / JHL

1 Britten 1911, p. 267.
2 Acc. no. 17.190.1468a, b. See Williamson 1912, p. 132, no. 136. The accession number for the other watch in the Metropolitan Museum's collection is 17.190.1483a, b. See Williamson 1912, p. 133, no. 137, and pl. LXII.
3 Jagger 1983, pp. 23–26.
4 See entry 17 in this volume.
5 Hackenbroch 1958, pl. 2.
6 Anderson Galleries 1926, pp. 50–51, no. XXVI, ill.
7 Inv. no. CAI-2115. See Thompson 2004, pp. 68–69. Our thanks to the staff of the Horological Students' Room at the British Museum for their gracious cooperation.

19. Watch

FRENCH (PARIS), CA. 1670–75
1½ × 1¼ × ⅝ in. (3.8 × 3.2 × 1.6 cm)
Gift of J. Pierpont Morgan, 1917
17.190.1600

CASE: gold, blued steel, rock crystal, partly gilded silver, and diamonds, possibly by Isaac Bergeron, dit d'Argent (French, active 1649–97)
DIAL: painted enamel and basse-taille enamel on gold
MOVEMENT: gilded brass, partly blued steel, and silver, signed: *F. Meybom Æparis / St. Germain* [F. L. Meybom, unknown, active ca. 1650–80]

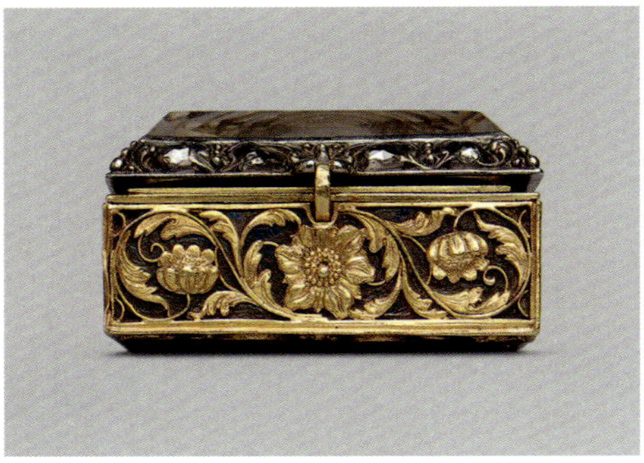

top: *The dial of the watch with the cover closed*
bottom: *The back of the watchcase*

ONE OF THE WAYS IN WHICH WATCHMAKERS WHO HAD NOT BEEN apprenticed to a Parisian master, and, therefore were not eligible to open an establishment in Paris, could circumvent the rules of the Guild of Master Clockmakers (*Corporation des maîtres horlogers*, established 1544) was by setting up a workshop outside the jurisdiction of the guild. The privileged close of the Abbey of Saint Germain-des-Prés on the left bank of the river Seine was one of the enclaves where the guild's rules did not apply, and in the eighteenth century, it would become the site of the workshops of such distinguished clockmakers as the Swiss Henri Enderlin (died 1753) and the German Michel Stollenwerck (died 1768).[1] From the signature on the back plate of the Metropolitan Museum's watch it can be certain that Meybom was one of the watchmakers working there in the seventeenth century. Aside from this exquisite watch, there is another watch with a similar square movement, signed "F. L. Meybom," and housed in a closely comparable case in the collection of the Fitzwilliam Museum in Cambridge, England.[2] Nothing more is known about Meybom.

The movement of the Metropolitan's watch consists of two square, gilded-brass plates that are held apart by four baluster pillars, which are pinned to the back plate. The watch is spring driven with a chain fusee and four wheels that end in a crown-wheel and verge escapement with a steel balance wheel. On the back plate, the worm-and-wheel setup for regulating the mainspring has blued-steel ornaments and a silver figure plate; below is the watchmaker's signature "F. Meybom Æparis / St. Germain." The mounting for the set-up regulation, the case bolt, and all of the screws are of blued steel.

The diminutive size of the watch created problems for the watchmaker. The small movement required a reduction in the size of the wheels and their pinions, which could not be achieved without decreasing the number of teeth on the wheels, therefore causing a reduction of the gearing ratios involved. To solve the problem, an extra wheel was often added to the train. The small movement also required a small balance at the end of the train, and a small balance tends to tick faster. In other words, a small movement needs a larger gear ratio in the train to accommodate the smaller balance, while the smaller size actually causes a reduction in the gear ratio. Finally, the movement requires a smaller-than-usual fusee with fewer turns of the fusee chain. The duration of the watch (the maximum period between windings) will thus be lessened, resulting in a watch that needs winding twice a day.

The exterior of the square gold case is covered with four side panels of delicately chased openwork of gold floral and foliate designs applied over blued-steel grounds. The same technique was used to

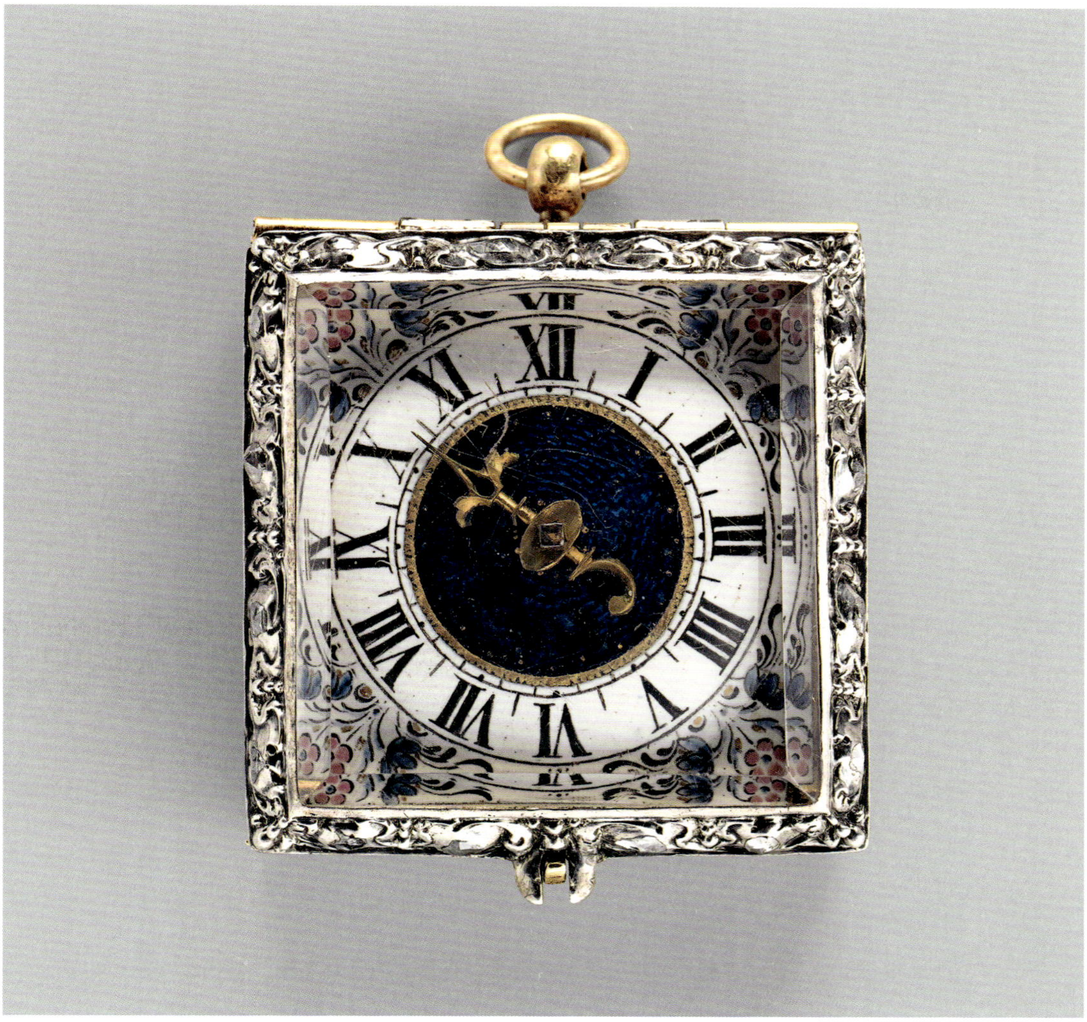

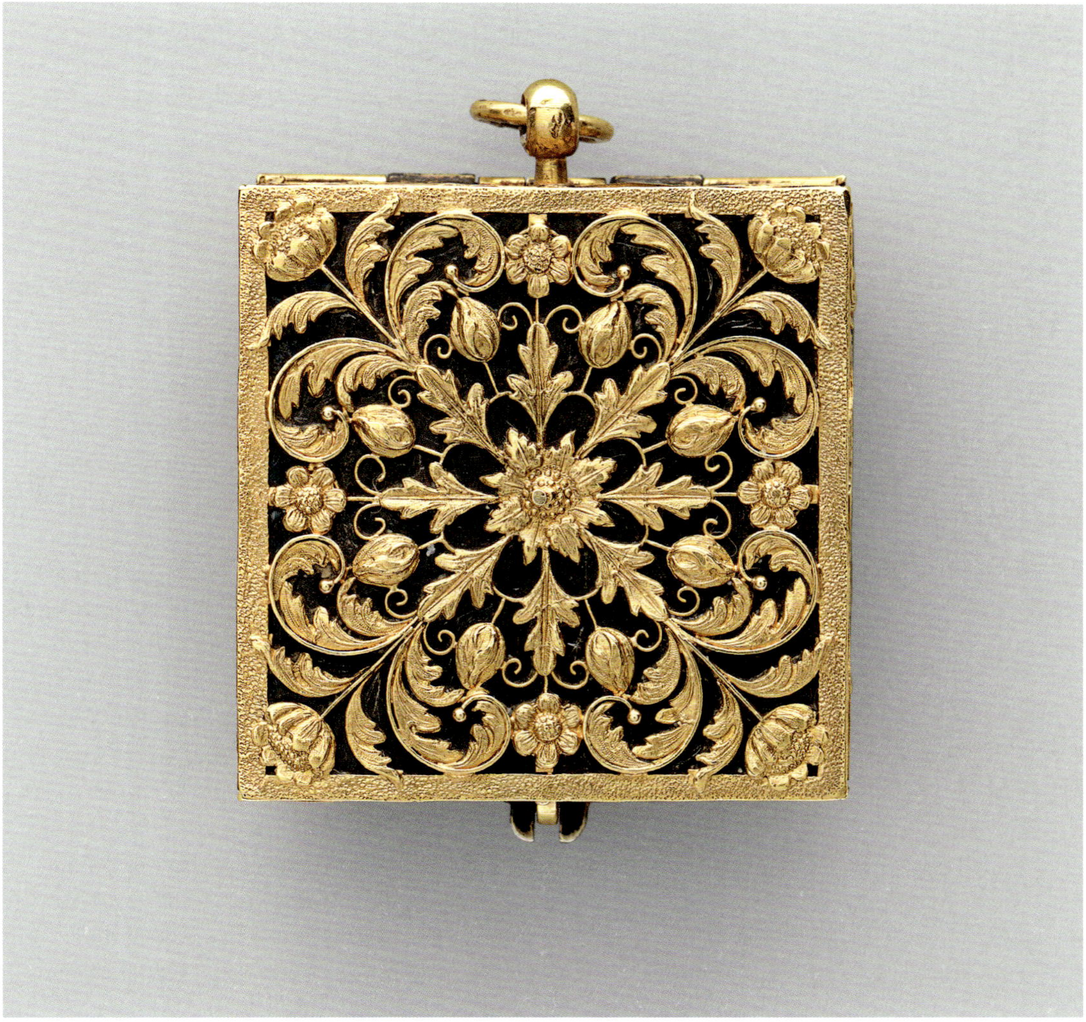

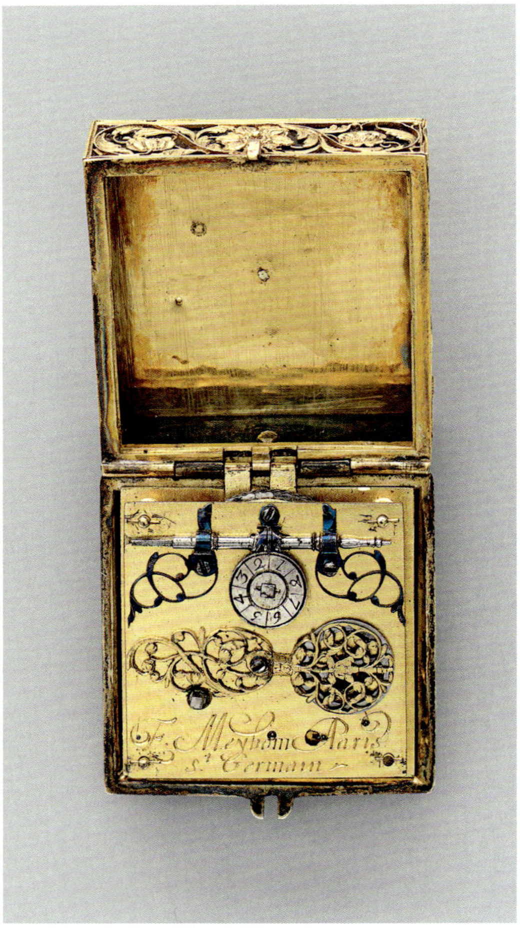

View of the watch with open case to show the back plate of the movement

create the openwork design of flowers and foliage radiating from a central blossom on the back of the case that, like the side panels, plays bright gold ornament against a dark blue ground. Hinged to the case is a square bezel with eight rose-cut diamonds set in silver and framing a beveled-edge plaque of rock crystal, the center polished as a lens through which the chapter ring on the dial can be viewed. The dial, pinned to the top plate of the movement, is made of white enamel with pink and blue floral designs painted in the spandrels and a dark blue basse-taille enameled center. The roman numerals (I–XII) of the chapter ring are painted in black enamel with half-hour divisions marked by radiating lines and quarter-hour divisions by lines painted on the inner edge of the chapter ring. The single hand is made of sculptured gold.

The design of the Museum's watchcase has been attributed by art historian Michèle Bimbenet-Privat to a Protestant goldsmith named Isaac Bergeron, who is first recorded to be living in Paris when his child was baptized in 1649.[3] Like the clockmakers, Parisian goldsmiths were required to be Catholic as one of the prerequisites to becoming a master in the guild. Bergeron would, therefore, have been forbidden to sign or to mark his work and could not lawfully sell it in Paris. But guild rules could be set aside if the king or his council wished. A record dated 1671 concerning the seizure by guild officials of a watchcase made by Bergeron for the watchmaker Guillaume de Beauvais (master 1630) demonstrates the advantage of royal influence: the watchmaker involved in the case was known to have the "care of watches and clocks of his Majesty's Council," and the seizure is recorded as having been overruled.[4] Bimbenet-Privat further proposed a square watch (now in the Musée du Louvre) with a movement signed by Balthazar Martinot (1636–1714), one of the king's clockmakers, as an example of Bergeron's watchcase making.[5] The Metropolitan Museum's Meybom watchcase closely matches the case of the Louvre's watch, and both belong to a small group of watches with similar cases that include another with a movement by Martinot that is also in the Louvre,[6] and still another by Auguste Bretonneau (active 1638–55) now in the Kremlin Armory, Moscow.[7]

The Revocation of the Edict of Nantes in 1685 removed the right of toleration for French Protestants. Evidence of the French king's special favor was found by Bimbenet-Privat in a record of 1686 in which "Isaac d'Argent," probably the same goldsmith as Isaac Bergeron, was now granted special dispensation by the king's council to continue making watchcases in Paris as he had been doing for the past eight years and without harassment from the guild.[8] D'Argent, his wife, Mary, and three children were last recorded in 1694 as émigrés in England,[9] so life as Protestants in Paris must have been difficult during these years.

While the evidence for the attribution of the case to Bergeron is not wholly convincing, and records of Meybom are evidently nonexistent, more is known about the other two watchmakers who signed watches in this group. Bretonneau can be found in Paris records working between 1638 and 1658.[10] He was the maker of movements for watches with painted enamel cases, one of which, in the Metropolitan Museum's collection, can be dated for stylistic and technical reasons to about 1645 or 1650.[11] It is not known how much later than 1658 he might have been active or even when he died, but he signed a silver traveling watch, also in the Museum's collection,[12] that displays more advanced watchmaking technology than does the enamel-cased watch.

In regards to the Balthazar Martinot case we are on firmer ground, because he belonged to a large and distinguished family of clockmakers. Born in Rouen in 1636, the son of the keeper of the Gros Horloge (the town clock of Rouen), Martinot had a career in Paris that included appointments as clockmaker to the queen mother, Anne of Austria (1601–1666), and later to King Louis XIV (1638–1715). While there was more than one Balthazar Martinot who made clocks, the one born in Rouen in 1636 is believed to be the only one authorized between 1660 and 1715 to sign his work "Balthazar Martinot à Paris," as the Louvre's watches are signed.[13]

The Martinot watches have been dated to the third quarter of the seventeenth century, but given Martinot's age, his watches are not likely to have been made before about 1660. In any case, they must have been made before about 1675 or 1676, for the Louvre's Martinot watches and the Metropolitan's Meybom watch all have pre–balance spring movements. In addition, the watches display a remarkably high degree of skill, finish, and attention to detail. It seems reasonable to suppose that they would have also incorporated the latest technical improvement: namely the spiral spring balance. Invented in late 1674 by Christiaan Huygens (1629–1695), the balance spring enormously increased the accuracy of a watch. Almost immediately Isaac II Thuret (1630–1706), another of the illustrious horologists of the reign of King Louis XIV, was given Huygens's instructions for making a model of the device, and by 1676, after a dispute over the possibility of obtaining a patent, Huygens granted free use of the invention to all watchmakers,[14] thus making the unregulated balance obsolete.

The blue enamel in the center of the dial of the Museum's watch displays areas of deterioration.[15] Otherwise, there are signs of light wear in the movement and on the case of the watch, but both are in a remarkably good state of preservation. It is not known where the donor, J. Pierpont Morgan, acquired the watch. CV / JHL

1 For further information about the clockmakers of the Abbey Saint Germain-des-Prés enclose, see Augarde 1996, p. 46.
2 Baillie 1929, p. 116, no. 5, and pl. xxv.
3 Bimbenet-Privat 2002, vol. 1, p. 244.
4 "Ayant le soin des monstres et horloges des conseils de Sa Majesté"; ibid.
5 Inv. no. OA 7030. See Cardinal 2000, p. 84, no. 53; Bimbenet-Privat 2002, vol. 2, pp. 490–91, no. 183.
6 For the second watch in the Musée du Louvre (inv. no. OA 8294), see Cardinal 1984b, p. 42, no. 17.
7 *Treasures of the Kremlin* 1997, p. 46, no. 9.
8 Bimbenet-Privat 2002, vol. 1, pp. 244–45.
9 See ibid., p. 245.
10 Vincent 2002, pp. 101, 105, n. 32.
11 Acc. no. 17.190.1626. See ibid., p. 96 and fig. 19, and p. 100, fig. 30.
12 Acc. no. 17.190.1628. See ibid., p. 101 and figs. 33, 34.
13 Augarde 1996, p. 368. See also Tardy 1971–72, vol. 2, pp. 442–44.
14 See Cardinal 1989, p. 79. See also entry 20 in this volume.
15 For a discussion of a reason for the tendency of translucent blue enamel to deteriorate, see Wypyski 2000, pp. 150–51.

20. Watch

CASE: FRENCH (PARIS), CA. 1676–80
MOVEMENT: DUTCH (THE HAGUE), CA. 1676–80
Diam. of case: 2¼ in. (5.7 cm)
Diam. of back plate: $1\frac{15}{16}$ in. (4.9 cm)
Gift of J. Pierpont Morgan, 1917
17.190.1417

CASE: painted enamel on gold, possibly by Henri Toutin (French, 1614–1684), and raised enamel on gold, possibly by Josias Belle (French, 1624–1695)
MOVEMENT: gilded brass, partly blued steel, and silver, signed (on back plate): *Johannes Van Ceulen Fecit Hagae* [Johannes van Ceulen the Elder, Dutch, active 1675–1715]

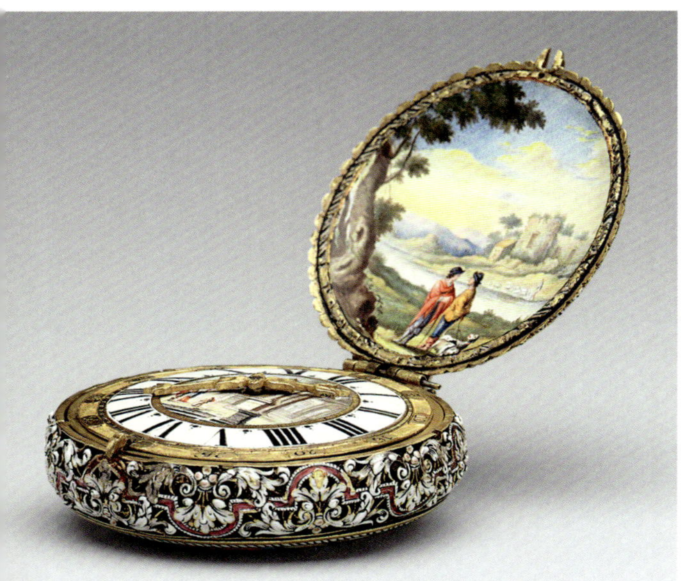

Case open to show dial and interior of the cover

Back plate of the movement of the watch with Huygens's balance spring attached to the balance

THE SECOND GREAT SEVENTEENTH-CENTURY ADVANCE IN timekeeping was the invention of the balance spring. When attached at one end to the balance staff of a spring-driven watch and attached at the other end to the back plate of the watch and set in motion, the oscillation of a spiral hair spring, like the swing of a pendulum, was discovered to be isochronous. Its employment increased the accuracy of a watch by an order of magnitude comparable to that achieved by the application of a pendulum to a clock. Both applications were the inventions of the Dutch mathematician, physicist, and astronomer Christiaan Huygens (1629–1695). Huygens's immediate family included his father, Constantijn I Huygens (1596–1687), who was secretary to the Dutch head of state, Stadtholder William II (1626–1650); and his elder brother, Constantijn II Huygens (1628–1697), who was secretary to Prince William of Orange (later to become King William III of England and Scotland; 1650–1702). Consequently Christiaan Huygens had entrée to the highest circles in the courts of The Hague and London, as well as to the court of King Louis XIV (1638–1715) in France. His aristocratic connections, together with his scientific genius, insured him a ready welcome in 1663 as the first overseas fellow of the Royal Society in England and secured him a salaried position from 1665–81 in France's Académie Royale des Sciences.[1]

Huygens's early letters written in 1675 to Henry Oldenburg (ca. 1618–1677), the first secretary of the Royal Society, contain his first disclosure of the secret of the balance spring. The letters were quickly followed by a published description and diagram of the mechanism in the February 25, 1675, issue of the Académie Royale's *Le journal des sçavans* (later renamed *Le journal des savants*).[2]

The news unleashed a torrent of complaint in England about the priority of the invention from the Royal Society's first Curator of Experiments, Robert Hooke (1635–1703), whose studies of the properties of springs were probably known to Huygens. In France, Huygens's collaborator for the construction of models of the invention was Isaac II Thuret (1630–1706), who was probably the best of King Louis XIV's clockmakers and also claimed to be the inventor of the mechanism.[3] In the end, Huygens never obtained a patent in England nor in France, thereby granting freedom to all to employ the invention.

As a result of the patent disputes, Johannes van Ceulen the Elder (active 1675–1715) became one of the first Dutch watchmakers to retain the right to make Huygens's balance springs. While little is known of Van Ceulen before 1675, two years later, he had moved to an address on the Plein, the prestigious square in The Hague where the Huygens family also had a residence.[4] By that time Van Ceulen had already received a commission for one of the new balance-spring watches from

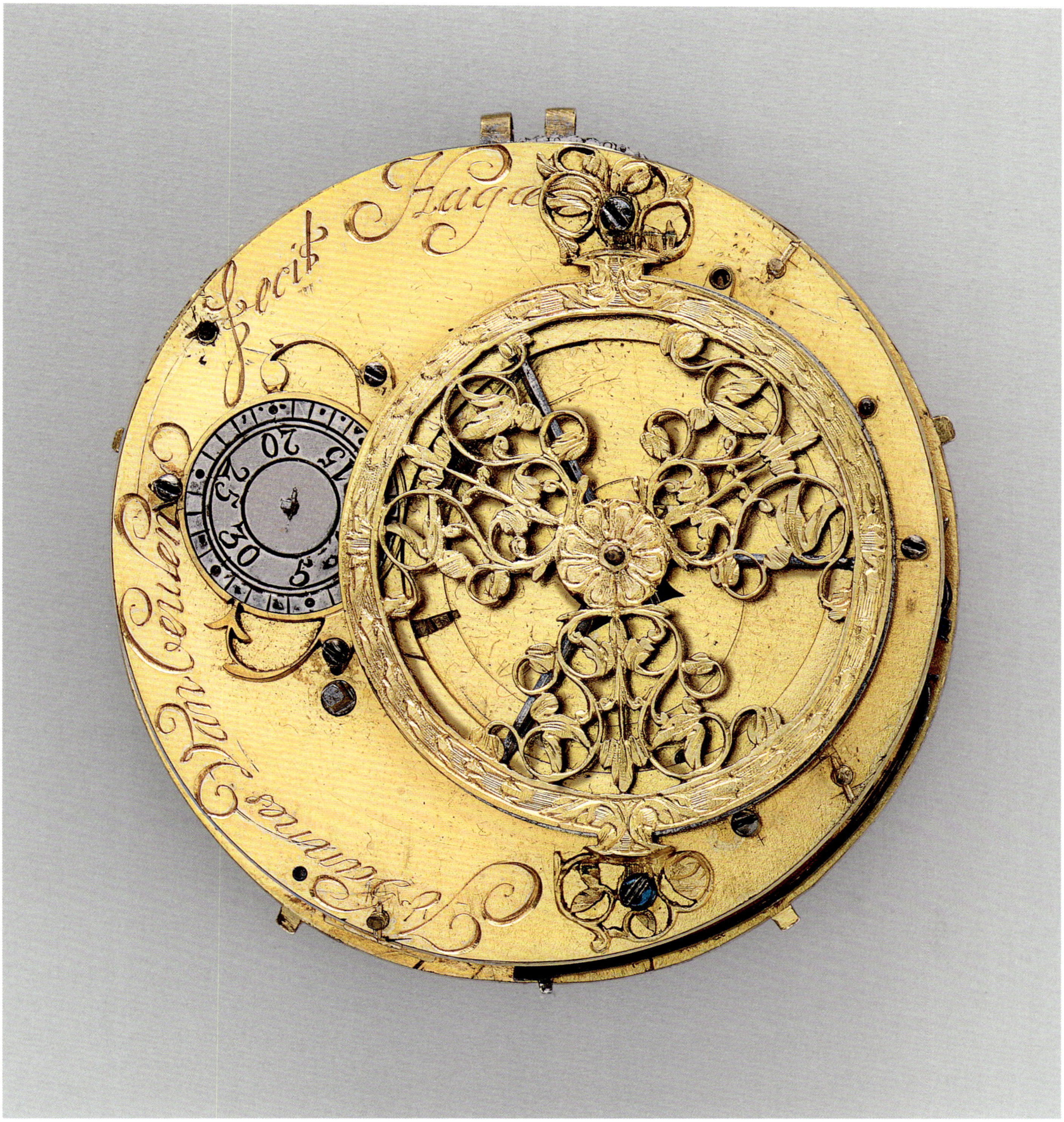
Johannes Van Ceulen
fecit Hag

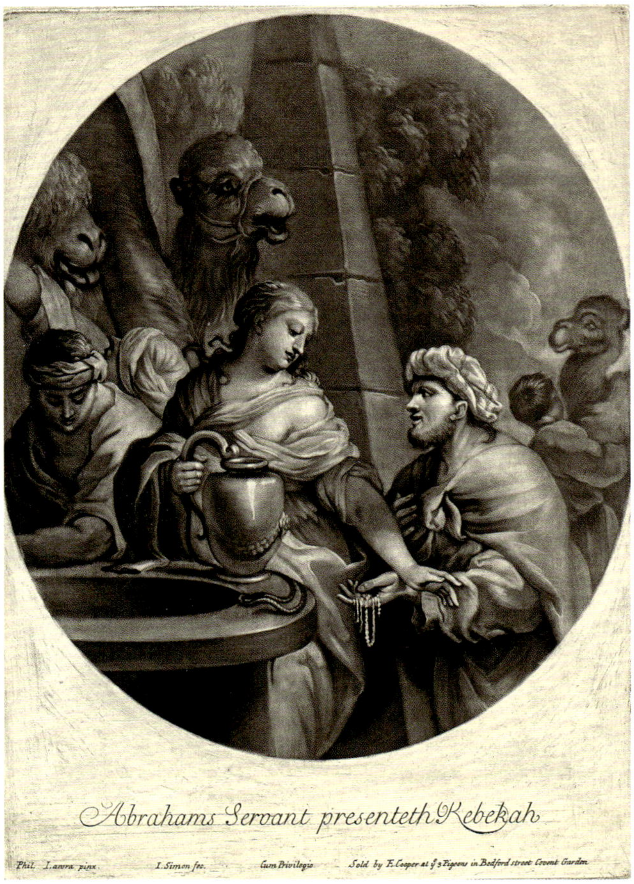

fig. 32 *John Simon (French, ca. 1675–1751), after Filippo Lauri (Italian, 1623–1694).* Abrahams Servant Presenteth Rebekah, *British (London), ca. 1700–1725. Mezzotint, 11⅞ × 8⅝ in. (30 × 22 cm). British Museum, London (1874,0808.1239)*

Huygens's brother Constantijn. The commission of the watch is mentioned in a letter from Constantijn to his wife (1676) while he was on military duty with Prince William on the French border, and receipt of the watch is recorded in his journal on July 18, 1676.[5] In 1688 Van Ceulen would become one of the founding members of the Clockmakers' Guild in The Hague,[6] and he is known to have been the maker of a large number of spring-driven clocks regulated by Huygens's short pendulums,[7] a type commonly known as a Hague clock (*Haagse Klok*).

The Metropolitan Museum's watch is of the variety that Van Ceulen was making in 1676, which incorporated the new balance spring. In the felicitously designed layout of its back plate the hair spring is barely visible underneath the balance bridge. The bridge, with its tripartite openwork of delicately scrolling vegetation that radiates from a central rosette, is screwed to the back plate through two openwork feet, and it occupies the greater part of the plate with only a silver figure plate (marked 5–30 by fives) for adjusting the spring. The engraved signature of the watchmaker, "Johannes Van Ceulen Fecit Hagae," completes the design. (Hidden between the mainspring barrel and the pillar plate of the watch is a worm-and-wheel regulator for setting up the mainspring.)

The movement consists of two thin, circular plates of gilded brass, which are held apart by four Egyptian-style pillars with pierced ornaments at their top ends, and a train of three gilded-brass wheels that end in a verge escapement with a balance wheel of three arms regulated by the newly invented hair spring. The fusee has grooves for seven turns and a fine steel chain. The dial plate has four feet that are pinned to the top plate (or pillar plate) of the movement, and it supports a painted-enamel chapter ring for the hours (I–XII) with dotted ornaments marking the half hours. Around the hour chapter is a circle of matte gold with polished gold reserves that emphasize five-minute periods (numbered 5–60 by fives) in incised and blackened numerals. The inner edge of the circle displays the minutes in carefully calibrated lines. The center of the dial is painted enamel and depicts an antique architectural ruin with human figures in the foreground that has been adapted from an etching by Gabriel Pérelle (1604–1677), a prolific French artist whose landscapes were among those most often used as models by the seventeenth-century enamelers of Paris and Blois. The scene and the chapter ring for the hours closely resemble French enamel-cased watches of the mid-seventeenth century.

The rest of the watchcase is more problematic. The circular cover and basin-shaped case, as well as the dial and movement, are hinged together at the twelve o'clock position. The thickness and diameter of the case allow a confident attribution to a French enameler, but the question of when

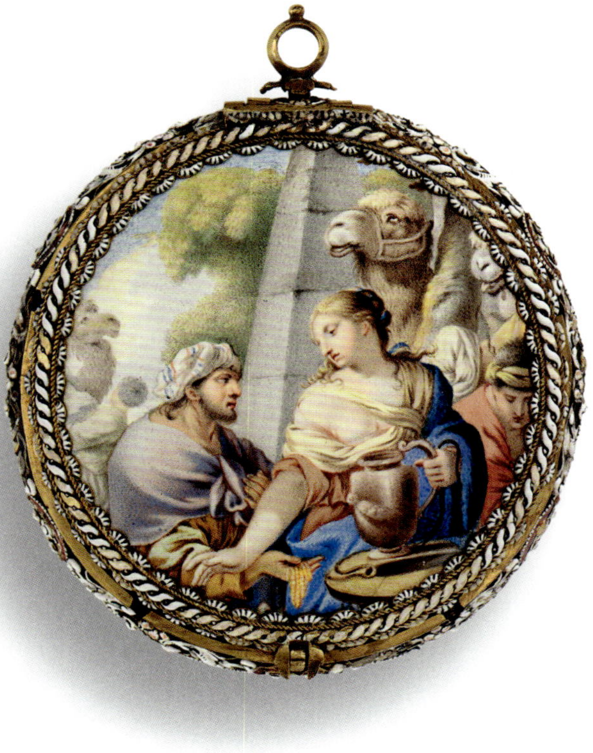

Elijah and Rebecca at the Well on the exterior of the cover of the watchcase

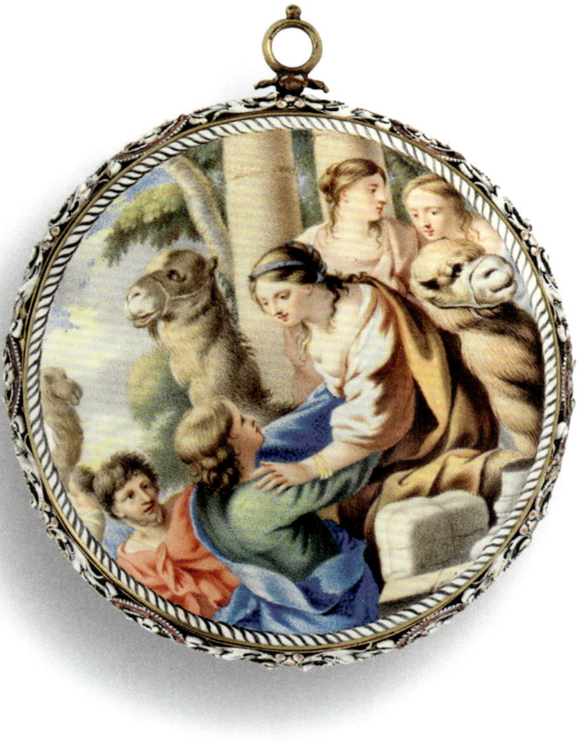

Isaac and Rebecca on the back of the watchcase

the case was made is more difficult. Most seventeenth-century French enameled watchcases are shaped from a single sheet of gold so that the side (or band) of the case and the bottom of the case are one piece. The band and bottom of this case are two separate elements, which are joined together by a series of bent gold lugs that were disguised by cold enameling. The advantage of this construction is that it allows the joining of two separate kinds of enamel: painted enamel for the bottom, and raised enamel, or enamel in relief, on the band. These two types of enamels are often the products of separate craftsmen. The cover, too, consists of a painted-enamel plaque with an added gold frame, or bezel, of white enamel in relief, attached, like the band, by means of gold lugs that are bent to attach the bezel to the plaque. The origin of the landscape on the interior of the cover has not been identified, but the man with two impatient dogs who has stopped to chat with a friend may have been the invention of the enameler.

While seventeenth-century enameled watchcases have not survived in quantity and were probably never made in great numbers, watchcases constructed in the manner of the Museum's Van Ceulen watch are remarkably rare. A watchcase cover in the collection of the Patek Philippe Museum in Geneva[8] displays a scene of Elijah and Rebecca at the Well; this same scene is on the cover of the Metropolitan Museum's watch, but the Geneva piece is painted in monochrome blue enamel. In addition, the cover has a bezel of raised enamel that is nearly identical to the Metropolitan's Van Ceulen watchcover bezel, and it has been dated to about 1650 or 1655. Another watchcase constructed in the same way as the Van Ceulen watchcase is in the Metropolitan's Robert Lehman Collection.[9] The interior side of the bottom of the case of the Lehman watch is enameled with the French Royal Arms; and the interior, or counter enamel, of the cover of the watch depicts King Louis XIV as a boy at the age of nine or ten on horseback, which lends support to a date of about 1645–48 for the watchcase. The movement, original to the case, is by Jacques Goullons (active 1626, died 1671), who is recorded working in Paris. Both objects tend to support a date of about 1650–55 for the Van Ceulen watchcase, but there is a further complication presented by the enamels.

The exterior of the cover of the Museum's Van Ceulen watch has an exquisitely painted scene of Elijah and Rebecca at the Well, and on the back of the case there is another scene of Isaac and Rebecca; both scenes are illustrative of the Old Testament story in the Book of Genesis. The two scenes were apparently quite popular as they appear on a number of surviving watchcases.[10] Enamel expert Hans Boeckh has grouped the watchcase cover in the Patek Philippe Museum with eleven other watches with various subjects that he believes were either influenced by or directly copied from models by the French painter Sébastien Bourdon (1616–1671).[11] No painting by Bourdon that could have served as a model for either scene of Rebecca has come to light, however, and there is some evidence that the model for Elijah and Rebecca at the Well might have been a painting not by Bourdon but by the Italian Filippo Lauri (1623–1694). Again, there is no trace of an original painting or even of a seventeenth-century print, the existence of which might be inferred from the number of enameled versions of the scene that survive. A reversed version of the scene does exist, however, in a print by engraver John Simon (ca. 1675–1751)

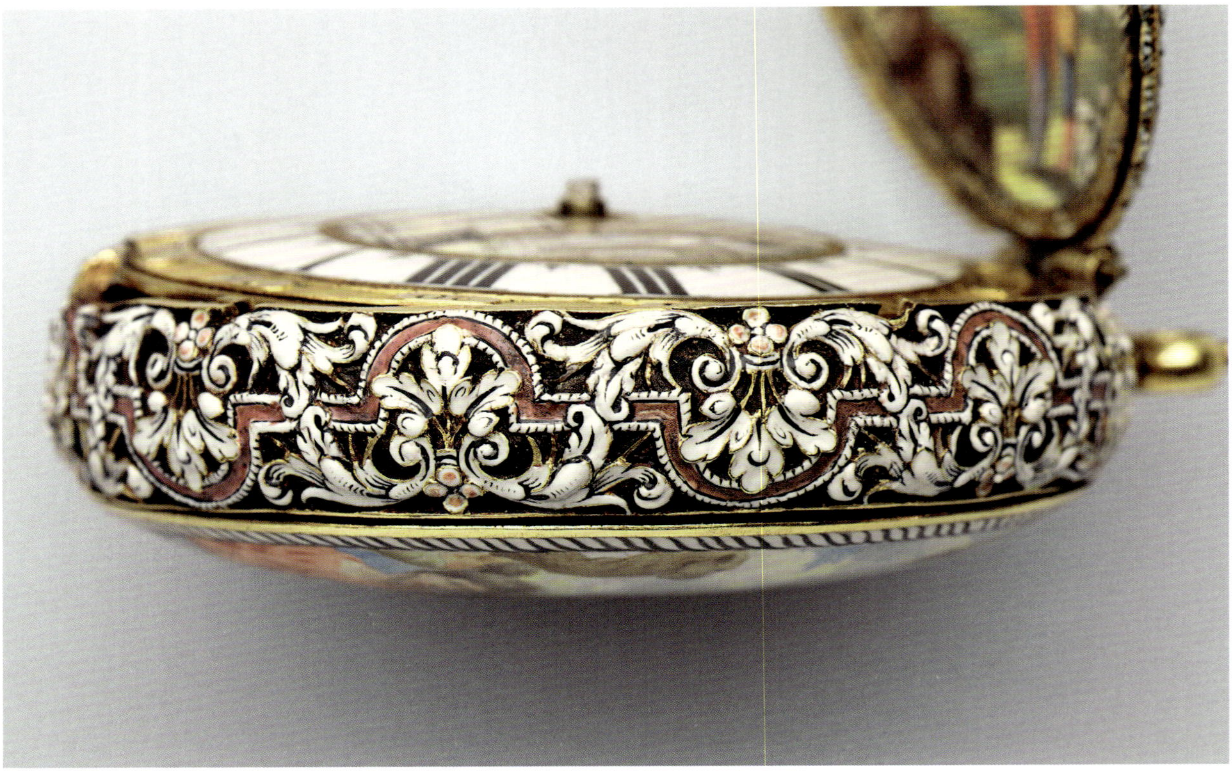

The band of the watchcase with the open cover to show a part of the dial

(fig. 32),[12] a Huguenot from Normandy, who was employed for a time as a copyist by London printseller Edward Cooper (active 1682–1725), and succeeded him in the trade in 1723.[13] The print of Elijah and Rebecca has multiple identifications: "Abrahams Servant Presenteth Rebekah," "Phil. Larvra pinx," "I. Simon fec," and "Sold by E. Cooper at ye 3 pigeons in Bedford street in Covent Garden." At some point before 1723 Simon must have seen and copied either a painting or a print, and he may have misread the name of the artist.

None of the foregoing helps very much in dating the enamels on the Van Ceulen watch, although Boeckh has suggested that the scene on the Patek Philippe Museum's fragment of Elijah and Rebecca is likely to have been enameled in Paris about 1650–55 by Henri Toutin (1614–1684). The convex band of raised enamel on the side of the case of the Van Ceulen watch is a mixture of strapwork and foliage that incorporates the type of occasional flower recorded in ornament prints by Daniel Marot (1661–1752).[14] These appeared in the early years of the eighteenth century, but reflected a style of ornament that was fashionable in his native France before Marot, a Protestant, left for the Netherlands in 1685 as the result of the Revocation of the Edict of Nantes that same year. The band of the Van Ceulen watchcase, therefore, seems to belong to the 1680s rather than the 1650s, and its raised enamel is technically comparable to that found on the mounts for cameos made in the 1680s by the Parisian goldsmith Josias Belle (1624–1695). Belle's jewelry for the French Royal Family has been identified by art historian Michèle Bimbenet-Privat, who also discovered a record of Belle as an embellisher of clocks with ornaments of various colored enamels.[15] One can only wonder whether enamel painting of the narrative variety that appears on the Museum's Van Ceulen watchcase went on longer in France than is usually thought, or whether the watchcase was simply modified and brought up to date by a highly skilled Parisian enameler, possibly Belle, who was active about 1676–80.

Taken together, the case is nearly as unusual as the movement, but some light may be shed on the problem of dating the watch by evidence that wealthy Dutch patrons were particularly enamored of watches with enameled gold cases and, with some notable exceptions, the enamelers of gold watchcases in the seventeenth century were either French or Swiss. The desired cases could be imported empty to be fitted with movements by Dutch watchmakers, as in the example of a watch by Pieter Klock (1665–1754) with a case by the Huauds of Geneva.[16] If it was especially treasured, a watchcase could be reused by a watchmaker who would supply a new and improved movement to fit the case, as was done with the Metropolitan Museum's watch movement by the eighteenth-century Dutchman Lambertus Vrythoff (died 1769) in a case of about 1645 originally made for the French courtier Louis Hesselin (1602–1662).[17] The reuse of such watchcases can be explained as a result of a simple desire for a new movement incorporating the Huygens balance spring, an improvement in technology that made older pre–balance spring watches obsolete as timekeepers.

The condition of the movement of the Metropolitan's Van Ceulen watch is excellent with the exception that the end of one pillar has been broken off. The center of the dial with the older markings for half hours may have been removed from an earlier watch, but the minute chapter ring was surely made to accommodate it, as well as to fit it to the case. The original hour hand and minute hand have been lost

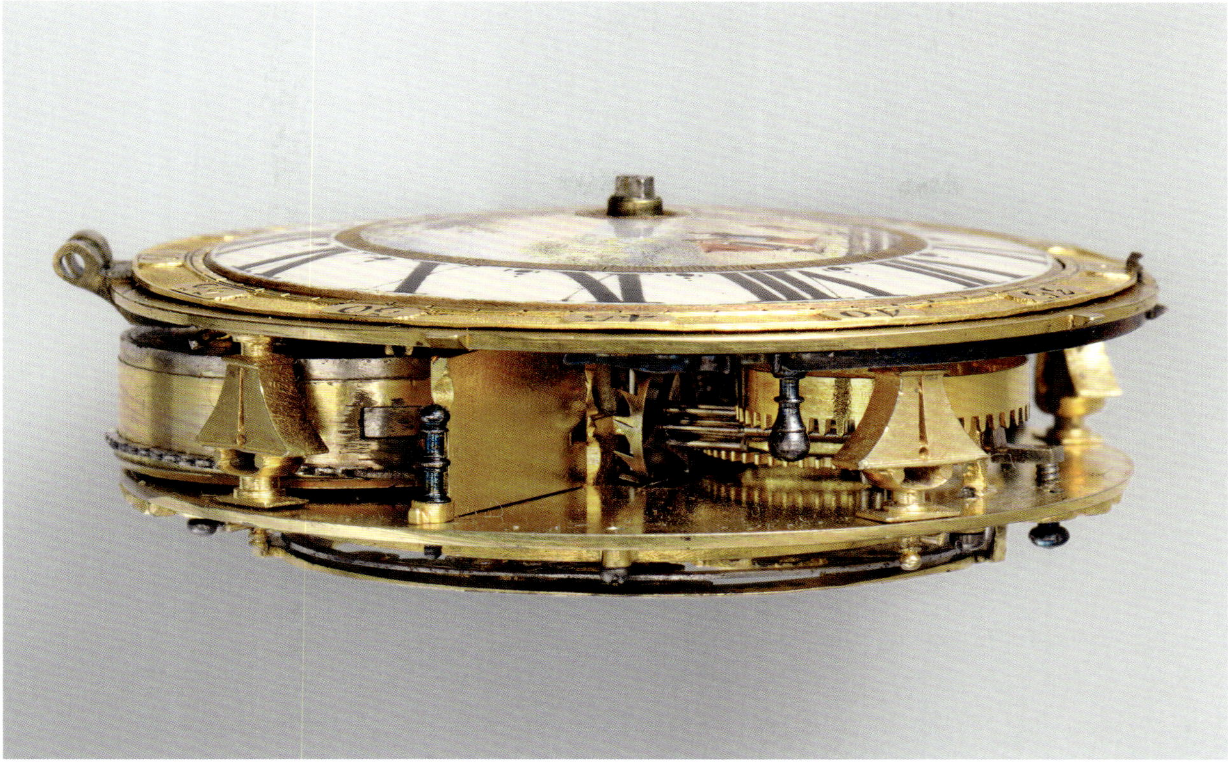

The left side of the movement with a partial view of the dial

and replaced by a single hand by someone who could not have understood the significance of the chapter ring on the dial for minutes. The central loop of the hinge is missing. The enamels on the case show the expected signs of normal handling: areas of stress have lost much of their original enamel. The band of raised enamel has sustained numerous losses. The frame around the front of the cover, too, has many areas of enamel loss. These losses have been replaced by one of the Museum's conservators. Many of the lugs that hold the frame to the cover of the case and the band (or side) of the case to the bottom have lost their enamel.

J. Pierpont Morgan acquired this watch from Carl H. Marfels of Frankfurt am Main and Berlin.[18] It was mentioned as being in Morgan's collection as early as 1911.[19] CV / JHL

1 For a fascinating account in English of Huygens, his family, and the society in which they flourished, see Jardine 2008; for his election to the Royal Society, see p. 309.

2 Huygens (Christiaan) 1675. See Leopold 1993, pp. 41–42; Leopold 1996, pp. 107, 108, n. 63; Jardine 2008, pp. 266–68. See also Thompson 2008, p. 52, for a good description of the device. The text of Huygens's publication of the invention in *Le journal des sçavans* is reproduced in Cardinal 1989, pp. 78–79, ill. no. 38, a–c. Robert Hooke's unsuccessful attempts to apply balance springs to watches are discussed in entry 23 of this volume.

3 For an account in English of the dispute, see Cardinal 1989, p. 79.

4 While most authors follow the biographical listing in Morpurgo 1970, pp. 25–26, more recent publications give Van Ceulen's birth as "before 1657 . . . a descendant of a family of clockmakers probably originating from Maastrict" (Vehmeyer 2004, vol. 2, p. 997) or in 1656 (Peeters 2012, p. 305).

5 Huygens (Constantijn) 1881, pp. 103, 114, quoting a manuscript in the Koninklijke Akademie van Wetenschappen, Amsterdam. Both entries appear in translation in Jardine 2008, p. 263.

6 For a reproduction of the charter of the guild in Jan. 1688, now in the Municipal Archives in The Hague, see Plomp 1979, p. 57.

7 For examples of Van Ceulen's Hague clocks, see ibid., pp. 88–101.

8 Inv. no. E 27. See Boeckh 2009, pp. 24–25 and figs. 17, 18.

9 Acc. no. 1975.1.1244. See Vincent 2012, pp. 78–83, no. 21.

10 They survive in various collections and include two more in the Metropolitan Museum's collection (acc. nos. 17.190.1558 and 17.190.1565).

11 Boeckh 2009, p. 25.

12 The authors are indebted to Maxime Préaud, formerly of the Cabinet des Estampes, Bibliothèque Nationale de France, Paris, for this discovery.

13 On John Simon, see Clayton 1997, pp. 20–21.

14 See, for example, Marot's designs for ornament published in his *Second livre d'orlogeries*, reproduced in *Ornamentwerk des Daniel Marot* 1892, ill. no. 183, and in *Oeuvre de Daniel Marot* n.d., vol. 1, pl. 47. The date of the original publication of this series is uncertain and opinions vary from about 1700 to about 1706. See Fuhring 2004, vol. 1, p. 375, no. 2224; see also Dee 1988, pp. 82–83.

15 Bimbenet-Privat 2000, pp. 76–79; Bimbenet-Privat 2002, vol. 2, p. 501.

16 See entry 26 in this volume.

17 See Leopold and Vincent 1993.

18 Williamson 1912, pp. 199–200, no. 222.

19 Britten 1911, p. 760.

21. Longcase Clock with Calendar

BRITISH (LONDON), CA. 1680–85
78¼ × 16⅜ × 9¼ in. (198.8 × 41.6 × 23.5 cm)
Width of dial plate: 10 in. (25.4 cm)
Bequest of Irwin Untermyer, 1973
1974.28.92

CASE: walnut and oak veneered with walnut
DIAL: gilded and silvered brass,
signed: *Ioseph Knibb London*
[Joseph Knibb, British, 1640–1711]
MOVEMENT: brass and steel

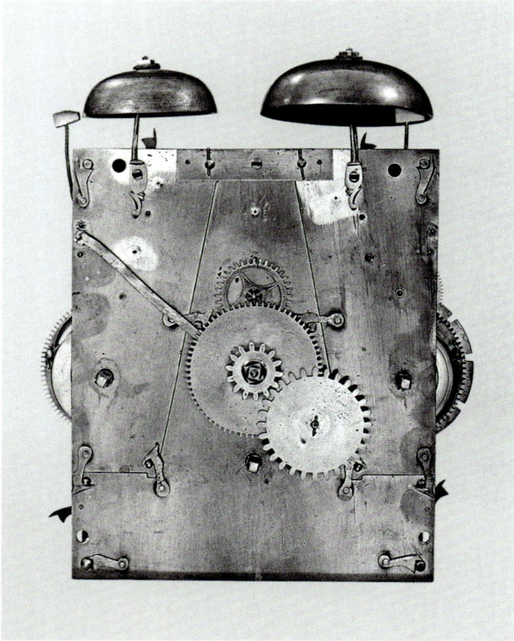

Front plate of the movement with three separately latched plates and motion work

WHEN THE EARLIEST PENDULUM CLOCKS WERE MADE, SHORT pendulums were directly attached to the crown-wheel and verge escapements. These early clocks were subject both to friction in the escapement and to a slight circular error in the pendulum's swing. Although they were far more accurate than almost all the clocks that had preceded them, they were not ideal timekeepers. While clockmakers tried various solutions, they found that it was sufficient to use a pendulum that swung in a small arc to obtain better results, but this improvement necessitated a new form of escapement. It remained for English clockmakers to develop a practical device that looks somewhat like a ship's anchor and is controlled by a longer pendulum of approximately thirty-nine inches that beats seconds (the so-called Royal Pendulum). The optimum shape of the anchor was not immediately determined. Several experimental shapes are illustrated by Tom Robinson,[1] and further evidence of early changes in the shape of the anchor can be found in the movement of one of the Metropolitan Museum's longcase clocks (see entry 22 in this volume).[2] Problems with the pendulum that were caused not only by changes in temperature and atmospheric pressure but also by the escapement, which produced a rocking motion of the anchor as it alternately advanced and slightly retarded the teeth of the escape wheel, a motion that created a slight recoil of the wheel. These problems were eventually solved during the course of the next century. Nonetheless, the anchor escapement and long pendulum contributed immensely to the enormous success of English clockmaking.

In the last decade of the seventeenth century, the London clockmaker William Clement (1633–1704)[3] was credited with the invention of the anchor escapement.[4] The priority of the invention had already been disputed by Robert Hooke (1635–1703), Curator of Experiments for the Royal Society of London, but while Hooke is known to have experimented with pendulums, there is little evidence that he attached them to an anchor escapement.[5] Joseph Knibb (1640–1711), however, is now recognized as having fitted an anchor escapement and long pendulum to a turret clock in Wadham College, University of Oxford, in 1670,[6] and he is credited with the conversion in the same year of the clock in the University Church of Saint Mary the Virgin, Oxford, to an anchor and long pendulum.[7] Historian C. F. C. Beeson, who did much of the original research on the Knibb family of Oxford, was probably the first to point out that the Wadham College's clock preceded by one year the clock with an anchor escapement by Clement for King's College, University of Cambridge, known to have been made in 1671.[8]

Born in Claydon, Oxfordshire, Joseph Knibb was not apprenticed in either Oxford or London. He may perhaps have learned the clockmaking craft in Newport Pagnell, Buckinghamshire, from his cousin

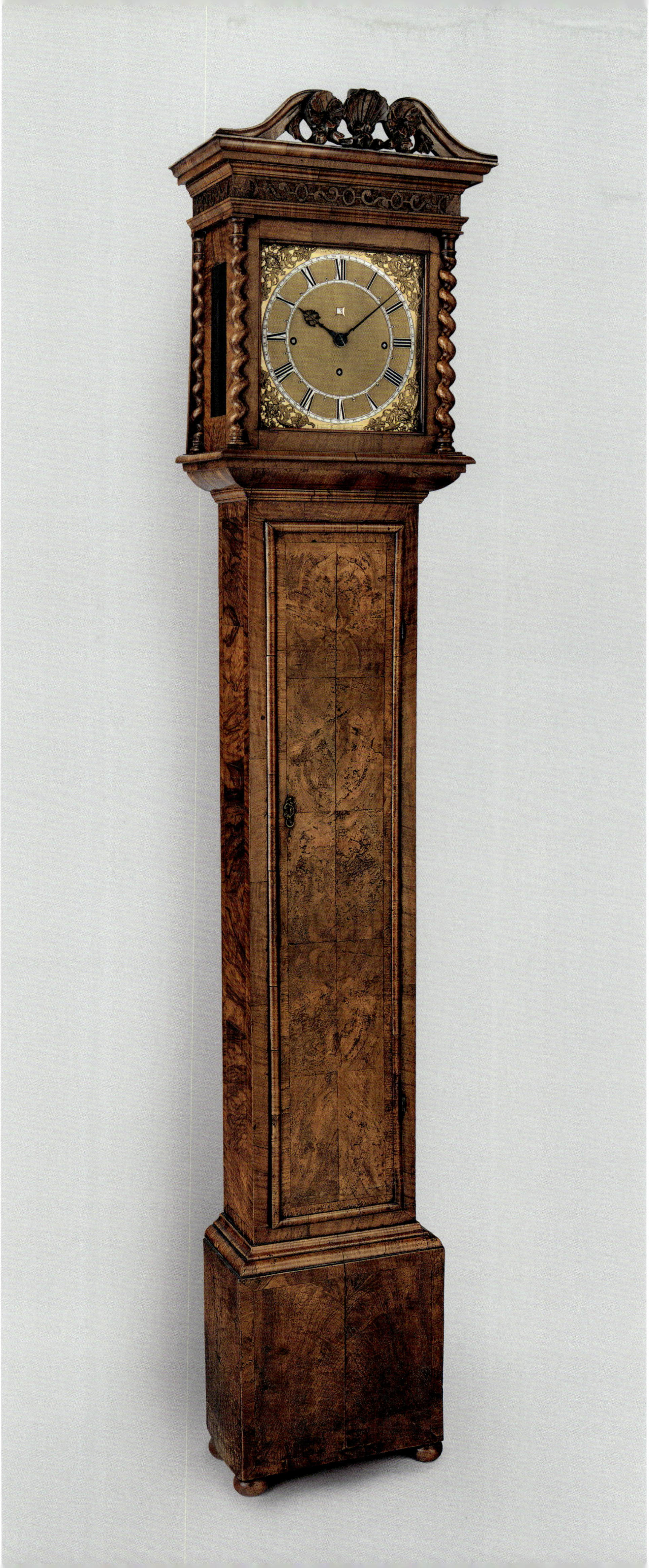

Samuel Knibb (1625–1690).[9] Although he is known to have worked in Oxford, Joseph was not granted freedom of trade there until 1668; instead, he became an employee of the university.[10] By 1663, Samuel had moved to London and paid a fee to become a member of the Clockmakers' Company. He died in London in 1670, perhaps providing the occasion for Joseph's subsequent move there.[11] Whatever the circumstances, Joseph was made free of the Clockmakers' Company in January 1670 (or 1671 in the new calendar),[12] leaving his brother, John, in charge of the Oxford business. Whether or not Joseph Knibb had a claim to the priority of the invention, his longcase clocks, with their anchor escapements and seconds-beating pendulums, assured his success in London, even in competition with such outstanding clockmakers as Thomas Tompion (1639–1713), John Fromanteel (1638–1692), and Daniel Quare (1647/49–1724).

The Metropolitan Museum's clock exemplifies the variety of longcase clock that made Knibb so successful. The case, developed in response to the improvements in the technology of the pendulum, now had wider proportions than the earliest longcase clocks, allowing the new, seconds-beating, long pendulum to swing undisturbed. The walnut-veneered plinth, with four bun feet that are rare survivals of seventeenth-century casemaking practice, supports a well-proportioned trunk. The trunk, in turn, supports a rising hood that rests on a convex molding typical of English clockcase design before about 1700, and consists of a protective pane of glass for the ten-inch-square dial framed in walnut veneer and flanked by baroque columns with simple Tuscan-style capitals made of carved walnut. The columns support an elegantly proportioned cornice that incorporates a fabric-backed wooden frieze of openwork scrolls. Above, the pediment consists of swan-necked baroque scrolls with floral swags, which frame a central block with a carved wooden cockle shell. Ten panels of matched walnut veneer on the door to the trunk are framed by half-round walnut strips that provide the sole decoration of the lower portion of the case.

The special delight of the exterior of the clock lies in the dial. One of Knibb's most felicitous, it has a silvered-brass skeleton chapter ring marked with roman numerals (I–XII) for the hours, with each individual minute in Arabic numerals (1–60) on the outer edge of the ring. On the interior edge, the quarters are marked by lines, and the half hours are marked by lozenge-shaped cutouts. The ring is applied to a finely matted area of the gilded-brass dial plate, and the remaining surface is polished and gilded brass with four applied reliefs of winged cherub heads in foliate ornament for the spandrels.[13] The remaining portions of the dial plate are enlivened by engraved foliate scrolls; at the center bottom edge, the clockmaker's name appears: "Ioseph Knibb London." A small aperture at the twelve o'clock position reveals the day of the month, and three holes for winding squares complete the dial. The two steel hands are described elsewhere as "hollow cut, bevelled and facetted."[14]

The weight-driven movement of the eight-day duration for this clock consists of a central going train of four wheels that end in an anchor escapement with a long pendulum. Two separate trains for hour striking and quarter-hour striking on two bells occupy the sides. The right side contains the hour-striking train that consists of four wheels and a fly, and the left side contains the quarter-striking train that also consists of four wheels and a fly. The front plate is divided into three latched sections and held apart from the back plate by twelve pillars in a system that greatly facilitates access to a single train, which makes repairs considerably easier for clockmakers. Other features facilitate repairs, including the latches on the interior of the front plate for ease in securing the feet of the dial plate, and the slot in the back plate that allows the removal of the anchor and its arbor without taking apart the entire movement. In the hour-striking train, the great wheel carries the count wheel that governs the number of blows struck by a hammer on the larger bell. The quarter-striking train is powered by a separate weight and has its own count wheel mounted, like the hour-striking count wheel, on the exterior of the back plate. It strikes quarters on the smaller bell. This arrangement makes it easy to adjust the cycle of striking.

Although the movement was made to have a seconds hand, instead it has a calendar for the day of the month in place of a seconds chapter ring. The cock for the pendulum crutch is a replacement, as is the pendulum spring. The small bell is probably not original, and the quarter-striking

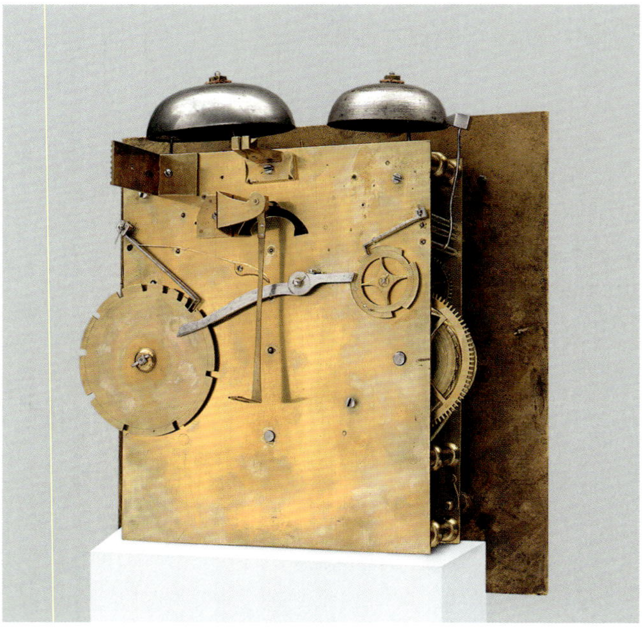

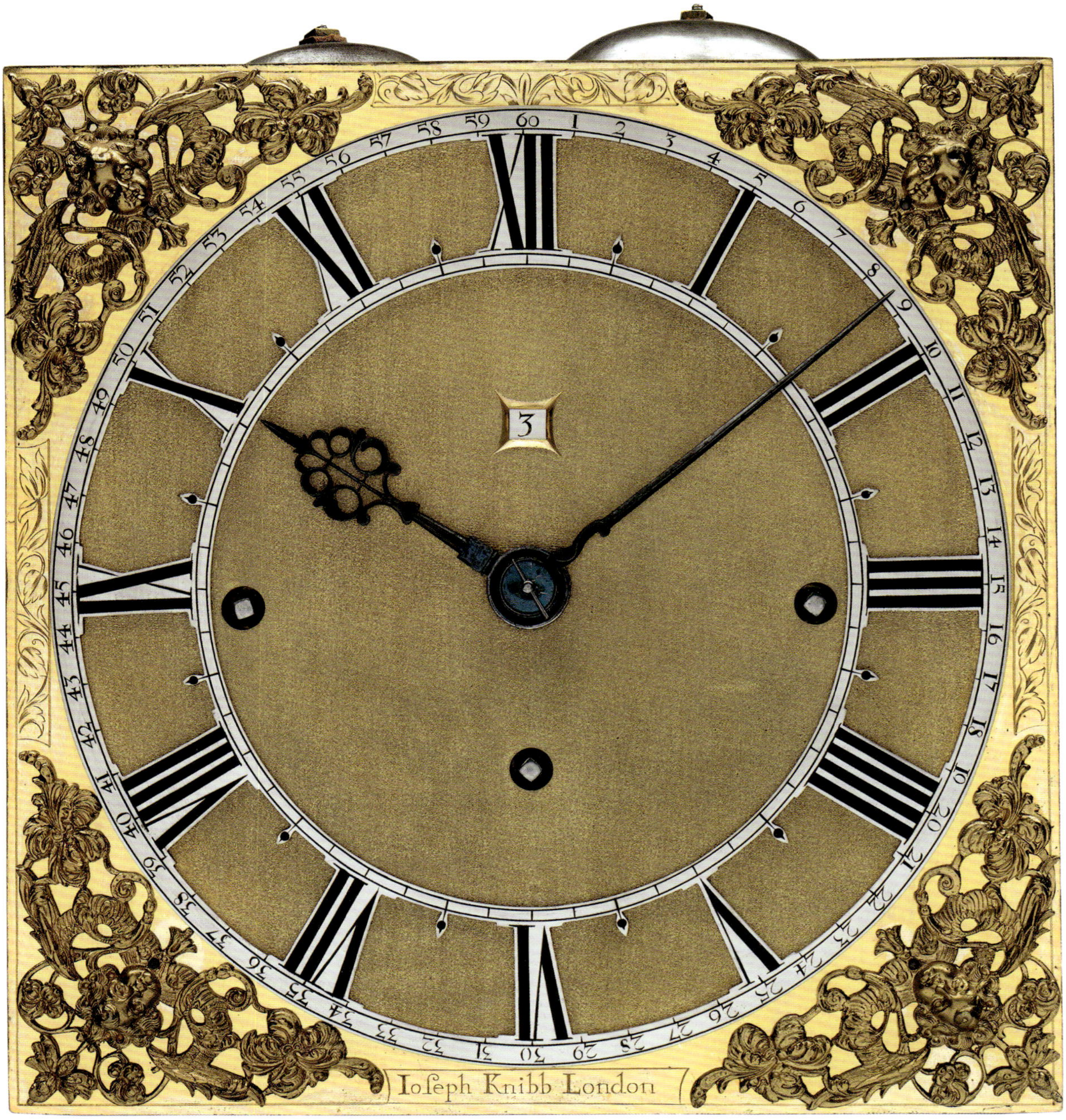

fly is a replacement. The twisted columns applied to the hood may at one time have been blackened.

Irwin Untermyer purchased the clock from a London auction,[15] and the accompanying catalogue states that it had been the property of one religious institution since the eighteenth century, though the name of the institution has not been disclosed. The clock was in running condition when it entered the Museum, and it has been running more or less continuously since 1975. CV / JHL

left: *Back plate of the movement, showing count wheels for hour striking and quarter striking, and part of the slot that allows for the easy removal of the anchor and its arbor*
above: *Skeleton dial with a partial view of the bells for quarter and hour striking*

1 Robinson 1981, p. 45, figs. 3/1, 3/2.
2 See entry 22 in this volume.
3 Loomes 1981, pp. 151–53. See also Penfold 1962.
4 J. Smith 1694 and Derham 1696, quoted in Robinson 1981, p. 44.
5 For further remarks about Hooke, see entry 23 in this volume. See also Hall 1978, p. 263.
6 See Beeson 1967, pp. 64–66, and pl. 5, figs. 7, 8. The clock is now in the Science Museum, London.
7 Ibid., pp. 61–62.
8 Ibid., p. 66. See also Thompson 2004, p. 76; Vehmeyer 2004, vol. 2, pp. 503–5.
9 Beeson 1967, pp. 122–23. Lee 1964, pp. 14–15, gives a slightly different account.
10 Beeson 1967, p. 122.
11 Ibid., pp. 124–25.
12 Ibid., p. 123; Loomes 1981, p. 343.
13 See Robinson 1981, p. 449, fig. G/6, no. 5, said by the author to have been rarely used before about 1685.
14 Lee 1964, p. 97, said by Lee to be typical of those used by Knibb for longcase clocks between 1680 and 1695.
15 Christie's 1972, p. 13, no. 17, ill.

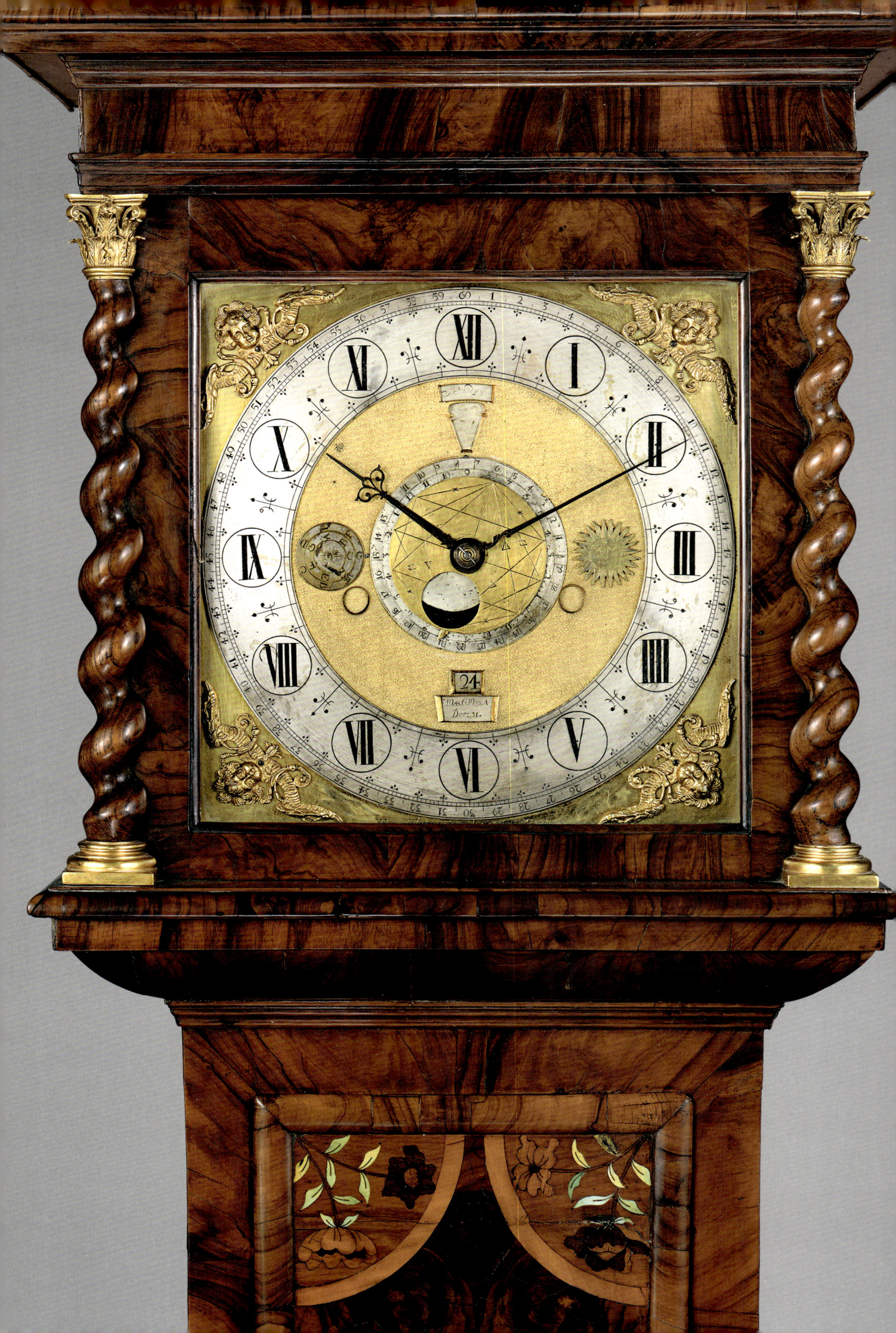

22. Longcase Clock with Calendar (The Graves Tompion)

BRITISH (LONDON), CA. 1677–80

77 × 17 × 8 in. (195.6 × 43.2 × 20.3 cm)
Width of dial plate: 10 in. (25.4 cm)
Bequest of Marilyn Preston Graves, 1999
1999.48.2

CASE: oak veneered with walnut, panels of oyster-cut olive wood; marquetry panels of green-stained bone, ivory, and various woods; gilded-brass mounts; attributed to Jasper Braem (Dutch, active ca. 1677–ca. 1696)
DIAL: gilded and silvered brass, signed: *Tho Tompion Londini Fecit* [Thomas Tompion, British, 1639–1713]
MOVEMENT: brass and steel

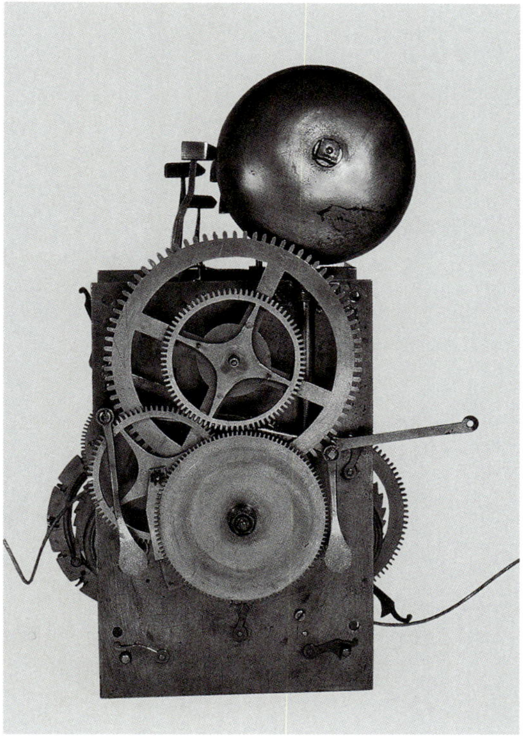

Movement showing the latched front plate and motion work

THOMAS TOMPION, THE MOST FAMOUS CLOCKMAKER IN LATE seventeenth-century and early eighteenth-century England, was baptized on July 25, 1639, the son of Bedfordshire blacksmith Thomas Tompion Sr. and his wife, Margaret.[1] Young Thomas presumably grew up in Bedfordshire, but the account of his early life by his biographer R. W. Symonds is based mostly on legend, as Symonds asserted.[2] More recently historian Jeremy L. Evans, in discussing the likelihood that Tompion did not enter the craft through the usual apprenticeship with an established clockmaker, has given a sober-minded summary of the several conjectures that have been proposed: that he might have worked for Samuel Knibb (1625–1690) in Newport Pagnell near Thomas Sr.'s blacksmith shop in Ickwell, or for either Edward East (1602–1697) or Ahasuerus I Fromanteel (1607–1693) in London.[3] What is, indeed, certain is that Tompion had a rare talent for perfecting mechanical devices and that he had acquired an extensive knowledge of metalworking by 1671, when records show not only that he was living in London but also that he had been admitted on September 4 as a "Great Clockmaker" (i.e., maker of turret clocks) by payment of a stiff fee of thirty shillings to the Clockmakers' Company. His admission was as a Brother. However, full freedom of the company and its privileges was not forthcoming until April 6, 1674, by payment of another ten shillings, the sizable fees indicating he had entered by redemption instead of by completing an apprenticeship.[4]

About 1676 Tompion moved his premises, later to be known as The Dial and Three Crowns, to the corner of Fleet Street and Whitefriars Street, then called Water Lane, in London. Evans has noted that in 1677 Tompion was subletting part of his building to a cabinetmaker Jasper Braem (or Bream; active ca. 1677–ca. 1696), who is known to have been skilled in the art of marquetry "done with several coloured woods in Resemblance of flowers, leaves etc.," and was the probable maker of the cases for some of Tompion's more decorative longcase clocks, including this one in the Museum's collection.[5]

Tompion's superb workmanship and ingenious designs undoubtedly contributed to his remarkable success in the late 1670s and 1680s, producing clocks, watches, barometers, sundials, and mathematical instruments in his Fleet Street workshop, as well as necessitating the outsourcing of commissions when he could not meet the demands for his work. His commissions from King William III (1650–1702) of England, Scotland, and Ireland include a year-going equation clock still in the British Royal Collections,[6] and the year-going spring-driven clock, extravagantly ornamented in silver that is known as The Mostyn Tompion, now in the British Museum, London.[7]

The Metropolitan Museum's longcase clock belongs to an earlier, less flamboyant period in the clockmaker's career. Nevertheless, the movement displays some of Tompion's inventiveness. The eight-day weight-driven movement consists of two rectangular plates held apart by six pillars latched throughout. It has a going train of three wheels ending in an anchor escapement that is regulated by a long pendulum, and it has bolt-and-shutter maintaining power.[8]

It is in the striking train of this clock that Tompion added an unusual embellishment. Consisting of four wheels and a fly, and controlled by a count wheel mounted inside the plates of the clock on the great wheel, the Museum's clock strikes hours, half hours, and quarters on four bells, which are mounted on two stands. The full hour is struck on a larger, lower-pitched bell mounted on the same stand as a smaller, higher-pitched bell that is struck on the half hour. The stand automatically swivels to present the correct bell, permitting both bells to occupy the relatively small space inside the hood of the clock, a space that was also required to accommodate a separate set of two bells, or ting tangs, for the quarters. Thus, in an hour, the clock strikes the full hour on the larger, lower-toned bell; the first quarter, once, on two bells; the half hour, as a repetition of the past hour, but on the smaller, higher-pitched bell; and the third quarter, twice, on the two bells.

The base, trunk, and hood of the case of the clock are of oak veneered with olive wood; the trunk door consists of oystershell-cut veneer and five panels of floral marquetry of green-stained bone, ivory, and various woods. The base has a front panel of oystershell-cut veneer that is arranged like the petals of a flower. The rising hood has a glass pane for viewing the dial flanked by Baroque spiral columns with crisply detailed Corinthian capitals and bases of gilded brass, repeated as quarter rounds at the back of the sides. The hood's structure is supported by a convex wooden molding, and, in turn, it supports a deep profile-molded wooden cornice.

The ten-inch dial is made of gilded brass with a silvered-brass chapter of ringed roman numerals for the hours (I–XII), the quarters marked. The minutes are indicated as individual Arabic numbers (1–60), and subdivided into ten-second intervals. A double aperture at the twelve o'clock position shows the day of the week and the planetary god who governs that day; a double aperture at the six o'clock position shows the day of the month and the month with the number of its days, and the number of the week within the year. A hand-manipulated disk at the nine o'clock position

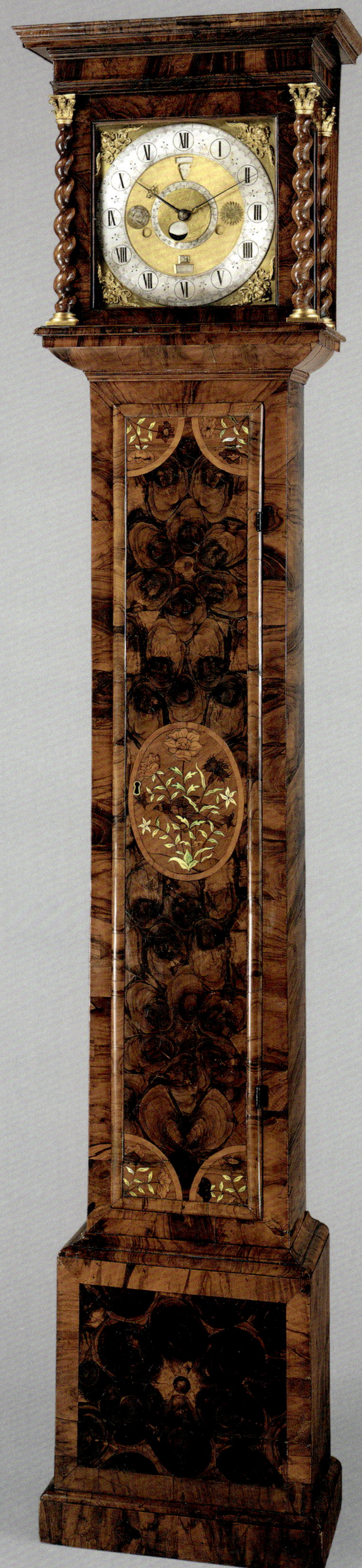

with a double ring of letters (A–G) can be set to indicate the Dominical Letters governing the year. The disk is balanced by a purely decorative sunburst at the three o'clock position. The revolving disk at the center of the dial shows the astrological aspects of the moon, its phases, its age within its monthly cycle (one–twenty-nine), and the tide times (one–twelve, one–twelve), probably for high tide at London Bridge. The early form of the standard cherub's head with wings fills the four corners of the dial, and the sculptured steel hands (the hour hand with an openwork scrolled design), are variants of hands used by Tompion, as well as by East and Knibb in the 1670s. The dial is signed at the lower edge, "Tho Tompion Londini Fecit."

The going train of the movement has its original wheels, but the present anchor replaces an earlier one of a somewhat different shape. The back cock for the pendulum and the crutch have also been replaced. When the clock entered the Metropolitan Museum's collection, the hood had been modified so it could slide forward. As the spring-latch for securing the rising hood in its open position was still in place, the hood was returned to its original state. Some areas of veneer on the trunk and plinth of the case had been replaced in an earlier period, yet more veneer was missing from the hood and trunk and replaced by the Museum's wood conservators. The present skirt probably replaces an original, but there is insufficient evidence to be certain about either an original skirt or feet.

There is no evidence of a serial number on the movement or on the case as these numbers, explained by Evans, were meant to correspond to entries in ledgers, which were kept by Tompion after his business had greatly expanded. The ledgers are now missing, but many of his surviving clocks and watches, including this example, predate his introduction of the numbering system,[9] which seems to have begun about 1682. If the attribution of the case to Jasper Braem is correct, Braem is likely to have made the case while he was renting a part of Tompion's Fleet Street premises. The Metropolitan Museum's clock should be dated, therefore, between 1677 and 1682, probably earlier in that five-year period than later.

In 1933 the clock belonged to Francis Herbert Green (died 1936), a liveryman in the Clockmakers' Company, when it was listed as number three in a loan exhibition at Mr. Green's establishment at 13, Royal Exchange, Cornhill, London.[10] The following year, Green sold the clock to the New York antiques dealer Arthur S. Vernay,[11] who, in turn, sold it to Henry Graves Jr. (1868–1953), a member of a prominent banking family in New York. Graves had several other remarkable horological items in his collection, notably a chronograph watch by the Geneva firm of Patek Philippe, said to be the most complicated mechanical watch ever made.[12] The Tompion clock remained in the Graves family until his granddaughter bequeathed it to the Metropolitan Museum in 1999. CV / JHL

1 Parish register of Northill, Bedfordshire Parish Transcripts, FG Emmison, vol. 13, Bedfordshire County Record Office, quoted in J. L. Evans 2006, p. 12.
2 Symonds 1951, pp. 10–12.
3 J. L. Evans 2006, pp. 14–16. See also Jagger 1983, pp. 53–54.
4 Clockmakers' Company, London, Court Minute Books, Ms. 2711/2, 1673–84, Guildhall Library, London, quoted in Symonds 1951, p. 13.
5 See J. L. Evans 2006, pp. 28–29, based in part on a bill describing a marquetry step for a bed for Mary of Modena, consort of the future King James II, published in Hope 1913, vol. 1, p. 328. See also Beard and Gilbert 1986, p. 104.
6 Symonds 1951, pp. 60, 268. See also Jagger 1983, p. 64, and p. 61, figs. 79–82.
7 Inv. no. 1982,0702.1. See Symonds 1951, pp. 257–58, figs. 135–39, and colorpl. II; Jagger 1983, pp. 66–67; Thompson 2004, pp. 84–87.
8 For a more complete description of the movement, see J. L. Evans, Carter, and Wright 2013, p. 505.
9 See J. L. Evans 2006, pp. 38–39, 66, no. 12, and p. 71.
10 The catalogue for the exhibition was reproduced in Jagger 1983, p. 292. See also F. Davis 1933.
11 A photocopy of the bill for the clock from Green to Vernay dated Feb. 8, 1934, is in the Metropolitan Museum's files. The authors thank Chris Jussel for the photocopy and for the clipping about the 1933 exhibition at Mr. Green's from the *Illustrated London News* (see F. Davis 1933).
12 Sotheby's 1999, pp. 54–77, no. 7, ill. See also Pritzker 2014, pp. 21–22.

23. Traveling Clock Watch with Alarm

BRITISH (LONDON), CA. 1680
Case: 5¾ × 4 × 2 in. (14.6 × 10.2 × 5.1 cm)
Diam. of back plate: 3¼ in. (8.3 cm)
Gift of J. Pierpont Morgan, 1917
17.190.1512

CASE AND DIAL: silver, by Nathaniel Delander (British, 1648–ca. 1691)
MOVEMENT: gilded brass, partly blued steel, and silver, signed on the back plate: *Tho Tompion London* [Thomas Tompion, British, 1639–1713]

THE ORIGINS OF THE ROYAL SOCIETY CAN BE TRACED TO A LOOSE association of Englishmen interested in science and technology, or what at the time was known as experimental philosophy. By 1645, one group was meeting in the rooms of the warden of Wadham College at Oxford University, while a second group met primarily at Gresham College in London. On November 28, 1660, twelve representatives from both groups (professors of mathematics, physics, and natural philosophy, doctors of medicine, and aristocratic amateurs and patrons of science) met in London to attend a lecture by the Gresham Professor of Astronomy, Christopher Wren (1632–1723). After Wren's lecture, the group decided to form "a Colledge for the promoting of Physico-Mathematicall Experimentall Learning."[1] In July 1662 King Charles II (1630–1685) of England granted the group their first royal charter. A second charter from 1663 designated the association "The Royal Society," the name by which it has been known ever since. Meetings during this early period were chiefly devoted to the performance and discussion of experiments. In 1665, a Curator of Experiments was duly appointed,[2] and Robert Hooke (1635–1703), Gresham Professor of Geometry, became the first member to hold this position.

There is some evidence that Hooke had been trying to develop a balance spring for watches as far back as 1658, but there is no written record of his efforts before 1665.[3] As late as 1675, he was sketching ideas for balance springs in his diary,[4] and contemplating the employment of a straight spring for the same purpose.[5] When and how he met Thomas Tompion (1639–1713) is not certain, although it was probably in connection with an astronomical quadrant that Tompion was making for the Royal Society based on Hooke's design.[6] Hooke's diary cites numerous meetings with Tompion in 1674, including their discussions about improvements in cutting and finishing the teeth of watch wheels.[7] Together, they produced a watch for King Charles with one of Hooke's balance springs. When initially presented to the king on May 17, 1675, Hooke reported that the king "Received the watch very kindly, it was locked up in his closet."[8] But a few months later, the king was no longer enthusiastic, citing the ill effects on the watch of a change in the weather.[9]

As a fellow of the Royal Society, Hooke was in a position to read the society's communications from its foreign correspondents. Three months prior to the presentation of their watch to the English king, Hooke noted in his diary that he had seen the design for a spiral balance spring from Christiaan Huygens (1629–1695) and had transcribed it.[10] This spring was the invention that Tompion soon adopted. As with several French watchmakers, Tompion went further by attempting to do away with the fusee, relying solely on the balance

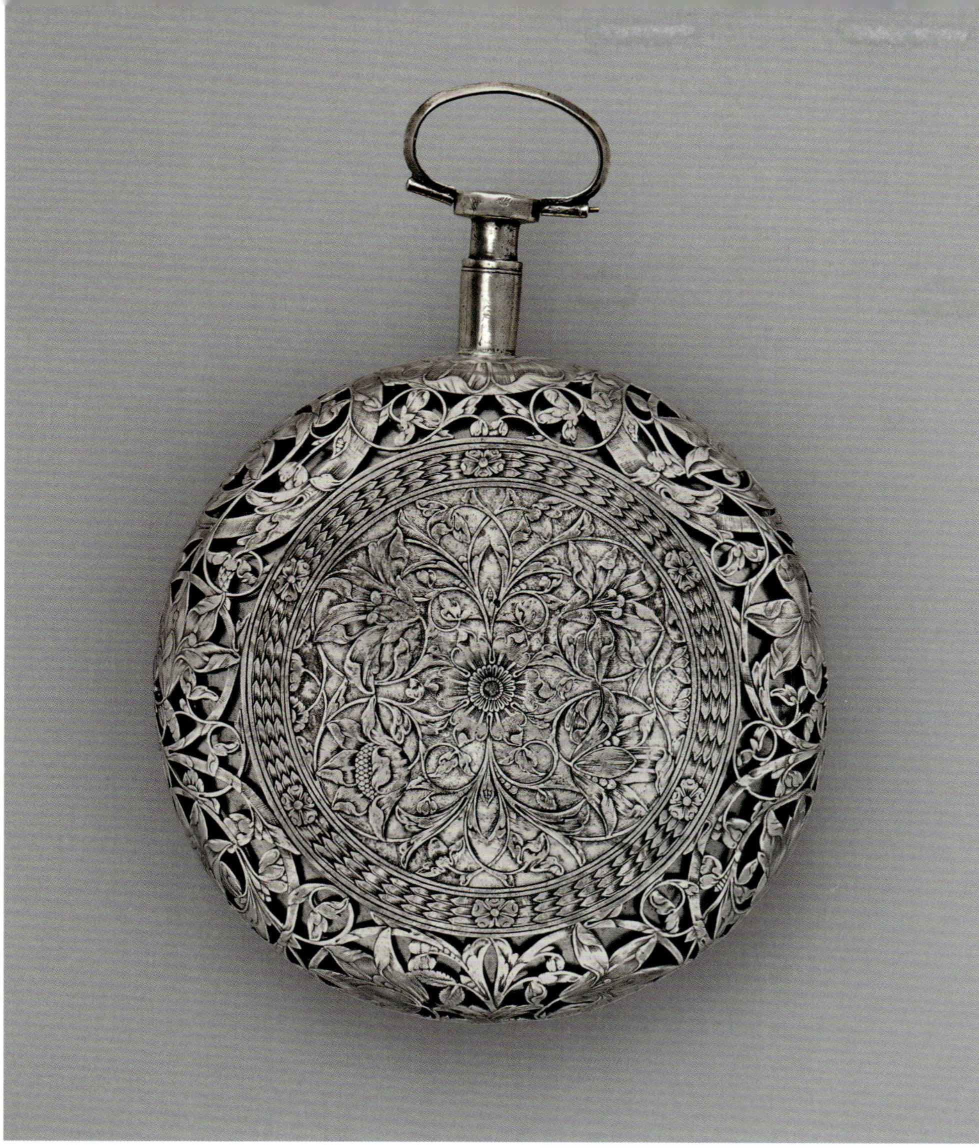

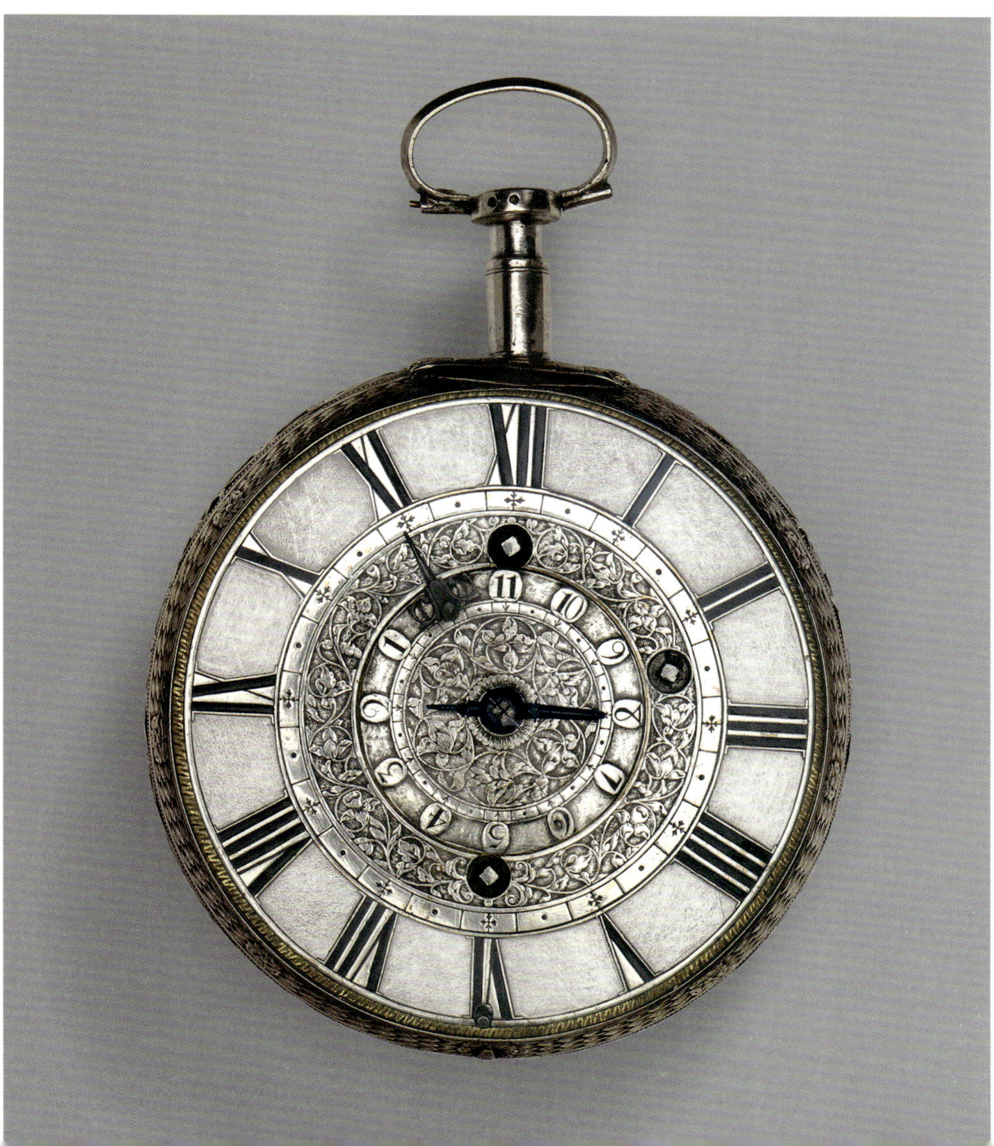

spring to regulate the changing force of the mainspring as it unwound. The Metropolitan Museum's traveling watch is a surviving example from this brief period of experimentation with the new invention.

Oversized watches with sturdy pendants for hanging them in moving conveyances became popular among the wealthy during the second half of the seventeenth century, and they are therefore often called coach watches. In this splendid example, there are separate going, striking, and alarm trains, each with its own power source. The movement consists of two circular brass plates held apart by five extraordinarily fine tulip pillars. The going train consists of three wheels ending in a verge escapement and balance spring. It is driven by a mainspring housed in a pierced and engraved brass barrel. The striking train is driven by a spring that is housed in a pierced and engraved brass going barrel, and it has a three-wheel train ending in a fly and controlled by a count wheel. The bracket for the count wheel is an elaborate openwork arm of blued steel. The alarm train is driven by a smaller spring in a pierced and engraved brass going barrel, which is installed between the barrels for the going and striking trains. It drives a brass wheel, a steel contrate wheel, and a steel escape wheel. A hammer mounted above the spring barrel of the striking train strikes hours on a bell mounted inside the case, and a crescent-shaped steel arm mounted on the opposite side of the movement strikes the alarm. The watch has a duration of thirty hours.[11]

The back plate has a large cock attached by a screw with a symmetrically pierced and engraved design of floral and foliate scroll ornament that ends in an unusual matte-finished rectangle enclosing a stylized flower. A circular figure plate marked (5–30) for adjusting the balance spring and a smaller silver figure plate (4–20) that indicates the setup of the mainspring of the going train flank the engraved signature: "Tho Tompion London." On the left side, above the figure plate for the balance spring adjustment, is a figure plate for the setup of the striking train, and above the figure plate is a silver count wheel (1-+) for the striking train.

The dial consists of a champlevé silver chapter of hours (I–XII), marked for quarters (lines) and half hours (dots). In the center, there is a circular revolving dial for the alarm with a chapter of Arabic numerals (1–11) for the hours and a single, openwork hand attached at the twelve o'clock position. A second single hand attached at the center sets the alarm. The two chapter rings are separated by a band of floral scrolls, and the motif is repeated in the center of the alarm dial. The case has a glass cover for the dial with a hinged silver bezel. The circular design in the center of the back of the case displays a subtle interplay between the engraved and chased floral scrolls incorporating lilies and anemones and the recessed ground of chiseled silver. The design is framed by a wreath made up of tripartite leaf forms that are punctuated by six rosettes, which are, in turn, encircled by an openwork ring of engraved floral scrolls composed of lilies, daffodils, and anemones. These same motifs appear, as well, on the dial, and the circle of leaves and rosettes repeats on the bezel for the glass cover of the dial. The initials "ND" conjoined (the casemaker's mark for Nathaniel Delander until at least 1682)[12] are punched on the interior of the case under the bell. The crab (a mark for small silver articles of .800 standard fineness used by provincial French assay offices beginning in 1838) appears twice on the pendant.[13]

There would have been a protective outer case for this watch, but it is missing. The pendant has been slightly bent. The figure plate for the setup of the spring of the alarm train is missing, and the figure plates for the setup of the springs of the going and striking trains have been repaired. The contrate wheel in the going train is a replacement. Otherwise, the watch is reasonably close to its original condition.

The presence of the French guarantee marks for silver indicates that the watch had at least one owner in France during the nineteenth century before it entered the collection of the British banker Frederick George Hilton Price in 1898. The watch became one of the glories of J. Pierpont Morgan's collection when he acquired it from Hilton Price.[14] CV / JHL

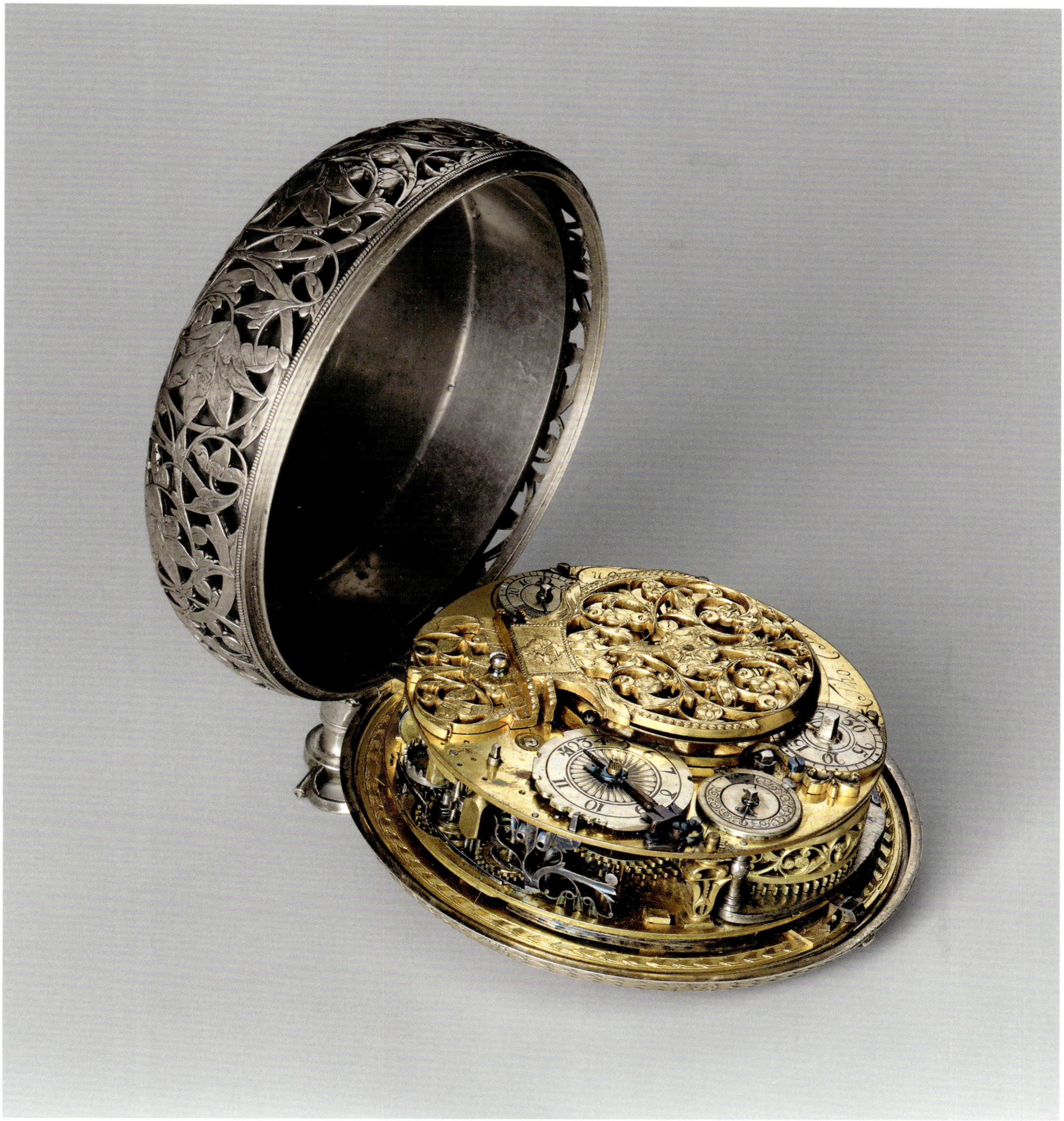

The watchcase open to show the movement

1 Harrison 1911, pp. 791–92.
2 Ibid., p. 792. See also Inwood 2002, pp. 30–33, for an extended account of Hooke's appointments in this period.
3 Hall 1978, pp. 262–63.
4 See Hooke 1968, p. 151, entry of Mar. 8, 1674/75, and p. 164, entry of June 13, 1675.
5 Ibid., p. 177, entry of Aug. 30, 1675.
6 J. L. Evans 2006, p. 22, and p. 19, fig. 18.
7 Hooke 1968, p. 100, entry of May 2, 1674.
8 Ibid., p. 161, entry of May 17, 1675.
9 Ibid., p. 185, entry of Oct. 5, 1675.
10 Ibid., p. 153, entry of Mar. 18, 1674/75. For further details of the Hooke-Tompion project and the subsequent dispute between Hooke and Huygens about the priority of the invention, see Hall 1951; Hall 1978, pp. 269–71; Inwood 2002, pp. 203–15. See also entry 20 in this volume.
11 For a more detailed description of the movement, see J. L. Evans, Carter, and Wright 2013, pp. 266, 565.
12 Priestley 2000, pp. 19, 66.
13 See Tardy 1981c, pp. 199–200.
14 Williamson 1912, p. 147, no. 159, and pl. LXXI.

24. Pair-Case Watch

BRITISH (LONDON), 1682–83
Diam. of outer case: 2 in. (5.1 cm)
Diam. of inner case: 1¾ in. (4.5 cm)
Diam. of back plate: 1½ in. (3.8 cm)
Gift of J. Pierpont Morgan, 1917
17.190.1489a, b

OUTER CASE: leather with gold studs, monogrammed: RWR or possibly GWR, surmounted by a coronet (unidentified)
INNER CASE AND DIAL: gold with blued-steel hands, marked: N[D] [Nathaniel Delander, British, 1648–ca. 1691]
MOVEMENT: gilded brass, partly blued steel, and silver, signed on the back plate: *Tho Tompion London* [Thomas Tompion, British, 1639–1713]

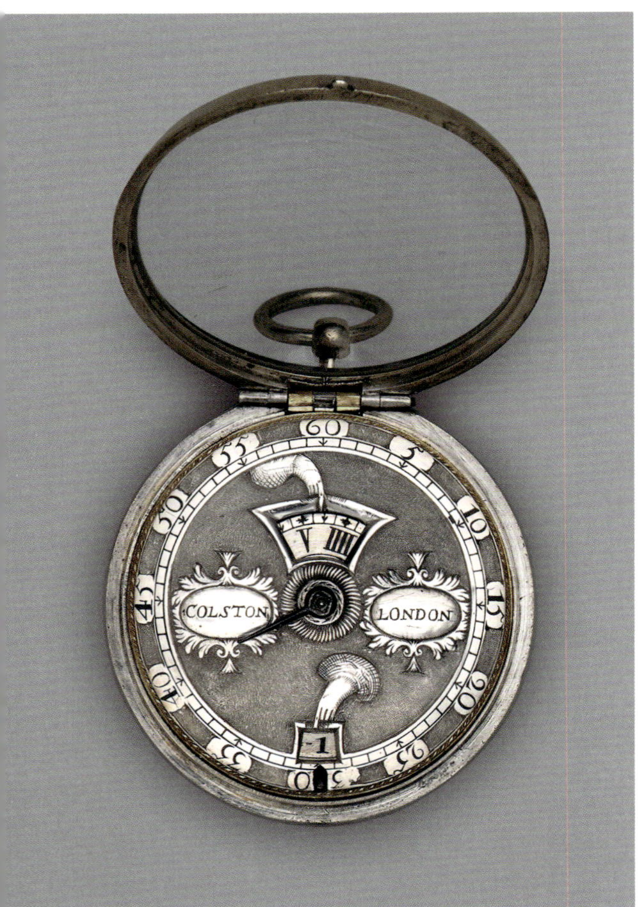

fig. 33 *Richard Colston (British, active 1682–1702). Pair-Case Watch, British (London), ca. 1680–90. Inner case and dial: silver, Diameter of inner case 1 13⁄16 in. (4.6 cm), diameter of back plate 1 7⁄16 in. (3.7 cm). The Metropolitan Museum of Art, New York, Gift of J. Pierpont Morgan, 1917 (17.190.1508)*

THE INVENTION OF THE SPIRAL BALANCE SPRING BY CHRISTIAAN Huygens (1629–1695) revolutionized the timekeeping properties of a watch in the same way that his application of the pendulum to a clock revolutionized the accuracy of the clock. It was the invention that dismayed the Englishman Robert Hooke (1635–1703) in early 1675,[1] as news of the spiral balance spring undoubtedly helped doom any hope of success of the experimental balance spring in a watch that he and Thomas Tompion (1639–1713) had presented to King Charles II (1630–1685) of England in May of that same year.[2] Three months earlier, Hooke had begun an extended battle for recognition of the priority of the invention,[3] a battle that was intensified by Huygens's attempt to register an English patent for the device.[4] Tompion, however, like many of his fellow watchmakers, seemed to have quickly grasped the advantage of Huygens's balance spring. Jeremy L. Evans, who deciphered Tompion's earliest efforts at serially numbering his watches, records the existence of only one pre–balance spring watch by Tompion, now missing its dial and cases.[5] The serial number 175 of the Metropolitan Museum's watch does not appear in the place that would later become usual on the back plate of a watch. Instead, it appears inside, on the pillar plate, leading Evans to propose a date of 1682 or 1683 for this watch.[6] By 1683, Tompion was using the spiral balance spring to make watches that were capable of registering hours, minutes, and seconds, but it was by no means new: on May 17, 1679, Hooke recorded that he had paid Tompion for a "Watch with seconds" destined for Christopher Wren (1632–1723).[7]

The movement is astounding for yet another reason. It contains a remarkably early stop mechanism that can be activated by pushing a lever that projects from under the dial at the forty-three-minute position, to measure short intervals of time. This particular movement consists of two circular plates, held apart by four exquisite tulip pillars, and the movement contains a three-wheel train that is driven by a mainspring and fusee and regulated by a verge escapement and three-armed balance with a balance spring. A large openwork cock with a table of delicate foliate scrolls dominates the back plate, leaving only a small area for the foot of the cock through which the cock is screwed onto the back plate. A quatrefoil, or flower, within a square serves as ornament at the neck of the cock, recalling the ornament of the cock in the Tompion traveling clock watch, also in the Museum's collection (see entry 23 in this volume). A silver figure plate for adjusting the balance spring and the watchmaker's signature, "Tho Tompion London" (engraved in script), fill the remaining space on the back plate.[8]

The inner case of plain gold is stamped on the interior with the letters "ND" conjoined, the "D" mostly effaced. Below is the number 175, apparently in keeping with Tompion's practice of using matching

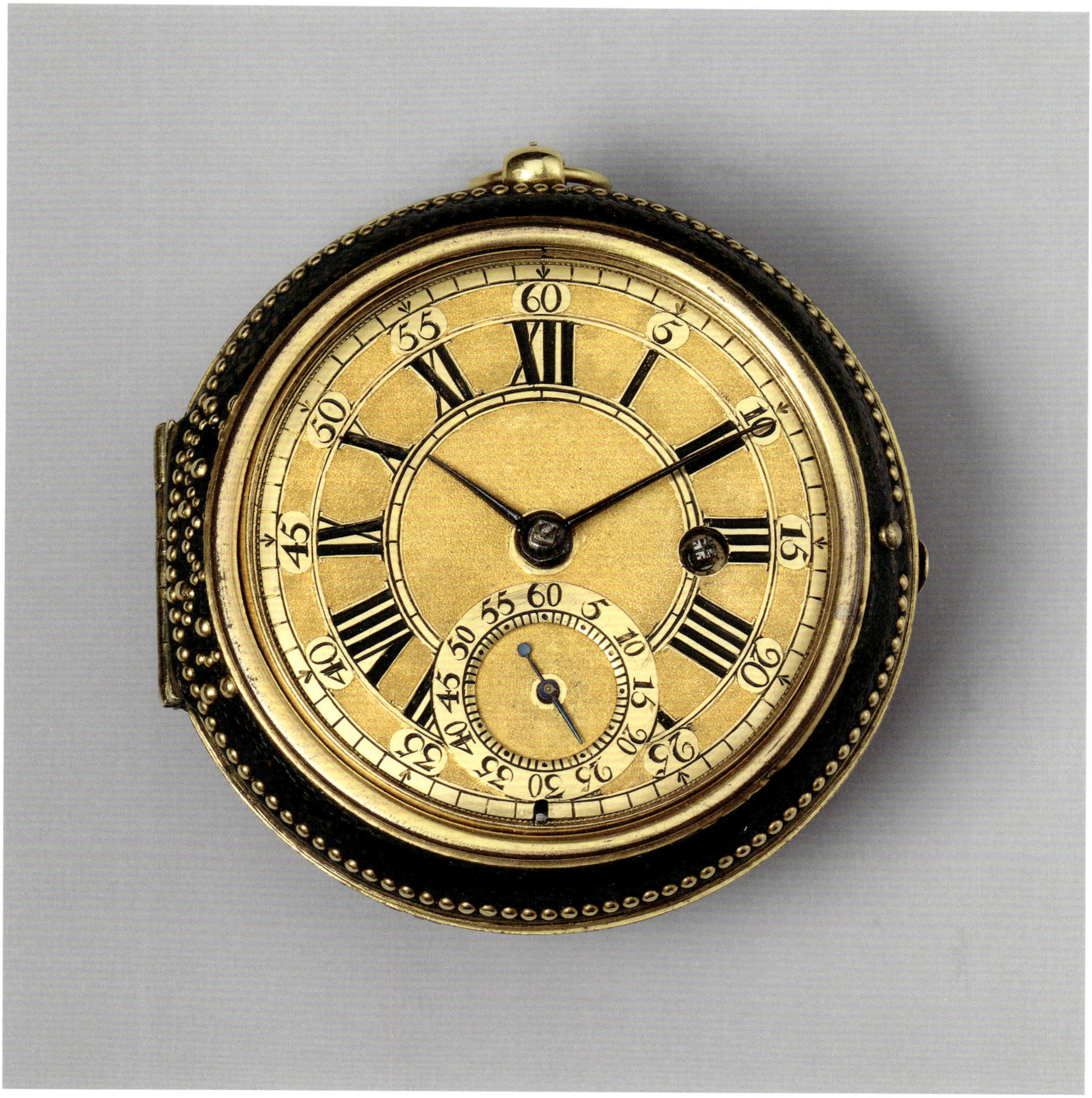

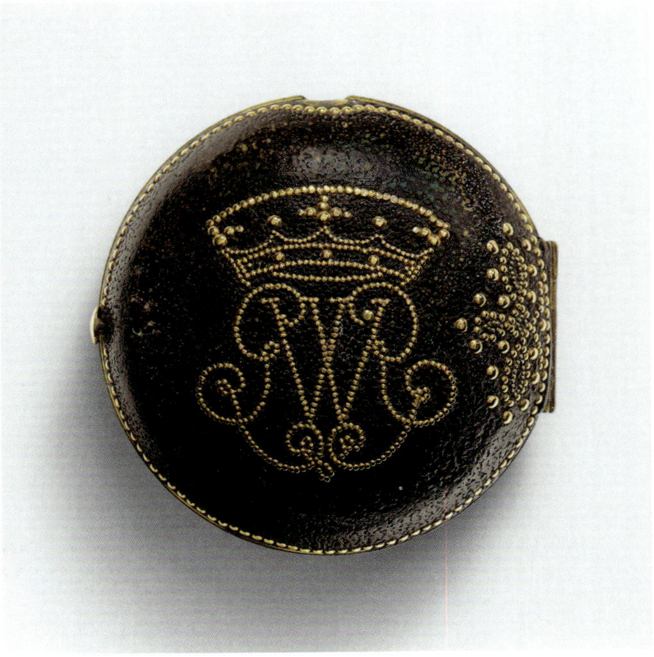

Back of the outer case

serial numbers for components of his production. Although there is evidence that the finishing of Delander's cases was sometimes done by specialist craftsmen,[9] the exquisite finish of the matte-gold ground and the finely engraved numerals filled with black wax on the dial of this watch are of a quality reached only by Delander's establishment, giving credence to the supposition that the "N" of the maker's mark does indeed stand for Nathaniel. More remarkable still is the design of the dial that records hours in roman numerals and minutes in Arabic numbers on its chapter ring, with separate concentrically mounted and easy-to-read hands for the hours and minutes, while incorporating a large chapter ring for seconds at the six o'clock position of the dial. The seconds chapter would have been necessary for the timing of short periods, perhaps for astronomical events such as an eclipse, or even a sporting event such as a horse race, but its prominence also suggests the watchmaker's pride in the new level of precision achieved by the movement.

How much of the design of the dial may be attributed to Tompion and how much to Delander is not known, but the evidence provided here and in the case of Tompion's traveling clock watch suggests that Delander had a special gift. Nothing certain is known of his early life and training, apart from the fact that he was admitted as a Free Brother into the Clockmakers' Company in London in January 1669, and as a Freeman by payment of a fee in March 1675.[10] There is no agreement about the probable date of his death, but his punched (incuse) "ND" conjoined mark is recorded on the Goldsmiths' Company's copperplate that registered maker's marks in 1682.[11] A second form of mark, which consists of a coronet above the "ND" conjoined and accompanied by a full set of London hallmarks for silver in 1683, appears on a Tompion watch in the Fitzwilliam Museum in Cambridge, England.[12] It seems likely that Delander had an unusual talent for design as well as for craftsmanship.

The visual logic of the design of this dial seems self-evident; however, in the period following the adoption of Huygens's balance spring, English watchmakers did not invariably make watches with two hands to indicate hours and minutes on concentric chapter rings. The dial of a paircase watch of the early 1680s in the Metropolitan Museum's collection by the London clock- and watchmaker Richard Colston (active 1682–1702)[13] is a good example of an alternative display (fig. 33). The minutes on Colston's watch are prominently indicated by a single hand on a chapter ring at the edge of the dial, while the hours appear singly and less easily read through an aperture near the top of the dial, leaving space for decorative cartouches that frame the maker's name and the place. Yet another aperture for a calendar appears at the bottom of the dial. A number of other alternatives were tried before most eighteenth-century English watchmakers adopted the familiar dial with concentric chapter rings and two hands: one for hours and one for minutes.

The outer case of the Museum's Tompion watch, with its design in gold nailheads, may also be the work of Delander, although little study has been devoted to the degree of specialization among casemakers during this period, and it may have been the work of another craftsman. The cipher and coronet have long remained unidentified.

The precociousness of the design and technical details of this watch so misled George C. Williamson, the author of the catalogue of J. Pierpont Morgan's watch collection, that he declared it to be a product of the eighteenth century.[14] Subsequent discoveries have proved him mistaken. Williamson asserted that Morgan bought it from Frederick George Hilton Price, who probably bought it from the sale of the collection of Claude Ashley Charles Ponsonby.[15] CV / JHL

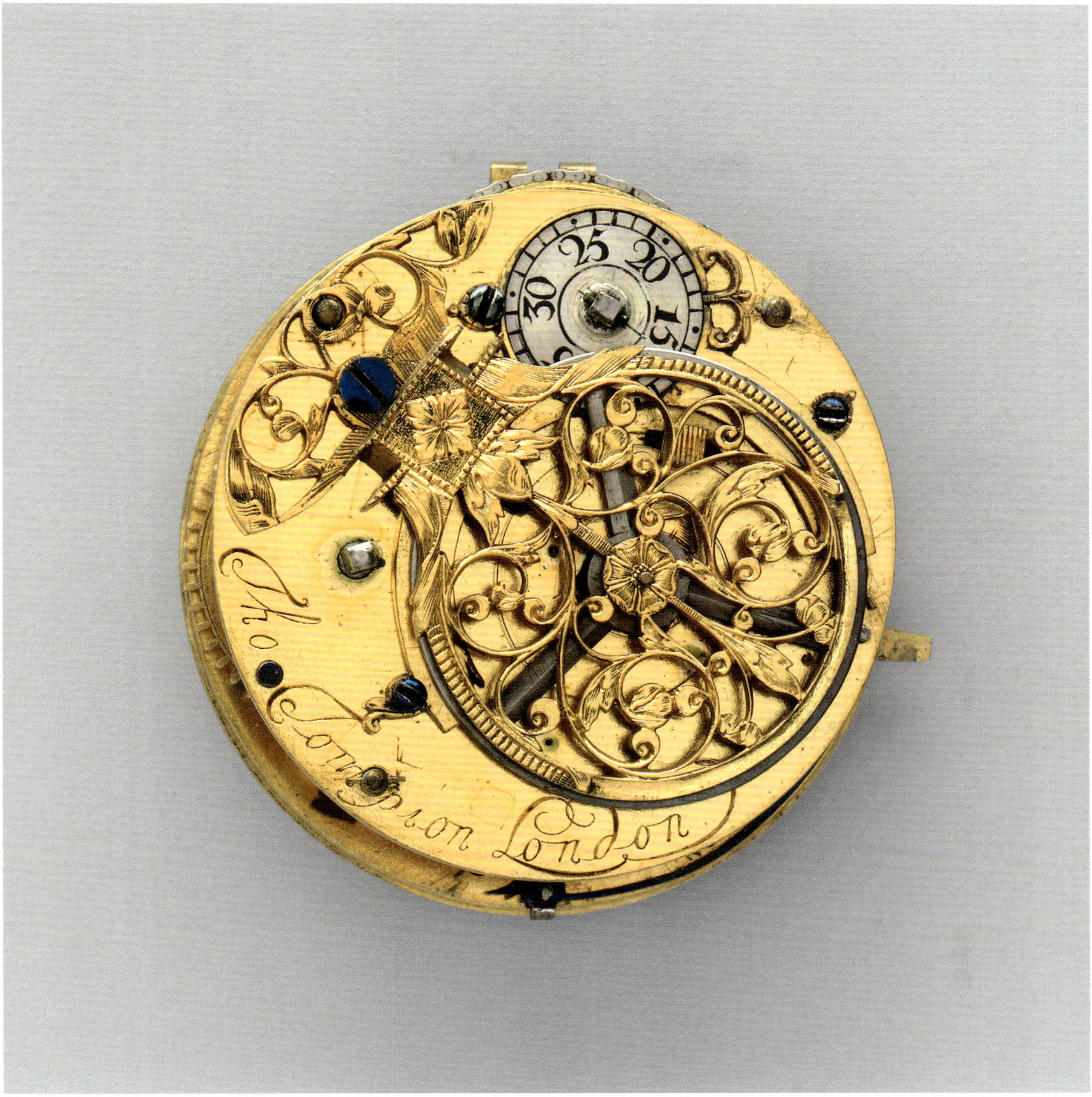

Back plate of the movement

1 See Hooke 1968, p. 148, entry of Feb. 18, 1674/75, and p. 153, entry of Mar. 18, 1674/75.

2 Ibid., p. 161, entry of May 17, 1675. See also entry 23 in this volume.

3 Ibid., p. 148, entry of Feb. 18, 1674/75. See also Howse and Finch 1976.

4 Hall 1951; Inwood 2002, pp. 200–215.

5 J. L. Evans 1984; J. L. Evans 2006, p. 87. See also Thompson 2008, p. 50.

6 J. L. Evans 2006, p. 87.

7 Hooke 1968, p. 412. The authors are indebted to Jeremy L. Evans, formerly of the British Museum, London, for bringing this fact to our attention.

8 For a more detailed description of the movement, see J. L. Evans, Carter, and Wright 2013, pp. 267, 568.

9 See Thompson 2007, pp. 42–43, no. 19, for a watch with a movement by Thomas Tompion in the Ashmolean Museum, Oxford (inv. no. WA1974.191.86).

10 Loomes 1981, p. 190.

11 Priestley 2000, p. 66, no. 40a.

12 Ibid., p. 6, fig. 8.

13 Acc. no. 17.190.1508. See Loomes 1981, p. 160. See also Thompson 2007, pp. 44–45, no. 20, for a Colston watch with a so-called sun and moon dial in the Ashmolean Museum (inv. no. WA1974.116).

14 Williamson 1912, p. 146, no. 157, and pl. LXX.

15 Christie's 1908, p. 3, no. 1. See also J. L. Evans, Carter, and Wright 2013, p. 568. The authors are indebted to Jeremy L. Evans for the latter information.

25. Longcase Clock with Calendar and Alarm

DUTCH (AMSTERDAM), CA. 1690–94

88 × 19¼ × 10⅞ in. (223.5 × 48.9 × 27.6 cm)

W. of dial plate: 10½ in. (26.7 cm)

Bequest of John Munro Woolsey, 1946

46.107a–h

CASE: walnut and rosewood veneer on oak, and partly gilded limewood

DIAL: gilded and silvered brass, signed (falsely): *Fromanteel / London*

MOVEMENT: brass and steel, by Ahasuerus II Fromanteel (British, 1640–1703)

WHILE THE FROMANTEEL FAMILY WAS INSTRUMENTAL TO introducing the pendulum clock into England, other English clockmakers subsequently made improvements. These improvements culminated in the widespread adoption of the seconds-beating or long pendulum with an anchor escapement, a much more accurate timekeeper than the earlier short pendulum with verge escapement. Whether the inventor was William Clement (1633–1704), Robert Hooke (1635–1703), or, most probably, Joseph Knibb (1640–1711), the development took shape in England after 1670. Within about five years, English clockmakers working in the Netherlands began making longcase clocks that incorporated the improved pendulum. One of the first of these expatriate clockmakers, Joseph Norris (1649/50–after 1696), probably settled in Amsterdam about 1675. As early as 1680, he was making weight-driven movements with long pendulums, which were housed in tall wooden cases. Some of his clocks had crests of carved acanthus leaves and freestanding baroque columns that flanked the doors to their almost, but not quite, English dials.[1] The identity of the Dutch cabinetmaker is not known, but similar cases contain movements by another English expatriate, Ahasuerus II Fromanteel (1640–1703), as well as the Dutchmen Steven Huygens (ca. 1653–1720) and Pieter Klock (1665–1754).[2] These clocks constitute a remarkable group of some of the earliest longcase clocks made in the Netherlands.

The tall, narrow trunk of the Metropolitan Museum's clock has a rectangular plinth and a double-skirted base. The trunk is made of walnut veneer, and the door is veneered with rosewood framed by walnut veneers and half-round moldings of walnut. The trunk is punctuated by an oval glass lenticule within a carved and gilded limewood frame. The plinth is similarly veneered with rosewood and walnut on the front and walnut on the sides. The hood is supported on three sides by concave moldings and framed by freestanding baroque columns with Corinthian capitals that flank the hinged glass door for the dial. The panel at the top of the door is carved in relief with ribbons caught up at each end and in the middle, as well as ornamented with bunches of fruit and flowers. The sides of the hood are fitted with carved openwork panels of acanthus backed by modern fabric. Quarter-round baroque columns attached at the back complete the housing for the movement. Above, the architrave is ornamented on three sides with stylized acanthus scrolls, which are carved in high relief and capped by a crest of plump acanthus leaves of carved and pierced limewood. Two gilded wooden eagles perch upon the front corners.

The square dial is made of gilded brass with a silvered chapter ring for the hours divided to show hours, half hours, quarter hours, and minutes. A smaller chapter ring records seconds (5–60, by fives) at the

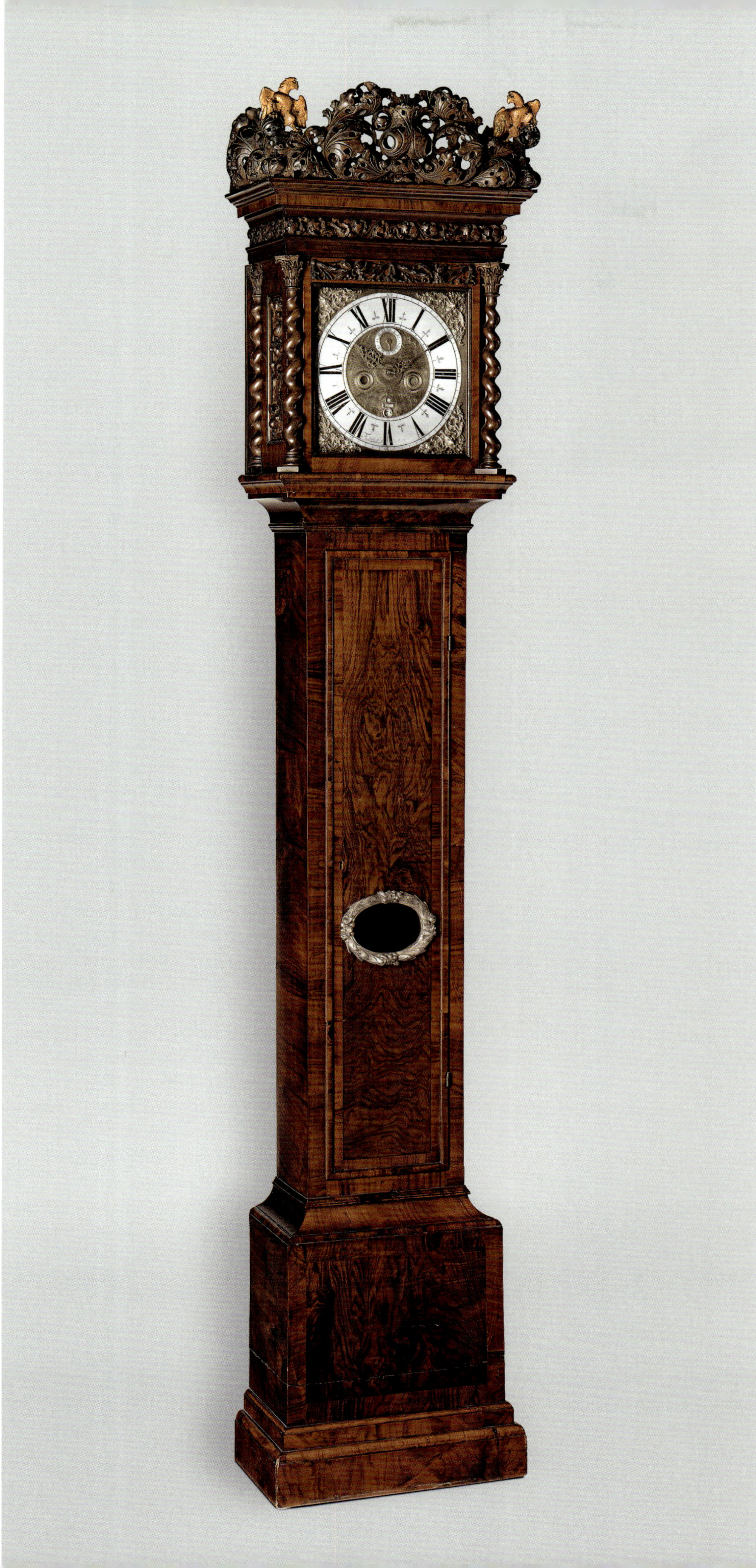

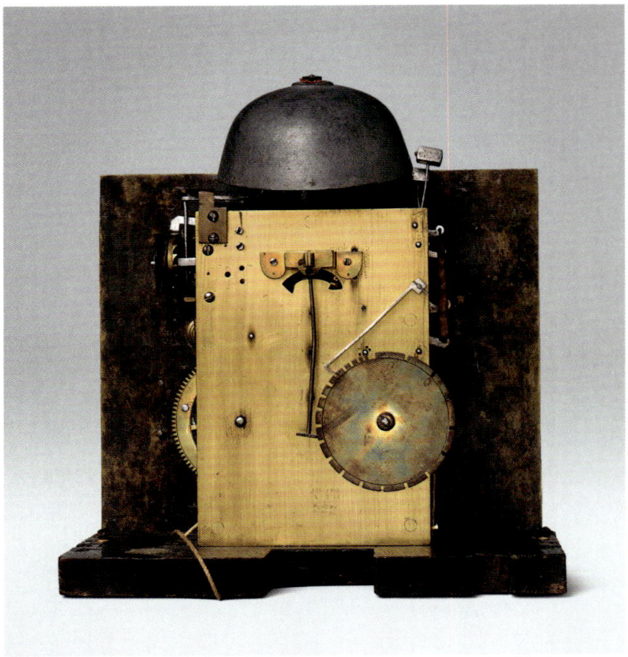

The back plate of the movement with the count wheel for Dutch striking, and the slot that allows for the easy removal of the anchor and its arbor

twelve o'clock position. Three apertures at the six o'clock position show the day of the month, the day of the week (in English), and the planetary sign governing the day. The signature and place appear on either side of roman numeral VI. The center of the dial is chased with a design of tulips, and cast heads of winged putti in foliage are attached to the four spandrels.

The eight-day, weight-driven movement has count-wheel striking and bolt-and-shutter maintaining power. The movement consists of two rectangular brass plates held apart by five turned pillars. It contains a going train of four wheels that are regulated by a seconds-beating pendulum (about forty inches in length), which is threaded for an adjustable nut at the end, and an anchor escapement. There is an anchor-shaped slot in the back plate that allows easy removal of the anchor assembly. The striking train activates hammers for two nested bells, the lower-toned bell for the hour and the higher-toned one for the half hour anticipating the next hour (known as Dutch striking). The alarm assembly is screwed to the back plate at the roman numeral I position, and it has its own set of two weights of unequal size. The plates are latched to the pillars throughout, and the dial plate is also latched.

While much of the construction reflects Fromanteel's English training, there are certain elements of the movement that are typically Dutch: the means of attachment of the hammers in the striking train and the sequence of their blows at the half hours, for example, as well as the layout of the calendar on the dial and the tulip pattern engraved in the center. The spandrel ornaments on the dial, on the other hand, may have been imported from London.

The history of the Fromanteel family of clockmakers remains a subject of contention, but Ahasuerus II Fromanteel, the second son of Ahasuerus I Fromanteel (1607–1693), was undoubtedly born in 1640 in London, where he apprenticed as a clockmaker. He moved to The Hague sometime between 1677 and 1681, as he is mentioned as being there at various times between 1677 and 1684. He became a burgher in 1683.[3] Alternatively, he is thought to have established a business in Amsterdam in 1681 with his brother John Fromanteel (1638–1692) in the Vijgendam, now part of the Dam Square near the Rokin.[4] The next record finds him in Amsterdam in 1693, and in the following year, his daughter, Anne, married the expatriate English clockmaker Christopher Clarke (1668–1734). Together, they operated in Amsterdam as Fromanteel and Clarke until Fromanteel's death in 1703, but Clarke apparently retained the double name until 1722.[5]

Most of the history of the Fromanteels in the Netherlands was not known in early twentieth-century England with the result that someone decided the original signature on the dial of the Museum's clock, "Fromanteel / Amsterdam," should read "Fromanteel / London." The new place-name and faint traces of the original "A" and "m" for Amsterdam can still be found on the chapter ring, and the depth of the newer engraving is noticeably shallower than that of the clockmaker's name.

The business letterhead of Percy Webster (ca. 1862–1938) at 24 Great Portland Street, London, who identified himself as "Clock-Maker and Dealer in Diamonds, Antique Plate, and Bric-a-Brac," is still attached to the inside of the door to the trunk of the clock, which provides fairly certain evidence of who changed the signatures. Webster's obituary in the *Times* further noted that "If anything ancient, like a skull watch or a Gothic clock came into Great Portland Street with a part missing or ignorantly misplaced, then the business could wait as far as Webster was concerned. He had to retire to his home workshop until that part had been replaced in the proper manner. He was a craftsman first and a dealer a long way after."[6] Such self-assurance had its consequences, regrettably, as the clock was bequeathed to the Metropolitan Museum as English, and the distinctly Dutch features remained a puzzle for more than forty years. It is not known where or when Percy Webster acquired the clock.

Parts of the crest are now missing, and others have been reattached. Some missing veneer has been replaced with mahogany. It is no longer possible to determine whether the case originally had the bun feet that are found on most of the other cases in this group of clocks. CV / JHL

1 Leopold 1989, pp. 160–61, 165, n. 25; Zeeman 1996, pp. 11, 472–73.
2 For examples, see Zeeman 1996, pp. 12, 20–31, 35–37, 50.
3 Leopold 1989, p. 160.
4 Zeeman 1996, p. 465; Vehmeyer 2004, vol. 2, pp. 965–66.
5 Leopold 1989, p. 160; Zeeman 1996, p. 462.
6 "Percy Webster" 1938.

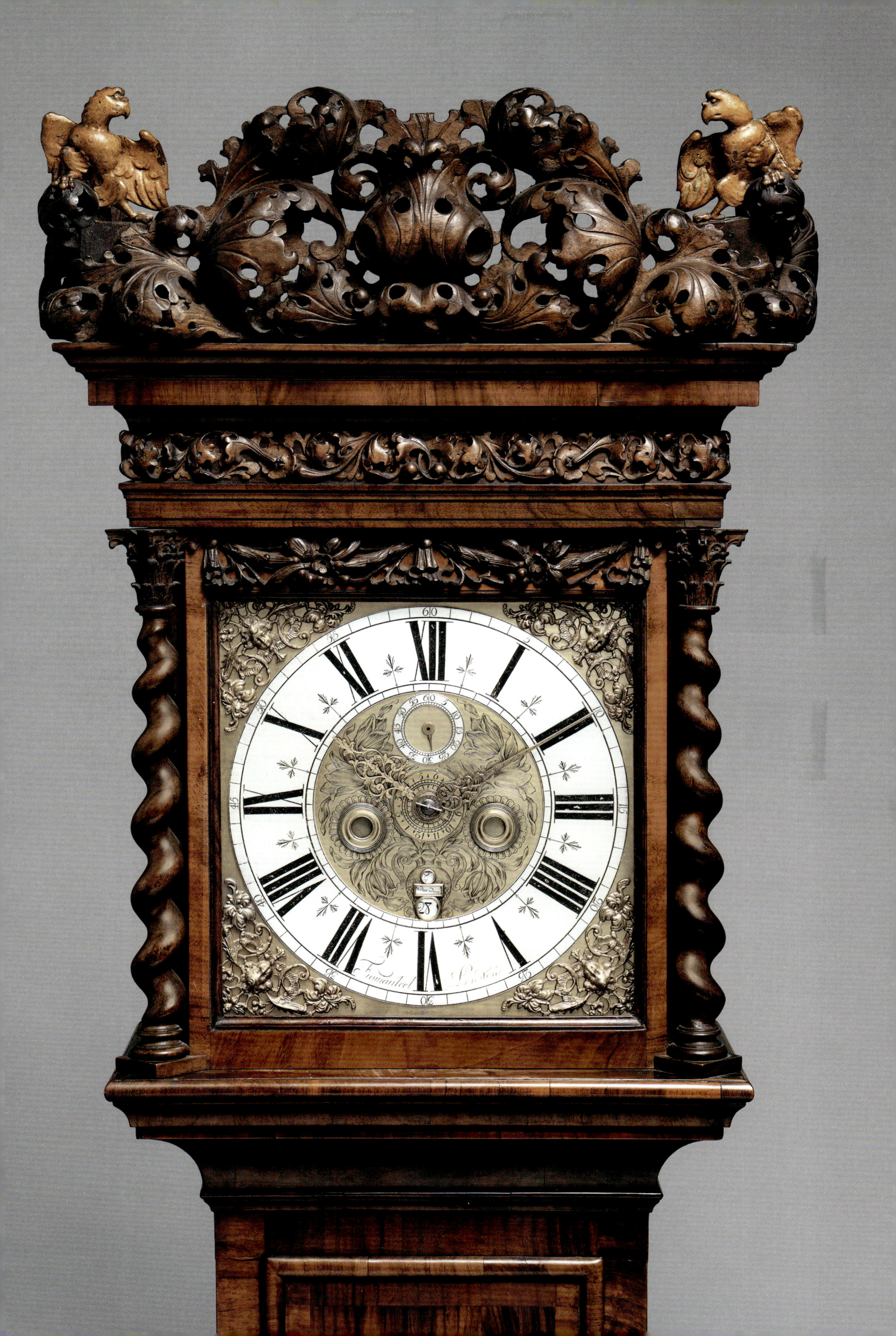
Fromanteel London

26. Watch

CASE: SWISS (GENEVA), CA. 1688;
MOVEMENT: GERMAN (BERLIN), CA. 1750
Diam. of case: 1 9/16 in. (4 cm),
Diam. of back plate: 1¼ in. (3.2 cm)
Gift of J. Pierpont Morgan, 1917
17.190.1522

CASE: painted enamel on gold, signed: *Huaut le puisné pintre de son A. E. aberlin* (Huaut the Younger, painter to his Highness Elector of Berlin) [Jean-Pierre Huaud, or Huaut, known as the Younger Huaud, Swiss, 1655–1723]
MOVEMENT: brass and steel, signed (on back plate): *Racine Berlin* [Johann G. Racine, Swiss, active Berlin, 1748]

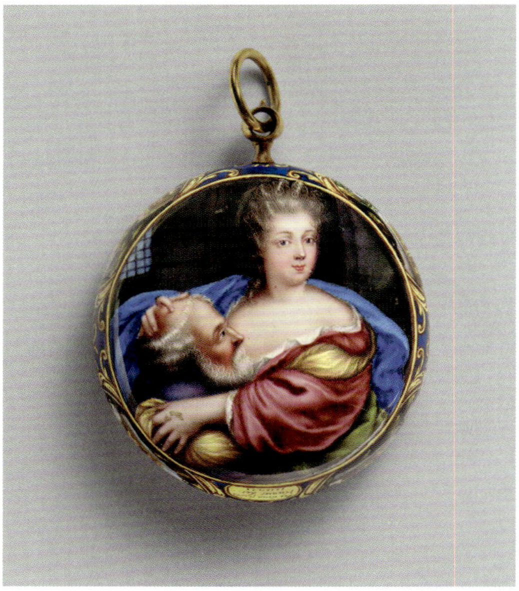

fig. 34 *Watch. Case: painted enamel on gold by Ami Huaud (Swiss, 1657–1724) and Jean-Pierre Huaud (Swiss, 1655–1723), Swiss (Geneva), ca. 1700–20; movement by Pieter Klock (Dutch, 1665–1754), Dutch (Amsterdam), ca. 1700–20. Diameter 1¾ in. (4.5 cm). The Metropolitan Museum of Art, New York, Gift of J. Pierpont Morgan, 1917 (17.190.1436a, b)*

IN SEVENTEENTH-CENTURY EUROPE SOME OF THE MOST TALENTED enamel painters of portrait miniatures worked in Geneva. Among the best known was Jean I Petitot (1607–1691), the son of a Protestant émigré from Villiers le Duc in Burgundy and whose early training in Geneva under his uncle Jean Royaume (died 1654), a goldsmith, lasted until 1626.[1] Paul Prieur (1620–1684), a grandson of the French sculptor Barthélémy Prieur (died 1611), was apprenticed to Geneva goldsmith Jean Planchant in 1635.[2] It is not known where Petitot and Prieur learned the technique of enamel painting, but it is thought that they both may have trained in France.

Petitot traveled to Paris in 1632 about the same time the Toutins are known to have moved from Châteaudun, France, and were producing enamels using their recently developed technique of painting in colored enamels on a pure white enamel ground.[3] Records show that Petitot then traveled to England and painted the exquisite miniature of Queen Henrietta Maria (1604–1669) of England that is now in the Dutch Royal Collection.[4] Later he returned to France, and, although a Protestant, he was appointed court painter in enamel to King Louis XIV (1638–1715).[5]

Prieur traveled to Denmark in 1655 or 1656,[6] where he became painter of miniatures to the court of King Frederick III (1609–1670), whose portraits by Prieur are among the treasures of Rosenborg Castle in Copenhagen.[7] Like Petitot, Prieur also spent some time in Paris, and it is believed that he knew the Toutins; later, he traveled to Prussia, Russia, and England.[8]

The Huaud family were descendants of Huguenots who settled in Geneva to escape increasing religious persecution in France.[9] Pierre I Huaud (1612–1680) was born in Châtellerault, France, and emigrated in 1630, becoming a master goldsmith in Geneva that same year. It is not known where he learned the technique of enamel painting, but it is possible that he learned his craft in Geneva by the late 1630s. In 1643, he married Françoise Mussard, the daughter of a Geneva lapidary, and they had three sons: Pierre II (1647–between 1696 and 1698), Jean-Pierre (1655–1723), and Ami (1657–1724), all of whom became well-known enamelers of miniatures, medallions, portrait cases, and the occasional cup and saucer, but a large majority of their enamels were watchcases. Like Petitot and Prieur, the Huauds were presented with the problem that the small Calvinist theocracy of Geneva did not contain a sufficient number of patrons to support the makers of luxury items such as their own. The Huauds, therefore, removed to Berlin. Pierre II is thought to have joined them in 1685.[10] By 1686, however, he was back in Geneva and succeeded in obtaining appointments for his brothers as painter-enamelists to Friedrich III (1657–1713),[11] who would become Duke of

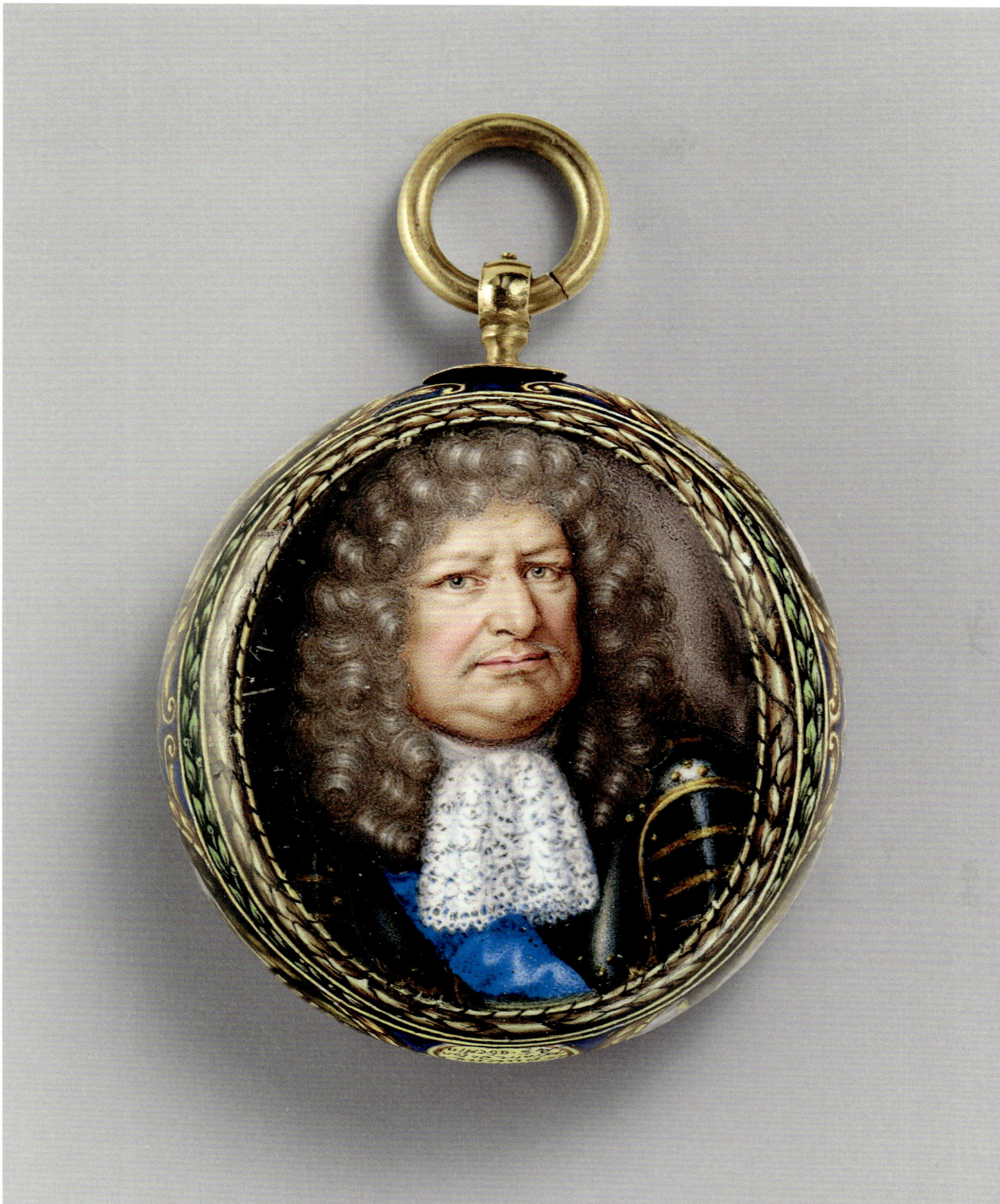

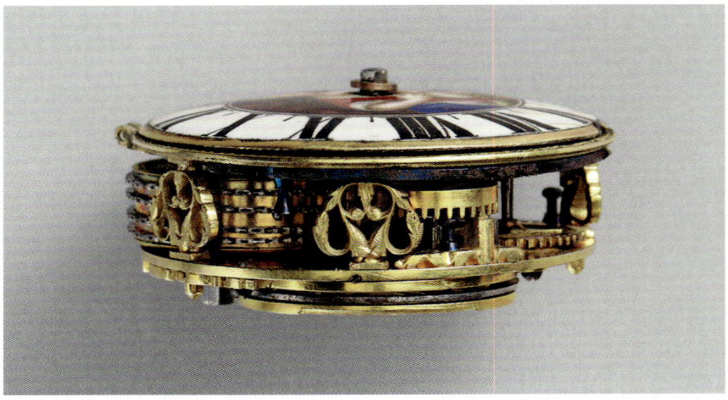

Detail showing movement by Pieter Klock

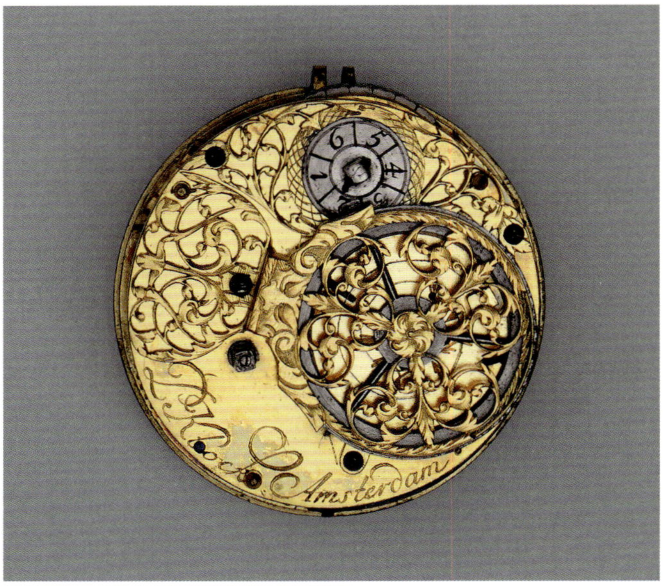

Back plate of movement by Pieter Klock

Prussia and Elector of Brandenburg upon the death of his father, Friedrich Wilhelm, in 1688, and then king of Prussia in 1701. Pierre II returned to Germany in 1689 and was appointed painter-miniaturist to Friedrick III; he died in Berlin between 1696 and 1698.[12] His enamels are often difficult to distinguish from those of Jean-Pierre and Ami, but all three artists customarily signed their work and adopted systematic forms of signatures: Pierre II, using "*Huaut l'âisné*" (Huaut the Elder); Jean-Pierre, using "*Huaut le puisné*" (Huaut the Younger) when working alone, as on a watchcase with a portrait of a man in military dress in the Museum's collection. When working with Ami, however, he and Ami signed "*Les deux frères Huaut*" (Two Huaut brothers) or "*Les deux frères Les jeunes*" (Two young brothers), sometimes adding the place as well. The latter signature appears on a second watchcase in the Museum's collection (see fig. 34).[13] The two younger brothers formed their partnership as early as 1682 in Geneva, and they left the service of the electors in Germany and returned to Geneva in 1700, where Jean-Pierre died in 1723 and Ami followed in 1724. The second watchcase appears to belong to the period after 1700, and to judge from the number of their surviving watchcases that contain movements by foreign watchmakers, they must have exported a large quantity of empty cases.

The signature, "*Huaut le puisné pintre de son A. E. aberlin*" (Huaut the Younger, painter to his Highness Elector of Berlin), appears in the cartouche on the band of the Huaud watchcase with the portrait. The painter was, thus, Jean-Pierre Huaud, and the portrait is of Friedrich Wilhelm, Elector of Brandenburg and Duke of Prussia (1620–1688), known as the Great Elector (*Der Grosse Kurfürst*).[14]

Ruled by the Holy Roman Emperor, Germany was a loose collection of territories and cities during the seventeenth century. By tradition, the emperor was elected by three prelates and four secular rulers who individually held the title Elector, which referred to their duty to choose the emperor. (From the end of the fifteenth century, however, the emperor was invariably a member of the Habsburg family.) Friedrich Wilhelm inherited land and the title Elector of Brandenburg from his father Georg Wilhelm (1595–1640), along with a number of separate territories throughout Germany that spanned from the Rhine to the Baltic Sea. While all territories were adversely affected by the Thirty Years' War (1618–1648), Brandenburg, in particular, was devastated by famine, plague, and pillage. It has been estimated that Brandenburg's population was reduced by half and that some parts of the territory had a loss of 90 percent.[15] At the time of his death in 1688 Friedrich Wilhelm had achieved a great deal to speed recovery of his domain and to elevate the position of both Brandenburg and Prussia within the Holy Roman Empire. He had created a standing army that was capable of defending its territory from attacks, and he had begun to turn Berlin into the permanent residence for the Electoral Court: hence the title of Great Elector. Among his efforts to repopulate the ruined city of Berlin, he welcomed Huguenot refugees who were fleeing King Louis XIV, of whom quite a few had skills in watchmaking.[16] It was in this context that the three Huaud brothers from Geneva were invited to Berlin to make some of their exquisite, painted-enamel watchcases, and it was by special permission of the council of Geneva that they were permitted to work for the electors.[17]

The portrait on the Museum's watchcase records a stout man of late middle age who looks out at the viewer somewhat warily. He wears a full-bottomed wig and military armor with a splendid lace cravat. This image was adapted from a half-length portrait by Gedeon Romandon (1667–1697), which is now in the Schloss Caputh, near Potsdam, Germany, the former country estate that belonged to Friedrich Wilhelm's second wife, Dorothea, daughter of Philip, Duke of Holstein-Glücksburg. As Romandon is thought to have arrived in Berlin only a year or two before the Great Elector died,[18] the painting probably reflects the effects of the ill health that preceded his death in 1688.

The miniature is tightly framed by a double border of painted wheat-ear decoration that separates the back of the case from its side. The side is one continuous band of enamel that has been divided into four zones of decoration, each with an oval that frames a tiny landscape. An even smaller cartouche at the six o'clock position encloses the signature of the enameler. The inside of the case is enameled with another landscape, this one with a human figure in front of a partly ruined castle that is typical of the Huauds' elegiac scenes, a number of which have been identified by Hans Boeckh as having been adapted from prints by the French artist Gabrielle Pérelle (1604–1677).[19]

A gold bezel hinged to the case holds a glass cover for the dial of the watch, now of white enamel with painted black roman numerals (I–XII) for the hours and Arabic numerals (5–60, by fives) for the minutes, and with a fine, openwork hour hand. (The minute hand must have been equally fine, but it has been awkwardly repaired.) The dial plate and movement, too, are hinged and open out of the case. The mainspring is wound from the front by a winding square that is accessed through the dial below the three o'clock position. The present movement, with a verge escapement, consists of two circular plates held apart by four cylindrical pillars and contains a train of three wheels. The back plate carries a large balance bridge with an openwork foliage design screwed to the plate and has a steel coqueret (or end plate) that secures the balance staff's pivot, and an equally large silver figure plate (labeled "Avant / Retard") for regulating the balance spring. The figure plate is flanked by the name of the watchmaker ("Racine"), the serial number of the watch ("110"), and his place of work ("Berlin"). Very little is known of the maker, but records show he came from Basel, Switzerland, and is believed to have been working in Berlin about fifty years after the Huauds returned to Geneva. Evidently, he made a new movement for a treasured watchcase.[20]

A second portrait watchcase, this one signed by Jean-Pierre and Ami, depicts Friedrich Wilhelm's daughter-in-law Sophie Charlotte of Brunswick-Hanover (1665–1705), who in 1684 married Friedrich III. The watch, now in the Theodore Beyer Collection in Zurich, has a movement signed "Huet a Berlin," and it is probably closer in date to the watchcase than would be the Metropolitan's Racine movement.[21]

A more typical variety of Huaud watchcase is represented in the Museum's collection by two examples,[22] each depicting the same scene from the well-known story in seventeenth- and eighteenth-century Europe of Roman Charity as recounted in Book 9 of *De factis dictisque memorabilis* by the Roman historian Valerius Maximus (ca. 20 B.C.–ca. A.D. 50). As an allegorical representation of filial piety, it was the subject of many paintings, including several by the Flemish Baroque painter Peter Paul Rubens (1577–1640). The origin of the Huaud version shown here (fig. 34) is unknown, however, and the female figure of Pero, who breastfed her incarcerated father, Cimon, in order to save him from starvation, may in fact record a living model. The watchcase, with its vivid blues and reds, was one of the Huauds' more popular designs, probably as much for its liberal exposure of feminine flesh as for the moral of the story. This one contains a beautifully made movement with a verge escapement by Pieter Klock (1665–1754), one of Amsterdam's finest clock- and watchmakers.[23]

J. Pierpont Morgan acquired the watch depicting the Great Elector from Carl H. Marfels of Frankfurt am Main and Berlin,[24] and the one depicting Roman Charity with his purchase of the Frederick George Hilton Price Collection.[25]

CV / JHL

1 See Clouzot 1928, p. 203, for a transcription from the Minutes of Etienne Demonthouz, notaire, vol. 40, fol. 204, Archives d'Etat de Genève.
2 Fuhring and Bimbenet-Privat 2002, p. 133; Hein 2009, vol. 2, pp. 86–87.
3 Schaffers-Bodenhausen and Tiethoff-Spliethoff 1993, p. 20. See also entry 12 in this volume.
4 Ibid., p. 199, no. 180.
5 Ibid., p. 21.
6 Schneeberger 1958, pp. 136–37.
7 Hein 2009, vol. 3, pp. 94, 95, no. 673, and vol. 2, pp. 86–87, nos. 150–65, dated 1663, 1666, 1668, and 1669.
8 One of his enamels is signed "Prieur à Londres" and dated 1682. See Schneeberger 1958, p. 137.
9 For a more extensive biography of the Huaud family, see Cardinal 1989, pp. 169–76. See also Tardy 1971–72, vol. 1, pp. 301–8; Patrizzi 1998, pp. 228–30.
10 Clouzot 1928, p. 104; Cardinal 1989, p. 169.
11 Clouzot 1928, pp. 212–13.
12 Cardinal 1989, p. 170.
13 Acc. no. 17.190.1436a, b.
14 For a good biography of Friedrich Wilhelm in English, see McKay 2001.
15 Ibid., pp. 49 and 96, n. 1. See also König 1988, p. 23, for figures on the population of Berlin.
16 McKay 2001, pp. 179–82.
17 See transcriptions from the Minutes of Gabriel Grosjean, vol. 22, fol. 525, entry of Sept. 18, 1682, and P.H. 3793, entry of June 7, 1686, Archives d'Etat de Genève. Clouzot 1928, pp. 212–15, doc. nos. LV, LVI.
18 Foerster 1934, p. 544.
19 Boeckh 1982, pls. 14, 15, 17–20, 22, 23, 26–29, 31, 36, 38, 39.
20 König 1988, p. 74.
21 Uhrenmuseum Beyer Zürich 1996, pp. 74–75, no. 31.
22 Acc. no. 17.190.1436a, b and 17.190.1414a, b.
23 Eugène Jaquet and Alfred Chapuis noted that the Huauds were collaborating with Amsterdam watchmakers even before 1700. See Jaquet and Chapuis 1970, p. 122.
24 Williamson 1912, pp. 104–6, no. 98, and pl. XLVIII.
25 Ibid., pp. 197–98, no. 219.

27. Pair-Case Watch with Alarm

BRITISH (LONDON), PROBABLY CA. 1695
Diam. of outer case: 2⁵⁄₁₆ in. (5.9 cm)
Diam. of inner case: 2 in. (5.1 cm)
Diam. of back plate: 1½ in. (3.8 cm)
Gift of J. Pierpont Morgan, 1917
17.190.1498a, b

CASE AND DIAL: silver with blued-steel hand
MOVEMENT: brass and steel, signed: *Massy / London*
[Nicholas II Massy, French, 1641–died probably ca. 1728, Clockmakers' Company, 1682; Henry Massy, British (London), active 1691–1745, Clockmakers' Company, 1692; or Nicholas Massey the Younger, active in The Hague ca. 1700, Clockmakers' Company, 1693]

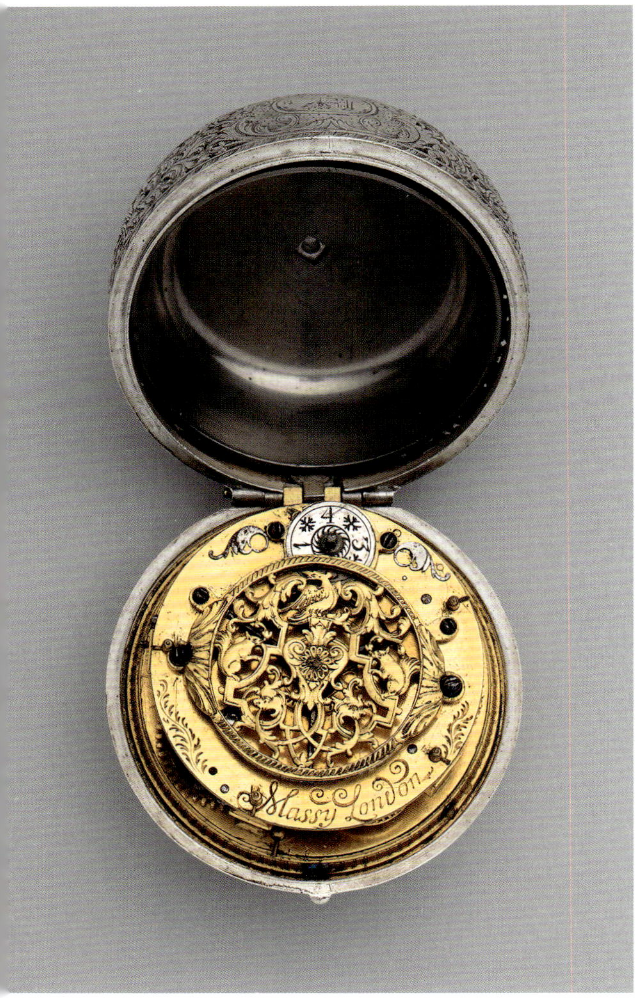

Back plate of the movement with the open inner case

THE REVOCATION OF THE EDICT OF NANTES IN 1685, BY WHICH French Protestants were no longer protected from religious persecution, came at the end of nearly a century of tolerance by the Catholic kings of France. A large number of seventeenth-century French clock- and watchmakers were Protestants and traditional centers of clock- and watchmaking, such as Blois and Rouen, had begun to be depleted by the exodus of Calvinist, or Huguenot, clockmakers even before the Revocation. In lesser-known cities, including Châtellerault and Gien, the craft was all but destroyed. Émigré French settled primarily in neighboring areas that were predominately Protestant, foremost among them Geneva, but also England, the Netherlands, and parts of Germany, bringing with them not only their technical skills but also French decorative designs. In England, the influence of the watchmakers on decorative design was reinforced by the contemporaneous influx of Huguenot goldsmiths, a number of whom would have successful careers in London.[1] By the last quarter of the seventeenth century, however, English clock- and watchmakers would develop a strong tradition of their own and became less influenced by the Huguenot watchmakers who had settled nearby. Thus, the watch signed "Massy / London" in the Metropolitan Museum's collection is probably an example of a collaboration between a Huguenot émigré watchmaker and a casemaker working in London or its environs, and it is unmistakably different from, for example, the watches by the Englishman Thomas Tompion and Nathaniel Delander (see entries 24 and 30 in this volume).

The central motif of the silver outer case is a cipher that can be read as either "CB" or "BC" bordered by a scale-patterned frame and a circle of scrolls; the cipher, circle, and scrolls are in relief. The side consists of a second circle, this one made of openwork and consisting of inhabited foliage that alternates with trifid-shaped ornaments. The inhabited-foliage motif is repeated on the sides of the inner case, and a cartouche with a landscape appears at the roman numeral VI position. A small hole in the center of the case permitted the insertion of a screw (now missing) for attaching the bell to the case. The champlevé dial is silver; the hour chapter is marked I–XII with raised lozenges at the half hours; and the dial has a single blued-steel hand. The alarm dial in the center is marked 1–5 and 7–11 in Arabic numerals with a knob attached at the 6 position for setting the alarm. The going train and the alarm are wound through the dial at the roman numeral IIII and IX positions of the hour chapter.

The movement consists of two circular brass plates that are held apart by four Egyptian pillars, and it contains a going train of three wheels with a verge escapement regulated by a balance spring, as well as an alarm train with a decorated barrel and double-armed hammer for

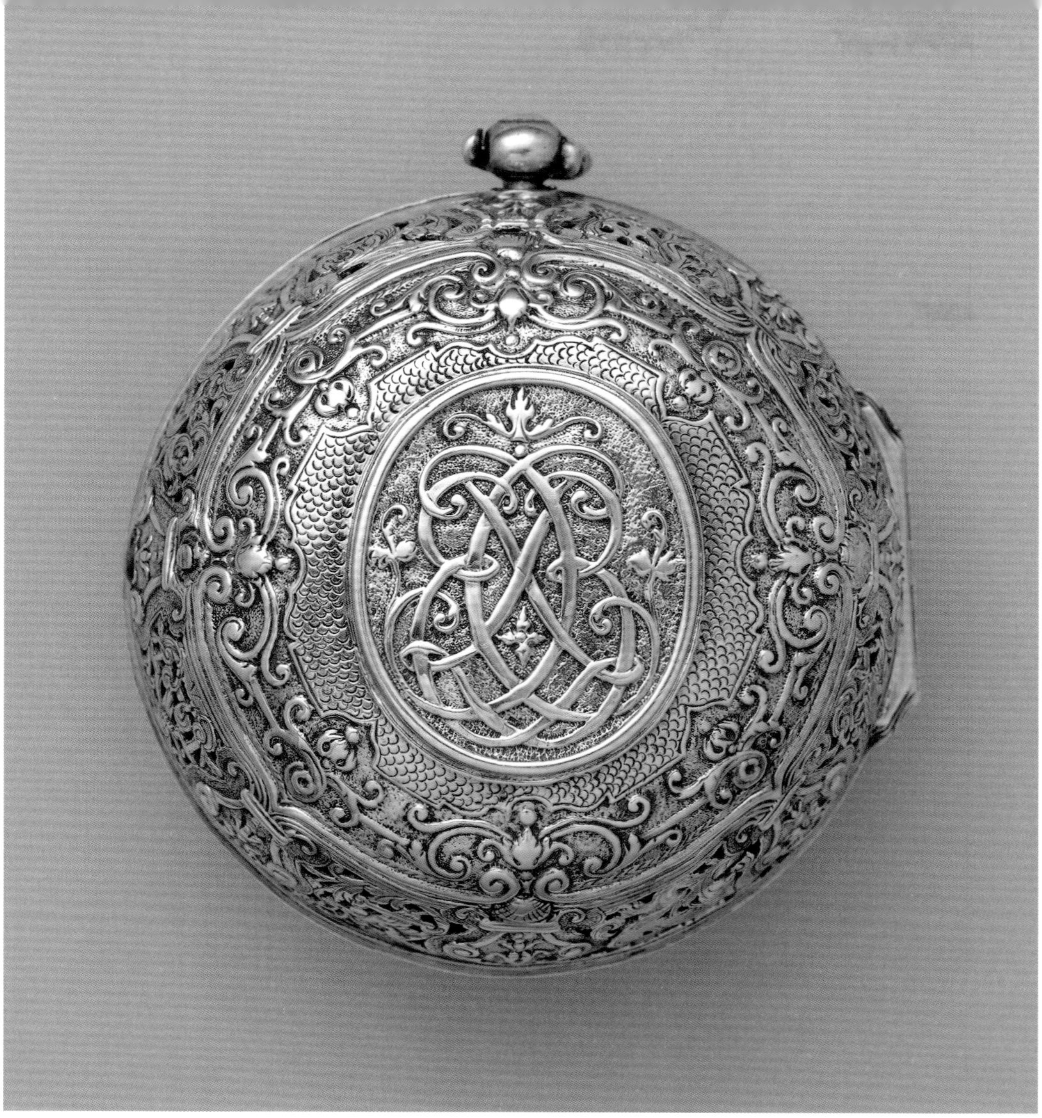

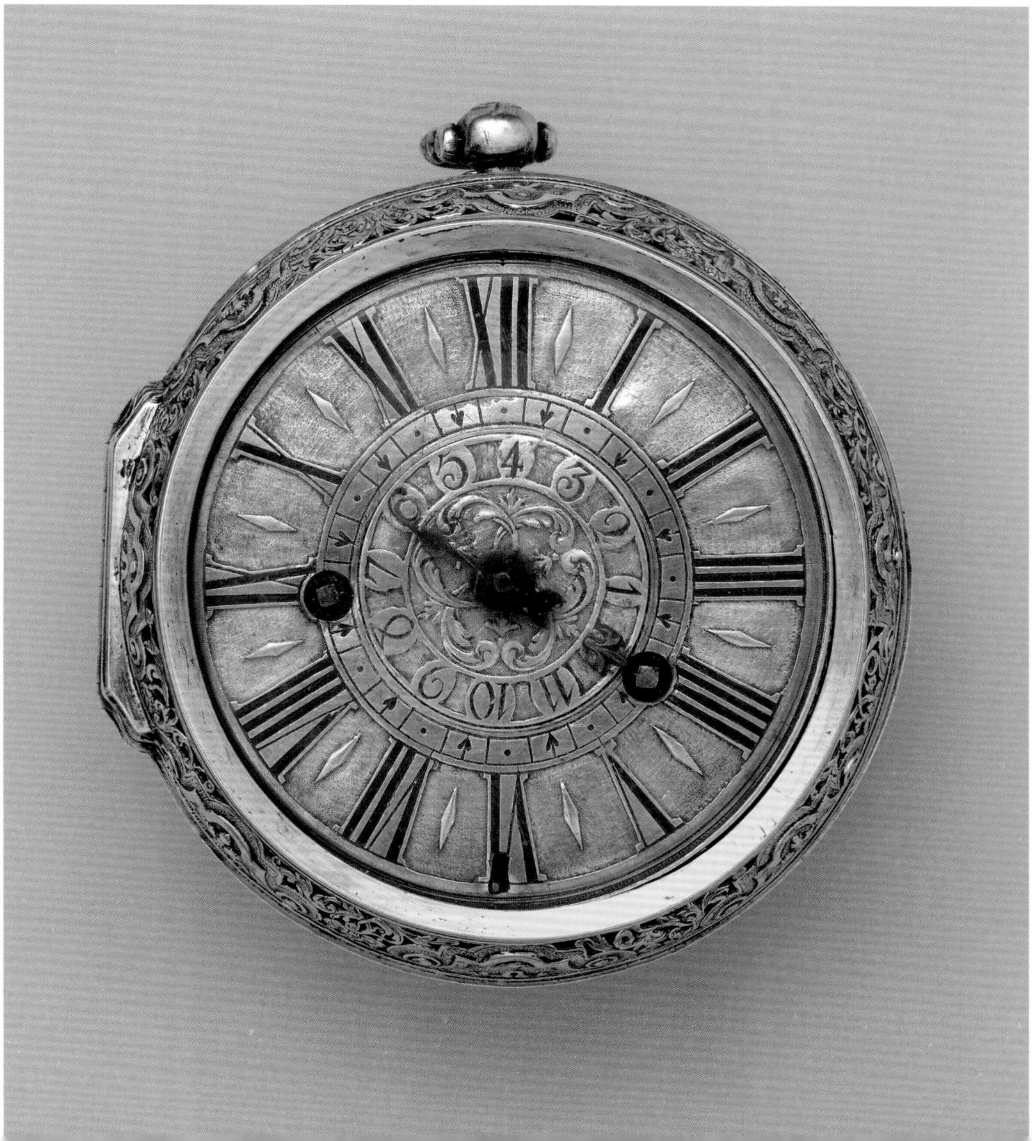

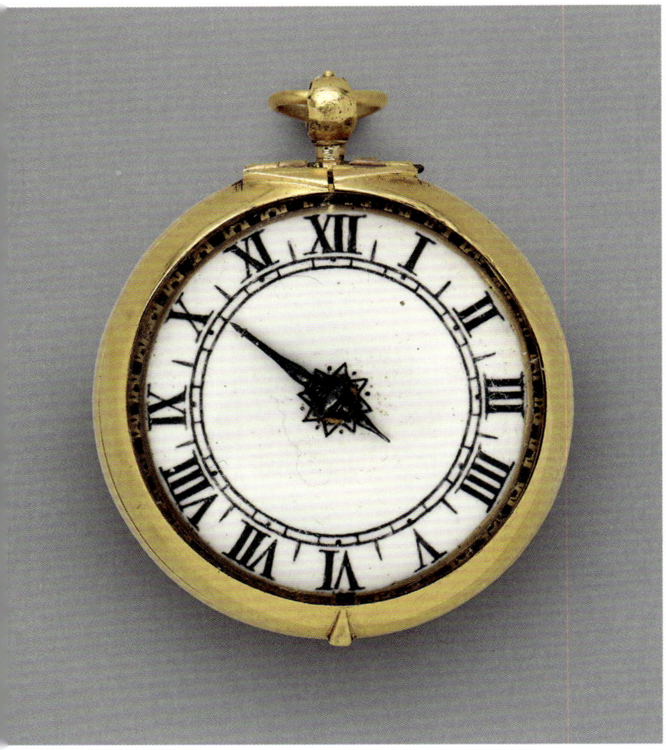

fig. 35 *Nicolas I Massy (or Massey, French, ca. 1600–before 1658). Watch, French (Blois), ca. 1650. Leather and gold, Diameter of inner case 1⅛ in. (2.9 cm), diameter of back plate ¹⁵⁄₁₆ in. (2.4 cm). The Metropolitan Museum of Art, New York, Gift of J. Pierpont Morgan, 1917 (17.190.1572)*

striking the bell mounted inside the inner case. Attached to the back plate is a large French-style balance bridge, pierced and chased with foliage that incorporates two squirrels and a bird. A silver figure plate for adjustment of the balance spring completes the attachments.

The enigmatic signature on the back plate of the watch, "Massy / London," is probably that of Nicolas II Massy (or Massey; 1641–ca. 1728), but previous accounts have erred because there were not two generations of Massys named Nicolas, as formerly thought, but three. Born in Blois, two Massys are recorded as working as watchmakers in London near the end of the seventeenth century. Nicolas II was the son of Nicolas I Massy (ca. 1600–before 1658), who was apprenticed to a clockmaker in Blois in 1611.[2] By 1617, Nicolas I was working in Blois as a companion clockmaker for Pierre II Cuper (born 1604, active in Constantinople in 1634),[3] a member of the large and well-known family of clockmakers established in Blois from the middle of the sixteenth century to the late nineteenth century. Nicolas I was undoubtedly the maker of a pre–balance spring watch (see fig. 35) in the Metropolitan Museum's collection.[4]

Born in Blois, Nicolas II (or Nicholas II) was in London by 1682 and is recorded in the Clockmakers' Company's Court Minute Books as "Nicholas Massy, Watchmaker, a French Protestant . . . admitted as a Brother of the company who paid nothing at present for his admission."[5] He was naturalized in London in 1685, and he may have died about 1728.[6] The same volume of the Court Minute Books records the admission of "Nicholas Massey the Younger Clockmaker admitted and Sworn a Brother of this Company" in 1693.[7] He was the son of Nicolas II and has in past accounts been confused with his father. It was probably Nicolas the Younger who immigrated to The Hague after 1700 and became a citizen in 1702, and it may have been he, not his father, who died about 1728. There is evidence that he remained in contact with his London-based brother Henry Massy (active 1691–1745) after 1702 and cooperated with supplying London-made gold watches for sale to Continental patrons.[8] This international trade fostered by a family relationship may help to explain the enigmatic character of the signature on the movement of the Metropolitan's watch, [9] but the use of elements like the balance bridge instead of a balance cock, the winding arrangement, and the ornamental design on the going barrel for the alarm train suggest that the maker of this watch had only recently left France, and long before 1702.

The case of the watch has been attributed to a member of a Huguenot émigré family from Marseille who might have been either Adam I (active 1687, died before 1698) or Adam II (recorded 1695/6–died after 1709) Roumeau. Both were members of the London Goldsmiths' Company and are believed to have used the same maker's mark: "AR."[10] There is no maker's mark on the case of the Museum's watch, however, nor is there evidence that the Roumeaus supplied watchcases for the Massys.[11] Another naturalized Huguenot, Alexander Leroux (active 1699–1722/3), did, in fact, make cases for Henry Massy.[12] Leroux, like the Roumeaus, was a member of the London Goldsmiths' Company, and he used a maker's mark. So the maker of the Metropolitan's watchcase was probably not Leroux. He may have been someone who worked outside of the City of London, where he could have avoided the rules of the Goldsmiths' Company for marking his work, as a number of Huguenot craftsmen are known to have done.[13]

The vocabulary of ornament employed by the casemaker is unquestionably of French origin and may have drawn upon the ornamental designs of another émigré from Blois to London, Simon Gribelin (1661–1733), who was admitted to the Clockmakers' Company in 1687 as an engraver.[14] No surviving watchcase or clockcase has been identified as his autograph work, but beginning with his publication *A Book of Severall Ornaments* (1682), his designs undoubtedly influenced a generation of craftsmen in London.

The design of the outer case centers around the cipher, a feature prized in Huguenot design as exemplified by Gribelin's *New Book of Cyphers* (1704), but prefigured in the Huguenot watchmaker Daniel de La Feuille's *Livre nouveau et utile pour toutes sortes d'artistes* (New and Useful Book for All Kinds of Artists, 1690). The trifid motif was favored by Huguenot goldsmiths working in London, including Pierre Platel and David Willaume, while the inhabited foliage on the inner case had a long history in French watchcase making. The variety of foliage appears, for example, on the case of a watch in the Museum's collection by Nicolas Forfaict, dating from about 1600 or 1610.[15] Although probably recording a style that was fashionable a few years earlier, it could still be found in London in Gribelin's *A Book of Ornaments Usefull to Jewellers, Watch-Makers and All Other Artists* (1697). Even later, in Gribelin's *A New Book of Ornaments Useful to All Artists* (1704) this same style is used to frame small engraved scenes in a way comparable to that on the inner case of the Metropolitan Museum's watch. But the influence of Parisian design was also direct. The pierced ornament for the brass balance bridge of the movement of the Museum's watch and the blued-steel ornaments of the screws that secure the regulator for the balance spring have their counterparts in a series of designs by the French engraver Pierre Bourdon (active 1703–8), which are designated for the use of watchmakers, goldsmiths, chasers, engravers, and others.[16] The better-known *Second livre d'orlogeries*, published about 1700 by the Paris-born Daniel Marot (1661–1752), also included comparable designs for parts of watches.[17] Like Bourdon's, these designs are thought to reflect French taste of a few years earlier. The relatively robust ornament of the outer case and the style of the movement probably place the date of the watch sometime in the mid-1690s and certainly not later than the first years of the eighteenth century.

There have been repairs to the inner case where it is joined to the pendant, and the side of the inner case is dented at the XI position. The hand is not original, nor is the bezel for the glass, perhaps made to accommodate a new glass.

The watch belonged to the British banker Frederick George Hilton Price, whose collection supplied many of the seventeenth-century British watches in J. Pierpont Morgan's collection. CV / JHL

1 See, for example, Hayward 1959.
2 Fourrier 2000, p. 46.
3 Ibid., pp. 8, 101.
4 Acc. no. 17.190.1572.
5 Clockmakers' Company, London, Court Minute Books, Ms. 2710/2, 1680–99, p. 13v, entry of Apr. 3, 1682, Guildhall Library, London.
6 Fourrier 2000, p. 46.
7 Clockmakers' Company, Court Minute Books, Ms. 2710/2, p. 141v, entry of July 3, 1693.
8 Leopold 1989, p. 162; see also Fourrier 2000, p. 46.
9 For more on this subject, see Leopold 2005a.
10 Priestley 2000, p. 71.
11 Ibid., pp. 25–26.
12 Ibid., pp. 23, 29. One hallmarked for 1710–11 is now in the British Museum, London (inv. no. CAI-0230). See Thompson 2008, pp. 66–67.
13 Oman 1978, p. 72. See also Vincent 1983, pp. 221–25.
14 Clockmakers' Company, Court Minute Books, Ms. 2710/2, p. 65v. For a discussion of Gribelin's engraving of salvers and seals dating from about 1690 to 1708, see Oman 1978, pp. 72–82.
15 Acc. no. 17.190.1606.
16 See Bourdon 1703, pl. 6.
17 *Oeuvre de Daniel Marot* n.d., vol. 1, pls. 43, 45–52.

28. Longcase Clock with Calendar

BRITISH (LONDON), CA. 1700

94 × 19 × 10½ in. (238.8 × 48.3 × 26.7 cm)
Width of dial plate: 11 in. (27.9 cm)
Gift of Irwin Untermyer, 1964
64.101.865

CASE: walnut; oak veneered with walnut; and string inlays of holly and stained holly
DIAL: partly gilded and partly silvered brass, signed: *Tho / Tompion Londini / Fecit* [Thomas Tompion, British, 1639–1713]
MOVEMENT: brass and steel

THE CONSTRUCTION OF THE ROYAL OBSERVATORY IN GREENWICH, England, begun in 1675, was based on designs by Christopher Wren (1632–1723), formerly Savilian Professor of Astronomy at Oxford University and architect of Saint Paul's Cathedral and most of the city churches that replaced those lost in the Great Fire of 1666, which destroyed much of London.[1] Late in 1675 Thomas Tompion (1639–1713) was commissioned by Jonas Moore to supply two clocks for use at the observatory by the royal astronomer John Flamsteed (1646–1719). The two year-going clocks, finished in 1676, are slow-beating and have thirteen-foot pendulums.[2] One clock is in the collection of the British Museum, London;[3] the other was returned to the Old Royal Observatory in 1994 after 275 years in private possession. These clocks are said to be accurate to two seconds a day.[4] Replicas are in place on the original site in the wainscoting of the Great Room, or Octagon Room, at Greenwich Observatory.

Pendulums of thirteen feet in length are impractical for most timekeeping; indeed, it proved remarkably difficult to make reliable pendulums longer than about thirty-nine inches, and only the best of the English clockmakers were able to employ them. Although they are extremely rare, Tompion was still making the occasional clock with a longer pendulum about 1700, when the Metropolitan Museum's longcase clock is thought to have been made.[5] The Museum's clock, beating at a rate of one and one quarter seconds, requires a pendulum about sixty inches long.

The eight-day, weight-driven movement, with bolt-and-shutter maintaining power, is composed of two rectangular plates that are held apart by six pillars, each latched to the front plate. The going train consists of three wheels and ends in an escape wheel and anchor. Peep holes in the back plate allow a view of the teeth of the escape wheel hitting the pallets of the anchor when the wheel is in motion. The holes are spaced to match the diameter of the small wheel required for a slow-beating pendulum. The striking train consists of four wheels and a fly, which are governed by a count wheel mounted inside the plates on the great wheel. It strikes the hours (I–XII) on a single bell mounted at the top of the front plate. The number "344" is stamped near the lower edge of the back plate, and it appears twice more scratched on the back of the dial plate.

The basic proportions of plinth, trunk, and domed hood of this clock conform to the evolving architectural design for longcase clocks, which was adopted by clockmakers in late seventeenth- to early eighteenth-century London. The design of the case is restrained but elegant in detail. Eight matched panels of walnut veneer on the door to the trunk are framed by half-round walnut moldings, and the geometry of their

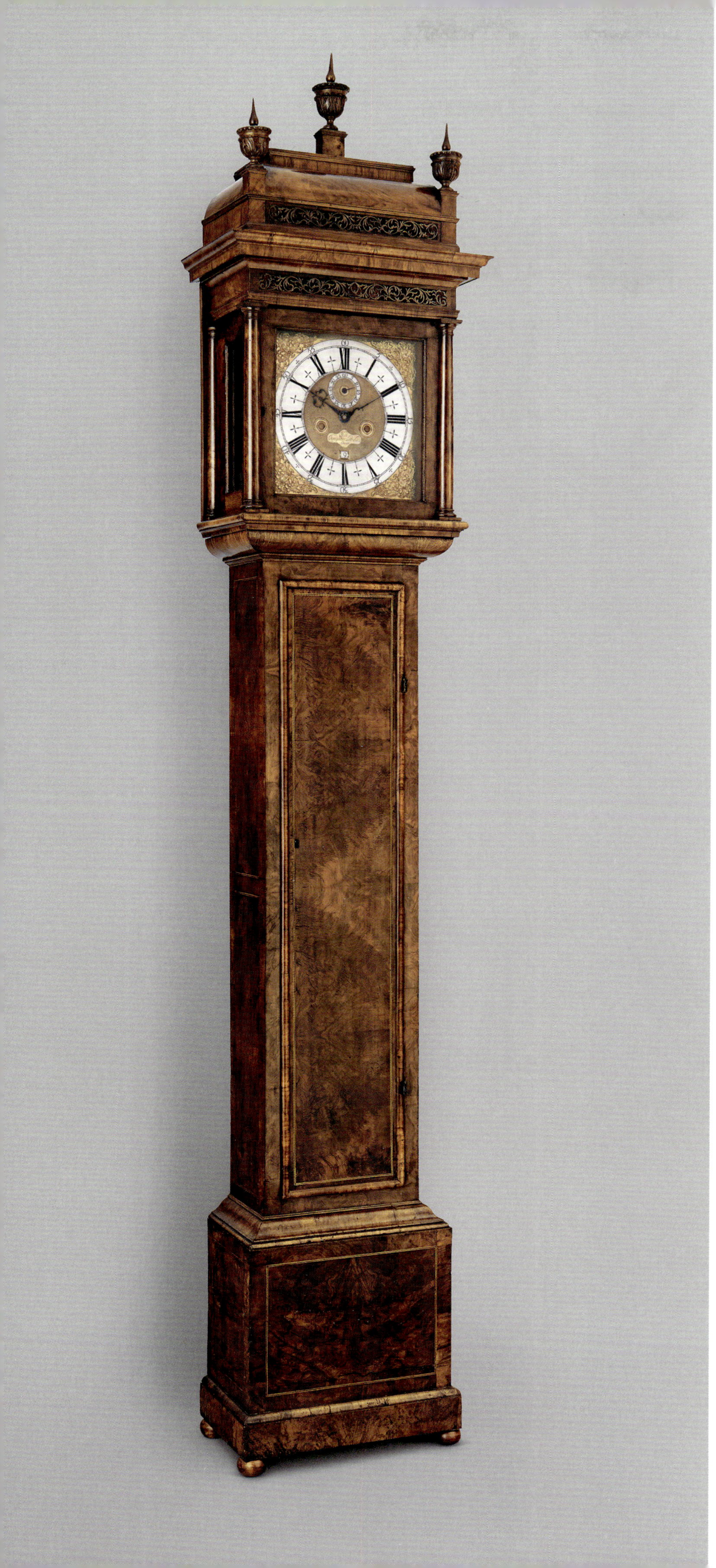

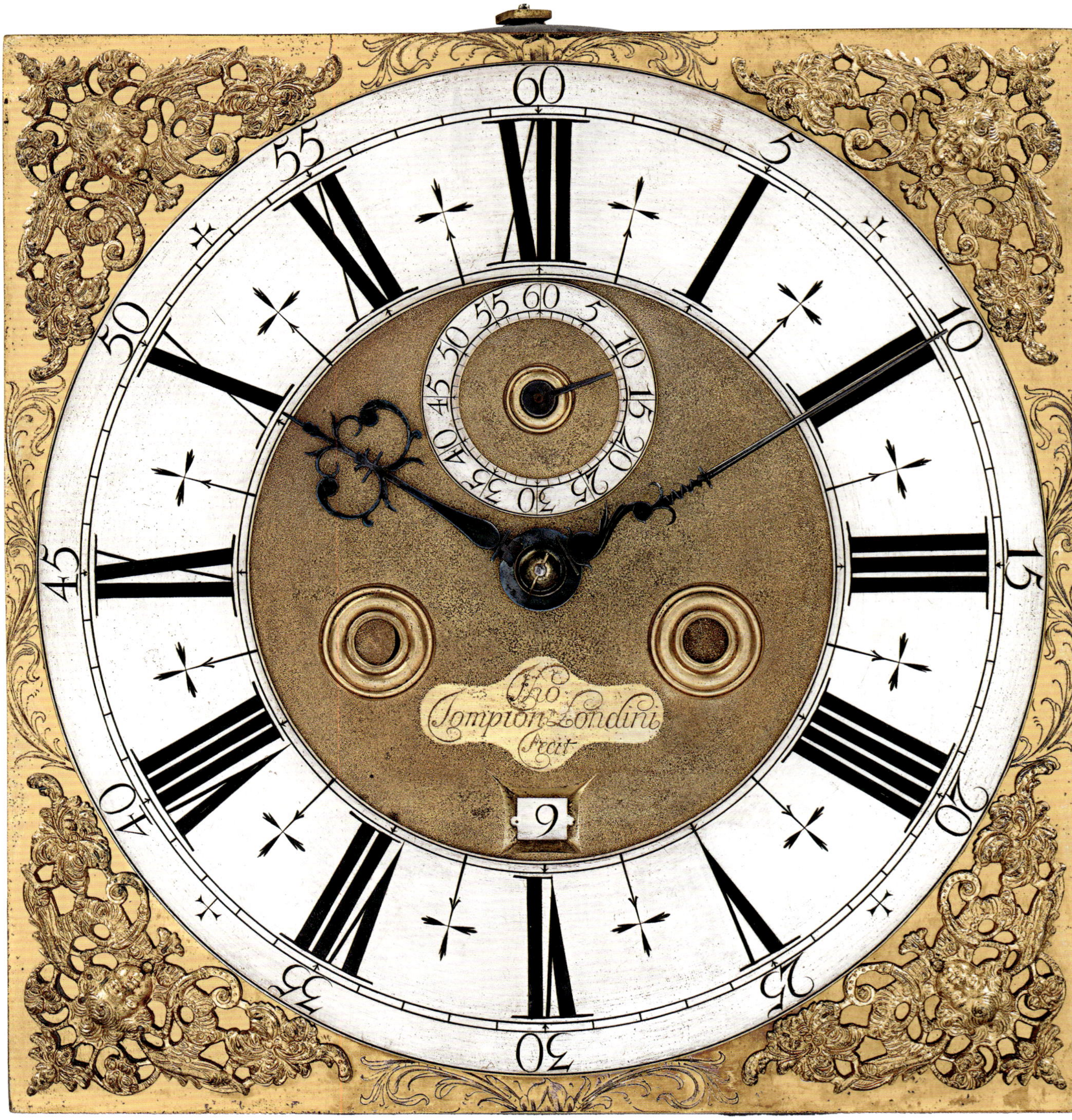

The dial plate with the clockmaker's signature

shape is emphasized by the continuous strings of inlaid dark and light woods. Comparable designs of veneer and inlay organize the surfaces of the two sides of the trunk and all three visible sides of the plinth. The forward-sliding hood has a hinged, wooden-framed glass door and is flanked by applied wooden columns with simple Tuscan capitals. Panes of glass and quarter-round columns complete the sides. These support a fretwork frieze surmounted by a cornice and a second fretwork frieze below an imposing double dome with three vase-shaped, carved wooden finials. The eleven-inch-square dial and the convex molding that supports the hood suggest that the case probably belongs to the same period as the movement, and the case is, in fact, numbered "27 / 344" on the upper edge of the door to the trunk. The cabinetmaker is unknown.

When the clock came as a gift to the Museum, the lower half of the pendulum shaft and the bob were missing. These elements were replaced by new parts. The holes for the arbors of the striking train were found to have been rebushed, but the wheels and pinions are original. A damaged spring for the bell hammer was noted, as was the replacement of the hour hand. Otherwise, the movement was intact, and it was put in running condition.

The hood of the case had suffered from an exceptionally dry atmosphere in New York, and it required reconstruction, as did the plinth. The latter was strengthened by the application of interior wooden supports. The skirting seemed original to the clock, but surviving evidence showed that the clock had originally had four bun feet. The present feet were made by the Museum's wood conservators. The two finials on the front of the hood are replacements.

The earliest known reference to this clock appears in the 1926 sale catalogue of the Frank Garrett Collection.[6] Irwin Untermyer acquired it from R. W. Symonds during the same year. CV / JHL

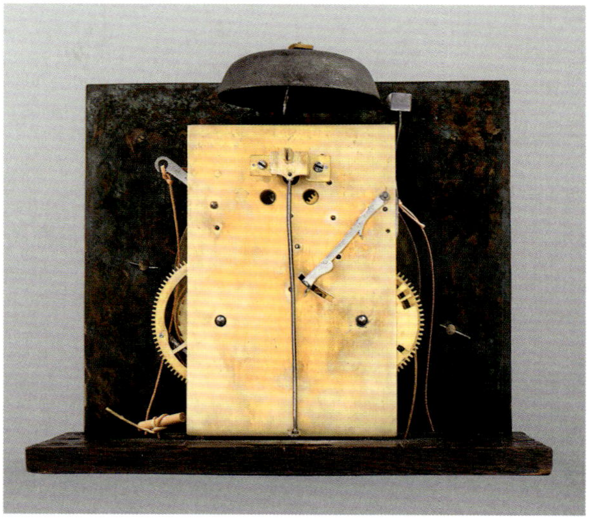

View of the back of the dial plate with the back plate of the movement

1 For a lively account of the founding of the Royal Observatory, see Howse 1980, pp. 19–44. See also entry 23 in this volume.
2 Howse 1970–71.
3 Inv. no. 1928,6-7.1. See Thompson 2004, pp. 80–83.
4 Ibid.
5 For the dating, see J. L. Evans 2006, pp. 71, 78, no. 344.
6 Anderson Galleries 1926, pp. 36–37, no. XVIII, ill.

29. Mantel Clock with Alarm

CASE: GERMAN (AUGSBURG), CA. 1710;
MOVEMENT: GERMAN (AUGSBURG), CA. 1760–70
31¾ × 17¼ × 11½ in. (80.6 × 43.8 × 29.2 cm)
Rogers Fund, 1946
46.162

CASE: tortoiseshell backed with brass leaf, pearwood veneered with rosewood; and partly gilded silver, signed: *J.A. Thelot* [Johann Andreas Thelot, or Thelott, German, 1655–1734]
MOVEMENT: gilded brass and steel, signed (on back plate): *Franz Xaveri Gegenreiner / Augsburg* [Franz Xavier Gegenreiner, German, active 1760–70]
ARMS (AT THE TOP OF CASE): shield with full-face, standing youth with wings dressed in a short tunic; crest: closed helmet with wings displayed between the letters M and F (unidentified)

SOME CLOCKS ARE VALUED AS MUCH FOR THEIR ORNAMENTAL cases as they are for their time-telling properties. One of the few clocks acquired by the Metropolitan Museum by purchase rather than as a gift falls securely into the category of decorative masterpieces. Its case displays five silver reliefs by an Augsburg goldsmith, Johann Andreas Thelot (or Thelott; 1655–1734), who is considered by many to be the best artist of his time in this medium.

Augsburg, his city, was severely afflicted by an outbreak of the plague in 1628. In 1632, the plague was followed by a siege of the forces of King Gustavus Adolphus (1594–1632) of Sweden during the Thirty Years' War (1618–48), which brought catastrophe to much of Germany. By the end of the war, Augsburg had lost more than half of its inhabitants. So great was the reputation and the commercial acumen of the city's goldsmiths, however, that when hostilities ceased, the export trade in ornamental silver plate recovered its vitality, and by the end of the century there were more goldsmiths at work in Augsburg than there had been before the outbreak of the war.[1] In the last quarter of the century, Augsburg goldsmiths specialized in mounting painted enamels, semiprecious stones, and gemstones on gilded silver or gold to create remarkable objects of baroque exuberance.[2] Side by side with this production there continued to exist an older tradition of working with silver in high relief, or repoussé, to create decorative or narrative scenes.

Thelot, who worked in the traditional technique,[3] came from a French Huguenot family that emigrated from Dijon in 1585. The son of Israel Thelot (1616–1696), a master in the Augsburg guild of goldsmiths, Johann made many of his early works in collaboration with his father. The first relief signed with his own name is dated 1679, but he did not become a master goldsmith in Augsburg for another ten years, time he spent partly in Italy.[4] More than 130 of his works are now known, nearly all of them finely detailed scenes worked in extraordinarily high relief, and many adopted from engravings and paintings by such well-known artists as Jacques Callot (1592–1635), Nicolas Poussin (1594–1665), and Charles LeBrun (1619–1690).[5] The original designs for the four vignettes illustrating mythological legends of the goddesses Venus and Diana that appear on the Metropolitan's clock, however, have never been identified. Perhaps they were original to the goldsmith. A fifth, smaller plaquette, with an allegorical scene attached to the base of the clock, is also surely the work of Thelot. The four figures in the scene, probably representing The Seasons, include (from left to right) a bouncing infant holding a wreath aloft; a seated female with pan pipes under her arm and a selection of fruit and vegetables beside her; a youthful Bacchus holding a

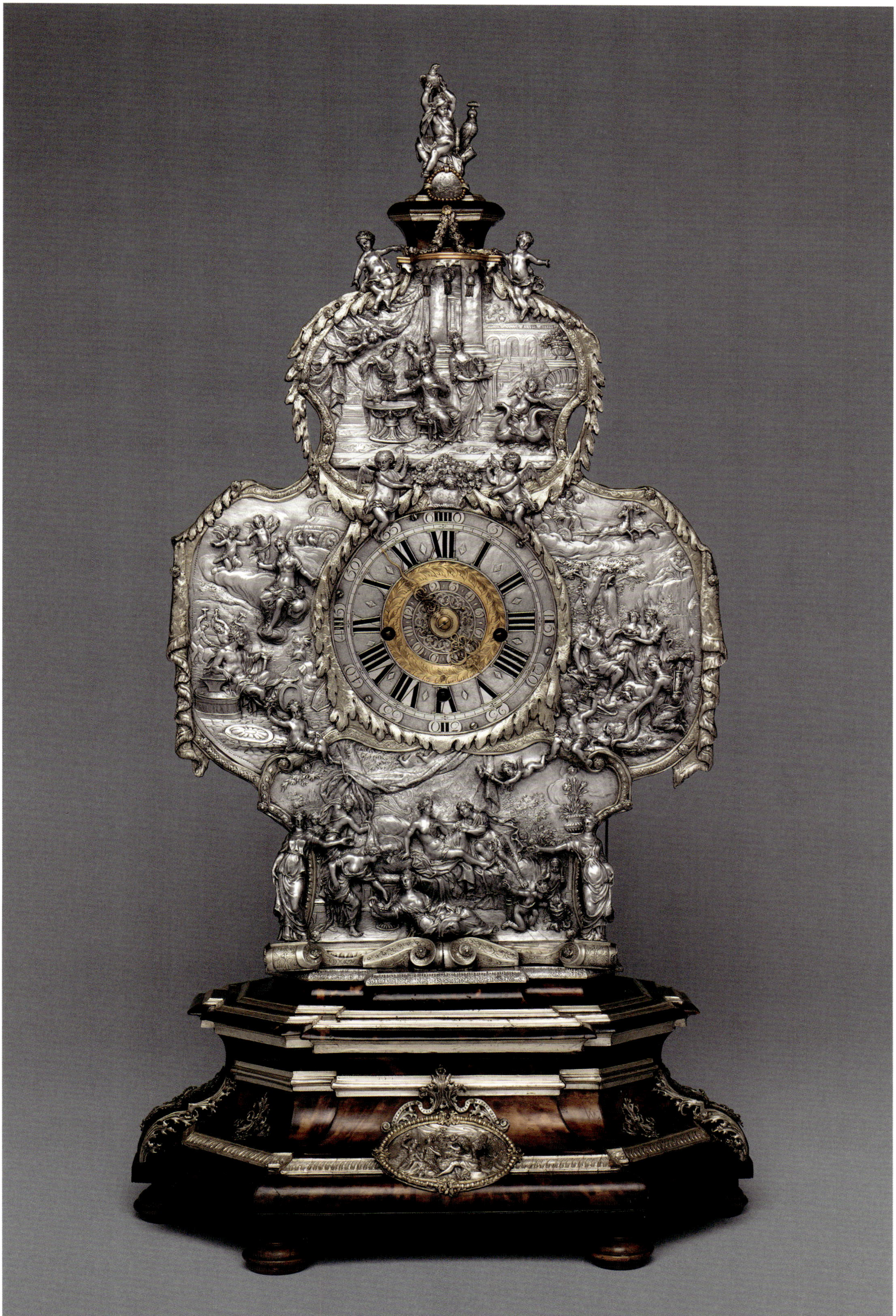

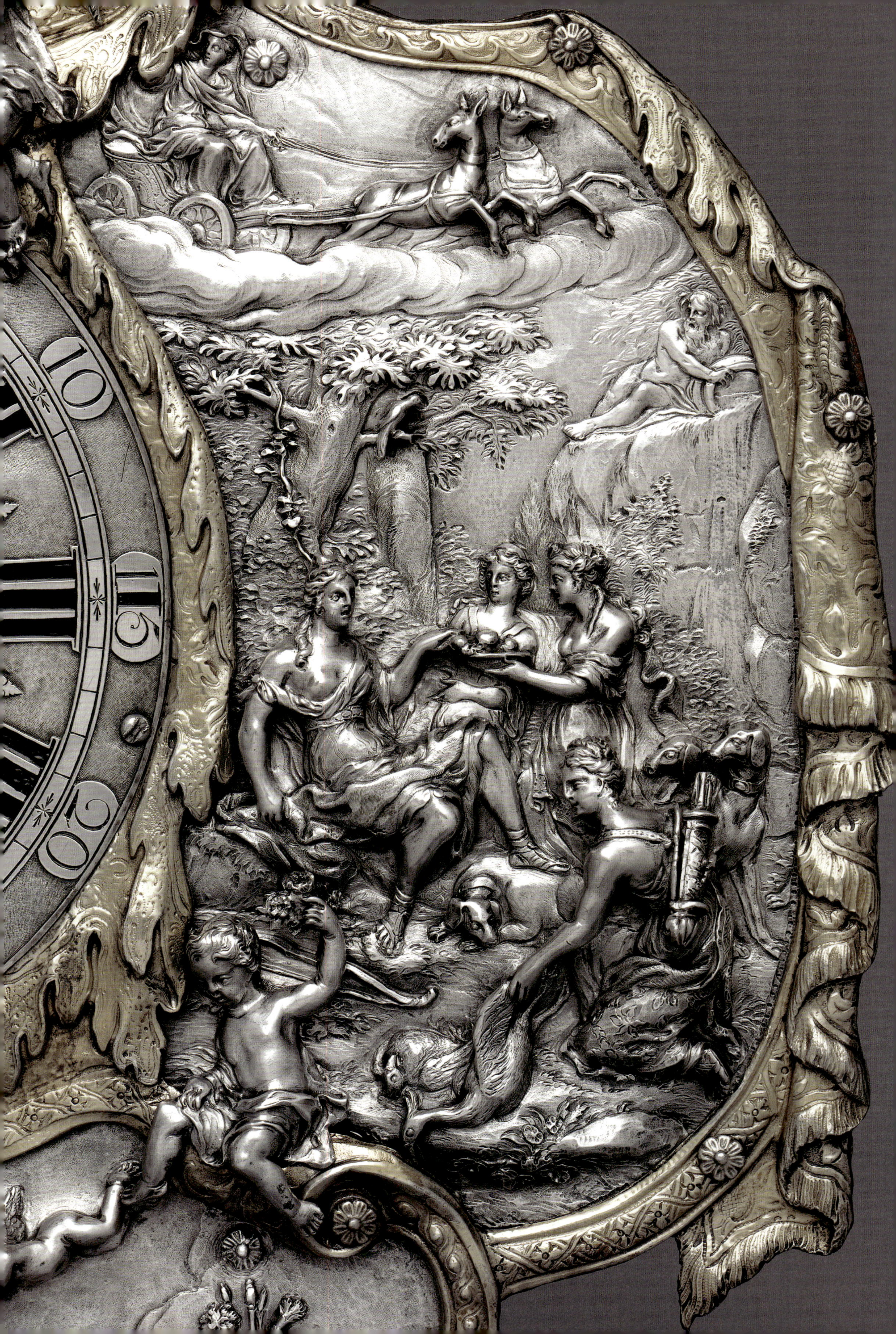

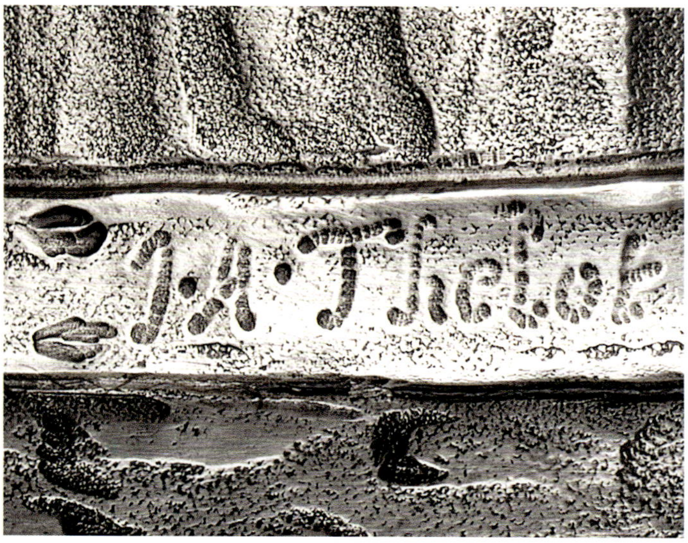

Detail showing signature of the goldsmith J. A. Thelot

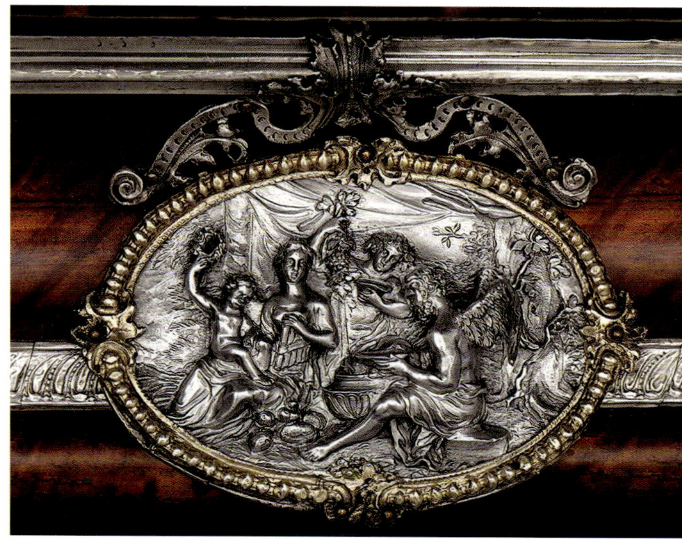

Detail with scene of the personifications of the Four Seasons

bunch of grapes and a wine cup; and an old man in the guise of Chronos warming a dish over a brazier.[6]

The four larger silver scenes, framed by curtains and foliate swags of gilded silver, surround the dial of the clock. They merit close attention as part of a group, two of which are signed by the goldsmith. Starting from the top, they illustrate Venus, or Aphrodite as the Greeks knew her, in a setting of classical architectural elements. She is seated at a round table near her swan-drawn chariot that is guarded by Cupid. Three of her handmaidens are bringing her the necessities of her toilette. Above the scene, two infants perch precariously at the top, and below it two winged putti present a basket filled with flowers. Moving clockwise, the next scene is most probably devoted to the goddess Diana (Artemis to the Greeks). She drives a chariot pulled by two female deer, and below a bank of clouds she appears again, seated in a wooded glen with a waterfall in the background. Accompanied by her hunting hounds, one snuggled at her feet, she is offered a dish of produce by two of her nymphs and a brace of game birds by a third. While she has formerly been identified as Venus,[7] she more closely resembles Diana, a deity who presides over game and hunting and whose habitat is the natural world. In addition, her long hair with loose-hanging curls, her Cretan hunting shoes, and her dress, caught up high on the waist but leaving one breast bare, mark her as Diana rather than Venus, goddess of love.

At the lower left of the Diana scene, still another infant, this one seated on the frame of the next scene, points to the dial of the clock. Below, in another stagelike setting, a curtain is pulled back to reveal Mars in a baroque version of Roman military dress and the nearly nude Venus reclining on a bed and attended by handmaidens and infants in various animated poses. One of them is kneeling at the bottom right and molesting a pair of birds nesting in the upturned helmet of Mars above the incised signature, "J. A. Thelot." On either side of the scene, standing female figures gesture toward the amorous pair. On the upper left still another infant calls attention to the last scene, where Vulcan greets his cloud-borne consort, Venus, who has alighted from her chariot, this time drawn by doves and accompanied by an animated infant Cupid leading a fellow cherub by the hand. On the stake supporting Vulcan's anvil is the incised signature "J. A. Thelot."

The center of all this activity, but no less impressive, is the champlevé silver dial with a chapter ring of hours (I–XII), the numerals filled with black wax, and a chapter ring of minutes (5–60, by fives, the quarters marked I–IIII). The half hours are further indicated by lozenges, and the individual minutes by incised lines. In the center there is a dial for setting the alarm (1–12). Openwork, scrolled brass hour and minute hands indicate the time.

As Klaus Maurice has demonstrated, the form of this part of the clock (the dial and the four plaquettes) descends from a variety of German wall clock, or plate clock (*Telleruhr*),[8] so called because the early examples resembled dinner plates. But here, supported by a hexagonal base with six bun feet, the silver "plate" is bolted to one of brass that is mounted on a wooden structure and veneered with tortoiseshell, and it has thin silver moldings typical of furniture made in Augsburg in the late seventeenth and early eighteenth centuries. The front of the base displays the repoussé silver allegorical scene in a frame with a baroque-scrolled crest; the back contains a drawer for the winding key; and the structure below serves as a container for the movement, as well as support for the silver plaquettes. At the top of the structure, an infant hunter releases a falcon, while a hooded falcon rests alongside him. Below the cherub with the falcon appears an oval plaque that displays the coat of arms for an unidentified owner, which is probably a later addition.

If the case of the clock reflects the height of baroque design in Augsburg, the present movement suggests that the turn of the eighteenth century was a less illustrious moment in the history of Augsburg's clockmaking. For during the course of the Thirty Years' War, the city that in the sixteenth century had been one of the chief suppliers of domestic clocks to all of Europe fell seriously behind other clockmaking centers. Unlike the goldsmiths and jewelers, the clockmakers never really recovered enough to regain their former status. Their reluctance to adopt the new technology can be demonstrated by the history of the reception in Augsburg of its native, Johann Philipp Treffler (1625–1698). As reconstructed by the American historian Silvio

Detail with scene of Diana and her nymphs

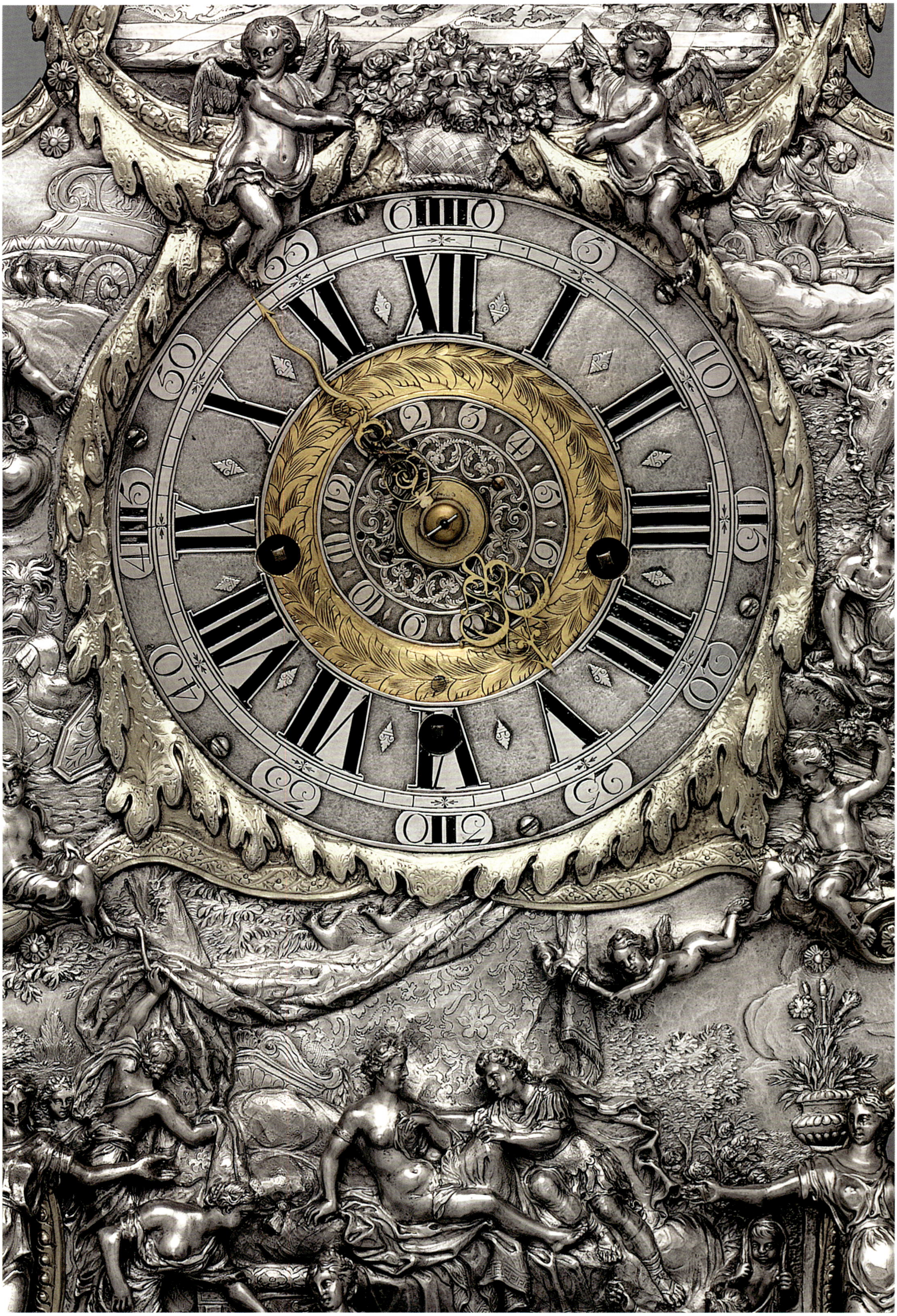

Detail of the clock dial with part of the scene of Venus and Mars

Bedini,[9] Treffler had been an active mechanician and clockmaker at the court of the Medici Granduke of Tuscany, Ferdinando II (1610–1670) in Florence, where experimentation with pendulums by Galileo Galilei (1564–1642) and his son Vincenzio (died 1649)[10] was recent, and where Italian pendulum clocks were being made independently of Huygens's invention by Galileo's pupil Vincenzo Viviani (1622–1703),[11] the brothers Giuseppe Campani (1635–1715), better known for his optical instruments, especially the telescope,[12] and Pietro Tomasso Campani (active 1655–after 1683),[13] and Treffler. In 1664 Treffler returned to Augsburg, only to be denied membership in the powerful guild of clockmakers and forbidden by them from making or even selling watches and clocks in Augsburg.[14]

The rectangular-plated spring-driven movement contained within the case of the Museum's clock is signed on the back plate: "Franz Xaveri Gegenreiner / Augsburg." It has a short pendulum and is quarter striking as well as quarter repeating on two bells attached to the back of the case. The movement fits the requirements dictated by the dial, and it is the work of a competent but comparatively unknown clockmaker, identified by Maurice in the records of the clockmakers' guild (*Schmiedzunftbuch*) in Augsburg.[15] He is listed as a maker of clocks (*Grossuhrmacher*) from Dölz in Bavaria on August 1, 1760,[16] and it is noted that he gained the right to make clocks in Augsburg by marrying the widow of one of the master clockmakers in the guild. Therefore, he would not have had the authority before 1760 to sign the Museum's clock in the way that he did. The dial of the clock is without doubt closer in style to 1700 than to 1760, and as the movement fits the dial precisely, the movement must have been made explicitly for this extraordinary clockcase.

Now missing from the case are two birds that were photographed before 1912 atop the scene of Venus and Vulcan and the scene of Diana. The arms of the infant on the left of the top plaque have been awkwardly repaired, and to judge from the illustration of the clock in the 1912 catalogue for the collection of Baroness James de Rothschild,[17] the standing female figure on the left side of the scene of Venus and Mars is a twentieth-century replacement. It differs from the others in that it is cast. Also, in 1912 there were only three tassels hanging from the lambrequin at the top of the Toilette of Venus plaquette; there are now four, and there is provision for a fifth, presumably long lost. The thumbs of several of the figures in relief are missing, the moldings around the base of the clock are chipped and dented, and a wing of a figure in the relief on the base was repaired at some time before 1912. Tortoiseshell veneer has been replaced and renewed in various places, particularly on the back of the clock. The ebonized board at the base and the feet are later replacements. The minute hand was broken and repaired.

Each of the four silver plaquettes is stamped with the French weavil mark for gold and silver that was imported between 1836 and 1864, but the identity of the French owner is unknown. The clock was in the London collection of Baroness James de Rothschild by 1912, and later sold by J. and S. Goldschmidt of Frankfurt am Main and London.[18] It was listed among the possessions of William Randolph Hearst by 1941,[19] and it appeared in a New York auction of property from private collections in 1946, at which time it was purchased by the Museum.[20] CV

1 Müller 1968; Seling 1994, p. 27.
2 See entry 16 in this volume for a watchcase exemplifying the style.
3 Recent authors have spelled his name Thelott, but signatures on his silver plaquettes are spelled Thelot.
4 Praël-Himmer 1978, p. 18; Schommers 1994, p. XXVI.
5 See, for example, Praël-Himmer 1978, pp. 41, 51, 53.
6 The author would like to thank Ellenor M. Alcorn, Curator, Department of European Sculpture and Decorative Arts, Metropolitan Museum, for suggesting the meaning of this unusual representation.
7 Jones 1912, p. 118; Praël-Himmer 1978, p. 88.
8 Maurice 1976, vol. 2, p. 91, nos. 750–60, and figs. 750–60.
9 Bedini 1956–57. See also Maurice 1976, vol. 1, pp. 182–84, 186. For some clocks by Treffler, see Maurice 1976, vol. 2, p. 85, nos. 679–81, and figs. 679–81.
10 Brusa 1978, pp. 115–16; Vehmeyer 2004, vol. 1, pp. 218–19, 222–23.
11 Vehmeyer 2004, vol. 2, pp. 942–43.
12 For two of Giuseppe Campani's telescopes, both in the Museo Galileo in Florence (inv. nos. 2556 and 3185), see Righini Bonelli 1968, p. 188, no. 424, and pl. 94 (bottom), and p. 189, no. 447. See also *Encyclopedia of Astronomers* 2014, pp. 357–58.
13 For one of his silent night clocks, now in the British Museum, London (inv. no. CAI-2128), see Thompson 2004, pp. 72–73. See also Stephanie Walker in *Baroque Palaces of Rome* 1999, pp. 196–98, no. 62, for more about the Campani family's work in Rome and a bibliography about the family.
14 Bedini 1956–57, p. 422.
15 Maurice 1976, vol. 1, p. 298.
16 Probably the spa Bad Tölz, south of Munich in Bavaria. See Abeler 1977, pp. 205–6, who gives a confusing account of the clocks attributed to this maker.
17 Jones 1912, pl. LX.
18 Ibid., p. 118 and pl. LX.
19 See *Hearst Collection* 1941, p. 307 (no. 1164-3).
20 See Parke-Bernet Galleries 1946, p. 30, no. 102, ill. p. 31.

30. Pair-Case Watch

BRITISH (LONDON), CA. 1715–19
Diam. of outer case: 2 in. (5.1 cm)
Diam. of inner case: 1¾ in. (4.5 cm)
Diam. of back plate: 1⅜ in. (3.5 cm)
Gift of J. Pierpont Morgan, 1917
17.190.1503a, b

OUTER CASE, INNER CASE, AND DIAL: silver, on each case: WI maker's mark [William Jaques, British, active 1679, died 1720] and numbered *623*
MOVEMENT: gilded brass and steel, signed (on back plate): *D. Delander / London* [Daniel Delander, British, 1678–1733] and numbered *623*

DURING THE FIRST QUARTER OF THE NINETEENTH CENTURY SWISS watchmakers began using gemstones with holes drilled in them to pivot the arbors of the wheels in their clock movements that were subject to the greatest wear.[1] A pocket watch in the Metropolitan Museum's collection is engraved on the inside cover for the movement with the signature: "A Vacheron Girod"; the serial number of the watch; the type of movement; and, significantly, the number of rubies in the movement (fig. 36).[2] The name A. Vacheron Girod was used by the Geneva firm of Vacheron Constantin beginning in 1786[3] until about 1832, the year of the manufacture of this watch, indicated by the serial number.

More than a century earlier, Swiss mathematician and polymath Nicolas Fatio de Duillier (1664–1753), or Facio de Duiller, as he is often called in horological literature, had visited England where he eventually settled. Fatio traveled extensively, and his colleagues included Jean-Dominique Cassini in France, Christiaan Huygens in the Netherlands, and Isaac Newton in England, for whom he translated Continental scientific publications and with whom he pursued alchemical experiments. By 1687, Fatio was in Oxford, and on May 2, 1688, he was granted membership in the Royal Society.[4] In 1693, he introduced a watch with a spiral-spring balance made by the watchmakers Peter and Jacob Debaufre. The Debaufres are believed to have been born in France, but by 1689 Peter had been admitted as a Brother in the Clockmakers' Company in London.[5] In association with the Debaufre brothers, in May 1704 Fatio petitioned the British Parliament for a patent to drill gemstones for use as bearings (i.e., endstones) in watches and clocks. At the time, this improvement consisted of embedding a half-drilled gemstone in the brass cock of a watch or clock movement, thus providing a durable hole for pivoting the end of an oscillating balance staff of a verge escapement. The advantage of using precious stones over brass or precious metal for this purpose was the hardness of the gems.

News of the patent (number 371) alarmed members of the Clockmakers' Company, and a December 11, 1704, entry in the company's Court Minute Books records the decision of the company to petition Parliament to stop any extension of the patent.[6] This petition was vigorously pursued, apparently somewhat disingenuously, and the story of the difficulties created by the company for Fatio has been told in the early editions of F. J. Britten's *Old Clocks and Watches and Their Makers* (1911).[7] Reports of the Clockmakers' opposition to the patent, their assertion that the invention was not new, and the account of their production as evidence against the grant of an "Old Watch" with "[t]he Maker's Name Ignatius Huggeford—That had a stone fixed in the Balance" appear in a January 15, 1704, entry of the Court Minute Books. There is more to the story, but it is interesting to note that a James Delander (active 1668–ca. 1706), a

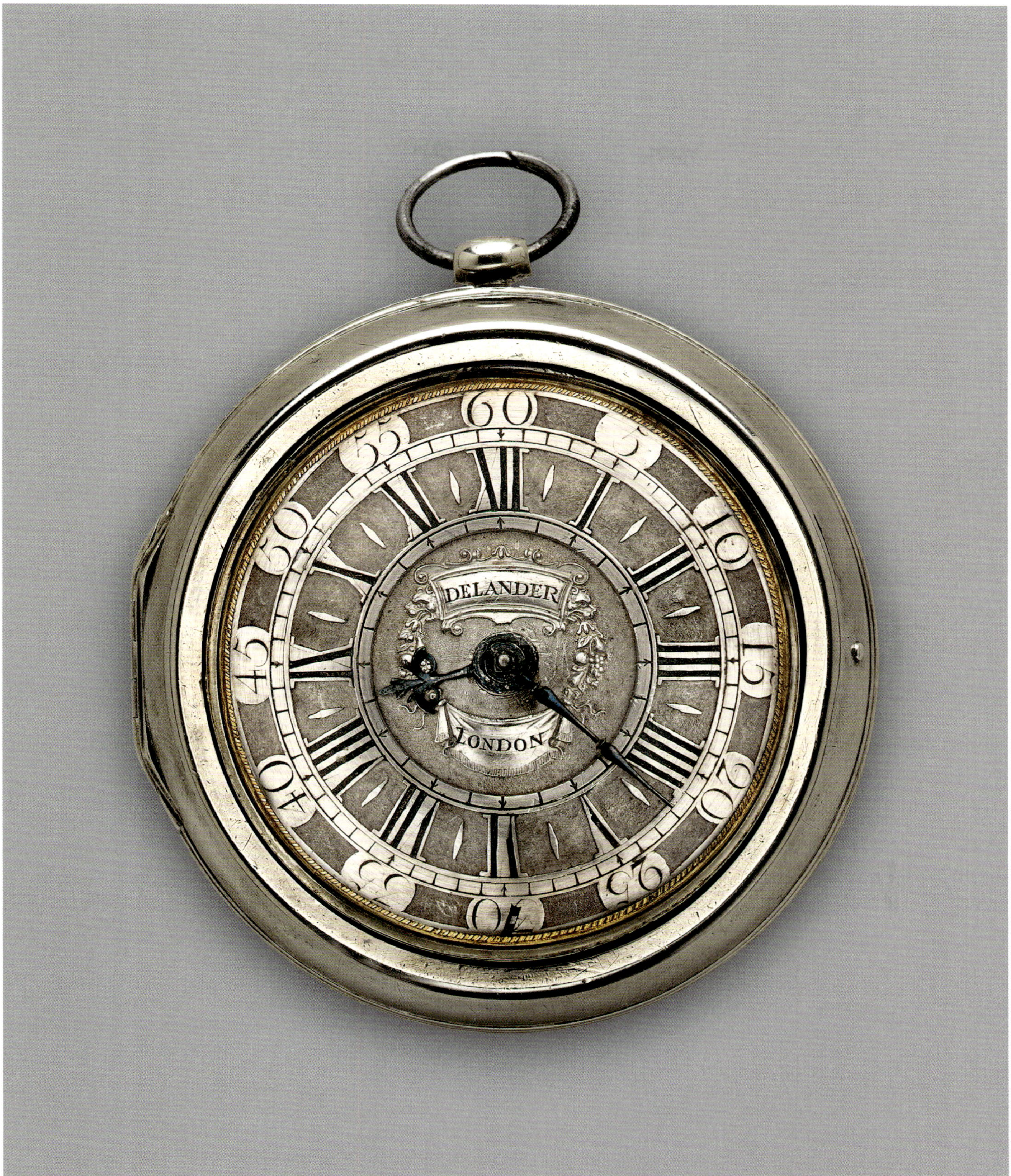
DELANDER
LONDON

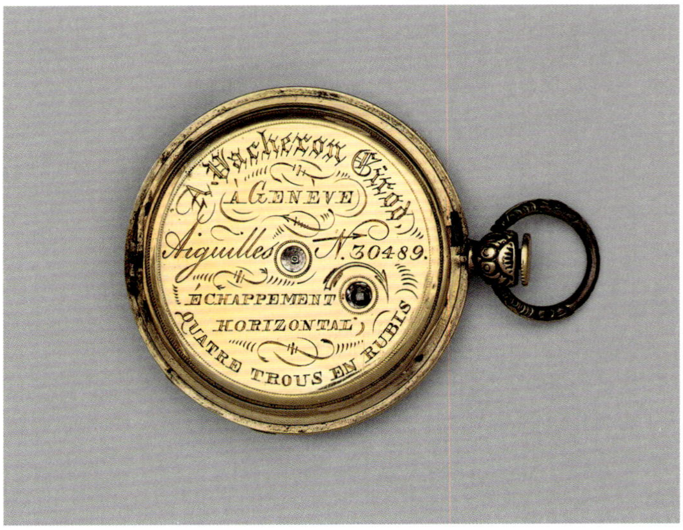

fig. 36 *Firm of Abraham Vacheron Girod later renamed Vacheron Constantin (Swiss, founded 1755). Watch, Swiss (Geneva), 1832. Enameled gold and silver, Diameter 1⁹⁄₁₆ in. (4 cm). The Metropolitan Museum of Art, New York, Anonymous Gift, in memory of Lady May Fletcher-Moulton, 1926 (26.267.18)*

London goldsmith who became a Free Brother in the Clockmakers' Company in 1669 and who was an uncle of Daniel Delander (1678–1733), was paid three guineas for this "information in opposing the Jewell Watch Bill in Parliament."[8]

It is, thus, probably not greatly surprising that a pair-case watch by Daniel Delander in the Metropolitan Museum's collection should be found to have a half-drilled diamond endstone. The watch can be dated with certainty before 1720, but many English watchmakers continued to use jeweled endstones throughout the eighteenth century, or about a hundred years before they were in general use by Swiss watchmakers.

The movement of the Museum's Delander watch consists of two circular plates held apart by four openwork, V-shaped pillars fashioned into a distinctive design that has been attributed to Delander. It contains a three-wheel train that is driven by a mainspring and fusee and regulated by a verge escapement with a balance spring. The most prominent feature of the watch is a large pierced and engraved balance cock screwed to the back plate. A pink diamond endstone with a tiny hole drilled halfway through is embedded in a silver frame held in place on the balance cock's table by three screws, the diamond pivots the balance staff of the watch. Engraved in script above the balance cock is the signature, "D. Delander," together with the serial number, 623, and the place of origin, London. Below, there is a silver figure plate for the adjustment of the balance spring. The winding square for the mainspring projects through the lower left of the back plate and can be accessed through a hole in the back of the inner case.

The champlevé silver dial has a chapter ring with concentric calibrations indicated for the hours (I–XII), half hours (diamond-shaped marks), and minutes (5–60, by fives, with single minutes marked by lines). The so-called beetle and poker hands are finely sculpted of blued steel. Their arbor divides a cartouche in the center of the dial that is signed, "DELANDER / LONDON."

The outer case and inner cases are made of plain silver, and both are stamped on their interiors with the serial number 623 and the initials "WI," partly effaced, but without question the maker's mark of William Jaques (active 1679, died 1720). Jaques was a specialist watchcasemaker who served part of his apprenticeship under Nathaniel Delander (1648–ca. 1691), the maker of the cases for three of the Thomas Tompion watches in the Museum's collection.[9] Jaques has been studied in some detail by historian J. A. Neale, who states that he began his apprenticeship with John Wright Sr. on December 1, 1679, before being turned over to Delander for the remainder of his training, that he became free of the Clockmakers' Company on September 29, 1687, and that his burial in London's Saint Sepulchre Holborn Church was recorded on January 24, 1719 (actually 1720 in the new calendar). An inventory made at the time of Jaques's death, and which was discovered by Jeremy L. Evans and quoted extensively by Neale, provides a great deal of information about the successful and prosperous London craftsman in the early eighteenth century.[10] While describing one of Jaques's more elaborately ornamented cases for a watch by Joseph Windmills (active 1671–ca. 1720) now in the British Museum, London, Neale noted that "many of Jaques's silver and some of his gold cases are plain. There is not much more to be said of these than that they are generally robust, well hinged, split bezelled—much as might be expected."[11] His description aptly fits the Metropolitan Museum's watchcase.

There is a small but deep dent in the bezel of the cover of the outer case near the pendant. There are signs of ordinary wear, especially on the outside of the inner case. The movement is in excellent condition. The watch entered the Museum's collection in 1917 as part of the gift of J. Pierpont Morgan, who acquired it from the British banker Frederick George Hilton Price.[12] CV / JHL

1 Jaquet and Chapuis 1970, p. 74; Cardinal 1989, p. 64.
2 Acc. no. 26.267.18.
3 See entry 51 in this volume, and Patrizzi 1998, pp. 386–89. See also Gibertini 1964, p. 244; *Treasures of Vacheron Constantin* 2011, p. 34.
4 Mandelbrote 2004.
5 Loomes 1981, p. 188.
6 Clockmakers' Company, London, Court Minute Books, Ms. 2710/3, 1699–1729, p. 55v, Guildhall Library, London.
7 See, for example, Britten 1911, pp. 587–88.
8 Clockmakers' Company, Court Minute Books, Ms. 2710/3, p. 56r.
9 Acc. no. 17.190.1487a, b; see also entries 23 and 24 in this volume. The authors are indebted to Jeremy L. Evans, formerly of the British Museum, London, for providing the birth date of Nathaniel Delander.
10 See Neale 1992.
11 Ibid., p. 346.
12 Williamson 1912, pp. 162–63, no. 173.

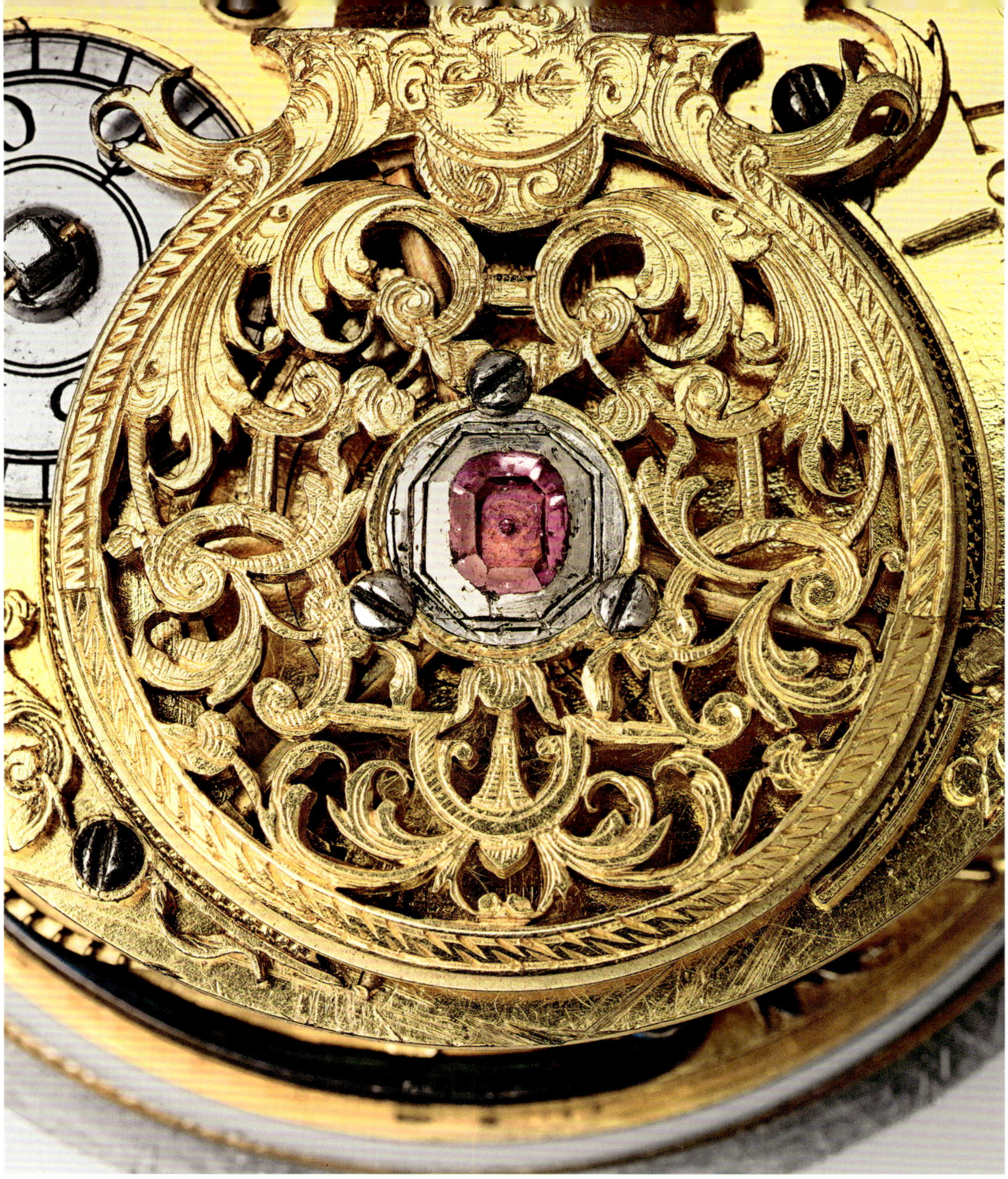

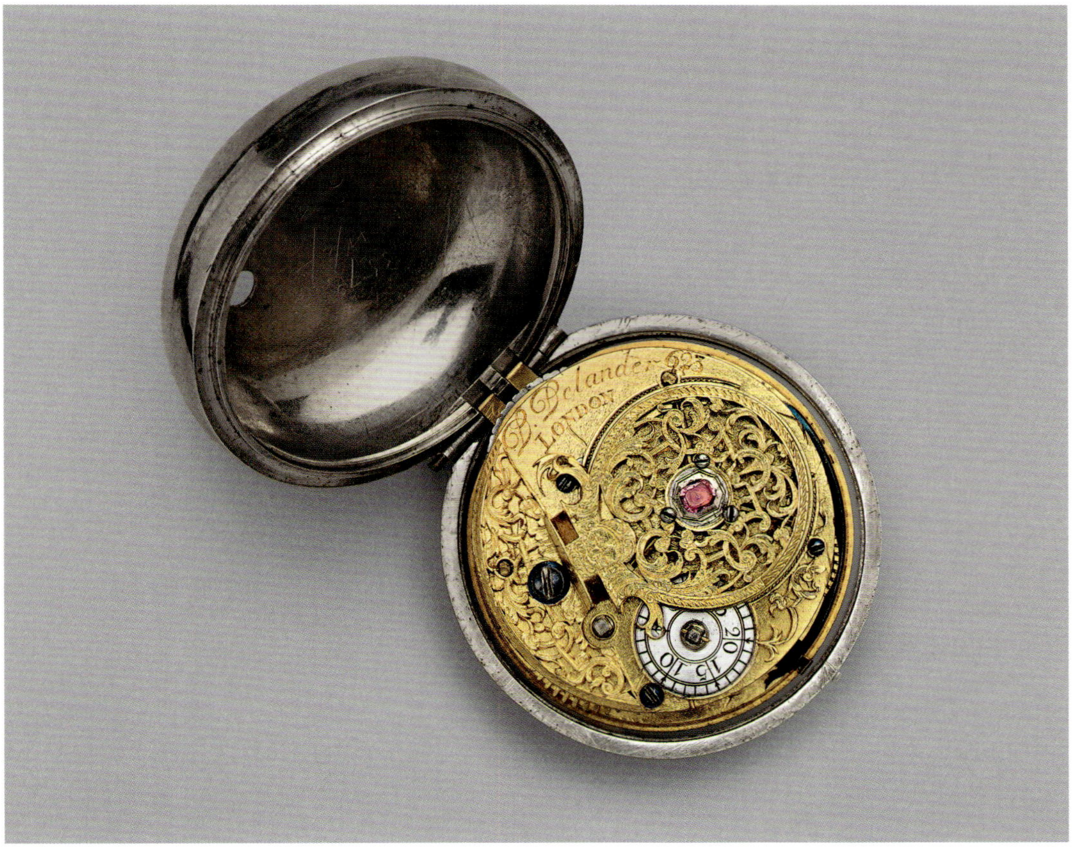

top: *Detail of the table of the balance cock with the half-drilled diamond endstone*
bottom: *View of the open watch to show the back plate*

31. Longcase Clock with Calendar

BRITISH (LONDON), PROBABLY CA. 1720
90⅜ × 17¾ × 9½ in. (229.6 × 45.1 × 24.1 cm)
Width of dial plate: 9¾ in. (24.8 cm)
Gift of Irwin Untermyer, 1964
64.101.864

CASE: oak veneered with burl walnut and walnut-herringbone inlay
DIAL: gilded and silvered brass, signed: *D. Delander / London / no. 13* [Daniel Delander, British, 1678–1733]
MOVEMENT: gilded brass and steel

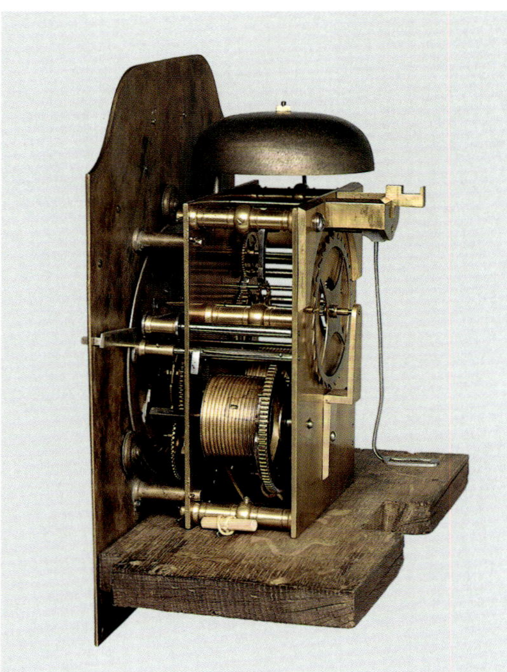

Movement showing the going train

IMPROVEMENTS TO THE TECHNOLOGY OF SECONDS-BEATING pendulum clocks by the English continued throughout the late seventeenth and early eighteenth centuries. The anchor escapement, probably the invention of Joseph Knibb about 1668–69,[1] was followed in 1676 by the rack-and-snail mechanism by Edward Barlow (1638–1719), whereby the striking of a clock was directly tied to the position of the hour hand that could be manipulated directly. Although the new mechanism no longer needed the more laborious adjustments to the striking required by a count wheel, several problems remained to be solved, including the effect of temperature changes on the pendulum. A few years before 1726 George Graham (1673–1751), Thomas Tompion's (1639–1713) former partner and successor to the firm, began experimenting with a pendulum ending in a cylinder of mercury that replaced the familiar brass-covered bob. Graham's publication of the invention appeared in the *Philosophical Transactions* of the Royal Society (1726–27).[2] A few years later John Harrison (1693–1776), better known for his invention of the marine chronometer, introduced his bimetallic gridiron pendulum. Although he probably devised it as early as 1732, John Ellicott (1706–1792) did not publish his compensation pendulum until 1753.[3] Ellicott's pendulum, however, was never as widely adopted by clockmakers as the first two.

Another problem in making the English longcase clock the remarkably accurate timekeeper it became was caused by the slight recoil of the early anchors of the escapement as they rocked back and forth, alternately giving impulse to and locking the escape wheel. Graham is usually credited with the invention of about 1730 of the recoilless, or dead-beat, escapement. There is evidence, however, that there had been attempts to overcome the problem as far back as Tompion's escapements of 1675 for the year-going clocks he made for the Royal Observatory in Greenwich (see entry 28 in this volume). Tompion's original escapements were apparently not successful, and they were soon replaced by Richard Towneley's, but these were subsequently modified by Tompion.[4] Nevertheless, the improved escapement for long pendulum clocks was not settled until Graham's time.

There is some evidence that other forms of recoilless escapements were being made.[5] One of them was the duplex, a device using two escape wheels that cut the amount of recoil in half. Escapements using the duplex principle, but in different configurations, were still being published as late as 1741, notably by Antoine Thiout l'aîné (1694–1767), whose technical treatise on horology (fig. 9) included, along with an example of the Graham dead-beat, a duplex escapement invented by the French clockmaker Jean-Baptiste Dutertre (1684–1734).[6] The duplex in the Metropolitan Museum's clock is usually called the

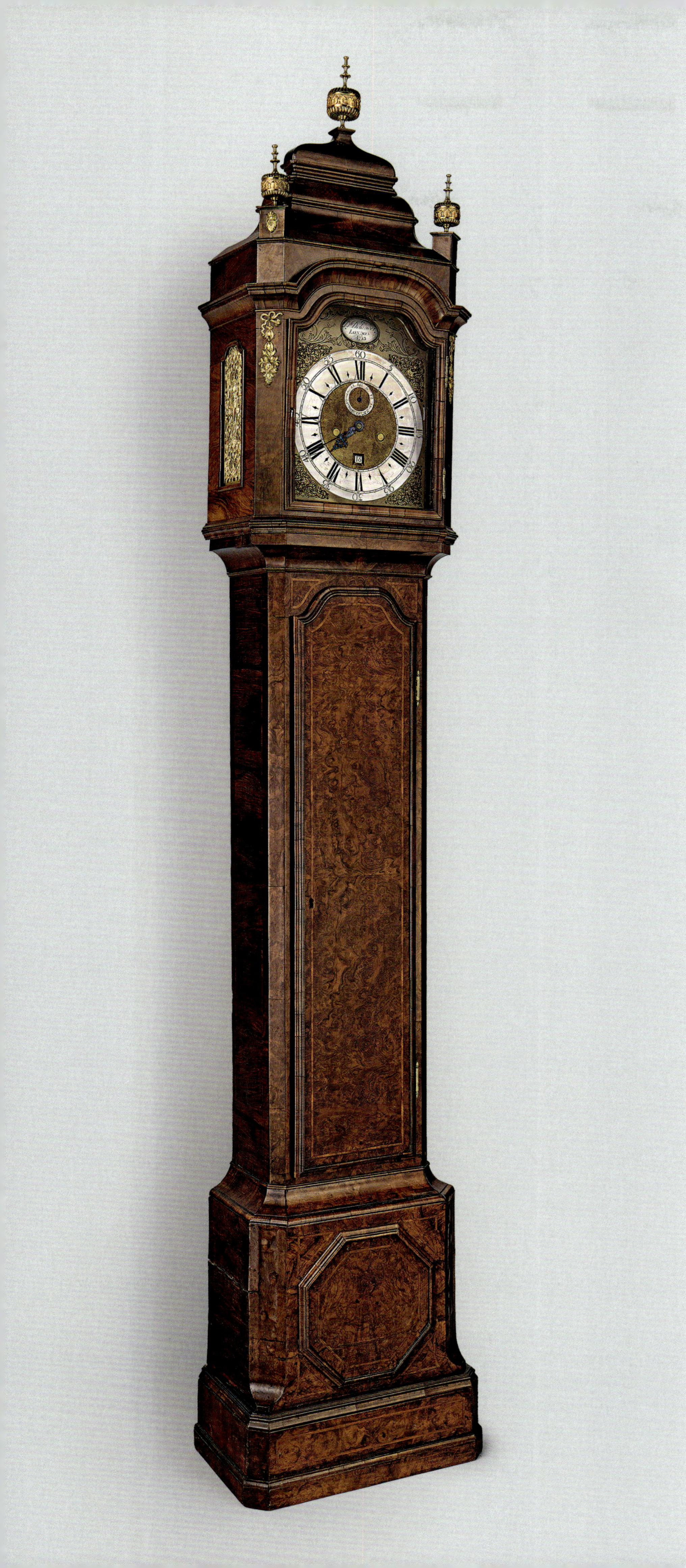

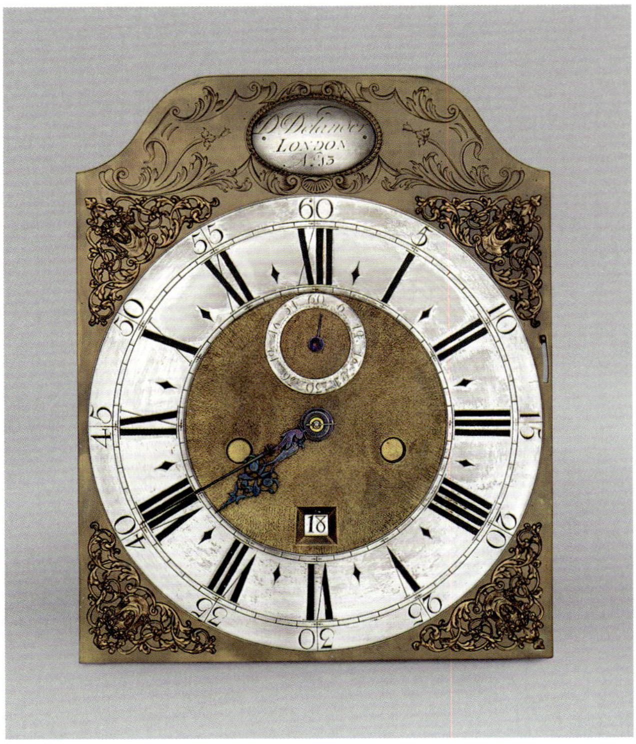

Dial plate with chapter ring

Delander duplex after its probable inventor, Daniel Delander (1678–1733).[7] Delander, the son of Nathaniel Delander, the maker of some of Tompion's most beautiful watchcases, was baptized at Saint Sepulchre, Holborn, in 1678.[8] His apprenticeship to the clockmaker Charles Halstead is recorded in April 1692 in the Clockmakers' Company Court Minute Books.[9] His admission to the company as a Freeman in July 1679 described him as still an apprentice of Halstead's,[10] but by July 1695, he had been turned over from Halstead to Tompion, for whom he apparently continued to work until setting up his own shop at The Dial in Deveraux Court about 1706.[11]

The Metropolitan Museum's longcase clock, numbered 13, belongs to a small group of clocks with numbers on their dials that apparently fall outside of Delander's regular production. Not all of the group can now be found, but number 18 is the highest numbered example recorded. The group is difficult to date. Delander apparently remained in close touch with Tompion's successor, Graham, however, and it seems likely that Delander's duplex predated Graham's deadbeat, which was capable of greater accuracy but required more precision in its construction. If Delander's escapement is earlier than Graham's, it is probably not by very much.

The eight-day, weight-driven movement of the Museum's clock consists of two rectangular plates, which are made of unusually thick brass and held apart by five turned pillars. A going train of three wheels and two separate escape wheels (a small wheel inside the movement for transmitting the impulse and a large one outside the back plate for locking) are mounted on a single arbor. The escape wheels are controlled by two pallets that are separately attached to the arbor of the pendulum crutch. Thus, the impulse is provided by only one pallet per excursion of the pendulum instead of two, which cuts the number of periods of recoil in half.

The striking train consists of four wheels and a fly. It is controlled by a rack-and-snail device with the rack mounted inside the front plate and the snail on the exterior of the plate. It strikes the hours on a bell that is mounted on the front plate.

The flat arched dial is of gilded brass. It has a wide, silvered-brass chapter ring for the hours (I–XII); for the minutes (5–60, by fives); and for the half hours, marked by diamonds. At the twelve o'clock position there is a silvered-brass chapter ring for seconds that reflects the period of the pendulum's excursion (6–60, by sixes) and at the six o'clock position an aperture for display of the day of the month. The center of the dial has a matte finish, and the spandrels are filled with human masks sporting bibs and surrounded by foliate ornament. The sculptured hour and minute hands are made of blued steel, and on the right side of the dial, located between the two and three o'clock positions, is a slot to accommodate the lever for connecting the clock's maintaining power.

The case is made of burl walnut veneered on oak. Applied wooden moldings outline the skirt, the hexagon on the plinth, and the door of the trunk. The inlays of herringbone-patterned walnut repeat the pattern on the plinth and trunk. The plinth, trunk, and hood have chamfered corners, and the flat arched motif of the dial is repeated on the door to the trunk, the door to the dial, and the molding above the dial. This design is extremely rare in English clockcases of the first quarter of the eighteenth century.

The forward-sliding hood has a hinged, glazed door with a lock. Applied gilded-brass ornaments of flowers and fruit are suspended from ribbon bows that adorn the chamfered surfaces and flank the door to the dial. Pierced and gilded-brass ornaments fill the openings in the sides of the hood. These ornaments consist of central term figures, which are flanked by seated infants and foliate ornaments punctuated by vases and masks, and backed by fabric, permitting the sound of the bell to escape the hood. The crest has three tiers at present: a platform supporting two pedestals with gilded

fig. 37 *Diagram of the Daniel Delander duplex escapement from Tom Robinson,* The Longcase Clock *(Woodbridge, Suffolk, 1981), p. 161*

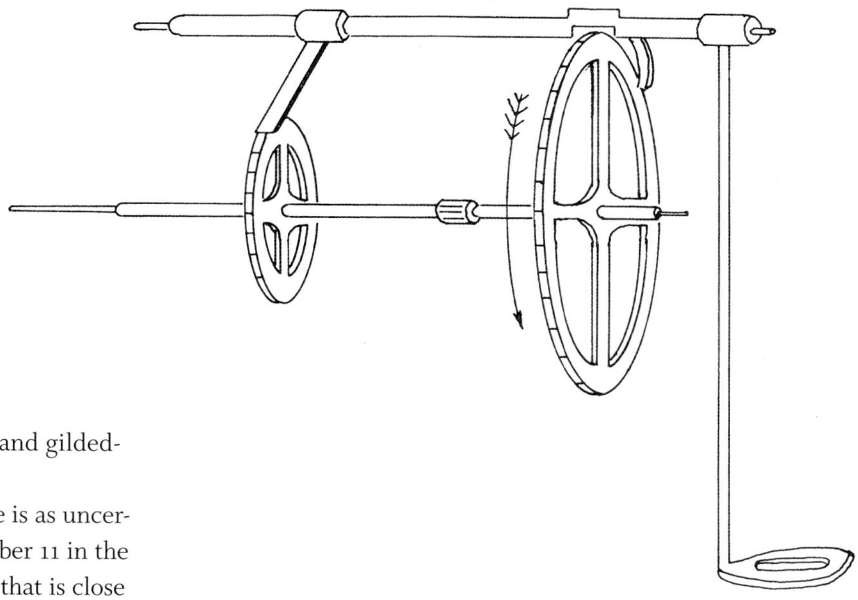

metal finials, an inverted bell top, and a pedestal and gilded-metal finial atop a domelike element.

The maker of the case is unknown, and its date is as uncertain as it is for the movement. Delander clock number 11 in the series with duplex escapements is housed in a case that is close in style to clocks with conventional escapements usually dated to the early eighteenth century.[12] Number 13 and number 17, as historian Percy Dawson has pointed out, have the distinct features found on the case of a clock by John Ellicott (1706–1792) probably not made before 1730.[13] Ellicott continued to use this design for clockcases that incorporated his compensated pendulums. But Dawson's conclusion that the Delander cases should be dated about 1730 seems too late if the correlation of Delander's experimental escapement with Graham's more successful dead-beat escapement of about 1720 is correct.

Inscriptions inside the movement of the Museum's clock indicate that it was repaired in 1840 and 1885. At some point, the functioning of the escapement was misunderstood, and the pallets were positioned in such a way that the arc of the swinging pendulum was wider than the trunk of the case. Openings were made in the sides of the trunk to accommodate the arc, and these were fitted with earlike wooden attachments. These additions are visible in an illustration of the clock published in 1937, when it was on loan to the Virginia Museum of Fine Arts, Richmond.[14] They were still evident in the 1948 sale catalogue for the collection of the clock's owner.[15] At some point, the two additions were removed by someone who apparently did not understand why they had been added. It remained for the Museum's conservator of clocks in the early 1970s to reposition the pallets of the escapement so that the pendulum could swing without hitting the trunk and stopping the clock.

The three finials and the extra dome atop the hood were in place in 1937, as the Virginia catalogue documents. It is not certain when they were added to the hood and not entirely certain what they replaced. Small losses to the wooden moldings and a missing gilded-metal ornament have been replaced by the Museum's conservators.

Henry P. Strause of Washington, D.C., placed his collection of clocks on loan to the Virginia Museum of Fine Arts in 1936.[16] The collection remained on view there until it was sold in 1948.[17] The clock was bought at the 1948 sale by Irwin Untermyer,[18] the donor to the Metropolitan Museum. CV / JHL

1 See entry 21 in this volume.
2 Graham 1726–27, p. 40.
3 Ellicott 1751–52. Like Graham, Ellicott was one of the very few clockmakers who were members of the Royal Society. For a summary of Ellicott's paper, with commentary on the Graham and Harrison inventions, see Baillie 1978, pp. 233–35. See also Foulkes 1960; Robinson 1981, pp. 387–89.
4 Howse 1970–71, pp. 22–24. See also J. L. Evans 2006, pp. 22–23.
5 Robinson 1981, pp. 45–46.
6 Thiout 1741, vol. 1, pp. 101–2, and pl. 41, figs. 15, 16.
7 See, for example, Robinson 1981, pp. 161–62.
8 The authors are indebted to Jeremy L. Evans, formerly of the British Museum, London, for the date and place of Delander's baptism as well as evidence of his relationship to Nathaniel Delander.
9 Clockmakers' Company, London, Court Minute Books, Ms. 2710/2, 1680–99, p. 126v, Guildhall Library, London.
10 Ibid., p. 230r.
11 The authors are indebted to Jeremy L. Evans for sharing evidence of the change of apprenticeship.
12 Phillips 1998, p. 64, no. 333, ill.
13 Dawson 1987.
14 Virginia Museum of Fine Arts 1937, p. 35, no. C-33, and pl. VII.
15 Parke-Bernet Galleries 1948, p. 62, no. 241, ill. p. 63.
16 Virginia Museum of Fine Arts 1937.
17 Parke-Bernet Galleries 1948.
18 Hackenbroch 1958, p. 7, and pl. 6, fig. 9.

32. Table or Bracket Clock with Calendar

BRITISH (LONDON), PROBABLY CA. 1720

22¼ × 14½ × 8¼ in.

Bequest of Irwin Untermyer, 1973

1974.28.94

CASE: walnut, oak veneered with walnut and burl walnut; stained wooden moldings; and brass fittings

DIAL: gilded and silvered brass, signed: *Dan Delander /* LONDON [Daniel Delander, British, 1678–1733]

MOVEMENT: brass and steel, signed (on back plate): *Dan Delander /* LONDON

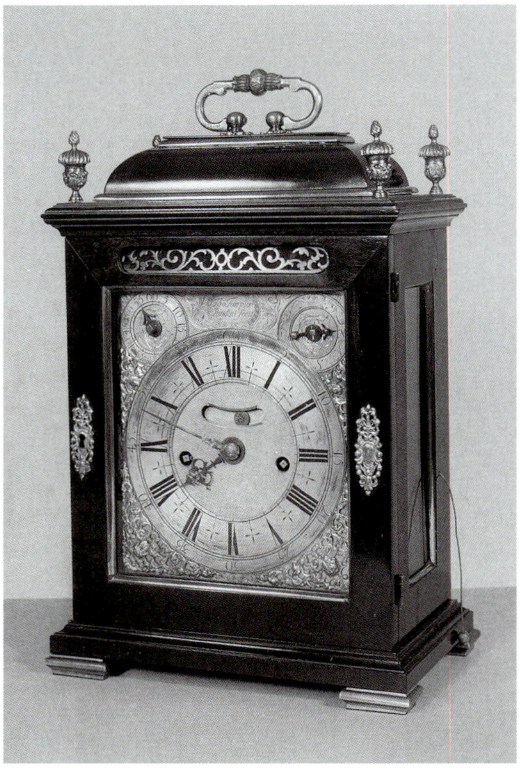

fig. 38 *Thomas Tompion (British, 1639–1713), Table Clock. British (London), ca. 1696. Case: ebony veneered on oak with gilded and silvered brass fittings. Movement: brass and steel. Height 16¼ × 10½ × 6¾ in. (41.3 × 26.7 × 17.2 cm). The Metropolitan Museum of Art, New York, Gift of Irwin Untermyer 1964 (64.101.867)*

THE DEVELOPMENT OF LONGCASE CLOCKS BY ENGLISH CLOCKMAKERS during the last quarter of the seventeenth century by no means discouraged them from producing spring-driven table clocks in wooden cases. These table clocks had short pendulums, most had verge escapements, and they did not require as careful leveling as longcase clocks. Above all, table clocks were portable and easily moved to wherever they might be needed. Many of these clocks also had the advantage of telling time at night in an era when lighting a candle in darkness could be difficult. One invention for this purpose was the dial with revolving openwork numerals, which were illuminated from behind by a candle. The pull-repeater, however, an application of a device invented by Edward Barlow (1638–1719) in 1676, was more practical. The repeating mechanism allowed the clock to strike the previous hour on a bell when a string that was attached to the device was pulled. Quarter repeaters, which required two separate bells, permitted the striking of the quarters as well as the previous hours when the string was pulled. Several other types of hour and quarter-hour striking mechanisms can also be found in English table clocks.[1] Among the seventeenth-century English table clocks in the Metropolitan Museum's collection is one by Thomas Tompion (1639–1713) that incorporates the more expensive string-pulled quarter-repeating mechanism in its movement (fig. 38).[2]

An account from 1710 for payment for "a shelf for my repeater"[3] explains the better-known name for these clocks: bracket clocks. These clocks could be placed on a shelf on a wall, but equally on a table or a desk. Their origin is traceable to the spring-driven, wooden-cased architectural clocks from the 1660s, but they soon began to develop a style of their own. During the course of the last quarter of the seventeenth century, domes were added to the top of their cases. Eventually, some domes were more elaborately shaped into forms that resembled bells, and sometimes they were made of openwork metal, when they were known as basket tops.[4]

About 1715, the square or rectangular dial plate began to give way to an arch or a break arch at the top of the plate, which allowed for a more comfortable accommodation of extra functions, such as calendars, dials for silencing the striking, and regulation of the pendulum. About twenty-five years earlier, a slot in the dial plate was introduced to reveal a small brass image connected to the pendulum, the motion of which it would mimic. Not only did it indicate at a glance whether the clock was running, but it also provided a way of starting the pendulum without turning the clock around.

At a little more than twenty-two inches in height, the Museum's clock by Delander is both taller and wider than the great majority of table clocks of the last quarter of the seventeenth century. It is even

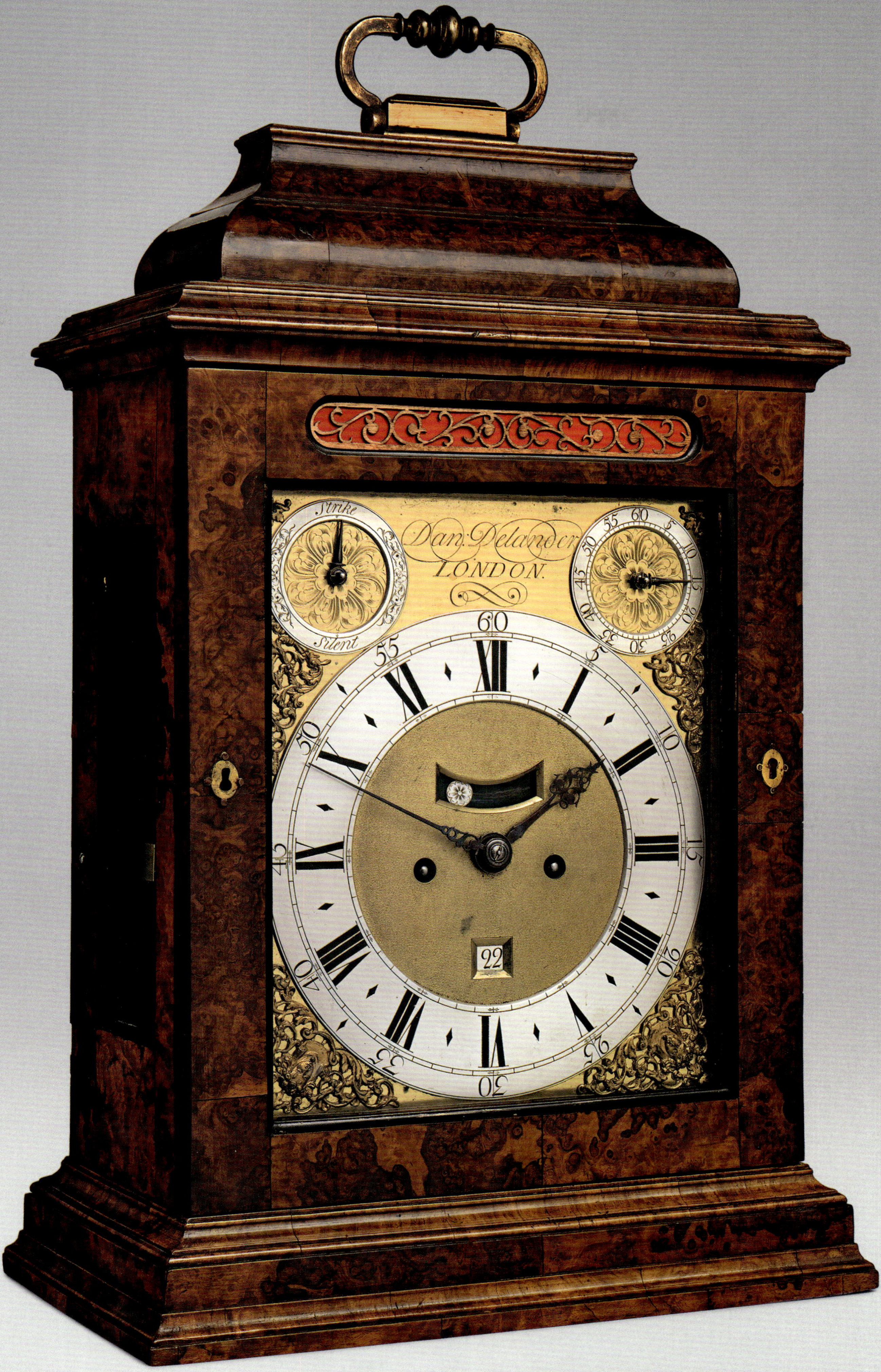
Strike
Silent
Dan: Delander
LONDON

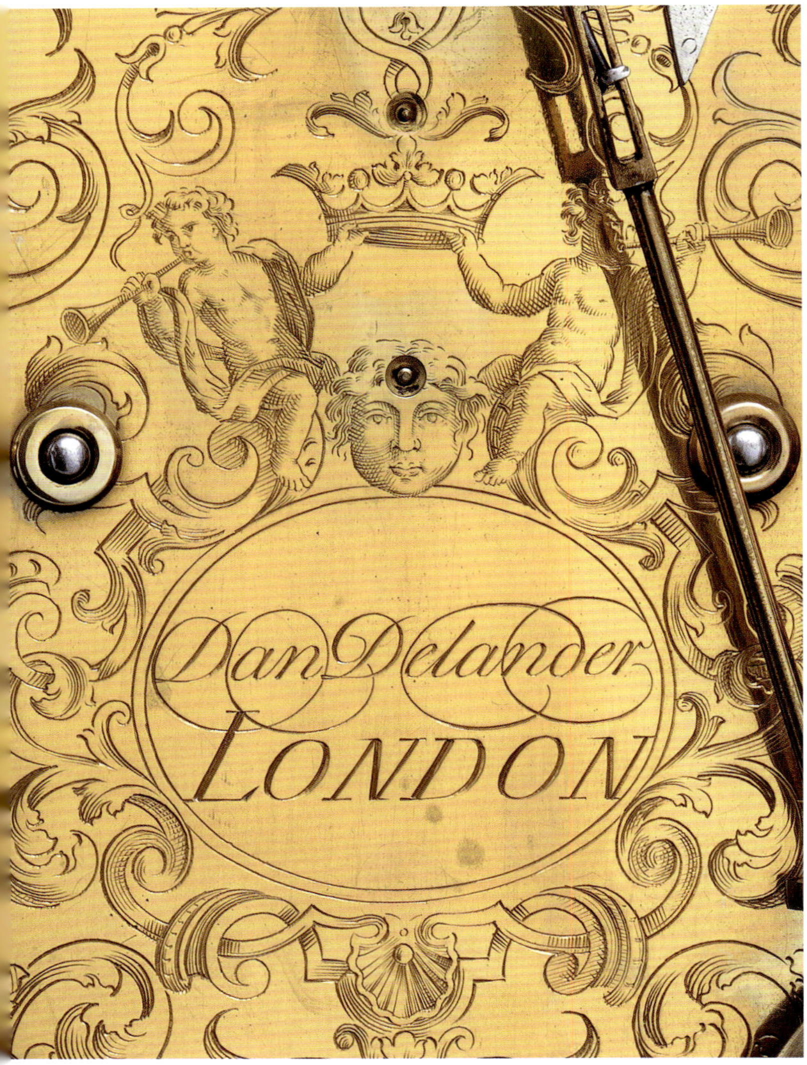
Dan Delander
LONDON

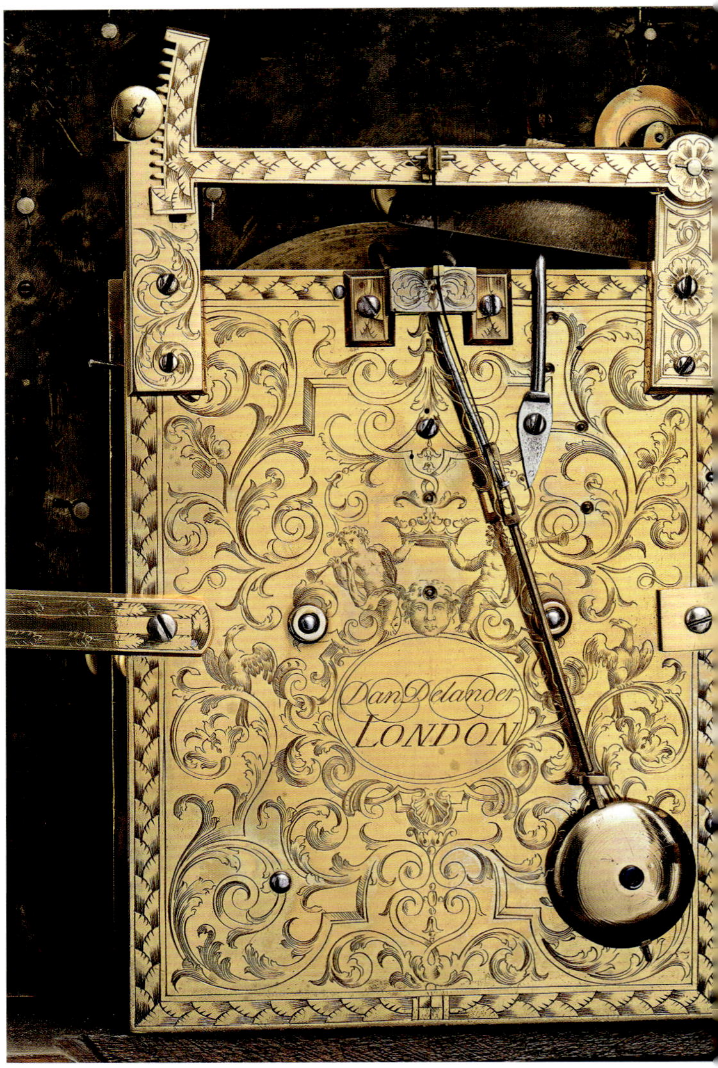
Dan Delander
LONDON

larger than most of the table clocks of the early eighteenth century, ordinarily recognized as being taller than earlier examples, which were approximately one foot in height. The case of the Museum's clock is essentially a rectangular wooden box with a framed glass door to the dial, another framed glass door in the back, and glass panels on the sides. The case rests on a molded wooden skirt and is fitted with an oak seat board inside. At the top, the clock is bordered on all four sides by a profile molding that is also veneered with matching burl walnut and supports an inverted bell top with a sturdy bail handle of brass. Two simple brass keyhole escutcheons ornament the hinged door to the dial: the escutcheon on the left is functional; the other is blind. A slot cut in the top of the door to the dial contains a delicately cut-out wooden fret backed with red silk that completes the relatively severe design of the case. The shape of the slot repeats that of one in the frame of the case that allows the sound of the bell to escape.

For all of its greater height, however, the door to the dial plate and the dial plate remain rectangular rather than arched at the top, as fashion in the new century increasingly demanded. The dial plate is of gilded brass with a matte center and a silvered-brass chapter ring for hours (I–XII), with lozenges marking the half hours, and an outer circle with minutes (5–60, by fives), each minute division marked by an engraved line, and each half-quarter hour marked by a lozenge. An aperture above the arbor for the hands displays the false pendulum, and another above the six o'clock position displays the day of the month. Above, on the left, is the hand for silencing or activating the striking train. The hand is encircled by an engraved ring of silvered brass marked "strike" and "silent." It is balanced on the right by another ring with a similar hand (marked 5–60, by fives), this one for the so-called rise-and-fall device for adjusting the length of the clock's pendulum. Between the two rings, the signature, "Dan Delander / LONDON" is engraved, and below are applied foliate scrolls, variants of the ornament that flanks the human masks in the spandrels below. The hour and minute hands are pierced and finely sculptured steel.

The eight-day, spring-driven movement consists of two rectangular brass plates, which are held apart by five turned pillars; a going train of three wheels; and a horizontal verge escapement controlled by a pendulum approximately nine and one-half inches long with spring suspension and a circular brass bob. Its length can be adjusted by moving the brass bar mounted at the top of the back plate. The striking train consists of four wheels and a fly. The hours, controlled by a rack-and-snail mechanism, are struck on a single bell mounted on the back plate. The clock was not provided with a repeating mechanism, although the "strike-silent" feature would have allowed convenient use of the clock in a bedroom, where unrestricted striking of the night hours would be an annoyance at the very least.

The back plate, visible through the glass door at the back of the clock, is a riot of engraved decoration that is typical until far into the eighteenth century. A cartouche placed a little below the midpoint of the plate displays the engraved signature, "Dan Delander / LONDON." Above the cartouche is the head of an infant and a coronet held aloft by two trumpet-blowing genies who are surrounded by leafy scrolls upon which two birds are perched. The edges of the plate are engraved with a trellis-like pattern that repeats on the surface of the rise-and-fall bar for the adjustment of the pendulum. The pattern appears again on the left bar for securing the movement to the case that is screwed at one end to the back plate and at the other end to the side of the case. The bar at the right is undecorated.

The right bar is undoubtedly a well-made replacement. The dial foot at the five o'clock position is broken near its end, and the escape wheel has been replaced. On the case, a piece of veneer is missing on the lower left side, and the end of the fretwork design at the right is a replacement. The veneer has undergone some shrinkage and cracking but retains its rich coloring that softens the severity of the design of the case.

The donor, Irwin Untermyer, acquired the clock in 1971 in London, where it was described as the "property of a lady of title."[5] Nothing further is known of its provenance. CV / JHL

1 These have been described in greater detail in Allix 1993.
2 Acc. no. 64.101.867.
3 Quoted in Barder 1993, p. 18.
4 For the progression of styles, see Cescinsky and M. R. Webster 1969, pp. 249–58; Barder 1993, pp. 24–72.
5 Christie's 1971, p. 14, no. 18, ill.

left: *Detail of back plate of clock with signature*
right: *Back plate*

33. Pair-Case Watch with Repeating Mechanism

BRITISH (LONDON), 1719–20
Diam. of case: $2\frac{3}{16}$ in. (5.6 cm)
Diam. of back plate: $1\frac{5}{16}$ in. (3.3 cm)
Gift of Captain Newton H. White Jr., U.S.N., 1952
52.62a–d

OUTER CASE: gold, marked: "WS" [William Sherwood Sr., British, active 1695–1740]; lion passant and leopard's head [London goldsmiths' marks]; and letter E [date letter for 1720]; numbered *467* [serial number for repeating watches by watchmaker George Graham; see below]
INNER CASE: gold, marked: WS, lion passant, leopard's head, letter D [date letter for 1719], and number *467*
DIAL: champlevé gold, signed: *Graham / London* [George Graham, British, 1673–1751]
MOVEMENT: gilded brass and partly blued steel, signed (on back plate): *Geo Graham / London 467*

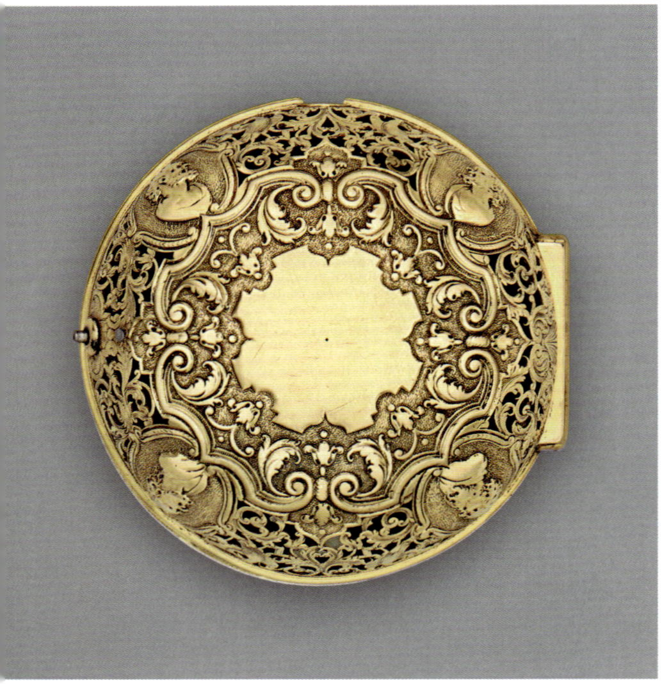

Exterior of the back of the outer case

ALTHOUGH STILL OFFICIALLY APPRENTICED TO THE LONDON clockmaker Henry Aske (active 1670–94), George Graham (1673–1751) began to work for Thomas Tompion (1639–1713) about 1696. In 1704, he married Tompion's niece Elizabeth; in 1711, he became Tompion's partner; and in 1713, he succeeded Tompion at The Dial and Three Crowns at number 67, Fleet Street.[1] In 1721, he became one of the rare clockmakers to be elected a fellow of the Royal Society.[2] Graham's most notable contributions to the technology of horology were the dead-beat, a recoilless escapement for clocks; the mercury pendulum that compensated for changes in temperature; and, for watches, the cylinder escapement, a recoilless escapement he perfected from the experimental virgule, or "tenterhook" escapement, that Tompion had introduced briefly in 1693.[3] The cylinder escapement replaced the verge escapement in all of Graham's watches after 1725 or 1726,[4] and it was widely adopted by other watchmakers. In 1755, the French treatise on clock and watchmaking by Jean-André Lepaute (1720–1789) could state that Graham's was the recoilless escapement most often employed for watches.[5]

The Graham watch in the Museum's collection has a verge escapement, and the London hallmarked gold outer and inner cases allow certainty in dating the watch to 1719 for the inner case (or box) and a year later for the repoussé-ornamented outer case. Graham continued Tompion's practice of giving serial numbers to his watches, and like Tompion, he separated ordinary watches from watches with repeating mechanisms, and gave each category its own series of numbers.[6] Thus, the number 467 on the Museum's watch identifies it as a repeating watch in a series begun by Tompion as early as 1692 and continued throughout both his and Graham's working life. Historian Jeremy L. Evans has noted that number 562 would have been the last Graham repeater with a verge escapement.[7]

The repeating mechanism was an English invention, but not one of Graham's. It is a device that allows the user to know the time without looking at the dial. The Museum's example, a quarter repeater, uses the long stem of the pendant as a plunger to cause the watch to strike the preceding hour followed by the preceding quarter hour on a bell attached to the inside of the inner case of the watch. Repeating watches exist for half-quarter hours, for five-minute periods, and even for minutes, and before the age of instant illumination, these watches were remarkably useful for telling time at night.

For a watch the repeating mechanism is a descendant of a device invented for clocks in 1676 by Edward Barlow (1638–1719). In 1685, Tompion made a repeating watch for Barlow, but when Barlow applied for a patent, he was opposed by Daniel Quare (1647/49–1724), whose own version of the mechanism not only won in a contest of the two

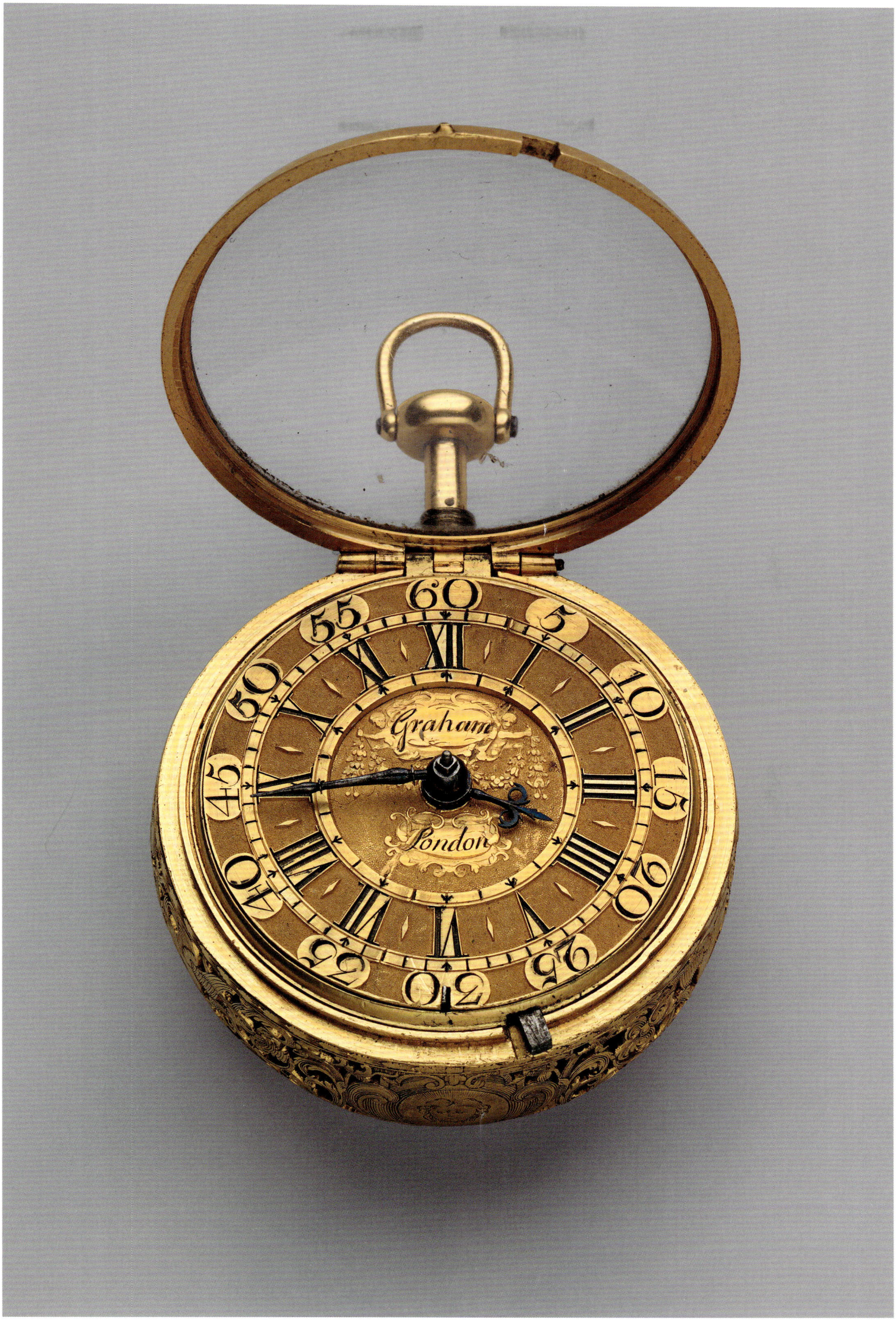
Graham
London

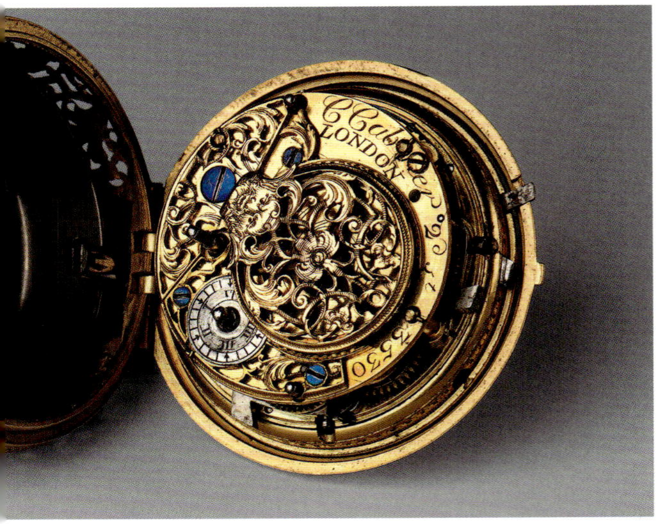

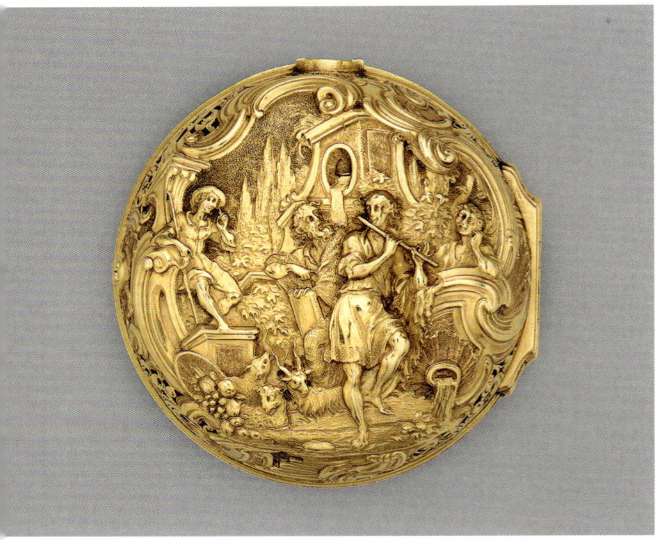

fig. 39 *Pair-Case Watch, British (London), 1741–42. Top: movement by Charles Cabrier II (British, 1719–1765); bottom: outercase by Frederick Wieland (British, active ca. 1731–after 1759), repoussé gold, Diameter 1⅞ in. (4.8 cm). The Metropolitan Museum of Art, New York, The Collection of Giovanni P. Morosini, presented by his daughter Giulia, 1932 (32.75.37a, b)*

devices that was held before the English king in 1687, but also ended Barlow's hopes for a patent. Horologist David Thompson's account of the contest appears in his discussion of a watch that may, in fact, be the actual watch entered by Quare in the contest.[8] The Metropolitan Museum's watch has a further refinement: a "pulse piece" between the five and six o'clock positions. On the side of the outer case it is hardly noticeable, but when pressed, it lifts the hammers so that they do not strike the bell, but instead create vibrations that can be felt, but not heard, whenever discretion is desired.

The movement of the watch consists of two circular gilded-brass held apart by four (?) pillars, and it contains a going train of three wheels ending in a verge escapement with a balance spring and repeating work. The back plate carries an openwork scrolled balance cock with a diamond end-stone in the table, a human mask at the neck, and a solid but engraved foot screwed to the back plate. Next to the balance is a silver figure plate for regulation of the hairspring, as well as the engraved signature, "Geo Graham / London" and the serial number 467.

The dial is laid out in a classic champlevé design, with the roman numerals I–XII in black enamel, the half hours marked by lozenges, and an outer ring of minutes (5–60, by fives), each minute marked by an engraved stroke. The concentric circles of the chapters are polished gold, and the ovals surrounding the numerals are of fine matte gold. The center has two cartouches: the top displays the name of the watchmaker, and the bottom displays the place, London. The beetle and poker hands are blued steel.

The inner case has a band with a cartouche framing a human mask and pierced foliage inhabited by four angry birds. The gold bezel for the glass cover of the inner case is hinged to the case at the nine o'clock position. The outer case is finely embossed and chased with four medallions, which enclose busts of bearded men who punctuate the openwork foliate motifs that allow the sound of the bell of the repeating mechanism to escape. The center, framed by bell flowers, foliage, and heavy baroque scrolls, is left plain, perhaps intended for a monogram if one was desired by the patron. The bezel for the outer case continues the embossed openwork design between two heavy, circular, profile moldings, but here it is divided by baskets of flowers and a shell motif at the hinge.

Both cases are signed with the initials "WS" for William Sherwood Sr. (active 1695–1740) known to have been a preferred casemaker for Graham, as well as Tompion and Quare.[9] Sherwood was one of the forerunners of a group of London goldsmiths who specialized in the embossing and chasing of small gold and silver objects, such as the snuffboxes, cane handles, and watchcases that became increasingly fashionable in late seventeenth- and eighteenth-century England. Narrative scenes were highly desirable in watchcases and in gold box lids, and among the makers of these prized objects who worked in London but came from Continental Europe were Augustin Heckel (died 1770), George Michael Moser (1706–1763), and to a lesser extent the Wieland family.[10]

By about 1742, a member of the Wieland family, Frederick Wieland (active ca. 1731, died after 1759), embossed a scene on the back of the outer case for a pair-case quarter-repeating watch (fig. 39) by Charles

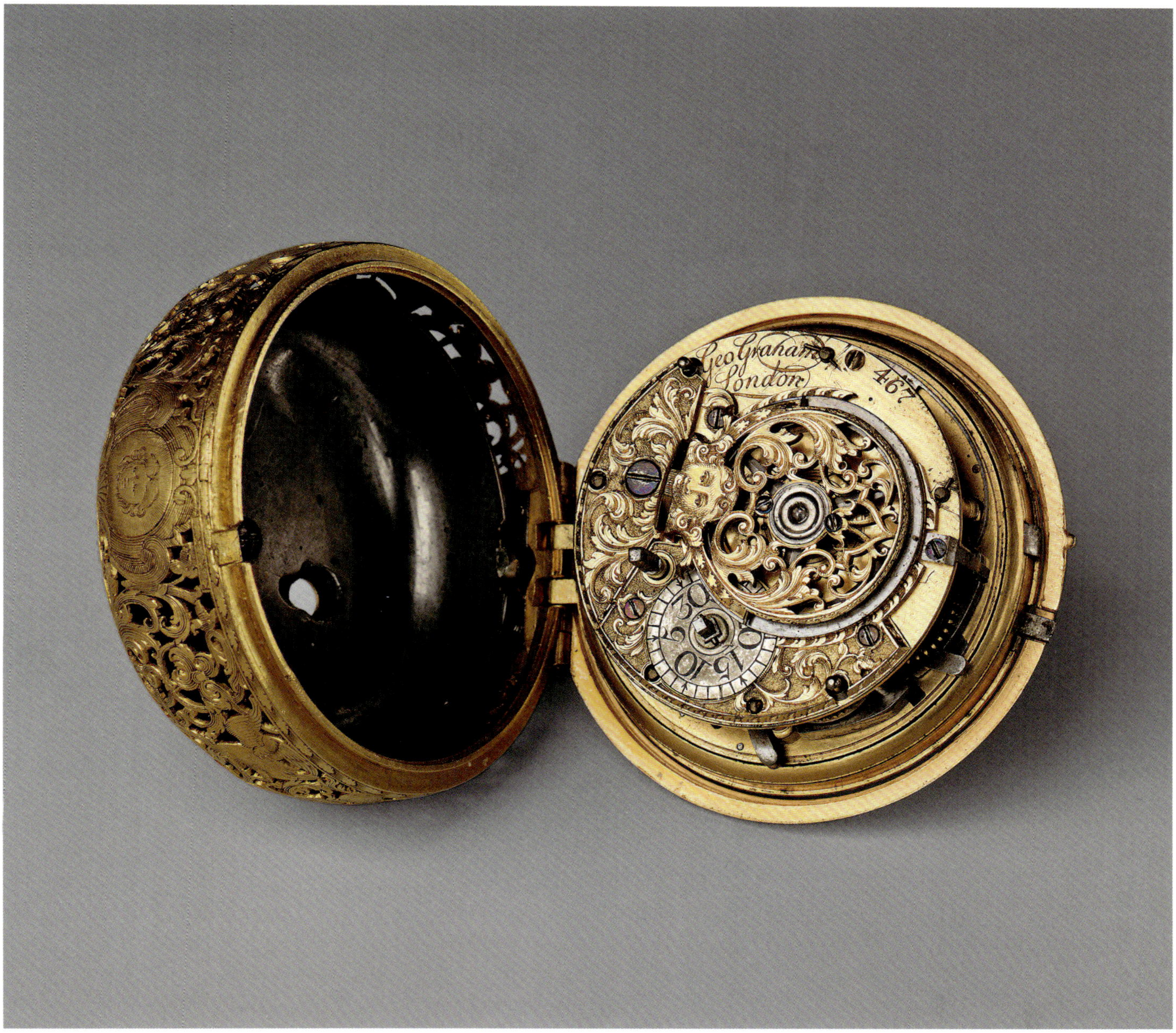

Inner case open to show the back plate of Graham watch

Cabrier II (1719–1765) in the Museum's collection.[11] Identified by historian Richard Edgcumbe as having been adapted from an etching by Sébastian Leclerc (1637–1714), the figure of a flute player and a shepherd with an old man seated in front of a fountain[12] illustrates a story of the Greek sun god Apollo, also regarded as lord of music and song (hence the flute). As shown here, he was serving the legendary mortal Admetus, King of Pherae in Thessaly and husband of the tragic Alcestis, as herdsman of the royal flocks in punishment for having killed the Cyclops. Thus, familiarity with Greek mythology, as well as conspicuous affluence and the discerning ownership of a timepiece signed by a member of a well-respected family of London watch-makers, could be demonstrated by the possession of one watch.

The dial of the Graham watch has been skillfully repaired after having been bent double at some point. The bezel for the glass cover for the inner case is a replacement. The end of the thumb piece of the outer case is missing. It is not known how or when Captain White acquired the watch. CV / JHL

1 "The Records of Famous Makers," in Britten 1982, pp. 326–29; J. L. Evans 2004, p. 178.
2 For a further discussion of the Royal Society, see entry 23 in this volume.
3 Britten 1982, pp. 148–50; J. L. Evans 2006, p. 38.
4 J. L. Evans 2004, p. 180; see also J. L. Evans 2006, p. 105.
5 J.-A. Lepaute 1755, p. 156, and pl. XIII.
6 J. L. Evans 2006, pp. 38, 102–7.
7 Ibid., p. 105, no. 567.
8 Ashmolean Museum, Oxford, inv. no. WA1947.191.85. See Thompson 2007, pp. 46–49, no. 21; see also Jagger 1983, pp. 48–49.
9 Priestley 2000, pp. 27, 45.
10 Edgcumbe 2000, pp. 56–66, 86–132, 148–51.
11 Acc. no. 32.75.37a, b. The outer case is signed "Wiela."
12 Edgcumbe 2000, p. 150, and figs. 137a, b.

34. Miniature Longcase Clock with Calendar

BRITISH (LONDON), CA. 1720–25
78 × 13¼ × 8⅜ in. (198.1 × 33.7 × 21.3 cm)
Width of dial plate: 7⅛ in. (18.1 cm)
Gift of Irwin Untermyer, 1964
64.101.870

CASE: walnut and oak veneered with walnut and figured walnut
DIAL: gilded and silvered brass, signed:
Danl: Quare & / Ste: Horseman / LONDON
[Daniel Quare, British, 1647/49–1724 & Stephen Horseman, British, died 1740, firm: British (London), ca. 1718–ca. 1730; and numbered *220*
MOVEMENT: gilded brass and steel

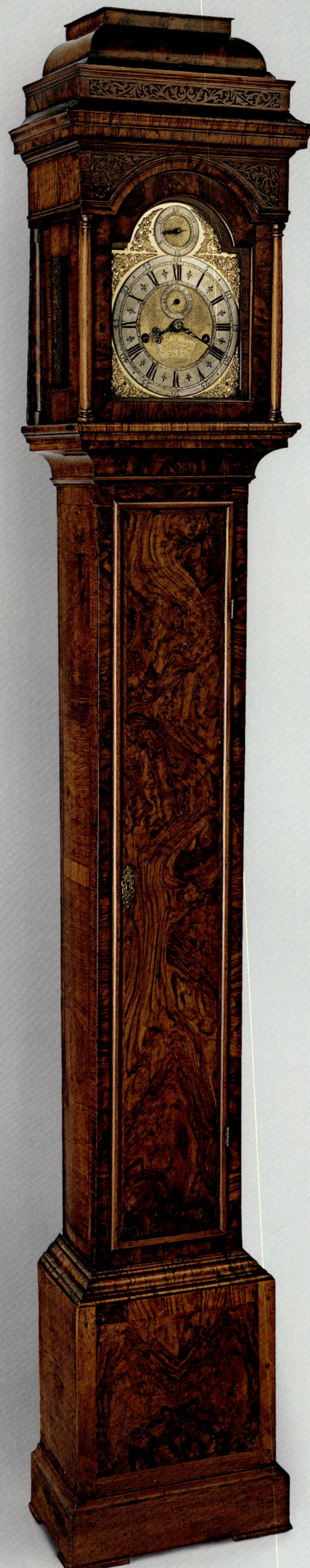

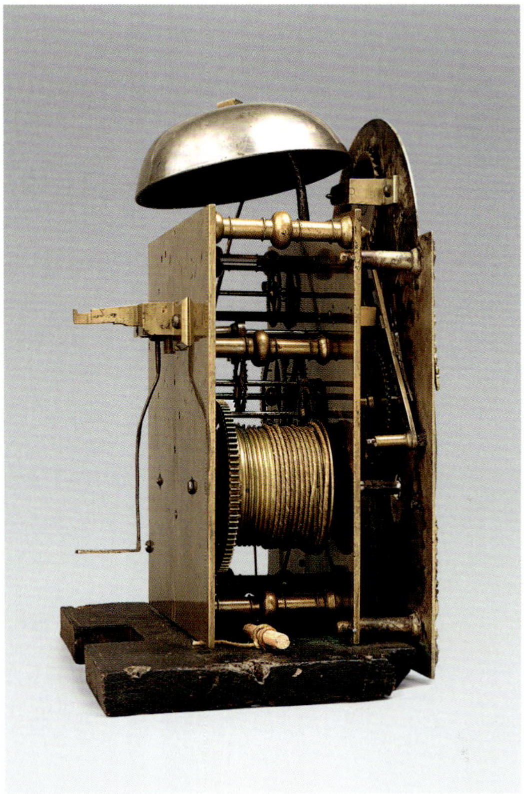

View of the month-going movement, showing the going train

DANIEL QUARE (1647/49–1724) WAS PROBABLY BORN IN SOMERSET, England. Like Edward East (1602–1697), Ahasuerus I Fromanteel (1607–1693), and Thomas Tompion (1639–1713), he was among the most successful seventeenth-century London clockmakers; however, he was considered a "foreigner" because he was not born in London. After 1631, when the Clockmakers' Company had obtained its charter, membership in the company was the usual method of gaining the privilege of doing business in the city. The opportunity to make and sell clocks and watches in the City of London was prohibited to those who were not members of a London company. Ordinarily, the aspiring clockmaker would serve an apprenticeship under a recognized member of the Clockmakers' Company, but the apprenticeship was long and the number of apprentices that a clockmaker could have at one time was usually severely limited. Alternatively, an aspiring clockmaker could gain work by becoming a member of one of the other London companies, such as the Goldsmiths' Company, where East was apprenticed,[1] or the Blacksmiths' Company, which accepted Fromanteel in 1631.[2] Others could be admitted by right of patrimony, and others who could purchase admission to a company were allowed entry if approved by that company, but the fee was high and nearly always more than that for a London-trained apprentice. Still, another alternative was to practice the craft outside the city limits or in certain nearby areas where foreigners such as French Huguenot craftsmen had settled.

It is not known where Quare was trained, but he became a Free Brother of the Clockmakers' Company in 1671 as a "Great Clockmaker" (turret clockmaker).[3] In January 1701, he took Stephen Horseman (died 1740) as an apprentice.[4] Horseman became Free Brother of the Clockmakers' Company in 1709,[5] and Quare's partner about 1718. He continued the firm after Quare's death in 1724 and until it went bankrupt in 1729 or 1730.[6]

While noting that Quare's Quaker religion prevented him from swearing an oath of allegiance to the English king, thus precluding an appointment as clockmaker to the king, historian Cedric Jagger outlined Quare's professional and social success, stressing that Quare gained direct access to aristocratic circles, both in England and on the European Continent.[7] Without question, Quare was among the most remarkably skilled and inventive clockmakers who came to seventeenth-century London in order to make their reputations. One of Quare's contributions to horology was the invention of a repeating mechanism for watches (see entry 33 in this volume). An early example, possibly the first of his watches with a quarter-repeating mechanism, is now in the Ashmolean Museum, Oxford.[8]

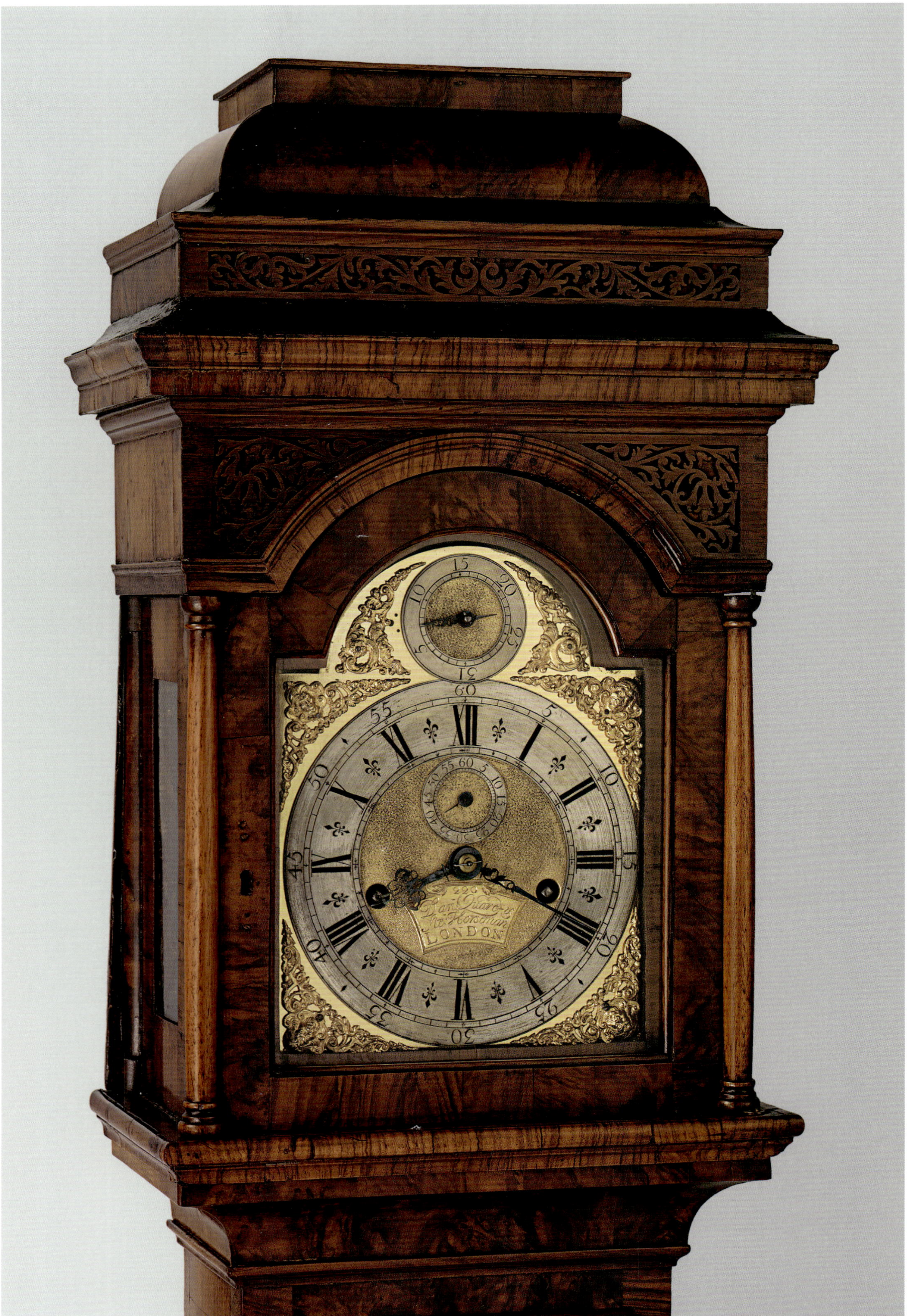

Clocks that went for long periods before needing to be rewound were another specialty. Quare's longcase clock, still in the Royal Collection at Hampton Court, near London, not only indicates both solar and mean solar time but also runs for a year on a single winding.[9] Another of Quare's year-going longcase clocks is now in the British Museum, London.[10] The month duration of the Metropolitan Museum's clock is, thus, not so surprising, but the fact that Quare and Horseman were able to create the movement and weights to fit into so small a case makes this clock remarkable. The case, in fact, barely accommodates the movement, and the door to the trunk had to be hollowed out to provide room for the free descent of the exceptionally heavy weights required by the clock's long duration.

The movement consists of two rectangular brass plates held apart by five turned pillars that are pinned to the front plate. It contains a going train of five wheels and an anchor escapement regulated by a long pendulum. It actually runs for thirty-five days before needing to be rewound. The striking train has four wheels and a fly, and it strikes hours on a bell that is mounted at the top of the front plate. It has rack-and-snail striking. The positions of the going and striking trains are reversed from those in an ordinary clock of the period, and both trains wind counterclockwise.

The semicircular arched (or break-arch) dial is seven and one-quarter inches wide. In the center of the arch is a calendar with a chapter ring (5–31, by fives), and below is a silvered-brass chapter ring for the hours (I–XII), minutes (5–60, by fives), and two-and-one-half-minute intervals marked by fleurs-de-lis. A separate chapter ring for seconds (5–60, by fives) appears at the twelve o'clock position, and a label above the six o'clock position is engraved with the signature, "Danl: Quare & / Ste: Horseman / LONDON."
The spandrels of the dial are filled with applied reliefs of a helmeted mask-and-scroll design that is thought to have come into use about 1710.[11] The calendar's chapter ring is framed by comparable scrolled reliefs, which incorporate masks in profile.

The case is a particularly felicitous version of the standard early eighteenth-century design for longcase clocks, only in reduced size. It relies on the use of richly figured walnut veneer, especially on the front of the plinth and on the door to the trunk, the latter framed by half-round molding that provides the only hint of ornament. Above the trunk, a convex molding supports the hood with a walnut-and-glass door to the dial of the clock, which is framed by applied wooden columns. These wooden elements support spandrels filled by fabric-backed fretwork, and a molded cornice with a fabric-backed fretwork frieze. An inverted bell-shaped dome completes the design. The sides repeat these motifs in less opulent fashion, but there is no additional fretwork, and the columns at the back of the hood are simply applied quarter rounds of wood.

There are serious signs of wear throughout the movement, and it has undergone extensive repair, some of it in London during the second half of the nineteenth century, as inscriptions on the interior document. The present anchor escapement does not fit the slot made to accommodate the easy removal of the original. The assembly for the pendulum suspension, too, has been replaced. The current hour hand was recently made to replace an earlier but clumsy substitute for the original steel hand. The minute hand is original but has been broken and repaired by soldering.

The fretwork on top of the hood and the right spandrel were replaced sometime before the clock entered the Museum. A number of areas of veneer had separated from the underlying oak carcass. The top of the trunk and the hood had seriously warped to the right, perhaps owing to the strain caused by the extra-heavy weight required by the striking train that furnishes power for approximately 4,881 blows in a single winding.

The clock had been in the possession of the American theatrical impresario David Belasco (1853–1931) when it was bought at auction by dealer Partridge, Inc., for Irwin Untermyer.[12] CV / JHL

1 Loomes 1981, p. 205.
2 Ibid., p. 236.
3 Ibid., p. 451.
4 Jagger 1983, p. 49.
5 Clockmakers' Company, London, Court Minute Books, Ms. 2710/3, 1699–1729, p. 98r, entry of Sept. 29, 1709, Guildhall Library, London. Horseman was admitted without payment.
6 An account of the bankruptcy of "Stephen Horseman, of Exchange Alley, London, Citizen and Clockmaker" appeared in the *London Gazette* (Nov. 28–Dec. 1, 1730), p. 2. An inventory of possessions for the bankruptcy of Robert Sutton, dated Jan. 1730, also indicates that Horseman was bankrupt at that time. See *Robert Sutton* 1732, p. 16.
7 Jagger 1983, pp. 49–51.
8 Inv. no. WA1947.191.85. See Thompson 2007, pp. 46–49, no. 21.
9 Inv. no. RCIN 1040. See Jagger 1983, pp. 49–51.
10 Inv. no. CAI-2098. See Thompson 2004, pp. 94–97.
11 Robinson 1981, p. 450, no. 12.
12 Anderson Galleries 1931, p. 187, no. 1233, ill.

35. Wall Clock (Cartel)

FRENCH, CA. 1735–40

19½ × 9½ × 4¾ in. (49.5 × 24.1 × 12.1 cm)
Diam. of back plate: 3 3/8 in. (8.6 cm)
The Jack and Belle Linsky Collection, 1982
1982.60.84

CASE: soft-paste porcelain, by the Chantilly Manufactory [French, founded, 1730]; and partly gilded brass
DIAL: white enamel, signed: ·ESTIENNE·LENOIR·/·A PARIS· [probably Étienne I Le Noir, French, 1675–1739]
MOVEMENT: brass and steel, signed (on back plate): *Etienne LeNoir / Æaris*

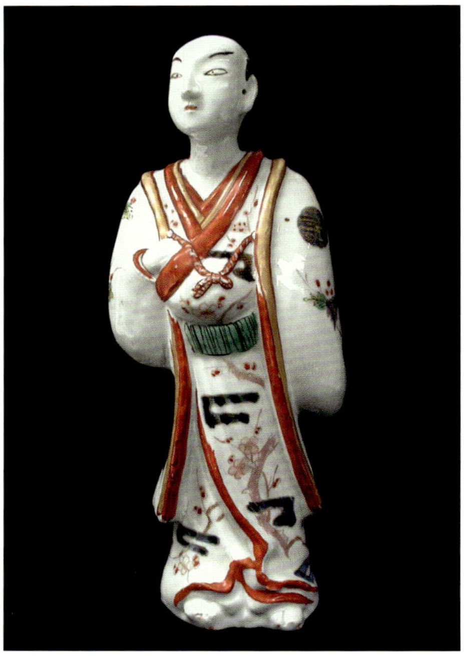

fig. 40 *Kabuki Actor, Japanese, Edo period (1615–1868), ca. 1700. Hard-paste porcelain painted with colored enamels over transparent glaze (Hizen ware, Imari type), Height 12 in. (30.5 cm). The Metropolitan Museum of Art, New York, The Hans Syz Collection, Gift of Stephan B. Syz and John D. Syz, 1995 (1995.268.235)*

DURING THE EIGHTEENTH CENTURY IN EUROPE ENTHUSIASM FOR exotica from Asia was far from new. Imported Chinese porcelain and Japanese lacquers had been highly prized throughout the seventeenth century, and a variety of fantastic ornament that drew heavily upon Chinese-inspired ornamental motifs began to appear on seventeenth-century European-made objects as diverse as English silver and French woven silks. The style came to be known as chinoiserie.

Japanese porcelain, too, appealed to European collectors, and the exportation of Imari and Kakiemon wares (fig. 40)—the latter produced in Arita on the Japanese island of Kyushu during the period after 1639 when the Tokugawa Shoguns closed the country to all but a very few foreign traders—is an interesting story in itself.[1] Nevertheless, we know that in an inventory made in 1688 of Burghley House, the Elizabethan country seat in Cambridgeshire built by William Cecil (1520–1598), there were Japanese porcelains that can still be identified.[2]

In France, a surviving inventory of the collection of Louis-Henri de Bourbon, Prince de Condé (1692–1740), lists more than two thousand porcelains, many of Japanese origin.[3] The prince, who had been minister to his cousin King Louis XV (1710–1774) of France, was exiled to the prince's estate at Chantilly in 1726, where he became the patron of a soft-paste porcelain manufactory initiated by Cicaire Cirou (born 1700).[4] By 1735 Cirou had been granted a patent by the king for the right to make porcelain specifically in imitation of Japanese porcelain. The Prince de Condé's collection was disbursed during the French Revolution (1789–99), and it is not now possible to identify precisely what it contained.[5] It is, however, possible to compare several of the Japanese figures known from the Burghley House inventory with the three human figures on the Metropolitan Museum's clock. Their egg-shaped heads, the pencil-thin black outlines of their features, and their small red mouths and pure white skin are recognizable, in particular, in the two boys seated on drums that are still at Burghley House.[6] The palette of burnt orange, light blue, sea green, coal black for the hair, and, especially, the whiteness of the skin achieved at Chantilly by the application of a white tin-glaze over the natural, yellow-tinted Chantilly clay, very closely resembles the coloring of the Japanese figures. The fabric designs for the kimonos worn by the French-made figures are not found on the Japanese examples at Burghley House, but they do derive from designs on Japanese Kakiemon hollowwares of the late seventeenth and early eighteenth centuries.[7] It is known that the Prince de Condé had a number of these in his collection, but taken together, these similarities lead one to believe that the collection also must have contained at least one comparable Japanese figure.

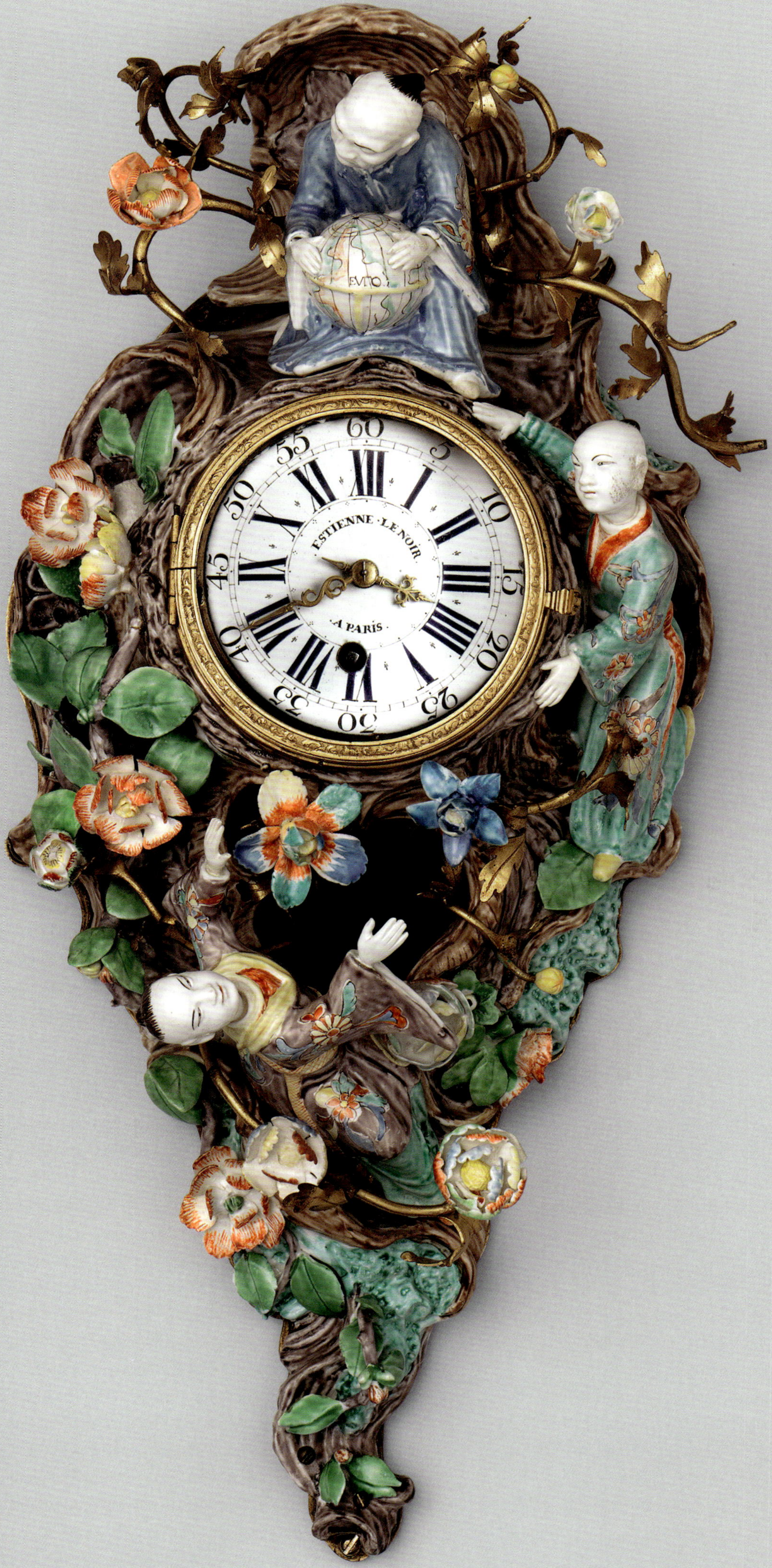
ESTIENNE LE NOIR
A PARIS

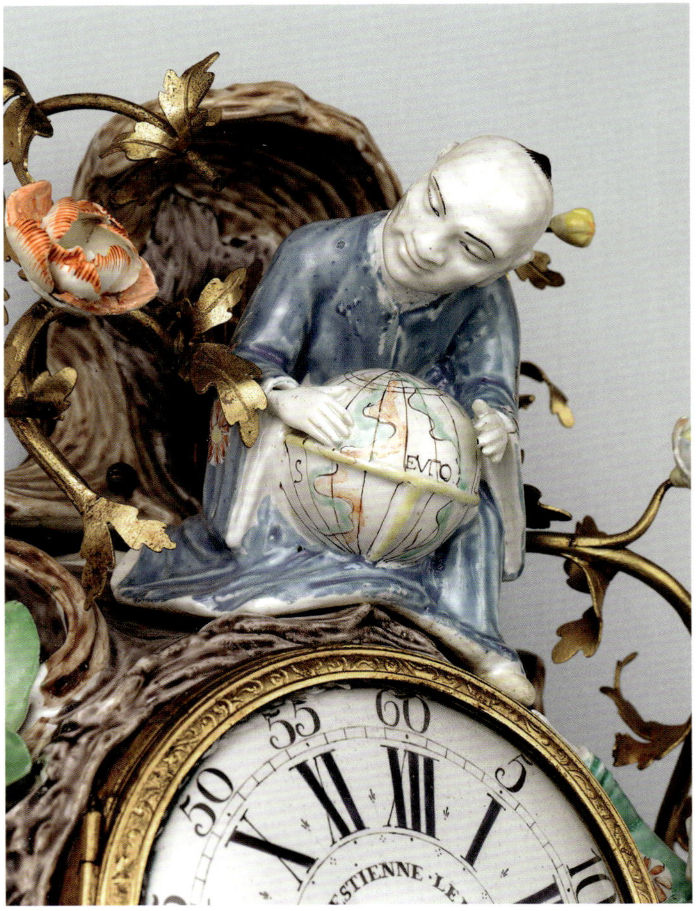

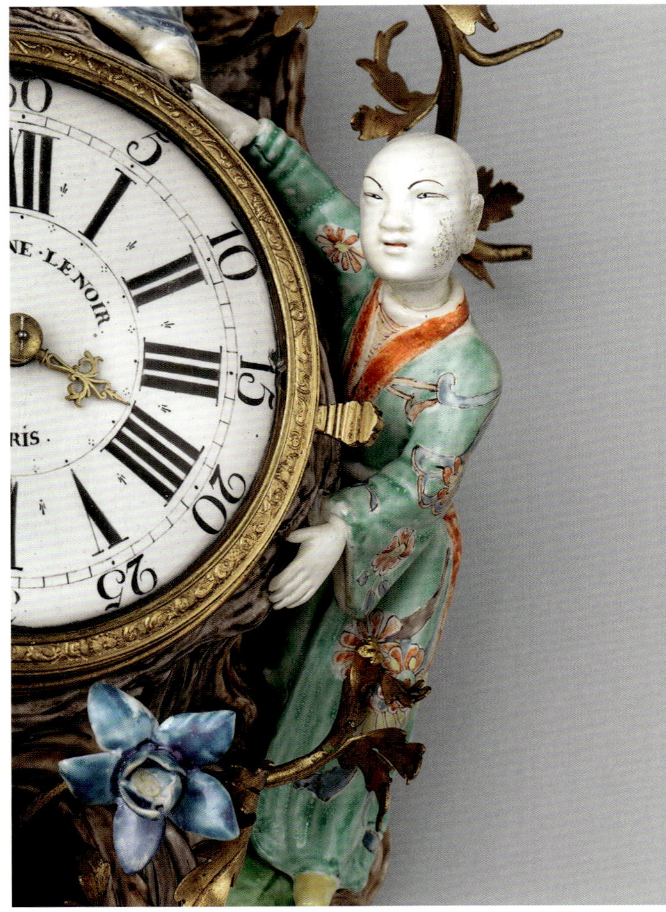

The three figures, *magots* in the parlance of the period,[8] on the case of this clock inhabit two pieces of asymmetrically shaped porcelain that are, in turn, bolted to a brass plate cut to fit the contours of the porcelain and gilded where visible. The porcelain ground consists of free-form rocaille ornament colored in shades of lavender and light brown, overlying brilliant green porous rockwork. Tendrils with burnt orange, lemon yellow, and white flowers and green leaves on the left side of the case are integral to the porcelain body, as are two of the human figures, one gesturing toward the dial of the clock and the second toward the pendulum. The rocaille crest and the figure with a globe are separate pieces, as are the more exotically colored blossoms. The blossoms are attached to double-stemmed branches of gilded brass, which are bolted to the brass plate that supports the porcelain body. One of these elements frames the *magot* with the globe; the second element covers most of the aperture below the dial that is meant to display the oscillation of the pendulum.

This highly decorative case frames a white-enamel dial with the hours (I–XII) painted in blue enamel and the minutes (5–60, by fives) painted in black. A hole at the six o'clock position allows the insertion of a key for winding the spring-driven movement of the clock, and two pierced-brass hands complete the requirements of time-telling. The clockmaker's name, "·ESTIENNE·LENOIR·," and place, "·Æparis·," are painted within the hour chapter.

Housed in a circular brass cylinder hidden inside the porcelain case is the movement, consisting of two circular brass plates containing a single train with a verge escapement and short pendulum. Due to the fact that the clock does not strike the hours, it probably would have been intended for installation on the wall of a sleeping alcove in the bedroom of a French mansion. Not all wall clocks, or cartels, of the kind were silent, however, and it is difficult to generalize about cartels made of Chantilly porcelain as there are only two other known examples: one in the J. Paul Getty Museum in Los Angeles, with both a going train and a repeating train, which could be released at will to strike the hours on a bell;[9] and the second in the Uhrenmuseum Beyer Zürich, with a movement striking both hours and half hours.[10]

"Etienne Le Noir," the signature on the back plate of the Metropolitan Museum's clock, probably refers to Etienne I Le Noir (1675–1739), who became a master clockmaker in Paris in 1698 and opened a shop called Aux Tuileries in the Place Dauphine the same year. He was the son of the Paris clockmaker Simon Le Noir (master in 1640), father of Etienne II Le Noir (1699–1778), and grandfather of Pierre-Etienne Le Noir (ca. 1724–after 1789).[11] According to historian Jean-Dominique Augarde, Etienne II signed his clocks "Etienne Le Noir le fils" until after 1740, when he, too, signed simply "Etienne Le Noir." Etienne II and Pierre-Etienne worked as partners from 1750 to 1771 making movements for lavishly decorated clockcases for aristocratic patrons in France and all over the rest of Europe.[12] A highly successful clockmaker, Etienne II died a rich man. He may have been the maker of the movement for the Museum's clock, but the probable early date of the porcelain case and the relative simplicity of the movement make the clock more likely to have been the work of Etienne I Le Noir.

While more or less similar in shape to the Metropolitan Museum's cartel, the cartel in the Beyer collection has an allover pattern of milky white morning glories set among leafy tendrils of gilded brass. The Getty Museum's cartel is somewhat closer in design to the Metropolitan's, having three polychrome figures at somewhat analogous points in the design, but these are not human. They derive instead from the Chinese world of animal motifs, being a dragon, a monkey, and a goose, and they inhabit a far more homogeneous array of porcelain flowers than the figures of the Metropolitan Museum's clock. A gilded-brass vine borders the entire case of the clock, adding to the comparative homogeneity of the rather dense ornament and perhaps allowing greater safety in handling the delicate porcelain.

With this example in mind, the edges of the Metropolitan's cartel were examined to see if there were traces of similar elements. Channels cut on either side of the edge of the plate near the lower edges of the porcelain crest were found to contain empty holes drilled and tapped to receive screws; traces of holes for screws on either side of the edge of the brass plate about three quarters of the way down from the top of the porcelain case would seem to indicate, at the least, a change of plan in the design. Close examination also revealed that the two double sprays of gilded-brass leafy branches with porcelain flowers are bolted directly to the brass plate in a rather careless manner by means of bolts that do not match the ones used to attach the porcelain elements to the plate. The flowers attached to these branches are of Chantilly porcelain, but most of their shapes and colors do not resemble those of the flowers that are integral to the body of the case, leading to the suspicion that the branches were additions, perhaps made to please the original patron or perhaps added at a later date but by someone who had a plentiful supply of Chantilly flowers. Seven of the intended blossoms are now missing, but the remaining ten seem less than coherent additions to the original design. Certainly, the flowers and animal figures on the case of the Getty Museum's clock are better integrated, as is the allover pattern of morning glories on the Beyer Museum's clock.

There is damage to the cheek and ear of the *magot* on the right side of the Metropolitan Museum's clock. The movement, which is held in place by means of four screws attached through four holes in the dial plate, has been repositioned, requiring three extra holes. Three of the screws are now stripped, and it is possible that a new bezel and lens for the dial may have been necessary when the position was changed.

Before entering the New York collection of Jack and Belle Linsky,[13] the clock belonged to Lady Margaret Fortescue, Castle Hill, Devonshire, England.[14] CV / ES

1 Impey 1990.
2 *Burghley Porcelains* 1986, p. 154, no. 51; pp. 220–21, no. 89; pp. 232–33, no. 95; pp. 238–39, no. 98.
3 Minutier central, XCII, 504, Archives Nationales, Paris.
4 Le Duc 1993, pp. 8–9.
5 Nelson and Impey 1994.
6 *Burghley Porcelains* 1986, pp. 220–21, no. 89.
7 Ballu 1958.
8 For a discussion of the meaning of the term in eighteenth-century France, see Kisluk-Grosheide 2002, p. 177.
9 Acc. no. 81.DB.81. The movement is by Charles Voisin (1685–1761). See Gillian Wilson in Wilson et al. 1996, pp. 42–47, no. VI.
10 By Julien Le Roy (1686–1759), probably the best clockmaker in eighteenth-century France and known to have had a very large workshop; see Jean-Nérée Ronfort and Jean-Dominique Augarde in Wilson et al., pp. 185–90. For the clock, see Museum der Zeitmessung Beyer 1982, pp. 64–65.
11 Tardy 1971–72, vol. 2, pp. 374, 376.
12 Augarde 1996, p. 347; Ronfort and Augarde in Wilson et al. 1996, p. 177. See also Tardy 1971–72, vol. 2, p. 376.
13 William Rieder in Metropolitan Museum of Art 1984, pp. 238–39, no. 147.
14 See Christie's 1966, p. 38, no. 145, and frontispiece.

36. Wall Clock (Cartel)

FRENCH (PARIS), PROBABLY CA. 1740–45
52½ × 24½ × 15½ in. (133.4 × 62.2 × 39.4 cm)
Gift of Mr. and Mrs. Charles Wrightsman, 1971
1971.206.27

CASE: gilded bronze, oak, and tortoiseshell on brass marquetry on oak, by Charles II Cressent (French, 1685–1768)
DIAL: white enamel and gilded brass with blued-steel hands
MOVEMENT: brass and steel, signed (on back plate): *Jean Godde l'aisné Æ Paris* [Jean Godde the Elder, French, ca. 1668–1748/49]

CHARLES II CRESSENT (1685–1768) LEARNED THE CRAFT OF bronze casting from his father, François Cressent (1663–ca. 1745), and probably served an apprenticeship as a cabinetmaker with his grandfather, Charles I Cressent (1625–1707), who was a master cabinetmaker in Amiens, France. He later moved to Paris, where he worked for the sculptors François Girardon (1628–1715) and Robert Le Lorrain (1666–1743), and in 1714, he became a master sculptor in the Parisian corporation of painters and sculptors, the Académie de Saint Luc. When he married the widow of a cabinetmaker who had been in the service of Philippe (1674–1723), the duc d'Orléans and Regent of France from 1715 to 1723, the marriage automatically admitted him to the Paris guild of cabinetmakers (*ébénistes*). Cressent's furniture, with its exotic veneers and beautiful gilded-bronze mounts, would probably have found great favor on its own, but the patronage of the duc d'Orléans assured his success as a cabinetmaker.[1]

With the death of the regent in 1723, Cressent lost protection from the rules of the Paris guilds, under which he was prohibited from engaging in making his own furniture mounts. It is probably no coincidence, therefore, that in the same year a large number of these were confiscated from his workshop by the officials of the corporations of the bronze founders (*bronziers / ciseleurs*) and the gilders (*doreurs*).[2] The medium, more often gilded brass than gilded bronze, was in fact quite practical for use in the serial casting of ornaments and for the small-scale sculpture that the better Parisian cabinetmakers were increasingly incorporating into their designs. The fashion for mounting furniture with ornaments, however, did not come without creating conflict between the cabinetmakers and the founders, chasers, and gilders, all of whom were instrumental in producing furniture mounts in accord with the guild rules.

Among the bronzes seized in Cressent's workshop in 1723 were two figures of Leda to be "placed below the dial [of a clock]" and a sphinx to be "used at the foot of a clock."[3] Some of the mounts on a clock in the Metropolitan Museum's collection (fig. 41) fit these descriptions, and they are fine enough to be the product of Cressent's hand.[4] Leda, according to classical myth, was one of the loves of the god Zeus, who visited her in the guise of a swan. The elegant figure of Leda is seated in a relief below the dial of the clock, and the front feet of the clock are exquisitely modeled sphinxes. The case is made of tortoiseshell and brass applied to an oak carcass. While the case is not signed, it is known that Cressent's admiration for the royal cabinetmaker André-Charles Boulle (1642–1732) resulted in his periodic use throughout his career of this kind of marquetry, often referred to as "Boulle work," combined with sculptural mounts of gilded bronze.[5] For comparison, a

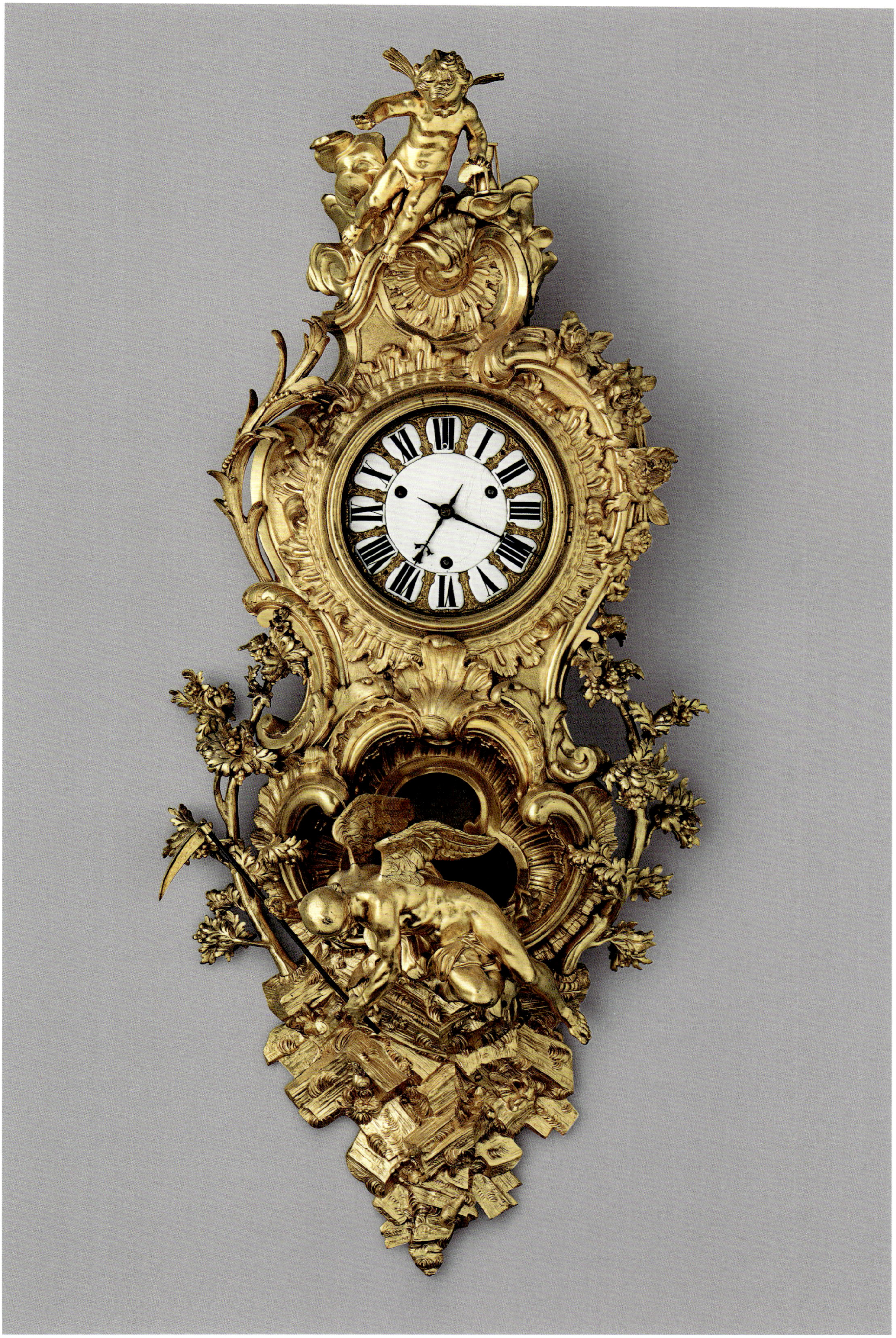

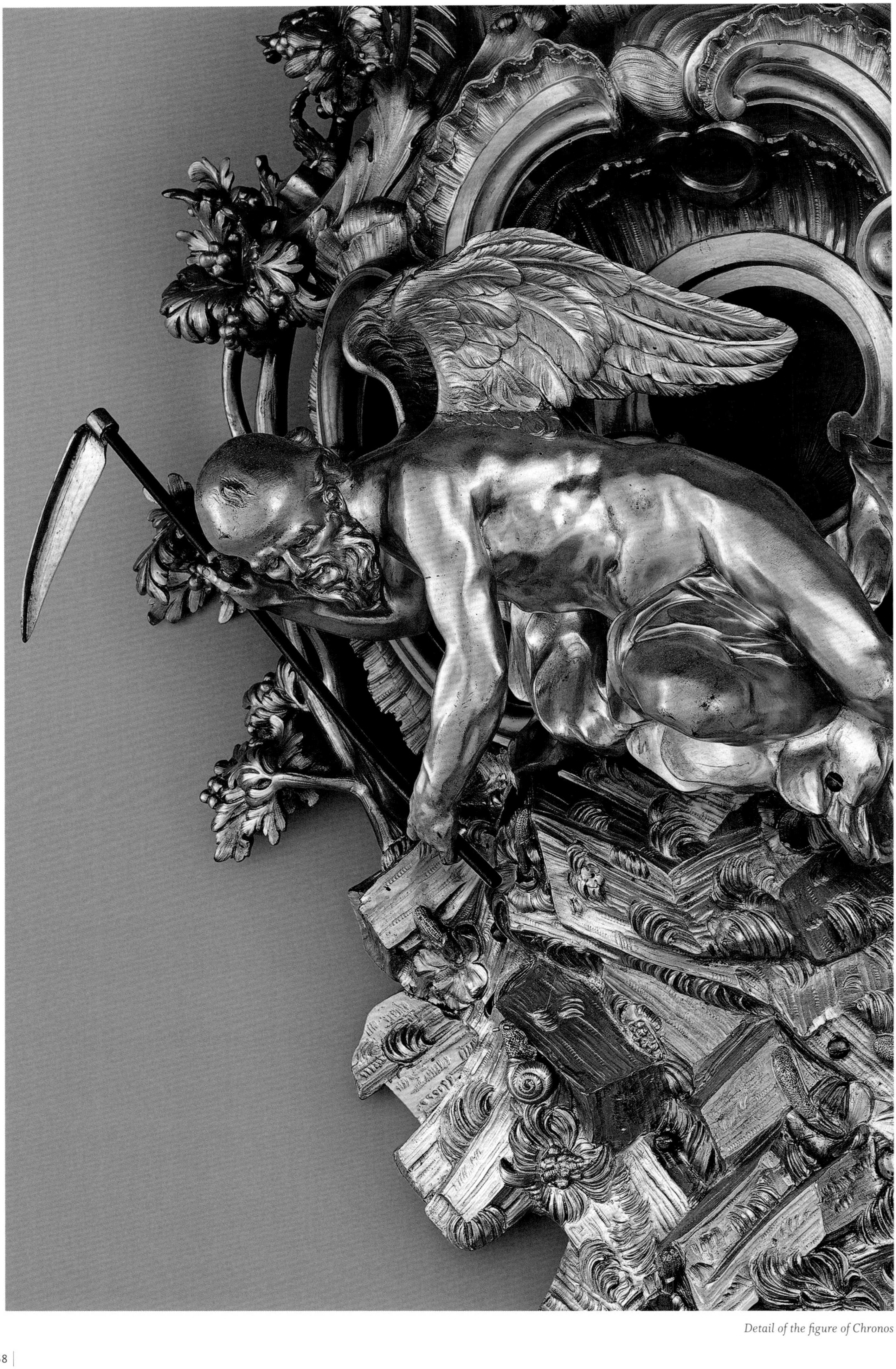

Detail of the figure of Chronos

clock and pedestal in the Museum's collection (fig. 12), with a case attributed to Boulle,[6] displays a similar pairing of tortoiseshell and brass marquetry with gilded-bronze sphinxes; these figures may be more earthbound than Cressent's strange creatures, but they serve the same function as supporters of a clock. As cabinetmaker to King Louis XIV and occupant of one of the workshops (or *logements*) given as favors to artists and craftsmen who held royal appointments, Boulle was free to work in whatever medium he wished. Not so with Cressent, at least not in 1723.

It comes as something of a surprise, therefore, that within ten years Cressent had begun a series of clockcases that on first sight seem to be made entirely of gilded bronze. They are largely wall clocks, or cartels, rococo in style. They were cast from models provided by Cressent, and they often are ornamented with allegorical figures connected with time. The appearance of many of these clocks is deceiving, for they are composed of a number of separate pieces of gilded bronze that are screwed to carved wooden cores. The compartments containing the clock's movement, too, have wooden sides veneered with Boulle marquetry.[7] Cressent's imposing example in the Museum's collection is unusually large. The construction may have been employed in part to lighten the weight of the clock, which, after all, had to be hung on a wall, but it may also have helped to satisfy some kind of compromise between Cressent and the Paris guilds. The result is a cabinetmaker's solution, not a sculptor's way of working.

It has been difficult to establish the sequence of Cressent's cartel clocks and even more difficult to date them. Historian Marie-Juliette Ballot's attempt[8] left much to be desired, and it was historian Theodore Dell who made order of the models based in part on descriptions of them in a series of eighteenth-century sales held by Cressent.[9] From evidence provided by the catalogues of these sales, it is certain that the model for the Museum's cartel was in existence before January 1749, when one of the clocks made from that model was described in detail. It was said to represent Cupid seated in clouds and leaning on a sandglass above the dial, and Time holding his scythe placed on the chaos of the world below, with a base framed by two large trees.[10] The catalogue does not mention the name of a clockmaker, and so it has not been possible to identify which of the clocks made from this model was the one in the sale.[11]

The Museum's clock has retained its original dial and movement, the latter signed on the back plate by Jean Godde the Elder. Not very much is known about him. According to historian Jean-Dominique Augarde, there is evidence that a Jean Godde did supply movements for cases made by Cressent,[12] but there were several Jean Goddes in Paris, and Augarde seems to have been confused about which of them might have identified himself as "the Elder." The maker is most likely to have been the one who became a master clockmaker in 1691, and who died in 1748 or 1749,[13] a good reason for dating the clock to earlier than 1749. Dell classified the Metropolitan's clock as "Type D" in a sequence of five models, but made no attempt at dating the model. The clock does not bear the tax mark on gilded bronze in use between 1745 and 1749, so it may, in fact, have been made before 1745.

The movement is spring driven, and it strikes hours and quarters on two separate trains. The dial is brass with a white enamel center and a gilded chapter of hours that is inlaid with separate plaques painted with roman numerals I–XII in blue on white enamel. The hour and minute hands are of blued steel.

Both the Triumph of Love and the Triumph of Time, based on the allegorical *I Trionfi* by the Italian poet Petrarch (1304–1374), would have been recognized immediately by many Europeans. These personifications appear in processions depicted in various visual media in the late Middle Ages and the Renaissance. A notable example in the Metropolitan Museum's collection is a Triumph of Time, depicted in a tapestry woven about 1500–1530 in the Southern Netherlands.[14] But the figures in the tapestry and in the rest of the series to which it belongs are not the gods of our wall clock.

In the eighteenth century the personifications of Love as the Greek god Eros, whether as the child Cupid or as a winged youth with bow and arrows, and Time as Chronos or, as the Romans knew him, Saturn, as an old man with a beard and scythe, were well known and the identities of the two human figures on the case of the clock would have needed no explanation. Their meaning, the Triumph of Love over Time or, alternatively, Love Vanquishing Time, would have been clear by their relative positions on the clock.

A series of clockcases either by or attributed to Boulle, with Boulle marquetry and gilded-bronze mounts representing Love and Time on their cases, began to appear about 1715.[15] The Saturnian figure of Time is especially interesting in light of Cressent's use of the symbolism for his wall-clock cases. It is a figure of an old man with beard and wings in a semi-reclining position who holds up a scale in his right hand. The origin of the design has been traced to an Italian woodcut, that, in turn, reproduces a design by Giovanni Antonio Pordenone (1484–1539).[16] But the model for the bronze version used by Boulle is known to have been supplied to him by the sculptor Girardon.[17] Cressent worked for Girardon during his early years in Paris, and he probably would have known Girardon's models and undoubtedly knew one or more of Boulle's clockcases. This knowledge must have played a role in Cressent's choice of subject for his own series of wall clocks and is visibly the inspiration for the lively infant and the old man with the scythe bent over a pile of rock work (rocaille) representing not only the "chaos of the world," as Cressent described it,[18] but also the influence of the fashionable rocaille or rococo style of ornament (fig. 41).

Cressent made several other versions of this clockcase. One, also described in the 1749 sale, had a figure of Time at the top threatening a frightened infant below, who is seemingly trying to escape the chaotic rockwork and a menacing C-scroll in the space below the dial.[19] He also used both the figure of Time and of Cupid separately on other clockcases.

The case of the Metropolitan Museum's clock is in excellent condition, even to the extent of preserving Cupid's sandglass, now missing on the example in the Musée du Louvre, Paris.[20] A later escapement has been substituted for an earlier one, which was probably a verge and crown wheel with a silk-thread suspension for a short pendulum.

A paper label attached to the inside of the case suggests that the clock was in Genoa, Italy, in the nineteenth century. Alexandre Pradère provides as provenance a sale in Paris in 1960 and to the art dealers Rosenberg and Stiebel in New York.[21] CV

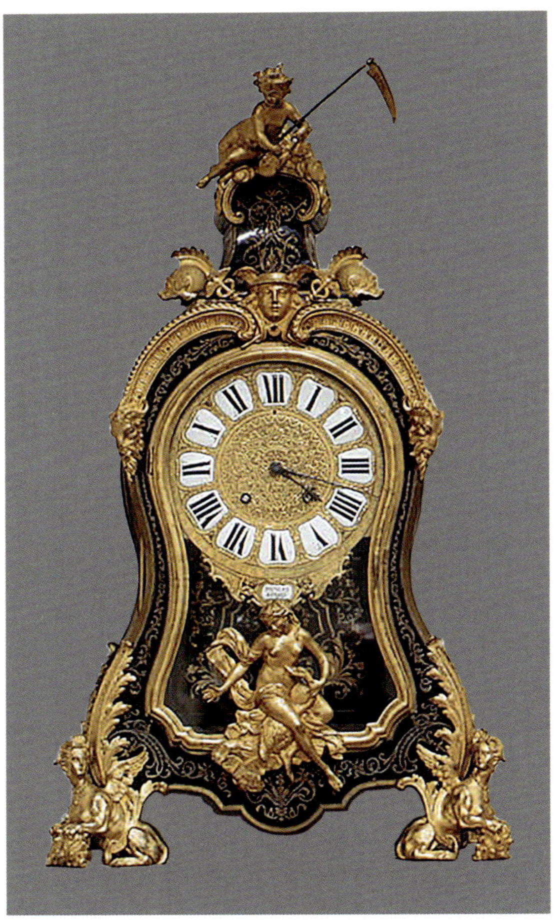

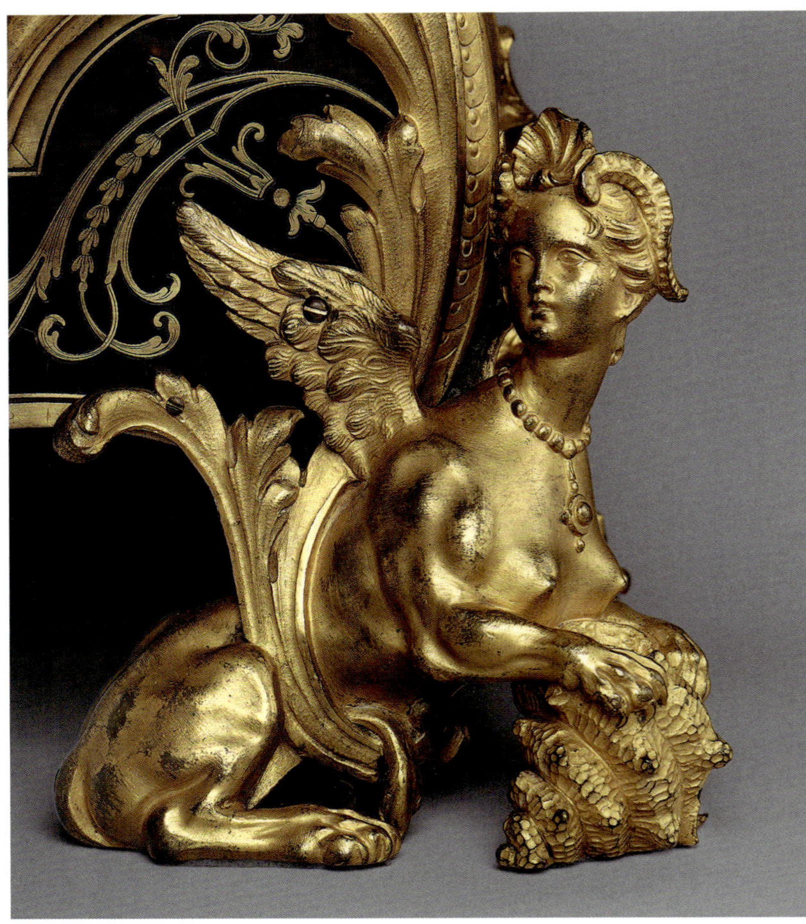

Detail of fig. 41 sphinx on the right foot of the clockcase by Charles II Cressent

fig. 41 *Louis Mÿnüel (French, ca. 1675/80–1742) and Charles II Cressent (French, 1685–1768). Clock, French (Paris), ca. 1720–23. Case [Cressent]: oak veneered with brass and tortoiseshell with gilded-bronze mounts; movement: [Mÿnüel]: brass and steel, 38¼ × 22½ × 9½ in. (97.2 × 57.2 × 24.1 cm). The Metropolitan Museum of Art, New York, Fletcher Fund, 1961 (61.69)*

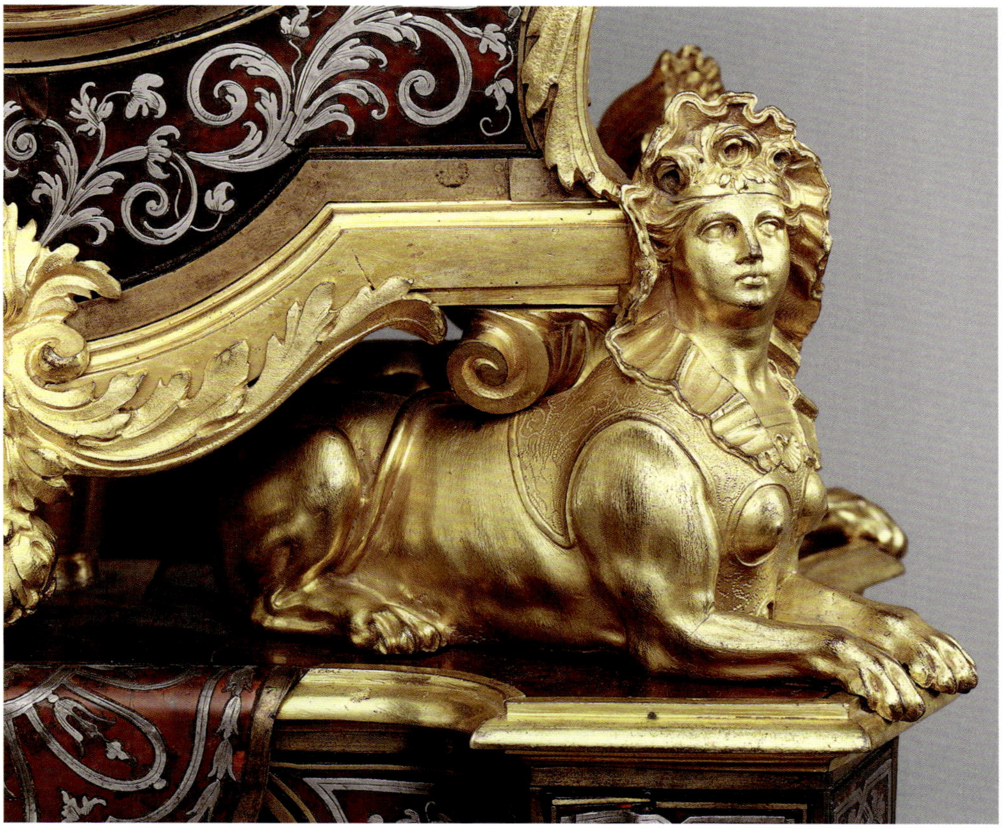

Detail of fig. 12 sphinx supporting clockcase by André-Charles Boulle

1 See Pradère 2003, pp. 19–21.
2 Part of the list of confiscated bronzes appears in ibid., pp. 201–4.
3 Ibid., p. 190, no. 17, "Plus deux figures . . . représentans Leyda, lequels sont pour mettre au-dessous de cadrans . . . ," and no. 41, "Plus un sphinx servant à mettre aux pieds de pendule."
4 Acc. no. 61.69. The movement is by Louis Mÿnüel (ca. 1675/80–1742).
5 See Watson 1956, p. 60.
6 Acc. no. 58.53a–c. The movement is signed "J. Thuret," probably for Isaac II Thuret (1630–1706). See James Parker in Parker et al. 1989, pp. 16–17; Jeffrey Munger in Kisluk-Grosheide and Munger 2010, pp. 52–54, no. 13. See also Ottomeyer and Pröschel 1986, vol. 1, p. 44, and vol. 2, pp. 483–85.
7 For illustrations of the disassembled parts of the case of a similar clock in the Wallace Collection, London, see Hughes 1994, p. 42; Hughes 1996, vol. 1, pp. 403, 404, 406.
8 Ballot 1919, pp. 1–96.
9 Dell 1967. See also Pradère 2003, pp. 176–99, 295–300.
10 See Pradère 2003, p. 333, no. 25, "Une magnifique pendule de bronze, dont la composition est du meilleur goût, il y a sur le haut un Amour qui est assis sur des nuages, il appuye son coude sur un sable. Au dessous du cadran, est la figure du Tems, tenant sa faulx, & posé sur le cahos du monde, les pieds sont formés par deux grandes arbres; le tout parfaitement sizelé, doré d'or moulu, de quatre pieds trois pouces de haut."
11 See ibid., p. 299, no. 228, for the clock in the Metropolitan Museum. At least three other extant clocks of the period fit the description of the case. They are now in the Musée du Louvre, Paris; the Wallace Collection; and the Hôtel de Ville, Marseille; ibid., p. 229, nos. 225–27. There are probably several more in private collections.
12 Augarde 1996, p. 327.
13 See Tardy 1971–72, vol. 1, p. 261.
14 Acc. no. 41.167.1. For a discussion of the tapestry and its iconography, see Cavallo 1993, pp. 463–78, no. 33, especially pp. 471–72.
15 For an example in the Wallace Collection, see Hughes 1994, pp. 18–19. For another example, in the J. Paul Getty Museum, Los Angeles, see Gillian Wilson in Wilson et al. 1996, pp. 20–27, no. IV. See also Ottomeyer and Pröschel 1986, vol. 1, pp. 38–40.
16 The woodcut has been attributed to Nicolò Vincentino or Andrea Andriani (or Andreani) after a finished drawing by Pordenone that was formerly in the collection of the Duke of Devonshire. See Ottomeyer and Pröschel 1986, vol. 1, p. 38, no. 1.2.2, ill. p. 39, and vol. 2, p. 475, and p. 474, fig. 4; Wilson in Wilson et al. 1996, pp. 23, 27, nn. 5, 6, and p. 25, fig. 4d.
17 See Wilson in Wilson et al. 1996, pp. 23, 27, n. 9.
18 See note 10 above.
19 Pradère 2003, p. 333, no. 47. For an example of this version now in the palace of Het Loo in the Netherlands, see Pradère 2003, pp. 188–89, 300, no. 233.
20 Ibid., p. 299, no. 225.
21 Palais Galliera 1960, no. 25, pl. XIV. See Pradère 2003, p. 299, no. 228.

37. Nécessaire with Watch

GERMAN, PROBABLY CA. 1745–50
Overall: 4¼ × 5 1/16 × 3¾ in. (10.8 × 12.9 × 9.5 cm)
Watch: Diam. of back plate: 1 ¼ in. (3.2 cm)
The Jack and Belle Linsky Collection, 1982
1982.60.135

CASKET: gold and mother-of-pearl, lined with dark-red velvet
WATCH: brass and partly blued steel, signed falsely (on back plate of movement): *Roth / Æparis*

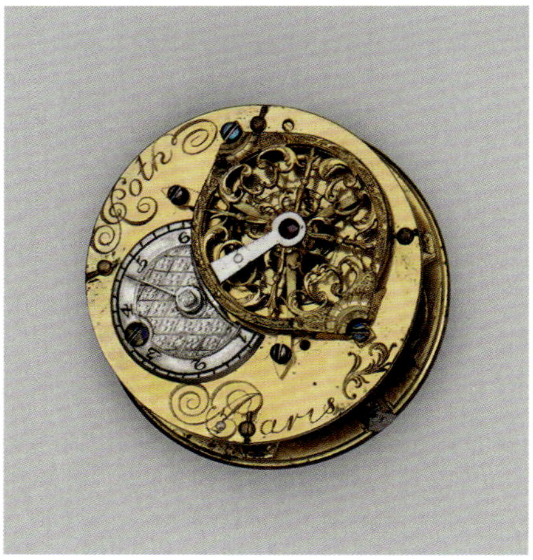

Back plate of the movement

THE ORNAMENT OF THIS EXQUISITE NÉCESSAIRE, A PORTABLE box, or casket, for the storage of small items needed in domestic life,[1] reflects the taste for chinoiserie, a European evocation of Chinese art. Chinoiserie usually incorporated figures of "Chinamen," the Chinese of European fantasy. When combined with rococo ornament with its rocaille—exotic rockwork, with seashells of various degrees of fidelity to nature—and with the ubiquitous C-scrolls, chinoiserie remained fashionable throughout much of the eighteenth century.

The Metropolitan Museum's nécessaire, shaped like a bombé commode, is made of gold to which sheets of white mother-of-pearl are attached by gold pins driven through artfully arranged ornaments of bright gold. It rests on four scrolled feet and has a hinged cover made of the same wonderfully lustrous materials. The sides of the casket are ornamented in high relief: a bird flies into the space between two seated human figures on the front side, a monkey sits on a tree branch on the left side, and the cover depicts a man presenting a garment to a woman who is turning away in distaste. Flaming C-scrolls, baskets of flowers, and bits of shrubbery from the vocabulary of chinoiserie ornament frame the scene on the cover, and comparable ornaments organize the space on each of the sides.

Included in a 1944 sale as the work of French goldsmith François Germain (1726–1791),[2] the nécessaire belongs to a group of caskets that use the same technique and is made from the same materials that are now thought to have been the work of an anonymous German goldsmith. Besides the Metropolitan's example,[3] there are three in the James A. de Rothschild Collection at Waddesdon Manor, near Aylesbury, Buckinghamshire, England;[4] one in the Cleveland Museum of Art;[5] and one in the Museum für Kunsthandwerk in Frankfurt am Main, where it has been related to eighteenth-century German designs for architecture and for ornament.[6] Several others are in private collections.

A closer look at the human figures on the Metropolitan's nécessaire reveals that the two figures on the cover and the two on the front side are neither Chinese nor even fantasy Chinese, but rather American Indians, as evidenced by the fact that they all wear feathers on their heads in the approved eighteenth-century European iconography for native Americans. Should there be any further doubt, however, the two seated figures with their commanding headgear each hold long-handled clubs, and of a particular origin: they are ceremonial objects used by natives of Brazil. Helmut Nickel has traced European acquaintance with the clubs to a report by Hans Staden (ca. 1525–ca. 1576), a sixteenth-century German sailor, who was stranded for a time among the Tupinamba people in Brazil. Staden described the clubs as "used for the ritual killing of a captive enemy, who was then eaten at a festive banquet."[7] Nickel

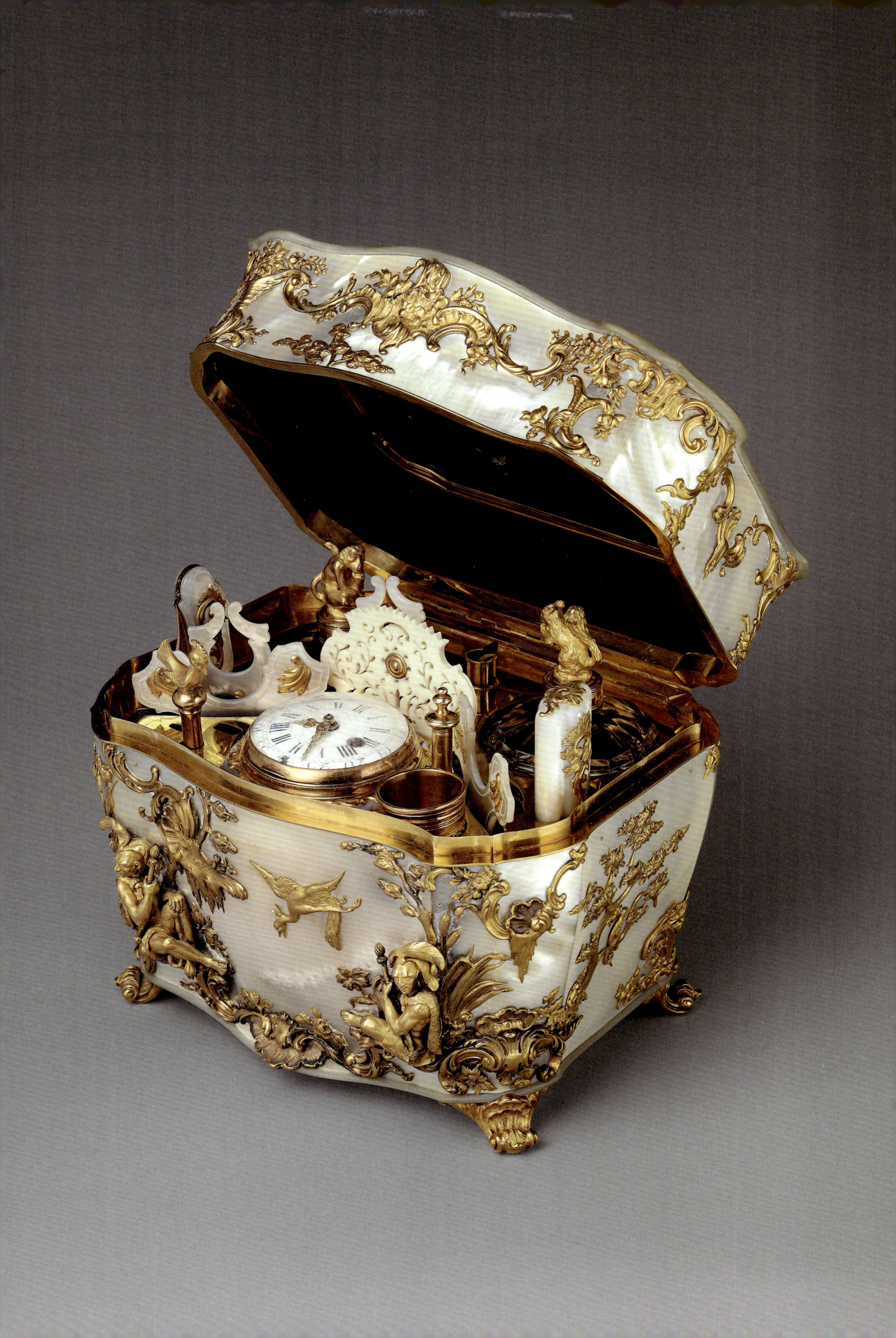

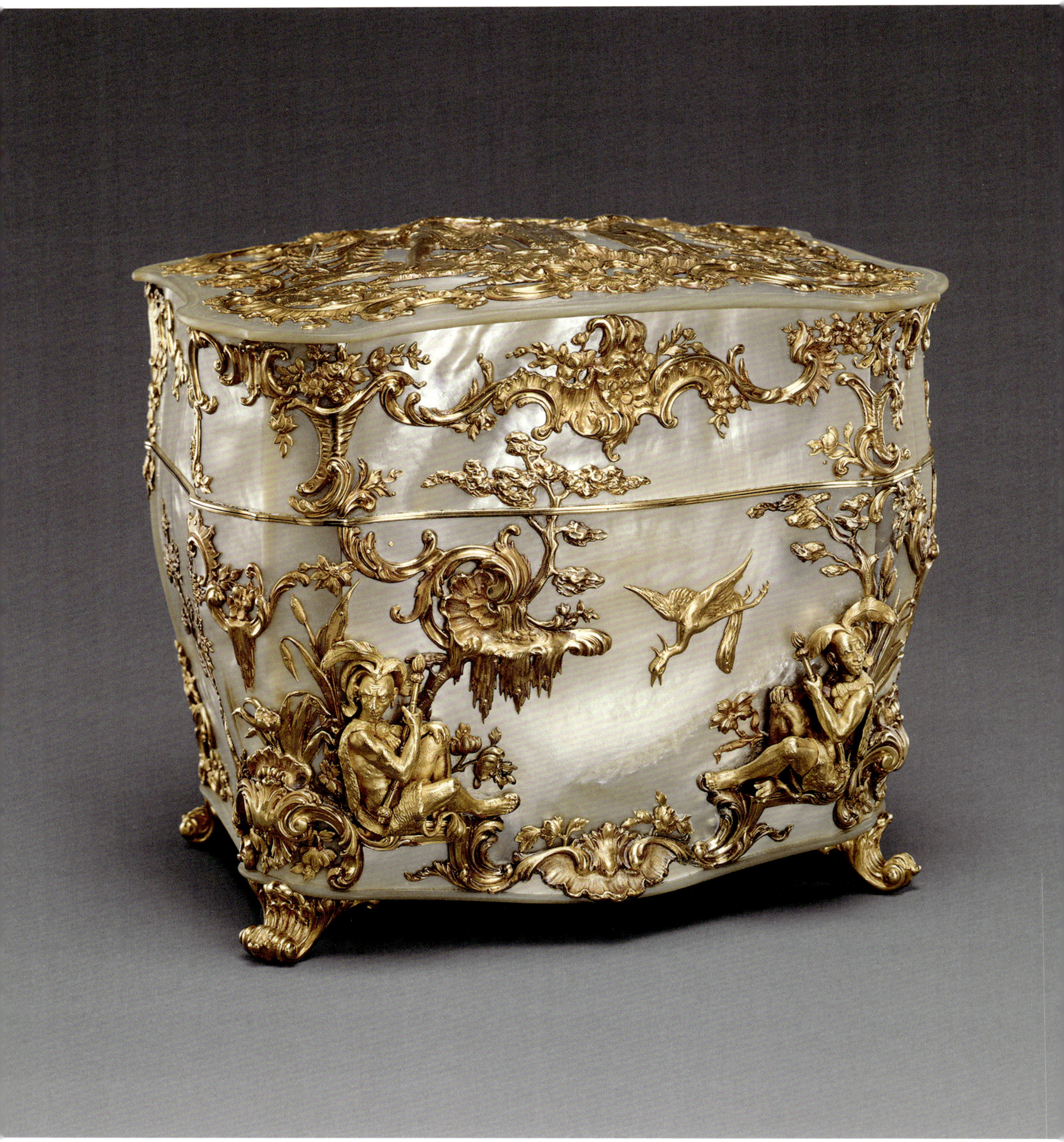

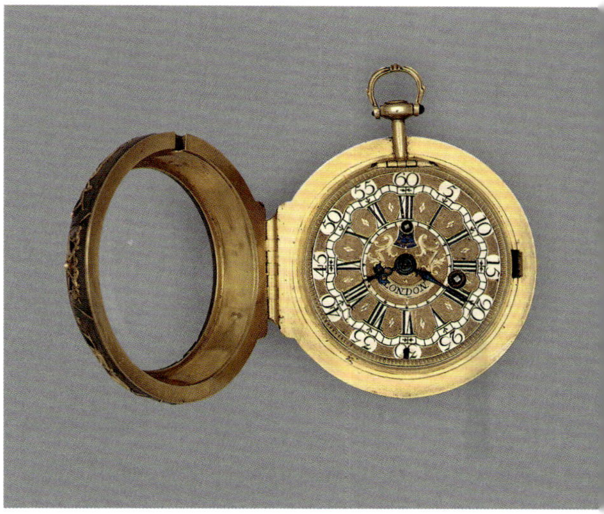

fig. 42 *Automaton Watch, falsely signed: "London," probably German, ca. 1710. Case: gold, mother-of-pearl, and enamel, Diameter 1⅞ in. (4.8 cm). The Metropolitan Museum of Art, New York, Gift of J. Pierpont Morgan, 1917 (17.190.1434)*

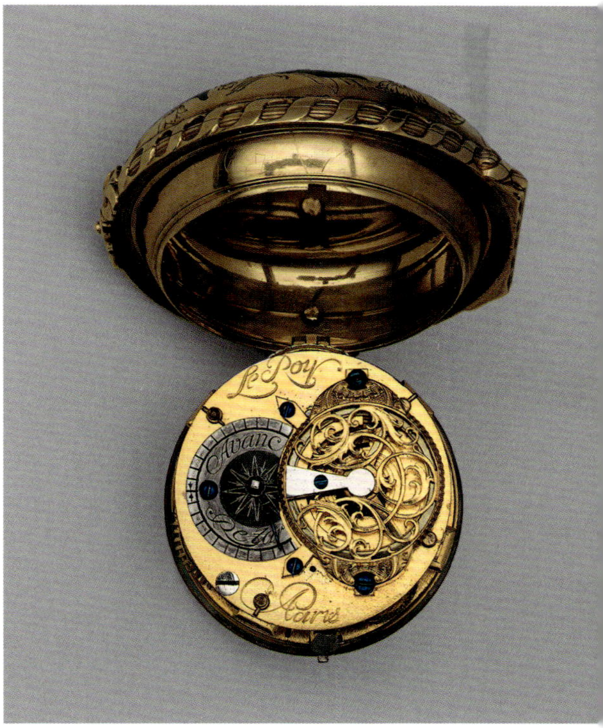

fig. 43 *Watch. Movement, falsely signed: "Le Roy / Æparis," probably German (Dresden), ca. 1770–80. Watchcase attributed to Christian Gottlieb Stiehl (German, 1708–1792). Case: gold inlaid with hardstones, Diameter 1 3/4 in. (4.5 cm). The Metropolitan Museum of Art, New York, Gift of J. Pierpont Morgan, 1917 (17.190.1567)*

found the particular club pictured in later German prints, such as the illustrations for the *Trachtenbuch* (1577) by Hans Weigel (active 1545–77), where, in addition, a Brazilian Indian man wears a cape[8] with fluffy feathers, and another wears what looks like ostrich feathers forming a sort of bustle. [9] Still later in the century, a man with the club was among the illustrations by Theodore de Bry (1528–1598) for part three of his influential *Historia Americae* (1590–92).[10] Nickel further recognized details from de Bry's illustrations as models for parts of the well-known figure of the *Moor with the Emerald Cluster* (*Mohr mit der Smaragdstufe*),[11] created shortly before 1725 by the Saxon Court goldsmith Johann Melchoir Dinglinger (1664–1731) and the court sculptor Balthasar Permoser (1651–1746).[12] The two seated figures on the nécessaire clearly have their origins in sixteenth-century German depictions of American Indians, and the German tradition is shown to have been current as late as 1725 or 1726, or only a few years earlier than the probable date when the fierce warriors of the Tupinamba people ended up as ornaments on the sewing kit that was intended for a *gnädige Frau* (gracious lady).

The interior of the cover of the Metropolitan Museum's nécessaire is fitted with a large mirror, and the box contains slots for sewing implements made of gold and mother-of-pearl, a spray of ivory leaves, a gold-tipped pencil for writing on the ivory, and two glass scent bottles with golden stoppers: one in the form of a squirrel, the other a monkey. In addition, the nécessaire features an embedded watch—the reason for including it in this volume. The dial of the watch is protected by a glass that is held in place by a hinged gold bezel. The dial is made of white enamel with painted roman numerals (I–XII) for the hours and Arabic numerals (5–60, by fives) for the minutes. It has hour and minute hands of sculptured brass and a hole between the three and four o'clock positions for winding the mainspring. The dial and movement are hinged to the interior of the casket at the twelve o'clock position, and the movement consists of two circular full plates held apart by four square-sectioned pillars. The movement also contains a train of four wheels regulated by a verge escapement. The back plate carries an openwork balance bridge, a silver figure plate for adjusting the balance spring, and the signature, "Roth Æparis." While the standard biographical dictionary of French clock- and watchmakers does list a watchmaker named "Roth" in Paris, first recorded in 1870,[13] the movement is consistent with eighteenth-century, not nineteenth-century, watchmaking practice.

The Museum has several eighteenth-century watches with signatures or place-names that do not match the style of the objects. One of them is a watch with a verge escapement in a pretty gold case inlaid

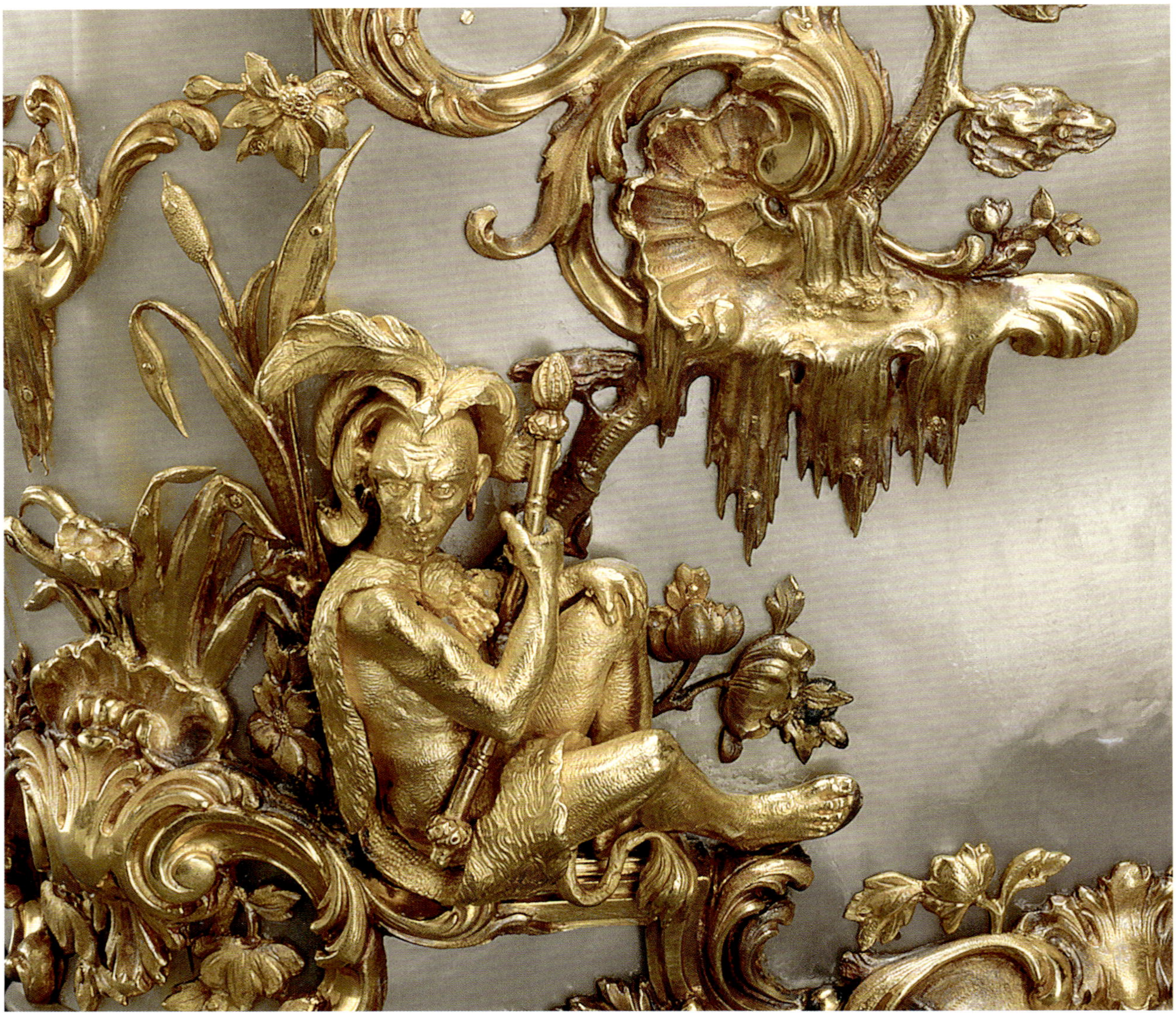

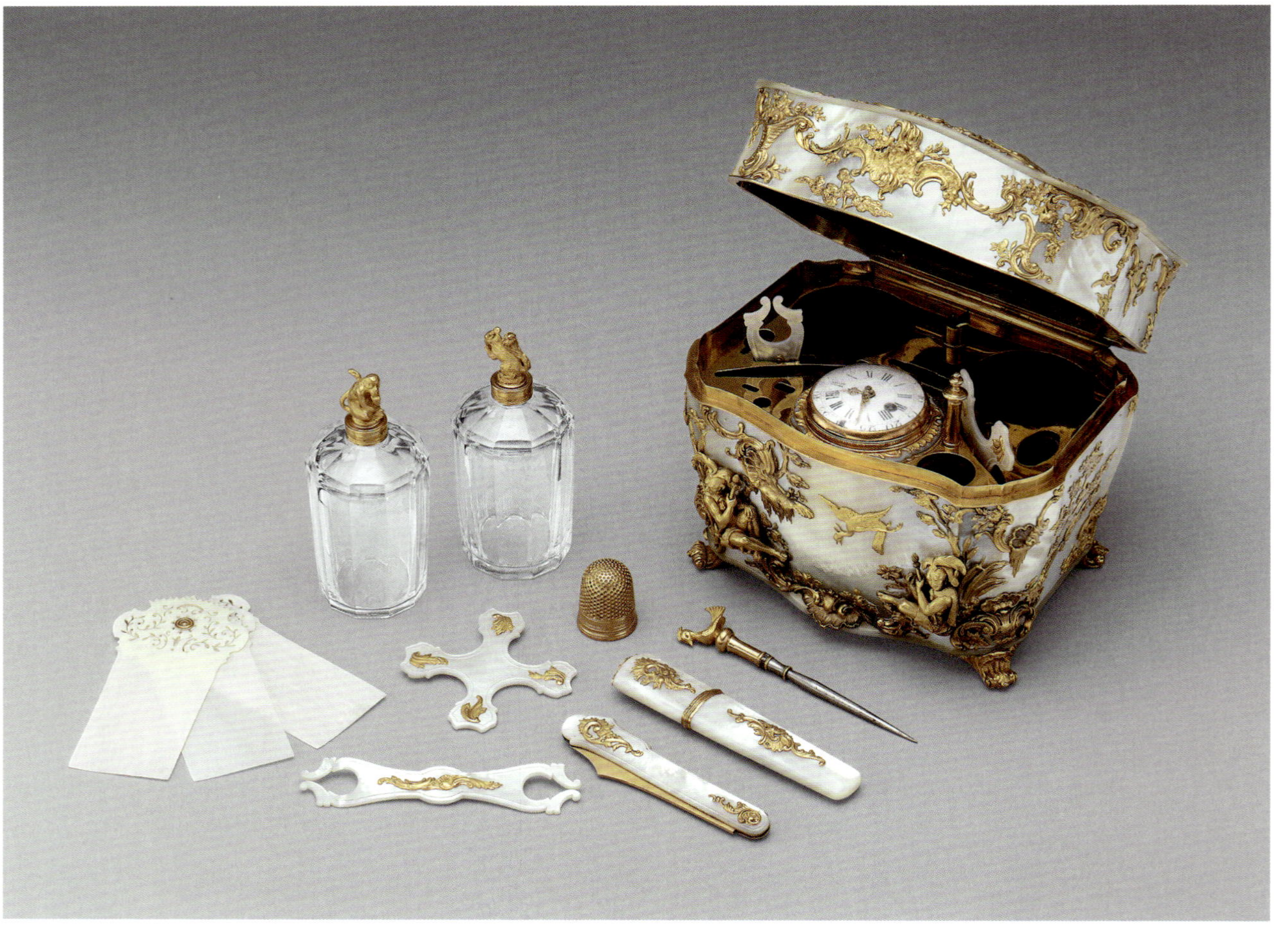

with colored hardstones in a floral pattern.[14] It displays a technique usually associated with Johann Christian Neuber (1736–1808) of Dresden.[15] Christian Gottlieb Stiehl (1708–1792), who also worked in Dresden and held an appointment to Augustus the Strong, King of Poland and Elector of Saxony (1670–1733), as well as to his successor Augustus III (1696–1763), is known for comparable lapidary work. His floral designs are freer and less geometrical than Neuber's,[16] and in the absence of a signature or maker's mark, it is to Stiehl that the Museum's watchcase can reasonably be attributed (fig. 43). The movement of the watch is a typical product of about the third quarter of the eighteenth century, except that it is signed "Le Roy / ÆParis," doubtlessly in the hope of benefiting from the excellent reputation of the Paris workshop of Julien Le Roy (1686–1759) and his son Pierre Le Roy (1717–1785). When compared with watches known to be products of the Le Roy workshop, the Museum's watch has been confidently identified as not among that select group.

One clue as to why a good watchmaker might feel the need to sign his work in this way may be inferred from the comments of a German author published in 1723 in both Dresden and Leipzig. Worried about the state of the horological trade in Germany, he lamented that "important and rich people buy most of their clocks and watches in the fairs, or from art dealers, or from London, Augsburg, Geneva, and other places where there are many watchmakers, which annually causes large amounts of money to leave the country."[17] Further on, he adds that German watchmakers ought to get organized and make proper masterpieces to insure a high quality of workmanship but

> if it were to be that in spite of this some important people and rich wastrels cannot appreciate anything that does not come from France or England, then a heavy tax could be levied on such foreign clocks and watches, and in addition the accredited [German] clockmakers [could be allowed] to engrave London or Geneva on their dials. . . .[18]

Such thinking may help to explain the signature on the watch inside the Museum's nécessaire, as well as the signature on another watch in the Metropolitan with a movement signed "Le Roy ÆParis" and a case attributed to Stiehl of Dresden.[19] A third watch in the Museum's collection incorporates a minuscule automaton equestrian hunt, which is housed in a gold case with panels of mother-of-pearl overlaid by partly enameled gold trophies and figures of military gentlemen brandishing weapons (fig. 42).[20] The dial of the watch is signed simply "London." In all probability, the three watches are German.

There are empty slots in the interior of the nécessaire, which suggests that a few of the implements are now missing. Otherwise, the object is in remarkably good condition. There are almost no signs that it was actually ever used. The nécessaire comes from the collection of J. Pierpont Morgan,[21] through the generosity of Jack and Belle Linsky.[22] It is not known where Morgan acquired the nécessaire.
CV / JHL

1 For an overview of the purpose of this nécessaire and comparable objects, see Kisluk-Grosheide 2011.
2 Parke-Bernet Galleries 1944, p. 152, no. 607, ill. p. 153.
3 See Clare Le Corbeiller in Metropolitan Museum of Art 1984, p. 190, no. 110. Le Corbeiller noted similarities of the ornament to designs by François Cuvilliés (1695–1768) working in Munich.
4 Serge Grandjean in Grandjean et al. 1975, pp. 94–102, nos. 45–47.
5 Acc. no. 67.157.
6 Inv. no. 12056. See Heidrun Zinnkann in Museum für Kunsthandwerk 1987, pp. 94–95. For an example of ornament by Johann Michael Hoppenhaupt II, see Maurice 1976, vol. 1, pp. 238–39.
7 Staden 1557, quoted in Nickel 2002, pp. 87–88; see also p. 87, fig. 9, for a woodcut depicting a long-handled club published in Staden's 1557 account.
8 Published by Weigel in Nürnberg in 1577. See Nickel 2002, p. 84, and p. 85, fig. 4.
9 Nickel 2002, pp. 84, 86, and p. 85, fig. 5.
10 A multivolume work published in Frankfurt am Main; part three, published in 1592, was titled *Americae Tertia Pars: Memorabile[m] Provinciae Brasiliae Historiam*. See Nickel 2002, pp. 87–88, and fig. 10. See also entry 48 in this volume.
11 In the collection of the Grünes Gewölbe in Dresden, inv. no. VIII 303. See Nickel 1980, p. 204, figs. 1, 2.
12 For the de Bry illustrations, see Nickel 1980, pp. 207–8, 210, and figs. 9, 10.
13 Tardy 1971–72, vol. 2, p. 572.
14 Acc. no. 17.190.1567.
15 For a scholarly appraisal of Neuber's work in inlaid hardstones by various authors, see *Gold, Jasper and Carnelian* 2012.
16 Somers Cocks and Truman 1984, pp. 282–83, no. 98. See also Poindront and Kugel 2012, pp. 223–25.
17 Marperger 1723, p. 152 (translation by J. H. Leopold).
18 Ibid., p. 154 (translation by Leopold).
19 Acc. no. 17.190.1586.
20 Acc. no. 17.190.1434.
21 Williamson 1910, pp. 151–52, no. 108, and pl. 45.
22 Le Corbeiller in Metropolitan Museum of Art 1984, p. 190, no. 110.

38. Mantel Clock

FRENCH, CA. 1750
17½ × 11¼ × 8¾ in. (44.5 × 28.6 × 22.2 cm)
Diam. of back plate: 3¾ in. (9.5 cm)
The Lesley and Emma Sheafer Collection,
Bequest of Emma A. Sheafer, 1973
1974.356.411

CASE: hard-paste porcelain (Meissen Manufactory, German, founded 1710) and soft-paste porcelain (Vincennes Manufactory, French, ca. 1740–56), with gilded-bronze mounts
DIAL: white enamel with blue numerals for hours and black numerals for minutes, signed: ·GUDIN·LEJEUNE·/·A PARIS·
[Paul Gudin, Gudin the Younger, French, active ca. 1739–55]
MOVEMENT: brass and steel, signed (on back plate): *Gudin Lejeune ÆParis*

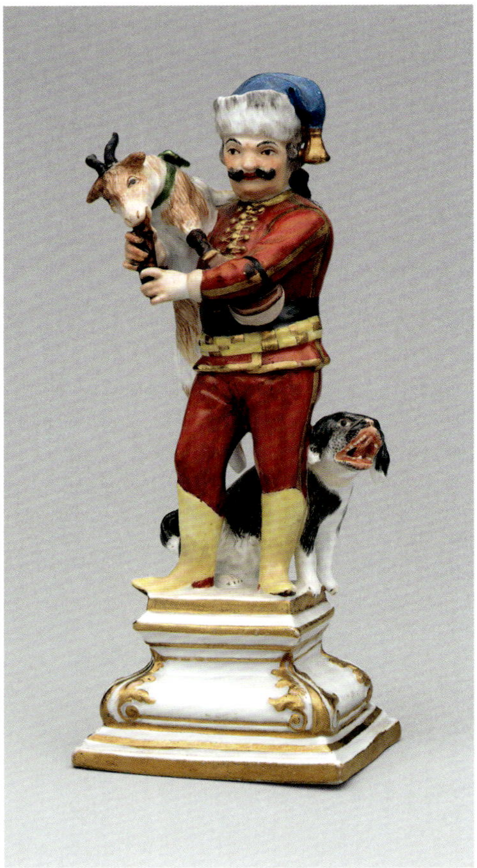

fig. 44 *Meissen Manufactory (German, founded 1710). Schindler (Court Jester and Hussar), German (Meissen), ca. 1735. Hard-paste porcelain, H. 6⅞ in. (17.5 cm). The Metropolitan Museum of Art, New York, Gift of Irwin Untermyer, 1964 (64.101.130)*

EIGHTEENTH-CENTURY FRENCH CLOCKMAKERS TOOK FULL ADVANTAGE of the luxury trades that flourished in Paris as they worked together to provide movements for domestic clocks with splendid cases in various media. This manner of working created difficulty within the community of clockmakers, especially among those who were masters in the clockmakers' guild. Up until the French Revolution in 1789, guild rules greatly restricted the kinds of cases that could be produced for clock movements. Nonetheless, various solutions had been proposed, including agreements between individual members of other guilds to cooperate with clockmakers; toleration of clockmakers who were not guild masters (a category known as *ouvriers libres* [free workers]); and the existence of special royal dispensations and privileges for these workers to accommodate the demand for decorative clocks.[1] Probably the most effective solutions, however, were attributed to the activities of members of the Paris corporation of *marchands-merciers* (merchants of luxury goods). Established in 1407, their corporation was by 1613 permitted to trade in many kinds of merchandise without interference from other corporations or guilds.[2] In the early eighteenth century, Jacques Savary des Brûlons (1657–1716), a former inspector general of French customs, noted that of the six corporations of Paris merchants, the *marchands-merciers* were considered the most important, regardless of their official ranking as third in line.[3] Further, he listed the twenty divisions within the *marchands-merciers* corporation, specifically mentioning clocks as belonging to the thirteenth division, which also included paintings, prints, and sculpture.[4] At the time of Savary des Brûlons's obvservations, the *marchands-merciers* were known as purveyors of creative designs who combined the products of various skilled craftsmen into a single object.

This clock, with its combination of German hard-paste porcelain figures, French soft-paste porcelain flowers, French gilded-bronze mounts, and French clockwork, is a fine example of the kind of object produced during this period. The movement, housed inside a gilded-brass cylinder supported on the gilded-bronze branch of a flowering shrub, is spring driven. It has a verge escapement and strikes the hours on a bell that is attached by means of a stand screwed to the circular back plate. The back plate also carries the signature: "Gudin le Jeune ÆParis" (Gudin the Younger), probably that of Paul Gudin (active ca. 1739–55).

The standard biographical dictionary of French clockmakers lists Jacques-Jérôme Gudin l'aîné (Jacques-Jérôme Gudin the Elder; 1732–after 1789) as a master clockmaker in Paris in 1750 and located on the Quai des Orfèvres in 1769–84. It also states that Jacques-Jérôme used the signatures "J. Gudin à Paris," "Gudin l'aîné à Paris," and "Gudin à Paris."[5] More recent research by art historian Jean-Dominique Augarde

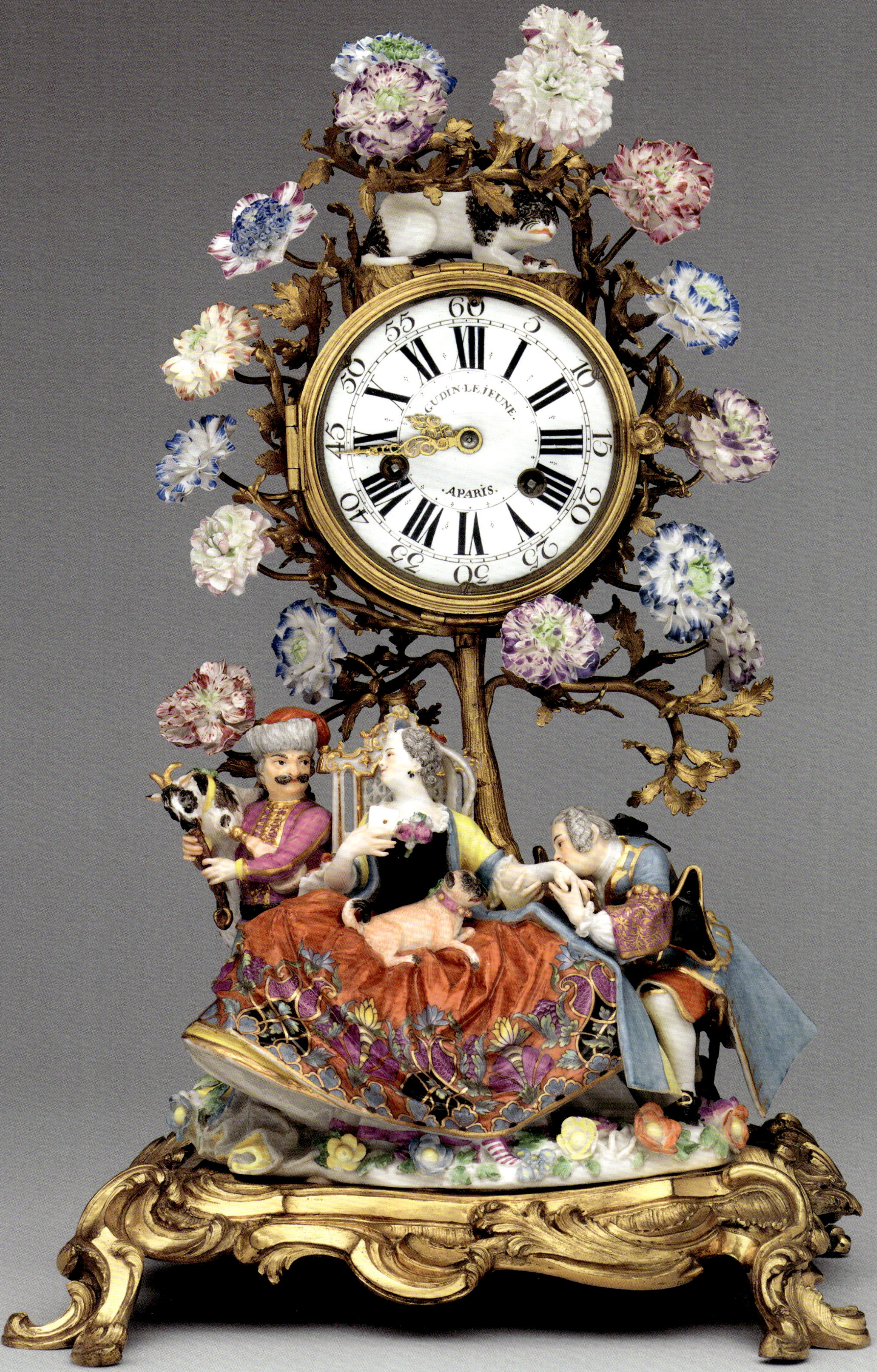
GUDIN·LE JEUNE
·A PARIS·

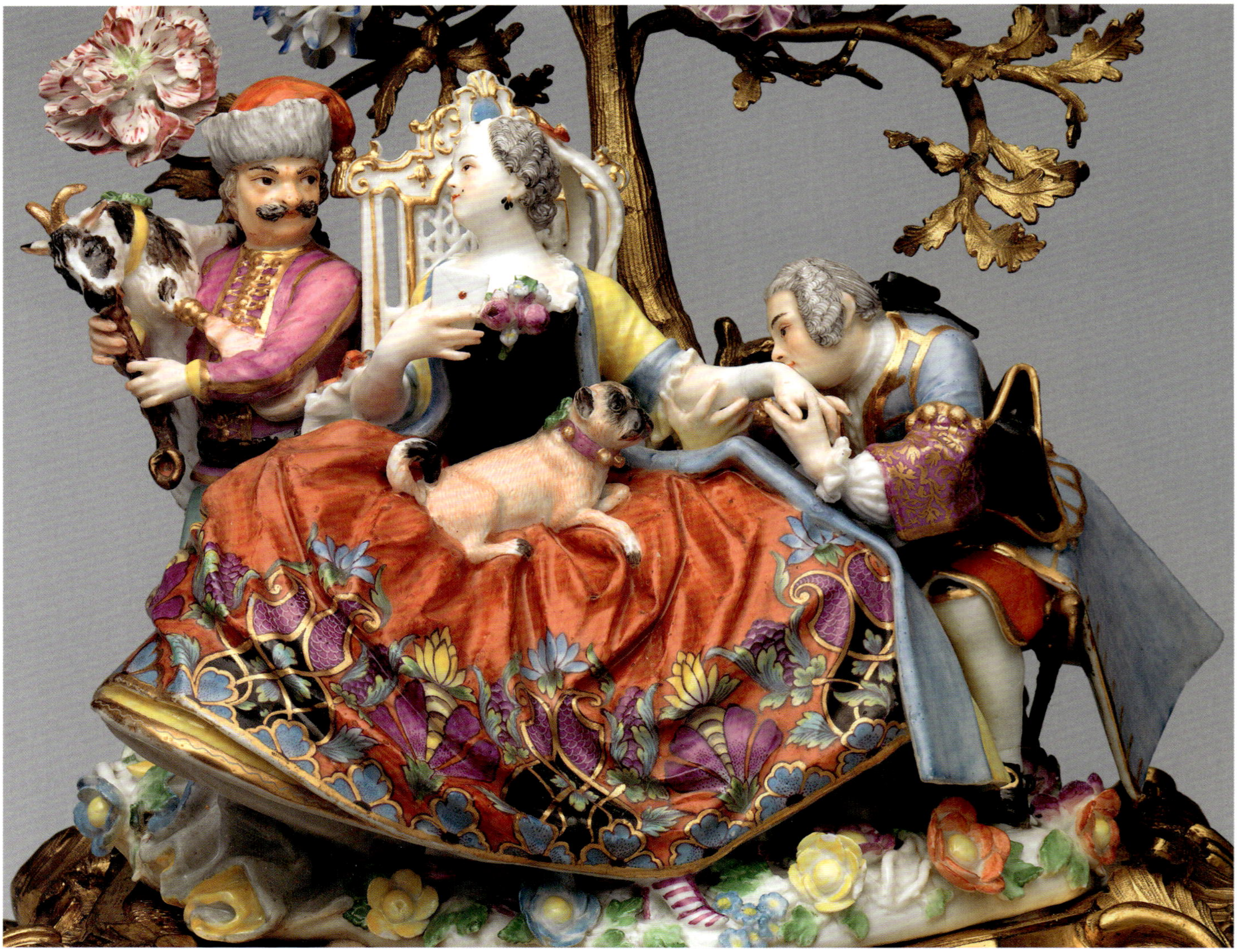

Detail of the Meissen porcelain group

has established that three members of the family were clockmakers, and, in fact, the widow of the first Gudin carried on his workshop long after his death. Paul Gudin (called Gudin le Jeune; Gudin the Younger), the uncle of Jacques-Jérôme, died about 1755, never having been a master clockmaker.[6] He belonged instead to the class of *ouvriers libres* and thus apparently not found in the records of the Paris guild. In 1739, Paul Gudin held a royal appointment as Marchand-Horloger Privilégié du Roi suivant la Cour et Conseils de Sa Majesté (Clock-Maker by Appointment to the King following his Court and Councils),[7] which carried with it certain privileges and duties to the royal court. As Augarde has pointed out, the appointment would have allowed Gudin to work undisturbed by complaints from the Paris clockmakers' guild.[8]

In 1725, Paul's brother Jacques Gudin (1706–1743) became a master clockmaker in Paris. At the time of his death, records indicate Jacques had an address on the Quai des Orfèvres in Paris, a locale with some of the best clockmakers and where Paul also rented a shop. It is Paul, however, who has been proposed as the maker of movements for clocks and watches for the highly decorative cases in various media, including porcelain, that are signed "Gudin le Jeune." There is evidence that clocks signed in this manner are for the most part to be found in rococo cases, some bearing the crowned "C" mark on their gilded-bronze mounts (a tax mark used in Paris in 1745–49 for metal alloys containing copper). As Jacques died in 1743 and Jacques-Jérôme did not have his own shop before 1754, Jean-Nérée Ronfort and Augarde reasoned that the signature "Gudin le Jeune" could only have been used by Paul Gudin.[9] One of the more successful *marchands-merciers* in eighteenth-century Paris was Lazare Duvaux (1709–1758), who held the title of Marchand-Bijoutier Ordinaire du Roy (Merchant Jeweler to the King) in 1748–58. Some of Duvaux's records have survived, and there is documentation of at least one payment from Gudin of 165 livres for a Meissen porcelain horse with a figure beside it.[10]

The Meissen group found on the Metropolitan Museum's clock has a complicated history. Commonly known as *The Hand Kiss* in English, the seated lady wearing a huge crinoline skirt has a pug dog on her lap. A cavalier kneels beside her and kisses her left hand. It has been suggested that these two figures have their origins in a print made by the French painter François Boucher (1703–1770), which also illustrates a scene from the Molière comedy *Le Sicilien, ou L'Amour peintre* (1667).[11] On the Museum's clock, however, the attention of the lady is directed to a third figure not found in the painting. This figure on the clock wears the colorful uniform of a Hungarian hussar and carries a remarkably lifelike goatskin bagpipe. As a separate porcelain piece, the third figure is

fig. 45 *Meissen Manufactory (German, founded 1710); modeler: Johann Joachim Kändler (German, 1706–1775). Lady with Attendant, German (Meissen), ca. 1740. Hard-paste porcelain with gilded-bronze mount, Height 7¼ in. (18.4 cm). The Metropolitan Museum of Art, New York, Gift of Irwin Untermyer, 1964 (64.101.59a, b)*

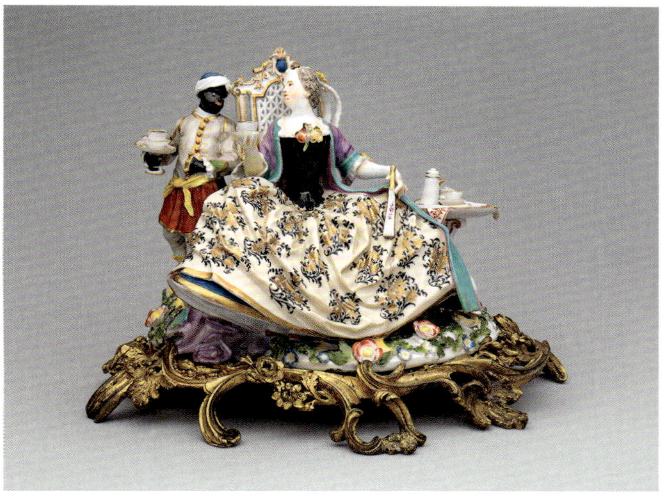

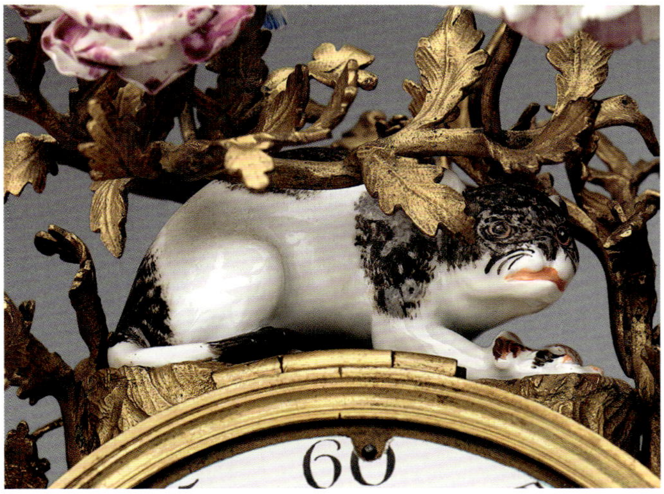

Detail of the cat from the crest of the clock

known as *Schindler (Court Jester and Hussar)*, or *Schindler the Liebhussar of Count von Brühl*, a reference to the real bodyguard of Count Heinrich von Brühl (1700–1763). Count von Brühl was prime minister to Augustus II (1670–1733), King of Poland, Elector of Saxony, and famously the patron of the porcelain manufactory at Meissen in Saxony. Count von Brühl became head of the Meissen Manufactory in 1733 and then the director in 1739. The meaning of this combination of *Schindler* with *The Hand Kiss* is far from certain, but the lady is clearly taken with the hussar, and her attitude prompts the thought that the situation may be closer to one of those found in a Mozart opera than in a Molière play.

Both *The Hand Kiss* and *Schindler* are the products of the chief modeler of Meissen, Johann Joachim Kändler (1706–1775). In April 1737, Kändler reported that his porcelain group depicted a lady with a cup of coffee in her right hand and a man kissing her left. She was also accompanied by an African servant with a salver (fig. 45). By August 1737, this porcelain group had grown, and the lady had now acquired a pug dog, and the African servant was serving coffee.[12] This version of the group seems to have been most popular, and it exists in a number of examples and permutations. Two of the variants appear on other clocks by "Gudin le Jeune."[13]

The group on the Metropolitan Museum's clock is mounted on an exuberantly rococo base of partly burnished and partly matte-finished gilded bronze. The base supports the stem of a bush laden with flowers that encircle the dial of the clock. The flowers are from the Vincennes porcelain manufactory (the predecessor to the Sèvres porcelain manufactory established by King Louis XV [1710–1774]), and peeping from the underbrush at the twelve o'clock position of the dial is a porcelain cat of uncertain origin with a dead bird between its front paws. The mounts are unmarked, the Vincennes porcelain was probably made about 1748 or shortly thereafter,[14] and the Meissen porcelain was modeled sometime after about 1737. Gudin is known to have purchased Meissen porcelain as late as 1753, therefore, it is plausible the clock may be dated about 1750 or slightly later.

A tooth that governs the striking of one o'clock on the count wheel is now missing, as is the pendulum. One of the flowers near the head of the cat is a replacement. Otherwise, the clock is in excellent condition.

The clock was in the possession of Maurice Kann, Paris, and also Joseph E. Widener at Lynnewood Hall, Elkins Park, Pennsylvania, before its acquisition by Lesley and Emma Sheafer.[15] CV / ES

1 For an expanded discussion, see Augarde 1996, pp. 13–49.
2 Sargentson 1998, pp. 99–105. See also Augarde 1996, pp. 179–82, 184, 186.
3 Savary des Brûlons 1761, p. 848. Savary des Brûlons's *Dictionnaire universel de commerce* was originally published in Paris, beginning in 1723.
4 Ibid., p. 849.
5 Tardy 1971–72, vol. 1, p. 279.
6 Augarde 1996, pp. 329–31.
7 See Jean-Nérée Ronfort and Jean-Dominique Augarde in Wilson et al. 1996, p. 176.
8 Augarde 1996, p. 36.
9 Ronfort and Augarde in Wilson et al. 1996, p. 176.
10 Courajod 1965, vol. 2, p. 162, no. 1443.
11 Jean-Richard 1978, p. 133, no. 429, ill.
12 From Kändler's work reports, quoted in Den Blaauwen 2000, p. 429.
13 *Frühes Meissener Porzellen* 1997, pp. 80–81, no. 51; Kjellberg 1997, p. 137, fig. F. See also Sotheby's 1978, no. 51, ill.
14 Préaud 2003, p. 51.
15 See Freeman's 1944, p. 79, no. 418, ill.

39. Mantel Clock

FRENCH (PARIS), CA. 1764–70
28 × 20¼ × 10 in. (71.1 × 51.4 × 25.4 cm)
Bequest of Ogden Mills, 1929
29.180.2

CASE: patinated bronze and gilded bronze
DIAL: white enamel, signed: LEPAUTE / APARIS [Jean-André Lepaute, French, 1720–1789, and Jean-Baptiste Lepaute, French, 1727–1802]
MOVEMENT: brass and steel

TIME AND ASTRONOMY ARE INEXTRICABLY LINKED: THE DAILY rotation of the earth and the apparent motion of the sun through the constellations of the zodiac provide the basis for the terrestrial day and the year. The months correspond loosely to the lunar cycle, but the motion of the moon is by no means easily determined. In the price list dated 1766 for the twenty-four clocks that Jean-André Lepaute (1720–1789) supplied to his clients, titled *Description de plusieurs ouvrages d'horlogerie* (Description of Several Clock Works), his model number one is described as *Pendule Uranie*, or a pendulum clock with a figure of Urania, the Muse of Astronomy.[1] In his description, Lepaute claims the figure of Urania is based on a model by the French sculptor Jean-Antoine Houdon (1741–1828).[2] With minor changes in some of the details, the description in the list matches that of a clock in the Metropolitan Museum's collection.

The case for the Museum's clock consists of a truncated pilaster made of gilded bronze that rests on a richly ornamented gilded-bronze base and supports a cylindrical movement with a white-enamel dial, the hours (I–XII) and the minutes (15–60, by fifteen-minute intervals) marked in black. The dial is signed, "Lepaute / Æparis," and below the six o'clock position, in tiny script, appears "Dubuis" (presumably the signature of the dial painter). The elegantly slim hour and minute hands are made of gilded brass. A swag of husks is draped below the dial. The figure of Urania, her right hand holding a scroll with the zodiacal symbols for Libra and Scorpio, leans against the movement. She wears a classical Greek dress that is bound at the waist with a contrasting belt with stars, and there is a second belt of undecorated gilded brass in her hair. Opposite Urania, a playful winged cherub, his drapery askew, turns away from the bird that he holds in both hands as he sits on a stack of heavy books. Behind him is a celestial globe, and beside him lies both a chart of a lunar eclipse, labeled "ECLIPSE DU 1.^{R} AVRIL / 1764," and a semicircle, labeled 10–100, by tens, with a projecting piece of something that might well be a sighting device. All of these elements are created from gilded bronze, and they are probably meant not only as attributes appropriate to an infant Genius of Astronomy[3] but also as allusions to the activities of Madame Jean-André Lepaute (1723–1788), the clockmaker's wife, who was an able mathematician also known by her maiden name Nicole-Reine Etable de la Brière.

A good theory that would accurately predict the moon's motion was lacking during the first part of the eighteenth century. Among the mathematicians who proposed solutions was the Frenchman Alexis-Claude Clairaut (1713–1765), whose *Théorie de la lune* (Theory of the Moon; 1752) won a prize given by the Imperial Academy of Sciences that same year.[4] His publications, as well as more successful ones by his

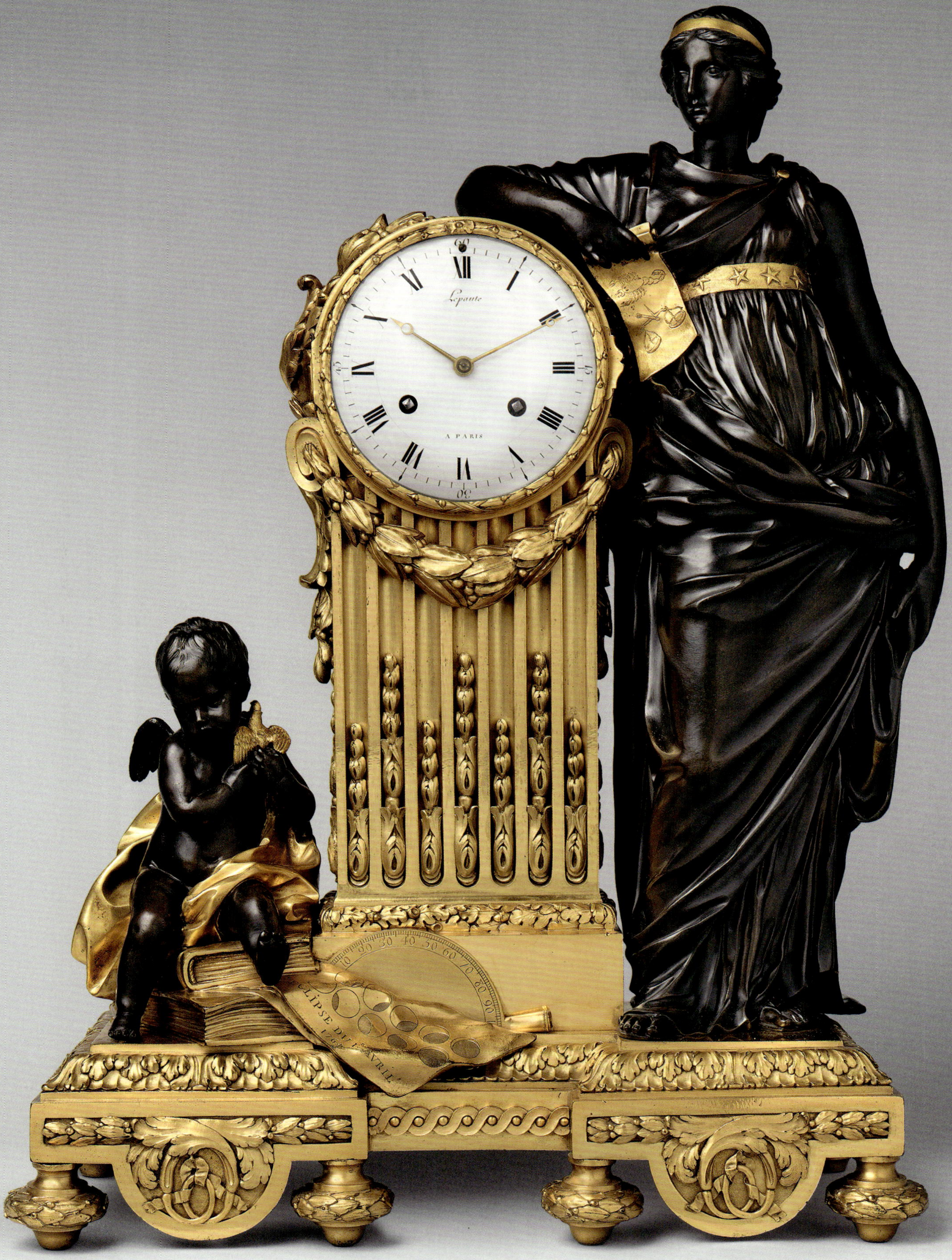
Lepaute
A PARIS

top: *Detail of the cherub and celestial globe*
bottom: *Detail of the chart depicting the course of the lunar eclipse, April 1, 1764, published by Madame Lepaute*

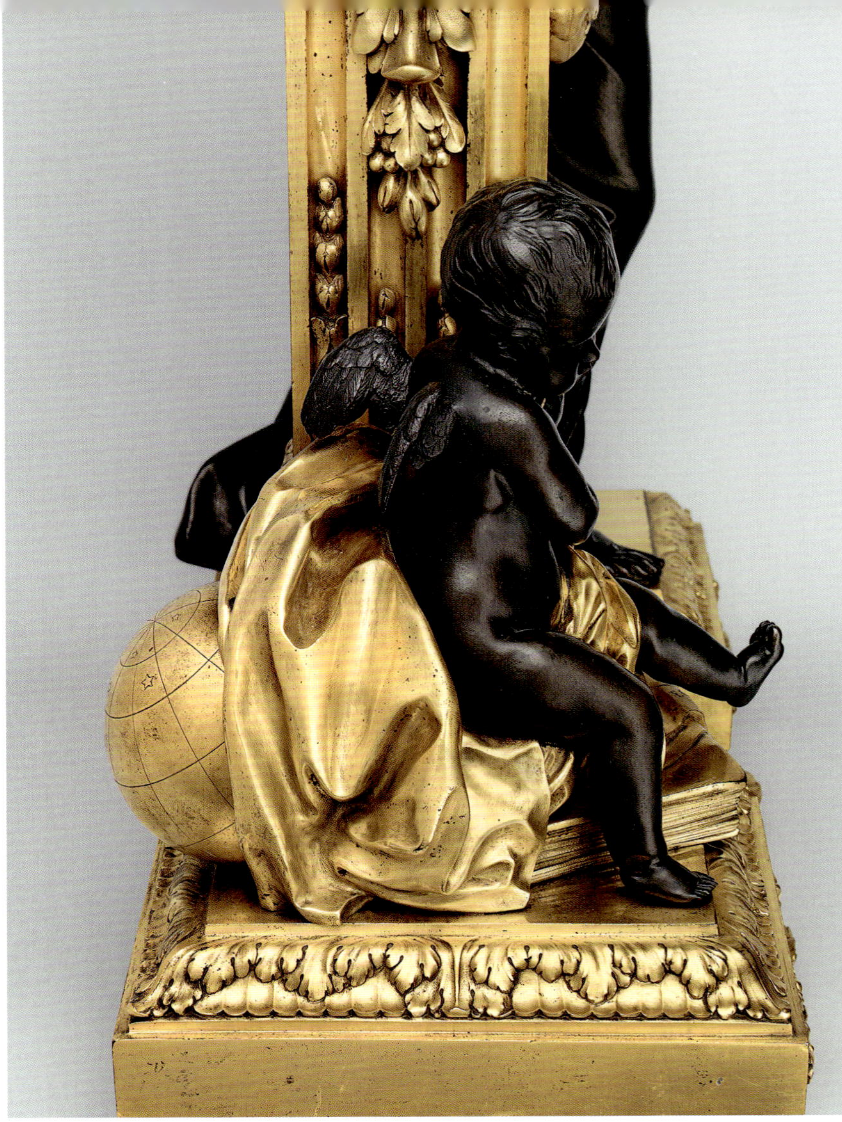

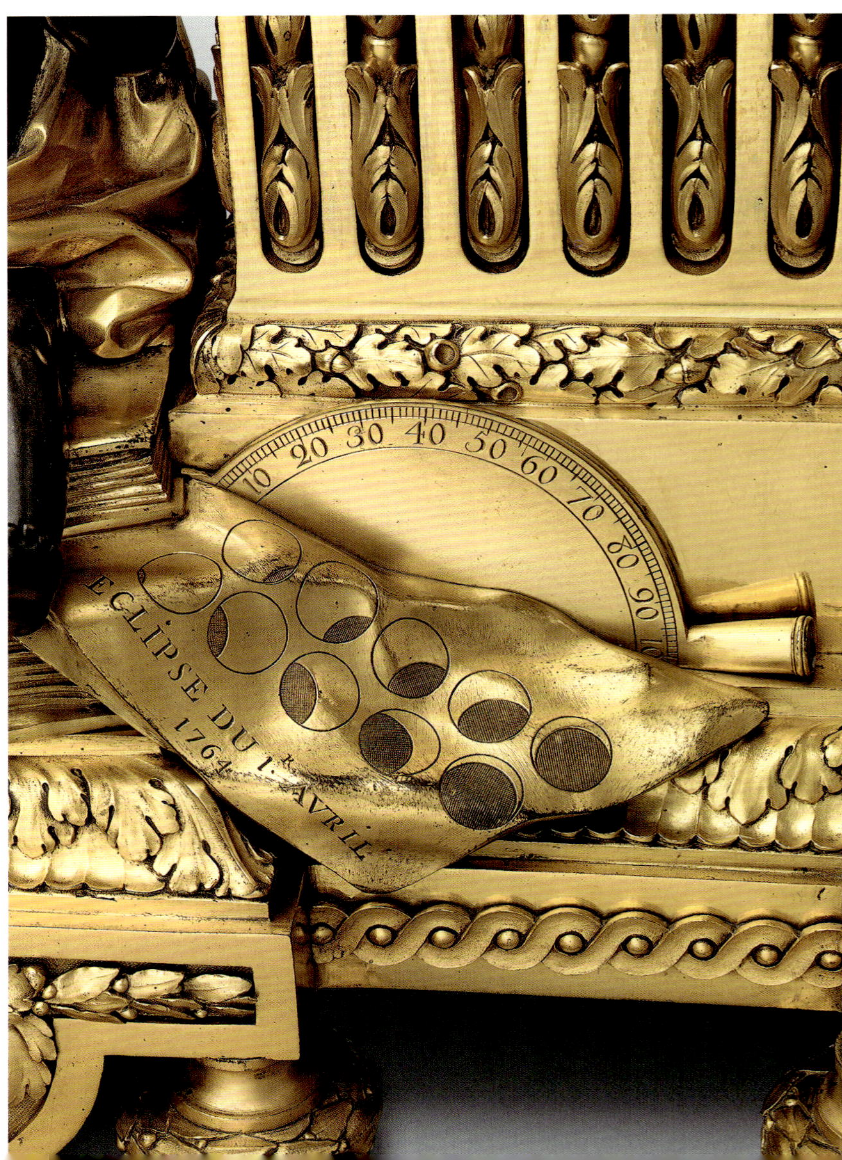

contemporaries Tobias Mayer (1723–1762) and Leonard Euler (1707–1783), who also attempted solutions to lunar theory, were not only important to theoretical science but also to the very practical problem of finding the longitude.[5] In the same period, the French astronomer Joseph-Jérôme Lalande (1732–1807) became the editor of the French almanac *Connaissance des temps* (Knowledge of Time), where some of Madame Lepaute's scientific work appeared. With Lalande, Madame Lepaute helped Clairaut with the laborious calculations leading up to the prediction of the return of Halley's Comet in 1761.[6] She also assisted Lalande with tracking the transit of Venus, the observation of the path of the planet across the face of the sun in 1769.[7] Her directions for the construction of pendulums appeared in her husband's treatise on clockmaking, the *Traité d'horlogerie* (Treatise on Clockmaking; 1755).[8] Her prediction of the lunar eclipse that occurred in 1764 was published in 1762 under her own name,[9] and it is Madame Lepaute's chart of the eclipse that appears on the base of the Museum's clock. The clock was destined in all probability for display on a mantelpiece in a Parisian mansion where it could suggest to the participants in a fashionable salon that its owner was cognizant of the importance of astronomy to the science of the period.[10]

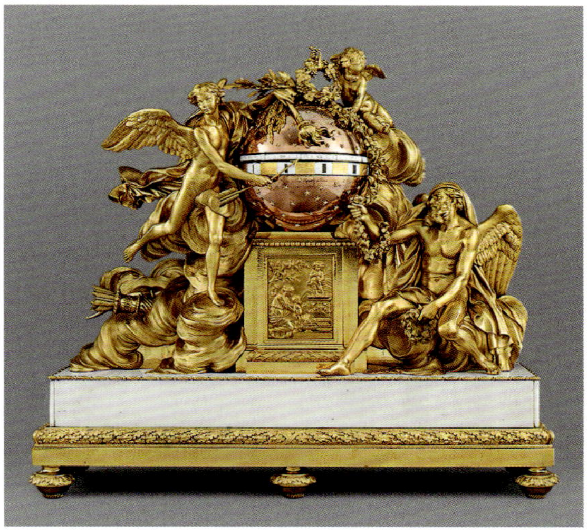

fig. 46 *Clockmaker: Lepaute workshop in this period consisting of Jean-Baptiste Lepaute (French, 1727–1802), Pierre-Henry Lepaute (French, 1748–1806), and Pierre-Basile Lepaute (French, 1750–1843); figure modeler: Augustin Pajou (French, 1730–1809); figure caster: Etienne Martincourt (French, active 1762–1800). Mantel Clock, French (Paris), ca. 1780–90. Gilded bronze, marble, and enamel, 37 × 41 × 12½ in., Weight 379 lbs. (94 × 104.1 × 31.8 cm, Weight 171.9 kg). The Metropolitan Museum of Art, New York, Gift of J. Pierpont Morgan, 1917 (17.190.2126)*

The movement attests to the competence of its makers, Jean-André Lepaute and his brother Jean-Baptiste. It is spring driven and consists of two circular brass plates held apart by four pillars, and it includes a going barrel with a train of four wheels regulated by a pinwheel escapement and a pendulum of approximately seventeen inches with spring suspension. The striking train, like the going train with a going barrel and no fusee, has four wheels and a fly, and it is controlled by a count wheel. It strikes hours on a bell that is mounted vertically on the back plate.

The pinwheel escapement, a variety of recoilless escapement, was the French answer to the Englishman George Graham's (1673–1751) dead-beat escapement and was probably invented about 1740 by the Paris clockmaker Louis Amant (master in 1725; died before 1753). Historians Jean-Nérée Ronfort and Jean-Dominique Augarde believe that Jean-André Lepaute had experimented with a form of dead-beat escapement before coming to Paris, and he probably showed his experiments to Amant when he first arrived.[11] It is not certain what experiments these may have been, but a diagram of the pinwheel escapement appears as the invention of Amant in the 1741 *Traité de l'horlogerie* by Antoine Thiout l'aîné.[12] In Jean-André Lepaute's own treatise on clock- and watchmaking, he describes an improved version of the pinwheel escapement of his own invention.[13] In this device a wheel with twenty-four pins—small cylinders attached on one flat side

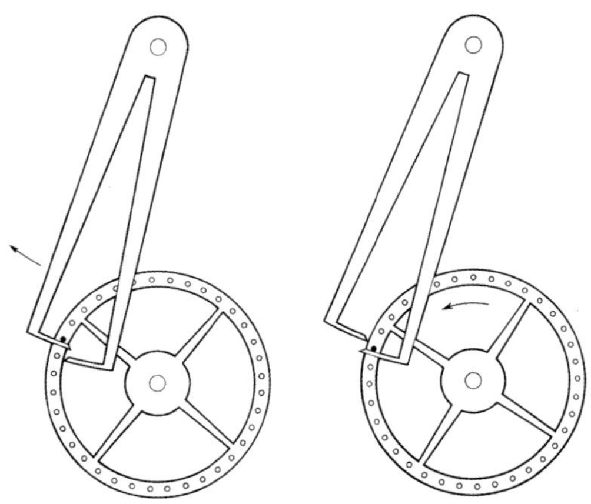

fig. 47 *Two views of a pinwheel escapement. Drawn by David Penney, British, 2014*

that catch and release two separate arms—mounted on the pendulum arbor, was modified so that the pins are placed alternately on both flat sides of the wheel, which are semicircular in section instead of circular. Lepaute asserted that his escapement was better than both Graham's and Amant's, and that it had met the approval of Lalande, member of the Académie Royale des Sciences in Paris[14] and the colleague and mentor of Madame Lepaute. In the succeeding chapter Lepaute gave directions on how to construct his version of the pinwheel. Nevertheless, it is Amant's original version of the pinwheel escapement that the Lepautes used in the Museum's clock.

Jean-André Lepaute was without doubt a skillful and inventive clockmaker. Augarde has affirmed that Lepaute was the son of André Lepaute, a locksmith in Thonne-la-Long in the Ardennes region of France from whom Jean-André probably learned metal casting, ironwork, and perhaps a variety of turret clockmaking.[15] When Jean-André arrived in Paris, he had not served the required period of apprenticeship to a Parisian clockmaker and therefore was not eligible for membership in the Paris guild of clockmakers. He seems, however, to have become a protégé of Amant's. His marriage to Nicole-Reine Etable de la Brière in 1747[16] brought him contact with both scientists and intellectuals, and his *Traité d'horlogerie* contains his wife's mathematical calculations. Among his inventions was a clock with a single wheel that he presented to the French King Louis XV (1710–1774) in 1751.[17] Ronfort and Augarde believe that Jean-André had already been appointed Clockmaker to the King, as evidenced by his occupation of a lodging in the royal palace of Luxembourg,[18] where he was engaged to make a turret clock for the palace. Among other privileges, the appointment usually carried an award of a lodging or workshop within the Galeries du Louvre, but according to Ronfort and Augarde, the award was not granted until 1756, when he was given lodging number fourteen.[19] He retired in 1775[20] and left the business to his brother Jean-Baptiste, who had joined him in Paris in the 1740s, as well as to two nephews, Pierre-Henry (1748–1806) and Pierre-Basile (1750–1843). Jean-Baptiste had received a royal appointment sometime before 1774 and the occupancy of the fourteenth lodging in the Louvre in 1775.[21] Due to their success, Jean-André and Jean-Baptiste had long outgrown the space in the Louvre; therefore, they had establishments elsewhere in Paris, including the prestigious rue Saint-Honoré in 1766 and the Place du Palais Royal by 1772.[22]

The Museum also has an example of model number two, the *Pendule Clio* (the Muse of History), from the 1766 price list,[23] as well as four clocks from the period in which the firm consisted of Jean-Baptiste, Pierre-Henry, and Pierre-Basile (fig. 46).[24] Three clocks have the revolving horizontal dials for which the Lepaute workshop was noted. One of the clocks is housed in an imposing case depicting the Triumph of Love over Time by the French founder Etienne Martincourt (active 1762–1800)[25] with figures cast after models by the French sculptor Augustin Pajou (1730–1809).

A number of variants of the case design were made for the Lepautes,[26] and the winged cherubs from the Urania and the Clio clocks appear together on yet another case for a clock with a movement by the Lepautes.[27]

The clock is in good condition. Nothing is known of its provenance before it was given to the Metropolitan Museum by Ogden Mills. It was one of five French clocks from the eighteenth century that entered the Museum's collection either as his gifts or by bequest,[28] including the *Pendule Clio*.
CV / JHL

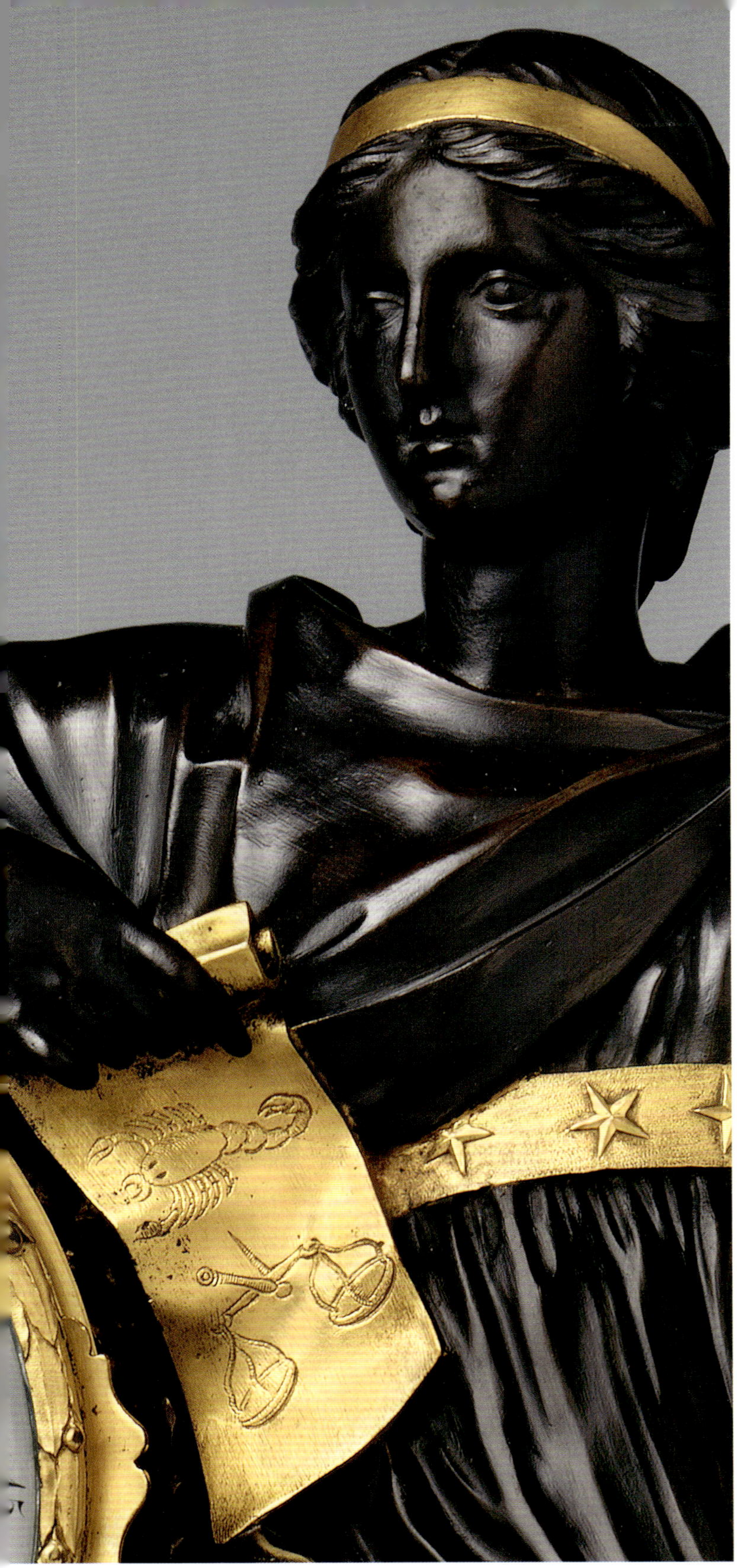

Detail of Jean-Antoine Houdon's Urania holding a scroll that depicts the zodiacal symbols of Libra and Scorpio

1. Quoted in Tardy 1971–72, vol. 2, p. 378. Some of the details and attributes are variations of those on the Museum's clock.
2. There is apparently no confirmation by Houdon scholars of this attribution.
3. It is so described (*Génie de l'Astronomie*) in Lepaute's price list. See Tardy 1971–72, vol. 2, p. 378.
4. Clairaut 1752.
5. For a further discussion of the lunar solution to finding longitude, see Chandler 1996.
6. See Clairaut 1760, in which Madame Lepaute's contributions were not acknowledged.
7. Lalande 1762, pp. 206ff.
8. J.-A. Lepaute 1755, pp. 282–97.
9. N.-R. Lepaute 1762, p. 8. According to Lalande, her chart was available from the printer Lattré on the rue de la Parcheminerie, Paris. See Lalande 1762, pp. 205–6.
10. Augarde 1996, p. 74.
11. Ronfort and Augarde in Wilson et al. 1996, p. 180.
12. Thiout 1741, vol. 1, p. 112, and pl. 44, fig. 38.
13. J.-A. Lepaute 1755, pp. 191–93, and pl. XIV.
14. Ibid., p. 192.
15. Augarde 1996, p. 351.
16. Ronfort and Augarde in Wilson et al. 1996, p. 179, give the date of the wedding as Aug. 27, 1747. Their evidence is based on a manuscript written by Gabriel-Joseph Lepaute (1793–1882), "Notice Historique sur la famille Lepaute," in the possession of Michel Henry-Lepaute (see p. 182, n. 2). Elsewhere the marriage year has been given as 1748 or 1749.
17. See Tardy 1971–72, vol. 2, p. 378.
18. Ronfort and Augarde in Wilson et al. 1996, p. 179.
19. Ibid., pp. 179, 182, n. 5. See also Guiffrey 1873, p. 132.
20. Augarde 1996, p. 351; Ronfort and Augarde in Wilson et al. 1996, p. 180.
21. Guiffrey 1873, p. 132. He was succeeded there in 1779.
22. Tardy 1971–72, vol. 2, p. 378.
23. Acc. no. 37.160.10. For the price list, see ibid., pp. 378–79.
24. Acc. nos. 17.190.2126, 29.180.4, 41.41, and 1972.284.16. The Lepaute firm continued to exist in Paris until 1952 see Tardy 1971–72, vol. 2, p. 385. For an extended account of the early Lepautes, see Ronfort and Augarde in Wilson et al. 1996, pp. 179–83.
25. A discovery of Jean-Dominique Augarde. See Augarde 1996, p. 136.
26. One example is in a private collection in Paris. See Kjellberg 1997, p. 250, fig. B.
27. Tardy 1971–72, vol. 2, p. 379, model number four. See Augarde 1996, p. 151, fig. 117; this clock was sold at Sotheby's, New York, Dec. 7, 1991, no. 10, ill.
28. Acc. nos. 29.180.3, 29.180.4, 37.160.9, and 37.160.10.

40. Automaton in the Form of a Chariot Pushed by a Chinese Attendant and Set with a Clock

BRITISH (LONDON), 1766

10¼ × 6⅜ × 3¼ in. (26 × 16.2 × 8.3 cm)

The Jack and Belle Linsky Collection, 1982

1982.60.137

CASE: gold with diamonds and paste jewels set in silver

DIAL: white enamel, signed: *J^a Cox / London* [James Cox, British, ca. 1723–1800]

MOVEMENT: partly gilded brass and steel; balance wheel and cock: silver set with paste jewels

DURING THE COURSE OF KING GEORGE III'S (1738–1820) EMBASSY to the Chinese emperor in 1792, the British emissary to China, Lord George Macartney (1737–1806), is reported to have viewed about forty or fifty buildings in the imperial establishment in Beijing that contained "every kind of European toys and sing-songs; with spheres, orreries, clocks, and musical automatons of . . . exquisite workmanship."[1] Lord Macartney was undoubtedly commenting on the fabled collection of clocks inherited, acquired, and commissioned by Emperor Qianlong (1711–1799). Among these European toys (or singsongs, as the Chinese are believed to have called them), there must have been a pair of automata that had been presented to the Chinese emperor by the English East India Company (1600–1708). The automata were earlier described in the December 1766 edition of the *Gentleman's Magazine*:

> These clocks are in [the] form of chariots, in which are placed, in a fine attitude, a lady leaning her right hand upon a part of the chariot, under which is a clock of curious workmanship, little larger than a shilling, that strikes and repeats, and goes eight days. Upon her finger sits a bird, finely modelled, and set with diamonds and rubies, with its wings expanded in a flying posture, and actually flutters for a considerable time, on touching a diamond button below it; the body of the bird (which contains part of the wheels that in a manner give life to it) is not the bigness of the sixteenth part of an inch.
>
> The lady holds in her left hand a gold tube, not much thicker than a large pin, on the top of which is a small round box, to which a circular ornament set with diamonds, not larger than a sixpence, is fixed, which goes round near three hours in a constant, regular motion. Over the lady's head (supported by a small fluted pillar, no bigger than a quill) is a double umbrella, under the largest of which a bell is fixed, at a considerable distance from the clock, and seems to have no connection with it, but from which a communication is secretly conveyed to a hammer, that regularly strikes the hour, and repeats the same at pleasure, by touching a diamond button fixed to the clock below.[2]

The *Gentleman's Magazine* continues with the description of two birds on spiral springs, which were attached to the front end of the chariot but are now missing from the Museum's automaton. The article also describes the boy who appears to be pushing the chariot from behind, and the bejeweled flowers atop the parasol that is crowned by a flying dragon. Notwithstanding the omission of the fact that the entire

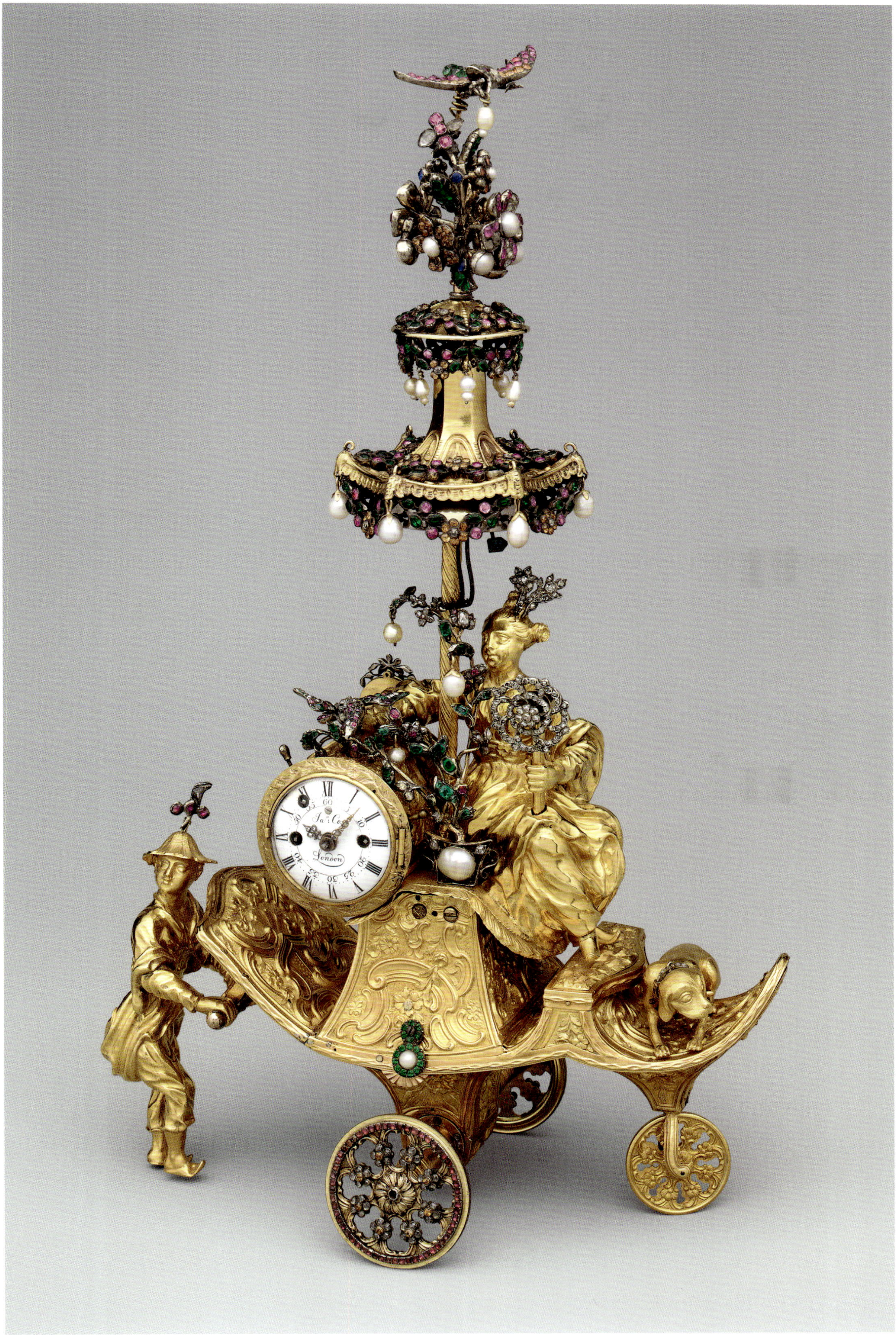

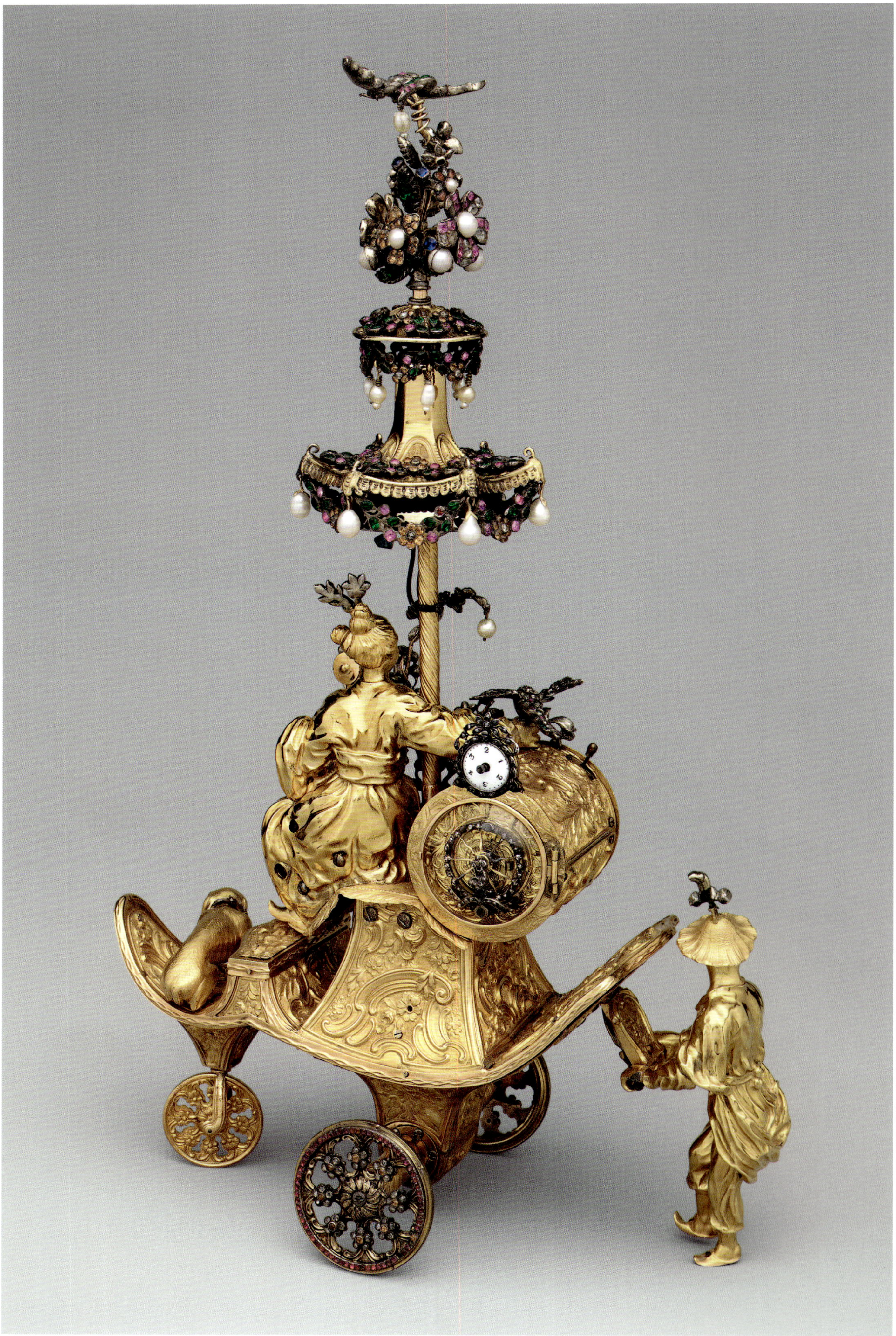

mechanism is propelled by a spring and fusee device and housed above the two central wheels of the chariot, *Gentleman's Magazine* provides a nearly exact description of the Museum's automaton, as recognized by the late Metropolitan Museum curator Clare Le Corbeiller in her catalogue entry for the object in *The Jack and Belle Linsky Collection in The Metropolitan Museum of Art* (1984).[3]

It may be noted that the date of the East India Company's gift in 1766 corresponds to the same year in which the company's monopoly on British trade to China expired. Presumably, the company hoped that this pair of automata, with its mandarins and flying dragons (European stereotypes of Chinese culture during the Qianlong era), might so delight the emperor that he would be disposed to welcome further British trade.

On a trade card bearing the London address "at the Golden Urn," from about the middle of the eighteenth century, James Cox proclaimed himself a goldsmith who "Makes Great Variety of Curious Work in Gold, Silver, and other Mettals. Also in Amber, Pearl, Tortoisshell and Curious Stones."[4] Yet Cox seems to have spent most of his career as an entrepreneur and in 1773, he was said to have "invented sundry pieces of uncommon and expensive workmanship, in the construction of which, employment had been afforded to numbers of ingenious artists and workmen. . . ."[5] Most of the craftsmen were part of a unique network of independent suppliers and craftsmen who resided in London during the second half of the eighteenth century.[6] These craftsmen rarely signed their work, and only a few of them have thus far been identified; nonetheless, their existence made possible the great variety of objects that Cox exported.

The clockmaker's name was required by law to be visible on watches with enameled dials that were made in London for export, a circumstance that explains the presence of Cox's name on the dials of watches and clocks that are incorporated into these objects. Cox would have had to depend upon skilled craftsmen in the watchmaking trade, because there is no evidence that he at any time made a watch movement. Beginning in the mid-1760s, Cox produced lavishly ornamented articles for trade with the Far East, first with India and then with China, where his toys were initially well received.[7] A later ban on shipment of his luxury goods to China, however, resulted in the establishment of the short-lived Spring Gardens Museum in London in 1772 and the publication of *A Descriptive Catalogue of the Several Superb and Magnificent Pieces of Mechanism and Jewellery, Exhibited in Mr. Cox's Museum* in several editions. In 1775, Cox disposed of his museum's contents by lottery.

The most spectacular survival of Cox's enterprise remains the ten-foot-high Peacock Clock in the State Hermitage Museum in Saint Petersburg, with its clockwork-driven automata, which was brought to the city in 1781, probably by one of Cox's clockmaker-suppliers, Frederick Jury.[8] Cox hoped to establish direct trade relations with Russia and attempted to sell jewelry to Catherine II, Empress of Russia (Catherine the Great) (1729–1796), although without success.

Cox's loss of reliable trade with China, the failure in Russia, and the fact that he never achieved royal patronage, in addition to suffering from the ill effects of the American Revolution (1775–83) on British foreign trade, together precipitated his second bankruptcy in 1778. The remaining stock from Canton, China, was sold at Christie's in London on February 16, 1792. In the meantime, Cox and his sons (one in Canton and the other in London) resumed business and began sending watches, mostly made by the Swiss firm of Jaquet-Droz et Leschot, to China.[9]

The emperor's second *Automaton in the Form of a Chariot* is not known to have survived, but the Metropolitan Museum's example has been traced to a publication titled *A Short Account of the Remarkable Clock Made by James Cox, in the Year 1766 . . . for the Emperor of China* (1868).[10] It next appeared in the collection of Alfred Charles de Rothschild,[11] and finally, in the collection of Jack and Belle Linsky in New York. CV / JHL

1 George Macartney, quoted in Pagani 2001, p. 83. See also Landes 1983, pp. 48–49.
2 "Description of Two Curious Clocks" 1766. The description was repeated verbatim in *Annual Register . . . for the Year 1766* 1785, pp. 230–31.
3 Clare Le Corbeiller in Metropolitan Museum of Art 1984, p. 191, no. 111.
4 The card is illustrated in R. Smith 2000, p. 353, fig. 16.
5 See "The Act for Enabling Mr. Cox to Dispose of His Museum by Way of Lottery," in *Descriptive Inventory . . . of Mechanism and Jewellery* 1773, p. ii.
6 For further discussion of these suppliers or subcontractors, especially to the furniture, coachmaking, and scientific instrument trades in eighteenth-century London, see Riello 2008, pp. 257–72.
7 See Pagani 2001, pp. 102–4. For the automata and clocks signed by Cox that are still in the collection of the Palace Museum in Beijing, see Harcourt-Smith 1933, pp. 13–18; *Clocks and Watches of the Qing Dynasty* 2002, nos. 51–57.
8 Zek and R. Smith 2005.
9 R. Smith 2000; Pagani 2001, pp. 105–9, 112–22. See also entry 46 in this volume.
10 *Short Account of the Remarkable Clock* 1868. Le Corbeiller in Metropolitan Museum of Art 1984, p. 191, no. 111, noted that the automaton had been acquired in Paris, recounting the story that it had been brought from China by a French sailor, after the looting of the Imperial Summer Palace near Beijing.
11 C. Davis 1884, vol. 2, no. 141.

41. Longcase Clock

ITALIAN (BOLOGNA), 1766

96½ × 23 × 15¾ in. (245.1 × 58.4 × 40 cm)
Height of dial plate: 19¼ in. (48.9 cm)
Gift of Madame Lilliana Teruzzi, 1971
1971.1.3

CASE: partly gilded walnut and pine with later additions of various woods
DIAL: brass, signed and dated: *Mario Gambelli da Montalboddo 1766* [Mario Gambelli, Italian, active 1766]
MOVEMENT: brass and steel

THE WEIGHT-DRIVEN, RECTANGULAR-FRAMED MOVEMENT OF THIS clock is not unlike some of those found in Rome during the last quarter of the fifteenth century. Firsthand descriptions of these clocks appear in the manuscript of Paulus Almanus (Paul the German), a lay brother and practical clockmaker who recorded his impressions of clocks that he saw in Rome beginning about 1475. A fifteenth-century model[1] has been brought up to date in the Museum's clock, also called a lantern clock in English, because of its perceived resemblance to a portable case for a light. It employs a pendulum in place of the foliot (or balance) for the regulation of its escapement that would have been found in a fifteenth-century clock, and an unequal-pin mechanism has been substituted for the older and more common count wheel to govern the striking of the hours.

In addition to hours and quarters, this clock strikes the previous hour on a lower-pitched bell before striking the first, second, and third quarters on a higher-pitched bell, a system known as *grande sonnerie*. Here, the *grande sonnerie* is employed in a four-times-six-hour division of the twenty-four-hour day, a division that was in use in eighteenth-century Italy.

The frame of the movement of the clock is made entirely of brass, with scalloped edges on the plates, pillars in the form of slender columns, and bars that are shaped to echo the architectural outlines of the columns. Cast finials, bun feet, and a handle for lifting the movement complete this extraordinary piece of clockmaking. The four brass wheels of the going train are regulated by a horizontal verge and short pendulum that ends in a bob shaped like a small bird. (It is likely that neither the pendulum shaft nor the bob is original to the clock.) Four wheels and a fly complete the striking train. The second wheel includes a double set of pins of unequal length, which controls the blows of the long-tailed hammers for two bells that are mounted on top of the hood and provide a visual display to accompany the arresting sound of the bells.

The dial plate, with applied rocaille-ornamented C-scrolls, is an exuberant example of Italian rococo design. The irregularly shaped piercing near the top permits a view of the urn-shaped finials mounted above the front pillars of the frame of the movement. These pierced openings flank a cartouche with a miniature painting of a bust-length figure of a woman (probably a later addition). A horizontal slot in a dial plate allows it to be pinned to the top plate of the movement. Below, the arc-shaped slot for the false pendulum permits an extension of the verge to swing back and forth with the movement of the pendulum. The applied chapter ring, introducing a note of sobriety, has easily distinguished roman numerals (I–XII) for the hours and Arabic numerals that label each five-minute interval.

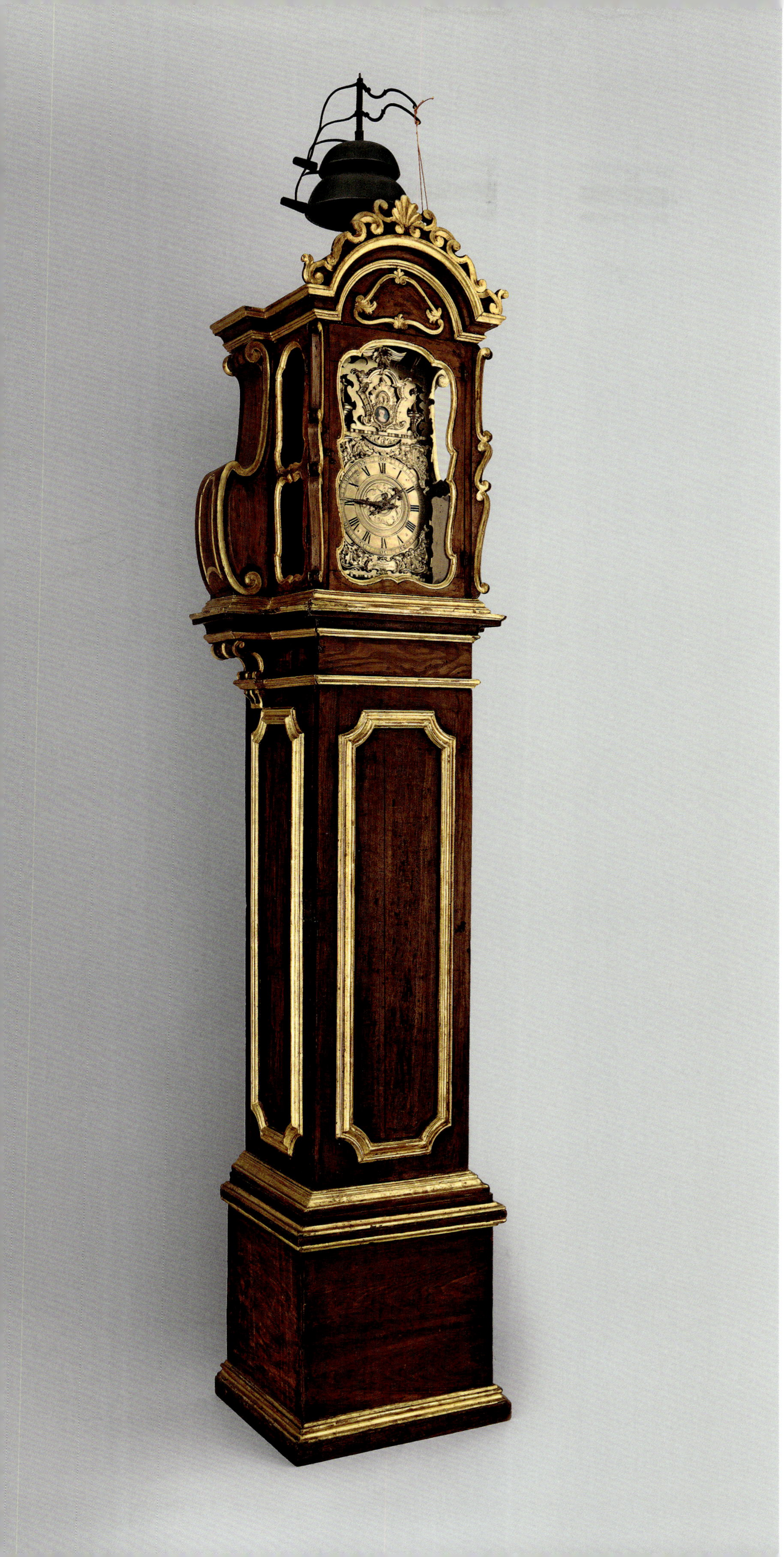

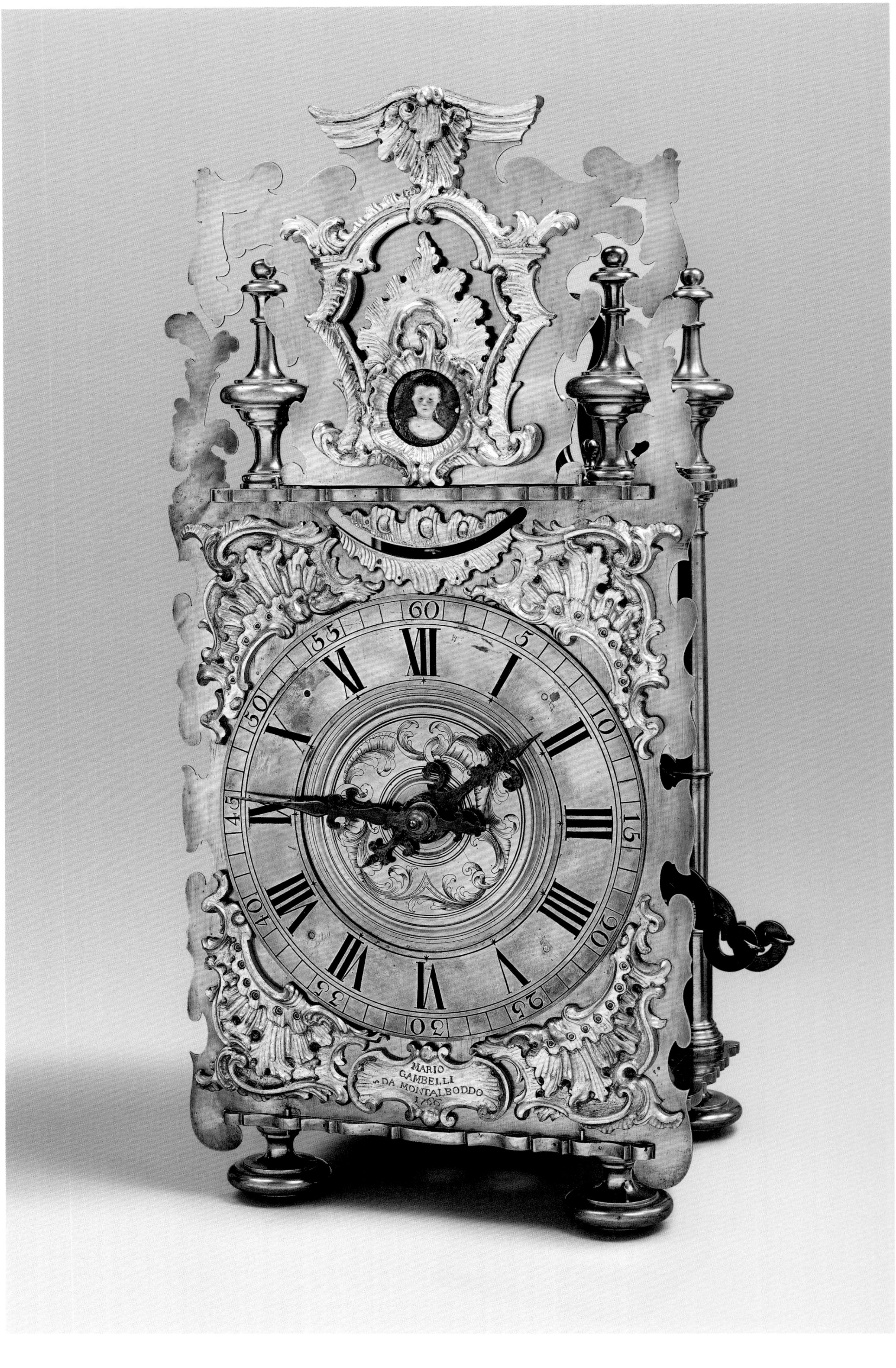
MARIO
GAMBELLI
DA MONTALBODDO
1766

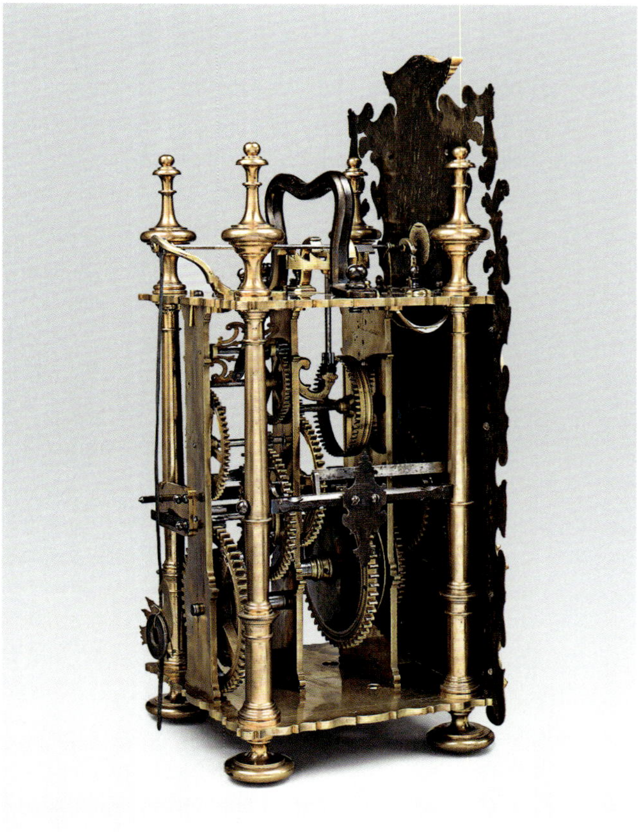

The lantern-shaped movement

The walnut hood of the case, with a break arch and gilded scrolling top, has console-shaped elements on both sides, which function as part of the doors that provide access to the movement. A glass-paneled door in the front gives access to the dial. Although the height of the case is more than eight feet, the trunk is made of different wood. It is relatively short, permitting a duration of only about fifteen hours, and lends support to the belief that the trunk is a later construction, perhaps made at two separate times. The hood, however, is original eighteenth-century cabinetry.

The clockmaker, Mario Gambelli (active 1766), is believed to have worked in Bologna, based on the Latinized name Marius Gambelli Bononiensis that appears on a lantern clock that also has an unequal-pin mechanism.[2] The location, Montalboddo, which is named on the Museum's clock, cannot be found on a modern map of Italy. However, the mystery was solved when it was learned that in 1881 a town known as Montalboddo, near Ancona on the Adriatic coast, had decided to revert to its ancient Roman name of Ostra.[3]

The clock belonged to Prince Cesare Ludovico Ottoboni in Rome when it is believed to have been sold about 1932 or 1933. The Museum acquired the clock as part of a larger gift of Italian decorative arts from Madame Lilliana Teruzzi, a former opera singer who lived in New York for many years until her death in 1987. CV / JHL

1 See, for example, Leopold 1971, pp. 46–51, clock no. 2. See also Leopold 2003, pp. 665–66, 671; Leopold 2005b.
2 Morpurgo 1974, p. 75. In a letter to Clare Vincent dated Feb. 25, 2002, Giancarlo Del Vecchio mentioned the Latinized name on the lantern clock. Its present location is unknown.
3 See http://www.comune.ostra.an.it. The authors are indebted to Del Vecchio for this identification.

42. Astronomical Regulator

FRENCH (PARIS), CA. 1768–70
90½ × 21 × 12¾ in. (229.9 × 53.3 × 32.4 cm)
The Jack and Belle Linsky Collection, 1982
1982.60.50

CASE: oak veneered with ebony and brass, with gilded-bronze mounts, stamped (on lower part of base, at back): B. LIEUTAUD [Balthazar Lieutaud, French, ca. 1720–1780]; mounts probably cast from models by Philippe II Caffiéri, French, 1714–1774
DIAL: white enamel, signed FERDINAND / BERTHOUD [Ferdinand Berthoud, Swiss, 1727–1807]
MOVEMENT: gilded brass and steel, signed (on back plate): *Ferdinand Berthoud Æaris*

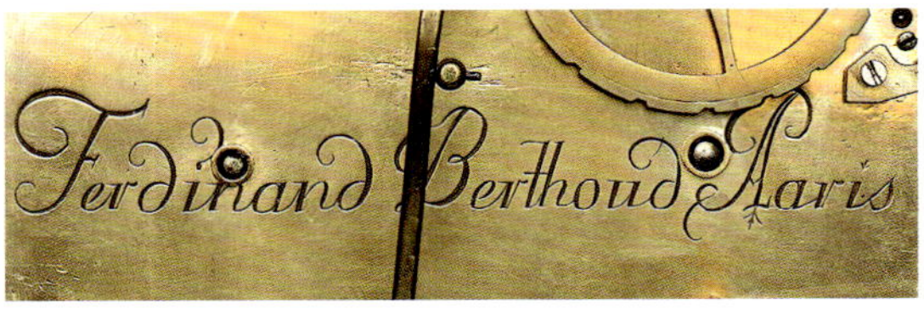

The signature on the back plate

FERDINAND BERTHOUD (1727–1807) LEFT HIS NATIVE VILLAGE OF Placemont, near Neuchâtel in the Swiss Jura region, in 1745 and moved to Paris after acquiring his clockmaking skills from an elder brother, Jean-Henri Berthoud (1710–1790).[1] Once in Paris, he encountered the difficulties posed by the restrictions of the guild of clockmakers who excluded anyone not apprenticed to a Parisian master. The guild's strictures discouraged some excellent clockmakers from opening shops in Paris,[2] but some of the cleverest were able to circumvent the rules by obtaining special dispensation granted by the French king,[3] by joining a category known as *ouvriers libres* (free workers),[4] or by working in certain places that were exempt from the jurisdiction of the guild (for more information, see entry 19 in this volume). One of these places was a small area on the Left Bank in Paris belonging to the Abbey of Saint-Germain-des-Prés.[5] Whether or not Berthoud worked in this enclosure during 1745–52 is not documented, but historian Jean-Dominique Augarde has suggested that he may have been working for Pierre-Joseph de Rivaz (1711–1772), a fellow Swiss maker of equation clocks and watches at this time.[6]

The situation changed in 1752, however, when Berthoud presented a treatise on the construction of his own equation clock to the Académie Royale des Sciences.[7] Unlike an ordinary clock that records only an arbitrary day of twenty-four hours of equal length (an average based on the length of all solar days in a year), an equation clock registers the time in a solar day (the day that results from one rotation of the earth measured from the sun's zenith on one day to the its zenith on the next). The period may be more or less than twenty-four hours, depending on the time of year. Solar time is measured by sundials, which were customarily used for setting eighteenth-century clocks. The utility of a clock that could simultaneously measure both twenty-four equal hours and true solar time was highly valued, therefore, if not so easily constructed. Mentioned in the list of "Machines ou inventions" approved by the Académie in 1752,[8] Berthoud's invention won the support of several influential members, which allowed him a special dispensation to become a master in the Paris guild.[9]

In the following decade Berthoud turned his attention to the construction of marine chronometers. He traveled to London twice during the continuous debates that concerned the award of the prize for a marine chronometer by the British Board of Longitude to John Harrison (1693–1776). While Berthoud apparently never met Harrison, he did see three of Harrison's chronometers during his first trip in May 1763.[10] Due to an oversight by the Board of Longitude in 1766, Berthoud learned a great deal about Harrison's last chronometer from Thomas Mudge (1715–1794),[11] the London clockmaker who was a

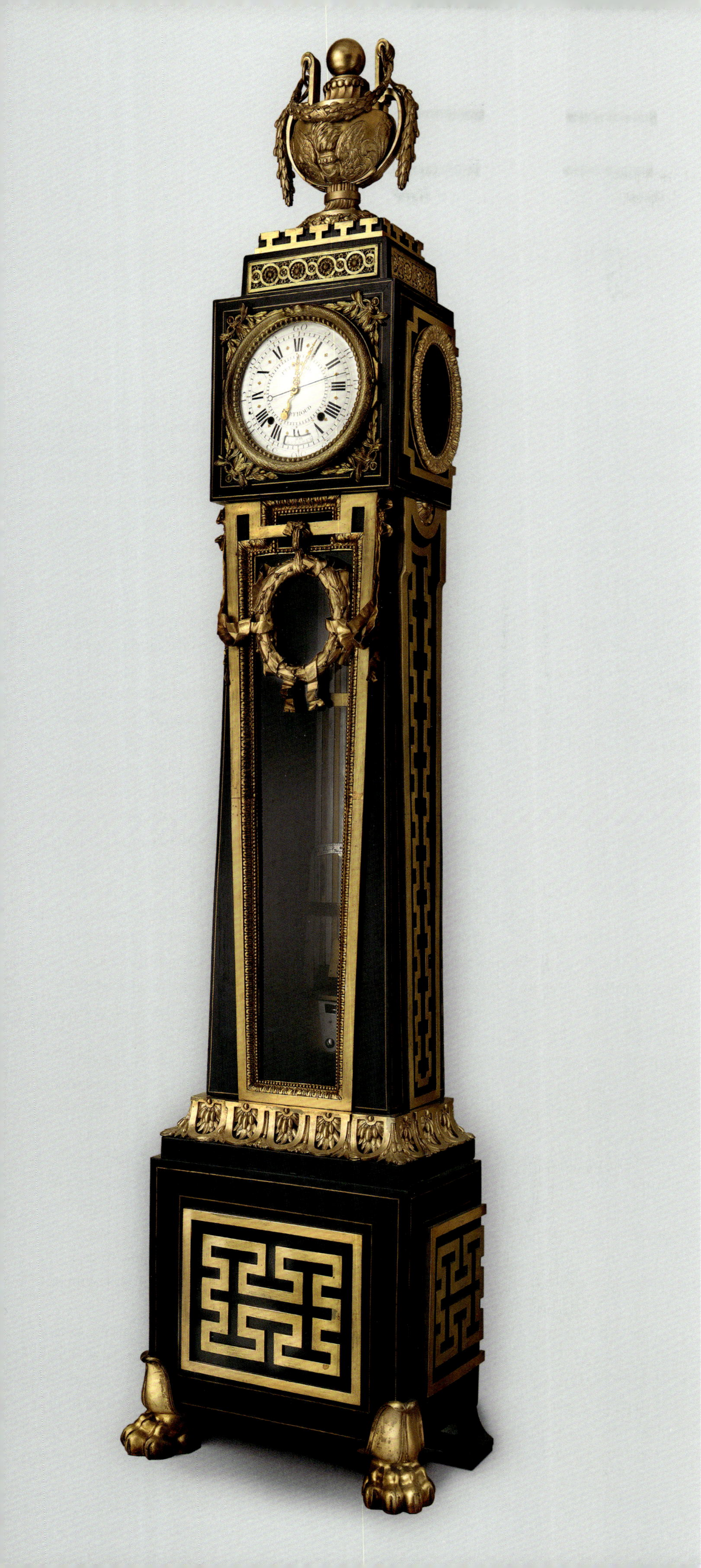

member of the committee convened by the board to judge the practicality of the Harrison chronometer, now commonly known as H.4.[12]

During Berthoud's second trip to London, in February 1766, the Parisian master clockmaker Pierre Le Roy (1717–1785), who held a royal appointment and occupied a prestigious, if not commodious, workshop in the Galeries du Louvre, presented a marine chronometer to King Louis XV (1710–1774). In 1769, Le Roy was awarded a double prize for his marine clocks and for describing the best method of determining the time at sea.[13] His rival Berthoud, however, produced two marine chronometers for the French king,[14] and it would be Berthoud, not Le Roy, who in 1770 was appointed clockmaker and mechanician to the king and to the navy.[15] In 1773, Berthoud was further commissioned to produce four marine clocks a year and to supervise all marine clocks made for the French Admiralty. In return, he received a liberal pension for life.[16] Berthoud published plans for a number of his marine timekeepers, including at least one timekeeper that he admitted was influenced by Harrison's inventions in the *Traité des horloges marines* (Treatise on Marine Clocks, 1773).[17]

Berthoud's work on equation clocks is only a little less known than his work on chronometers. In fact, he published a remarkable amount of information about horology between 1753 and 1807, including entries on the equation of time and equation clocks in volume five of the *Encyclopédie* (1755) by Denis Diderot (1713–1784) and Jean Le Rond d'Alembert (1717–1783). The illustration of the movement of an equation clock shown here, appeared in the second edition of the *Essai sur l'horlogerie* (Essay on Timekeeping) in 1786 (fig. 48). In the etching, the kidney-shaped element superimposed on the calendar dial of the clock modified the motion of an extra hand (with sunburst), allowing the hand to register true solar time. This system is employed in the Museum's astronomical regulator with the kidney-shaped piece attached to the back of the calendar dial. In the Museum's clock, a pin on a spring-loaded arm that is connected to the calendar and incorporated into the clock rides along the edge of the kidney-shaped piece and regulates the motion of the solar hand.

Whatever Berthoud may or may not have appropriated from Harrison's chronometers, it is certain that the giant pendulums he employed in longcase astronomical regulators owed a great deal to Harrison and his brother James, whose bimetallic, or gridiron, pendulums were made to prevent the expansion or contraction of the pendulum caused by temperature changes, which influenced the length of the pendulum and the accuracy of its timekeeping. Berthoud's version of the device did less for temperature compensation than Harrison's version, as the alternating rods of brass and steel were too thick and mounted too closely together in Berthoud's pendulums to be wholly effective.

Visually, however, the compensated pendulums were a great success. Berthoud made a series of precision regulators with glass panels in their trunks, which displayed the full length of their pendulums' ponderous swing. Two of the most elaborate cases for such clocks are in the Frick Collection, New York,[18] and the Château de Versailles, France.[19] These two clocks have sculptural groups atop their hoods that evidently were inspired by a sculptural group by Jean-Baptiste Tuby (1635–1700) of the sun god driving his chariot in the *Bassin d'Apollon* at Versailles, plaques with scenes of infant personifications of the Four Seasons on their bases, and decorative Neoclassical mounts. A plaque on the Frick Collection's regulator is signed by the founder Philippe II Caffiéri (1714–1774) and dated 1767. Another regulator in the series, now in the Wallace Collection, London,[20] like the Metropolitan's regulator, has a classicizing vase atop its hood, but is more generously supplied with heavy, gilded-bronze mounts. The Frick and Wallace regulators incorporate barometers in gilded-bronze laurel wreaths at the top of the glazed panels on their trunks. The Versailles, Wallace, and Metropolitan cases are made of ebony veneer, whereas the Frick regulator, probably the first in the series, is veneered with tulipwood and kingwood. All four clocks are signed by Balthazar Lieutaud (ca. 1720–1780), a master *ébéniste* in the Paris guild of cabinetmakers in 1749 who specialized in making clock-cases.[21] Probably beginning about 1767, he and Caffiéri created the cases for Berthoud's regulators, mostly in a severely linear style, but lightened by such departures as the lively crests or the surprising Chinese fret motifs on the base of the Metropolitan's regulator.

The Museum's example originally had four hands: one for the hour, two for the minutes, and one for the seconds. The hand for mean time (twenty-four equal hours) is missing; the original gilded-brass hand with the sun image for solar time has been substituted for it. Like the seconds hand, the missing hand would have been made of blued steel.

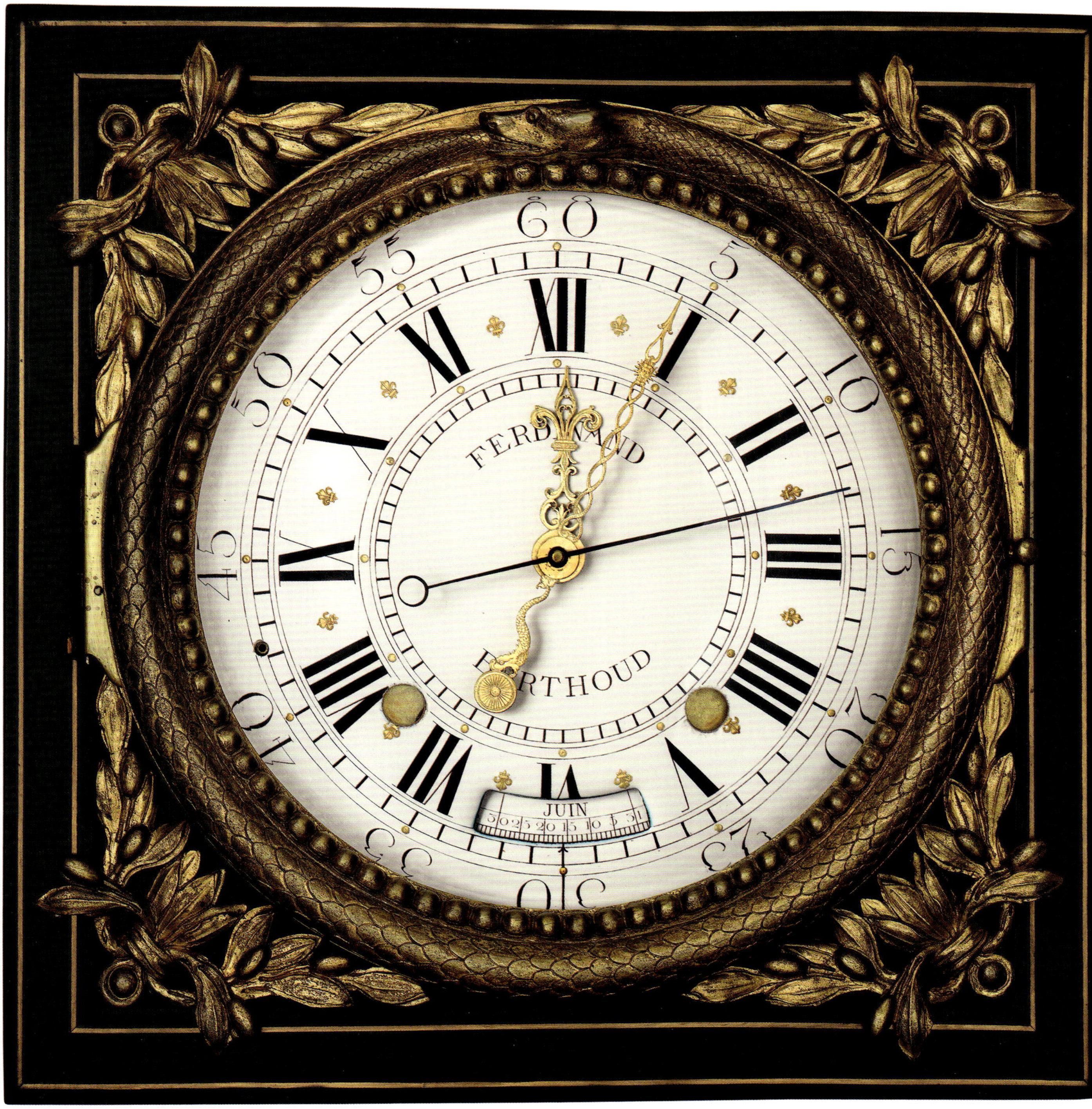
FERDINAND
BERTHOUD
JUIN

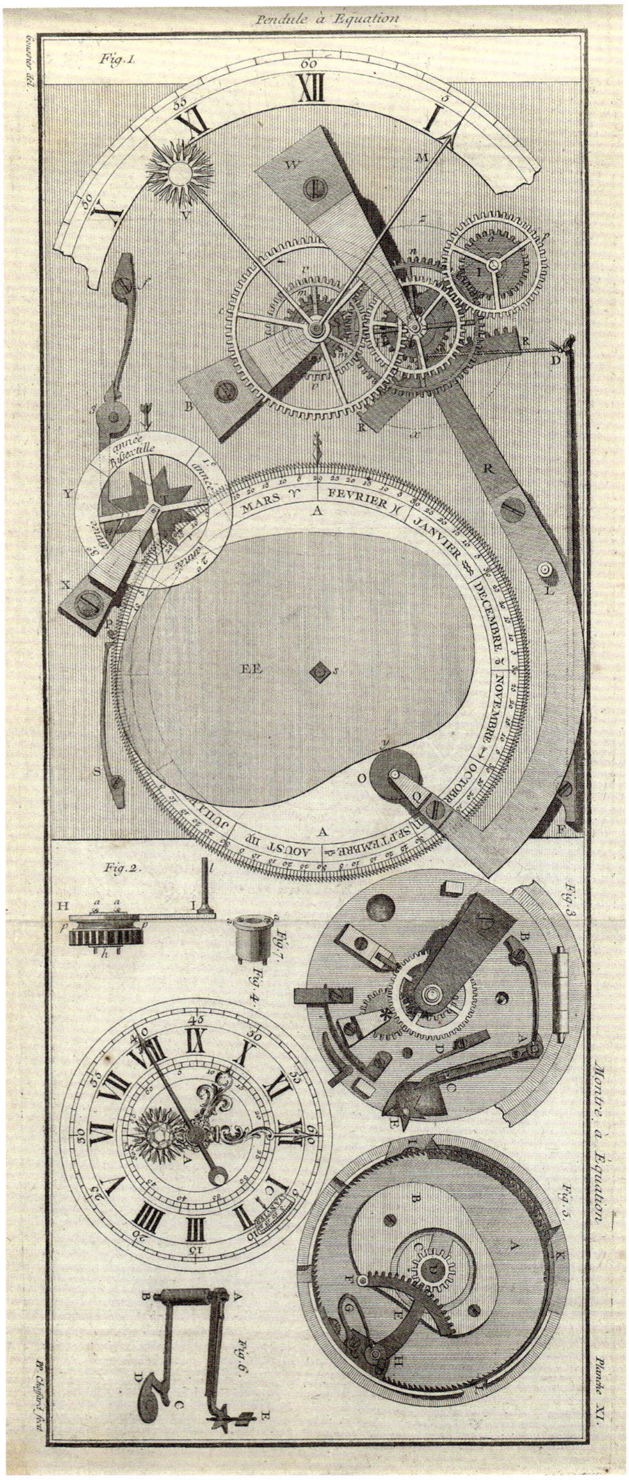

fig. 48 *"Pendule à équation" (Equation Clock), pl. XI, fig. 1, from vol. 1 of Ferdinand Berthoud,* Essai sur l'horlogerie; Dans lequel on traite de cet art, relativement à l'usage civil, à l'astronomie & à la navigation, en établissant des principes confirmés par l'expérience, dédié aux artistes & aux amateurs *(Paris: J. G. Merigot le jeune, 1786). The Metropolitan Museum of Art, New York, Thomas J. Watson Library, Special Collections*

The white enamel dial registers the hours (I–XII) in black enamel and the minutes (5–60, by fives) with individual lines for each minute along both the inner and the outer circumference of the chapter ring. Applied gold fleurs-de-lis mark each two-and-one-half-minute period. Below the eleven–one o'clock position and above the five–seven o'clock position, the clockmaker's name, "Ferdinand Berthoud," appears, and an aperture at the six o'clock position reveals the day of the month. The revolutions of the calendar plate govern the opening and closing of the shutters for winding squares at the four and eight o'clock positions. The dial is protected by a glass lens in a hinged bezel in the form of a snake biting its tail that encircles a beaded border. Vegetal ornament fills the spandrels.

The movement is held in place by two brass arms to which it is secured by means of screws that operate from below the arms. The movement consists of two square plates held apart by five cylindrical pillars. On the right-hand side, it has a weight-driven going train with maintaining power, regulated by a Graham-type dead-beat escapement and the heavy gridiron pendulum that rests on a knife-edge when in service. A screw on the bottom end of the pendulum permits some adjustment to the beat. As the clock has a duration of thirty-four and one half days, it requires a heavy weight with a long fall, the drop lengthened by running its cord over a pulley attached above the back plate. The train drives the epicyclic system for the equation mechanism that is described in principle in Berthoud's *Essai sur l'horlogerie*.[22]

The left-hand train of the regulator is the striking train. It is spring driven and strikes both mean-time hours and a single blow at the half hours by means of a hammer and a bell mounted on the back plate. It is governed by a single count wheel mounted on the back plate above the signature of the clockmaker.

The ball finial on top of the vase is probably a replacement. When the clock entered the Museum's collection, the bottom of the wooden base was found to have been shattered, and it needed replacement. The movement was cleaned and put in running condition. The equation mechanism's indexing arm was tied off with a wire because if it were put back into service, the clock could be wound only during the few days of the month when the movement of the calendar disk permitted access to the winding squares. As the clock needed a more solid installation than it could be given in the present Jack and Belle Linsky Galleries, it frequently stopped in the course of a month. Therefore, the decision was made not to try to keep it running either with or without engaging its equation mechanism. When properly installed, this regulator, like those mentioned earlier, would have been sufficiently precise to have been usable by astronomers for timing most celestial events.

The earliest record of the regulator appears in the "Art Treasures Exhibition" held in New York in 1955.[23] In 1959, it was sold by Thelma Chrysler Foy in New York, and it is described in the sale catalogue as having been owned by Madame Jacques Balsan in New York.[24] CV / JHL

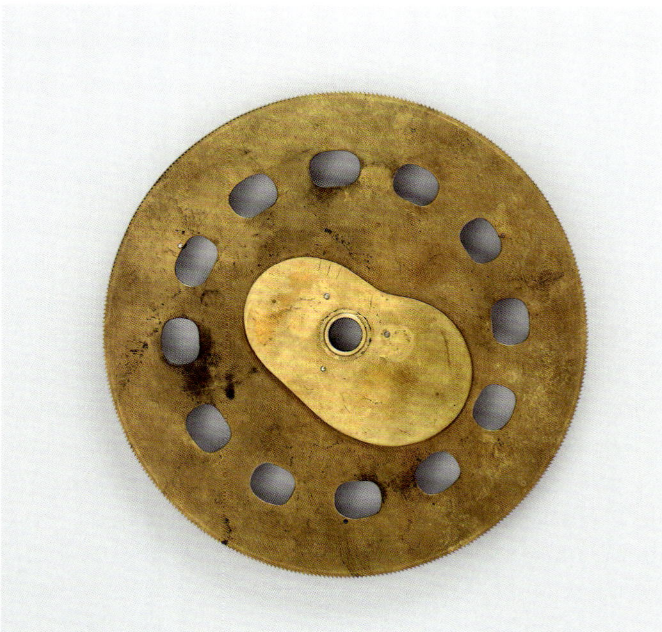

The reverse side of the calendar plate with the kidney-shaped element, allowing the solar hand to register true solar time

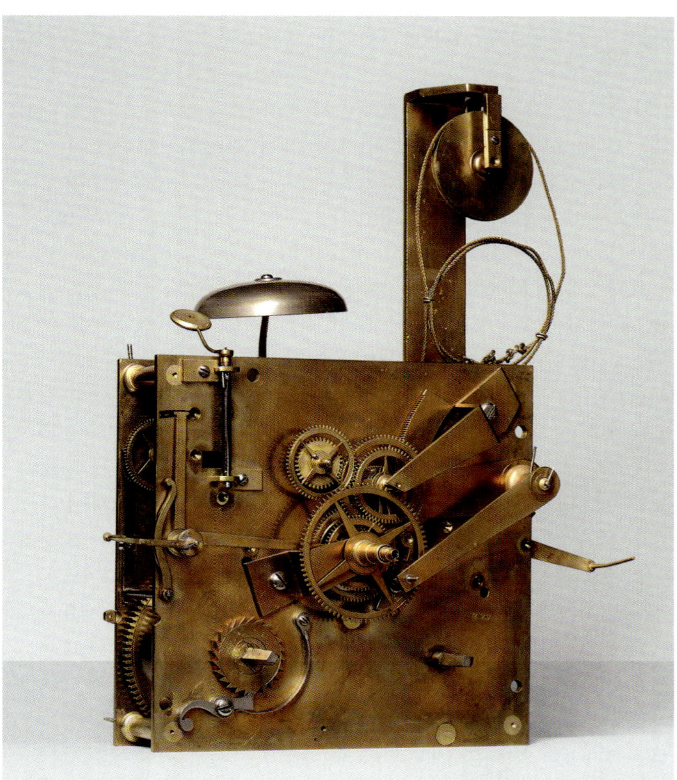

The view of the movement, showing the front plate with the epicyclic system for the display of both the true solar time and mean time

1 For details of Berthoud's apprenticeship and later life, see Cardinal 1984a. A copy of his certificate of apprenticeship appears in *Ferdinand Berthoud* 1984, p. 303. See also Augarde 1996, pp. 280–82.
2 Augarde 1996, pp. 15–16.
3 Ibid., p. 38.
4 Ibid., p. 14.
5 Ibid., pp. 40–49, especially p. 46.
6 Ibid., p. 280. The Swiss-born Henri Enderlin and German-born Michel Stollenwerck, both distinguished clockmakers, were established in the enclosure of Saint-Germain-des-Prés in the 1740s. Ibid., pp. 311, 398.
7 Established in 1666 by a decree of King Louis XIV for the promotion of French scientific matters.
8 "Machines ou inventions" 1756, p. 147, cited in Cardinal 1984a, pp. 21–22.
9 See Cardinal 1984a, p. 23, based on a document of the Conseil d'Etat du Roy, Y 9327, in the Archives Nationales, Paris. The document is dated Dec. 31, 1753; see *Ferdinand Berthoud* 1984, p. 325.
10 The first three are now in the Royal Observatory in Greenwich, England, inv. nos. ZAA0034, ZAA0035, and ZAA0036. The fourth is in the National Maritime Museum in Greenwich, inv. no. ZAA0037. For more about the four Harrison chronometers, see Gould 1960; see also Betts 1993, pp. 10–16; Randall 1996. For a lively account of the attempts to make a practical marine chronometer, see Sobel and Andrewes 1998.
11 Randall 1992, p. 21.
12 For a brief account of what Berthoud adapted from Harrison's inventions, see Turner 1984a, pp. 154–58; also Sabrier 1984, pp. 165–70. See also note 17 below.
13 Le Roy 1770. See also Baillie 1978, pp. 280–83.
14 Cardinal 1984a, p. 31.
15 Ibid., pp. 32–33; *Ferdinand Berthoud* 1984, p. 313.
16 Cardinal 1984a, pp. 36–37. For the quarrel over the priority of the invention, see Cardinal 1996.
17 See Berthoud's timekeeper Horloge Marine No. 2 in the Musée National des Techniques, Paris (inv. no. 1387). See Catherine Cardinal and Jean-Claude Sabrier in *Ferdinand Berthoud* 1984, p. 191, and p. 164, fig. 60.
18 See Edey 1982, pp. 69–70, 72–75, and cover. See also Heuer and Maurice 1988, pp. 111–13, figs. 200–202.
19 Inv. no. V 1679VBM 1055. See Calin Demetrescu in *Decorative Furnishings* 2014, p. 417, no. 171. See also Watson 1960, p. 112, no. 50, and fig. 50; Augarde 1996, pp. 266–67.
20 Hughes 1994, pp. 57–58.
21 For more about Berthoud, Lieutaud, and Caffiéri's collaboration, see Jean-Nérée Ronfort in *Ferdinand Berthoud* 1984, pp. 253–54; Ronfort 1984, pp. 113–15. See also Edey 1982, pp. 72–74; William Rieder in Metropolitan Museum of Art 1984, p. 244, no. 150.
22 Berthoud 1786, vol. 1, pp. 66–72. The horologist Jean-Claude Sabrier has pointed out that Berthoud's descriptions are so full of detail that his designs can be executed even today by following his instructions. See Sabrier 1984, p. 165.
23 *Art Treasures Exhibition* 1955, no. 290.
24 Parke-Bernet Galleries 1959, p. 186, no. 352, ill. p. 187.

43. Pair-Case Quarter-Repeating Watch

BRITISH (LONDON), MADE FOR CHINESE MARKET, CA. 1770–72
Diam. of outer case: 1 13/16 in. (4.6 cm)
Diam. of back plate: 1 1/8 in. (2.9 cm)
Gift of J. Pierpont Morgan, 1917
17.190.1440a, b

OUTER CASE: glass and gold set with diamonds, pearls, emeralds, and rubies
INNER CASE: gold, casemaker's mark: H. T. [unidentified]
DIAL: white enamel with black painted Chinese characters and blued-steel hands
MOVEMENT: gilded brass and partly blued steel, signed (on back plate): *Jn° Champion / London* [John Champion, 1730–1779] and numbered *1995*

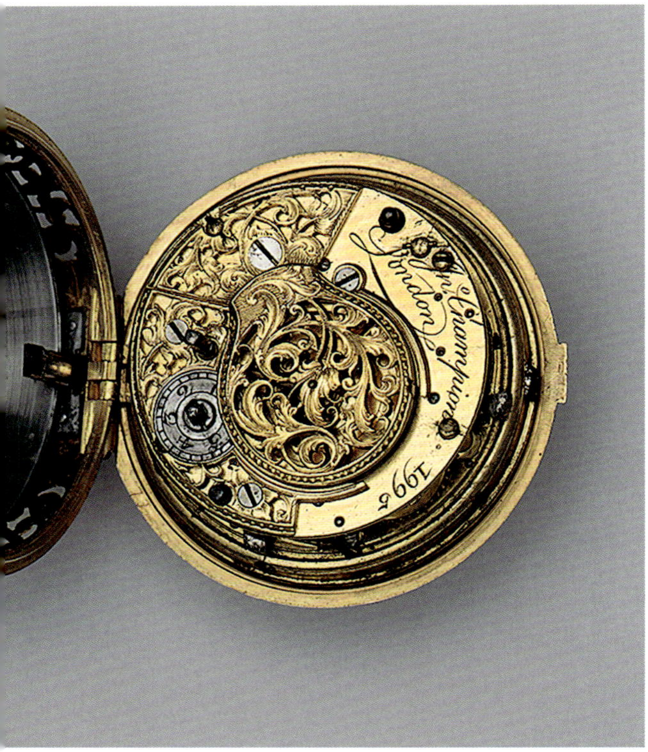

The inner case open to show the back plate of the Champion watch

WELL BEFORE THE FIRST MECHANICAL CLOCK APPEARED IN Europe, the Chinese were constructing water clocks.[1] None of the early Chinese clocks survive, but a description of a remarkably sophisticated example, known as the *Xin Yi Xiang Fa Yao* (New Design for a [Mechanized] Armillary [Sphere] and [Celestial] Globe, 1089), was discovered in the twentieth century and translated by Wang Ling, Joseph Needham, and Derek J. de Solla Price.[2] The clock was constructed under the direction of the diplomat and astronomer Su Song (1020–1101) during the reign of Emperor Zhezong (or Zhou Xuz) (1042–1100) from the Northern Song dynasty. The description is so detailed that a half-sized working model could be built in 1970 for the Time Museum in Rockford, Illinois.[3] There are other reconstructions, including one in Beijing.[4] The purpose of the clock was primarily astronomical. Finished in about 1090, it is estimated to have been between thirty and forty feet high, supporting an armillary sphere for the observation of heavenly bodies and a revolving celestial globe.[5] Below was a pagoda-like structure in which appropriate figures representing the Chinese hours appeared in sequence, accompanied by the sound of bells and drums. The most surprising feature, however, was a device that, although water-driven, performed a function analogous to the escapement of a European mechanical clock.[6] Like other early Chinese timekeeping and astronomical instruments, the clock vanished as the result of the vicissitudes of war.[7] No known connection has been made between these vanished timekeepers and the mechanical clocks introduced into the Chinese imperial court by the seventeenth-century missionaries of the Society of Jesus. Matteo Ricci (1552–1610), working at the court in 1601–10, is often cited as the earliest of the missionaries who presented European clocks to the Chinese emperor[8] and is believed to have brought two clocks to China in 1601.[9] These clocks needed maintenance and repair, a need that probably added to the welcome reception of Ricci and the Jesuit mechanicians and clockmakers who journeyed to China in the course of the seventeenth century. Scholar Catherine Pagani states that there were four foreigners, and that even in the reigns of the eighteenth-century emperors there were only eleven.[10]

But the relatively few number of foreign specialists is misleading, because the imperial household had a tradition of setting up its own workshops within the precincts of the Forbidden City to make luxury goods for the imperial court. Pagani states that although there is more to be learned about these workshops, as their number and activities changed periodically, we do know that they were formally established in 1693, during the reign of Emperor Kangxi (1654–1722). By 1758, one of the fourteen workshops thought to have then been in existence was devoted to clockmaking.[11] In addition, timepiece manufacturing had

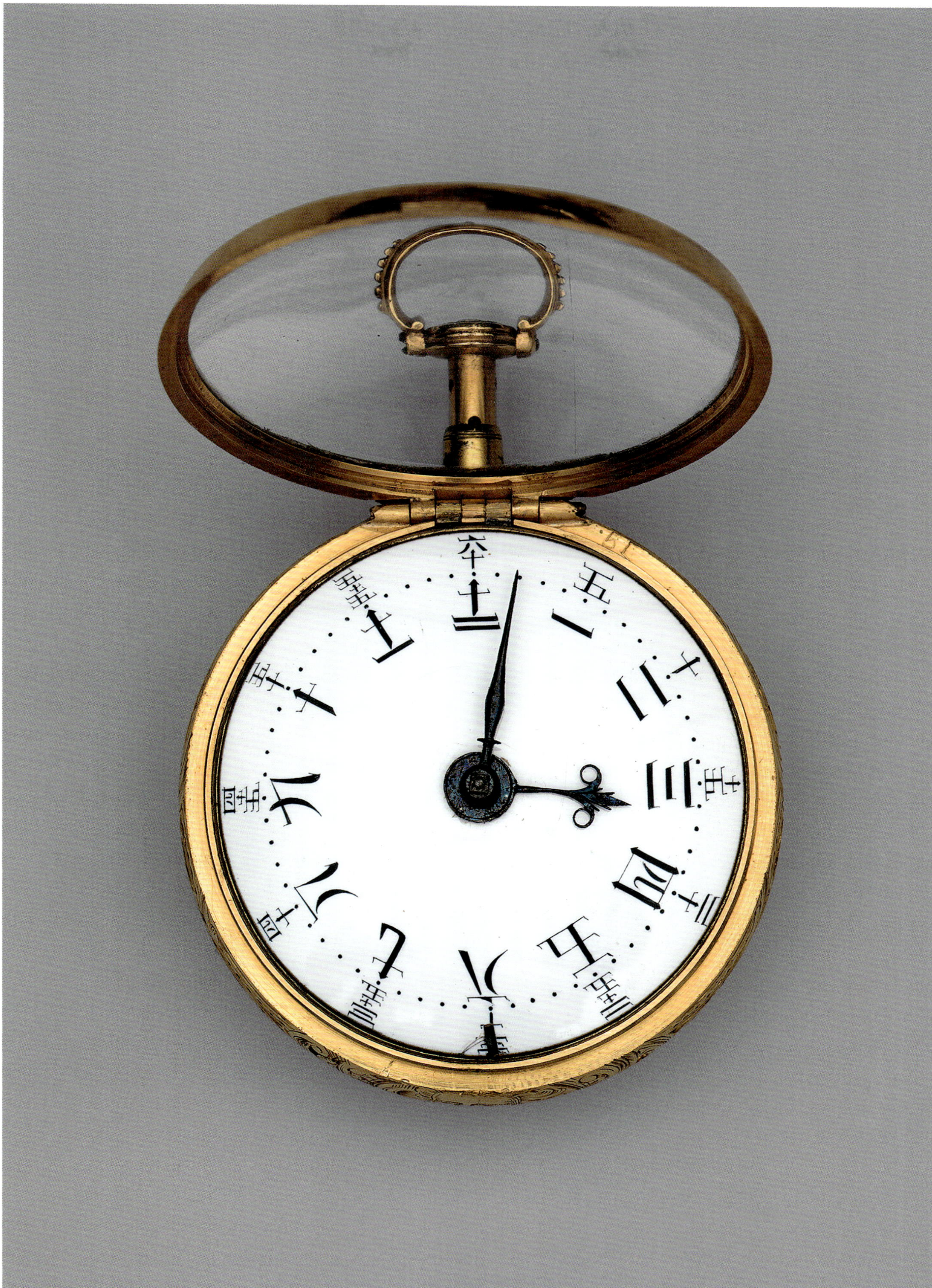

begun in Guangzhou (Canton), the coastal city where European clocks were shipped for further distribution to Chinese patrons. Guangzhou became an important source of Chinese clockwork during the Qianlong period (1736–1795), as did clockmaking factories in Suzhou and Macao, the latter said to have employed one hundred craftsmen.[12]

The real impetus driving the success of these workshops, however, was the enthusiasm of two Chinese emperors, Kangxi and Qianlong. Eighteenth-century reports describe the imperial palace as filled with horology.[13] The two emperors set the taste for their courtiers, as well as for officials and mandarins, creating demand for decorative clocks with moving figures and self-sounding bells.[14]

Into this rarefied market came British clock- and watchmakers. They delivered their wares to the port of Guangzhou via the ships of the East India Company,[15] as well as in other, less officially sanctioned vessels. The best known of these English entrepreneurs is James Cox (ca. 1723–1800),[16] but others who catered to the Chinese trade were Paul Barbot (1720–after 1766), Timothy Williamson (active 1769, died before 1799), and two Francis Perigals,[17] all of whom are still represented by clocks in Chinese palace collections. John Champion (1730–1779) seems to have contributed far fewer timekeepers to this trade, but there is a belief that the Metropolitan Museum's watch once belonged to Emperor Qianlong.[18]

Champion's pair-case watch in the Museum's collection has a repeating movement, meaning that when a plunger in the stem of the watch was pushed, it would strike the last hour and last quarter on a bell nested inside the box, or inner case, of the watch. The movement consists of two gilded circular brass plates held apart by four cylindrical pillars. The going train is spring driven and regulated by a verge escapement. The back plate has a balance cock with an asymmetrical openwork, leafy-scroll design on its table, and an openwork foot screwed to the back plate. A silver figure plate for adjusting the balance spring completes the "furniture" of the back plate, as the worm-and-wheel regulation of the setup of the mainspring lies between the two plates instead of on the exterior side of the back plate. Below the balance cock the plate is engraved "Jn° Champion / London" and numbered 1995. The movement is provided with a dust cover that bears the same signature and serial number as the back plate.

The dial marks the watch as one intended for export, as Chinese characters in place of the usual roman or Arabic numerals encircle the white enamel disk. These characters have been identified as correct for the twice-twelve division of the day customary in the West and painted by someone who was not entirely comfortable with Chinese calligraphy.[19] They are not related, however, to traditional Chinese methods of dividing the day,[20] which would not have been suitable for representation on a simple watch dial. The outer case further supports the identification of the watch as one made for the China trade. It consists of glass made to resemble the figured agates framed by openwork

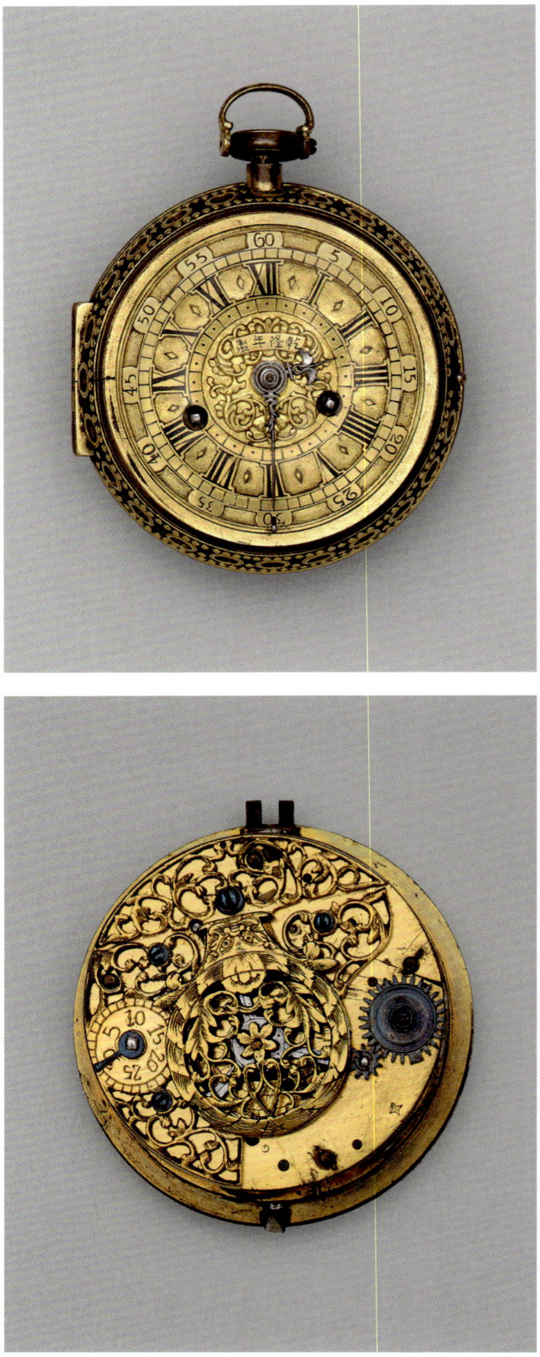

fig. 49 *Watch. Chinese, Qianlong period (1736–95). Case: partly gilded brass and black leather, fish skin, with gold studs; dial (top): gilded brass; movement (bottom): gilded brass, partly blued steel, Diameter of case 2¼ in. (5.7 cm), Diameter of back plate 1½ in. (3.8 cm). The Metropolitan Museum of Art, New York, Gift of J. Pierpont Morgan, 1917 (17.190.1447a, b)*

rococo scrolled designs that were popular among London jewelers and "toy" makers. A similar combination in the Museum's collection, but employing genuine pink agate in a framework of gold rococo scrolls and floral swags, can be found on a James Cox "toy," a miniature secretary incorporating a watch.[21] It is uncertain whether the glass in the watchcase was meant as an alternative to the more desirable agate or whether the glass was regarded as an ingenious substitute. The gold on the outer case that frames the glass panels is set with diamonds, emeralds, rubies, and pearls, and it has a large pearl thumb-piece, suggesting that the second possibility is the correct one. (By contrast, the butterflies and flowers that adorn the miniature secretary consist of colored paste.) While the Museum's miniature secretary is known to have come from the collection of Princess Z. M. Youssoupof in Saint Petersburg, Russia, and a second version survives in the State Hermitage, also in Saint Petersburg, a third version is still in the collection of the imperial palace in Beijing.[22] In all likelihood, the combined gold-and-pink glass of the Champion watchcase was intended for export and probably made about 1770 or 1772. (The latter date appears on the key for the Hermitage Museum's example.[23])

The Metropolitan Museum has yet another reminder of Chinese enthusiasm for European horology, this one a watch that at first glance seems to be of European origin and that George C. Williamson, the author of the catalogue of J. Pierpont Morgan's watch collection, published as the work of an unknown Englishman (fig. 49).[24] The case is brass, partly gilded and partly covered with fish skin, and leather studded with gilded brass. The gilded-brass dial has qualities that are not conventionally European: it is cast, and the foliate ornament in its center shows no trace, however faint, of the antique Roman heritage to be expected in a European design. The movement, also, is not exactly European, although it demonstrates a sporting attempt at a repeating watch. The suspicion that the watch might be one of those made in China, perhaps in Guangzhou or Suzhou, or less likely in the imperial palace workshop in Beijing, is confirmed by the Chinese characters inscribed on the dial and translated as "Made in the Qianlong years." The back plate of the movement is laid out in European fashion, but in place of a traditional European motif on the neck of the balance cock, the engraver has substituted the age-old Chinese decorative animal mask, the *Taotie*. A European-style mask derived from the Roman grotesque tradition would probably have puzzled a Chinese patron in a way that the *Taotie* would not.

The movement of the Champion watch shows signs both of normal wear and signs of past neglect. The watch was purchased by the donor from Carl H. Marfels of Frankfurt am Main and Berlin. The traditional belief that it was looted from the imperial palace in Beijing may be correct but cannot now be substantiated.[25] CV

1 See Needham, Wang Ling, and Price 1960, pp. 70–131; Pagani 2001, pp. 10–11; *Clocks and Watches of the Qing Dynasty* 2002, unpag. (foreword).

2 Needham, Wang Ling, and Price 1960, pp. 28–47.

3 Turner 1984b, pp. 59–65.

4 Pagani 2001, p. 8, fig. 1, and p. 9, fig. 2.

5 Needham, Wang Ling, and Price 1960, pp. 24, 44–45.

6 Ibid., pp. 34–41, 48–51; Turner 1984b, pp. 62–63, figs. 32a–d.

7 Needham, Wang Ling, and Price 1960, pp. 131–33; Landes 1983, pp. 17–19; Pagani 2001, p. 10.

8 See, for example, Landes 1983, pp. 38–40; Zheng Xin Miao in *Moments of Eternity* 2004, p. 30.

9 Pagani 2001, pp. 2, 31–32, based on Ricci 1953, pp. 371–72. For an English translation of excerpts from Ricci's account, see Cipolla 1967, pp. 83–85.

10 Pagani 2001, pp. 2, 35.

11 Ibid., pp. 36–37, 181, 182–83. Some of Pagani's information is based on studies of ivory carvers and cloisonné enamelers (p. 246, nn. 13, 14). There is a short account of the work of the clockmakers in the Qing Dynasty period in *Clocks and Watches of the Qing Dynasty* 2002, unpag. (foreword). See also Chapuis 1919, pp. 42–44.

12 Guan Xue Ling 2004, p. 241. Products of both Macao and Guangzhou (Canton) are illustrated.

13 See White 2012, pp. 33–35. See also entry 40 in this volume.

14 For examples, see entry 40 in this volume. See also ibid., pp. 158–260.

15 For a great deal more about the China trade, see Harcourt-Smith 1933. See also Pagani 2001, pp. 58–124; R. Smith 2008; White 2012, pp. 29–45, 75–157, 208–60. For Swiss participation in eighteenth-century trade with China, see Chapuis 1919, pp. 45–79.

16 See entry 40 in this volume. See also R. Smith 2008; White 2012, pp. 158–207. For Cox's clocks and watches in the Metropolitan Museum's collection, see Vincent and Leopold 2008.

17 See entry 45 in this volume. See also White 2012, p. 347.

18 Williamson 1912, p. 190, no. 207.

19 The author is indebted to Pengliang Lu, Andrew W. Mellon Fellow, 2012–13, in the Department of Asian Art, Metropolitan Museum, for this evaluation.

20 For an explanation of the traditional Chinese methods, see Needham, Wang Ling, and Price 1960, app., "Chinese Horary Systems," pp. 199–205.

21 Acc. no. 46.184a–c.

22 White 2012, p. 167, fig. 7.3, and p. 173, fig. 7.12.

23 The key is illustrated in White 2012, p. 167, fig. 7.3.

24 Acc. no. 17.190.1447a, b. See Williamson 1912, pp. 195–96, no. 216, and pl. LXXXVI.

25 Ibid., p. 190, no. 207.

44. Musical Longcase Clock

GERMAN (NEUWIED), CA. 1774–75
10 ft. 2½ in. × 27 in. × 16 in. (309.9 × 68.6 × 40.6 cm)
Gift of Mrs. Edgar Worch, in memory of her husband, 1975
1975.101

CASE: oak veneered with maple, burl woods, holly, and hornbeam (all partly stained), and other woods; mother-of-pearl; gilded bronze; and brass; by David Roentgen, German, 1743–1807
DIAL: partly gilded and partly silvered brass and enameled and painted copper, signed: *Achenbach & Schmidt à Neuwied* [Hermann Achenbach, German, born 1730, active before 1759–92, and Johann Schmidt, German, 1735–1795]
MOVEMENT: brass and steel

THE GERMAN TOWN OF NEUWIED LIES SOUTH OF COLOGNE ON the right bank of the Rhine river. In the eighteenth century it was home to a community of Moravian brethren, Protestants of pietist belief, who settled there under the protection of the overlord of the region, Count Johann Friedrich Alexander zu Wied-Neuwied (1706–1791). Two of the most successful and inventive cabinetmakers in all of Europe, Abraham Roentgen (1711–1793) and his son David (1743–1807), were members of this colony. Trained by his father in Mühlheim, Germany, Abraham became a journeyman cabinetmaker, first in the Netherlands and then in London, before returning to Germany. He opened a workshop in Neuwied in 1750. The count exempted him, as a member of the Moravian colony, from the rules of the Neuwied guild that pertained to the number of craftsmen that a master cabinetmaker could employ.[1] As the result of the initial success of his products, Abraham and his son greatly expanded their firm, creating a manufactory that at one time employed more than two hundred people, making exuberantly rococo and, later, more soberly architectural furniture. David Roentgen's last series of clocks, made in partnership with Peter Kinzing (1745–1816), would anticipate the relative simplicity of the nineteenth-century Biedermeier style. The Roentgens' patrons would eventually include Marie Antoinette; her uncle Duke Charles Alexander of Lorraine and governor of the Austrian Netherlands in Brussels; Frederick the Great in Berlin; Catherine the Great in Saint Petersburg; and many other clients from the German aristocracy.[2]

Similar to the Roentgens, the Kinzing family of clockmakers were Mennonites, adherents of an unorthodox variety of Protestantism, who also found a home in eighteenth-century Neuwied. Christian I Kinzing (1707–1804), son of a miller in Rengsdorf, settled in Neuwied about 1740.[3] He and his son Peter made clocks as well as automata, mechanical devices of various kinds, and musical mechanisms, many of them for installation in the Roentgens' cabinetry. In 1753, Christian was joined by Hermann Achenbach (born 1730), a clockmaker from Marienborn, near Siegen in the North Rhine-Westphalia district, who subsequently married Christian's sister Elisabeth.[4] For at least a part of his long association with the Kinzings, Achenbach had his own workshop in Neuwied's Zweifelshof,[5] where in 1761 he had begun putting his name on his clocks.[6] Johann Schmidt (1735–1795) was a clockmaker who in 1758 married into the Kinzing family and became Achenbach's foreman.[7] Their double signature began to appear as early as 1774 or 1775, as it does on the dial of the Museum's clock. Their last double signature is believed to be datable to about 1785.[8] The firms of the Roentgen and Kinzing families continued their collaboration until the last decade of the eighteenth century, when the outbreak of the

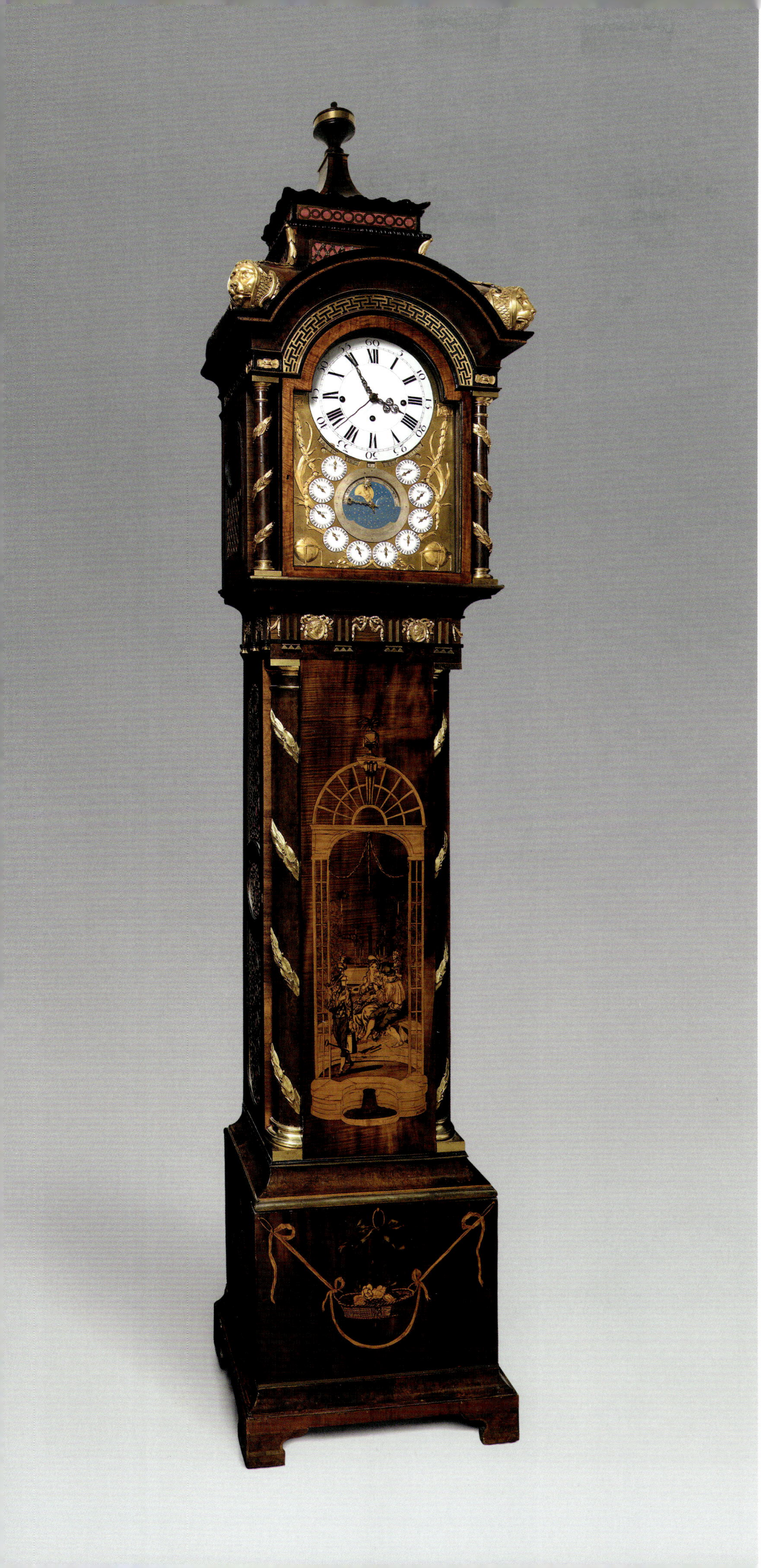

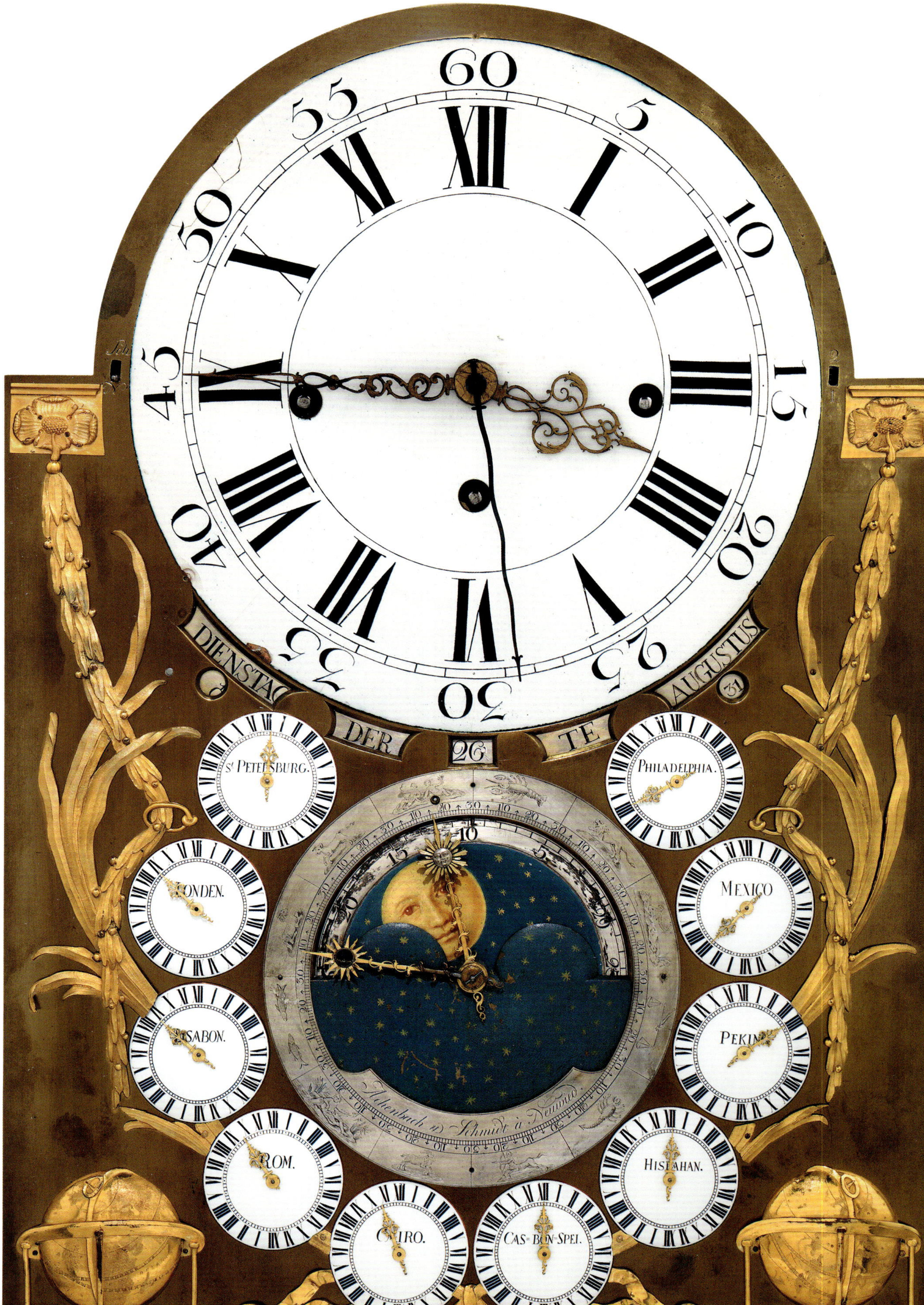
DIENSTAG
DER
26
TE
AUGUSTUS
31
St PETERSBURG.
PHILADELPHIA.
LONDEN.
MEXICO
LISABON.
PEKIN
ROM.
HISPAHAN.
CAIRO.
CAS-BON-SPEI.

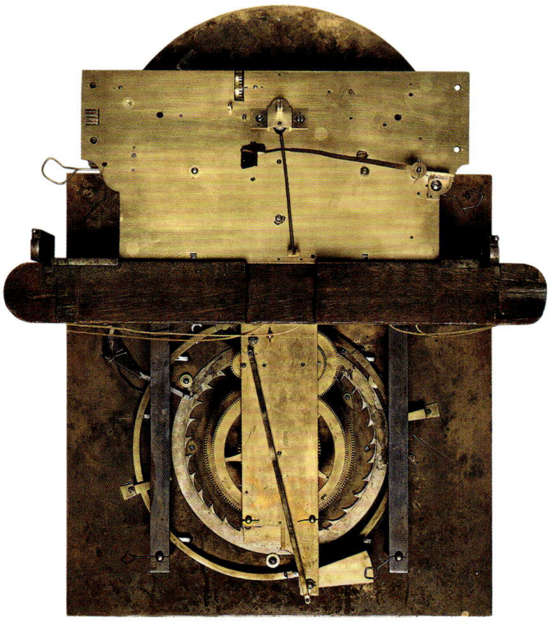

View of the movement from the back showing the back plate, part of the mechanism for the calendar, and for the time in ten cities

French Revolution in 1789 and the subsequent French Revolutionary wars (1792–1801) enveloped continental Europe in turmoil.

Abraham Roentgen's experience as a journeyman cabinetmaker in London must have been reinforced by the trip that he and David made in 1765.[9] In London they were able to purchase new and exotic materials. They also found new ideas for their Neuwied firm, doubtlessly among them the designs published by Thomas Chippendale (1718–1779), the cabinetmaker who gave his name to the English style of rococo furniture. A design on a page from Chippendale's *Gentleman and Cabinet-Maker's Director* has been identified as the probable inspiration for the case of the Metropolitan's Roentgen clock.[10] The Museum's clock has the same stately proportions of plinth, trunk, and hood as the clock in the Chippendale design, and the similarity of the hood, with its broken arch and hint of chinoiserie in the pagoda-like crest, is not likely to be accidental.

But Roentgen parted company with Chippendale in his use of the elaborate marquetry, the so-called marquetry *à la mosaïque*, in which various colored and shaped woods are inlaid to create both form and shadow that produces a painterly effect. The scene on the front of the trunk of the clock depicts two lovers seated on a garden bench in front of a fountain and framed by a tall trellis through which a third figure carrying a watering can exits to the left while pointing to the lovers. The scene has been identified as an adaptation of a painting by Januarius Zick (1730–1797),[11] who supplied designs for a number of marquetry panels incorporated into the furniture of the Roentgens' manufactory. The marquetry panel on the Museum's clock is signed "Reusch" at the lower right side of the panel. Johann Anton Reusch (1740–1821) is known to have had his own workshop in Neuwied, but he is not thought to have been skilled enough nor to have possessed the proper tools to have produced the graceful design on the clock.[12] The trunk itself is massive, owing to the need for room to install a weight-driven pin-cylinder organ and a dulcimer. These musical instruments and the pin-cylinders that would have governed the tunes played on them are now missing, but as the clock belongs to a series of at least six with cases by the Roentgen manufactory, some of which have retained their original musical instruments, it is possible to be fairly certain of what the Museum's clock originally contained.[13]

A detailed description of the case by Metropolitan Museum curator Wolfram Koeppe appears in the Museum's exhibition catalogue *Extravagant Inventions: The Princely Furniture of the Roentgens* (2012),[14] in which both he and Reinier Baarsen have made a convincing proposal that the clock was originally commissioned by Charles Alexander, Duke of Lorraine, for his palace, the Court of Nassau, in Brussels. If this is,

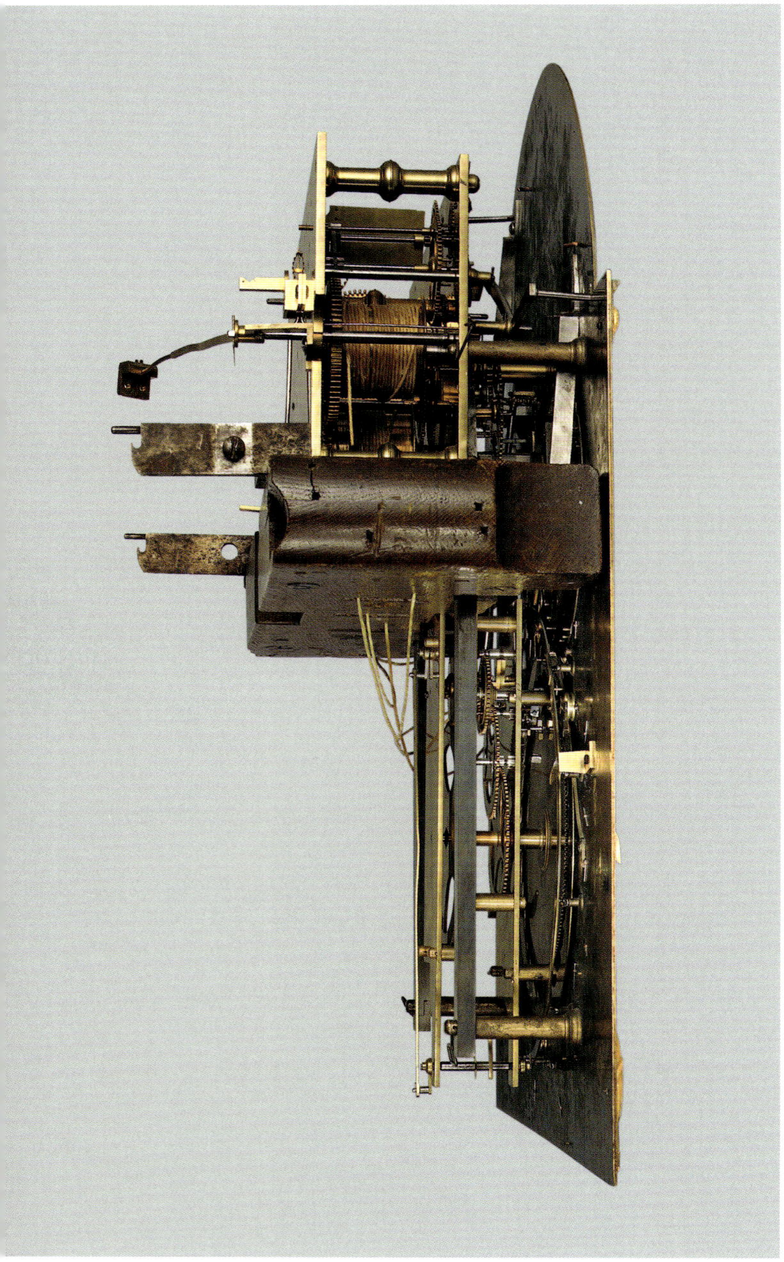

The movement seen from the left side, showing the pin cylinder (now missing) and part of the motion work for the calendar

indeed, the same clock, then it was returned to Roentgen in 1776 in partial exchange for an extravagant secretary cabinet that incorporated another clock.[15]

The dial plate of the clock is one piece of gilded brass with attached dials and mechanisms that display the time in eleven places, as well as calendrical and astronomical information. The dials are organized into two large circles, the upper circle consisting of a large white enamel disk that displays local time with chapter rings for hours (I–XII); for minutes (5–60, by fives), each minute marked by a line radiating from the central arbor; and for seconds. The hour and minute hands are openwork scrolls in brass; the seconds hand is made of iron. On either side are apertures for regulating the striking of the clock (Sch [lag], N [icht schlag]) and for the pin cylinders (1, 2) that were originally installed in the clock. Below the enamel dial, and from left to right, are apertures for displaying the day of the week in German above the symbol of the planetary ruler of the day, followed by an aperture for the article in German for the numerical day of the month, the correct preposition in German, and the month by name with the number of days in the month in a circular aperture below. All these change automatically and adjust for months of twenty-eight, thirty, and thirty-one days, as well as for leap years.

The lower circle consists of a central disk that displays the moon's phases in a painted simulation of the heavens, as well as the moon's age within its monthly cycle. Two hands, one with a miniature crescent moon and the other with a sunburst, revolve to show the movement, or apparent movement, of these bodies against the zodiac with a calendar that is engraved on the circular frame. The signature, "Achenbach & Schmidt à Neuwied," appears prominently at the bottom on an arc inside the circle. Ten small subsidiary dials of white enamel surround the astronomical dial, each painted I–XII twice and each with a single hand that points to the hour in ten geographical locations. Reading clockwise, they are named PHILADELPHIA; MEXICO; PEKING (Beijing); HISPAHAN (Isfahan); CAS • BON • SPEI (Cape of Good Hope); CAIRO; ROM (Rome); LISABON (Lisbon); LONDEN (London); and ST PETERSBURG. If the clock is accepted as the one traded in by Duke Charles Alexander of Lorraine in 1776, the applied ornaments in the lower corners, a celestial globe on the right, a terrestrial globe on the left, and above them the leaf-and-berry swags intertwined with wispy palm fronds may perhaps be attributed to the duke's court goldsmith, Michel-Paul-Joseph Dewez (1742–1804). Certainly, they are far from typical ornaments found on German clock dials of the period. Further, they complement the gilded-bronze medallions on the trunk of the case that have been convincingly attributed to Dewez.[16]

The eight-day, weight-driven movement of the clock consists of a thick, irregularly shaped brass back plate and an equally thick, rectangular front plate held apart by four turned brass pillars. The movement contains a going train, a striking train, and the remains of a musical train. The going train has three wheels ending in an escape wheel and anchor escapement regulated by a long pendulum. The striking train has four wheels and a fly. It is regulated by a rack-and-pinion device mounted outside on the front plate, and the device activates a hammer that strikes the hours on a bell, which is mounted on the back of the case. This part of the movement rests on a thick seat board of oak that is secured to the case of the clock by two pins. To this more or less routine unit of clockwork, a large number of complications have been added, which tax the power provided by the going train nearly to its limits. Below the seat board and within their own pair of plates are the trains of wheels, or motion work, for the lunar disk, the lunar hand, and the solar hand, as well as the large wheel with pins attached to the interior flat side that in one revolution governs the time shown in each of the ten foreign locations displayed on the front of the dial plate. The wheel carrying the day of the week in the calendar is activated by the going train of the clock; the wheel of the day of the month is activated by the lunar train; and the wheel of the months is activated by the date ring.

With the exception of the prodigious clock with calendrical and astronomical dials made by a member of the Kinzing family from a plan by Wilhelm Friedrich Hüsgen,[17] no other known clock by the same family or their in-laws has the number of complications as the Museum's clock. The complexities of this clock add further strength to the supposition that it was originally intended to complement an exceptionally elegantly furnished study of Duke Charles Alexander in Brussels.

The wooden case shows normal signs of wear. The fabric behind the openwork brass panels in the sides of the case has probably been renewed, and the glass in the arched doors on the sides of the hood has been added. The urn finial on top of the hood is not original to the clock. The edge of the large white enamel dial has chips and a repair. The musical instruments have been removed and the musical train partly lost. The present bell, a product of the Whitechapel Bell Foundry in London, replaces a nineteenth-century wire gong. The motion work for the calendar has been repaired at various times, and the minute hand was broken into two pieces and soldered together at some point before the clock entered the Museum's collection.

Edgar Worch bought the clock from the Hessen family sometime after World War I. The clock is believed to have been in possession of the landgraves of Hessen-Kassel, although this supposition cannot be documented. CV / JHL

1 See Koeppe 2012, pp. 5–6.
2 For details of their lives and patrons, see Baarsen 2012; Koeppe 2012, pp. 3–15, 239–40; Rappe 2012; Rondot 2012; Stiegel 2012; Willscheid 2012.
3 D. Fabian 1984, p. 45, gives the date as 1740, when he abandoned milling and took up clockmaking in Neuwied, but elsewhere (p. 51) he gives the dates of the Kinzing workshop as 1738/41 to 1838.
4 Ibid., p. 66.
5 Ibid.
6 See Sauer-Kaulbach 2003, p. 10. The authors would like to thank Wolfram Koeppe for bringing this publication to our attention.
7 D. Fabian 1984, p. 67.
8 Ibid., p. 66.
9 Koeppe 2012, p. 7.
10 See D. Fabian 1984, p. 188, ill. no. 41, for the design published in the 1754 edition of Chippendale's *Director*. The original drawing for Chippendale's design is in the Metropolitan Museum (acc. no. 20.40.1[95]); see Koeppe 2012, pp. 114–15, and fig. 68.
11 D. Fabian 1984, p. 203, ill. no. 72. The painting was in a private collection in Schweinfurt at the time of Fabian's publication.
12 See Koeppe 2012, pp. 115, 246, n. 10, under no. 26.
13 For the five others, see D. Fabian 1984, pp. 316–17, nos. 28–31, 33.
14 Koeppe 2012, pp. 113–15, no. 26.
15 Baarsen 2012, pp. 26–28; Koeppe 2012, pp. 12, 113–15.
16 See Baarsen 2012, pp. 27–28; Koeppe 2012, p. 113.
17 Now in the collection of the Goethehaus, Frankfurt am Main. See Maurice 1976, vol. 2, pp. 102–5, no. 888, and fig. 888; D. Fabian 1984, pp. 162–71, ill. nos. 5–9, and p. 298, no. 1.

45. Pair-Case Quarter-Repeating Watch

BRITISH (LONDON), MADE FOR THE TURKISH MARKET, PROBABLY CA. 1770

Diam. of inner case: 1 9/16 in. (4 cm)
Diam. of outer case: 1 7/8 in. (4.8 cm)
Diam. of back plate: 1 1/8 in. (2.9 cm)
Gift of J. Pierpont Morgan, 1917
17.190.1427 and 17.190.1568

OUTER CASE AND INNER CASE: partly enameled gold, outer case: set with diamonds, casemaker's mark: GH [possibly George Harrison, British, active beginning 1760, or Gyles Hooper, British, active beginning 1773]
DIAL: white enamel with black numerals and silver hands set with diamonds, signed: PERIGAL / ROYAL / EXCHANGE / LONDON [Francis Perigal, British, active 1741–67, or Francis Perigal Jr., British, active 1778–1809]
MOVEMENT: gilded brass and partly blued(?) steel, signed (on back plate): *Fras Perigal* / LONDON, and numbered *17389*

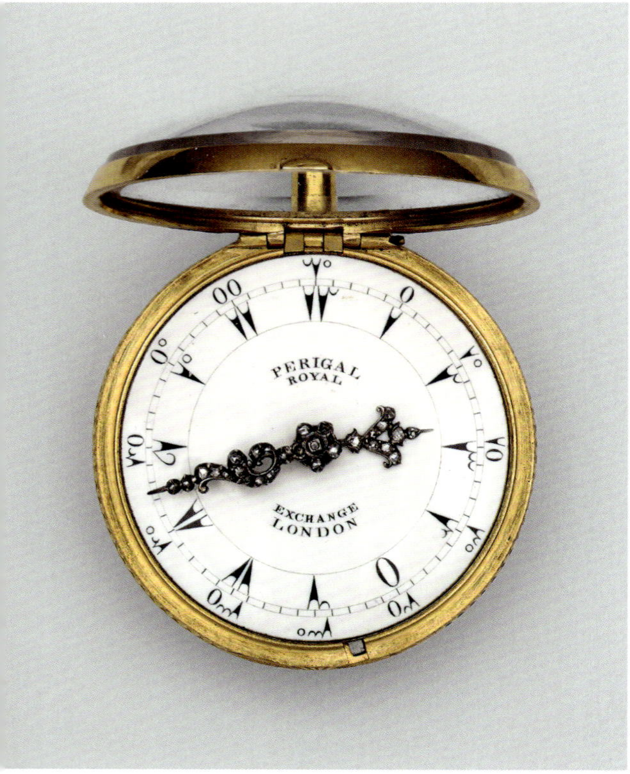

THERE IS A TRADITION THAT HĀRŪN AL-RASHĪD (763 OR 766–809), the fifth Abbasid caliph of Baghdad, perhaps best known to the Western world as the caliph in the *One Thousand and One Nights*, sent a water clock as a gift to the Frankish King and Roman Emperor Charlemagne (742–814).[1] Some twentieth-century historians have seriously questioned the veracity of the story,[2] but the existence of water clocks, some of them quite remarkable, in Muslim-ruled parts of the Near East and North Africa is unquestionable. The illustrated treatise *Kitab fi ma'rifat al-hiyal al-handasiyya* (The Book of Knowledge of Ingenious Mechanical Devices), finished in 1206 by Ibn al-Razzāz al-Jazarī (1136–1206), describes water clocks that came in fanciful shapes, sounded the hours, and caused automaton figures to function. The descriptions and illustrations are accompanied by detailed instructions on how to make them.[3]

For various reasons, mechanically driven clockwork was apparently not introduced into the empire of the Ottoman Turks until the sixteenth century. In 1531, however, a watch that reportedly struck the hours embedded in a gold ring made by the Italian clock and automaton maker Giorgio da Capobianco (1511–1550) was bought by the Ottoman Sultan Süleyman I (1494–1566).[4] Ten years later, the Habsburg Holy Roman Emperor Charles V (1500–1558) instituted the custom of giving yearly gifts to the sultan in exchange for peace on his borders. An early list of these gifts included a clock, a planetarium, and objects made of silver.[5] By 1548, the "gifts," or, more accurately, the tribute, consisted not only of clocks but also the clockmakers to care for them. Further documents indicate that the clocks were chiefly made in the Habsburg-ruled, imperial city of Augsburg and that many were made by some of the best clockmakers of the time.[6] In 1568 Gerhard Emmoser (active 1556–84), Court Clockmaker to Holy Roman Emperor Maximilian II (1527–1576), was paid for two small clocks or watches that were sent to Turkey.[7]

The Peace of Zsitvatorok in 1606 produced a new agreement between the Holy Roman Emperor and the Ottoman sultan that ended the yearly tribute. By that time Galata, a suburb of Istanbul (Constantinople), had become a colony of foreign goldsmiths, engravers, and clockmakers,[8] in addition to native-born Turkish clockmakers who already resided there. No clocks apparently survive in Turkey of either European or Turkish origin from this period,[9] however, well-known astronomer and chief astrologer to Sultan Murad III (1546–1595), Taki-al-Din, or Takiyüddin (1526–1585), was the founder of the short-lived observatory in Galata in 1575.[10] His treatise, *Al-Kawakib al-durriyya fi wadh' al-bankamat al-dawriyya* (The Brightest Stars for the Construction of the Mechanical Clocks),[11] describes in detail the technology of European mechanically driven clocks that he had seen. The treatise is thought to have been used as a manual of construction by native Turkish clockmakers.[12]

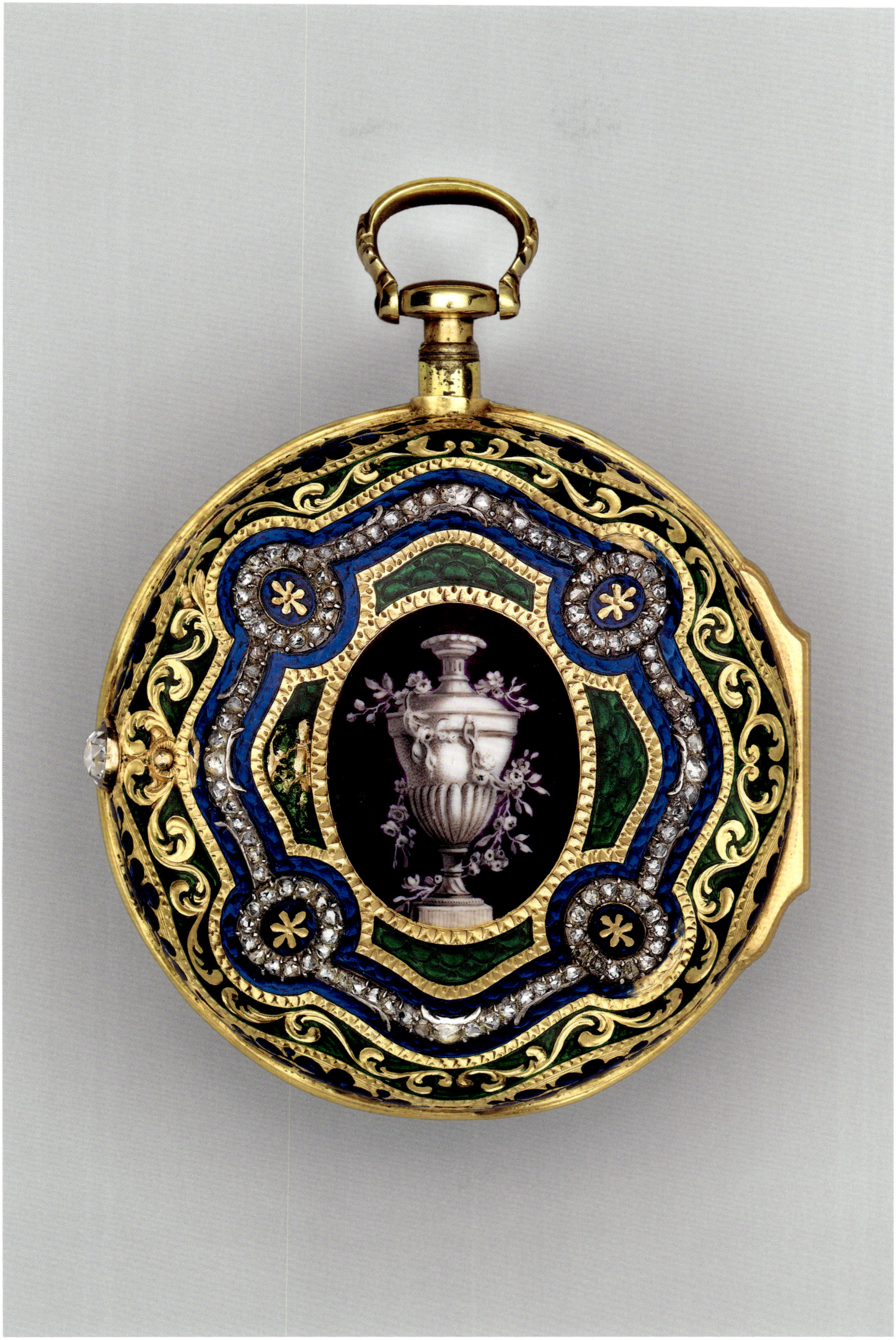

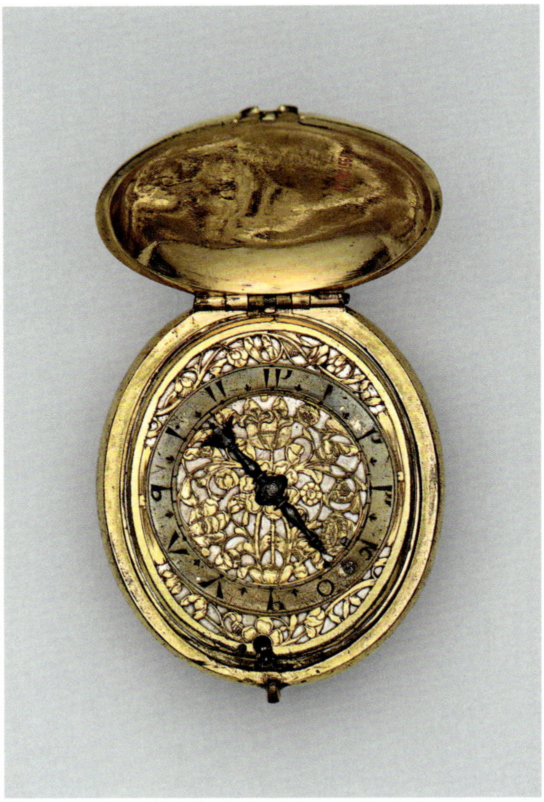

fig. 50 *Watch, Turkish (probably Galata), mid-17th century. Gilded metal, 2¼ × 1⅞ in. (5.7 × 4.8 cm). The Metropolitan Museum of Art, New York, Gift of J. Pierpont Morgan, 1917 (17.190.1560)*

Information about foreigners in seventeenth-century Galata is scant, but it is known that both French and Swiss watchmakers were among them.[13] A watch in the Musée International d'Horlogerie, La Chaux-de-Fonds, Switzerland,[14] has an inscription identifying it as having a movement by a member of the Arlaud family of Genevan watchmakers. Several members of that family are recorded as having been in Galata during the middle of the seventeenth century.[15] The case of the watch, looking a great deal more Turkish than Swiss, resembles a watchcase in the Metropolitan Museum's collection (fig. 50),[16] and the similarity provides evidence that the Museum's watch is likely to have been the product of the Galata colony.

The Metropolitan's watch has a closely comparable dial with an allover pattern of vegetal ornament, some of it suggesting the strawberry-leaf designs used by mid-century European watchmakers for watch cocks. The chapter ring is applied and has numerals representing the hours and a single, sculptured hand. The numerals are adaptations made by European clockmakers of the numbers used in Arabic arithmetic, and eventually they were adopted by Turkish watch- and clockmakers as well.[17] The back plate of the watch is covered almost entirely by an openwork pattern of flowers. The watch is fitted with a later balance cock that is undoubtedly European-made.

Both watchcases in New York and in La Chaux-de-Fonds could conceivably have been made by Turkish craftsmen, however, the movements tell a different story. Casual examination of the Metropolitan's watch identifies its movement as a rather clumsy version of an Arlaud movement. The watch is not signed, but there are a small number of known watches that are signed by makers with Turkish names, such as Dūnā[18] or Şeyh Dede.[19] Wolfgang Meyer, writing in the catalogue of the collection of the Topkapı Sarayı Müzesi, Istanbul, lists the names of nine Turkish clockmakers working between 1650 and 1780 whose works are now in Istanbul.[20]

By the 1780s, a flood of English and, to a lesser extent, French watches had captured the high-end Turkish market.[21] The English Levant Company (1581–1825), founded as a monopoly for trading with Turkey and the lands ruled by the Ottoman sultans, was older than the English East India Company, which had held the monopoly on English trade with China. Similar to the Chinese emperors, the Ottoman sultans appreciated gifts in return for the right to trade.[22] As early as 1599, the Levant Company presented to Mehmet III an elaborate, English-made organ clock by Thomas Dallam (ca. 1570–after 1614) with clockwork attributed to John Harvey (active 1594–99, died before 1608) of Oxford.[23] During the 1600s, the Swiss and French overshadowed English imports in Turkish lands, but by 1786 English watches had become the dominant imports.[24]

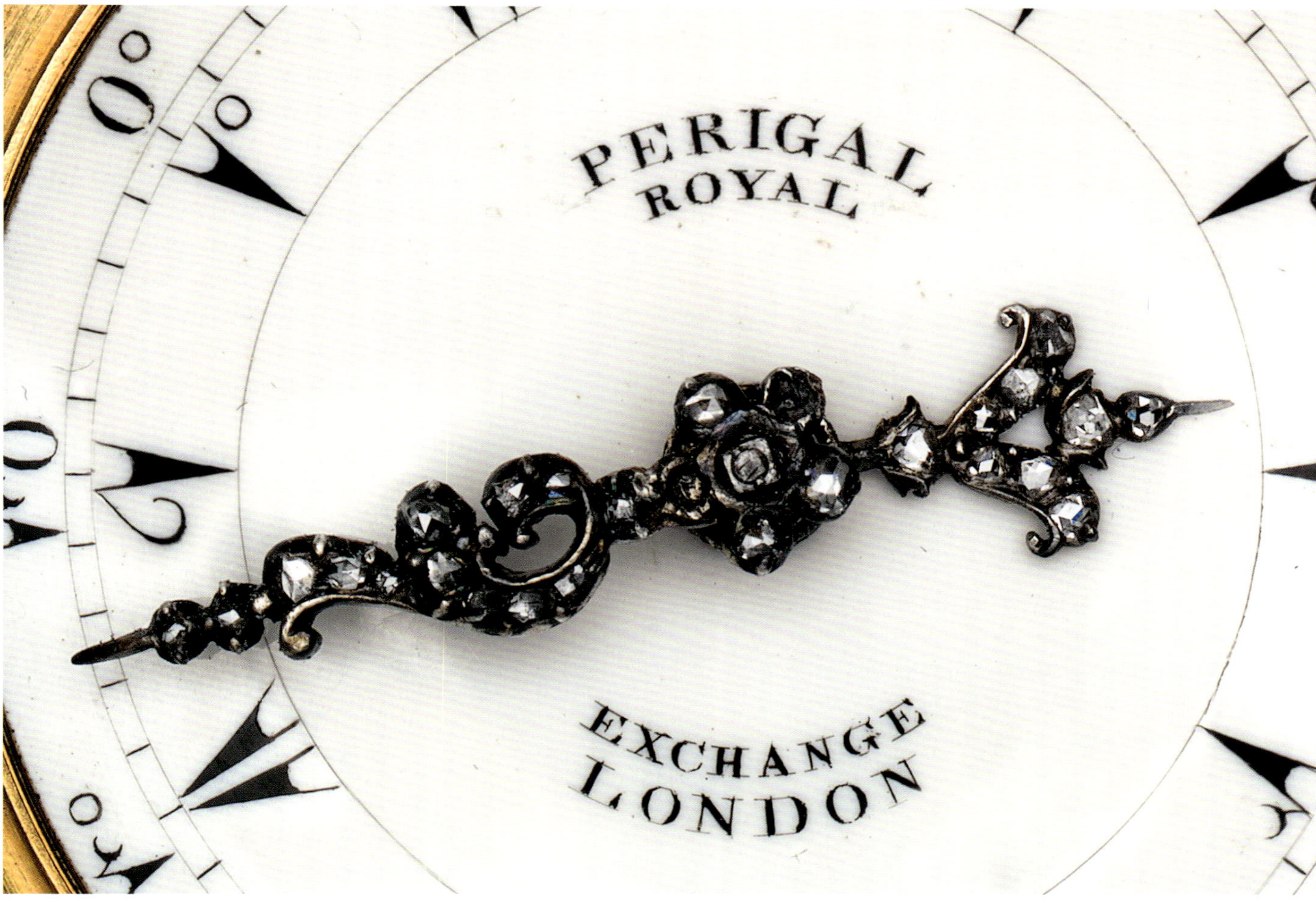

Detail of the diamond-set hour and minute hand

The success of the English was probably due to their ability to produce quantities of high-quality watch movements in cases exhibiting the fine workmanship provided by a network of independent suppliers of craftsmen, which existed in London during this period. The enameled gold and diamond pair-case quarter-repeating watch in this entry is an excellent example of the type of watch intended to please a luxury-loving Turk. The white enamel dial painted with "Turkish" numerals (1–12) for the hours and the minutes (5–60, by fives) marks it as intended for the Ottoman trade. The elaborately sculptured silver hands are set with tiny diamond chips.

Most watches for this market had not one but two, and sometimes three, outer cases, the outermost of leather, shagreen, or silver filigree to protect their delicate inner cases. This watch now has only one outer case, and in fact, had none when it entered the Museum's collection as the gift of J. Pierpont Morgan. The outer case had become separated at some time between its possession by Carl H. Marfels[25] and the inclusion of the rest of the watch in the catalogue of the Morgan watch collection.[26] For this reason, the watch acquired two separate accession numbers: one for the watch and inner case, and one for the outer case, which had been misidentified as French.

The outer case is in fact a tour de force of English craftsmanship. Wavy edged, the case is made of chased gold ornamented with concentric bands of translucent, basse-taille enamels in emerald green and royal blue, one band set with a circle of diamond chips, which is punctuated by ovals at the four corners and contains gold stars. In the center, a panel with a flower-draped Neoclassical vase enameled in shades of gray and lavender is set against an oval chocolate-colored ground. The case is hinged at the nine o'clock position and opened by applying pressure to a large rose-diamond thumb-piece. The interior of the case bears an incuse mark "GH" below a coronet. The bezel repeats the design of the outermost band of ornament on the case, yet is framed by another circle of diamond chips. Hidden within the design, tiny openings allow the sound of the bell for the repeating mechanism to escape.

The gold inner case has a glass cover with a plain gold bezel. The case has a band of chased, openwork scrolling issuing from a stylized shell motif at the six o'clock position. The exterior of the back of the case sports rows of chased-gold and white-enameled lozenges, each containing a six-petal flower in green enamel with the rows separated by a zigzag pattern of translucent blue enamel. The whole design is enclosed by a wavy, circular frame of translucent blue enamel, which completes a perfect candy-box effect. Engraved at the twelve o'clock position is the number 17389. A separate dust cover for the movement and fitting is engraved: "Fra^{s} / Perigal / LONDON" and numbered 17389.

The movement consists of two circular plates of gilded brass held apart by four cylindrical pillars. It is quarter repeating and has a cylinder escapement. As usual for this period, the worm-and-wheel setup for the mainspring is located between the two plates. The back plate supports a balance cock with a solid, engraved foot that is screwed to the plate, and a diamond endstone for pivoting the balance staff, as well as a silver figure plate for adjusting the balance spring. The back plate is also signed "Fra^{s} Perigal / LONDON" and numbered 17389. The mainspring is wound through keyholes in the back of the inner case and the dust cover.

Of the five Francis Perigal watchmakers known to have worked in eighteenth-century London, it is possible to identify "Perigal Royal / Exchange London" on the dial of this watch to either "Francis Perigal at the Royal Exchange," a member of the Clockmakers' Company, mentioned in an extant list of freemen of the company between 1766 and 1773, or the "Francis Perigal jr," also at the Royal Exchange during the same period.[27] According to historian Ian White, the first Francis Perigal established himself at the Royal Exchange in 1740 and was succeeded by his son and grandson, both of the same name. The founder's son became apprenticed to his father in 1748, and according to White, in the third generation, Francis Jr. was apprenticed to his father in 1778 and became a freeman in the Clockmakers' Company in 1786. The latter two Perigals are the ones believed by White to have been engaged in providing watches for both the Chinese and Turkish trades.[28]

From the high serial number engraved on this watch, it would seem that the signature probably stands for Francis Perigal Jr. How much of any movement from the workshop of a successful London watchmaker in the 1770s is the actual work of the watchmaker who signed it may be questioned, however. The production of another watchmaker, George Prior (1735–1814), to the Chinese and Turkish trades, perhaps the most prolific, has been compiled by White. Prior's workshop is estimated to have produced more than 10,000 watches between about 1765 and 1780, or soon thereafter.[29]

The Museum's Perigal watch is of very high London quality. The mainspring is unfortunately now broken and the fusee chain has come loose. There are numerous losses of enamel on both the outer and the inner cases. The most extensive damage is on the outer case, where the element that frames the left side of the painted enamel vase is largely missing its translucent green enamel. CV / JHL

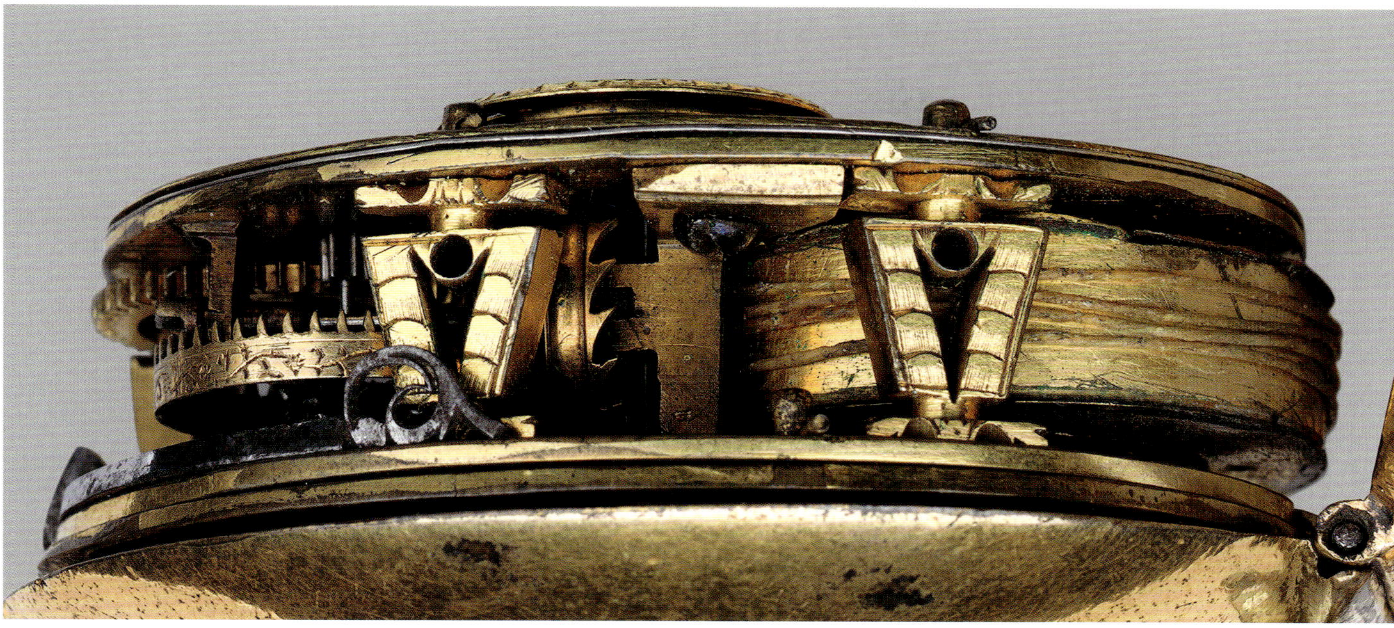

Side view of the Turkish movement

1 See Kurz 1975, p. 7; White 2012, p. 16.
2 See North 1975, pp. 382, 395, n. 16; see also Beliaev 1969, p. 221.
3 See al-Jazarī 1974; Turner 1984b, pp. 21–22; Turner 2002.
4 Kurz 1975, p. 22; Morpurgo 1950, pp. 41–42.
5 Kurz 1975, p. 23.
6 Mraz 1980, pp. 39–40. See entries 1, 9, 11, and 29 in this volume for more about Augsburg clocks.
7 Hofzahlamts-Rechnung, 1568, fol. 93, entry of Sept. 10, 1568, quoted in Boeheim 1888, p. cxxix, no. 5136. See also entry 4 in this volume for more about Gerhard Emmoser.
8 Kurz 1975, p. 49.
9 Özdemir 1993, pp. 99–109.
10 For more about the observatory, see Sayılı 1960, pp. 289–305.
11 One manuscript is in the Bibliothèque Nationale de France in Paris; another is in the Bodleian Library in Oxford. For an English translation, see Tekeli 1966.
12 White 2012, p. 59.
13 Kurz 1975, p. 49. See also Jaquet 1948b; Jaquet and Chapuis 1970, pp. 27–28.
14 Inv. no. I-555. See Cardinal and Piguet 2002, pp. 120–21, no. 117. See also Chapiro 2001, p. 32, figs. 3, 4.
15 Patrizzi 1998, pp. 75–76.
16 Acc. no. 17.190.1560.
17 For an example with more nearly correct Turkish numerals, see a plate clock by the Turkish clockmaker Bulugat from about 1650; illustrated in Meyer 1975, no. 2/1239.
18 Kurz 1975, pl. VIII, fig. 15a, b, and fig. 16a–d, and pl. IX, fig. 17a, b.
19 Ibid., p. 59; Özdemir 1993, pp. 115, 117. For a selection of European-made and Turkish-made watches of the seventeenth and early eighteenth centuries, see Chapiro 2001; Kremer 2014.
20 Meyer 1975, p. 6.
21 Kurz 1975, pp. 72–79, citing contemporaneous evidence of the quantity of English exports.
22 See White 2012, pp. 48–58, for a history of the clock and watch trade through the Levant Company.
23 Ibid., pp. 49–52.
24 Ibid., pp. 60–74.
25 Marfels 1889, pl. X, figs. 1a–d.
26 Williamson 1912, p. 192, no. 210. The outer case was not included in the catalogue but was part of the Morgan gift to the Museum.
27 Clockmakers' Company, London, Ms. 3941, unpag., Guildhall Library, London.
28 White 2012, p. 347.
29 Ibid., p. 69.

46. Mantel Clock with Musical Movement

FRENCH (PARIS), CA. 1784
29 × 16¼ × 9 in. (73.7 × 41.3 × 22.9 cm)
Gift of Samuel H. Kress Foundation, 1958
58.75.127

CASE: gilded and lacquered bronze and marble, signed (on enameled plaque at base of bust): *Furet H^{GER} du Roi* [Jean-Baptiste-André Furet, French, ca. 1720–1807)
MOVEMENT (IN BUST): brass and steel with enameled hour and minute chapter rings (in head); miniature organ with pipes and bellows (in base): brass, steel, and leather

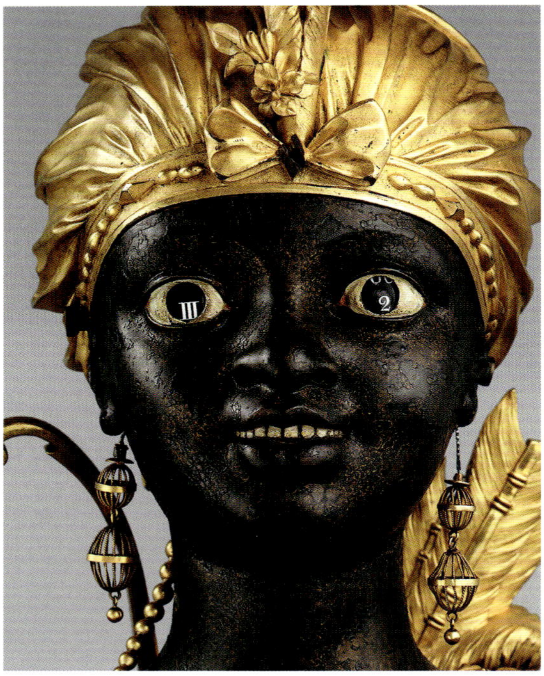

Detail of figure with eyes open to show the hour (left) and minute (right)

IN PARIS IN JANUARY 1775, A DISPLAY OF THREE MARVELOUS automata created a sensation. One automaton wrote a sentence of forty letters; the other automaton drew portraits of the King Louis XV, King Louis XVI, Queen Marie Antoinette, and a small dog; and the third automaton played a keyboard instrument. These nearly lifesize automata were the creation of Swiss clockmakers Pierre Jaquet-Droz (1721–1790) and his son Henri-Louis Jaquet-Droz (1752–1791), with assistance from the mechanician Jean-Frédéric Leschot (1746–1824); their association would last until the end of the eighteenth century.[1] The lady musician, who not only played five tunes, but also batted her eyes and turned her head from side to side, no doubt fueled French enthusiasm for musical automata. In fact, about the end of 1784 the French queen acquired a musical automaton playing a dulcimer, which was made by the Germans David Roentgen (1743–1807) and Christian I Kinzing (1707–1804) of Neuwied.[2]

Thus, it is understandable that one of the contributing authors to the *Mémoires secrets pour servir à l'histoire de la République des Lettres en France, depuis* MDCCLXII *jusqu'à nos jours* (Secret Memoirs Serving as a History of the Republic of Letters in France from 1762 until Our Day), a thirty-six volume record of notable events literary, scientific, and otherwise, paid a visit to the clockmaker Jean-Baptiste-André Furet (ca. 1720–1807) on July 4, 1784, and in whose shop three clocks of special interest were seen.[3] The author, who was probably Barthélemy-François-Josephy Mouffle d'Angerville (1728–1795), was impressed with the first clock, in part, because of its beautifully ornamented case that included the bust of an African woman wearing long earrings, but also because when one earring was pulled, the hour appeared in her right eye and the minute in her left. When the other earring was pulled, the organ played six different airs. The second clock, a hanging birdcage with a clock dial on its bottom, was almost certainly one of the variety for which the Jaquet-Droz et Leschot firm was well known. Indeed, in a Parisian trade publication from 1786, the mechanical musician and the birdcage clocks with avian automata were described as precious works to be obtained from "Monsieur Droz, the celebrated mechanician of Neuchâtel."[4] The third clock, now lesser known, was a terrestrial globe that displayed the time in Paris and numerous other places around the world.

The Museum's clock more or less matches the description of the first clock. The case of the clock consists of the bust of an African woman, perhaps a princess, as she has sometimes been called, resting on a black-and-white marble base that is supported by six gilded-bronze feet. Details of the Neoclassical ornament that adorns the case have been exhaustively described by the Metropolitan Museum's late Curator Emeritus James Parker in the catalogue of the Samuel H.

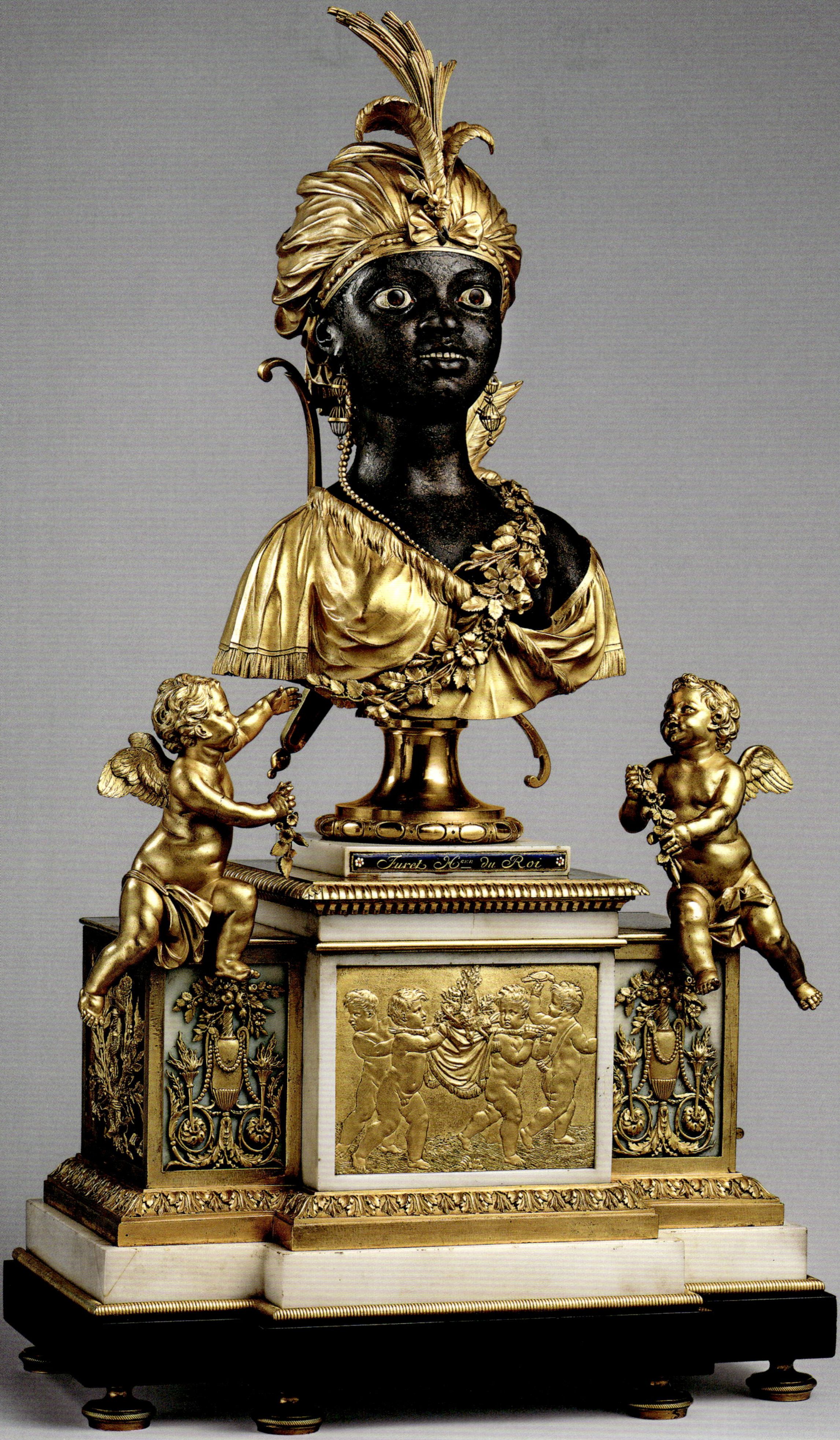
Furet Hger du Roi

Kress Collection.[5] The sculptor who provided the model for the bust, with its exquisite floral swag, bow and arrows, and feather-decorated cap, remains unknown. Nor is it known who executed the decorative plaque on the front of the base, with its procession of child huntsmen, or the two winged cherubs perched precariously on either side. The matte and burnished surface of the gilded-bronze elements is meticulously finished, but the lacquer on the skin of the bust has suffered extensive deterioration.

The time-telling mechanism of the clock is related to that of the revolving dials that had recently become the fashion for French clocks during this period, and especially but not exclusively, favored by the Paris workshop of the Lepaute family (see entry 39 in this volume). Essentially, the mechanism in Furet's clock consists of an arbor with two revolving wheels, which are attached vertically instead of horizontally, the more common construction. One wheel is enameled with the hours in roman numerals; the other wheel with the minutes in Arabic numerals by twos. The wheels are concealed inside the head of the figure, and for most of the time they are completely invisible and covered by shutters. The gearing for the two wheels is attached to two shafts that are in turn driven by a movement containing a single train with a verge escapement and spring balance, which is concealed inside the shoulders of the figure. Its spring is wound through a hole in the back of one shoulder, and a second hole in the other shoulder permits adjustments to the setting of the hours and minutes.

The base of the clock houses a spring-driven cylinder organ that has been identified by curator Jan Jaap L. Haspels as a type described by Dom François Bedos de Celles (1709–1779), a master builder of French pipe organs and Benedictine monk, in a treatise on the construction of organs titled *L'art du facteur d'orgues* (The Art of the Organ Builder), published in Paris in four volumes between 1766 and 1778 (fig. 51).[6] Haspels noted that the author of the treatise believed that a spring-driven cylinder organ could support only one rank of ten pipes, but recognized that with the application of certain devices, or transmissions, enough power could be supplied to operate organs with as many as three ranks of pipes. One of these devices is to be found in the Museum's clock in which the entire musical train is driven by two barrels containing mainsprings that act in tandem to produce greater force on a single fusee. Together, the two springs power a bellows and two ranks of pipes with fifteen keys. The music played by the organ that closely resembles the cylinder organ found in clocks made by the firm of Jaquet-Droz et Leschot has not been studied.[7]

It is quite likely that the clock was originally made to open the eye shutters and play a selected tune on the hour and to shut them again when the tune stopped, but the connection for activating the music no longer exists. The hours and minutes can still be seen by pulling at will the earring on the right side of the figure; the hours appear in the left eye and the minutes in the right eye. The earring on the left side originally activated the cylinder organ.

It cannot be certain that the Museum's clock was the one described by the author of the entry in the *Mémoires secrets*, because at least three

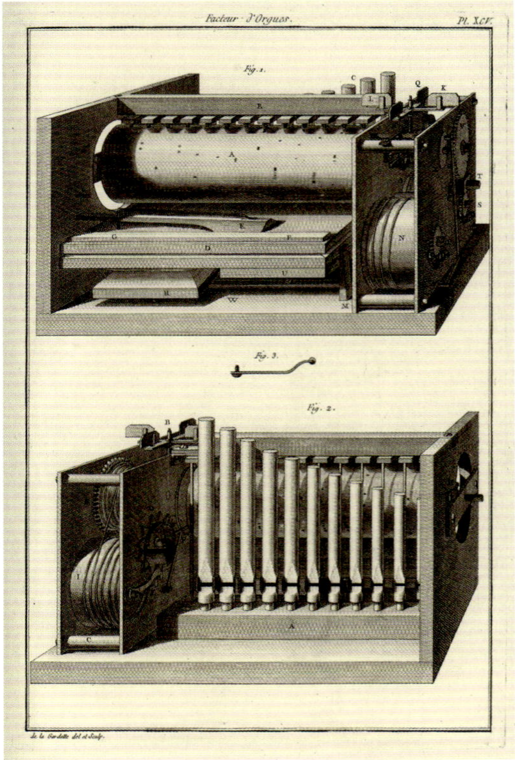

fig. 51 *François Bedos de Celles (French, 1709–1779). Plate XCV from* L'art du facteur d'orgues, *Description des arts et métiers 11–12 (Paris: L. F. Delatour, 1766–78), part IV, chap. III. The Metropolitan Museum of Art, New York, Thomas J. Watson Library, Special Collections*

other examples of the model are known. One, now in a private collection in Paris, was acquired for Marie Antoinette (1755–1793) by Thierry de Ville d'Avray (1732–1792), the director general of the Garde-Meuble de la Couronne (or keeper of the Royal Furniture and Moveable Possessions), who apparently kept the clock in his office for his own amusement and had the mechanism repaired several times between 1787 and 1792, until the French Revolution put an end to such amusements.[8]

A second example, this one signed "L^{e} pine H^{er} du Roy ÆParis 4195" (Jean-Antoine Lépine [1720–1814]), is in the British Royal Collection Trust, where it has been since before 1807 when another royal clockmaker, Benjamin Lewis Vulliamy (1780–1854), cleaned and refurbished the movement and regilded parts of the case.[9] This clock is nearly an exact duplicate of the Metropolitan Museum's clock, so closely related that the author of the exhaustive study of Lépine's work, Adolphe Chapiro, has attributed the clock to Furet regardless of the Lépine signature.[10] It seems likely, therefore, that either Furet supplied the equally busy and highly successful Lépine with the entire clock, or they each patronized the same subcontractors.

Parker reported the existence of another clock in the private collection of Mrs. Herbert A. May (formerly Marjorie Merriweather Post,[11] best known for her collection of Russian decorative arts) in Washington, D.C., and a fourth clock with a movement signed "J.S. Bourdier, 1817 ÆParis" appeared on the Paris auction market in 2007.[12] The clockmaker, Jean-Simon Bourdier (active 1787–1829), is known as a maker of ingenious musical clocks and automata.[13]

The clockmaker Furet, who signed the Metropolitan Museum's clock, was one of the very few clockmakers who were visited by the authors of the *Mémoires secrets*. He belonged to the third generation of Furets who were clockmakers in Paris, the earliest being André, whose shop was recorded in the rue des Gesvres in 1699. His son Jean-André became a master clockmaker in 1710, and his son Jean-Baptiste-André was born about 1720. Jean-Baptiste-André was made a master clockmaker in 1746, and a year later, he is recorded with his father at an establishment in the rue Saint-Honoré, presumably the one visited by Mouffle d'Angerville. By 1758, he had been granted a royal appointment (Horloger Ordinaire du Roi pour sa Bibliothèque [Clockmaker to the King and for His Library]), and about 1784 or 1785, he briefly became an associate of the Spanish clockmaker François-Antoine Godon (ca. 1740–1800).[14]

According to historian Jean-Dominique Augarde, Furet ceased paying his bills in 1785, and by March 4, 1786, he was bankrupt, declaring a stock of ninety-eight clocks valued at 63,903 livres, including one "African princess" (*Tête de négresse*) clock. There were more than ninety creditors, and a list reveals that Furet was subcontracting most of his production by the time of his bankruptcy. More than a third of the total was owed to Swiss suppliers and clockmakers.[15] This record strengthens the evidence to be seen by examining the cylinder organ and probably also the movement inside of the Metropolitan Museum's clock, suggesting that both Furet and Lépine, who signed the clock now in the British Royal Collection Trust, did indeed obtain their movements from the same Swiss supplier.

Sold in 1881 at the Paris sale of the collection of Léopold Double,[16] the Metropolitan Museum's clock was later owned by the Marquis de Lambertie and by C. Ledyard Blair of Peapack, New Jersey.[17] CV / JHL

1 All three automata are now in the Musée des Beaux-Arts in Neuchâtel, Switzerland. See Chapuis and Droz 1958, pp. 279–83, and pl. 1; Droz 1971. For further illustrations and discussion of the mechanism of the musician, see Jan Jaap L. Haspels in *Royal Music Machines* 2006, pp. 239–43, no. 47.

2 D. Fabian 1984, p. 345, no. 92; Haspels in *Royal Music Machines* 2006, pp. 182–86, no. 33; Koeppe 2012, pp. 146–48, no. 38.

3 *Mémoires secrets* 1786, p. 78. The *Mémoires secrets* are thought to have been started by Louis-Petit de Bachaumont (1690–1771).

4 "M. Droz, célèbre méchanicien de Neuf-Châtel"; *Tablettes royale de renommée* 1786, unpag. ("Nouvel étalon, ou Mesure universelle").

5 James Parker in Dauterman, Parker, and Standen 1964, pp. 268–72, no. 65, and figs. 226–28.

6 See Haspels 1987, pp. 69–79, and pls. 107–9.

7 Haspels 1994, pp. 58–59.

8 Christian Baulez in *Marie-Antoinette* 2008, p. 210, no. 149.

9 Jagger 1983, pp. 161–63. Cedric Jagger suggested that the clock may have been bought in 1790 by King George III's eldest son, later to become King George IV (1765–1820).

10 Chapiro 1988, p. 231.

11 Parker in Dauterman, Parker, and Standen 1964, p. 269.

12 See Rouge 2008, p. 85.

13 Tardy 1971–72, vol. 1, p. 74; Augarde 1996, pp. 285, 287.

14 Tardy 1971–72, vol. 1, pp. 240–41; Augarde 1996, pp. 317–18.

15 Augarde 1996, pp. 317–18.

16 *Collection Double* 1881, p. 86, no. 274.

17 Parker in Dauterman, Parker, and Standen 1964, pp. 269, 272.

47. Watch

PROBABLY SWISS (GENEVA) MADE FOR THE FRENCH MARKET, CA. 1783–90

Diam. of case: 1½ in. (3.8 cm)
Diam. of back plate: 1³⁄₁₆ in. (3 cm)
Gift of J. Pierpont Morgan, 1917
17.190.1587

CASE: partly enameled gold set with pearls, gold bezel with diamonds set in silver
DIAL: white enamel with openwork brass hands
MOVEMENT: brass and steel, signed (on back plate): *Vaucher Æparis* [Daniel Vaucher, or Vauchez, French, 1716–active 1767–90] and numbered *2065*

FRENCH ENTHUSIASM FOR BALLOONING WAS SPARKED BY THE June 4, 1783, ascent of a hot air balloon made by the Montgolfier brothers, Joseph (1740–1810) and Etienne (1745–1799). On September 19 of the same year, a Montgolfier balloon with crew of a sheep, a duck, and a rooster was launched at Versailles in the presence of King Louis XVI (1754–1793) and Queen Marie Antoinette (1755–1793).[1] The first human flight, which took place a few weeks later in Paris on November 21, was witnessed by Benjamin Franklin (1706–1790), among others.

By January 10, 1784, the members of the French Académie Royale des Sciences were invited by Louis XVI's director of buildings and gardens, Charles-Claude La Billarderie, Comte d'Angiviller (1730–1810), to a competition for a commemorative monument to the achievement of flight. The proposed monument was to be erected in the Tuileries Palace in Paris.[2] The monument was never completed, but a model for it, one of two submitted by the sculptor Claude Michel, known as Clodion (1738–1814), survives. Depicting the Montgolfiers' balloon, heralded by a trumpet-blowing genius and attended by putti bearing straw and lighted torches with which to ignite the flame that heated the air in the balloon, the Metropolitan Museum's model is one of the gems of the Museum's collection of eighteenth-century French terracottas (fig. 53).[3]

The Museum's watch, although a more modest novelty, nevertheless demonstrates how great early attempts at human flight captured the French imagination. In the enameled scene on the back of the Museum's watchcase, two men precariously perched atop ladders secure a balloon, which is about to be launched by three men on the ground. One of the three men wields a lighted torch that identifies the balloon as a true *montgolfière*, the French word for a hot-air balloon.

Daniel Vaucher (or Vauchez; born 1716, active 1767–90), was a master watchmaker in Paris in 1767. His shop is recorded to have been located in the rue Saint-Pierre aux Boeufs between 1769 and 1790. His son Jean-Henri-David Vaucher became a master clockmaker in 1779 and a member of the Juraude, a governing body of the Corporation des Horlogers de Paris, in 1786. He is recorded as having been located on rue Saint-Pierre aux Boeufs from 1790 to 1791[4] and described not as a watchmaker, however, but as a maker of gold and silver watchcases (*monteur des boites*).[5] It seems that Jean-Henri-David was apparently involved with the infamous affair of the queen's necklace.[6]

The rue Saint-Pierre aux Boeufs evidently vanished around the same time in 1837 when the tenth-century church of Saint-Pierre aux Boeufs was demolished in order to enlarge the open space on the north side of the Notre-Dame Cathedral, Ile Saint-Louis, Paris.[7] The nearby Place Dauphine, on the northwest end of the island, was the location

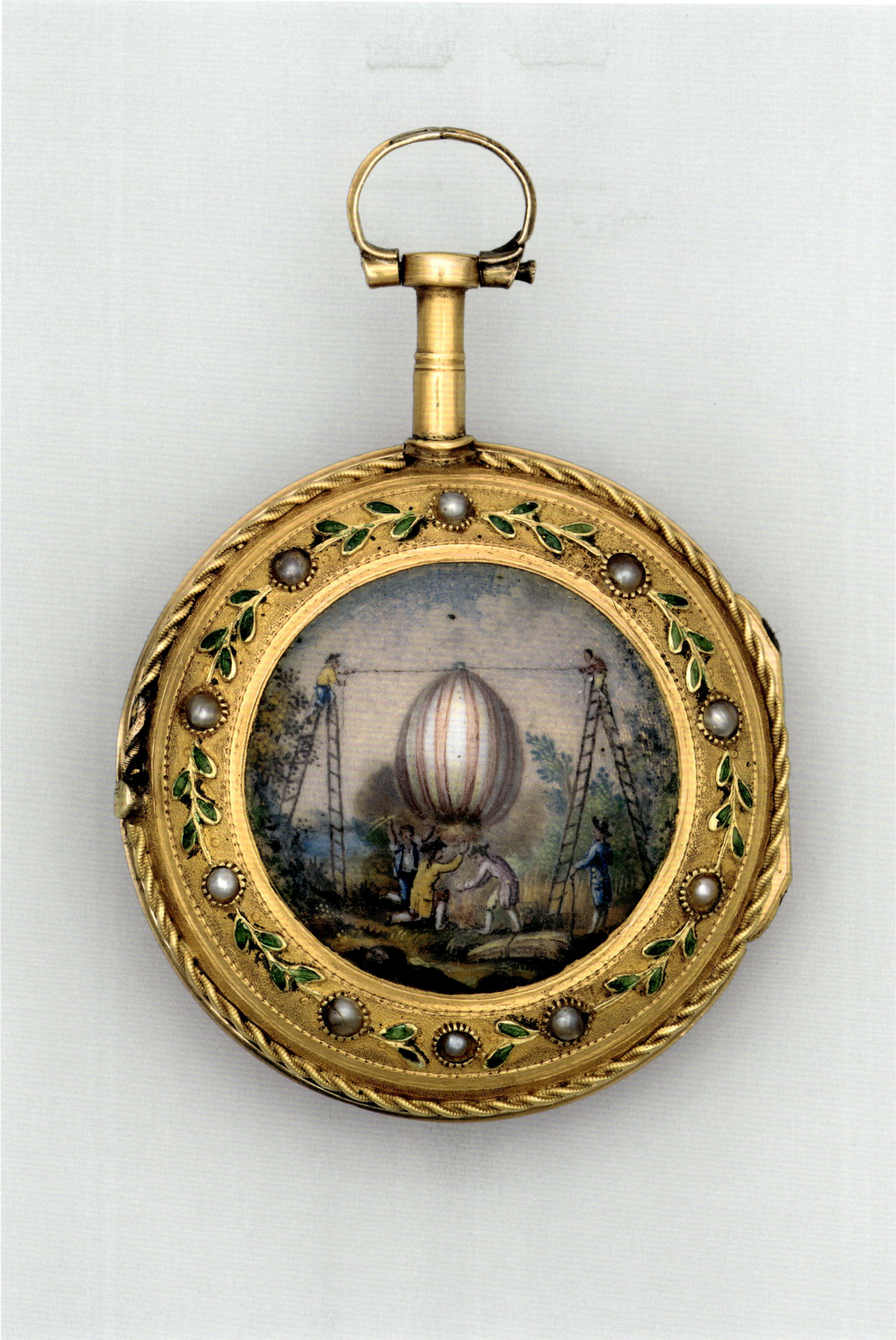

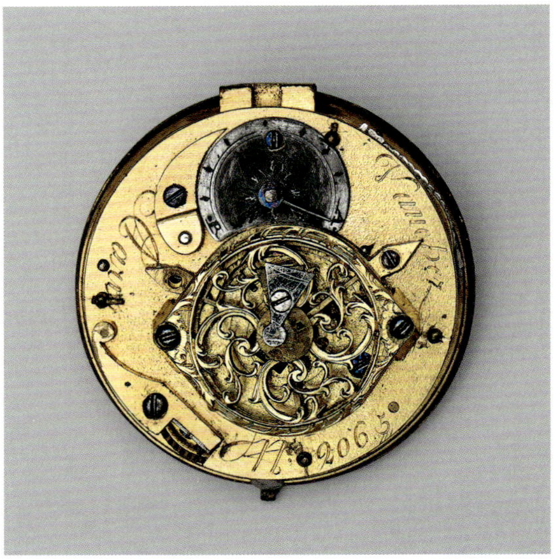

The back plate of the movement

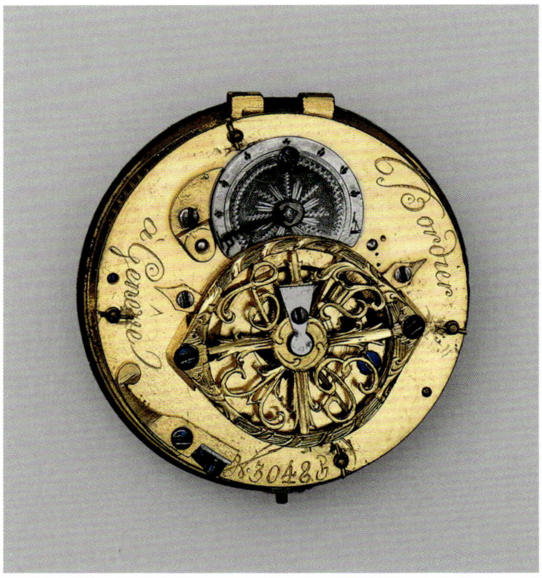

fig. 52 *Watch with calendar, Swiss (Geneva), ca. 1780–90. Case: varicolored gold, partly enameled; dial: white enamel, signed "Bordier / A. GENEVE," movement: brass and steel, signed "Bordier / à Genève." Diameter back plate 1³⁄₁₆ in. (3 cm). The Metropolitan Museum of Art, New York, Gift of Mrs. Lucy W. Drexel, 1889 (89.2.83)*

of some of the best watch- and clockmakers in eighteenth-century Paris, including Ferdinand Berthoud (1727–1807), Abraham Breguet (1747–1823), Julien Le Roy (1686–1759), and Pierre Le Roy (1717–1785).[8] The Cité was thus a prestigious location for a watchmaker, and it seems likely that the Metropolitan Museum's watch, seven watches belonging to the Musée du Louvre, Paris,[9] two watches in the Musée International d'Horlogerie, La Chaux-de-Fonds, Switzerland,[10] and one watch in the Musée Paul Dupuy, Toulouse, France,[11] variously signed "Vaucher ÆParis," "Vauchez ÆParis," or "Vauchez en la Cité ÆParis," were all sold by Daniel or Jean-Henri-David Vaucher at some point during this same time period.

The movement of the Metropolitan Museum's Vaucher watch is a standard type made during the second half of the eighteenth century with full plates, a fusee, and a verge escapement, the back plate with a balance bridge and silver figure plate for the regulation of its balance spring. It was customary for eighteenth-century watchmakers in France and England to number their products consecutively, and it is often possible to estimate the date of a watch by its number. Thus, it is important to note that in author Catherine Cardinal's careful descriptions of the seven Vaucher watches in the Musée du Louvre, the enameled gold cases of the watches with lower numbers bear full sets of Parisian goldsmiths' marks, and that those with higher numbers, like the Metropolitan Museum's watchcase, bear no maker's marks at all.[12] The explanation for this observation probably lies in a passage in *L'art de conduire et de régler les pendules et les montres*, first published in Paris in 1759 by the illustrious clockmaker Ferdinand Berthoud, in which he bemoans the fact that Parisian sellers of horology were purveyors of watches with poor-quality Genevan movements in French cases, their movements signed with the names of respected French watchmakers.[13]

It is only a single step further to import both case and movement and to sell the product under the name of a French watchmaker. With this in mind, examination of the Metropolitan Museum's Vaucher watch, as well as another in the Museum's collection,[14] signed "Bordier à Genêva," reveals that, while the subject of the scenes on their enameled cases differs, the two scenes are stylistically comparable, and neither case is marked. Further, the movements are nearly identical, except for the ornament of the figure plates and the balance bridges, which in the Bordier watch incorporates the initials "PABF" in its openwork design of the balance bridge. As there were numerous watch- and clockmakers named Bordier in Geneva, these initials may have identified the true makers of the watch as Pierre IX Bordier (1712–1789) and his brother Ami II (1722–1811), or Pierre, Ami, Bordier et Fils.[15] The use of identifying initials in the table of a balance bridge or a

fig. 53 *Clodion (Claude Michel, French, 1738–1814). Model for a Proposed Monument to Commemorate the Invention of the Balloon, French (Paris), ca. 1784. Terracotta, 43⅛ × 24¾ × 20⅜ in. (109.5 × 62.9 × 51.8 cm). The Metropolitan Museum of Art, New York, Purchase, Rogers Fund and Anonymous Gift, 1944 (44.21a, b)*

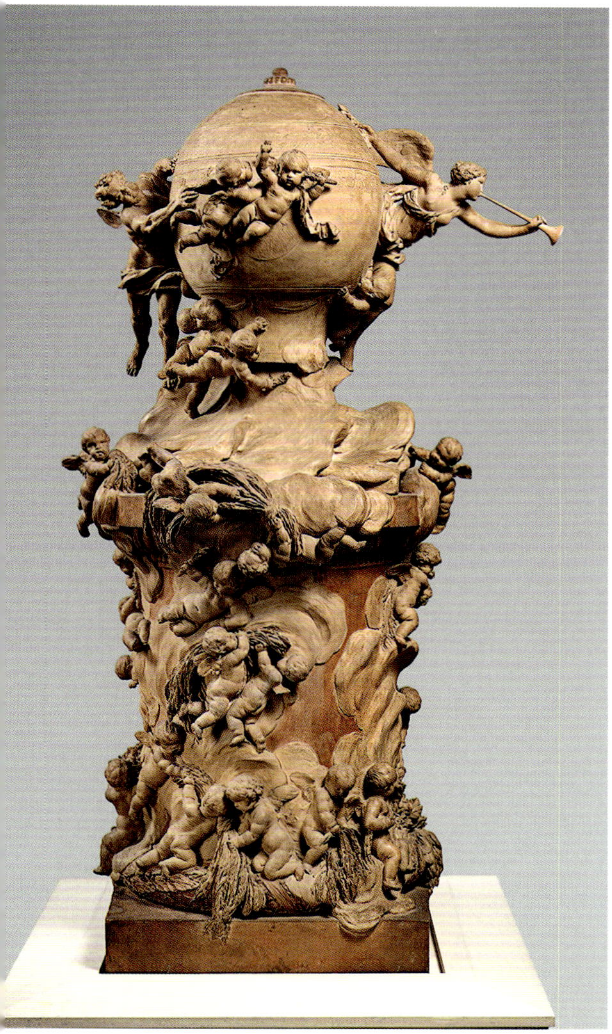

balance cock was not unique to the Bordiers; they can also be found in both Swiss and English watches beginning in the second half of the eighteenth century.

The greater interest in the Metropolitan Museum's Vaucher watch lies, however, in the probable date of its creation as a novelty, for example, as a reflection of the passion of the moment. That moment can be dated with reasonable certainty: 1783, when the Montgolfiers launched their first balloon, or shortly thereafter, when wholly Swiss-made watches were being sold in Paris under French names. The practice is hard to document, but it would continue until well into the nineteenth century.

This watch was in the collection of Frederick George Hilton Price before it appears in the Morgan watch collection in 1912.[16] CV / JHL

1 Gillispie 1983, p. 20.
2 Furcy-Raynaud 1925–26, pp. 217, 419–20.
3 Wardropper 2011, pp. 200–202, no. 69.
4 Tardy 1971–72, vol. 2, p. 631.
5 See Diderot and d'Alembert 1765, p. 308, for this specialization.
6 Tardy 1971–72, vol. 2, p. 631.
7 Hillairet 1954, p. 15.
8 Chapiro 1991, pp. 144–48.
9 Cardinal 1984b, pp. 187–88, nos. 239, 240; pp. 189–90, nos. 244, 245; p. 191, no. 249; pp. 194–95, no. 256; and p. 196, no. 258.
10 Musée International d'Horlogerie 1974, pp. 73, 75.
11 Hayard 2004, p. 244.
12 Cardinal 1984b, pp. 194–95, no. 256, and p. 196, no. 258.
13 Cardinal 1984a, p. 53.
14 Acc. no. 89.2.83.
15 Patrizzi 1998, pp. 111, 113; see also Gibertini 1964, p. 221, for dates (1775–89) when watches were signed in this way.
16 Williamson 1912, pp. 68–69, no. 64, and pl. XXVI.

48. Mantel Clock with Calendar

FRENCH (PARIS), CA. 1800
22⅛ × 17½ × 6 in. (56.2 × 44.5 × 15.2 cm)
Diam. of back plate: 4¾ in. (12.1 cm)
Gift of Estate of James Hazen Hyde, 1959
59.208.79

CASE: partly patinated and partly gilded bronze, gilded brass, and paste jewels, by Jules-Simon Deverberie [French, active 1788–1820, died ca. 1824]
DIAL: white enamel with gilded brass and steel hands, signed: *Ridel à Paris* [Laurent Ridel, French, active 1789]
MOVEMENT: brass and steel

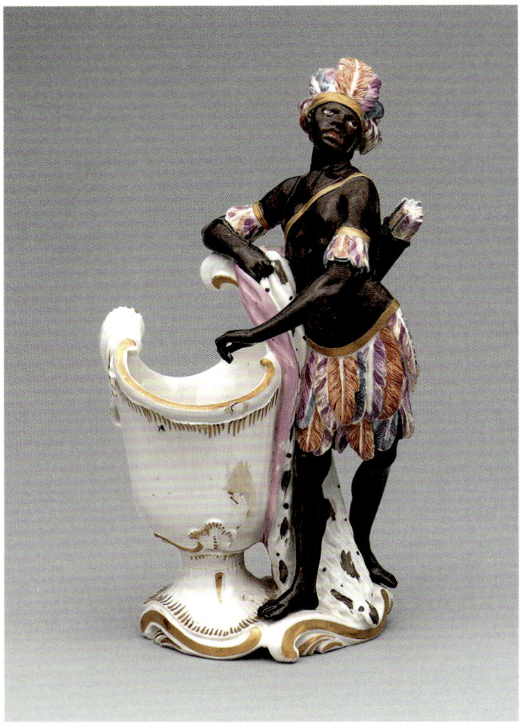

fig. 54 *Frankenthal Porcelain Manufactory (German, founded 1755); modeler: Franz Konrad Linck (German, 1730–1793). Figure of America, German (Frankenthal), ca. 1765. Hard-paste porcelain, Height 8 in. (20.3 cm). The Metropolitan Museum of Art, New York, Gift of Estate of James Hazen Hyde, 1959 (59.208.14)*

THE TWO HUMAN FIGURES, MALE AND FEMALE, EACH DRESSED IN feathered headdresses and skirts, posed in erotic positions and framing the dial of the clock, come out of a long history of European fascination with foreign lands and peoples. The recording of such knowledge was in the beginning often incomplete and sometimes quite inaccurate. One of the most influential sixteenth-century publications with text and illustrations of the newly discovered Americas was based on information provided by a German sailor, Hans Staden (ca. 1525–ca. 1576), who was captured in 1557 by the Tupinamba people of Brazil.[1] At about the time of Staden's capture, two Frenchmen participated in the short-lived French colony near present-day Rio de Janeiro. They returned to France and, like Staden, reported their experiences in the New World.[2] The Englishman John White recorded what he saw of the Algonquians of the North Carolina coast and Roanoke Island during his voyages to America in the 1580s; his watercolors were the basis of engravings published by Theodore de Bry (1528–1598) in Frankfurt am Main beginning in 1590.[3]

Knowledge, however fragmentary, of the natives of America was already current even before the middle of the sixteenth century. One of the wooden panels from a choir screen carved about 1510 for the chapel of the Château de Gaillon in Normandy,[4] for example, incorporates two male figures wearing feathered skirts and headdresses. Further evidence that this information was current well before mid-century lies in the existence of German graphic illustrations, such as an engraving that pictures the Tupinambas wearing feathered skirts and headdresses as early as 1505 (fig. 56).[5] Similar to the figures on the Metropolitan's Gaillon panel, the men are bearded and carry bows and a spear. Women and children also appear in the woodcut, and one of them has begun feasting on an arm from the mangled body of a European sailor roasting over an open fire. In the distance, two ships, one with Portuguese emblems on its sails, suggest the means of the unfortunate's arrival on the coast of Brazil. In 1550, as part of the pageantry celebrating the entry of King Henri II (1519–1559) of France into Rouen, a tableau composed of Brazilian flora, fauna, and living "naked savages" was reportedly created on the banks of the river Seine.[6]

Before the beginning of the seventeenth century another line of representations portrayed native American Indians as personifications of America, one of the Four Continents—Africa, Asia, and Europe being the others (Australia was as yet undiscovered by Europeans). America was presented in the graphic arts as an Indian princess, sometimes wearing bejeweled anklets and feathered skirts, and sometimes—as, for example, in an engraving of about 1595 by Adriaen Collaert (ca. 1560–1618)—armed with bow and arrows and a long-handled ax and wearing

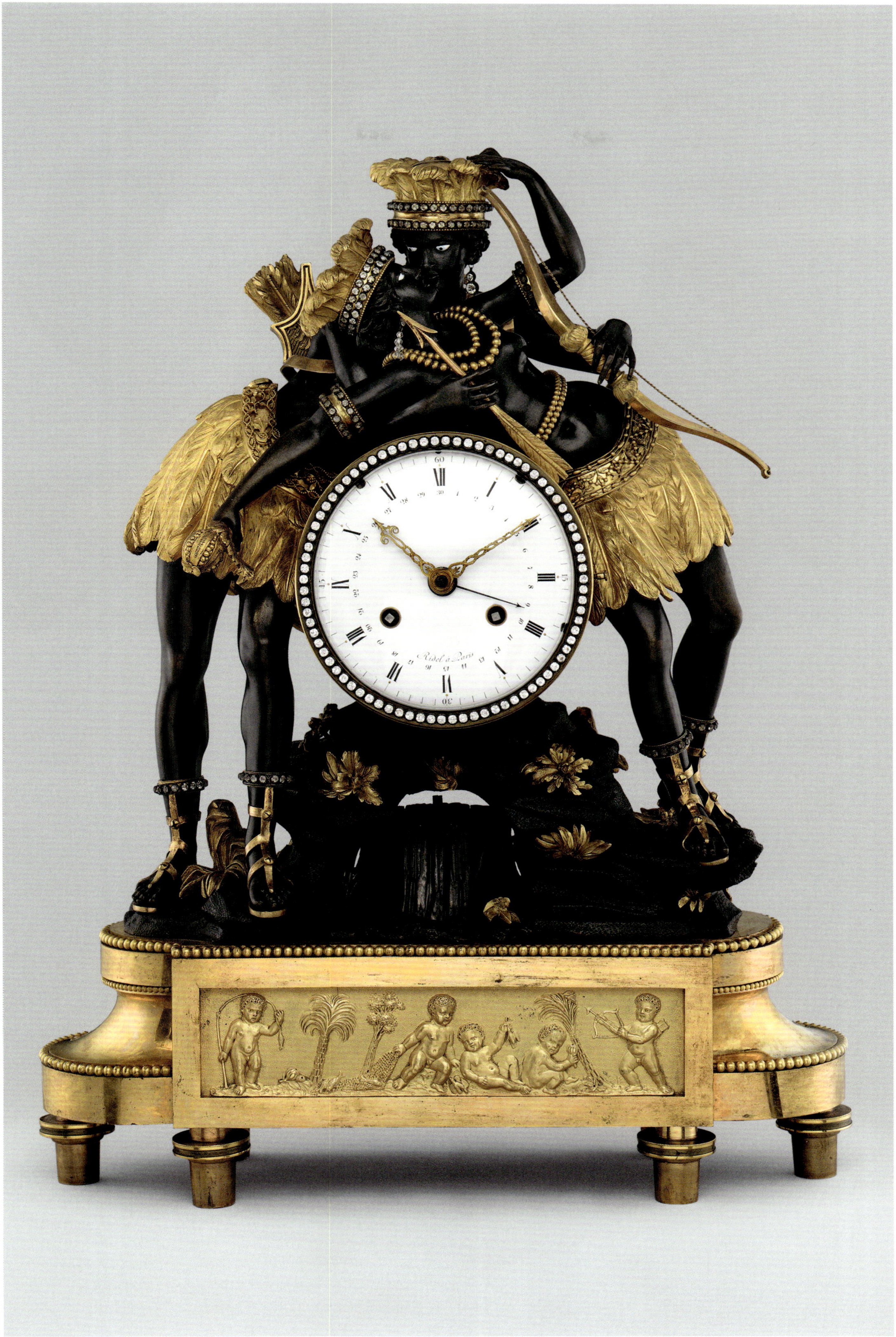

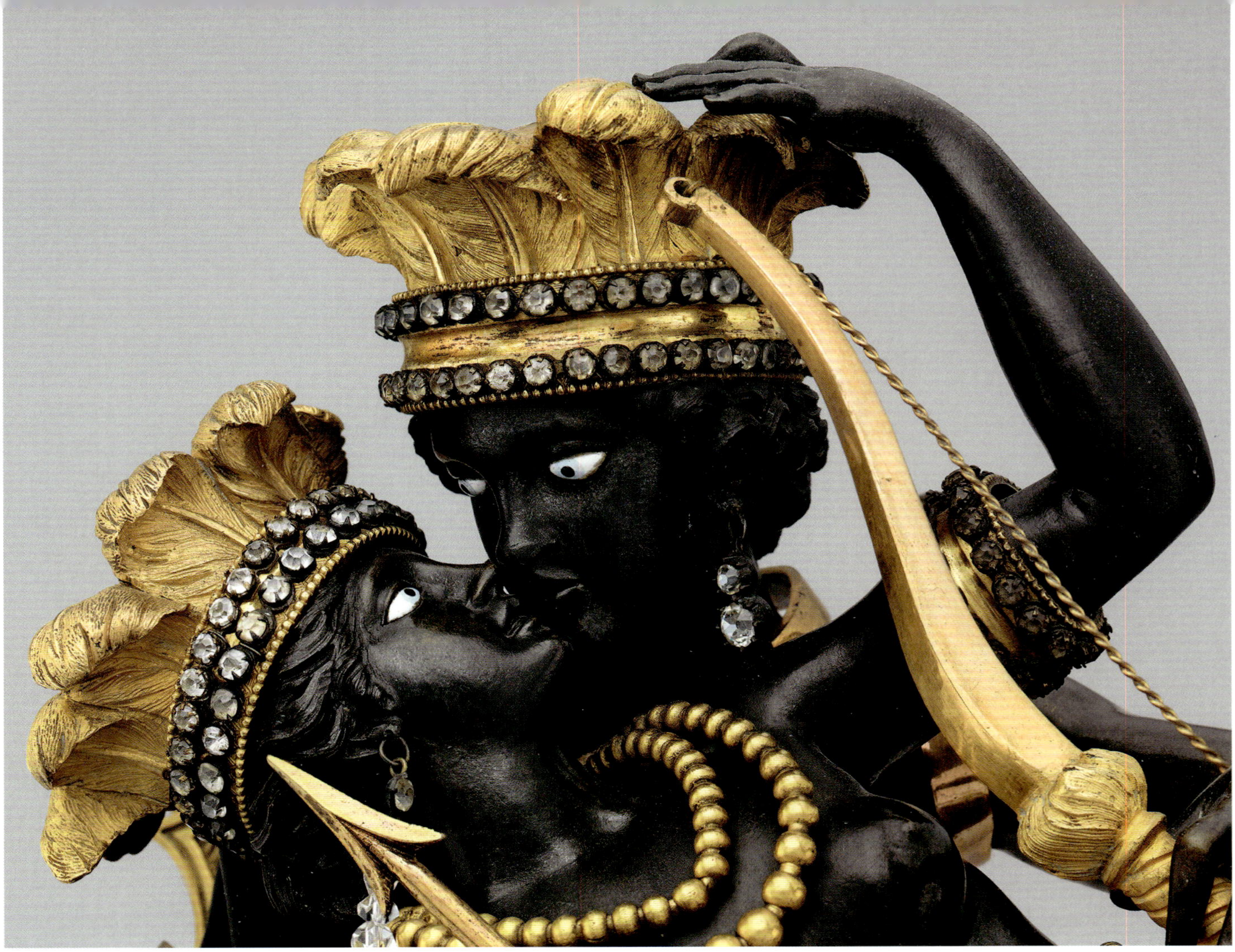

only a feathered headdress and a loincloth.[7] In a pen and wash drawing of about 1587–89 by Jan van der Straet (1523–1605), she wears little but a crown and a leg ornament, her scanty woven wrapper having fallen away from her body (fig. 55).[8]

Eventually these two traditions coalesced, producing a dark-skinned figure personifying America, with facial features that often appear more sub-Sahara African than American Indian. These portrayals can be found, for example, in eighteenth-century European porcelain, including one in the Metropolitan Museum from the collection of James Hazen Hyde, the donor of the Museum's mantel clock. A product of the Frankenthal Porcelain Manufactory and made from a model by Franz Konrad Linck (1730–1793), the black-skinned, beardless figure wears a feathered skirt, headdress, and armlets, and he carries a quiver full of arrows on his back (fig. 54).[9] It is doubtful that either Linck or the maker of the case of the Museum's clock, Jules-Simon Deverberie (active 1788–1820; died ca. 1824), were aware of the lugubrious origin of their figures: a tribe of South American cannibals.

Deverberie is known to have been the owner of a foundry and metalwork manufactory during the last years of the eighteenth century, after the events of the French Revolution had destroyed the ancient Paris guilds that formerly presided over the strict separation of Parisian crafts. Bronze founders, chasers, gilders, and metalworkers of all kinds, many of them trained in their skills during the ancien régime, could now work together in one establishment where models were provided, various components assembled, and the resulting products sold without interference by the authorities.[10] Curator Charlotte Vignon has given a fascinating account of Deverberie's firm and of the milieu in which the company operated.[11] She has illustrated a series of thirty-one etchings of designs for clocks that are now in a volume in the library of the Institut National d'Histoire de l'Art, Paris,[12] which constitutes a catalogue of the clocks that were for sale in about 1800, not only throughout France but also in foreign markets. Number 24 illustrates the prototype for the Metropolitan Museum's clock, identified by Vignon as a "Native American couple embracing."[13] (Among the other clocks described were a "Clock with allegory of America" and a "Clock with allegory of Africa,"[14] each with a single, seated female figure.)

Noted also is the existence of a group of drawings now in the Bibliothèque Nationale de France, Cabinet des Estampes, one of which depicts the same clock in pen and wash and is signed: "N° 3 DeVerberie Du trois pluviose an Sept,"[15] "an Sept" corresponding to the period between September 22, 1798, and September 22, 1799, in the Revolutionary French calendar. Although it is uncertain whether Deverberie was the draftsman, the signature confirms the identity of the author of the model and the date. The drawing was displayed at the Musée de l'Hôtel Sandelin, Saint-Omer, in a 1978 loan exhibition of clocks with African figures on their cases but titled *Indien et Indienne enlacés* ("Indian man and Indian woman embracing"). It accompanied an example of a clock from a private collection[16] by then recognized as depicting native Americans, not native Africans. The clock's dial is signed "Deverberie à Paris / Rue Barbete N° 483," presumably indicating that both the movement and the case are the work of Deverberie. Where he might have learned his clockmaking skills is unknown, and there is little firm evidence about the origin of his foundry training. Perhaps he was able to enlist the skills of others, for the period about 1800 was one of increasing prosperity in France but of great and unsettling changes in the traditional crafts.

The clock in the loan exhibition is one of a number derived from the same model as the Metropolitan Museum's clock. A comparison is instructive insofar as the human figures and the base of the clock, with its gilded relief of infants hunting and fishing in a tropical landscape, are almost identical. There are differences, however, the most immediately striking of which is the circle of paste jewels that surrounds the dial of the Museum's clock but is not present on the clock in the loan exhibition. Details such as the clumps of greenery on the rocky hillock under the feet of the figures are neither the same nor arranged in the same way. The female on the Museum's clock wears sandals that are not present on the other clock; the sandals, armlets, and headdresses on the Museum's clock are all enriched with circlets of paste jewels; and both male and female figures sport long earrings.[17]

fig. 55 *Jan van der Straet, called Stradanus (Netherlandish, 1523–1605).* Discovery of America: Vespucci Landing in America, *Netherlandish, ca. 1587–89. Pen and brown ink and brown wash, heightened with white, over black chalk, incised, 7½ × 10⁹⁄₁₆ in. (19.1 × 26.9 cm). The Metropolitan Museum of Art, New York, Gift of the Estate of James Hazen Hyde, 1959 (1974.205)*

fig. 56 *After an engraving by Johann Froschauer (German). "The First Representation of the People of the New World," from Amerigo Vespucci,* Von der neüw gefunden Region; Die wol ain welt genent mag werden; Durch den Cristenlichen; Künig von portugal; Wunderbarlich erfunden, *second edition of Mundus Novus (Augsburg: Johann Schönsperger, 1505). New York Public Library, Rare Book Collection*

Taken together, the clocks demonstrate that although the models were cast in quantity, parts could be modified or added to suit the taste of the customer. The same apparently held true of the movements: the clock in the loan exhibition that is signed with the name of the firm does not have a calendar, whereas the Museum's clock does. The signature, however, does lend credence to the supposition that Deverberie was indeed a clockmaker, or at least must have had some training in the craft. The volume of demand had already led to the custom in pre-Revolutionary France of filling cases made from one model with movements by several different clockmakers. Vignon lists a number of Paris clockmakers to whom Deverberie owed money by the beginning of the new century in addition to more than twenty clockmakers whose names appear on the dials of clocks with cases made by Deverberie. Some, like Jean-Antoine Lépine (1720–1814) and Pierre-Henry Lepaute (1745–1806), are well known, but Laurent Ridel (active 1789) is more elusive. The earliest record of a clock by him is that of a cartel made for the sisters of King Louis XVI (1754–1793) before 1789. Historian Jean-Dominique Augarde has added that he found evidence that Ridel supplied movements to a number of casemakers, including Deverberie.[18]

Ridel's spring-driven movement for the Museum's clock consists of two circular brass plates held apart by four cylindrical pillars. It has a going train consisting of three wheels, which end in an anchor escapement that is regulated by a short pendulum with silk thread suspension. A series of holes in the arbor that secures one end of the thread permits anchoring the other end of the thread at various positions, thus changing the length of the pendulum. The striking train consists of four wheels and a fly, which are regulated by a count wheel mounted on the back plate and marked 1–12; a hammer strikes hours on a single bell. There is little in the way of complication besides an unexceptional calendar, but it is a well-made, serviceable movement.

The dial is of white enamel with an hour chapter (I–XII), each hour with a gold dot at the exact moment of the hour; minutes enumerated (15, 30, 45, and 60) and marked by a stroke for each minute; and days of the month (1–30). The signature, "Ridel à Paris," appears above the six o'clock position. The dial is fitted with a glass lens encircled by a bezel that supports the ring of paste gems. The back of the movement can be seen through a glass cover set in a hinged bezel of gilded bronze, which provides a view of the hammer and the bell attached to the back plate. The back of the base consists of a rectangle that is framed in gilded bronze, and in the center appears a lozenge in the same medium applied to the patinated bronze ground.

The lens covering the dial was replaced in 1960, and a missing paste jewel on the bezel of the dial was replaced in 2007. Several of the paste jewels from various garments are missing, as is a section of the man's openwork waistband. The separately cast arms, plants, quiver, and border are now loose, but perhaps they always were.

James Hazen Hyde, a well-known collector of images personifying the Four Continents,[19] bequeathed the clock, and some 150 such objects in various media, to the Metropolitan Museum in 1959. The Cooper Union Museum for the Arts of Decoration (now the Cooper Hewitt, Smithsonian Design Museum), New York, however, received even more of his collection. CV

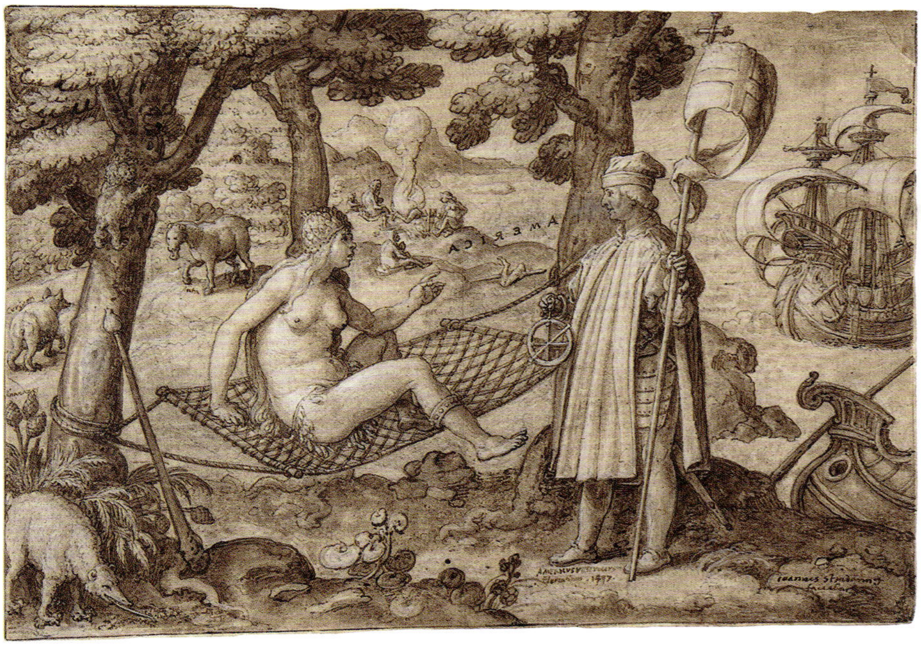

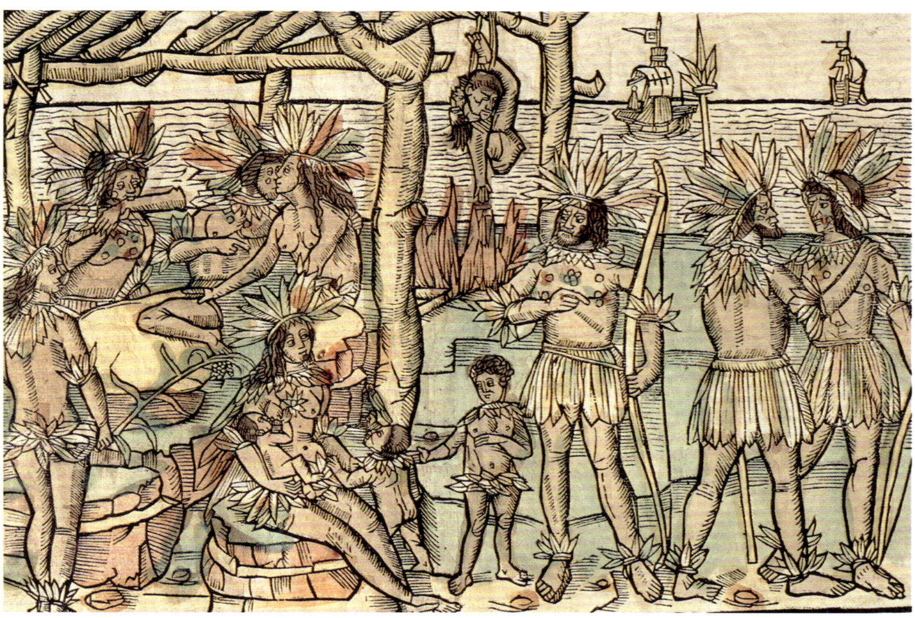

1 See entry 37 in this volume. For more about Staden, see Jantz 1976, p. 95; Sturtevant 1976, p. 433, and p. 434, fig. 21, and p. 435, fig. 22.

2 These publications were André Thevet's *Les Singularitez de la France antarctique, autrement nommée Amerique* (Paris, 1557) and Jean de Léry's *Histoire d'un voyage fait en la terre du Bresil, autrement dite Amerique* (La Rochelle, 1578).

3 Seventy-five of White's watercolors were included in Sloan 2007. For a more extensive investigation of the representation and sources for De Bry's *India Occidentalis*, see Van Groesen 2008, especially pp. 175–217, 390–94.

4 Acc. no. 16.32.301.

5 A surviving example is now in the Bayerische Staatsbibliothek, Munich. See Sturtevant 1976, p. 420, and p. 422, fig. 2.

6 Stanley Appelbaum in *Triumph of Maximilian I* 1964, p. 19, n. 71.

7 Fleming 1965, p. 67, fig. 1.

8 Le Corbeiller 1961, p. 211, fig. 1.

9 Acc. no. 59.208.14.

10 See entry 36 in this volume for Charles II Cressent's difficulties with the guilds and entry 38 for the role of the *marchands-merciers* in the creation of luxury goods combining various media.

11 Vignon 2003.

12 Inv. no. 4e, Rés. 121; the volume was formerly in the Bibliothèque Doucet in Paris.

13 Vignon 2003, p. 173, fig. 1.24.

14 Ibid., p. 172, figs. 1.14, 1.15.

15 For an illustration of the drawing, see *Pendule au "nègre"* 1978, p. 26; Ottomeyer and Pröschel 1986, vol. 1, p. 381, no. 5.15.29.

16 *Pendule au "nègre"* 1978, pp. 26–27, no. 15.

17 Other examples of the model, each with individual differences, are illustrated in Tardy 1981b, p. 245, in which the author noted its similarity to another model said to depict Cupid and Psyche; Kjellberg 1997, pp. 356–57, figs. B, C; Niehüser 1999, pp. 154–55, fig. 252.

18 Augarde 1996, p. 390.

19 For an extended account of Hyde and his collecting activities, see Arizzoli 2013.

49. Longcase Clock

BRITISH (BOSTON), CA. 1807

8 ft. 5 in. × 18 in. × 9⅛ in. (256.5 × 45.7 × 23.2 cm)
Bequest of Cecile L. Mayer, 1962
62.171.17

CASE: rosewood, coniferous wood veneered with mahogany and inlaid with bands of holly, stained holly and bone, and brass, signed (on interior of trunk): *Jas Fielding / Clock Maker / 1807 / Boston / Lincolnshire* [possibly James Fielding, British, active 1804–after 1820]
DIAL: painted enamel on copper with brass hour hands, signed: *Dickinson / Boston* [Thomas Dickinson, British, active 1790–1827]
MOVEMENT: brass and steel

BOTH FORM AND ORNAMENT COMBINE TO MAKE THIS CLOCK AN unusually elegant example of an English country clock, as well as an exceptionally good timekeeper. The tall, narrow case has a high rectangular plinth with a Hepplewhite-style apron and two carved front feet but no back feet. The trunk is flanked by applied quarter-round columns that are mounted with brass bases and capitals. Its door is arched at the top and ornamented with inlays of light-colored wooden strips forming a large oval, and the keyhole escutcheon is a lozenge-shaped inlay of bone. The hood has a pagoda top with three brass finials, the center finial on a wooden plinth with ornamental fretwork attached to the sides. In the center of the top appears a patera-like aperture with openwork ornament. The elliptical wooden-framed glass door for the dial is flanked by freestanding mahogany colonettes with brass bases and capitals. Like the quarter-round columns, the colonettes are inlaid with strips of light-colored wood in imitation of fluting, and all of the architectural elements of the case are accented by comparable inlays. A printed paper label for the equation of time, titled "MOORE 1826," with a notice of its intended use for the regulation of clocks and watches in 1823, is attached to the inside of the door to the trunk,[1] and the back board of the trunk has four holes intended for securing the clock to a wall.

The dial of the clock is laid out within a larger ellipse, not with a chapter ring of hours, but with a ring of minutes (labeled 5–60, by fives). A subsidiary ring painted with Arabic numerals 1–12 below the arbor for the minute hand records the hours, and a third ring above the arbor is painted with Arabic numerals 15–60, for fifteen-second intervals, but also marked for each second. All of the hands are made of sheet brass, the minute hand being the most prominent, and the hole for the single winding square is bordered with brass.

The movement consists of two trapezoidal plates formed from unusually thick brass and held apart by six pillars. The movement has a single train of three wheels and a Graham-type dead-beat escapement. The braided brass wire (a replacement) for suspending the single weight has a small hook at one end, and a wire loop is attached to the seat board, to which the end of the wire can be attached.[2] The original pendulum is lost, but the position of a long scar on the interior of the back of the trunk suggests that the clock might originally have been fitted with a simple, but rare, pendulum with a wooden shaft for temperature compensation. The clock beats seconds and runs for eight days on a single winding.

Although there are no clocks among the compilation of furniture designs made by George Hepplewhite's widow and published in three editions beginning in 1788, the design of the Dickinson clockcase owes

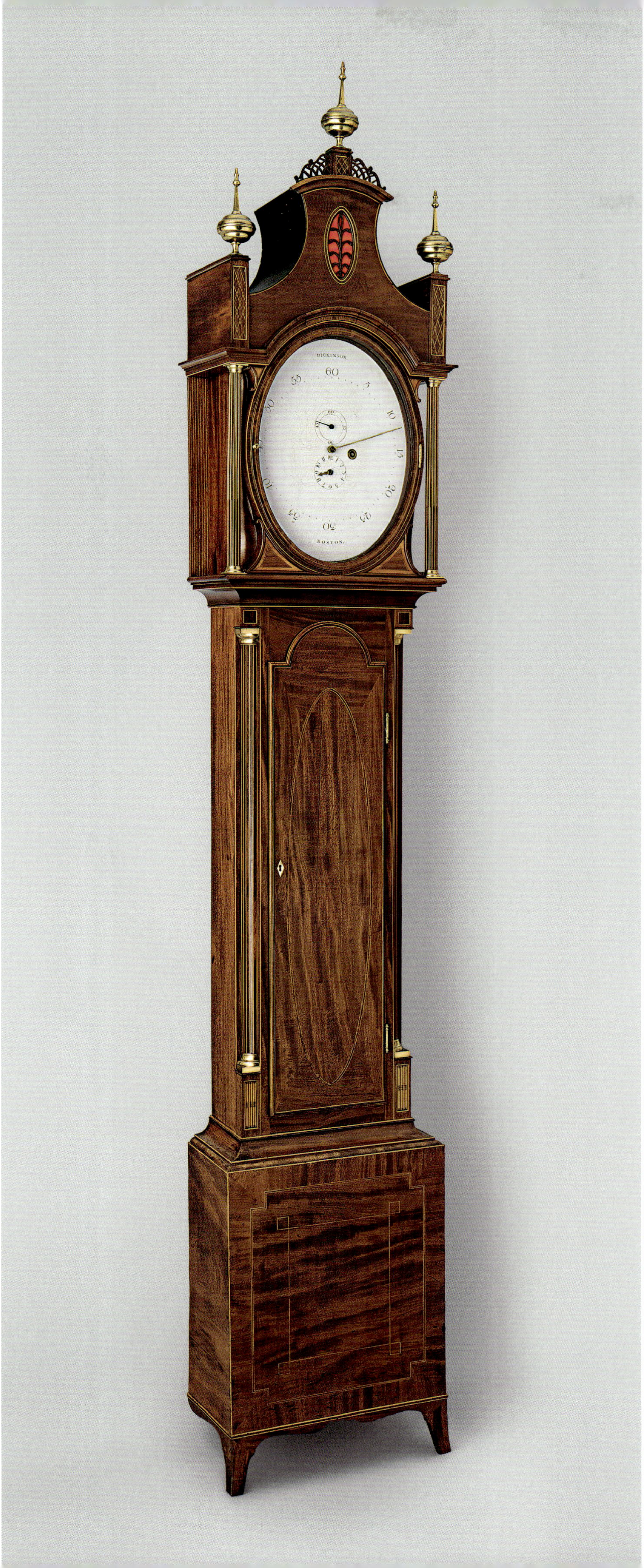
DICKINSON
BOSTON.

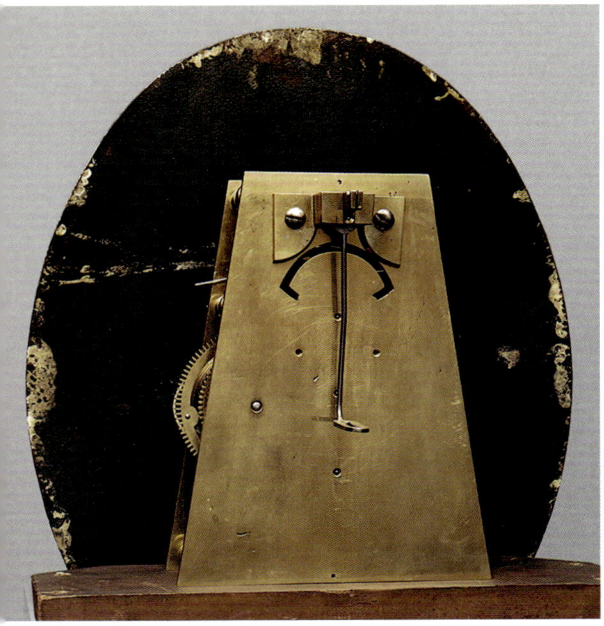

The back plate of the movement

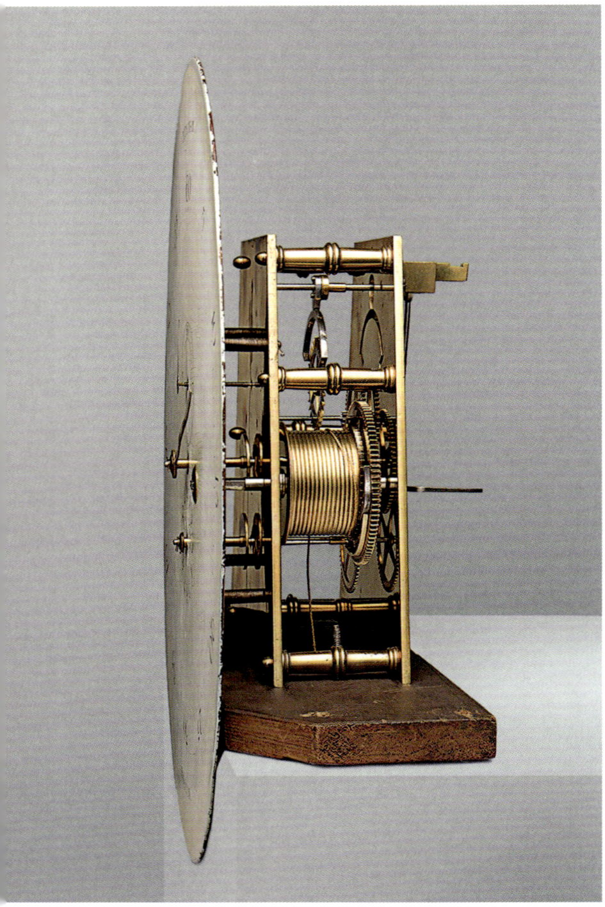

The movement from the right side, showing the dead-beat escapement

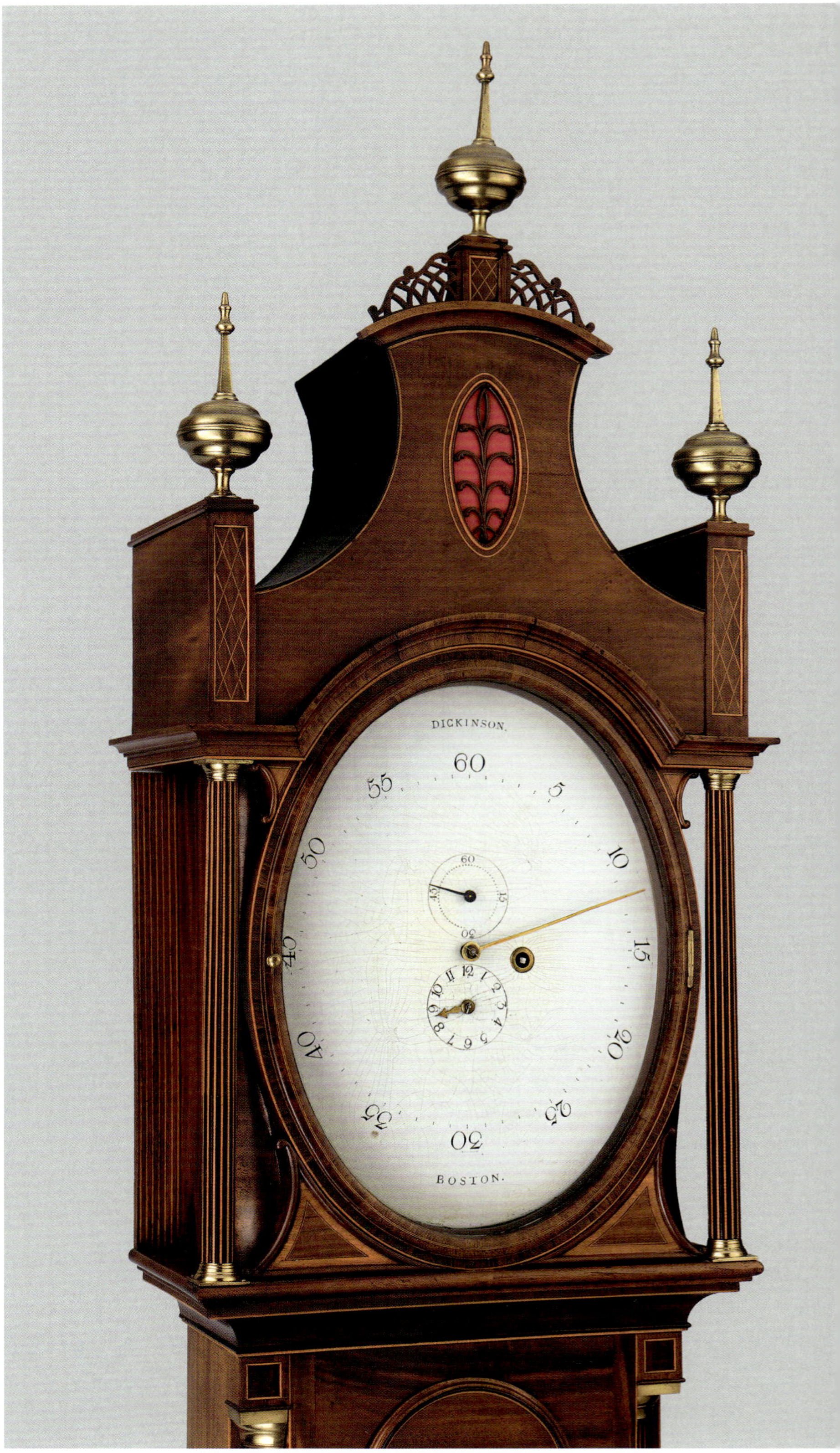

a great deal to some engravings included in Hepplewhite's *The Cabinet-Maker and Upholsterer's Guide*. Aside from the apron and feet of this clock, a preference for the ellipse clearly apparent in the design of the case surely derives from such case pieces as the wardrobe illustrated in plate 88 of the third edition (1794) of the *Guide*, although the ellipses may ultimately have descended from designs for elliptical furniture ornament and for pier glasses by the great English Neoclassicist Robert Adam (1728–1792).[3] More elaborately ornamented ellipses, such as those in the designs of tops for Pembroke tables, are to be found in plate 63 of the third edition of Hepplewhite's *Guide*, as well as prototypes for the vegetal ornament in the aperture of the hood of the Dickinson clock. Furthermore, the fashion for elliptical pier glasses in Adam's designs and in Hepplewhite's publications must have influenced the shape of the dial of the Dickinson clock, at least indirectly.

Painted elliptical dials, in themselves, do occur in late eighteenth-century English country clocks. Many of them are known to have been made in Birmingham or Liverpool and to have been adapted for use in clocks made in various parts of the country. But these dials ordinarily consisted of two distinct portions, the bottom containing a true circular chapter of hours and the top ornamented with painted landscapes, arrangements of fruit and flowers, or lunar displays.[4] In contrast, the dial of the Dickinson clock has no ornament and allows especially easy reading of minutes and seconds. In fact, its deceptively simple layout owes more to the standard designs for regulators, the very accurate clocks made for the use of natural philosophers and astronomers. Such layouts are not usually found on ordinary longcase clocks, either London-made or provincial. They are quite rare and probably ought to be understood as having been specially made for precision clocks. Coupled with the fact that the Dickinson clock has a finely made movement with a loud-ticking dead-beat escapement and probably once had a temperature-compensated pendulum, it seems possible that it was intended for use by an amateur astronomer, especially since small, private observatories were very much in vogue in the later eighteenth and early nineteenth centuries following the construction in 1760 of King George III's private observatory at Kew.[5]

There is some evidence that the maker of the movement, Thomas Dickinson (active 1790–1827), was a member of the Clockmakers' Company in London about 1799.[6] The authors of a monograph on Lincolnshire clockmaking, A. S. H. Wilbourn and R. Ellis, have found no evidence, however, for his presence in Boston (Lincolnshire) before April 26, 1804, when he advertised in the *Lincoln, Rutland & Stamford Mercury* as the local purveyor of mathematical instruments manufactured by the London establishment of Joseph and James Cox.[7] His advertisements in the regional newspaper continued until May 25, 1827.

Dickinson was an active clockmaker, rather than simply a retailer, as indicated by a record of July 28, 1807, that bound James Fielding (active 1804–after 1820) as an apprentice clock- and watchmaker to him for the customary seven years.[8] The somewhat puzzling signature of "Jas Fielding Clock Maker" on the interior of the trunk of the Museum's clock is difficult to explain in light of the record of his apprenticeship to Dickinson in the same year. By November 10, 1809, however, Dickinson was advertising for a journeyman clock- and watchmaker, and again on May 24, 1810, for another.[9] He married in 1809, and records indicate that from 1804 until at least as late as 1820 his place of work was at the Market Place in Boston, but local directories were still listing him there until as late as 1829.[10]

Wilbourn and Ellis remark that by the early nineteenth century complete movements were not commonly made in Lincolnshire and that it is not known who actually made the movements in most Lincolnshire clocks of the period.[11] To judge from the evidence that Dickinson took an apprentice clockmaker and that he had at least one journeyman assistant, if not more, it is probable that he was, in fact, making the movements for his longcase clocks.

Cecile L. Mayer owned this clock until it was bequeathed to the Museum in 1962. CV / JHL

1 John Hamilton Moore (1734–1807), author of *The Practical Navigator and Seaman's New Daily Assistant* (London, 1772), gave practical instruction and sold maps, charts, and mathematical instruments on Little Tower Hill in London. After his death, Moore's sons and his son-in-law Robert Blachford (flourished 1804–40) carried on the business at the same address. See Taylor 1966, pp. 240–41, no. 512, and p. 357, no. 1086. Further history of the firm appears in Howse and Sanderson 1973, p. 127.

2 Wilbourn and Ellis 2001. The authors note (p. 160) that this arrangement is typical of South Lincolnshire and, thus, Boston clockmaking.

3 See, for example, an engraving of furniture for Kenwood House, dated 1774, illustrated in Ward-Jackson 1958, p. 59, no. 229. Adam's influence was undoubtedly responsible for the elliptical forms to be found in the engraved designs in Hepplewhite's *Guide*.

4 Loomes 1975, p. 25.

5 See Taylor 1966, p. 103, who noted the contributions to the catalogue of stars made by private individuals, stating that one James South (1785–1867) alone added 458 stars to the catalogue he had compiled with John F. W. Herschel (1792–1871), son of William Herschel (1738–1822), King George III's astronomer. For the king's interest in astronomy and timekeeping and his patronage of clockmakers, see Jagger 1983, pp. 90–119. See also Morton and Wess 1993, pp. 17–37.

6 See Britten 1982, p. 425.

7 Wilbourn and Ellis 2001, p. 36. Joseph Cox (active 1789–1822) was a maker of optical and mathematical instruments in London. He was apparently succeeded by James Cox (active 1822–55) at 5 Barbican in London. See Clifton 1995, pp. 68–69.

8 Moore 2003, p. 99.

9 Wilbourn and Ellis 2001, pp. 36–37.

10 Ibid., p. 37.

11 Ibid., p. 157.

50. Pocket Watch

BRITISH (LIVERPOOL), 1820–21

2 7/8 × 2 × 1 3/16 in. (7.3 × 5.1 × 3 cm)
Diam. of back plate: 1 5/8 in. (4.1 cm)
Anonymous Gift, in memory of
Henry L. Phillips, 1944
44.18

CASE: gold with assay marks: for Chester office, C [1820–21] and crowned *18* [eighteen-carat gold], and casemaker's mark (inside bottom of case and inside back cover): T·H over J·H [Thomas Helsby, or Hilsby, British, and John Helsby, British, 1796–died after 1891]
DIAL: gold with gold and steel hands
MOVEMENT: partly gilded brass, partly blued steel, and diamond, signed (on back plate): *Liverpool* / ROB^{T} ROSKELL [Robert Roskell, British, active 1790–1847] and numbered *29664*

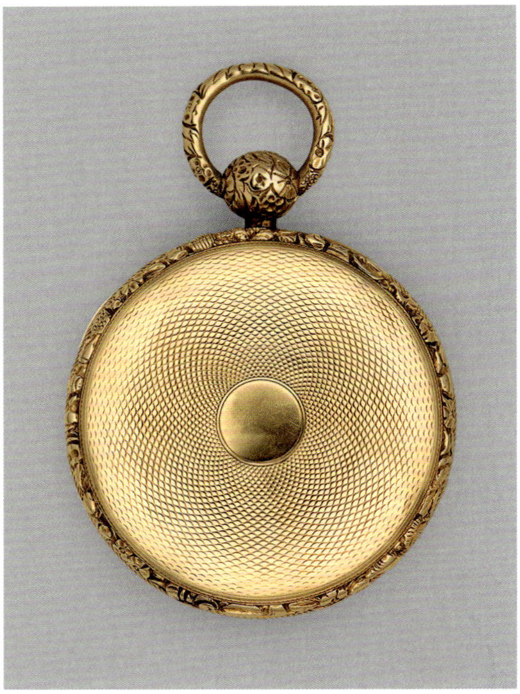

The back of the case

top: *View of the front cover open to display the dial*
bottom: *View with the case open to display the back plate*

THE RIVALRY IN THE EIGHTEENTH AND NINETEENTH CENTURIES between the watchmakers of the two major European watch-exporting nations, the British and the Swiss,[1] has been discussed at length by David S. Landes.[2] An economist with a deep interest in the history of watchmaking, Landes drew attention to the factors that he perceived as being responsible for nineteenth-century Swiss primacy despite major British and French contributions to technological improvements in both pocket watch and chronometer making.[3]

By the end of the eighteenth century, London makers of ordinary pocket watches had begun to lose ground to Swiss competition. The situation was made worse by the imposition of an annual tax by Parliament on watches and clocks in 1797.[4] The tax, promoted by King George III (1738–1820) and imposed by Prime Minister William Pitt the Younger (1759–1806), with the aim of financing Britain's military engagement in the Napoleonic Wars (1803–15), only succeeded in rewarding a flourishing trade in smuggling. In addition, the tax managed to drive British possession of watches underground.[5] In 1802, a memorial to the Clockmakers' Company's Court of Assistants could state that the repeal of the tax in 1798, as well as the duty on gold and silver cases, put the "trade on the best footing to increase Home and Foreign Consumption."[6] Concurrently, the increasing division of labor in the making of watches, together with a flood of émigré watchmakers (largely Swiss), had made many of the old rules of the Clockmakers' Company obsolete; such rules, "considered hostile to the present mode of manufacturing watches . . . would decrease sales thereof as well as produce endless litigation & bring distress to a great number of useful and industrious Workmen."[7]

An exception to this apparently distressed state of English watchmaking was to be found in early nineteenth-century Lancashire, where at least as far back as 1713 specialists had been making unfinished movements (blanks or *ébauches*) to be completed by London watchmakers. Watchmakers in Liverpool, the main city of Lancashire, adopted some of the newer practices of manufacturing,[8] and by about 1800, they were producing reliable watches in considerable quantity for a market that is believed to have consisted in no small part of merchants and manufacturers made remarkably prosperous by the flourishing industries in the British Midlands.

One of the most successful of Lancashire watchmakers was Robert Roskell (active 1790–1847). Relatively little is known about his early life; some accounts are contradictory, and it is apparently uncertain when he was born. His early watches contain both lever and rack-lever escapements,[9] and in 1832, he patented a repeating mechanism.[10] Historian John Culme has traced Roskell's partnerships in later life, first

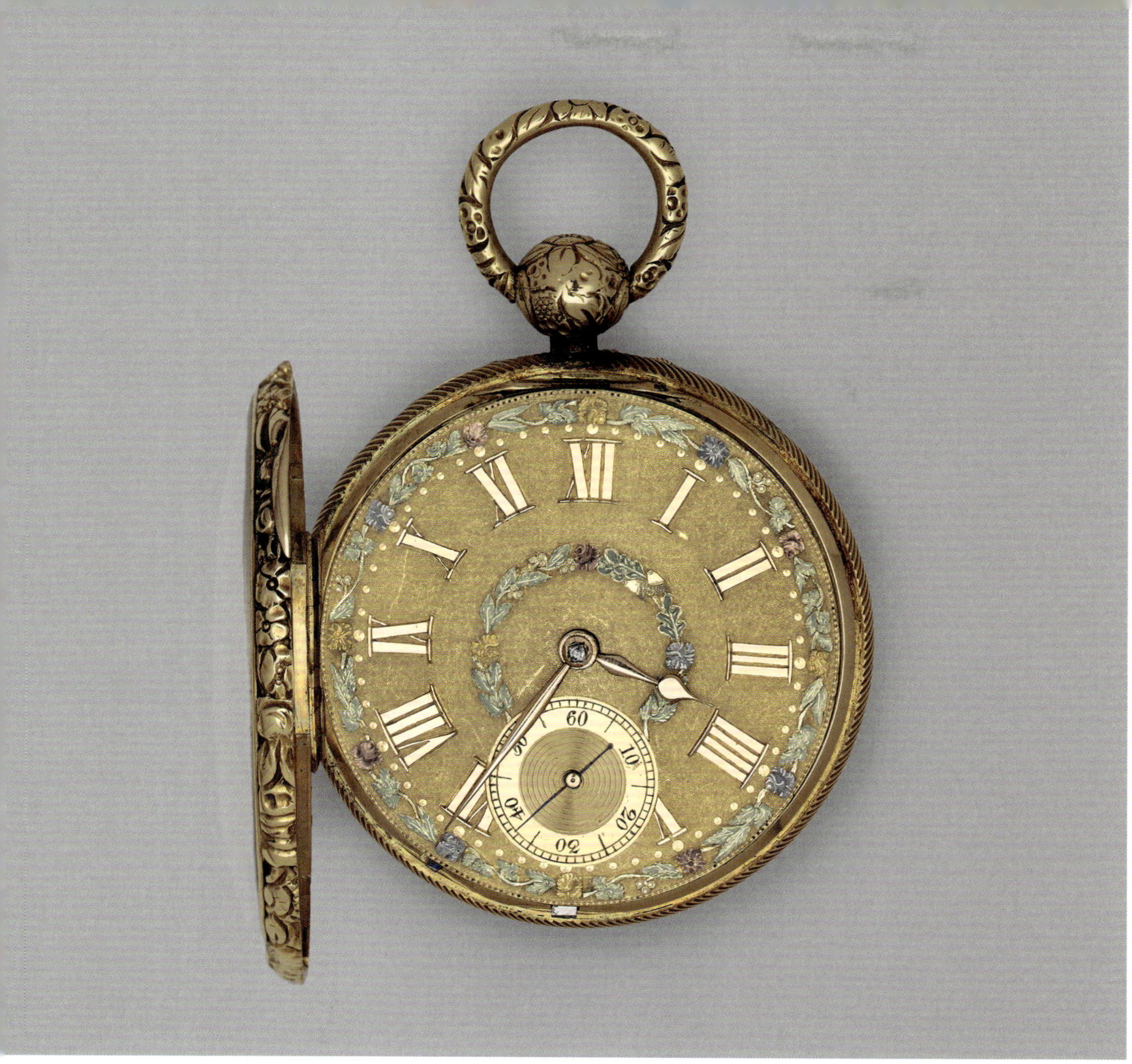

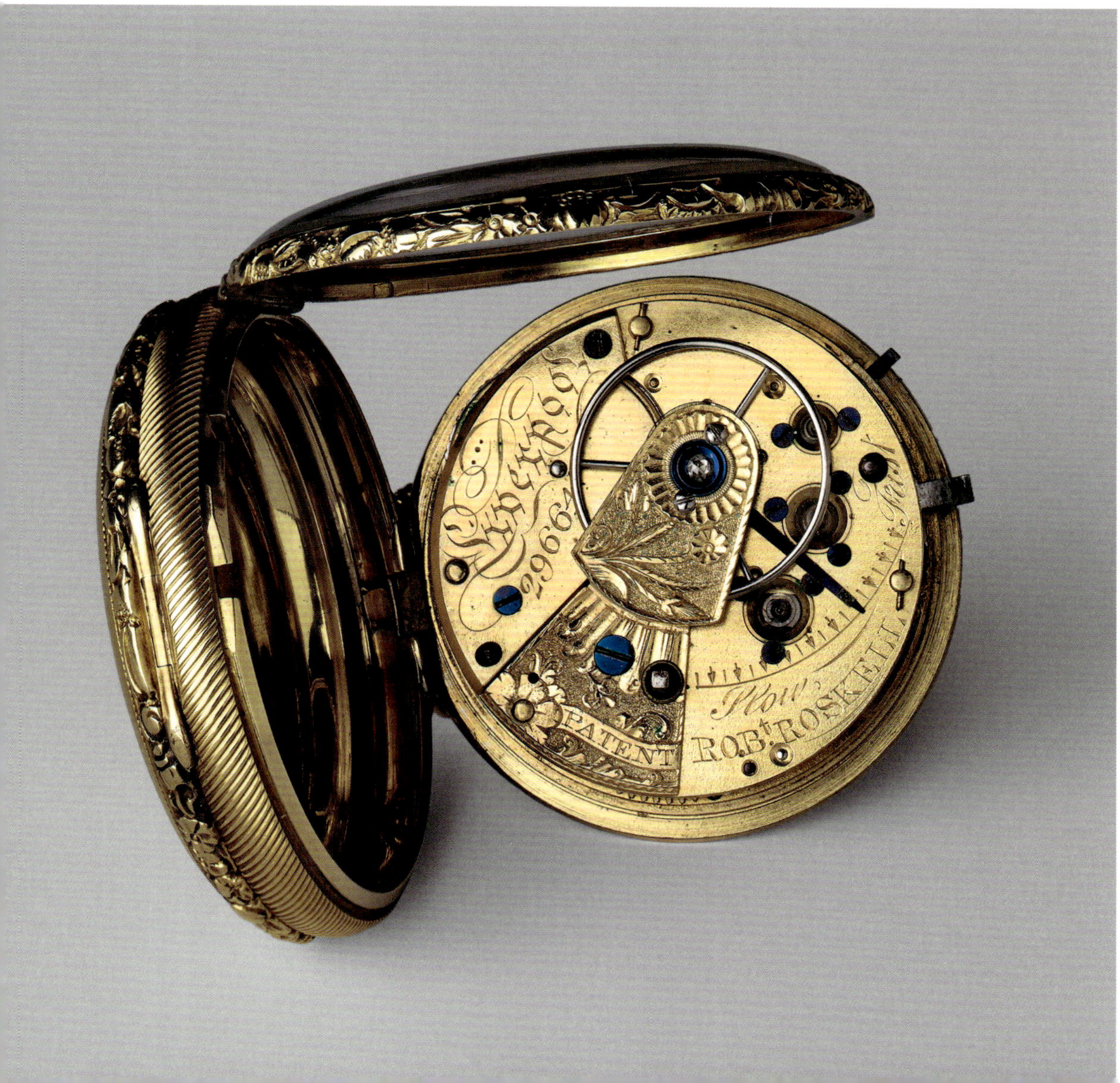
PATENT
ROB^t ROSKELL

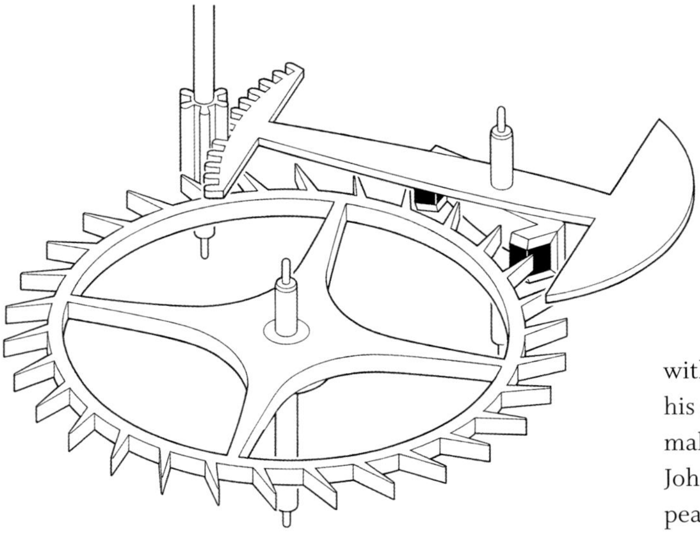

fig. 57 *An English lever escapement. Drawn by David Penney, British, 2014*

with Nicholas Roskell (partnership dissolved in 1832); afterward with his son Robert Roskell Jr. (died 1888) as Robert Roskell and Son, watchmakers and merchants, in Liverpool (dissolved in 1842); and with John Roskell Jr. (dissolved in 1847). After 1847, Robert Roskell Sr. disappears from Culme's record, but Roskell and Company continued in Liverpool as a partnership between William Roskell and Richard Roskell, manufacturers and sellers of chronometers and watches, until 1877. By 1897 the firm had become Robert Roskell and Company Ltd., claiming to have been established in 1790,[11] presumably by Robert Roskell Sr.

In 1843, Robert Roskell Jr., following the dissolution of the partnership with his father, joined John Samuel Hunt (died 1865), a nephew by marriage of the highly successful London goldsmith Paul Storr (1771–1844), as a partner in the London firm that became Hunt and Roskell, jewelers, goldsmiths, and silversmiths to Queen Victoria (1819–1901).[12] Surviving watches signed "Hunt & Roskell" indicate that the firm also dealt in watches.[13]

The foot of the balance cock to the Robert Roskell watch in the Museum's collection prominently displays the word "PATENT," evidently referring to the rack-lever escapement. It is widely agreed, however, that the origin of the rack lever should be credited to a French mechanician, the Abbé Jean de Hautefeuille (1647–1724), who was also chaplain of the church of Saint Aignan in Orléans, France. Hautefeuille published his idea in 1722, an invention that is not to be confused with the detached lever escapement that Thomas Mudge (1715–1794), a former apprentice of George Graham (1673–1751), invented sometime about 1750.[14] Other forms of watch escapements, including various types of levers, proliferated in the course of the century[15] in continuing attempts to create a wholly recoilless escapement and, thus, a watch that was a better timekeeper.

Lever escapements in England had a different history than the varieties made on the Continent, but Hautefeuille's rack lever was taken up not by French watchmakers but by Peter Litherland (1756–1804) in Liverpool, who obtained patents in 1791 and 1792 for two versions of the device.[16] His rack lever continued to be favored by Lancashire watchmakers, including Robert Roskell, until well into the nineteenth century. Roskell incorporated both rack levers and detached levers in watches that, like many others of the period, whether of Lancashire or London origin, are relatively substantial, retaining chain fusees and full-plate construction. These were in marked contrast to the fashionably thin watches with movements based on the inventions of Jean-Antoine Lépine (1720–1814) and Abraham-Louis Breguet (1747–1823),[17] which were being produced by French and Swiss watchmakers at this time.

The Museum's watch is open-faced, the front cover consisting of glass within a circular gold bezel that is hinged to the band of the watch at the nine o'clock position. The dial and movement together are hinged to the band at the twelve o'clock position and can be released by a spring at the six o'clock position. The back cover swings open at the twelve o'clock position to reveal a domelike piece, really the bottom of the case, through which the watch is wound. The exterior of the back cover is ornamented by a geometric pattern of engine-turned engraving,[18] the band is reeded, and the bezels, ball pendant, and ring are of cast and chased gold with an allover pattern of shell and floral ornament.

The dial provides the salient impression of the watch, however, with large roman numerals (I–V and VII–XII) of polished gold set against a fine matte gold ground and bordered by concentric circles of intricately fashioned vegetation in appropriate shades of white, blue, pink, and green made of gold alloys. The minutes are indicated by polished-gold dots that are located around the interior circumference of the hour chapter. The hands are made of gold: the hour hand with the so-called spade tip, and the minute hand with a finely proportioned baluster shape. A subsidiary dial for seconds in the six o'clock position (marked 10–60, by tens) has a polished gold chapter ring, an engine-turned center, and a needle-like steel hand. Altogether, the dial is easily read and creates a handsome effect, meriting its conspicuous display behind the glass cover.

The hallmarks on the case are those used for gold at the assay office in Chester during the years 1820–21. The incuse initials are those of the goldsmiths Thomas Helsby, or Hilsby,[19] and John Helsby (born 1796–died after 1891),[20] who are known to have worked in Liverpool until 1831 as "Watch-Case Manufacturers and Merchants," after which time Thomas, with various members of the family doing business in Liverpool, as well as Argentina and Peru, declared bankruptcy.[21] John Helsby is believed to have used an incuse mark with his initials alone after about 1823 until at least 1871.[22]

The movement of the Museum's watch consists of two gilded-brass plates, which are held apart by four cylindrical pillars. It contains a mainspring, a chain fusee, and a three-wheel train ending in a three-armed steel balance wheel that is regulated by the rack lever. The back plate supports a solid balance cock marked "PATENT" on its foot, and the cock has a bell-shaped table that incorporates a diamond endstone for the pivoting of the balance's arbor. The plate is engraved with a scale and has a hand for adjusting the balance spring. It is also engraved with the city name, Liverpool, the number 29664, and the watchmaker's name "ROB^T ROSKELL" that is repeated on the back of the case.[23] When in place, a protective dust cover for the movement that is fitted to the back plate permits a view of the bell-shaped table of the balance cock.

There are scratches in the areas of matte on the dial. The spring on the dust cover bears traces of rust. Otherwise, the watch is in excellent condition. CV

1 If, in the earlier years, we include the Genevan Republic as part of Switzerland.
2 Landes 1983, chaps. 14–18.
3 Ibid., pp. 300–301.
4 Britten 1922, pp. 594, 595.
5 Landes 1983, pp. 274–75.
6 Clockmakers' Company, London, Ms. 3951, no. 23, Guildhall Library, London. Among the rules felt to be obsolete was the requirement that the name engraved on a watch movement had to be the name of the actual maker.
7 Ibid. For more about the state of British watchmaking at this time, see Weiss 1982, pp. 232–45.
8 Ibid., p. 51.
9 The Metropolitan Museum also has one of his watches with a detached lever escapement numbered 2056 and datable from the hallmarks to 1802 (acc. no. 10.24). It is perhaps the earliest surviving Roskell watch. See Shenton 1995, p. 77.
10 T. C. Cuss 2009, p. 394.
11 Culme 1987, vol. 1, p. 393.
12 Ibid., p. 245.
13 See T. C. Cuss 2009, p. 412, pl. 264, for a pocket watch hallmarked for 1877–78. See also Thompson 2008, p. 118.
14 Much has been written about this complicated subject; see Thompson 2008, p. 98.
15 For further information about these, see T. P. C. Cuss 1967, pp. 78–92; Britten 1978, pp. 190–99, for lever escapements; Britten 1982, pp. 188–95. For a wider variety of watch escapements, see Clutton and Daniels 1979, pp. 67–80. See also Tardy n.d., with numerous helpful diagrams.
16 Mercer 1962; Clutton and Daniels 1979, p. 279.
17 See entry 51 in this volume. See also Clutton and Daniels 1979, pp. 59–66. For more about Lépine, see Chapiro 1988; about Breguet, see Daniels 1975.
18 For a brief discussion of the technique, as well as the lathes required for engine turning that were available in early nineteenth-century England, see Jagger 1988, pp. 86–87.
19 Ridgway and Priestley 2004, pp. 410–11, nos. 8271, 2, and 8273. See also Priestley 1994, pp. 51–52.
20 Ridgway and Priestley 2004, pp. 254–55.
21 *London Gazette*, Feb. 28, 1832, p. 454.
22 Ridgway and Priestley 2004, p. 255, no. 4819.
23 For an attempted correlation between known numbered Roskell watches and hallmarked dates on their cases, see D. M. W. Evans 1976.

51. Hunter-Case Pocket Watch

SWISS (GENEVA), CA. 1844
2 3/8 × 1 5/8 × 5/16 in. (6 × 4.1 × 0.8 cm)
Diam. of movement: 1 5/16 in. (3.3 cm)
Anonymous Gift, in memory of Lady May Fletcher-Moulton, 1926
26.267.49

CASE: gold
DIAL: white enamel with gold hands, signed: VACHERON&CONSTANTIN [Swiss (Geneva), founded 1755; partnership of Jacques Barthélémi Vacheron, Swiss, 1787–1864, and François Constantin, Swiss, 1788–1854]
MOVEMENT: brass and steel, signed (on third wheel bridge): VACHERON&CONSTANTIN

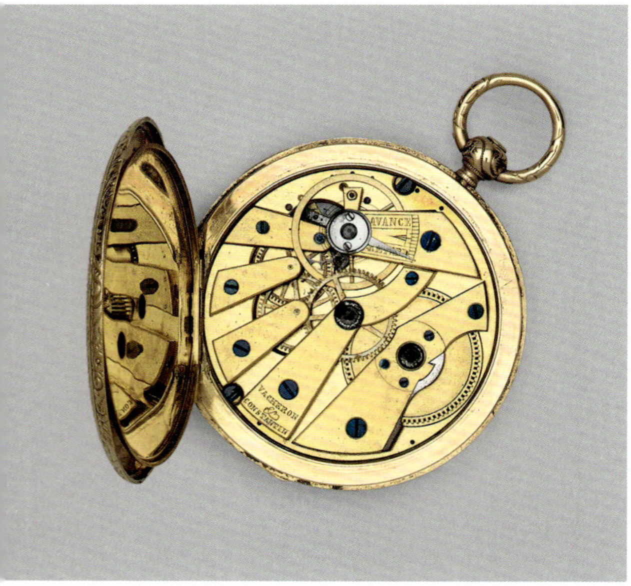

View with the back cover open to display the back plate

AN EXTENDED TRIP, COMMONLY KNOWN AS THE GRAND TOUR, WAS intended to acquaint wealthy young Englishmen and Europeans, many of them recent recipients of classical educations, with firsthand knowledge of the monuments of Greek and Roman antiquity, as well as the splendors of Italian Renaissance art and architecture.[1] The custom began in the late sixteenth century, and by the eighteenth and nineteenth centuries many notable English and Northern European collectors of paintings and classical antiquities had enriched their collections with purchases made in the course of a tour. One of the more ambitious purchases, a third-century Roman marble sarcophagus now in the Metropolitan Museum, was transported in 1728 from Rome by the English third Duke of Beaufort and installed in his country estate in Badminton, Gloucestershire (fig. 59).[2] Such sightseeing came to a halt in the unsettled times of the late eighteenth century when the French Revolutionary Wars (1792–1802) were followed by the Napoleonic Wars (1803–15). Travel became practical again after the defeat of Napoleon at Waterloo in 1815, when travelers flocked to Italy, especially Rome, and brought back mementos, though rarely on the scale of the Badminton sarcophagus.

Several watches in the Museum's collection belong to this period of travel, among them the gold pocket watch with a bird's-eye view of Saint Peter's Square in Rome on the cover. Another watch in the collection by the same makers depicts the Campidoglio, also in Rome,[3] providing evidence that the Saint Peter's watch was primarily intended not as a souvenir for a religious pilgrim (although certainly appropriate for that market) but for travelers making a Grand Tour. Still another watch displays the Roman Colosseum on its cover.[4] The demand for these watches coincided nicely with the rise of watchmaking firms in Switzerland that could supply merchants in Italy and France with handsome souvenirs, sporting scenes of the monument visited or the object viewed that could remind the traveler of the journey and impress his acquaintances. Many of these watches were, in fact, the products of improved manufacturing techniques that allowed the Swiss to make respectable timekeepers in quantity that could be bought at relatively reasonable prices.

One of the most successful Swiss firms and certainly the longest surviving is Vacheron (eventually Vacheron and Constantin), which was founded by Jean-Marc Vacheron (1731–1805), who opened a workshop in Geneva in 1755.[5] He was succeeded by his son Abraham Vacheron (1760–1845), who married Anne-Elisabeth Girod in 1786, forming a partnership with his father-in-law.[6] Their watches were signed "A. Vacheron Girod."[7] By 1816, Jean-Marc's grandson, Jacques Barthélémi Vacheron (1787–1864), was traveling to Italy and soon

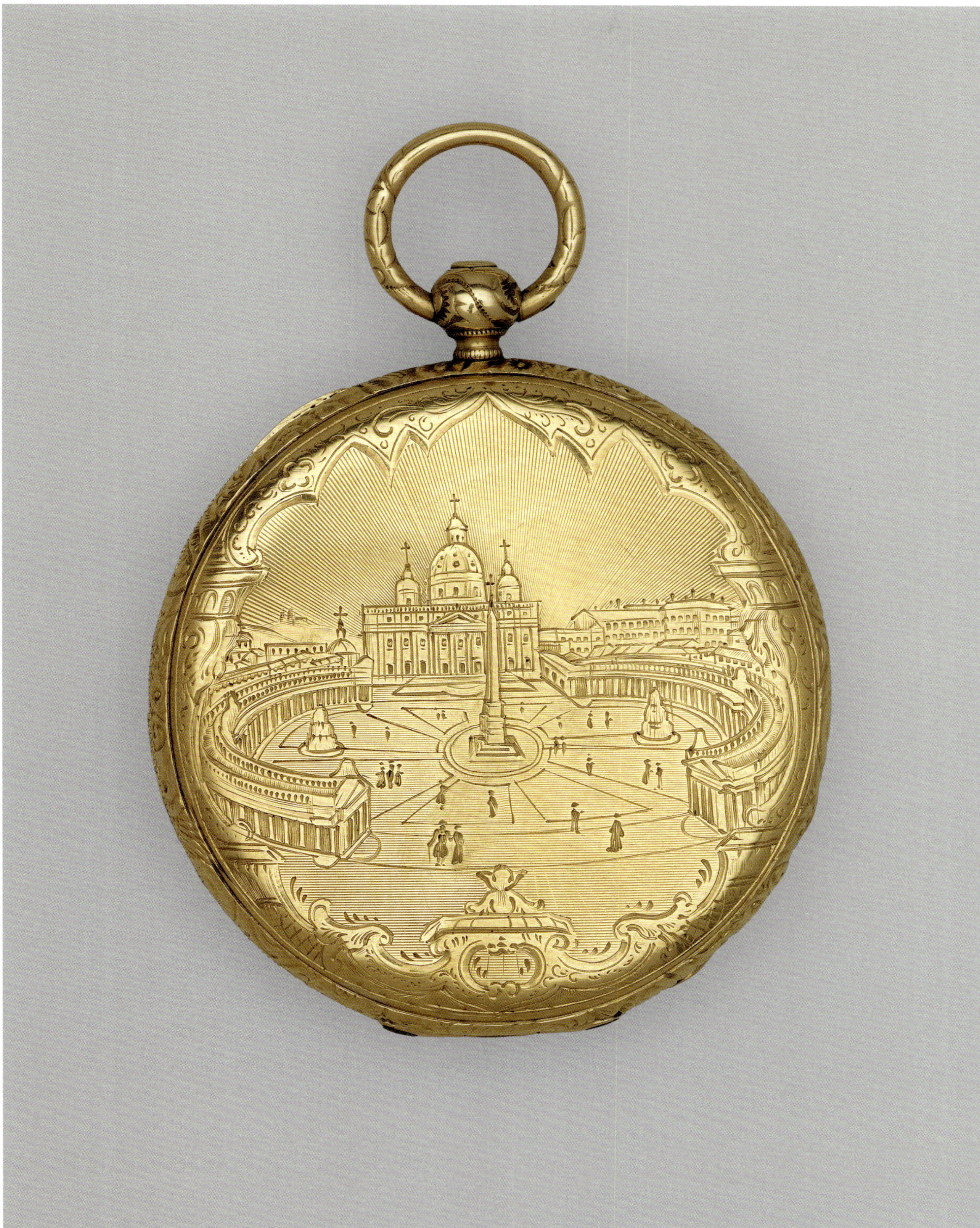

selling watches in Turin and Milan.[8] Shortly thereafter, in 1819, he entered into partnership with François Constantin (1788–1854) and the firm became known as Vacheron and Constantin. Records show that a carriage was bought for trips to France and Italy, [9] and as the representative abroad, Constantin began traveling with a large trunk full of the firm's products.[10]

In 1839, George-Auguste Leschot (1800–1884), the son of Jean-Frédéric Leschot (1746–1824), who was the automaton maker and partner of Henri-Louis Jaquet-Droz (1752–1791), was contracted by the Vacheron and Constantin firm to supply technical improvements to the manufacturing of their watches.[11] While specialists had long made blanks (*ébauches*), or plates, for individual watch movements, these and other watch parts often needed considerable adjustments and other hand-finishing when a watch was assembled. Other specialists made individual parts of the movement, while still others specialized in escapements. The components were assembled in one place, fitted together, polished, gilded, and cased under the supervision of a master watchmaker, who was often the marketer of the watch as well.

Much of this time-consuming work changed with the adoption of standardized sizes and layouts (calibers) of movements. Vacheron and Constantin, like many other watchmakers, adopted layouts of movements that were invented by the French clockmaker Jean-Antoine Lépine (1720–1814), who radically diminished the thickness of a watch in 1770 (or 1772). He did so by doing away with the fusee and relying on a going barrel alone for the regulation of the power produced by the mainspring as it uncoiled, and substituting a relatively flat, or horizontal, escapement (usually a cylinder or virgule) for the verge in some of his watches. In place of a back plate, Lépine's layout pivoted the wheels of the train on a series of separate cocks (bridges, or bars), each one screwed to the front plate of the watch.[12] These parts were produced in standardized sizes so that a watch could be assembled and finished in considerably less time than under the old, so-called putting-out system. The layout employed in the Museum's watch is similar to the one Lépine began using about 1795.[13]

Leschot became a full-time member of the Vacheron and Constantin firm in 1844.[14] Among his contributions were the application of a pantograph for precisely duplicating the plates of watches in standardized sizes based directly on a single technical drawing or template.[15] He also developed machinery for manufacturing uniform components for the chosen size (or caliber) of the watch, and he added improvements and promoted the adoption of the detached lever escapement, more durable and more easily made than the cylinder escapement in general use at the time. His watchmaking machinery enabled Vacheron and Constantin

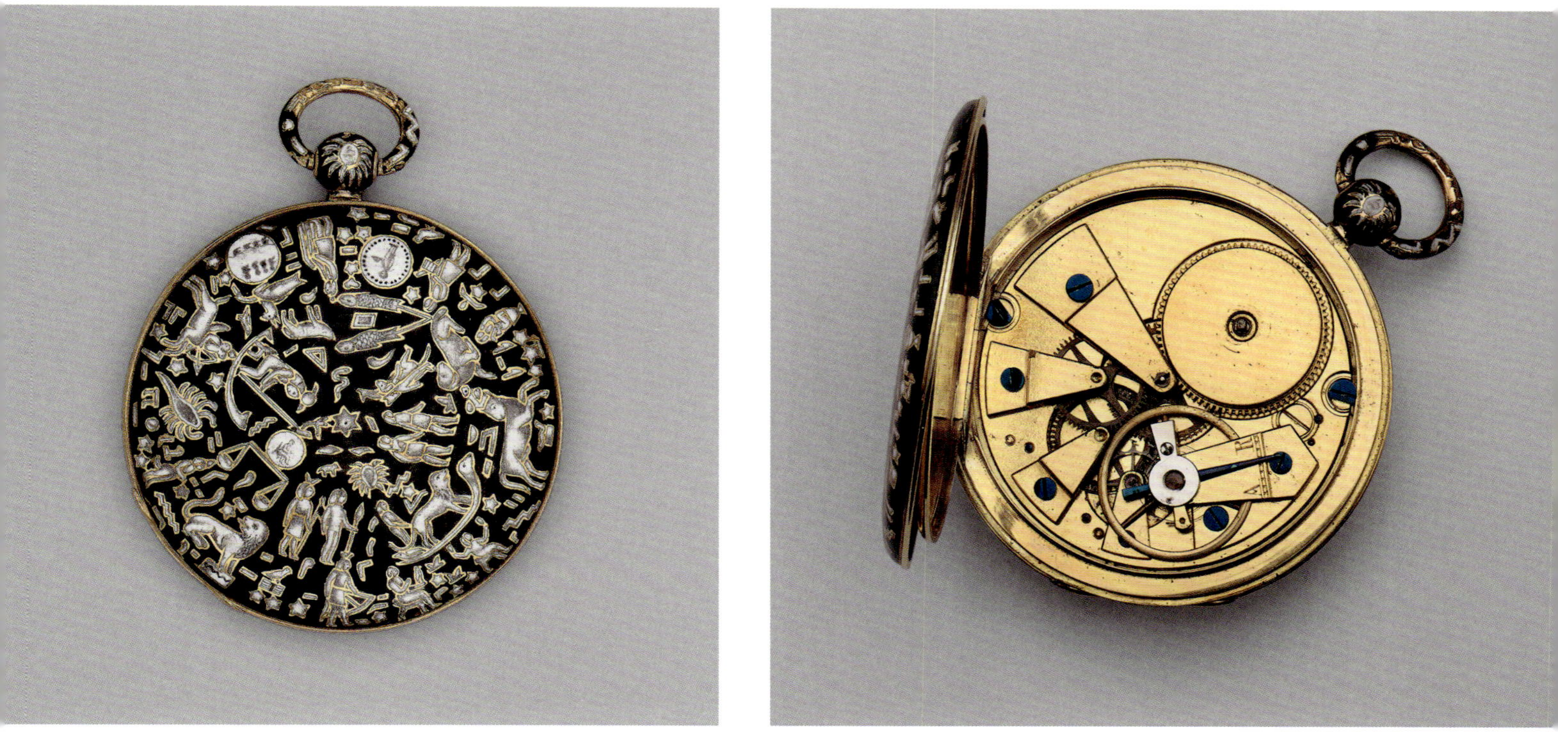

fig. 58 *Bautte and Moynier (Swiss [Geneva], 1826–31). the partnership of Jean-François Bautte (Swiss, 1772–1837) and Jean-Gabriel Moynier (1772–1840). Pocket watch, case (left): enameled gold; movement, Swiss (Geneva) 1823–31 (right): gilded brass and steel with ruby endstones, Diameter of case 1 11/16 in. (4.3 cm). The Metropolitan Museum of Art, New York, Anonymous Gift, in memory of Lady May Fletcher-Moulton, 1926 (26.267.14)*

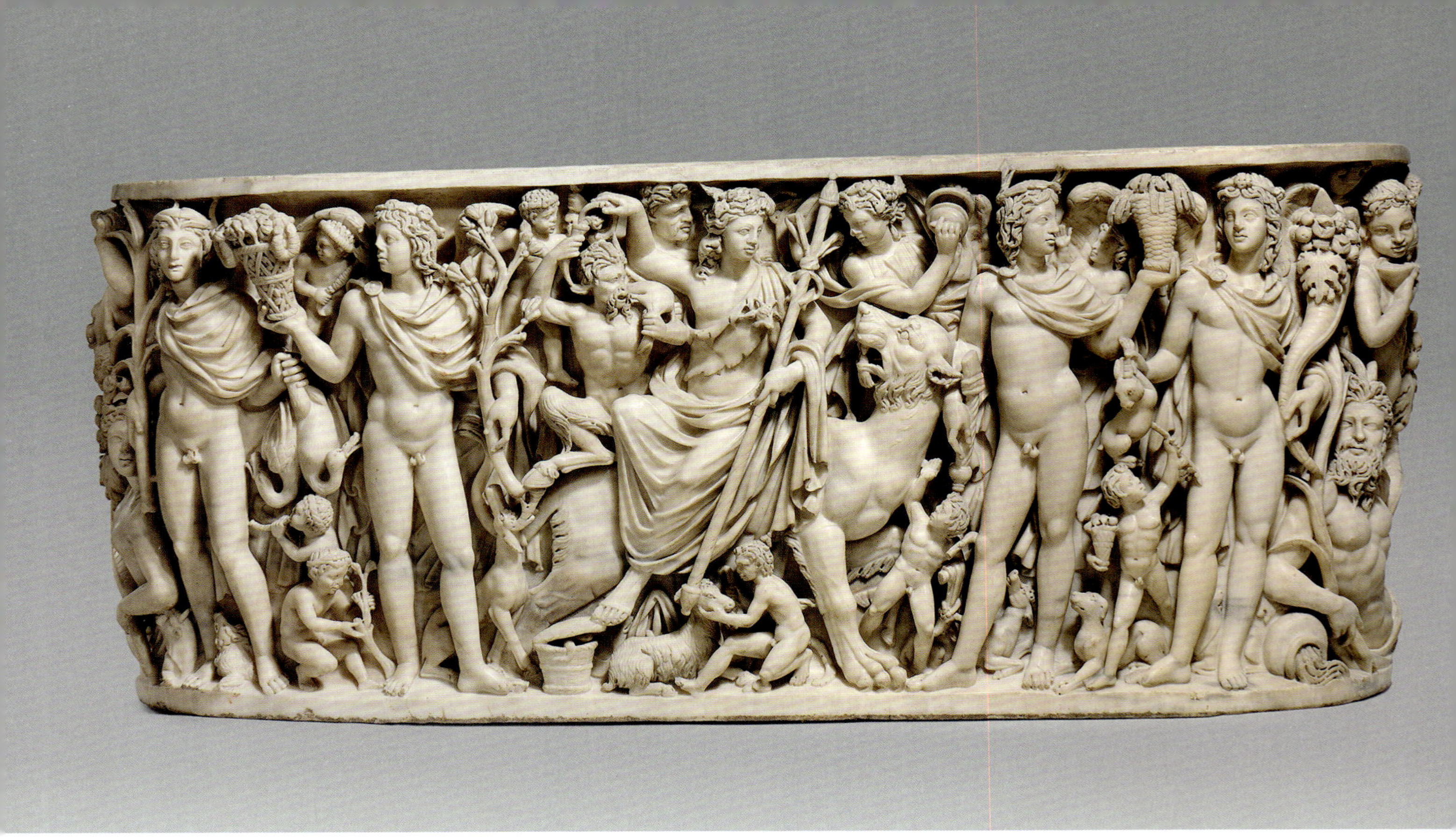

fig. 59 *Sarcophagus, Roman, Late Imperial, Gallienic period (ca.* A.D. *260–270). Marble, 34 × 85 × 36¼ in. (86.4 × 215.9 × 92.1 cm). The Metropolitan Museum of Art, New York, Purchase, Joseph Pulitzer Bequest, 1955 (55.11.5)*

to produce watches of standardized sizes that needed much less fitting than before. While the first use of truly interchangeable parts for watches and their incorporation into a factory system was probably by the American watchmakers Aaron L. Dennison (1812–1895) and Edward Howard (1812–1904) in the 1850s,[16] or perhaps by the itinerant Swiss watchmaker and mechanician Pierre Frédéric Ingold (1787–1878) in the 1840s,[17] the new speed and ease of production at Vacheron and Constantin in the 1840s enabled the firm to expand their output greatly. Swiss and American production eventually outstripped all others.[18]

The Museum's watch was finished, according to the firm's records, in 1844.[19] Housed in a thin Hunter-style case, the movement has a Lépine layout but retains a cylinder escapement instead of the more up-to-date lever escapement. The front cover of the case is engraved with a view of Saint Peter's Square, bordered at the top by a Gothic-inspired ornamental design, and at the bottom by one reminiscent of the baroque. It is hinged to the reeded band of the case at the nine o'clock position, and when opened it reveals a white enamel dial covered by glass held in place by a thin gold bezel. The dial is painted with black enameled roman numerals (I–XII) for the hours and individual strokes for the minutes. Remarkably slim gold hands of the Breguet type and the firm's name, "VACHERON ET CONSTANTIN," painted at the four o'clock position complete the simple but elegant design.

The back cover is hinged at the seven–eight o'clock position and is engraved with two winged, airy spirits holding up a large basket of flowers. A gold inner cover has an engine-turned pattern and the polished gold label of Vacheron and Constantin at the top. Another label of polished gold at the bottom is engraved "a Geneve" and, in between, a decorative cartouche has the words ECHAPPEMENT / HORIZONTAL (cylinder escapement); "Aguilles" (hands); "N. 44631" (serial number); and QUATRE TROUS / RUBIS (four ruby endstones). There are also two holes in the cover, one for setting the hands, as indicated, and one for winding the mainspring with a key. The cover, too, is hinged to the band of the case at the seven–eight o'clock position.

The ball-shaped pendant and the ring are suitably shaped and ornamented, and they are attached to the movement at the three o'clock position so that when the front cover is released, the watch can easily be held in one hand and read in a horizontal position, or Hunter-style.

The Lépine-type layout of the movement consists of a going barrel for the mainspring and a three-wheel train held in place by four brass bridges screwed to the single plate. The bridge for the balance is engraved with a scale marked "AVANCE / RETARD" accompanied by a hand for adjusting the hair spring; the bridge for the first wheel of the train (the center bridge) is marked "VACHERON & CONSTANTIN"; and the escapement is indeed a cylinder.

Interests similar to those that prompted visits to Italy also inspired sojourns in Paris, another of the traditional destinations of seekers of cultural enrichment and all but required of those on the Grand Tour. By the 1830s, the newly constructed galleries of the Cour Carrée additions to the old royal palace of the Louvre permitted the public to view sculptures and other antiquities from Greece and Rome, but also from Egypt. Egyptian antiquities had fostered a fashion in late eighteenth-century France of Egyptian motifs in decorative designs, a taste further encouraged by the French invasion of Egypt in 1798 and the ensuing survey of its antiquities, some of them ending in French possession. An Egyptian motif appears on another pocket watch (fig. 58) in the Museum's collection that belongs to the category of upscale mementos for travelers.[20] It was made by the Geneva firm of Bautte and Moynier, the partnership of Jean-François Bautte (1772–1837) and Jean-Gabriel Moynier (1772–1840) that existed from 1826 to 1831.[21] It seems that Bautte, with an earlier partner, Jacques-Dauphin Moulinié (or Moulinier; active 1793–1828), had specialized in luxury watches with enameled and gemstone-ornamented cases, and he was selling his watches in Paris as early as 1795.[22] The back of the case of the Museum's watch depicts a Ptolemaic (305–30 B.C.) sandstone bas-relief representing the constellations of the Egyptian zodiac, which was brought to France in 1821 from the Temple of Hathor in Dendera, Egypt, and given to the Bibliothèque Nationale de France, Paris.[23] The image is a fine example of the art of champlevé enamel then available in Geneva, and a document of Greco-Egyptian astronomy for both foreign and French cognoscenti.

The enamel at the top of the three o'clock numeral of the dial of the Vacheron and Constantin watch is damaged; there is a small scratch in the gold above the Vatican portion of the Saint Peter's Square scene; and slight scratches appear on the cartouche with the serial number. There is a small piece of enamel missing from the two o'clock position on the back of the case of the Bautte and Moynier watch and several areas of enamel loss on both the pendant and ring. Both watches have been carefully preserved and are part of a large gift of nineteenth-century Swiss watches by an anonymous donor made in 1926 in memory of Lady May Fletcher-Moulton. CV

1 For an entertaining account of the custom, written largely from a British viewpoint, see Black 2003, pp. 3–16, 23, 46–67. See also Buzard 2002.
2 Acc. no. 55.11.5.
3 Acc. no. 26.267.71.
4 Signed "D. Bachelard & Fils / A GENEVE." Acc. no. 26.267.22. Little is known about the makers.
5 For a watch of this date signed "J:M:Vacheron A GENEVE" in the collection of the present-day firm, see *Treasures of Vacheron Constantin* 2011, p. 25.
6 See Pritchard 1997, vol. 2, p. V-3; Patrizzi 1998, p. 386. For genealogical tables of the family, see Pritchard 1997, vol. 2, p. V-4; *Treasures of Vacheron Constantin* 2011, pp. 32–33. A chronology of the company is provided in Cologni 2005.
7 For the full range of signatures and trademarks used by the firm, see Pritchard 1997, vol. 2, pp. V-1, V-2; *Treasures of Vacheron Constantin* 2011, p. 34. See also entry 30 in this volume for one of the watches signed "A. Vacheron Girod" in the Museum's collection.
8 Patrizzi 1998, p. 387; Cologni 2005, p. XXVIII.
9 Cologni 2005, p. XXVIII. See also Jaquet and Chapuis 1970, p. 119, for an account of earlier Vacheron trade with Italy.
10 *Treasures of Vacheron Constantin* 2011, p. 27.
11 Jaquet and Chapuis 1970, p. 158. See also *Treasures of Vacheron Constantin* 2011, pp. 28–29.
12 Chapiro 1980; Chapiro 1988, pp. 46, 93–106.
13 Chapiro 2006, pp. 6–7, and fig. 3.
14 Cologni 2005, p. XXIX.
15 An illustration of the pantograph together with eight examples of the same layout in eight sizes made possible by the machine appears in Jaquet and Chapuis 1970, pl. 111; see p. 158 for a more detailed description of the pantograph. See also Pritchard 1997, vol. 2, p. L-52.
16 Harrold 1984, pp. 16–21; Hoke 1990, pp. 181, 188–89, 198; Hoke 1991, pp. 61–63.
17 R. F. Carrington and R. W. Carrington 1978; Thompson 2008, pp. 124–25. See also Landes 1983, pp. 283–85.
18 Landes 1983, p. 326, and app. B, pp. 380–84.
19 The authors would like to thank the officials at Vacheron Constantin for providing this information from their records.
20 Acc. no. 26.267.14.
21 For more about Bautte and his various partnerships, see Pritchard 1997, vol. 1, pp. B-26 to B-30, and vol. 2, pp. M-106, M-107. See also Patrizzi 1998, p. 96.
22 Jaquet and Chapuis 1970, pp. 146–47.
23 Now in the Musée du Louvre, Paris, inv. no. D 38. For further discussion of the meaning of the constellations, see J. Evans 1998, pp. 39–40.

52. Pocket Chronometer

SWISS (GENEVA), CA. 1850–55
2½ × 1¾ × ½ in.(6.4 × 4.5 × 1.3 cm)
Diam. of plate: 1⁹⁄₁₆ in. (4 cm)
Bequest of Vladimir M. Eitingon, in memory of his parents, Michail and Betty Eitingon, 1982
1983.183.5

CASE: partly enameled gold, signed (on inside of back cover): *Czapek & Cie* [François, or František, Czapek, born Bohemia (present-day Czech Republic), 1811–before 1895; firm, Swiss (Geneva), 1845–69]
DIAL: white enamel with gold hands
MOVEMENT: gilded brass and steel, signed (on bridge of going barrel): *Czapek & Cie* / A GENÈVE 2478

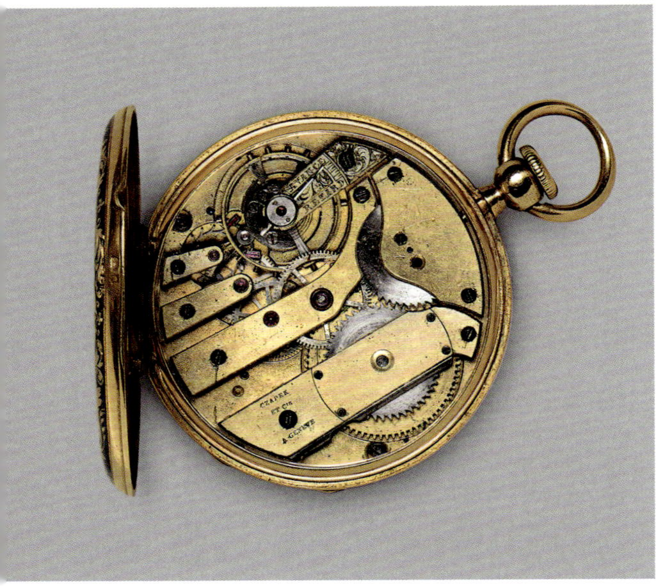

The back cover of the watch open to show the movement

WATCHES WITH PORTRAITS PAINTED ON THEIR CASES HAVE A history that is almost as long as watches with painted enamel cases of any kind. One with portraits of the French King Louis XIII (1601–1643) and his minister, Cardinal Richelieu (1585–1642), inside the front and back covers has been attributed to Henri Toutin (1614–1684)[1] and confidently dated to about 1640.[2] The Metropolitan Museum has an exquisitely enameled gold watchcase that contains a portrait of Louis Hesselin (1602–1662), appointed *surintendant des plaisirs du roy* (organizer of entertainments) to King Louis XIV (1638–1715), painted about 1645 inside the bottom of the case.[3] A second watch, in the Robert Lehman Collection at the Metropolitan, has an even more exquisitely enameled case that depicts King Louis XIV as a boy astride a rearing horse, painted about 1645–48.[4] All three watchcases may have been made in Paris or Blois, but more likely Paris. By the 1660s the locus of fine enameled portrait painting had moved to Geneva, where the enamels of Jean I Petitot (1607–1691) and Paul Prieur (1620–1684) set a remarkably high standard. Later in the century others, including Jean-Pierre Huaud (1655–1723), with his rare but penetrating portraits[5] continued the tradition (see entry 26 in this volume).

It has usually been assumed that the watches with portraits of kings and those of high status in their courts were given as rewards for loyalty or service. This was not invariably the case, however, for the watch with Hesselin's likeness, for example, is known to have been in his own possession at the time of his death.[6] Still, it is probable that most such timepieces were, indeed, more commonly commissioned as tokens of princely, royal, or imperial favor. This watch in the Museum's collection with a portrait of Czar Nicholas I of Russia (1796–1855) on the back of the case surely belongs to the tradition of gifts or awards. Providing additional evidence, at least one other with the identical portrait survives most probably in Russia.[7]

The half-length portrait of the czar depicts a man in military uniform with a blue sash and gold epaulets. The upper part of the Imperial Russian arms is visible below, lest there be any doubt about his identity. The portrait is made of enamel painted on gold within a frame of leafy scrolls chiseled in low relief partly filled with enamel and contrasted with a black enamel ground. Like the portrait, the frame has a coating of colorless transparent enamel that adds to the brilliance of both portrait and frame. The technique, perfected about 1780 by Geneva enamelers,[8] was widely used throughout the nineteenth century, owing to the protection it gave to the delicate surfaces of painted enamels.

The white enamel dial of the watch has a cover of glass in a plain gold bezel. The dial has unusually slim roman numerals (I–XII) for

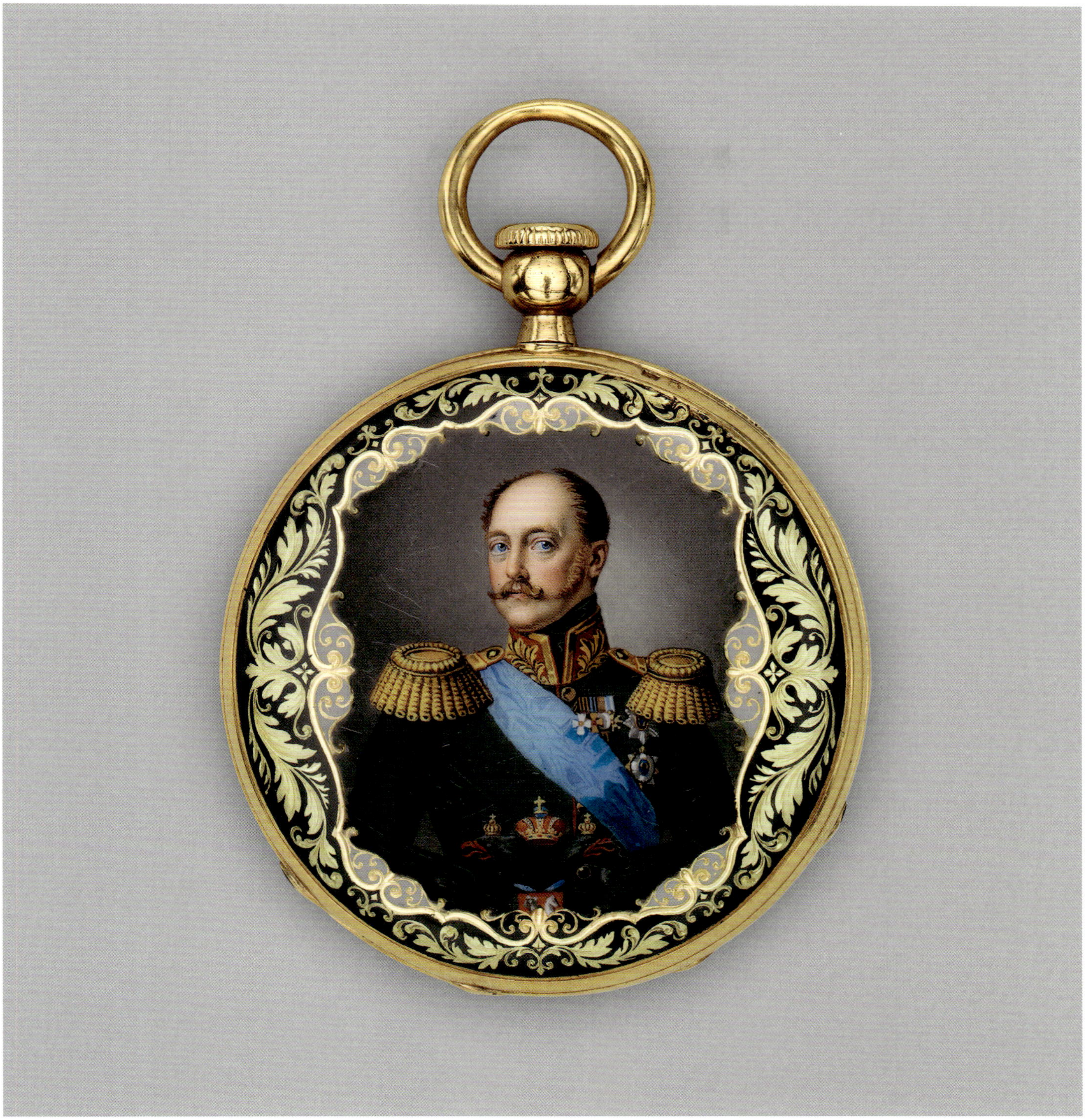

the hours and strokes for the minutes, each five-minute interval indicated by a dot. The gold hour hand with a spade-shaped ending and a subtly shaped gold minute hand complete the spare but elegant design. The back cover opens on a hinge at the four-five o'clock position, and it is signed on the interior side "Czapek & Cie / A GENÈVE," numbered 2478, and labeled *cronometre de poche* (pocket chronometer). A pocket chronometer, a different timekeeper from a marine chronometer,[9] is a very accurate pocket watch with a variety of lever escapement[10] and temperature compensation.

When the back cover of the watch is opened, the jeweled movement is seen to be covered not with a dust cover or a dome but with glass. As seen through the glass, the movement has a Lépine-type,[11] single full plate and bridges for securing the going barrel (on the right) and the three wheels of the train. A bridge on the left of the train is screwed to the plate and secures the escape wheel of the lever escapement. On the upper left is another bridge marked "AVANCE / RETARD" and calibrated for the regulation of the temperature-compensated balance and flat spiral hairspring. The large bridge on the right of the train is marked "CZAPEK & CIE / A GENÈVE." At the top, a bridge screwed at both ends to the full plate secures a wheel that engages with a second wheel, which is mounted on the arbor of the going barrel. These two wheels are part of the mechanism for winding the mainspring of the watch, which is manipulated by the flat disk on top of the pendant instead of by a key.

The principle of the mechanism was used by several watchmakers in the late eighteenth and early nineteenth centuries,[12] but the version used in this watch was the invention of Frenchman Jean-Adrien Philippe (1815–1894) in 1842.[13] His invention was seen by Count Norbert-Antoine de Patek (1812–1877) in the Paris Exposition Universelle of 1844, where Patek, a Polish-exile-turned-watch-seller in Geneva, offered Philippe a position as technical director in his Geneva firm to begin in 1848, as soon as Patek's contract with Czapek expired. Thereafter, Czapek, a Bohemian-born watchmaker of Polish descent and Patek's partner in 1836–48, began his own company. The new company specialized in souvenir and portrait watches, including watches with patriotic or religious themes.[14] In 1854, Czapek opened a shop in Warsaw, and in 1860, another in the Place Vendôme, Paris, the latter catering not only to Polish émigrés but also to the imperial court of Napoleon III (1808–1873). Czapek and Company was liquidated in 1869, and it is said that Czapek died in poverty.[15] Patek Philippe, however, founded by Patek, Philippe, and their financial partner, Vincent Gostrowski, still flourishes in Geneva to this day.

The enamelists who supplied portraits for Czapek apparently remain unknown, as do the watchcase makers. The keyless, or stem-winding, mechanism in the Museum's watch, which was Philippe's invention, is the earliest practical keyless watch to have been produced in quantity.

Except for a hairline crack in the enameled dial that appears between the seven and eight o'clock positions and runs to the ten o'clock position, slight scratches all over the portrait, damage at the eleven o'clock position, and a screw missing from the bridge that secures the top winding wheel, the watch is in excellent condition.

Vladimir Eitingon, who bequeathed the watch to the Museum, lived in New York at the time of his death in 1982. CV

1 Now in the Victoria and Albert Museum, London, inv. no. 7543-1861. See T. P. C. Cuss 1967, p. 25, pl. 18; Cardinal 1989, pp. 152–53, ill. no. 116.
2 See entries 12 and 20 in this volume for more about these early enamels.
3 Acc. no. 17.190.1413. See Leopold and Vincent 1993.
4 Acc. no. 1975.1.1244. See Vincent 2012, pp. 78–83, no. 21.
5 See entry 26 in this volume.
6 See Leopold and Vincent 1993, p. 103.
7 The watch is illustrated in Maziarkin and Iudkevich 2011, p. 48.
8 Cardinal 1989, pp. 196–201; see also Clutton and Daniels 1979, p. 76, in which the invention is dated to 1760.
9 For more about marine chronometers, see Randall 1992, especially pp. 33–35. See also Sobel and Andrewes 1998, pp. 187–95.
10 For a more detailed discussion of lever escapements, see Clutton and Daniels 1979, pp. 119–29.
11 See entry 51 in this volume.
12 For an earlier variety invented by John Roger Arnold about 1821, see Clutton and Daniels 1979, figs. 253a–c; another, invented by Abraham-Louis Breguet, appears in figs. 265a–c. Others were by Louis Audemars & Sons (possibly as early as 1838) and Antoine Lecoultre (1847); Clutton and Daniels 1979, p. 76. See also Huber and Banbery 1982, pp. 40–48.
13 For the Philippe system, see Huber and Banbery 1982, pp. 49–52.
14 Ibid., p. 16. See also Pritchard 1997, vol. 1, p. C-107, and vol. 2, pp. P-10, P-11; Patrizzi 1998, p. 147; *Timepieces for Royalty* 2005, pp. 13–15.
15 *Timepieces for Royalty* 2005, p. 15; a brief biography of Czapek also appears on pp. 14–15.

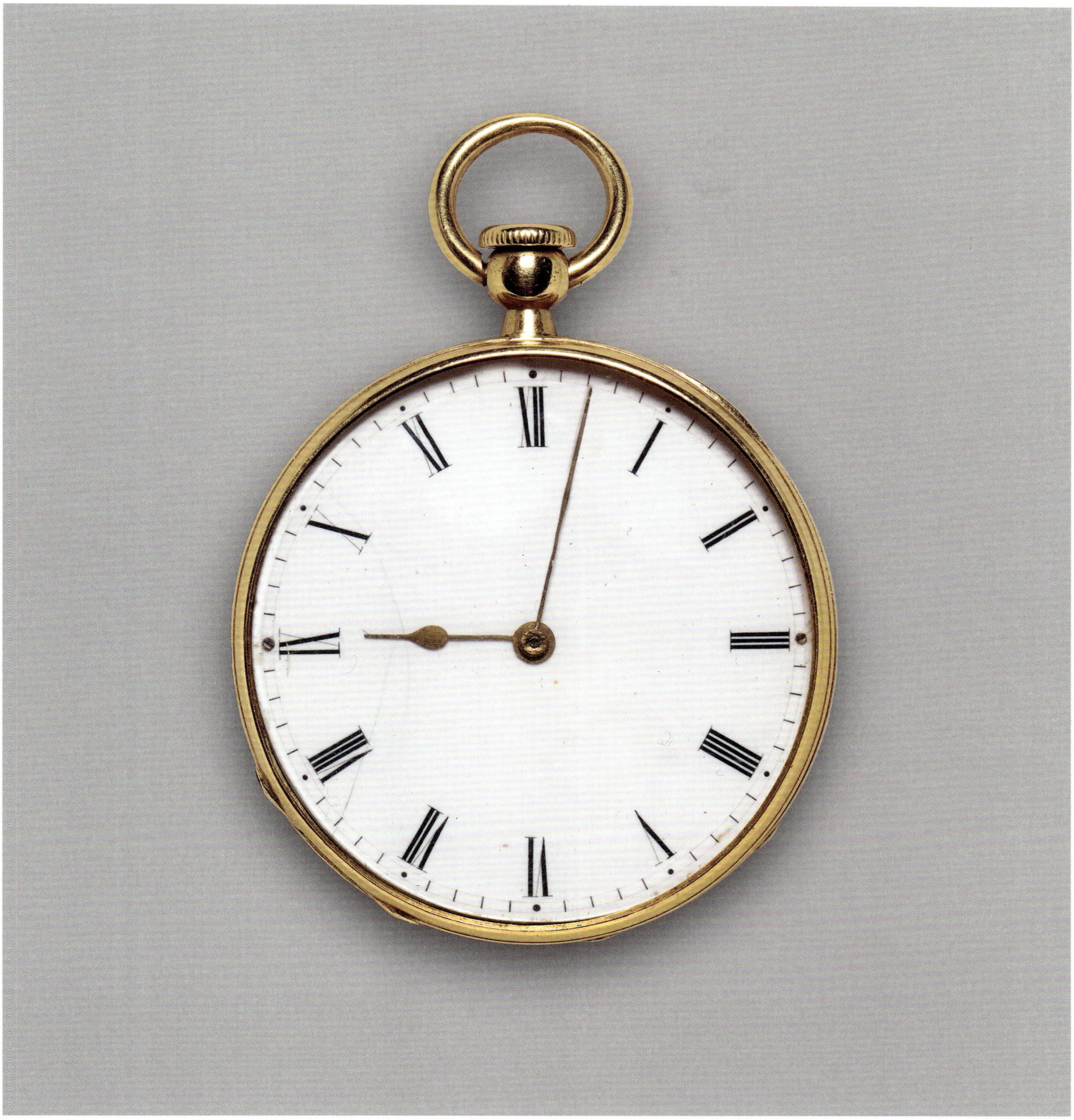

The dial of the watch with the front cover removed

53. Watch and Chatelaine

FRENCH (PARIS), CA. 1875–78
6¼ × 2⅜ in. (15.9 × 6 cm)
Diam. of back plate: 1¹⁄₁₆ in. (2.7 cm)
Gift of Cele H. and William B. Rubin, 1959
59.43a–c

CHATELAINE: partly enameled gold and platinum set with diamonds, stamped (on back of chatelaine, incuse): HIPPTE TETERGER / H. T. DÉPOSE [trademark, Hippolyte Téterger, French, 1831–after 1891]; gold chased by Jules Paul Brateau, French, 1844–1923
WATCHCASE: gilded brass and steel, signed (on dome): *Téterger* / 31 RUE S^T AUGUSTIN / *Paris*

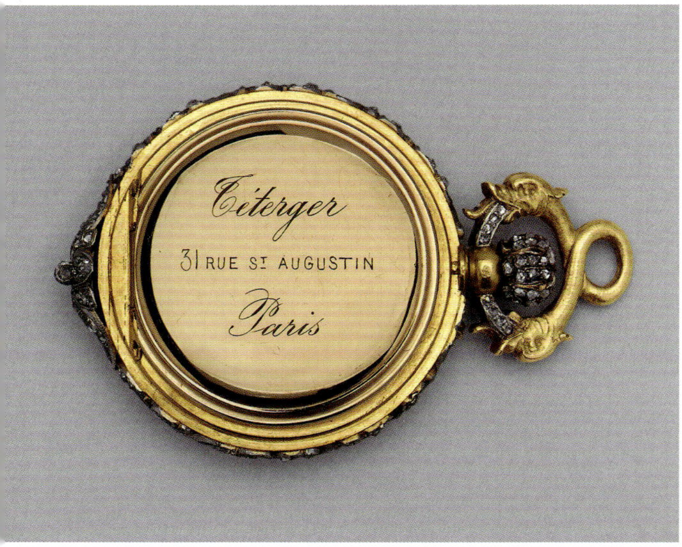

Watch with back cover removed to display the dome with the jeweler's signature

DURING THE NINETEENTH CENTURY IN FRANCE, A VARIETY OF ornament known as grotesque was understood to be a revival of Italian Renaissance design. Derived ultimately from Roman wall decorations discovered during the excavations begun in Rome about 1480 in the Domus Aurea (Golden House) of the emperor Nero (37–68) the style was quickly adopted by Italian artists and soon widely disseminated through the medium of prints.[1]

An etching from a series titled *Petits Panneaux Grotesques* (1562) by Jacques Androuet Du Cerceau (ca. 1520–1585/86)[2] displays both the vertical organization and the fanciful inhabitants of the grotesque style, which took its name from the grottoes or underground areas where the motifs were originally found. Du Cerceau's etchings or similar ornament prints must have inspired the designer of a French watch and chatelaine in the Metropolitan's collection. The object is a product of a Parisian jeweler at work during a period of eclectic taste when a sixteenth-century vocabulary of ornament could comfortably be combined with a watch suspended from an elaborate chatelaine, itself a revival of a fashion current a century earlier than the Museum's watch and chatelaine.

The watch was illustrated in a report by Lucien Falize (1839–1897) of the Exposition Universelle in Paris in 1878, which appeared in the influential *Gazette des beaux-arts*.[3] A great deal more is known about Falize than about Hippolyte Téterger (1831–after 1891), the maker of the case and chatelaine. Henri Vever (1854–1942), author of a three-volume history of nineteenth-century French jewelry, had little to say of Téterger other than that after their apprenticeships with the prominent Parisian jeweler Jean-Paul Robin the Elder (1797–1869), Hippolyte and his brother Eugène had hoped to join Robin's firm. The opportunity never arose, and the two brothers opened their own establishments, sometimes separately and sometimes together.[4] The date of Hippolyte's birth remained unknown to historians of jewelry until it was discovered in a French police report in 1891.[5] It is still not known when he moved to the address engraved on the Museum's watch, when he retired, or when he died. Vever illustrated a bracelet in the Art Nouveau style attributed to the "Maison Henri Téterger" that was displayed in the Paris Exposition Universelle of 1900.[6] He noted, as well, that a son, Henri, had been trained by Hippolyte, and he seems to imply that Henri was born in 1862.[7] Some later historians have apparently remained uncertain of Vever's meaning and have assumed that 1862 was the date when Henri took charge of his father's firm (Maison Téterger).[8] The assumption is most unlikely, however, given the age that Hippolyte would have been at the time, to say nothing of Henri. Moreover, Falize,[9] writing in 1878, felt free to describe the Museum's

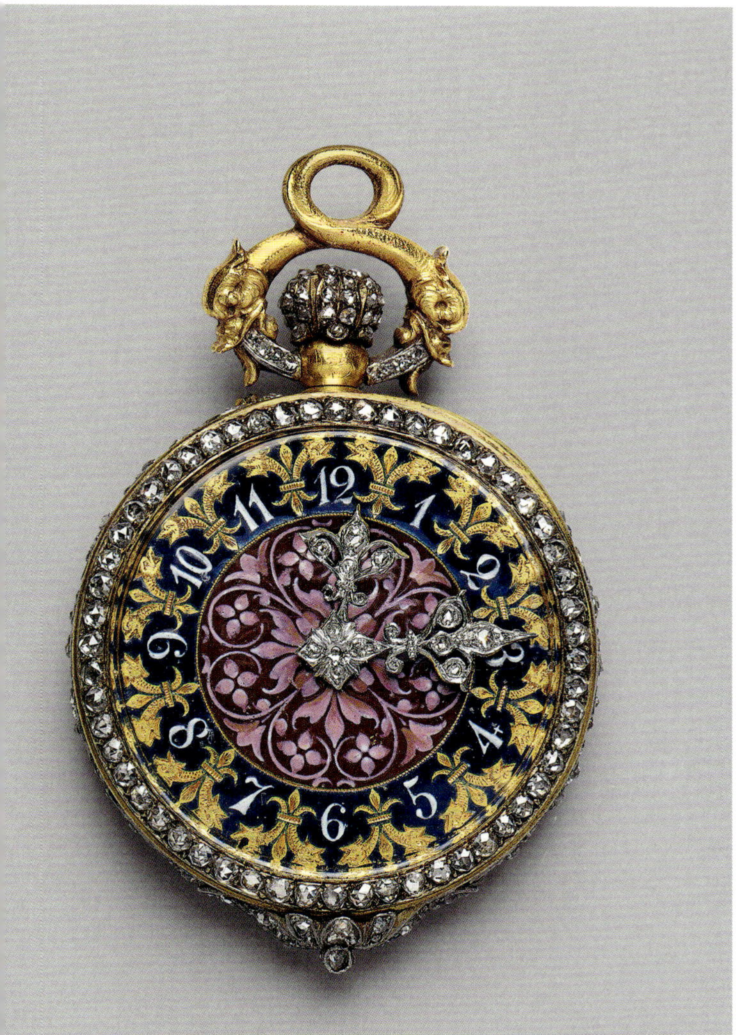

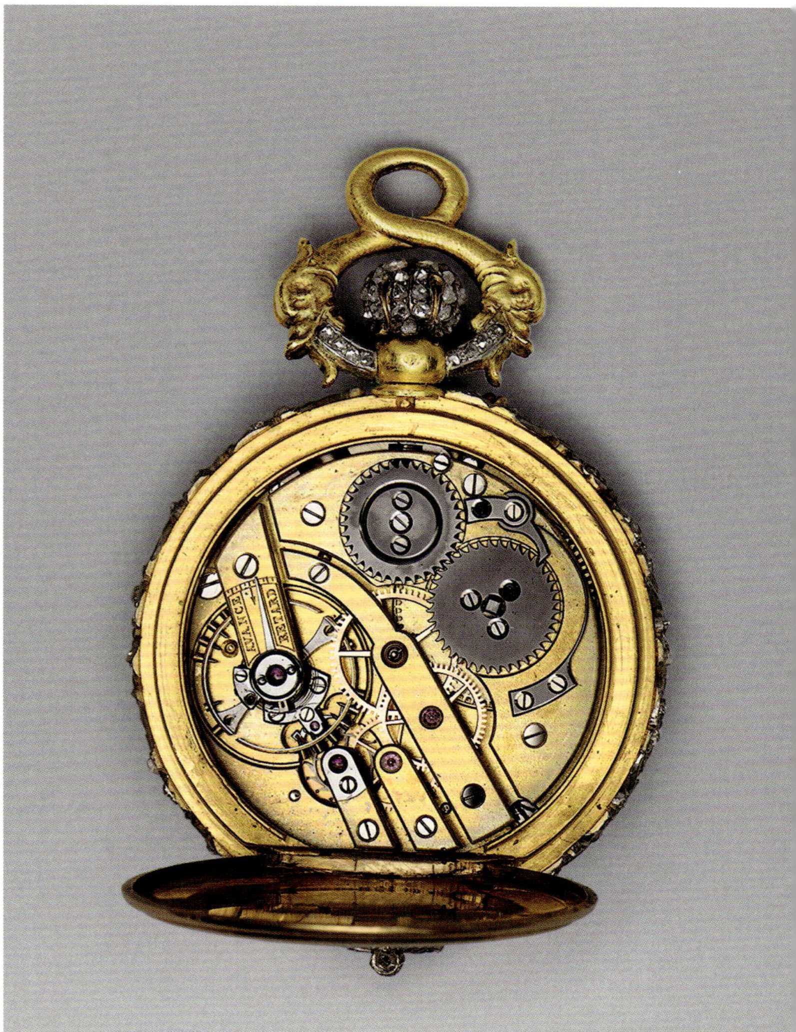

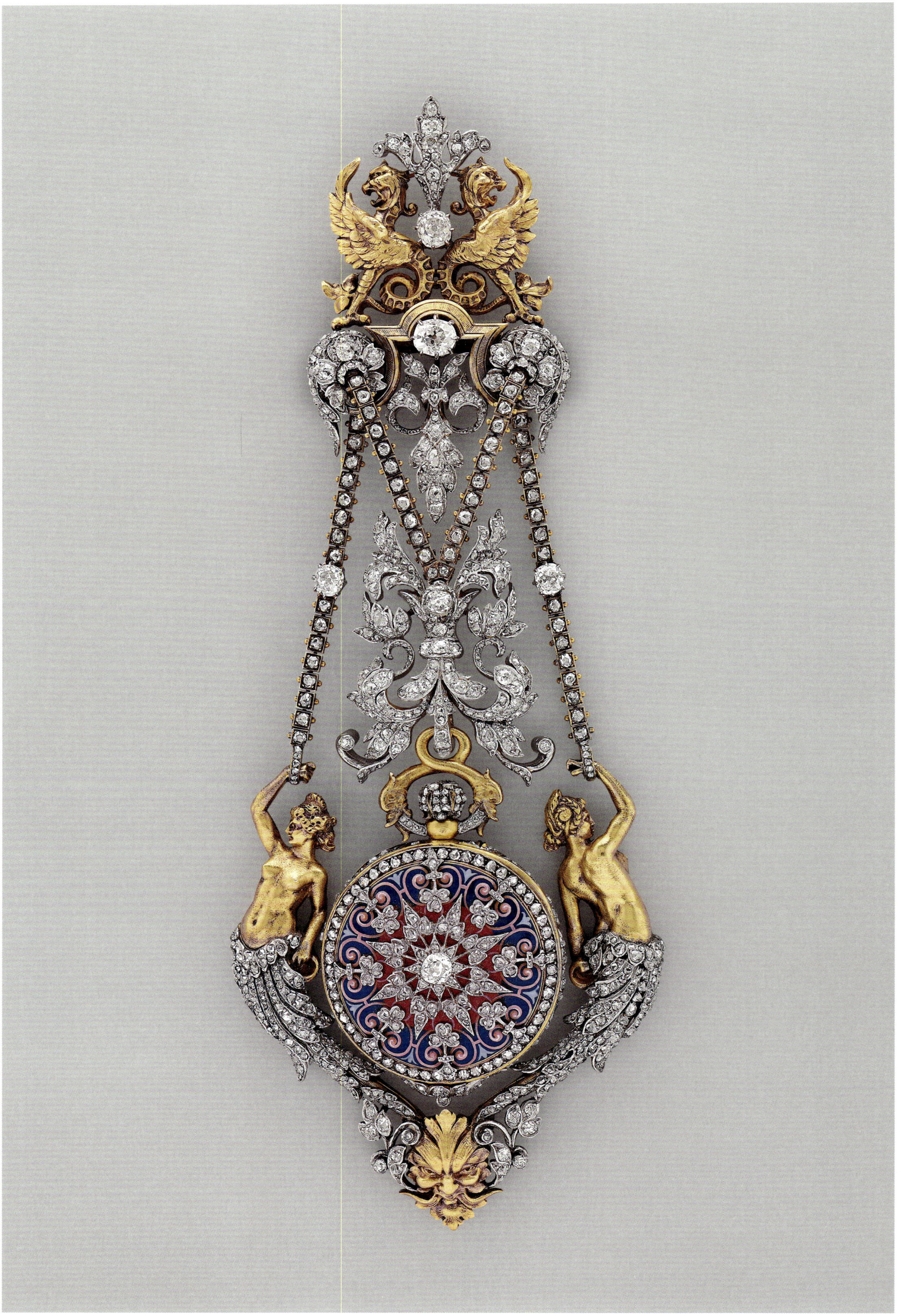

chatelaine as among the best works of "Monsieur Téterger," seemingly indicating that at that time Hippolyte was still the only Téterger to be credited with its creation, but in the same sentence crediting Jules Brateau (1844–1923) with chasing the gold elements.[10]

The mythological griffins, the half-human females, and the mask at the bottom of the chatelaine are beautifully executed, but most of the effect of the piece depends upon the setting of the diamonds, which were cleverly chosen to emphasize the separate parts of the design. From the top, the design begins with a three-leaved ornament reminiscent of the French lily, or fleur-de-lis, that grows out of a large diamond flanked by the gold figures of addorsed griffins. The griffins are seated upon a larger diamond that anchors a cascade of diamond-encrusted foliage and is flanked by diamond-petaled flowers from which depend a continuous diamond-set, M-shaped chain. Punctuated by large diamonds, the chain forms the attachment for the raised arms of the two half-nude females, their tails ending in a golden grotesque mask with diamond-set tendrils issuing from its mouth. The diamond-encrusted foliage that hangs below the center of the "M" serves to disguise the hook by which the pendant of the watch can be attached so that either the dial of the watch or the back of its case is visible. A gold tongue-shaped clip with openwork neoclassical ornament derived in part from Greek honeysuckle motifs is attached to the back at the level of the two diamond-petaled flowers and stamped "HIPPTE TETERGER / H. T. DÉPOSE."

The watchcase displays an exquisite use of enamel combined with gemstones, another greatly admired skill of Téterger's. The back of the case, the side that would ordinarily be visible when the watch was worn, consists of a large central diamond set within an eight-pointed star and eight spade-shaped ornaments, all set with diamond trefoils on a ground of dark and light blue, pink, and mauve enamel encircled by a band of small diamonds. The back snaps off to reveal the gold dome of the inner case that is signed "Téterger / 31 RUE S^{T} AUGUSTIN / Paris."

Lest any part of the case appear to have been neglected, the side of the gold case, or band, supports applied foliate designs of platinum set with diamond sparks. The front cover is glass with a bezel set with yet another circle of small diamonds. The glass cover allows a clear view of the dial with its hour circle (1–12) in blue and white enameled Arabic numerals that are separated by gold fleurs-de-lis. The center of the dial consists of a pink and mauve enameled design of quatrefoils issuing from a cluster of foliage, against which the openwork hands with diamond chips set in platinum inspire admiration not only for their exquisite craftsmanship but also for the ease by which the time can be read. The winding stem, too, is pavé-set with tiny diamonds, more diamonds adorn the dolphins that form the pendant of the watch, and yet another cluster of diamond-set foliage is applied to the band at the six o'clock position. Altogether, the object is a prime example of nineteenth-century French extravagance that might be dismissed as mere exhibition showmanship except for the fact that the craftsmanship it displays is exquisite.

The movement is unsigned, but it is a high-quality example of single-plate bridge construction with ruby endstones pivoting the arbors of its three wheels, a lever escapement, and a spring balance with temperature compensation. It features the two steel wheels necessary to wind the mainspring by manipulation of the stem,[11] a commonplace occurrence in Continental watches made in both France and Switzerland by the 1870s. The anonymity of its maker suggests that the prestige of the jeweler far surpassed the reputation of the watchmaker.

A few small diamonds on the chatelaine are missing. CV

1 See Dacos 1969, pp. 78–99; see also entry 2 in this volume.
2 The Metropolitan Museum of Art, New York (acc. no. 21.10.1[11]), from the Paris edition of 1562.
3 See Falize 1878, pp. 253–54.
4 See Vever 1906–8, vol. 1 (1906), p. 208. See also Gere and Rudoe 2010, pp. 286–87, 289, 519, n. 166.
5 *Mémoires de M. le Préfet de la Seine* 1892, p. 752, Procès-verbal of Dec. 27, 1891, naming Hippolyte Téterger, born in 1831, a jeweler living at rue des Mathurins, 3. The author thanks Rose Whitehill, former Research Associate, Department of European Sculpture and Decorative Arts, Metropolitan Museum, for bringing this information to my attention.
6 Vever 1906–8, vol. 3 (1908), p. 616. See also Duncan 1994, vol. 2, p. 233, in which the bracelet and a neck ornament, both displayed in the Exposition Universelle in 1900, appear as the work of Henri Téterger.
7 Vever 1906–8, vol. 3, p. 645.
8 See, for example, Gere 1998–99, p. 40.
9 See entry 54 in this volume for more about Falize.
10 See Falize 1878, p. 254. Jules Brateau is well known for his skill in metalworking. The Museum has seven of his designs in pewter (acc. nos. 1985.110.1, .2, 1992.16.1, .2, 1995.396.1, .2, and 2001.657).
11 See entry 52 in this volume.

54. Table Clock with Calendar

FRENCH (PARIS), 1881
18⅝ × 7 × 7 in. (47.3 × 17.8 × 17.8 cm)
Purchase, Mrs. Charles Wrightsman Gift, 1991
1991.113a–f

CASE: silver, partly enameled gold, hardstones, rock crystal, amethysts, and diamonds, signed (in center of upper dial, on calendar side): BF flanking a ring and pendant pearl [mark, Lucien Falize, French, 1839–1897, and Germain Bapst, French, 1853–1921; Bapst and Falize partnership, 1879–97]; design and enamels by Lucien Falize; figures modeled by Léon Chédeville, French, active 1875, died 1883, and chased by Claudius Marioton, French, 1844–1919
MOVEMENT: brass and steel, signed: LE ROY ET FILS [firm of Casimir Halley Desfontaines, French, 1794–1838]

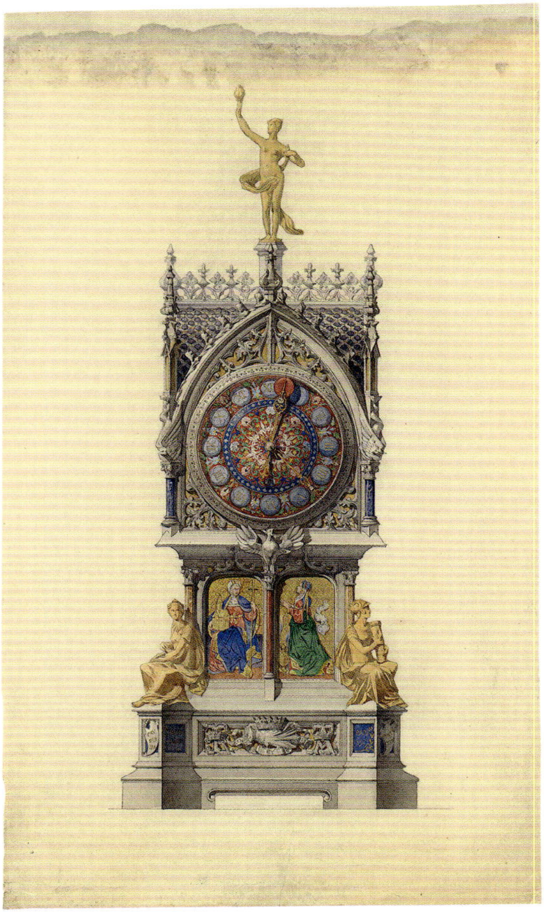

fig. 60 *Lucien Falize (French, 1839–1897). Design for Enameled Clock, French, ca. 1881. Pen, ink, and watercolor, 23 × 13¾ in. (58.4 × 34.9 cm). The Metropolitan Museum of Art, New York, The Elisha Whittelsey Collection, The Elisha Whittelsey Fund, 1991 (1991.1254)*

THE PUBLICATION IN 1831 OF VICTOR HUGO'S NOVEL *NOTRE DAME de Paris*, known in its English translation as *The Hunchback of Notre Dame*, was hugely successful. Hugo's success further ignited an already nascent enthusiasm for France's medieval past, and it gave support to the revival of Gothic design in the decorative arts as well as in architecture. One of the most celebrated exponents of this essentially romantic taste was the architect and designer Eugène-Emmanuel Viollet-le-Duc (1814–1879).[1] Beginning in the 1840s as the rebuilder of the Romanesque abbey church at Vézelay in Burgundy,[2] Viollet-le-Duc subsequently became the architect and designer of many of what are now regarded as quintessentially French Gothic elements of the Notre-Dame Cathedral, Ile Saint-Louis, Paris,[3] the setting of Hugo's tragic romance. English enthusiasm for Gothic design long predated the French, however. Horace Walpole's domesticated country house at Twickenham, Strawberry Hill (1749–1776),[4] and William Beckford's newly created abbey at Fonthill in Wiltshire (1796–1822)[5] are prime examples of the Gothic revival in English architecture.

The Museum's clock is the design of a nineteenth-century Frenchman, Lucien Falize (1839–1897), and the product of French craftsmen made expressly for a nineteenth-century Englishman. It was Alfred Morrison (1821–1897),[6] the son of James Morrison (1789–1857), who was made extraordinarily wealthy in the textile business.[7] James Morrison purchased many of the furnishings and objets d'art from Beckford and eventually the remains of the abbey, whose imposing central tower had collapsed in 1825, taking with it the vast Great Western Hall at its base. The surviving structure became one of Morrison's country residences, and it was inherited by his second son, Alfred, for whom the Museum's clock was created. Alfred continued the tradition of collecting begun by his father, but he specialized in autograph letters and manuscripts, which were much admired by his contemporaries, as well as becoming a patron of a wide variety of contemporary craftsmen, Lucien Falize among them.

The son of Alexis Falize (1811–1898) and the second in three generations of jewelers and makers of small, precious objects, Lucien came of age in a period in which Paris became famous for luxury goods produced by such firms as Cartier, Boucheron, and Lalique, as well as Falize.[8] The clock that Falize created for Morrison is a miniature late-Gothic-style tower, but it is unlike any surviving Gothic clock of similar size. Falize may have been inspired by an actual Gothic church tower, or he may have been influenced by the structures that house clockwork inside Gothic churches. No more than fifteen years before Falize's design, a new clock by Auguste-Lucien Verité (1806–1887) was housed in a Gothic Revival structure inside the Cathedral of Saint-Etienne in

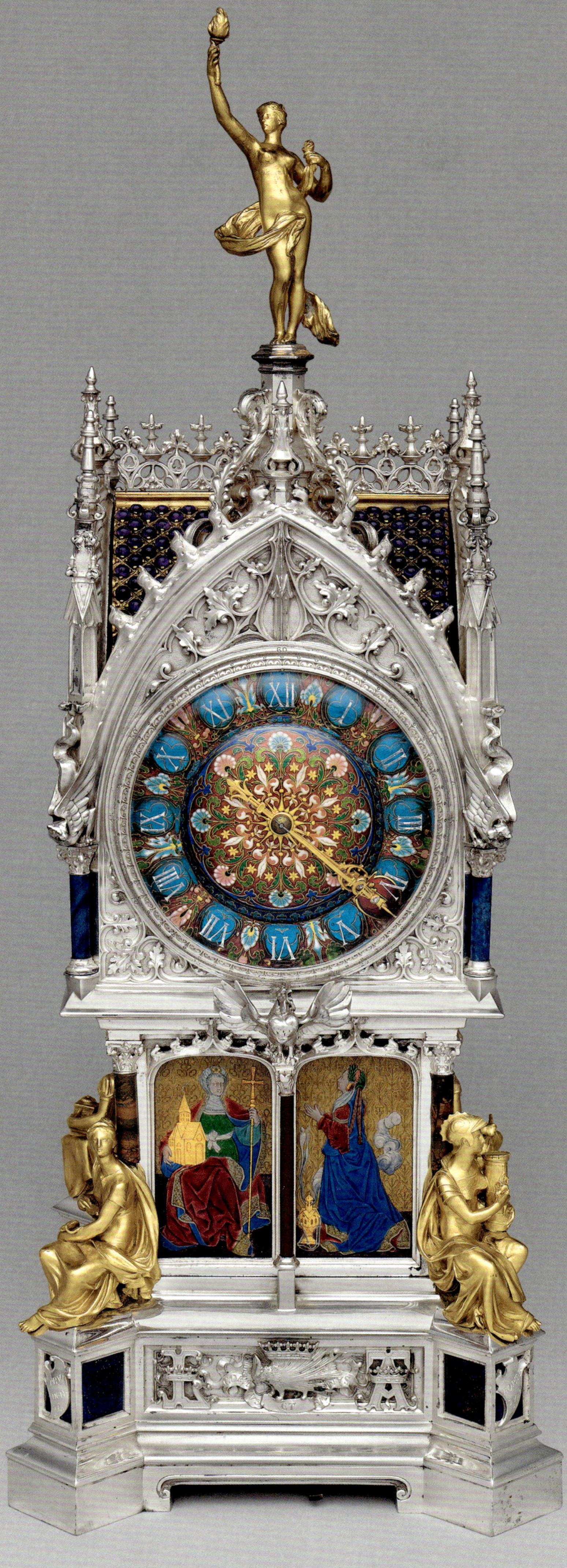

Detail of calendar dials on the reverse of the clockcase

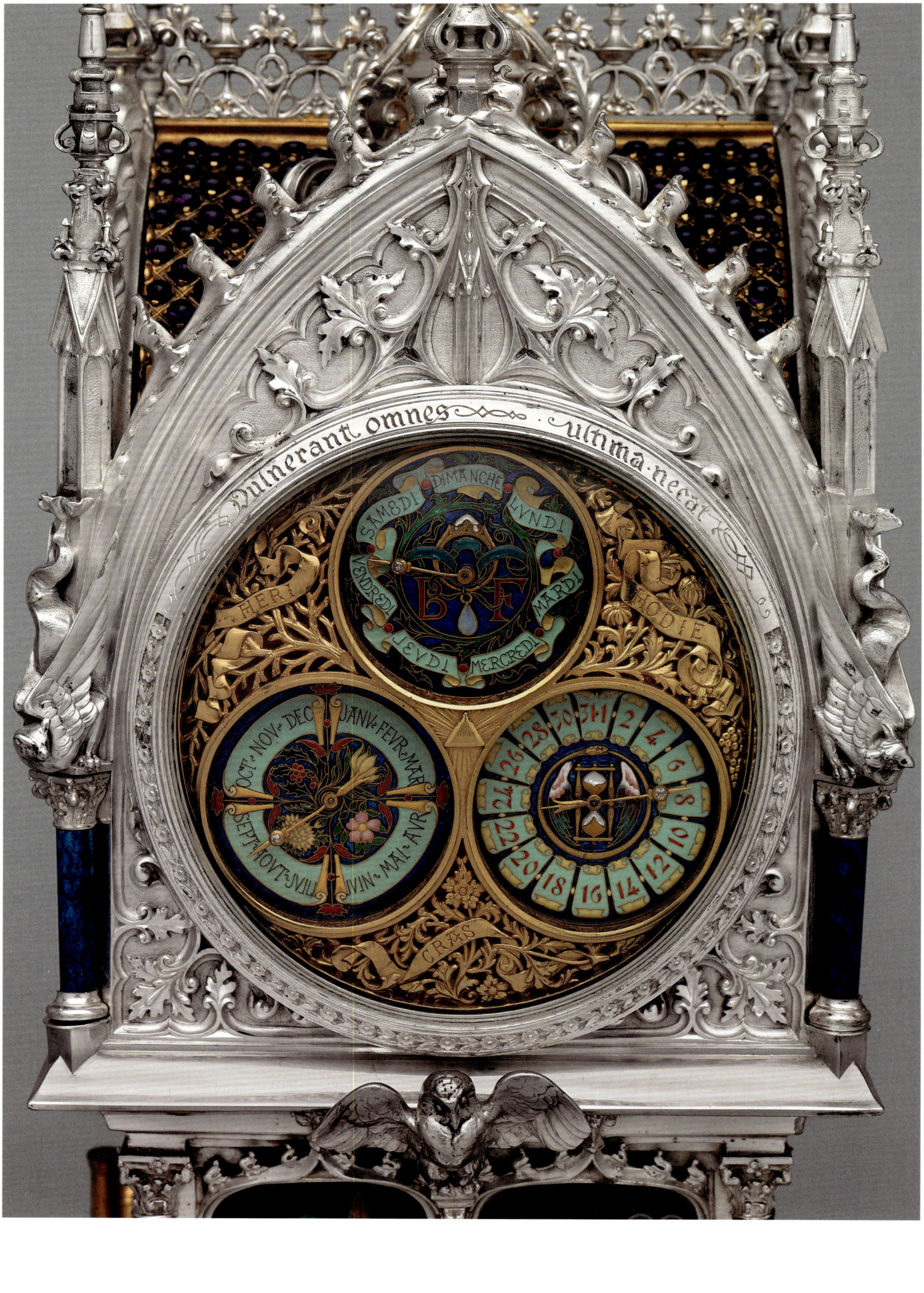

Beauvais, France. More comparable to Falize's clock in form is the housing of a timepiece that stands in the Cathedral of Saint-Jean in Lyon.[9] However, the elaborate structure above the dials of the four-sided Lyon clock is quite unlike Falize's extravagant golden roof studded with cabochon-cut amethysts and surmounted by a svelte figure of Truth, minimally clothed in a windblown scarf. The Falize case also displays a brief compendium of heraldic references and late-medieval iconography, some of it updated to include later developments. All of it is labeled to provide certainty to the meaning of each element.[10]

The case is divided into three tiers. The base is of cast silver with heraldic reliefs on all four sides and gold figures seated on the corners. The midsection has windowlike silver frames for eight basse-taille enameled plaques. The top carries two more plaques on the sides and time and calendar dials on the front and back sides. These are within Gothic pointed arches complete with silver crockets and finials and with winged gargoyles at the corners. The midsection is further enriched with carnelian and jasper colonettes, and the top section with lapis lazuli colonettes.

The principal dial registers the time (I–XII for the hours) engraved on the interior of a convex lens of rock crystal. The minutes (5–60, by fives) are marked on the silver bezel for the lens, where each minute is indicated by tiny circular punchmarks. In the closed position of the lens the hour numerals cover translucent blue enamel trefoils on the dial, which are separated from each other by various floral ornaments in colored enamels. The center of the dial is a mixture of cloisonné and painted enamel ornaments depicting pink fleurs-de-lis, pink and green blossoms, and tiny yellow six-pointed flowers in a sunburst pattern. Radiating from the central arbor are sculptured gold hour and minute hands, both set with tiny diamonds. Directly below the dial, a three-dimensional crowing cock presides over the time side of the clock.

The reverse side carries a comparable lens-covered circle encompassing three smaller circular dials that register calendrical information. These are separated by openwork gold branches incorporating ribbon scrolls with the Latin words "Heri" (yesterday), "Hodi" (today), and "Cras" (tomorrow). The top dial consists of a ribbon with the days of the week identified in French and in the center the emblem of the firm of Bapst and Falize: a ring and a pendant pearl flanked by the initials "B" and "F" in cloisonné enamel.[11] Moving clockwise, the second dial is marked 1–31 by twos for the days of the month and includes in the center a winged sandglass encircled by the serpent representing eternity, all in colored enamels. The third is divided into four segments, with the months marked in French and an enameled flower representing each season. Each dial has a diamond-set gold hand. Below these dials an owl presides over this side of the clock.

Here the time and calendrical functions of the clock end. The remaining spaces on the clockcase are filled with ten gold plaques incised with allegorical images covered with translucent enamels in a riot of brilliant color: blue, green, red, yellow, pale green, lavender, flesh colors, and more. The subject of each is labeled in Latin: FIDES (Faith), SPES (Hope), CARITAS (Charity), ECCLESIA (Church), ORAGIO (Prayer), SAPIENSIA (Wisdom), LIBERAGIO (Liberty), INVESGIGAGIO (Inquiry), LABOR (Industry), and LEX (Law). Falize was reported to have been particularly proud of these enamels as they represented for him the reinvention of a variety of basse-taille enameling that had flourished in France and Italy in the fourteenth and fifteenth centuries.[12] His pride in these enamels probably accounts for his inclusion of the clock eight years after its completion in the firm's display at the Paris Exposition Universelle of 1889.[13]

Two panels of lapis lazuli that flank the Morrison silver relief on the base are marked "·L·FALIZE· / ·INV· / ·EXECUT·" and "·PARIS· / ·1881·," respectively. A watercolor design in the Metropolitan Museum's collection for the clock (fig. 60) by Falize[14] displays the Gothic-style initials of King Louis XII (1462–1515) of France, and his wife, Anne, heiress of Brittany (1476–1514), below the enameled plaques depicting ECCLESIA and ORAGIO on the time-telling side of the clock. This is the configuration now on the clock, but there is evidence that the enameled plaques were rearranged at least twice in the past, no doubt to match their symbolism with the silver reliefs on the four sides of the base of the clock that refer to King Louis XII, Pope Julius II (1442–1513), King Henry VIII of England (1491–1547), and Alfred Morrison (1821–1897), respectively. The personifications of the Cardinal Virtues that sit at the corners of the lower rank of the plaques have also been rearranged.

The plaques on the clock are superb. Elegant, too, are the four Cardinal Virtues (Temperance, Prudence, Fortitude, and Justice). These were recognized at the time to have been inspired by the early sixteenth-century sculptures seated on the four corners of the monumental tomb of King Louis XII and Anne in the Abbey of Saint Denis, and they amplify the legacy of the royal couple commemorated on what is now the front, or time-telling side, of the clock. The four seated females on the clock are cast in gold, each identified by her customary attributes and by the name engraved on a shield on the front of her pedestal. They were modeled by Léon Chédeville (died 1883),[15] a sculptor who exhibited his work in the Paris Salons between 1875–83. His signature appears on the clock on the silver frame below the enamel depicting Temperance. An article written soon after the clock was created has further identified the artist who chased the details on these figures as Claudius Marioton (1844–1919),[16] another of the sculptors now best remembered as participants in the Paris Salons of the last quarter of the nineteenth century.

The spring-driven movement of the clock consists of two rectangular plates held apart by four cylindrical pillars. It has a going and a striking train wound in tandem by means of a single winding square concealed under the figure of Truth at the top of the clock. Governed by a rack-and-snail system, it strikes hours and quarters by means of four hammers on four coils of a gong mounted on the back plate of the clock. A lever in the base of the clock activates a repeating mechanism. Apparently, the sound was intended to evoke memories of the pealing bells of a late-Gothic church.[17]

On the underside of the base, the maker's name appears: "LE ROY ET FILS / Horlogers / fournisseurs brevétas / de S. M. la Reine à Londres." This mention of an appointment to Queen Victoria aids in certain identification of the firm. Although there existed two firms named Le Roy et fils or Leroy et fils during this period, both with establishments in Paris (at 15 Palais Royal and 115 Palais Royal, respectively) and branches in London,[18] the firm that held the Royal Warrant from the English queen was the one at 15 Palais Royal listed among the privileged clockmakers between 1864 and 1893.[19] Tardy's *Dictionnaire des horlogers français*[20] supplies the further information that the founder of this firm, Bazile Le Roy (1731–1804), was unrelated to Julien and Pierre Le Roy, the illustrious Paris clockmakers of the eighteenth century. Bazile's son was Bazile-Charles (1765–1839), also a clockmaker, who managed to stay in business during the French Revolution by spelling his name backwards. Later, he supplied clocks to Napoleon and in 1829 moved the shop to the Palais Royal, where he was associated with his son Charles-Louis (1794–1865/6) in the establishment then called Le Roy et Fils.[21] By 1835, they had become clockmakers to the French king and to the Ministère de la Marine, but by 1845 Charles-Louis had sold the firm to Casimir Halley Desfontaines (1794–1838) on condition that he would keep the name. In 1866, Desfontaines also became clockmaker to the French navy, followed by appointments to the queen of England and the emperor of Brazil.[22] The London branch of the firm opened in 1856 at 215 Regent Street.

Cedric Jagger's research into the history of the British Royal Collection of clocks confirms that this was, indeed, the firm with the Royal Warrant beginning in 1864 and continuing as late as 1893.[23] In 1883 Casimir was succeeded by his son Georges, who died in 1888, leaving the firm to his brother Jules. He became associated the next year with Louis Leroy, and the firm then became known as the Ancienne Maison LeRoy et fils. L. Leroy et Cie.[24]

Possession of the clock continued in the Morrison family until 1938, when it was sold in London by John Granville Morrison.[25] It was then sold in New York in 1955 as the property of Antique Dome, Inc., of Miami Beach, Florida,[26] and in 1991, it was sold in New York as the property of Harry J. Reicher.[27] It was bought for the Museum by Mrs. Charles Wrightsman, who, together with her husband, donated a large part of the Museum's distinguished collection of French decorative arts. CV

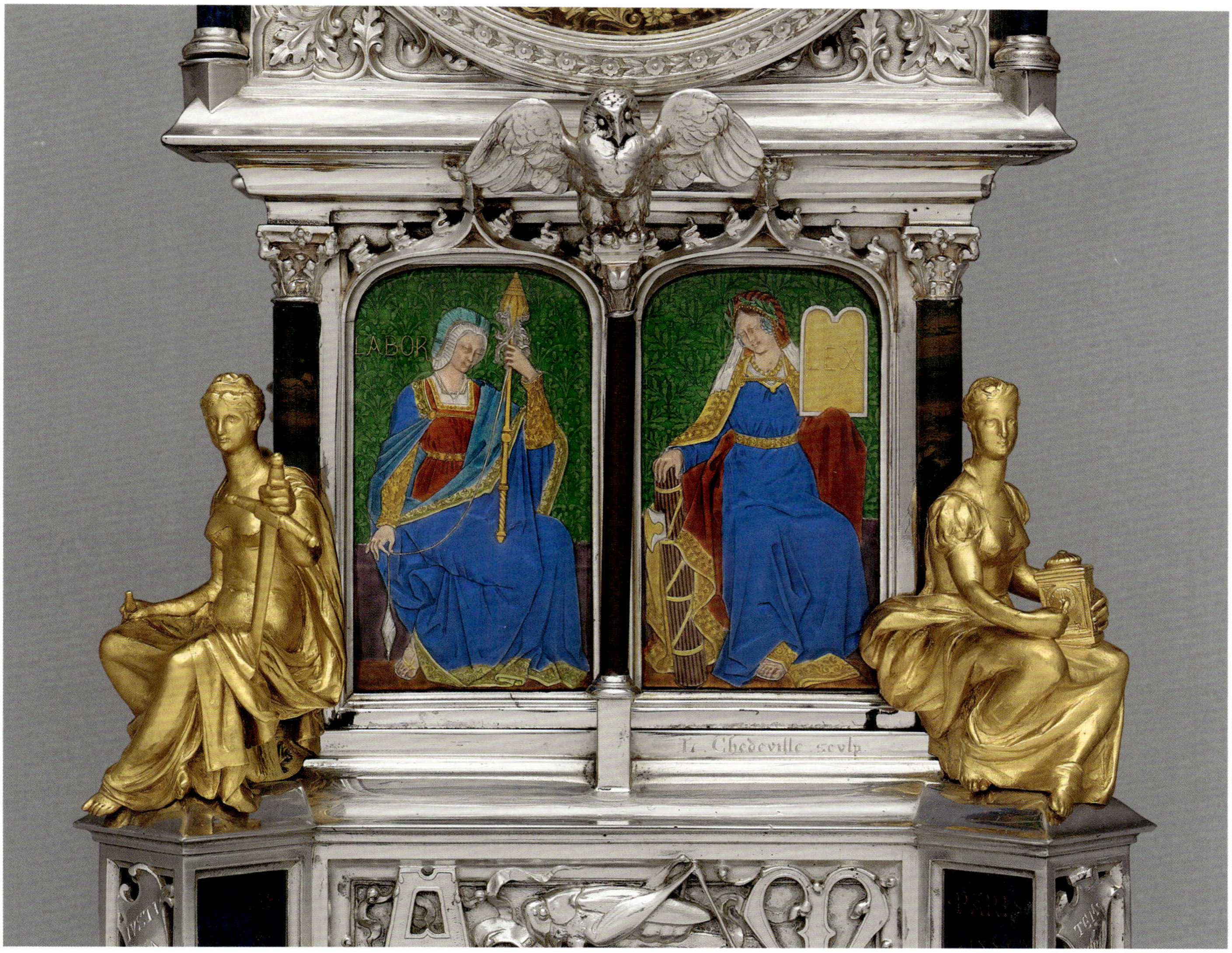

Detail of reverse side of the clockcase with figures personifying Justice and Temperance and enameled plaques depicting Labor and Law

1 For the wide variety of his designs and architectural drawings together with an extensive bibliography, see *Viollet-le-Duc* 1980.
2 Saulnier 1980.
3 Erlande-Brandenburg 1980.
4 Wainwright 1989, pp. 70–107; Clarke 2009; Snodin 2009, pp. 15–17, 20–31.
5 Wainwright 1989, pp. 108–16. See also Gemmett 2003.
6 Dakers 2011, pp. 225–47. See also Bell 2004; Dakers 2010, pp. 201–14, and p. 189, fig. 2, for a portrait of Morrison by John Brett (1831–1902).
7 Gatty 1977; Dakers 2011, pp. 82–112. See also Dakers 2010, pp. 189–201, for details of his possession of Fonthill Abbey.
8 For details of the lives and products of the three generations of Falize jewelers, see Purcell 1999.
9 See "L'Horloge Astronomique de la Cathédrale Saint-Jean de Lyon," http://www.ens-lyon.fr/RELIE/Cadrans/Musee/HorlogesAstro/Lyon/Cathedrale.htm.
10 For more complete descriptions of these elements, see Sotheby's 1991, no. 233; Purcell 1999, pp. 92–95.
11 See Le Corbeiller 1996, who states that this mark was not registered until 1892 but was used during the period of the partnership from 1880 to 1892.
12 "Oeuvres nouvelles" 1882–83, p. 30, with a steel engraving of the clock on p. 29.
13 Falize 1889–90, p. 5.
14 Acc. no. 1991.1254.
15 Lami 1914–21, vol. 1 (1914), pp. 364–65.
16 "Pendule artistique" 1882, p. 202; see also Kjellberg 1987, pp. 457–58.
17 "Pendule artistique" 1882, p. 204.
18 Allix 1974, pp. 120–24.
19 Jagger 1983, pp. 214–15, 316–18.
20 Tardy 1971–72, vol. 2, pp. 406–7.
21 Ibid., p. 407.
22 Ibid.
23 Jagger 1983, pp. 316–18.
24 Tardy 1971–72, vol. 2, p. 409.
25 Christie's 1938, p. 8, no. 30.
26 Parke-Bernet Galleries 1955, p. 72, no. 342, ill. p. 73.
27 Sotheby's 1991, no. 233, ill.

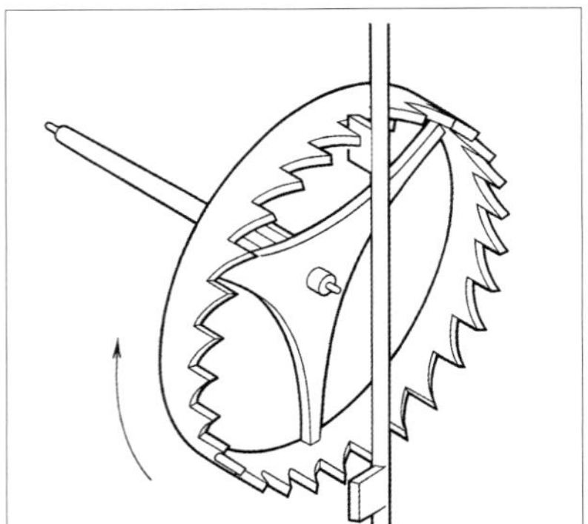
1.

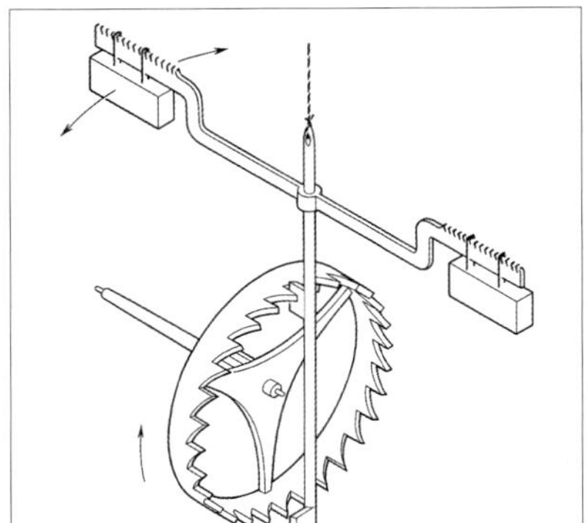
2.

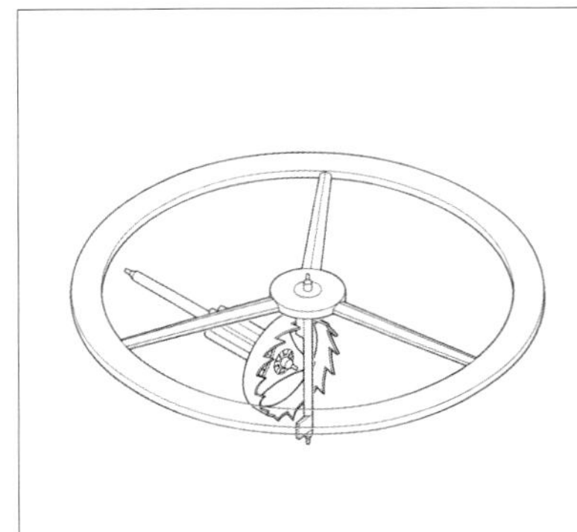
3.

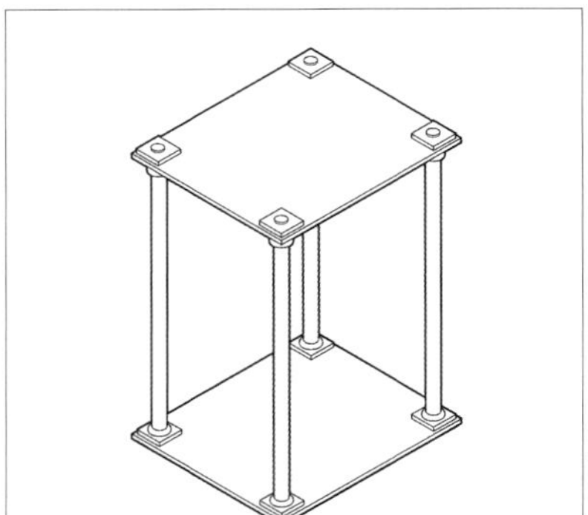
4.

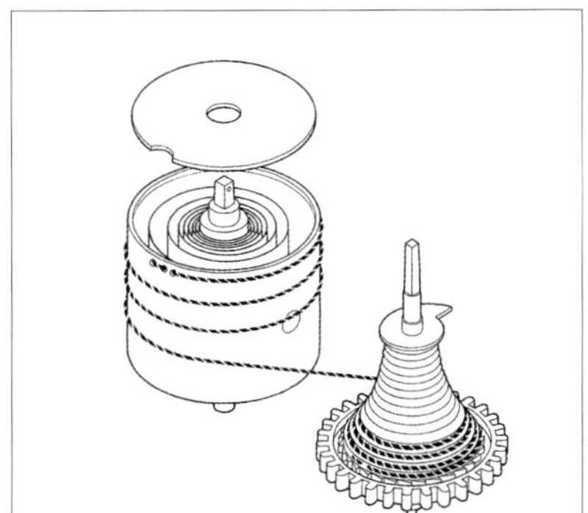
5.

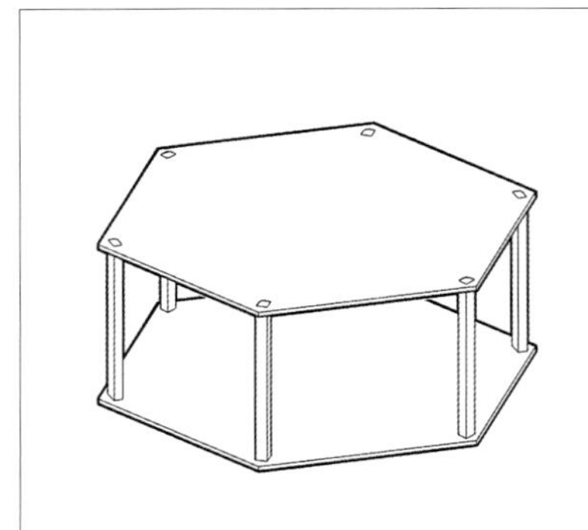
6.

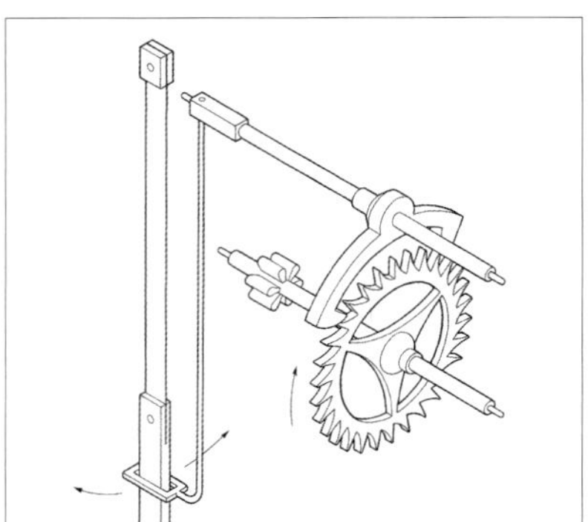
7.

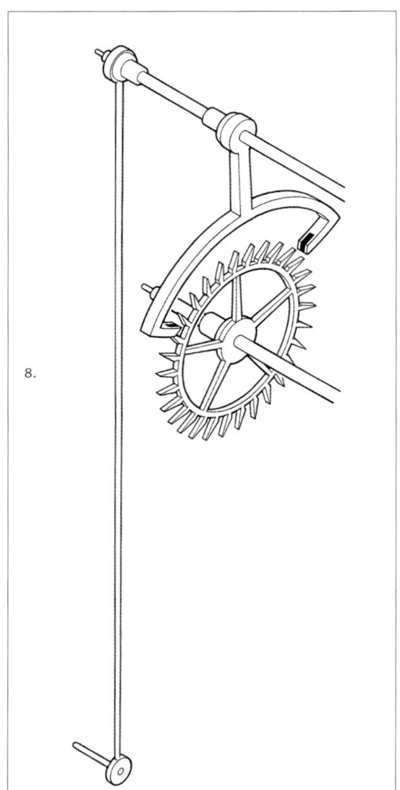
8.

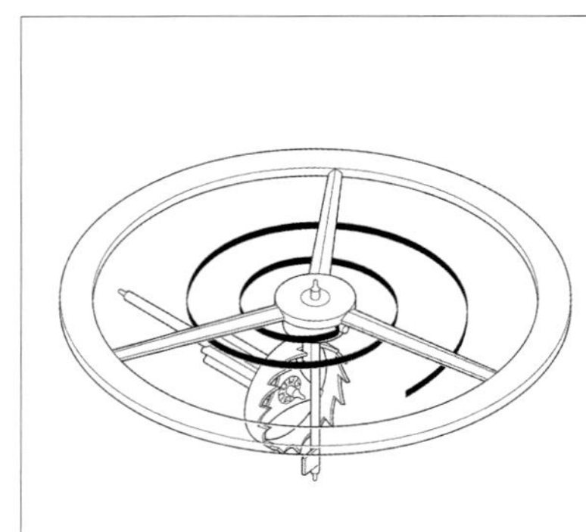
9.

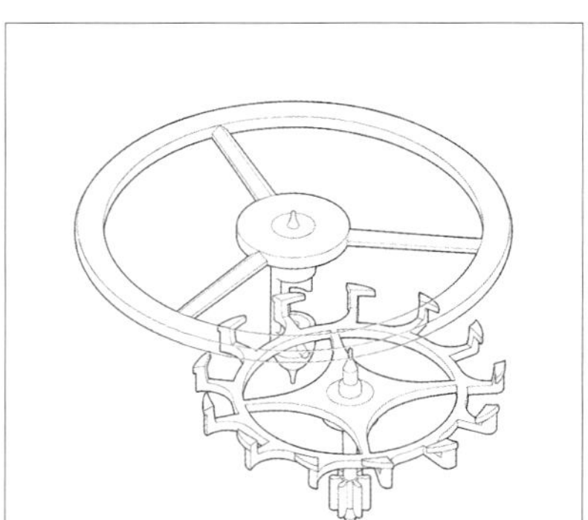
10.

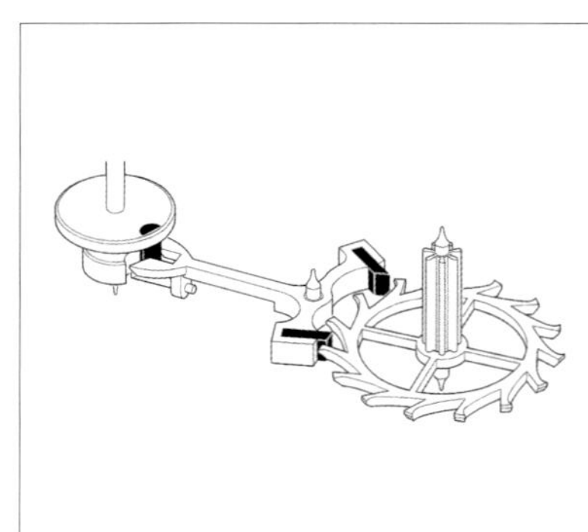
11.

1. *A verge and escape wheel*
2. *A foliot with a verge and escape wheel*
3. *A balance with a verge and escape wheel*
4. *A posted frame for a clock movement*
5. *A mainspring within a barrel connected by a cord to a fusee*
6. *A plated frame for a clock*
7. *An anchor escapement with a crutch for a clock with a long pendulum (pendulum is shown in part)*
8. *A Graham dead-beat escapement shown here with a crutch for a pendulum*
9. *A spiral balance spring and balance with a verge and escape wheel*
10. *A cylinder escapement*
11. *A Swiss lever escapement*

Glossary diagrams by **DAVID PENNEY**

Note: The great wheel and the escape wheel have not been included in the ennumerations of wheels (train counts) of the clocks and watches in this publication.

Cross references are indicated by SMALL CAPITAL LETTERS.

anchor escapement. A device consisting of a flat toothed wheel that is mounted at the end of the going train of a clock, and a separate semicircular piece of steel with pallets at each end of the semicircle that somewhat resembles a sea anchor. When set in motion by the pendulum to which it is attached, the anchor rocks back and forth, releasing one tooth of the wheel and catching another, thus releasing the energy of the going train at small intervals. The interval is usually one second in late seventeenth- or eighteenth-century longcase clocks.

arbor. A shaft, axle, or spindle upon which the wheels of a train are mounted.

aspectarium. A diagram showing the changes in the angular distance between the sun and moon in the zodiac for astrological purposes.

astrolabe. A multifunctional instrument used among other things to measure the altitudes, positions, and movements of celestial bodies.

automaton. An animated mechanical figure often associated with clocks and sometimes with watches.

back plate. The plate that is farthest away from the dial of a clock or watch.

balance, or balance wheel. A wheel, usually with two or three spokes, when attached to the top of an oscillating verge and coupled with a power source, controls the going train of a clock or a watch.

balance cock. The component on the back plate of a watch or a spring-driven clock with a foot attached to the exterior side of the plate and a raised portion called a table at the opposite end in which there is a small hole for securing the pivot of the arbor of a balance staff.

balance spring. A spiral spring that regulates timekeeping in watches and spring-driven clocks. It is attached to the balance staff at its inner end and to the back plate of the movement at its outer end. Invented by Christiaan Huygens (1629–1695) in late 1674.

balance staff. An arbor, or shaft, on which the balance is mounted.

band. The side of a watchcase or a clock case.

basse-taille. A technique of enameling on metal in which a large surface of the metal is cut away and filled with enamel. The cutout area is typically incised with a decorative design that is then covered with colored translucent enamel, fired, and polished.

bezel. The rim that holds a glass, hardstone, or rock crystal cover of a watch or a clock in place.

bob. The part of a pendulum at the farthest end of the rod from the suspension. As a rule the bob accounts for most of the weight of a pendulum.

bolt-and-shutter maintaining power. A flat spring or weight-loaded lever that when activated ensures the continuance of power during the period of winding a clock. The device is activated by raising the shutters behind the holes in a dial for winding, especially used in seventeenth- and eighteenth-century clocks.

bracket clock. A type of spring-driven clock introduced in the mid-seventeenth century, which originally would have been placed on a shelf or a wall-mounted bracket. Now more commonly termed a table clock, owing in part to the ease by which it can be moved and placed on a table.

bridge. A metal bar for securing the pinion of the arbor of the balance of a watch or a clock. In early clocks and watches, both sides of the bridge are attached to the back plate of the movement. In nineteenth-century single-plated movements, bridges secure the arbor of each wheel in the train.

cartel. A French wall clock.

champlevé. A technique of cutting away or stamping large surface areas of a metal watch or clock dial so that the numerals can be filled with colored wax or enamel. The term is not to be confused with champlevé enameling.

champlevé enameling. A technique in which powdered enamel is poured into hollowed-out grooves or cells on the surface of objects made of gold, silver, brass, or copper, then fired and polished down to be level with the surrounding metal.

chapter ring. The circle on which the hours and, later, minutes are indicated. Sometimes the ring is a separate piece applied to the dial; sometimes it is engraved or painted directly on the dial.

chasing. A method of decorating metal objects with designs incised from the front surface.

chronometer. In modern usage, a timekeeper of great precision or a timepiece used to determine longitude in navigation.

cloisonné enameling. A technique in which powdered enamel is fired within compartments formed by metal wires separating areas of colored enamel from one another. It is one of the earliest techniques of decoration on metal surfaces.

cock. The support of the pendulum in a clock. See also BALANCE COCK.

contrate wheel. A wheel in which the teeth stand up at right angles to the plane of the wheel.

count wheel. A wheel that is driven by the striking train and controls the number of bell or gong strokes for each hour or part of an hour. The count wheel has a number of notches on its circumference spaced at increasingly wider intervals to enable the clock to strike in the correct sequence.

crown wheel. An escape wheel in a verge escapement with teeth that stand up at right angles to the plane of the wheel, resembling a crown.

crutch. In a pendulum clock, an arm fixed to the pallet arbor, which connects the escapement to the pendulum, usually by means of a pin or a fork.

dead-beat escapement. A recoilless escapement.

dial. The part of a clock or a watch against which the hands indicate the time. Sometimes, it is called a face.

Dominical Letters. A system by which the date of Easter as well as of each Sunday in a year can be determined. They are also called Day Letters.

duplex escapement. A device using two separate escape wheels, one with a pallet for supplying impulse and the other with a pallet for locking the going train in a clock (not to be confused with the watch escapement by the same name).

ecliptic. The apparent path traveled by the sun through the constellations of the zodiac circle during the course of a year.

enamel. A vitreous substance, essentially pulverized glass with or without colorants fused to a metal surface under heat to form a brilliant, glossy surface. Enamel can also be applied to surfaces other than metal.

en ronde-bosse**.** A technique of enameling on metal with a raised surface, either in relief or fully in the round. The enamel may be either opaque or translucent, and it is often varicolored.

equation clock. A clock made to display true solar time, the time measured by a sundial, which is governed by the diurnal revolutions of the earth in relation to the sun. Usually, such clocks also display mean solar time, or mean time, which is an average drawn from the length of all the solar days in the year and results in a day of exactly twenty-four equal hours. The difference between the two reaches a maximum of a little more than sixteen minutes.

escape wheel. The final wheel in a going train. Also known as a 'scape wheel.

escapement. The mechanism that converts the continuous motion of the series of wheels and pinions, or going train, of a clock or watch to the back-and-forth motion of its regulator. In the oldest form of escapement an arbor (a balance staff with two pallets or flags) is placed across the last wheel in the going train and attached in such a way that when the wheel revolves, the teeth of the wheel alternately engage a pallet, releasing a train in short, measured intervals.

fly. The last component in a striking train or a musical train that employs the air resistance of a rotating radial fan to control the speed of the train when striking takes place.

foliot. In early clocks, a heavy bar with adjustable weights at each end that is fixed at right angles to the top of a vertical arbor, or staff, and used to control the release of power in a clock.

fusee. A cone with a spiral groove in its surface that accommodates a cord or, later, a chain that is attached at one end to the barrel containing the mainspring and at the other end to the cone. It is inserted between the spring and the wheel train that drive the hands of a clock or a watch, and it is used to even out the spring's decreasing force as it unwinds.

going train. The series of toothed wheels and pinions that connects with a power source and drives a timekeeping mechanism.

grande sonnerie**.** A type of striking in which the hour is repeated before each quarter is struck.

great wheel. The first and usually the largest toothed wheel in a going train. In a spring-driven timepiece, it is often directly attached to the barrel or else fitted below the end of the fusee. In a weight-driven clock it is usually attached to the winding drum.

gridiron pendulum. A pendulum consisting of multiple rods made of two metals (usually brass and steel) with differing coefficients of expansion that are arranged so that the total length of the pendulum remains constant and unaffected by changes in temperature.

grotesque ornament. A variety of ornament derived from antique Roman wall decorations that were discovered in the late fifteenth century in Italy buried underground or in grottoes. Typically, it consists of fantastic beasts, birds, and hybrid figures amid scrolling foliate motifs.

Harrison's maintaining power. The system for providing constant power to the going train of a clock or watch while the timekeeper is being wound, invented by John Harrison (1693–1776).

hog's bristle regulator. Two hog's hairs attached to a movable lever used to regulate the arc of an oscillating balance wheel.

hood. The top section of the case of a longcase clock, usually removable, which encases the movement and dial.

horology. The art and science of keeping time.

horror vacui. Ornament in which elements are closely piled next to one another.

isochronous motion. The equal period of oscillation of a pendulum or spiral spring.

Italian hours. An early system of counting equal hours from one to twenty-four, beginning at sundown.

lantern clock. A weight-driven wall clock.

lenticle. A glass panel in a longcase clock through which the pendulum can be seen.

longcase clock. A tall wooden case that contains the movement, pendulum, and weights. Also known as a grandfather clock.

mainspring. The coiled spring that acts as the driving force for a watch or a spring-driven clock.

maintaining power. A mechanism incorporated into a clock or a watch designed to keep it running while it is being wound.

marquetry. A technique that employs small pieces of wood or precious materials arranged in floral or figurative patterns on the surface of a piece of furniture to form a decorative veneer.

masterpiece clock. An admission piece demonstrating a clockmaker's skill required for membership in a guild.

monstrance clock. A clock in a case that resembles the container that displays the wafer for the Catholic mass.

moresque ornament. A style of ornament that Italian artists derived from Islamic sources and disseminated throughout Europe by means of the medium of prints.

motion work. Wheels that transfer power from the going train to the hands of a clock or a watch. Used to assure that the hour hand and minute hand travel at the appropriate rates.

movement. Clockwork, usually consisting of a source of power, a train of wheels and pinions, an escapement, and motion work driving hands that indicate the time. The mechanism of a clock or a watch without the case.

niello. An alloy of silver, copper, and lead to which sulphur and often borax have been added. In pulverized form, this composition is applied to a silver plaque that has been prepared with an incised design and heated until the composition and the silver fuse. When cool, the plaque is scraped until the blackened composition remains in the incised areas alone.

Nürnberg hours. An early system of reckoning time by which the twenty-four-hour day is divided into daylight and nighttime hours beginning at one o'clock at each sunrise and sunset. In this system, the hours vary in number according to the season.

pair-case watch. A type of watch introduced in the seventeenth century with an additional outer case to protect the watchcase.

pallet. The part of a clock or a watch movement that alternately gives impulse to the teeth of an escape wheel or locks them.

pendant. A stem fitted to a watchcase by which the watch can be hung from a ring, or bow, at the top end. In a repeating watch the mechanism is operated through a hollow stem.

pendulum. A swinging rod, or shaft, weighted at the lower end and used to regulate timekeeping in clocks.

pillar. The component of a clock or watch used to separate and secure the back plate and front plate of the movement.

pinion. The smaller revolving elements of a train, with teeth that are called leaves. They are placed between the wheels of a train in such a way that their leaves connect to the teeth of a wheel and are driven by the wheel. Usually a pinion has a low number of leaves, seldom more than fourteen or fifteen.

plinth. Typically a square or rectangular base for a column, pillar, or pilaster, but in horology, the base of a longcase clock.

rack-and-snail striking. A mechanism that controls the number of blows struck by the striking train by the position of a rack, or toothed segment of a wheel, governed by a stepped snail-like cam, replacing the earlier count-wheel system.

Rathaus. The German word for city hall. Thus, a *Rathaus* clock is a turret clock with a dial visible on an exterior wall or on a tower.

recoil. The backward motion of an escapement.

regulator. A stationary clock of great precision. It usually has a seconds-beating, temperature-compensated pendulum of the gridiron variety or some other type, such as the mercury-filled jar. Some have specially designed escapements as well.

repeater clock. Often called a pull-repeater clock, it strikes hours, quarter hours, or rarely minutes when a cord connected to the striking train is pulled. Most repeaters are quarter repeaters and are useful for telling the time at night, when it is difficult to read a dial.

repeating watch. A watch that will audibly sound the time by means of a mechanism operated by pushing a button or a plunger. There are various types of repeaters, including simple repeaters that sound the hours, quarter repeaters that sound hours on one note and nearest quarters on another, as well as five-minute and minute repeaters.

repoussé. In metalwork, designs done in relief that are produced by raising the metal from the back.

rod. The part of a pendulum between the suspension and the bob.

setup. The construction in a watch or spring-driven clock that allows the mainspring to retain a certain amount of its tension after the fusee has run down. The setup can be adjusted in various ways in order that a suitably regular portion of a coiled spring is selected for use.

spandrels. Ornamental reliefs used to decorate the space outside the chapter ring at the four corners of a dial plate.

stackfreed. A controlling device used to equalize the pulling power of the spring in a watch or clock. It consists of a flat spring that presses against a cam to provide greater opposition to the fully wound mainspring and lessens pressure as the spring unwinds. A more efficient mainspring equalizer was found in the fusee.

stopwork. A mechanism that limits the extent to which a spiral spring can be wound or allowed to run down.

strapwork. A variety of ornament consisting of narrow interlaced bands.

striking train. The series of toothed wheels and pinions that connects a source of power with a hammer that in seventeenth- and eighteenth-century clocks usually strikes a bell.

train. A sequence of wheels and pinions that transfer power from a falling weight or an unwinding spring to the controlling escapement and ultimately to the hands of a clock or a watch. The striking train differs from the going train in that it has no escapement and connects to a hammer and bell instead of to the hands. In this book, the great wheel and the escape wheel have been omitted from the count of the wheels in a train.

tympan. In an astrolabe, it is a circular plate engraved with a projection of terrestrial latitudes and longitudes that form the grid for a map of stars from the horizon to the zenith as seen from a given latitude on earth.

verge. The balance staff and pallets of a verge escapement.

verge escapement. A toothed contrate wheel that is the last wheel in the going train of a clock or a watch across which is placed an arbor, or balance staff, with two pallets or flags attached to it in such a way that when the wheel revolves, the teeth of the wheel alternately engage a pallet, stopping and releasing the energy of the going train in short measured intervals. It is the oldest practical form of escapement for a portable clock and can be used with balance wheels as well as with short pendulums.

winding square. The squared end of a shaft where a key is fitted in order to wind the spring of a clock or a watch or to raise the weight of a weight-driven clock.

Bibliography

Abeler 1977
Jürgen Abeler. *Meister der Uhrmacherkunst: Über 14000 Uhrmacher aus dem deutschen Sprachgebiet mit Lebens- oder Wirkungsdaten und dem Verzeichnis ihrer Werke*. Wuppertal, 1977.

Aghib and Leopold 1974
E. G. Aghib and J. H. Leopold. "More about the Elusive Fromanteel." *Antiquarian Horology* 8, no. 8 (Sept. 1974), pp. 890–94.

Alcouffe 2001
Daniel Alcouffe. *Les gemmes de la Couronne*. Exh. cat. Musée du Louvre. Paris, 2001.

Allix 1974
Charles Allix. *Carriage Clocks: Their History & Development*. Woodbridge, Suffolk, 1974.

Allix 1993
Charles Allix. "English Silent Pull and Pull Quarter Repeating Work." In Barder 1993, pp. 22–24. [Originally published in Charles Hobson, with Laurence Harvey and Charles Allix, *Hobson's Choice: English Bracket Clock Repeating Work; the Working Sketches Made over More Than Seventy Years*. Sevenoaks, Kent, 1982.]

Anderson Galleries 1926
English Long-Case & Bracket Clocks: Being a Collection Made by the Late Frank Garrett . . . London, England. Sale cat. Anderson Galleries, New York, Feb. 16, 1926.

Anderson Galleries 1931
The Collection of the Late David Belasco. Sale cat. American Art Association, Anderson Galleries, New York, Dec. 8–12, 1931.

***Annual Register . . . for the Year 1766* 1785**
The Annual Register; or, A View of the History, Politics and Literature for the Year 1766. 4th edition. London, 1785.

Antiquorum 1996
Ulysse Nardin, Jubilee & Important Collectors Watches, Wristwatches, Clocks and Horological Documents / Ulysse Nardin, jubilé & importantes montres, montres-bracelet de collection, pendules et documents d'horlogerie. Sale cat. Antiquorum, Geneva, Oct. 12–13, 1996.

Arizzoli 2013
Louise Arizzoli. "James Hazen Hyde and the Allegory of the Four Continents: A Research Collection for an *Amateur* Art Historian." *Journal of the History of Collections* 25, no. 2 (July 2013), pp. 277–86.

***Art Treasures Exhibition* 1955**
Art Treasures Exhibition. Exh. cat. Parke-Bernet Galleries. New York, 1955.

Artcurial 2012
Mobilier et objets d'art. Sale cat. Artcurial Briest, Poulain, F. Tajan, Paris, June 19, 2012.

Ashmole 1672
Elias Ashmole. *The Institution, Laws & Ceremonies of the Most Noble Order of the Garter*. London, 1672.

Augarde 1996
Jean-Dominique Augarde. *Les ouvriers du temps: La pendule à Paris de Louis XIV à Napoléon 1er / Ornamental Clocks and Clockmakers in Eighteenth Century Paris*. Geneva, 1996.

Avery 1927
C. Louise Avery. "A New Collection of Watches." *Bulletin of The Metropolitan Museum of Art* 27, no. 2 (Feb. 1927), pp. 46, 48–50.

Baarsen 2012
Reinier Baarsen. "A Unique Relationship: Charles Alexander of Lorraine and David Roentgen." In Koeppe 2012, pp. 25–29, 240–41.

Baillie 1929
G. H. Baillie. *Watches: Their History, Decoration and Mechanism*. London, 1929.

Baillie 1978
G. H. Baillie. *Clocks and Watches: An Historical Bibliography*. London, 1978. [Originally published in 1951.]

Ballot 1919
Marie-Juliette Ballot. "Charles Cressent: Sculpteur, ébéniste, collectionneur." *Archives de l'art français*, n.s., 10 (1919). [Repr., Paris, 1969.]

Ballu 1958
Nicole Ballu. "Influence de l'Extrême-Orient sur le style de Chantilly aux XVIIIe siècle." *Cahiers de la céramique et des arts du feu*, no. 11 (1958), pp. 100–112.

Barder 1993
Richard C. R. Barder. *The Georgian Bracket Clock, 1714–1830*. Woodbridge, Suffolk, 1993.

***Baroque Palaces of Rome* 1999**
Life and the Arts in the Baroque Palaces of Rome: Ambiente Barocco. Exh. cat. edited by Stefanie Walker and Frederick Hammond. Bard Graduate Center for Studies in the Decorative Arts. New York, 1999.

Bauer and Haupt 1976
Rotraud Bauer and Herbert Haupt, eds. "Das Kunstkammerinventar Kaiser Rudolfs II., 1607–1611." *Jahrbuch der Kunsthistorischen Sammlungen in Wien* 72 (1976).

Beard and Gilbert 1986
Geoffrey Beard and Christopher Gilbert, eds. *Dictionary of English Furniture Makers, 1660–1840*. Leeds, 1986.

Bedini 1956–57
Silvio A. Bedini. "Johann Philipp Treffler: Clockmaker of Augsburg." *Bulletin of the National Association of Watch and Clock Collectors, Inc.* 7, no. 6 (Dec. 1956), pp. 361–74; 7, no. 7 (Feb. 1957), pp. 415–27; 7, no. 8 (Apr. 1957), pp. 481–92; 7, no. 9 (June 1957), pp. 541–47.

Beeson 1967
C. F. C. Beeson. *Clockmaking in Oxfordshire, 1400–1850*. Oxford, 1967.

Beeson 1971
C. F. C. Beeson. *English Church Clocks, 1280–1850: History and Classification*. Antiquarian Horological Society, Monograph 5. London, 1971.

Beliaev 1969
E. A. Beliaev. *Arabs, Islam, and the Arab Caliphate in the Early Middle Ages*. Translated by Adolphe Gourevitch. London, 1969.

Bell 2004
Alan Bell. "Morrison, Alfred (1821–1897)." In *Oxford Dictionary of National Biography*, vol. 39, pp. 329–30. Oxford, 2004.

de Bellaigue 1974
Geoffrey de Bellaigue. *Furniture, Clocks, and Gilt Bronzes*. 2 vols. The James A. de Rothschild Collection at Waddesdon Manor. Fribourg, 1974.

Beringen 2012
John Beringen. *Horloges van Nederlandse uurwerkmakers, 1600–1800*. Schoonhoven, 2012.

Berliner and Egger 1981
Rudolf Berliner and Gerhart Egger. *Ornamentale Vorlageblätter des 15. bis 19. Jahrhunderts*. 3 vols. 2nd edition. Munich, 1981.

Berthoud 1786
Ferdinand Berthoud. *Essai sur l'horlogerie; dans lequel on traite de cet art, relativement à l'usage civil, à l'astronomie & à la navigation, en établissant des principes confirmés par l'expérience, dédié aux artistes & aux amateurs*. 2 vols. 2nd edition. Paris, 1786.

Betts 1993
Jonathan Betts. *John Harrison*. Illustrations by David Penney. Exh. cat. Old Royal Observatory. Greenwich, England, 1993.

Bimbenet-Privat 2000
Michèle Bimbenet-Privat. "Josias Belle: Orfèvre virtuose de Louis XIV." *Estampille / L'objet d'art*, no. 347 (May 2000), pp. 74–82, 87.

Bimbenet-Privat 2002
Michèle Bimbenet-Privat. *Les orfèvres et l'orfèvrerie de Paris au XVIIe siècle*. 2 vols. Paris, 2002.

Den Blaauwen 2000
Abraham L. den Blaauwen. *Meissen Porcelain in the Rijksmuseum*. Catalogues of the Decorative Arts in the Rijksmuseum, Amsterdam, 4. Zwolle and Amsterdam, 2000.

Black 2003
Jeremy Black. *Italy and the Grand Tour*. New Haven, 2003.

Bobinger 1966
Maximilian Bobinger. *Alt-Augsburger Kompassmacher: Sonnen- , Mond- und Sternuhren, astronomische und mathematische Geräte, Räderuhren*. Abhandlungen zur Geschichte der Stadt Augsburg 16. Augsburg, 1966.

Bobinger 1969
Maximilian Bobinger. *Kunstuhrmacher in Alt-Augsburg*. Abhandlungen zur Geschichte der Stadt Augsburg 18. Augsburg, 1969.

Boeckh 1982
Hans Boeckh. *Emailmalerei auf Genfer Taschenuhren von 17. bis zum beginnenden 19. Jahrhundert*. Freiburg im Briesgau, 1982.

Boeckh 2009
Hans Boeckh. "Sur les traces du peintre Sébastien Bourdon (1616–1671): À travers des émaux de son époque." *Sèvres*, no. 18 (2009), pp. 18–39.

Boeheim 1888
Wendelin Boeheim. "Urkunden und Regesten aus der K. K. Hofbibliothek." *Jahrbuch der Kunsthistorischen Sammlungen des Allerhöchsten Kaiserhauses* 7 (1888), pp. XCI–CCCXIII.

Bourdon 1703
Pierre Bourdon. *Livre second. Essais de gravûre. . . . Ou, l'On voit de beaux contours et listels d'ornemens traités dans le goût de l'art, utiles aux horlogeurs, orfévres, cizeleurs, graveurs et autres persones*. Paris, 1703.

***British Clockmaker's Heritage Exhibition* 1952**
British Clockmaker's Heritage Exhibition. Exh. cat. Science Museum. London, 1952.

Britten 1894
F. J. Britten. *Former Clock & Watchmakers and Their Work*. London, 1894.

Britten 1911
F. J. Britten. *Old Clocks and Watches & Their Makers.* 3rd edition. London, 1911.

Britten 1922
F. J. Britten. *Old Clocks and Watches & Their Makers.* 5th edition. London, 1922.

Britten 1978
F. J. Britten. *Britten's Watch & Clock Maker's Handbook: Dictionary and Guide.* 16th edition. Revised by Richard Good. New York, 1978.

Britten 1982
F. J. Britten. *Britten's Old Clocks and Watches and Their Makers.* 9th edition. Edited by G. H. Baillie, Courtenay Ilbert, and Cecil Clutton. Revised by Cecil Clutton. London, 1982.

Brusa 1978
Giuseppe Brusa. *L'arte dell'orologeria in Europa: Sette secoli di orologi meccanici.* Arte e tecnica. Busto Arsizio, Italy, 1978.

***Burghley Porcelains* 1986**
The Burghley Porcelains: An Exhibition from the Burghley House Collection and Based on the 1688 Inventory and 1690 Devonshire Schedule. Exh. cat. Japan Society, New York, and High Museum of Art, Atlanta. New York, 1986.

Burke 2006
Jill Burke. "Meaning and Crisis in the Early Sixteenth Century: Interpreting Leonardo's Lion." *Oxford Art Journal* 29, no. 1 (2006), pp. 79–91.

Buzard 2002
James Buzard. "The Grand Tour and After (1660–1840)." In *The Cambridge Companion to Travel Writing*, edited by Peter Hulme and Tim Youngs, pp. 37–52. Cambridge, 2002.

Byrne 1981
Janet S. Byrne. *Renaissance Ornament Prints and Drawings.* Exh. cat. The Metropolitan Museum of Art. New York, 1981.

de Caluwé 2008
Jean-Pierre de Caluwé. "Pour une reconnaissance de l'horlogerie 'Belge.'" *Bulletin de l'Association Nationale des Collectionneurs et Amateurs d'Horlogerie Ancienne et d'Art*, no. 113 (Autumn–Winter 2008), pp. 61–74.

Cardinal 1984a
Catherine Cardinal. "Biographie." In *Ferdinand Berthoud* 1984, pp. 19–55.

Cardinal 1984b
Catherine Cardinal. *Catalogue des montres du Musée du Louvre.* Vol. 1, *La collection Olivier.* Paris, 1984.

Cardinal 1989
Catherine Cardinal. *The Watch: From Its Origins to the XIXth Century.* Translated by Jacques Pages. Bristol, 1989.

Cardinal 1996
Catherine Cardinal. "Ferdinand Berthoud and Pierre Le Roy: Judgement in the Twentieth Century of a Quarrel Dating from the Eighteenth Century." In *The Quest for Longitude: The Proceedings of the Longitude Symposium, Harvard University, Cambridge, Massachusetts, November 4–6, 1993*, edited by William J. H. Andrewes, pp. 282–92. Cambridge, Mass., 1996.

Cardinal 2000
Catherine Cardinal. *Les montres et horloges de table du Musée du Louvre.* Vol. 2. Paris, 2000.

Cardinal and Piguet 2002
Catherine Cardinal and Jean-Michel Piguet. *Catalogue of Selected Pieces.* Musée International d'Horlogerie. La Chaux-de-Fonds, Switzerland, 2002.

R. F. Carrington and R. W. Carrington 1978
R. F. Carrington and R. W. Carrington. "Pierre Frederic Ingold and the British Watch and Clock-making Company." *Antiquarian Horology* 10, no. 6 (Spring 1978), pp. 698–714.

Cavallo 1993
Adolfo Salvatore Cavallo. *Medieval Tapestries in The Metropolitan Museum of Art.* New York, 1993.

Cescinsky and M. R. Webster 1969
Herbert Cescinsky and Malcolm R. Webster. *English Domestic Clocks.* London, 1969. [Originally published in 1913.]

Chandler 1996
Bruce Chandler. "Longitude in the Context of Mathematics." In *The Quest for Longitude: The Proceedings of the Longitude Symposium, Harvard University, Cambridge, Massachusetts, November 4–6, 1993*, edited by William J. H. Andrewes, pp. 34–42. Cambridge, Mass., 1996.

Chandler and Vincent 1980
Bruce Chandler and Clare Vincent. "To Finance a Clock: An Example of Patronage in the 16th Century." In *Clockwork Universe* 1980, pp. 103–13.

Chapiro 1980
Adolphe Chapiro. "Evolution des calibres de montres à ponts de 1770 (Lépine) à 1850." *Bulletin de l'Association Nationale des Collectionneurs et Amateurs d'Horlogerie Ancienne*, no. 28 (Summer 1980), pp. 45–54.

Chapiro 1988
Adolphe Chapiro. *Jean-Antoine Lépine: Horloger (1720–1814). Histoire du développement de l'horlogerie en France, de 1760 à l'Empire.* Paris, 1988.

Chapiro 1991
Adolphe Chapiro. *La montre française du XVIe siècle jusqu'à 1900.* Paris, 1991.

Chapiro 2001
Adolphe Chapiro. "Les montres 'Turques' du 17e siècle." *Bulletin de l'Association Nationale des Collectionneurs et Amateurs d'Horlogerie Ancienne et d'Art*, no. 92 (Autumn–Winter 2001), pp. 31–42.

Chapiro 2006
Adolphe Chapiro. "Influence de la technique de construction des mouvements sur le style des montres de la premiere moitié du XIXe siècle." *Bulletin de l'Association Nationale des Collectionneurs et Amateurs d'Horlogerie Ancienne et d'Art*, no. 107 (Autumn–Winter 2006), pp. 5–18.

Chapuis 1919
Alfred Chapuis. *Relations de l'horlogerie suisse avec la Chine: La montre "chinoise."* With Gustave Loup. Introduction by Léopold de Saussure. Neuchâtel, 1919.

Chapuis and Droz 1958
Alfred Chapuis and Edmond Droz. *Automata: A Historical and Technological Study.* Translated by Alec Reid. New York, 1958.

Christie's 1908
Catalogue of Porcelain & Faience, Objects of Art and Vertu. . . . Sale cat. Christie, Manson & Woods, London, Mar. 27, 1908.

Christie's 1938
Catalogue of Porcelain and Objects of Art, Decorative Furniture, Eastern Rugs and Carpets. Sale cat. Christie, Manson & Woods, London, Dec. 8, 1938.

Christie's 1966
Catalogue of Fine Continental Porcelain and Faience. Sale cat. Christie, Manson & Woods, London, Mar. 28, 1966.

Christie's 1971
Fine English Furniture, English Clocks and Objects of Art, Tapestries, Eastern Rugs and Carpets. Sale cat. Christie, Manson & Woods, London, Dec. 9, 1971.

Christie's 1972
Fine English Furniture, Important Clocks, Eastern Rugs and Carpets. Sale cat. Christie, Manson & Woods, London, Mar. 16, 1972.

Christie's 2009
Collection Yves Saint Laurent et Pierre Bergé. 5 vols. Sale cat. Christie's, Paris, Feb. 23–25, 2009.

Christie's 2015
The Abbott Guggenheim Collection: A New York Kunstkammer. Sale cat. Christie's, New York, Jan. 27, 2015.

***Christina* 1966**
Christina, drottning av Sverige: En europeisk kultur-personlighet. Exh. cat. Nationalmuseum. Stockholm, 1966.

Cipolla 1967
Carlo M. Cipolla. *Clocks and Culture, 1300–1700.* New York, 1967.

Clairaut 1752
Alexis-Claude Clairaut. *Théorie de la lune, déduite du seul principe de l'attraction réciproquement proportionnelle aux quarrés des distances.* Saint Petersburg, 1752.

Clairaut 1760
Alexis-Claude Clairaut. *Théorie du mouvement des comètes, dans laquelle on a égard aux altérations que leurs orbites éprouvent par l'action des planètes; avec l'application de cette théorie à la comète qui a été observée dans les années 1531, 1607, 1682 & 1759.* Paris, 1760.

Clarke 2009
Stephen Clarke. "*A Description of . . . Strawberry Hill.*" In *Horace Walpole's Strawberry Hill*, edited by Michael Snodin, with Cynthia Roman, pp. 18–19. Exh. cat. Yale Center for British Art, New Haven, and Victoria and Albert Museum, London. New Haven, 2009.

Clayton 1997
Timothy Clayton. *The English Print, 1688–1802.* New Haven, 1997.

Clifton 1995
Gloria C. Clifton. *Directory of British Scientific Instrument Makers, 1550–1851.* London, 1995.

***Clocks and Watches of the Qing Dynasty* 2002**
Clocks and Watches of the Qing Dynasty: From the Collection in the Forbidden City. With texts by Lang Xiuhua and Qin Xiaopei. [In English and Chinese.] Beijing, 2002.

***Clockwork Universe* 1980**
The Clockwork Universe: German Clocks and Automata, 1550–1650. Exh. cat. edited by Klaus Maurice and Otto Mayr. Bayerisches Nationalmuseum, Munich, and National Museum of History and Technology, Smithsonian Institution, Washington, D.C. Washington, D.C., and New York, 1980. [German ed., *Die Welt als Uhr: Deutsche Uhren und Automaten, 1550–1650.* Munich, 1980.]

Clouzot 1928
Henri Clouzot. *La miniature sur émail en France.* Paris, [1928].

Clutton and Daniels 1979
Cecil Clutton and George Daniels. *Watches: A Complete History of the Technical and Decorative Development of the Watch.* Rev. edition. London, 1979.

***Collection Double* 1881**
Catalogue des objets d'art, tableaux anciens, livres, composant la collection Double. Sale cat. Rue Louis-le-Grand, 9, Paris, May 30–June 1, 1881.

***Collection of Watches* 1907**
Collection of Watches Loaned to The Metropolitan Museum of Art of the City of New York by Mrs. George A. Hearn. Exh. cat. The Metropolitan Museum of Art. New York, 1907.

"Collection of Watches" 1914
"Collection of Watches." *Horological Journal* 56, no. 670 (June 1914), p. 161.

***Collection Spitzer* 1891–93**
La collection Spitzer: Antiquité, Moyen-Âge, Renaissance. 6 vols. Paris, 1891–93.

Cologni 2005
Franco Cologni. "The Chronology of Vacheron Constantin." In *The Quarter Millennium of Vacheron Constantin, 1755–2005 / Le quart de millénaire de Vacheron Constantin, 1755–2005*, pp. XXVIII–XXX. Sale cat. Antiquorum, Geneva, Apr. 3, 2005.

de Conihout et al. 2001
Isabelle de Conihout, Julia Fritsch, Jan Jaap L. Haspels, J. H. Leopold, Eric Rieth, and Nadja Zweigler. *Ships of Curiosity: Three Renaissance Automata.* Exh. cat. Musée National de la Renaissance, Ecouen. Paris, 2001.

Courajod 1965
Louis Courajod. *Livre-journal de Lazare Duvaux: Marchand-bijoutier ordinaire du Roy, 1748–1758.* 2 vols. Repr., Paris, 1965. [Originally published in 1873.]

Culme 1987
John Culme. *The Directory of Gold & Silversmiths: Jewellers & Allied Traders, 1838–1914; from the London Assay Office Registers.* 2 vols. Woodbridge, Suffolk, 1987.

Cunningham 1559
William Cunningham. *The Cosmographical Glasse, Conteinyng the Pleasant Principles of Cosmographie, Geographie, Hydrographie, or Nauigation.* London, 1559.

T. C. Cuss 2009
Terence Camerer Cuss. *The English Watch, 1585–1970: A Unique Alliance of Art, Design and Inventive Genius.* Woodbridge, Suffolk, 2009.

T. P. C. Cuss 1967
Theodore Patrick Camerer Cuss. *The Country Life Book of Watches.* London, 1967.

Dacos 1969
Nicole Dacos. *La découverte de la Domus Aurea et la formation des grotesques à la Renaissance.* Studies of the Warburg Institute 31. London, 1969.

Dakers 2010
Caroline Dakers. "Furniture and Interior Decoration for James and Alfred Morrison." *Furniture History* 46 (2010), pp. 189–216.

Dakers 2011
Caroline Dakers. *A Genius for Money: Business, Art and the Morrisons.* New Haven, 2011.

Daniels 1975
George Daniels. *The Art of Breguet.* London, 1975.

Daston and Park 1998
Lorraine Daston and Katharine Park. *Wonders and the Order of Nature, 1150–1750.* New York, 1998.

Dauterman, Parker, and Standen 1964
Carl Christian Dauterman, James Parker, and Edith Appleton Standen. *Decorative Art from the Samuel H. Kress Collection at The Metropolitan Museum of Art: The Tapestry Room from Croome Court, Furniture, Textiles, Sèvres Porcelains, and Other Objects.* London, 1964.

C. Davis 1884
Charles Davis, comp. *A Description of the Works of Art, Forming the Collection of Alfred de Rothschild.* 2 vols. London, 1884.

F. Davis 1933
Frank Davis. "An Exhibition of Tompion Clocks." *Illustrated London News*, Nov. 18, 1933, p. 822.

Dawson 1987
Percy G. Dawson. "Long Case Clocks of a Distinctive Design." *Antiquarian Horology* 16, no. 5 (Mar. 1987), pp. 479–81.

***Decorative Furnishings* 2014**
Decorative Furnishings and Objets d'Art in the Louvre, from Louis XIV to Marie-Antoinette. Edited by Jannic Durand, Michèle Bimbenet-Privat, and Frédéric Dassas. Paris, 2014.

Dee 1988
Elaine Evans Dee. "Printed Sources for the William and Mary Style." In *Courts and Colonies: The William and Mary Style in Holland, England, and America*, pp. 80–85. Exh. cat. Cooper-Hewitt Museum, New York, and Carnegie Museum of Art, Pittsburgh. New York, 1988.

Dell 1967
Theodore Dell. "The Gilt-Bronze Cartel Clocks of Charles Cressent." *Burlington Magazine* 109 (Apr. 1967), pp. 210–15, 217.

Derham 1696
William Derham. *The Artificial Clock-Maker: A Treatise of Watch, and Clock-Work.* London, 1696.

"Description of Two Curious Clocks" 1766
"A Description of Two Curious Clocks." *Gentleman's Magazine* 36 (Dec. 1766), p. 586.

***Descriptive Inventory . . . of Mechanism and Jewellery* 1773**
A Descriptive Inventory of the Several Exquisite and Magnificent Pieces of Mechanism and Jewellery . . . for Enabling Mr. James Cox, of the City of London, Jeweller, to Dispose of His Museum by Way of Lottery. London, 1773.

Develle 1913
Edmond Develle. *Les horlogers blésois au XVIe et au XVIIe siècle.* Blois, 1913.

Diderot and d'Alembert 1765
Denis Diderot and Jean-La Rond d'Alembert. *Encyclopédie; ou, Dictionnaire raisonné des sciences, des arts et des métiers.* Vol. 8. Neuchâtel, 1765.

Droz 1971
Edmond Droz. "Les automates." In François Faessler, Samuel Guye, and Edmond Droz, *Pierre Jaquet-Droz et son temps*, pp. 73–92. La Chaux-de-Fonds, Switzerland, 1971.

Duncan 1994
Alastair Duncan. *The Paris Salons, 1895–1914.* Vols. 1 and 2, *Jewellery: The Designers.* Woodbridge, Suffolk, 1994.

Edey 1982
Winthrop Kellogg Edey. *French Clocks in North American Collections: The Frick Collection.* Exh. cat. Frick Collection. New York, 1982.

Edgcumbe 2000
Richard Edgcumbe. *The Art of the Gold Chaser in Eighteenth-Century London.* Oxford, 2000.

Ellicott 1751–52
John Ellicott. "A Description of Two Methods, by Which the Irregularity of the Motion of a Clock, Arising from the Influence of Heat and Cold upon the Rod of the Pendulum, May Be Prevented." *Philosophical Transactions* (Royal Society, London) 47 (1751–52; pub. 1753), pp. 479–94.

***Encyclopedia of Astronomers* 2014**
Biographical Encyclopedia of Astronomers. Edited by Thomas A. Hockey. 2nd edition. New York, 2014.

***English Pendulum Clock* 1969**
The First Twelve Years of the English Pendulum Clock; or, The Fromanteel Family and Their Contemporaries, 1658–1670. Exh. cat. Ronald A. Lee. [London], 1969.

Erlande-Brandenburg 1980
Alain Erlande-Brandenburg. "Paris: La restauration de Notre-Dame." In *Viollet-le-Duc* 1980, pp. 72–81.

D. M. W. Evans 1976
David M. W. Evans. "Liverpool Watchmakers." [Letter to the Editor.] *Antiquarian Horology* 9, no. 6 (Mar. 1976), p. 705.

J. Evans 1998
James Evans. *The History & Practice of Ancient Astronomy.* New York, 1998.

J. L. Evans 1984
Jeremy L. Evans. "The Numbering of Tompion's Watches Series and System." *Antiquarian Horology* 14, no. 6 (June 1984), pp. 585–97.

J. L. Evans 2004
Jeremy L. Evans. "Graham, George (*c.* 1673–1751)." In *Oxford Dictionary of National Biography*, vol. 23, pp. 177–82. Oxford, 2004.

J. L. Evans 2006
Jeremy L. Evans. *Thomas Tompion at the Dial and Three Crowns, with a Concise Check List of the Clocks, Watches and Instruments from His Workshops.* Ticehurst, East Sussex, 2006.

J. L. Evans, Carter, and Wright 2013
Jeremy L. Evans, Jonathan Carter, and Ben Wright. *Thomas Tompion, 300 Years: A Celebration of the Life and Work of Thomas Tompion.* Stroud, Gloucestershire, 2013.

D. Fabian 1984
Dietrich Fabian. *Kinzing und Roentgen, Uhren aus Neuwied: Uhren, Uhrenmöbel, Musikinstrumente, Spielwerk. Leben und Werk der Uhrmacherfamilien Kinzing und der Kunstschreiner Abraham und David Roentgen.* Bad Neustadt, 1984.

L. Fabian 1977
Larry L. Fabian. "Could It Have Been Wren?" *Antiquarian Horology* 10, no. 5 (Winter 1977), pp. 550–70.

Fairholt and Wright 1857
Frederick W. Fairholt and Thomas Wright. *Miscellanea Graphica: Representations of Ancient, Medieval, and Renaissance Remains in the Possession of Lord Londesborough.* London, 1857.

Falize 1878
Lucien Falize. "Exposition Universelle: Les industries d'art au Champ de Mars. I. Orfèvrerie et bijouterie." *Gazette des beaux-arts*, 2nd ser., 18, no. 3 (Sept. 1878), pp. 217–55.

Falize 1889–90
Lucien Falize. "Exposition Universelle de 1889: Orfèvrerie et bijouterie." *Revue des arts décoratifs* 10 (1889–90), pp. 1–12.

***Ferdinand Berthoud* 1984**
Ferdinand Berthoud, 1727–1807: Horloger Mécanicien du Roi et de la Marine. Exh. cat. Musée International d'Horlogerie. La Chaux-de-Fonds, Switzerland, 1984.

Finch 2004
Adrian Finch. "Newsam, Bartholomew (*c.* 1530–1587)." In *Oxford Dictionary of National Biography*, vol. 40, pp. 677–78. Oxford, 2004.

Fleming 1965
E. McClung Fleming. "The American Image as Indian Princess, 1765–1783." *Winterthur Portfolio* 2 (1965), pp. 65–81.

Foerster 1934
C. F. Foerster. "Romandon, Gedeon." In *Allgemeines Lexikon der bildenden Künstler*, edited by Ulrich Thieme and Felix Becker, vol. 28, pp. 543–44. Leipzig, 1934.

Foulkes 1960
R. K. Foulkes. "The Ellicotts." *Antiquarian Horology* 3, no. 4 (Sept. 1960), pp. 102–10.

Fourrier 2000
Thibaud Fourrier. *Dictionnaire des horlogers de Blois.* Mosnes, 2000.

Fourrier 2001
Thibaud Fourrier. *Les maîtres horlogers de Blois.* Vol. 1, *Les origines.* Mosnes, 2001.

Fourrier 2004
Thibaud Fourrier. *Les maîtres horlogers de Blois.* Vol. 2, *Le XVIIe siècle: L'âge d'or de l'horlogerie blésoise.* Mosnes, 2004.

Fraiture 2002
Eddy Fraiture. *Uurwerkmakers en uurwerknijverheid in Vlaanderen.* Leuven, 2002.

Fraiture 2009
Eddy Fraiture. *Belgische uurwerken en hun makers, A–Z / Horloges et horlogers belges, A–Z.* Leuven, 2009.

Fraiture and Van Rompay 2011
Eddy Fraiture and Paul van Rompay. "Clock and Watchmaking in Belgium, 1300–1830." *Antiquarian Horology* 33, no. 1 (Sept. 2011), pp. 27–45.

Freeman's 1944
The Valuable Furnishings and Objects of Art at "Lynnewood Hall," the Residence of the Late Joseph E. Widener. Sale cat. Samuel T. Freeman & Co., Philadelphia, June 20–24, 1944.

***Frühes Meissener Porzellen* 1997**
Frühes Meissener Porzellen: Kostbarkeiten aus deutschen Privatsammlungen. Exh. cat. Hetjens-Museum, Deutsches Keramikmuseum, Düsseldorf, and Staatliche Kunstsammlungen Dresden. Munich, 1997.

Fuhring 2004
Peter Fuhring. *Ornament Prints in the Rijksmuseum, II: The Seventeenth Century.* 3 vols. Studies in Prints and Printmaking 5. Amsterdam and Rotterdam, 2004.

Fuhring and Bimbenet-Privat 2002
Peter Fuhring and Michèle Bimbenet-Privat. "Le style 'Cosses de pois': L'orfèvrerie et la gravure à Paris sous Louis XIII." *Gazette des beaux-arts*, 6th ser., 139 (Jan. 2002), pp. 1–224.

Furcy-Raynaud 1925–26
Marc Furcy-Raynaud, ed. "Inventaire des sculptures exécutées au XVIIIe siècle pour la Direction des Bâtiments du Roi." 2 vols. *Archives de l'art français*, n.s., 14 (1925–26; pub. 1927).

Galerie Georges Petit 1886
Catalogue des objets d'art et de haute curiosité . . . collection de M. Ch. Stein. Sale cat. Galerie Georges Petit, Paris, May 10–14, 1886.

Galerie Georges Petit 1891
Catalogue des objets d'art composant la précieuse et importante collection de M. L. de M. . . . [Georges-Louis-Claude Lebeuf, comte de Montgermont]. Sale cat. Galerie Georges Petit, Paris, May 25–30, 1891.

Galerie Georges Petit 1910
Galerie Georges Petit. *Ancienne collection Charles Mannheim: Objets d'art.* Paris, 1910.

Garai 2007
Luca Garai. *Gli automi di Leonardo / Leonardo's Automata*. Bologna, 2007.
Gatty 1977
Richard Gatty. *Portrait of a Merchant Prince: James Morrison, 1789–1857*. Northallerton, North Yorkshire, 1977.
Gemmett 2003
Robert J. Gemmett. *Beckford's Fonthill: The Rise of a Romantic Icon*. Norwich, 2003.
Gere 1998–99
Charlotte Gere. "European Decorative Arts at the World's Fairs, 1850–1900." *The Metropolitan Museum of Art Bulletin*, n.s., 56, no. 3 (Winter 1998–99).
Gere and Rudoe 2010
Charlotte Gere and Judy Rudoe. *Jewellery in the Age of Queen Victoria: A Mirror to the World*. London, 2010.
Gibertini 1964
Dante Gibertini. "Liste des horlogers genevois du XVIe au milieu du XIXe siècle." *Genava*, n.s., 12 (1964), pp. 217–46.
Gillispie 1983
Charles Coulston Gillispie. "The Invention of Aviation." In *The Balloon: A Bicentennial Exhibition*, pp. 20–33. Exh. cat. University Art Museum, University of Minnesota, Minneapolis; David and Alfred Smart Gallery, University of Chicago; and Albuquerque Museum, Albuquerque, N. Mex. Minneapolis, 1983.
Giraldi 1541
Lilio Gregorio Giraldi. *De Annis et Mensibus, Caeterisque Temporum Partibus*. Basel, 1541.
Girod 1975
François Girod. "Un précurseur: Frédéric Japy (1749–1812)." *Bulletin de l'Association Nationale des Collectionneurs et Amateurs d'Horlogerie Ancienne*, no. 14 (May 1975), pp. 32–48.
Glanville 1990
Philippa Glanville. *Silver in Tudor and Early Stuart England: A Social History and Catalogue of the National Collection, 1480–1660*. Victoria and Albert Museum. London, 1990.
Gobiet 1984
Ronald Gobiet. *Der Briefwechsel zwischen Philipp Hainhofer und Herzog August d. J. von Braunschweig-Lüneburg*. Munich, 1984.
***Gold, Jasper and Carnelian* 2012**
Gold, Jasper and Carnelian: Johann Christian Neuber at the Saxon Court. Exh. cat. edited by Alexis Kugel. Grünes Gewölbe, Dresden, and Frick Collection, New York. London, 2012.
Gould 1960
Rupert T. Gould. *The Marine Chronometer: Its History and Development*. Foreword by Frank W. Dyson. Repr., London, 1960. [Originally published in 1923.]
Graham 1726–27
George Graham. "A Contrivance to Avoid the Irregularities in a Clock's Motion, Occasion'd by the Action of Heat and Cold upon the Rod of the Pendulum." *Philosophical Transactions* (Royal Society, London) 34 (1726–27; pub. 1728), pp. 40–44.
Grandjean et al. 1975
Serge Grandjean, Kirsten Aschengreen Piacenti, Charles Truman, and Anthony Blunt. *Gold Boxes and Miniatures of the Eighteenth Century*. The James A. de Rothschild Collection at Waddesdon Manor. Fribourg, 1975.
Grieb 2007
Manfred H. Grieb, ed. *Nürnberger Künstlerlexikon: Bildende Künstler, Kunsthandwerker, Gelehrte, Sammler, Kulturschaffende und Mäzene vom 12. bis zur Mitte des 20. Jahrhunderts*. 4 vols. Munich, 2007.
Van Groesen 2008
Michiel van Groesen. *The Representations of the Overseas World in the De Bry Collection of Voyages (1590–1634)*. Library of the Written Word, Handpress World 2. Leiden, 2008.
Groiss 1980
Eva Groiss. "The Augsburg Clockmakers' Craft." In *Clockwork Universe* 1980, pp. 57–86.
Guan Xue Ling 2004
Guan Xue Ling. "A fábrica de relógios do Palácio Qing / Qing Palace Clock-Making Factory." In *Moments of Eternity* 2004, pp. 240–41.
Guicciardini 1581
Lodovico Guicciardini. *Descrittione . . . di tutti i Paesi Bassi, altrimenti detti Germania Inferiore*. Antwerp, 1581.
Guiffrey 1873
J. J. Guiffrey. "Logements d'artistes au Louvre." *Nouvelles archives de l'art français* 2 (1873), pp. 1–221.
Hackenbroch 1958
Yvonne Hackenbroch. *English Furniture, with Some Furniture of Other Countries in the Irwin Untermyer Collection*. The Metropolitan Museum of Art, New York. Cambridge, Mass., 1958.
Hall 1951
A. Rupert Hall. "Robert Hooke and Horology." *Notes and Records of the Royal Society of London* 8, no. 2 (Apr. 1951), pp. 167–77.
Hall 1978
A. Rupert Hall. "Horology and Criticism: Robert Hooke." In *Science and History: Studies in Honor of Edward Rosen*, pp. 261–81. Studia Copernicana 16. Institute for the History of Science, Education, and Technology, Polish Academy of Sciences. Wrocław, 1978.
Hamburger Kunsthalle 1995
Hamburger Kunsthalle. *Hamburg Kunsthalle*. Munich, 1995.
Harcourt-Smith 1933
Simon Harcourt-Smith. *A Catalogue of Various Clocks, Watches, Automata, and Other Miscellaneous Objects of European Workmanship Dating from the XVIIIth and the Early XIXth Centuries, in the Palace Museum and the Wu Ying Tien, Peiping*. [Beijing], 1933.
Harrison 1911
Robert William Frederick Harrison. "Royal Society, The." In *Encyclopaedia Britannica*, 11th edition, vol. 23, pp. 791–93. New York, 1911.
Harrold 1984
Michael C. Harrold. *American Watchmaking: A Technical History of the American Watch Industry, 1850–1930*. National Association of Watch and Clock Collectors Bulletin Supplement 14. Columbia, Pa., 1984.
Haspels 1987
Jan Jaap L. Haspels. *Automatic Musical Instruments, Their Mechanics and Their Music, 1580–1820*. N.p., 1987.
Haspels 1994
Jan Jaap L. Haspels. *Musical Automata: Catalogue of Automatic Musical Instruments in the National Museum "From Musical Clock to Street Organ."* Nationaal Museum van Speelklok tot Pierement. Utrecht, 1994.
Hayard 2004
Michel Hayard. *Chefs-d'oeuvre de l'horlogerie ancienne: Collection du Musée Paul-Dupuy de Toulouse*. Paris and Toulouse, 2004.
Hayward 1959
John F. Hayward. *Huguenot Silver in England, 1688–1727*. Faber Monographs on Silver. London, 1959.
Hayward 1969
John F. Hayward. *English Watches*. 2nd edition. Victoria and Albert Museum. London, 1969.
Hayward 1975
John F. Hayward. "Four Carved Wood Models for a Clock-Case." *Anzeiger des Germanischen Nationalmuseum*, 1975, pp. 65–71.
***Hearst Collection* 1941**
Art Objects and Furnishings from the William Randolph Hearst Collection: Catalogue Raisonné Comprising Illustrations of Representative Works, Together with Comprehensive Descriptions of Books, Autographs and Manuscripts and Complete Index. Dealer's cat. Hammer Galleries. New York, 1941.
Hein 2009
Jørgen Hein. *The Treasure Collection at Rosenborg Castle: The Inventories of 1696 and 1718, Royal Heritage and Collecting in Denmark—Norway, 1500–1900*. 3 vols. Copenhagen, 2009.
Hellman and Swerdlow 1978
C. Doris Hellman and Noel M. Swerdlow. "Peurbach (or Peuerbach), Georg." In *Dictionary of Scientific Biography*, edited by Charles Coulston Gillispie, vol. 15, suppl. 1, pp. 473–79. New York, 1978.
Heuer and Maurice 1988
Peter Heuer and Klaus Maurice. *Europäische Pendeluhren: Dekorative Instrumente und Zeitmessung*. Munich, 1988.
Hillairet 1954
Jacques Hillairet. *Connaissance du vieux Paris*. Vol. 2, *Rive Gauche & les îles*. Paris, 1954.
Himmelheber 1980
Georg Himmelheber. "The Clock and Its Base." In *Clockwork Universe* 1980, pp. 121–24.
***Hoe laat was het?* 1956**
Hoe laat was het? Het Nederlands uurwerk. Exh. cat. Museum Willet-Holthuysen. Amsterdam, 1956.
Hoke 1990
Donald Robert Hoke. *Ingenious Yankees: The Rise of the American System of Manufactures in the Private Sector*. New York, 1990.
Hoke 1991
Donald Robert Hoke. *The Time Museum Historical Catalogue of American Pocket Watches*. Rockford, Ill., 1991.
Hollstein, *Dutch and Flemish*, 1949–2010
F. W. H. Hollstein et al. *Dutch & Flemish Etchings, Engravings and Woodcuts, 1450–1700*. 72 vols. Amsterdam, Rotterdam, and Ouderkerk aan den IJssel, 1949–2010.
Hollstein, *German*, 1954–2014
F. W. H. Hollstein et al. *German Engravings, Etchings and Woodcuts, ca. 1400–1700*. 82 vols. Amsterdam, Rotterdam, Blaricum, and Ouderkerk aan den IJssel, 1954–2014.
Hooke 1968
Robert Hooke. *The Diary of Robert Hooke, 1672–1680*. Edited by Henry W. Robinson and Walter Adams. Repr., London, 1968. [Originally published in 1935.]
Hope 1913
William Henry St. John Hope. *Windsor Castle: An Architectural History, Collected and Written by Command of Their Majesties Queen Victoria, King Edward VII & King George V*. 2 vols. London, 1913.
Hôtel Drouot 1858
Catalogue des objets d'art et des curiosités composant la collection de feu M. Daugny. Sale cat. Hôtel Drouot, Paris, Mar. 8–11, 1858.
Hôtel Drouot 1981
Horlogerie ancienne: Livres et documents. . . . Sale cat. Nouveau Drouot, Paris, Nov. 23, 1981.
Howse 1970–71
Derek Howse. "The Tompion Clocks at Greenwich and the Dead-Beat Escapement." *Antiquarian Horology* 7, no. 1 (Dec. 1970), pp. 18–34 (pt. 1, "1675–1678"); 7, no. 2 (Mar. 1971), pp. 114–33 (pt. 2, "1678–1971"), with an appendix, "Technical Descriptions," by Beresford Hutchinson.
Howse 1980
Derek Howse. *Greenwich Time and the Discovery of the Longitude*. Oxford, 1980.
Howse and Finch 1976
Derek Howse and Valerie Finch. "John Flamsteed and the Balance Spring." With an addendum by J. H. Leopold. *Antiquarian Horology* 9, no. 6 (Mar. 1976), pp. 664–73.
Howse and Sanderson 1973
Derek Howse and Michael Sanderson. *The Sea Chart: An Historical Survey Based on the Collections in the National Maritime Museum*. New York, 1973.
Huber and Banbery 1982
Martin Huber and Alan Banbery. *Patek Philippe, Genève*. Zurich, 1982.
Hughes 1994
Peter Hughes. *French Eighteenth-Century Clocks and Barometers in the Wallace Collection*. London, 1994.
Hughes 1996
Peter Hughes. *The Wallace Collection: Catalogue of Furniture*. 3 vols. London, 1996.

Hutchinson 2011
Robin Hutchinson. "Meeting on 2 March 2011." *Antiquarian Horology* 32, no. 6 (June 2011), pp. 870–71.
Huygens (Christiaan) 1658
Christiaan Huygens. *Christiani Hugenii à Zulichem, Const. F. Horologium*. The Hague, 1658.
Huygens (Christiaan) 1675
Christiaan Huygens. "Extrait d'une lettre de M[r]. Hugens." *Le journal des sçavans*, Feb. 25, 1675, pp. 68–70.
Huygens (Christiaan) 1889
Christiaan Huygens. *Oeuvres complètes de Christiaan Huygens*. Vol. 2, *Correspondance, 1657–1659*. Edited by the Société Hollandaise des Sciences. The Hague, 1889.
Huygens (Constantijn) 1881
Constantijn Huygens. *Journaal van Constantijn Huygens, den zoon, gedurende de veldtochten der jaren 1673, 1675, 1676, 1677 en 1678*. Utrecht, 1881.
Impey 1990
Oliver Impey. "Japanese Export Porcelain." In John Ayers, Oliver Impey, and J. V. G. Mallet, *Porcelain for Palaces: The Fashion for Japan in Europe, 1650–1750*, pp. 25–34. Exh. cat. British Museum. London, 1990.
Inwood 2002
Stephen Inwood. *The Man Who Knew Too Much: The Strange and Inventive Life of Robert Hooke, 1635–1703*. London, 2002.
Irmscher 1997
Günter Irmscher. *Der Breisgauer Bergkristallschliff der frühen Neuzeit: "Natur und Kunst beisamen haben."* Exh. cat. Augustinermuseum, Freiburg im Breisgau. Munich, 1997.
Israel 1995
Jonathan Israel. *The Dutch Republic: Its Rise, Greatness, and Fall, 1477–1806*. Oxford History of Early Modern Europe. Oxford, 1995.
Jagger 1983
Cedric Jagger. *Royal Clocks: The British Monarchy and Its Timekeepers, 1300–1900*. London, 1983.
Jagger 1988
Cedric Jagger. *The Artistry of the English Watch*. Newton Abbot, Devon, 1988.
Jantz 1976
Harold Jantz. "Images of America in the German Renaissance." In *First Images of America: The Impact of the New World on the Old*, edited by Fredi Chiappelli, vol. 1, pp. 91–106. Berkeley, Calif., 1976.
Jaquet 1938
Eugène Jaquet. "Horlogers genevois du XVIIme siècle." *Bulletin de l'Institut National Genevois* 51, no. 2 (1938), pp. 1–51.
Jaquet 1948a
Eugène Jaquet. "La généalogie de la famille Penard au XVIIe siècle." *Revue internationale de l'horlogerie*, Nov. 15, 1948, unpag.
Jaquet 1948b
Eugène Jaquet. "Horlogers genevois à Constantinople au XVIIe siècle." *Journal suisse d'horlogerie et de bijouterie*, 1948, nos. 5–6 (May–June), pp. 241–44.
Jaquet 1948c
Eugène Jaquet. "Travaux d'orfèvres au XVIIe siècle: Les montres 'tête de mort.' / Het werk van zilversmeden in de XVIIe eeuw: De doodskophorloges." *Belgica: Revue belge de la bijouterie, joaillerie, orfèvrerie, horlogerie*, Dec. 1948, pp. 565–72.
Jaquet 1949
Eugène Jaquet. "Les Bobinet à Genève." *Revue internationale de l'horlogerie*, Jan. 1, 1949, unpag.
Jaquet and Chapuis 1970
Eugène Jaquet and Alfred Chapuis. *Technique and History of the Swiss Watch*. [Rev. edition.] London, 1970.
Jardine 2008
Lisa Jardine. *Going Dutch: How England Plundered Holland's Glory*. New York, 2008.
al-Jazarī 1974
Ibn al-Razzāz al-Jazarī. *The Book of Knowledge of Ingenious Mechanical Devices*. Translated and edited by Donald R. Hill. Dordrecht, 1974.
Jean-Richard 1978
Pierrette Jean-Richard. *L'oeuvre gravé de François Boucher dans la collection Edmond de Rothschild*. Cabinet des Dessins, Musée du Louvre. Paris, 1978.
Jones 1912
E. Alfred Jones. *A Catalogue of the Objects in Gold & Silver and the Limoges Enamels in the Collection of the Baroness James de Rothschild*. London, 1912.
Kisluk-Grosheide 2002
Daniëlle O. Kisluk-Grosheide. "The Reign of Magots and Pagods." *Metropolitan Museum Journal* 37 (2002), pp. 177–97.
Kisluk-Grosheide 2011
Daniëlle O. Kisluk-Grosheide. "Inside the Box and Out: European Cabinets, Caskets, and Cases." *Magazine Antiques* 178, no. 2 (Mar.–Apr. 2011), pp. 124–31.
Kisluk-Grosheide and Munger 2010
Daniëlle O. Kisluk-Grosheide and Jeffrey Munger. *The Wrightsman Galleries for French Decorative Arts, The Metropolitan Museum of Art*. New York, 2010.
Kjellberg 1987
Pierre Kjellberg. *Les bronzes du XIXe siècle: Dictionnaire des sculpteurs*. Paris, 1987.
Kjellberg 1997
Pierre Kjellberg. *Encyclopédie de la pendule française du Moyen Age au XXe siècle*. Paris, 1997.
Knappe 1965
Karl-Adolf Knappe. *Dürer: The Complete Engravings, Etchings and Woodcuts*. New York, 1965.
Koeppe 2008
Wolfram Koeppe. "Pietre Dure North of the Alps." In *Art of the Royal Court: Treasures in Pietre Dure from the Palaces of Europe*, edited by Wolfram Koeppe, pp. 54–69. Exh. cat. The Metropolitan Museum of Art. New York, 2008.
Koeppe 2012
Wolfram Koeppe. *Extravagant Inventions: The Princely Furniture of the Roentgens*. With contributions by Reinier Baarsen et al. Exh. cat. The Metropolitan Museum of Art. New York, 2012.
König 1988
Gerhard König. *Uhren and Uhrmacherei in Berlin: Geschichte der Berliner Uhren und Uhrmacher, 1450–1900*. Miniaturen zur Geschichte, Kultur und Denkmalpflege Berlins 24. Berlin, 1988.
Kremer 2014
Birgit Kremer. "Taschenuhren mit astronomischen Zifferblättern." Pt. 5, "Für die Türkei und aus der Türkei." *Klassik Uhren*, 2014, no. 1, pp. 32–37.
Kurz 1975
Otto Kurz. *European Clocks and Watches in the Near East*. Studies of the Warburg Institute 34. London, 1975.
Lalande 1762
Joseph-Jérôme Lalande. *Connoissance des mouvemens célestes, pour l'année bissextile 1764*. Paris, 1762.
Lami 1914–21
Stanislas Lami. *Dictionnaire des sculpteurs de l'école française au dix-neuvième siècle*. 4 vols. Paris, 1914–21.
Landes 1983
David S. Landes. *Revolution in Time: Clocks and the Making of the Modern World*. Cambridge, Mass., 1983.
Le Corbeiller 1961
Clare Le Corbeiller. "Miss America and Her Sisters: Personifications of the Four Parts of the World." *The Metropolitan Museum of Art Bulletin*, n.s., 19, no. 8 (Apr. 1961), pp. 209–23.
Le Corbeiller 1996
Clare Le Corbeiller. "Falize, Lucien." In *The Dictionary of Art*, edited by Jane Turner, vol. 10, p. 771. New York, 1996. [Also published in *Grove Art Online*.]
Le Duc 1993
Geneviève Le Duc. "The Porcelain of Chantilly: The Collections of the Duke and Duchess of Bourbon Condé and the Inventory of the Factory in the Middle of the 18th Century." In *The International Ceramics Fair and Seminar, 11, 12, 13, 14 June 1993*, pp. 8–18. London, 1993.
Le Roy 1770
Pierre Le Roy. *Mémoire sur la meilleure manière de mesurer le tems en mer. . . . Contenant la description de la montre à longitudes, présentée à Sa Majesté le 5 août 1766*. Paris, 1770.
Lee 1964
Ronald A. Lee. *The Knibb Family: Clockmakers; or, Automatopaei Knibb Familiaei*. Byfleet, Surrey, 1964.
Leopold 1971
J. H. Leopold, ed. *The Almanus Manuscript: Staats- und Stadtbibliothek Augsburg, Codex in 2° No. 209, Rome circa 1475–circa 1485*. London, 1971.
Leopold 1974
J. H. Leopold. *Die grosse astronomische Tischuhr des Johann Reinhold: Augsburg, 1581 bis 1592*. Lucerne, 1974.
Leopold 1986
J. H. Leopold. *Astronomen, Sterne, Geräte: Landgraf Wilhelm IV. und seine sich selbst bewegenden Globen*. Lucerne, 1986.
Leopold 1989
J. H. Leopold. "Clockmaking in Britain and the Netherlands." *Notes and Records of the Royal Society of London* 43, no. 2 (July 1989), pp. 155–65.
Leopold 1990
J. H. Leopold. "L. G. Giraldi." [Letter to the Editor.] *Antiquarian Horology* 18, no. 5 (Spring 1990), pp. 54–55.
Leopold 1993
J. H. Leopold. "Christiaan Huygens, the Royal Society and Horology." *Antiquarian Horology* 21, no. 1 (Autumn 1993), pp. 37–42.
Leopold 1995
J. H. Leopold. "Collecting Instruments in Protestant Europe before 1800." *Journal of the History of Collections* 7, no. 2 (1995), pp. 151–57.
Leopold 1996
J. H. Leopold. "The Longitude Timekeepers of Christiaan Huygens." In *The Quest for Longitude: The Proceedings of the Longitude Symposium, Harvard University, Cambridge, Massachusetts, November 4–6, 1993*, edited by William J. H. Andrewes, pp. 102–14. Cambridge, Mass., 1996.
Leopold 2002
J. H. Leopold. "Some Early Clocks from Nuremberg." *Antiquarian Horology* 26, no. 5 (Mar. 2002), pp. 505–26.
Leopold 2003
J. H. Leopold. "Almanus Re-examined." *Antiquarian Horology* 27, no. 6 (Dec. 2003), pp. 665–72.
Leopold 2005a
J. H. Leopold. "Huguenot Watchmaking in the Netherlands / L'horlogerie huguenote aux Pays-Bas." *Huguenot Heritage*, no. 14 (2005), pp. 1–3.
Leopold 2005b
J. H. Leopold. "Orologi italiani nel *Manoscritto Almanus*." In *La misura del tempo: L'antico splendore dell'orologeria italiana del XV al XVIII secolo*, edited by Giuseppe Brusa, pp. 119–27. Exh. cat. Castello del Buonconsiglio. Trent, 2005.
Leopold 2005c
J. H. Leopold. "Some More Notes on the Coster-Fromanteel Contract." *Antiquarian Horology* 28, no. 5 (Mar. 2005), pp. 568–70.
Leopold and Vincent 1993
J. H. Leopold and Clare Vincent. "A Watch for Monsieur Hesselin." *Metropolitan Museum Journal* 28 (1993), pp. 103–19.
Leopold and Vincent 2000
J. H. Leopold and Clare Vincent. "An Extravagant Jewel: The George Watch." *Metropolitan Museum Journal* 35 (2000), pp. 137–49.
J.-A. Lepaute 1755
Jean-André Lepaute. *Traité d'horlogerie, contenant tout ce qui est nécessaire pour bien connoitre et pour regler les pendules et les montres*. Paris, 1755.
N.-R. Lepaute 1762
Nicole-Reine Lepaute [Nicole-Reine Etable de la Brière]. *Explication de la carte, qui représente le passage de l'ombre de la lune au travers de l'Europe dans l'eclipse du soleil centrale & annulaire, du premier avril 1764*. Paris, [1762].

Lloyd and Drover 1955
H. Alan Lloyd and Charles B. Drover. "Nicholas Vallin (c. 1565–1603)." *Connoisseur Year Book*, 1955, pp. 110–16.
Loomes 1975
Brian Loomes. *The White Dial Clock*. New York, 1975.
Loomes 1981
Brian Loomes. *The Early Clockmakers of Great Britain*. London, 1981.
"Machines ou inventions" 1756
"Machines ou inventions approuvées par l'Académie en M. DCCLII." In *Histoire de l'Académie Royale des Sciences; année M. DCCLII*, pp. 147–50. Paris, 1756.
McKay 2001
Derek McKay. *The Great Elector*. Profiles in Power. Harlow, Essex, 2001.
Mandelbrote 2004
Scott Mandelbrote. "Fatio, Nicolas, of Duillier (1664–1753)." In *Oxford Dictionary of National Biography*, vol. 19, pp. 136–40. Oxford, 2004.
Marfels 1889
Carl H. Marfels. *Marfels'sche Uhrensammlung*. Frankfurt am Main, 1889.
Marfels 1921
Carl H. Marfels. "Wie ich Sammler wurde." *Der Kunstwanderer*, Oct. 1921, pp. 51–56.
***Marie-Antoinette* 2008**
Marie-Antoinette. Exh. cat. Galeries Nationales du Grand Palais. Paris, 2008.
Marperger 1723
Paul Jacob Marperger. *Paul Jacob Marpergers Horologiographia; oder, Beschreibung der Eintheilung und Abmessung der Zeit*. Dresden, 1723. [Repr., Leipzig, 1975.]
Maurice 1975
Klaus Maurice. "Entwurf zu einer planetarischen Uhr für Kardinal Albrecht IV. von Brandenburg." *Pantheon* 33, no. 2 (Apr.–June 1975), pp. 111–13.
Maurice 1976
Klaus Maurice. *Die deutsche Räderuhr: Zur Kunst und Technik des mechanischen. Zeitmessers im deutschen Sprachraum*. 2 vols. Munich, 1976.
Maziarkin and Iudkevich 2011
G. Maziarkin and V. Iudkevich. *Podarochnye, nagradnye i prizovye karmannye chasy Rossiiskoi imperii* [Gift, Presentation, and Prize Watches of the Russian Empire]. Vol. 1, *"Vsemilostiveishe pozhalovany . . ."* ["Graciously Bestowed . . ."]. Mozhaisk, 2011.
Meis 1980
Reinhard Meis. *Les montres de poche: De la montre-pendentif au tourbillon*. Paris, 1980.
Melanchthon 1999
Philip Melanchthon. *Orations on Philosophy and Education*. Edited by Sachiko Kusukawa. Translated by Christine F. Salazar. Cambridge Texts in the History of Philosophy. Cambridge, 1999.
***Mémoires de M. le Préfet de la Seine* 1892**
Mémoires de M. le Préfet de la Seine & de M. le Préfet de Police et procès-verbaux des délibérations. 2nd and 3rd sessions of 1891. Pt. 2, *Procès-verbaux*. Conseil Général du Département de la Seine. Paris, 1892.
***Mémoires secrets* 1786**
Mémoires secrets pour servir à l'histoire de la République des Lettres en France, depuis MDCCLXII jusqu'à nos jours; ou, Journal d'un observateur. Vol. 26. London, 1786.
Mercer 1962
R. Vaudrey Mercer. "Peter Litherland & Co." *Antiquarian Horology* 3, no. 11 (June 1962), pp. 316–23.
Metropolitan Museum of Art 1984
The Metropolitan Museum of Art. *The Jack and Belle Linsky Collection in The Metropolitan Museum of Art*. New York, 1984.
Meyer 1975
Wolfgang Meyer. *Topkapı Sarayı Müzesindekl saatların kataloğu / Catalogue of Clocks and Watches in the Topkapı Sarayı Museum / Katalog der ausgestellten Uhren im Topkapı Sarayı Museum zu Istanbul / Catalogue des pendules et montres exposées au musée de Topkapı Sarayı à Istanbul*. Istanbul, 1975.
***Moments of Eternity* 2004**
Momentos da eternidade: Colecção de relógios do Museu do Palácio / Moments of Eternity: Timepieces Collection from the Palace Museum. [In Chinese, Portuguese, and English.] Exh. cat. Museu de Arte de Macau. [Macao], 2004.
Moore 2003
Dennis Moore. *British Clockmakers & Watchmakers Apprentice Records, 1710–1810*. Ashbourne, Derbyshire, 2003.
***Morgan Collection* 1914**
Guide to the Loan Exhibition of the J. Pierpont Morgan Collection. Exh. cat. The Metropolitan Museum of Art. New York, 1914.
"Morgan's Collection of Watches" 1913
"Mr. Pierpont Morgan's Collection of Watches." *Horological Journal* 56, no. 663 (Nov. 1913), p. 34.
"Morgan's Watches" 1912
"Mr. Morgan's Watches. The Superb Catalogue of a Collection That Has No Equal." *New York Times*, Nov. 25, 1912, p. 12.
Morpurgo 1950
Enrico Morpurgo. *Dizionario degli orologiai italiani (1300–1880)*. Rome, 1950.
Morpurgo 1970
Enrico Morpurgo. *Nederlandse klokken- en horlogemakers vanaf 1300*. Amsterdam, 1970.
Morpurgo 1974
Enrico Morpurgo. *Dizionario degli orologiai italiani*. 2nd edition. Milan, 1974.
Mortimer 1964
Ruth Mortimer, comp. *Catalogue of Books and Manuscripts*. Pt. 1, *French 16th Century Books*. Vol. 2. Harvard College Library, Department of Printing and Graphic Arts. Cambridge, Mass., 1964.
Morton and Wess 1993
Alan Q. Morton and Jane A. Wess. *Public & Private Science: The King George III Collection*. Oxford, 1993.
Mraz 1980
Gottfried Mraz. "The Role of Clocks in the Imperial Honoraria for the Turks." In *Clockwork Universe* 1980, pp. 37–48.
Müller 1968
Hannelore Müller. "Augsburger Goldschmiedekunst, 1620–1720." In *Augsburger Barock*, pp. 279–81. Exh. cat. Rathaus and Holbein Haus. Augsburg, 1968.
Musée International d'Horlogerie 1974
Musée International d'Horlogerie. *Collections du Musée International d'Horlogerie, La Chaux-de-Fonds, Suisse: Une sélection parmi 3100 objets*. La Chaux-de-Fonds, 1974.
Museum der Zeitmessung Beyer 1982
Museum der Zeitmessung Beyer. *Antike Uhren: Das Museum der Zeitmessung / Le Musée de la Mesure du Temps / The Museum of Time Measurement / Beyer Zürich*. Munich, 1982.
Museum für Kunsthandwerk 1987
Museum für Kunsthandwerk. *Museum für Kunsthandwerk Frankfurt am Main: Aus den Sammlungen*. Auswahlkatalog 1. Frankfurt am Main, 1987.
Neale 1992
J. A. Neale. "The Case of William Jaques (William Jaques, CC, Watch Case Maker)." *Antiquarian Horology* 20, no. 4 (Winter 1992), pp. 340–55.
Needham, Wang Ling, and Price 1960
Joseph Needham, Wang Ling, and Derek J. de Solla Price. *Heavenly Clockwork: The Great Astronomical Clocks of Medieval China*. Antiquarian Horological Society Monograph 1. Cambridge, 1960.
Nelson and Impey 1994
Christina Nelson and Oliver Impey, with Clare Le Corbeiller. "Oriental Art and French Patronage: The Foundation of the Bourbon-Condé Ceramics Collection." In *The International Ceramics Fair and Seminar, 10, 11, 12, 13 June 1994*, pp. 36–43. London, 1994.
Neumann 1961
Erwin Neumann. "Die Tischuhr des Jeremias Metzker von 1564 und ihre nächsten Verwandten: Bemerkungen zur Formengeschichte einer Gruppe süddeutscher Stutzuhren der Renaissance." *Jahrbuch der Kunsthistorischen Sammlungen in Wien* 57 (1961), pp. 89–122.
Neumann 1966
Erwin Neumann. "Das Inventar der rudolfinischen Kunstkammer von 1607/1611." In *Queen Christina of Sweden: Documents and Studies*, edited by Magnus von Platen, pp. 262–65. Analecta Reginensia 1. Nationalmusei skriftserie 12. Stockholm, 1966.
Nickel 1980
Helmut Nickel. "The Graphic Sources for the *Moor with the Emerald Cluster*." *Metropolitan Museum Journal* 15 (1980), pp. 203–10.
Nickel 2002
Helmut Nickel. "Miss America's Brother and His Club." *Metropolitan Museum Journal* 37 (2002), pp. 83–88.
Niehüser 1999
Elke Niehüser. *French Bronze Clocks, 1700–1830: A Study of the Figural Images*. Atglen, Pa., 1999.
North 1975
John D. North. "Monasticism and the First Mechanical Clocks." In *The Study of Time II: Proceedings of the Second Conference of the International Society for the Study of Time, Lake Yamanaka, Japan*, edited by Julius Thomas Fraser and Nathaniel M. Lawrence, pp. 381–98. New York, 1975. [Reprinted in John D. North, *Stars, Minds and Fate: Essays in Ancient and Medieval Cosmology*, pp. 171–86. London, 1989.]
O'Dell-Franke 1977
Ilse O'Dell-Franke. *Kupferstiche und Radierungen aus der Werkstatt des Virgil Solis*. Wiesbaden, 1977.
O'Dell-Franke 1996
Ilse O'Dell-Franke. "Zündt, Matthias." In *The Dictionary of Art*, edited by Jane Turner, vol. 33, pp. 727–28. London, 1996. [Also published in *Grove Art Online*.]
***Oeuvre de Daniel Marot* n.d.**
L'oeuvre de Daniel Marot, architecte de Sa Majesté Britannique et des Etats de Hollande: Epoque Louis XIV. Edited by A. Guérinet. 2 vols. Paris, n.d.
"Oeuvres nouvelles" 1882–83
"Oeuvres nouvelles." *Revue des arts décoratifs* 3 (1882–83), pp. 29–30.
Oman 1978
Charles Oman. *English Engraved Silver, 1150 to 1900*. London, 1978.
***Ornamentwerk des Daniel Marot* 1892**
Das Ornamentwerk des Daniel Marot. Foreword by Peter Jessen. Berlin, 1892.
von Osterhausen 2003
Fritz von Osterhausen. "Der Uhrenhändler und -Sammler Carl Marfels." *Klassik Uhren*, 2003, no. 3 (May–June), pp. 14–31.
Ottema 1923
Nanne Ottema. *Bijdrage tot Uurwerkmakerskunst in Friesland*. Leeuwarden, 1923.
Otto 1929
H. Otto. "Carl Marfels." *Horological Journal* 72, no. 856 (Dec. 1929), pp. 62–63.
Ottomeyer and Pröschel 1986
Hans Ottomeyer and Peter Pröschel. *Vergoldete Bronzen: Die Bronzearbeiten des Spätbarock und Klassizismus*. 2 vols. Munich, 1986.
Özdemir 1993
Kemal Özdemir. *Ottoman Clocks and Watches*. Translated by Priscilla Mary Işin. Istanbul, 1993.
Pagani 2001
Catherine Pagani. *"Eastern Magnificence & European Ingenuity": Clocks of Late Imperial China*. Ann Arbor, 2001.
Palais Galliera 1960
Tableaux anciens, dessins, orfèvrerie ancienne: Objets d'art et de bel ameublement du XVIIIe siècle. . . . Sale cat. Palais Galliera, Paris, Dec. 14, 1960.

Palustre 1892
Léon Palustre. "Les horloges et les montres." In *Collection Spitzer* 1891–93, vol. 5 (1892), pp. 25–62.

Pannekoek 1961
Anton Pannekoek. *A History of Astronomy*. London, 1961.

Parke-Bernet Galleries 1944
Furniture and Objects of Art . . . Property of the Estate of the Late J. P. Morgan. Pt. 2. Sale cat. Parke-Bernet Galleries, New York, Mar. 22–25, 1944.

Parke-Bernet Galleries 1946
Fine French Furniture and Objects of Art . . . from Private Owners. Sale cat. Parke-Bernet Galleries, New York, Nov. 22, 1946.

Parke-Bernet Galleries 1948
Old English Clocks, Georgian Furniture, from the Distinguished Collection of the Late Henry P. Strause, Washington, D.C. Sale cat. Parke-Bernet Galleries, New York, Oct. 22–23, 1948.

Parke-Bernet Galleries 1955
Furniture & Works of Art. Pt. 1. Sale cat. Parke-Bernet Galleries, New York, Oct. 7–8, 1955.

Parke-Bernet Galleries 1959
French Modern Paintings & Drawings, Eighteenth Century French Furniture . . . Objects of Art. Pt. 1. Sale cat. Parke-Bernet Galleries, New York, May 13, 15–16, 1959.

Parker et al. 1989
James Parker, Alice M. Zrebiec, Jessie McNab, Clare Le Corbeiller, and Clare Vincent. "French Decorative Arts during the Reign of Louis XIV, 1654–1715." *The Metropolitan Museum of Art Bulletin*, n.s., 46, no. 4 (Spring 1989).

Patrizzi 1998
Osvaldo Patrizzi. *Dictionnaire des horlogers genevois: La "fabrique" et les arts annexes du XVIe siècle à nos jours*. Geneva, 1998.

Peeters 2012
Cees Peeters. *Hollandse horloges*. Zaandam, 2012.

"Pendule artistique" 1882
"Orfèvrerie.—Beaux-arts. Une pendule artistique." *Revue britannique*, n.s., May 1882, pp. 201–4.

***Pendule au "nègre"* 1978**
La pendule au "nègre." Exh. cat. Musée de l'Hôtel Sandelin. Saint-Omer, 1978.

Penfold 1962
John B. Penfold. "The Life of William Clement." *Antiquarian Horology* 3, no. 12 (Sept. 1962), pp. 354–56.

Penney 2009
David Penney. "The Earliest Pendulum Clocks: A Re-evaluation." *Antiquarian Horology* 31, no. 5 (Sept. 2009), pp. 614–20.

"Percy Webster" 1938
"Mr. Percy Webster: An Authority on Clocks." [Obituary.] *Times* (London), Nov. 25, 1938, p. 8.

Phillips 1998
Clocks & Watches, including Scientific Instruments and Barometers. Sale cat. Phillips, London, Mar. 10, 1998.

Plomp 1979
R. Plomp. *Spring-Driven Dutch Pendulum Clocks, 1657–1710*. Schiedam, 1979.

Poindront and Kugel 2012
Philippe Poindront and Alexis Kugel. "Heinrich Taddel and Christian Gottlieb Stiehl." In *Gold, Jasper and Carnelian* 2012, pp. 220–25.

Ponsford 2008
Clive N. Ponsford. "Wills of Clock and Watchmakers On-line from the National Archives, Part III: The City of London and Middlesex (K–Z)." *Antiquarian Horology* 30, no. 6 (June 2008), pp. 804–17.

Pradère 2003
Alexandre Pradère. *Charles Cressent: Sculpteur, ébéniste du Régent*. Dijon, 2003.

Praël-Himmer 1978
Heidi Praël-Himmer. *Der Augsburger Goldschmied Johann Andreas Thelot*. Munich, 1978.

***Prag um 1600* 1988**
Prag um 1600: Kunst und Kultur am Hofe Rudolf II. Exh. cat. Kulturstiftung Ruhr, Villa Hügel, Essen, and Kunsthistorisches Museum, Vienna. Freren, 1988.

Préaud 2003
Tamara Préaud. "The Origins and History of Porcelain Flowers." *French Porcelain Society Journal* 1 (2003), pp. 47–55. [Issue titled *French Porcelain of the Eighteenth Century: A Symposium in Honour of Geneviève Le Duc (1930–1999)*, edited by Oliver Fairclough and Aileen Dawson.]

Price 1955
Derek J. de Solla Price. "Clockwork before the Clock." *Horological Journal* 97, no. 1167 (Dec. 1955), pp. 810–14.

Priestley 1994
Philip T. Priestley. *Watch Case Makers of England: A History and Register of Gold & Silver Watch Case Makers of England, 1720–1920*. National Association of Watch and Clock Collectors Bulletin Supplement 20. Columbia, Pa., 1994.

Priestley 2000
Philip T. Priestley. *Early Watch Case Makers of England, 1631 to 1720*. Columbia, Pa., 2000.

Pritchard 1997
Kathleen H. Pritchard. *Swiss Timepiece Makers, 1775–1975*. 2 vols. West Kennebunk, Maine, 1997.

Pritzker 2014
Bob Pritzker. "The Most Complicated Watch in the World." *Watch & Clock Bulletin* (National Association of Watch and Clock Collectors) 56, no. 1, no. 407 (Jan.–Feb. 2014), pp. 17–24.

Purcell 1999
Katherine Purcell. *Falize: A Dynasty of Jewelers*. London, 1999.

Randall 1992
Anthony G. Randall. *The Time Museum Catalogue of Chronometers*. Illustrations by David Penney. Rockford, Ill., 1992.

Randall 1996
Anthony G. Randall. "The Timekeeper That Won the Longitude Prize." In *The Quest for Longitude: The Proceedings of the Longitude Symposium, Harvard University, Cambridge, Massachusetts, November 4–6, 1993*, edited by William J. H. Andrewes, pp. 236–54. Cambridge, Mass., 1996.

Rappe 2012
Tamara Rappe. "Neuwied Furniture and the Russian Luxury Market." In Koeppe 2012, pp. 45–48, 243.

Raulet 1999
Sylvie Raulet. *Rock Crystal Treasures, from Antiquity to Today*. New York, 1999.

Remmert 2009
Volker R. Remmert. "On Picturing the Past: Arithmetic and Geometry as Wings of the Mind." *Mathematical Intelligencer* 31, no. 3 (June 2009), pp. 42–47.

Ricci 1953
Matteo Ricci. *China in the Sixteenth Century: The Journals of Matthew Ricci, 1583–1610*. Translated by Louis J. Gallagher. New York, 1953.

Richard of Wallingford 1976
Richard of Wallingford. *Richard of Wallingford: An Edition of His Writings*. Translated and edited by John D. North. 3 vols. Oxford, 1976.

Ridgway and Priestley 2004
Maurice H. Ridgway and Philip T. Priestley. *The Compendium of Chester Gold & Silver Marks, 1570 to 1962, from the Chester Assay Office Registers*. Woodbridge, Suffolk, 2004.

Riello 2008
Giorgio Riello. "Strategies and Boundaries: Subcontracting and the London Trades in the Long Eighteenth Century." *Enterprise and Society* 9, no. 2 (June 2008), pp. 243–80.

Righini Bonelli 1968
Maria Luisa Righini Bonelli. *Il Museo di Storia della Scienza a Firenze*. Gallerie e musei di Firenze. Milan, 1968.

***Robert Sutton* 1732**
The Particular and Inventory . . . of the Right Honourable Sir Robert Sutton. London, 1732.

Robinson 1981
Tom Robinson. *The Longcase Clock*. Woodbridge, Suffolk, 1981.

Rondot 2012
Bertrand Rondot. "David Roentgen and the Court of Versailles." In Koeppe 2012, pp. 31–37, 241–42.

Ronfort 1984
Jean-Nérée Ronfort. "Art et horlogerie à l'époque de Ferdinand Berthoud: Du rocaille au néo-classicisme." In *Ferdinand Berthoud* 1984, pp. 103–27.

Rosen 1986
Edward Rosen. *Three Imperial Mathematicians: Kepler Trapped between Tycho Brahe and Ursus*. New Horizon Series. New York, 1986.

Rosenfeld 1980
Rochelle S. Rosenfeld. "Celestial Maps and Globes and Star Catalogues of the Sixteenth and Early Seventeenth Centuries." PhD diss., New York University, 1980.

Rouge 2008
Françoise Rouge. "Adjugé: Mobilier et objets d'art." *Estampille / L'objet d'art*, no. 431 (Jan. 2008), pp. 84–85.

***Royal Music Machines* 2006**
Royal Music Machines. Exh. cat. edited by Jan Jaap L. Haspels. Nationaal Museum van Speelklok tot Pierement, Utrecht. Zutphen, 2006.

***Rudolf II and Prague* 1997**
Rudolf II and Prague: The Court and the City. Exh. cat. edited by Eliška Fučíková et al. Prague Castle. London, 1997.

Sabrier 1984
Jean-Claude Sabrier. "La contribution de Ferdinand Berthoud aux progrès de l'horlogerie de marine." In *Ferdinand Berthoud* 1984, pp. 165–84.

Sargentson 1998
Carolyn Sargentson. "The Manufacture and Marketing of Luxury Goods: The *Marchands Merciers* of Late 17th- and 18th-Century Paris." In *Luxury Trades and Consumerism in* Ancien Régime *Paris: Studies in the History of the Skilled Workforce*, edited by Robert Fox and Anthony J. Turner, pp. 99–137. Aldershot, 1998.

Sauer-Kaulbach 2003
Lieselotte Sauer-Kaulbach. "Vom Mühlrad zum Uhrwerk: Die Erfolgsgeschichte der Neuwieder Uhrenmacherfamilie Kinzing." In Lieselotte Sauer-Kaulbach et al., *Kinzing & Co.: Innovative Uhren aus der Provinz*, pp. 6–27. Exh. cat. Kreismuseum. Neuwied, 2003.

Saulnier 1980
Lydwine Saulnier. "Vézelay: La restauration de l'église de la Madeleine." In *Viollet-le-Duc* 1980, pp. 59–65.

Savary des Brûlons 1761
Jacques Savary des Brûlons. *Dictionnaire universel de commerce: D'histoire naturelle, & des arts & métiers contenant tout ce qui concerne le commerce. . . .* Vol. 3. New edition. Copenhagen, 1761.

Sayılı 1960
Aydın Sayılı. *The Observatory in Islam and Its Place in the General History of the Observatory*. Publications of the Turkish Historical Society, ser. 7, no. 38. Ankara, 1960.

Schaffers-Bodenhausen and Tiethoff-Spliethoff 1993
Karen Schaffers-Bodenhausen and Marieke Tiethoff-Spliethoff. *The Portrait Miniatures in the Collections of the House of Orange-Nassau*. Zwolle, 1993.

Schneeberger 1958
P.-F. Schneeberger. "Les peintres sur émail genevois au XVIIe et au XVIIIe siècle." *Genava*, n.s., 6, nos. 2–3 (July 1958), pp. 77–216.

Schommers 1994
Annette Schommers. "Biographien der Augsburger Goldschmiede." In *Silber und Gold: Augsburger Goldschmiedekunst für die Höfe Europas*, edited by Reinhold Baumstark and Helmut Seling, vol. 1, pp. VIII–XXIX. Exh. cat. Bayerisches Nationalmuseum. Munich, 1994.

Schroder 2009
Timothy Schroder. *British & Continental Gold & Silver in the Ashmolean Museum*. 3 vols. Oxford, 2009.

Schuckman and Luijten 1997
Christiaan Schuckman, comp., and Ger Luijten, ed. *Gerard van Groeningen*. 2 pts. The New Hollstein Dutch & Flemish Etchings, Engravings and Woodcuts, 1450–1700. Rotterdam, 1997.

Seling 1994
Helmut Seling. "Einleitung." In *Silber und Gold: Augsburger Goldschmiedekunst für die Höfe Europas*, edited by Reinhold Baumstark and Helmut Seling, vol. 1, pp. 17–31. Exh. cat. Bayerisches Nationalmuseum. Munich, 1994.

Shenton 1995
Alan Shenton. *Pocket Watches, 19th & 20th Century*. Woodbridge, Suffolk, 1995.

Shirley 1869
"An Inventory of the Effects of Henry Howard, K.G., Earl of Northampton, Taken on His Death in 1614, Together with a Transcript of His Will; Prefaced by a Letter . . . from Evelyn Philip Shirley, Esq., F.S.A., Local Secretary for Warwickshire." *Archaeologia* 42, no. 2 (1869), pp. 347–78.

***Short Account of the Remarkable Clock* 1868**
A Short Account of the Remarkable Clock Made by James Cox, in the Year 1766, by Order of the Hon. East India Company for the Emperor of China: Illustrated. London, 1868.

Sloan 2007
Kim Sloan. *A New World: England's First View of America*. With contributions by Joyce E. Chaplin, Christian F. Feest, and Ute Kuhlemann. British Museum. London, 2007.

J. Smith 1694
John Smith. *Horological Disquisitions Concerning the Nature of Time*. London, 1694.

J. C. Smith 1983
Jeffrey Chipps Smith. *Nuremburg: A Renaissance City, 1500–1618*. Exh. cat. Archer M. Huntington Art Gallery, University of Texas at Austin. Austin, 1983.

R. Smith 2000
Roger Smith. "James Cox (c. 1723–1800): A Revised Biography." *Burlington Magazine* 142 (June 2000), pp. 353–61.

R. Smith 2008
Roger Smith. "The Sing-Song Trade Exporting Clocks to China in the Eighteenth Century." *Antiquarian Horology* 30, no. 5 (Mar. 2008), pp. 629–58.

Snodin 2009
Michael Snodin. "Going to Strawberry Hill." In *Horace Walpole's Strawberry Hill*, edited by Michael Snodin, with Cynthia Roman, pp. 15–17, 20–31, 34–37, 40–57. Exh. cat. Yale Center for British Art, New Haven, and Victoria and Albert Museum, London. New Haven, 2009.

Sobel and Andrewes 1998
Dava Sobel and William J. H. Andrewes. *The Illustrated Longitude*. New York, 1998.

Somers Cocks and Truman 1984
Anna Somers Cocks and Charles Truman. *Renaissance Jewels, Gold Boxes, and Objets de Vertu: The Thyssen-Bornemisza Collection*. London, 1984.

Sotheby's 1960
Medieval Works of Art; . . . Important English Clocks; Fine English Furniture. Sale cat. Sotheby & Co., London, July 8, 1960.

Sotheby's 1978
Highly Important French Furniture, Decorations, Continental Porcelain, Works of Art and Gold Boxes from the Collection of Henry Ford II. Sale cat. Sotheby Parke Bernet, New York, Feb. 25, 1978.

Sotheby's 1991
Important English and Continental Silver. Sale cat. Sotheby's, New York, Apr. 19, 1991.

Sotheby's 1999
Masterpieces from the Time Museum. Sale cat. Sotheby's, New York, Dec. 2, 1999.

Sotheby's 2002
Masterpieces from the Time Museum. Part Two. Sale cat. Sotheby's, New York, June 19, 2002.

Speckhart 1904
Gustav Speckhart. *Kunstvolle Taschenuhren der Sammlung Marfels*. Berlin, [1904].

Spierdijk 1973
Cornelis Spierdijk. *Horloges en horlogemakers*. Amsterdam, 1973.

Sponsel 1925
Jean Louis Sponsel. *Geräte und Gefässe*. Das Grüne Gewölbe zu Dresden: Eine Auswahl von Meisterwerken der Goldschmiedekunst 1. Leipzig, 1925.

Staden 1557
Hans Staden. *Warhaftige Historia und beschreibung eyner Landtschafft der Wilden, Nacketen, Grimmigen Menschfresser Leuthen, in der Newenwelt America gelegen*. Marburg, 1557.

Stiegel 2012
Achim Stiegel. "David Roentgen under the 'Special Protection' of the King of Prussia." In Koeppe 2012, pp. 39–43, 242–43.

Sturtevant 1976
William C. Sturtevant. "First Visual Images of Native America." In *First Images of America: The Impact of the New World on the Old*, edited by Fredi Chiappelli, vol. 1, pp. 417–54. Berkeley, Calif., 1976.

***Sun King* 1984**
The Sun King: Louis XIV and the New World. Exh. cat. Louisiana State Museum, New Orleans, and Corcorcan Gallery of Art, Washington, D.C. Studies in Louisiana Culture 3. New Orleans, 1984.

Symonds 1951
R. W. Symonds. *Thomas Tompion: His Life & Work*. London, 1951.

***Tablettes royale de renommée* 1786**
Tablettes royale de renommée; ou, de Correspondance et d'indication générales des principales fabriques, manufactures et maisons de commerce . . . de Paris & autres villes du royaume & des pays étrangers. Paris, [1786].

Tait 1987
Hugh Tait. *Catalogue of Watches in the British Museum*. Vol. 1, *The Stackfreed*. With technical descriptions by P. G. Coole. Revised by David Thompson. London, 1987.

Tardy n.d.
Tardy. *Les échappements des montres*. Paris, n.d. [ca. 1940–65].

Tardy 1971–72
Tardy. *Dictionnaire des horlogers français*. 2 vols. Paris, 1971–72.

Tardy 1981a
Tardy. *French Clocks the World Over*. 5th edition. Pt. 1, *From Their Beginnings to the Louis XV–Louis XVI Transition Period*. Paris, 1981.

Tardy 1981b
Tardy. *French Clocks the World Over*. 5th edition. Pt. 2, *From Louis XVI Style to Louis XVIII–Charles X Period*. Paris, 1981.

Tardy 1981c
Tardy. *International Hallmarks on Silver*. Paris, 1981.

Taylor 1966
Eva G. R. Taylor. *The Mathematical Practitioners of Hanoverian England, 1714–1840*. London, 1966.

Tekeli 1966
Sevim Tekeli. *16'ıncı asırda Osmanlılarda saat ve Takiyüddin'in "Mekanik saat konstrüksüyonuna dair en parlak yıldızlar" adlı eseri / The Clocks in Ottoman Empire in 16th Century and Taqi al Din's "The Brightest Stars for the Construction of the Mechanical Clocks."* [In Arabic, Turkish, and English.] Ankara, 1966.

Thiout 1741
Antoine Thiout l'aîné. *Traité de l'horlogerie, méchanique et pratique, approuvé par l'Académie Royale des Sciences*. 2 vols. Paris, 1741.

Thoma and Brunner 1964
Hans Thoma and Herbert Brunner. *Schatzkammer der Residenz München: Katalog*. Munich, 1964.

Thompson 2004
David Thompson. *The British Museum Clocks*. London, 2004.

Thompson 2007
David Thompson. *Watches in the Ashmolean Museum*. Ashmolean Handbooks. Oxford, 2007.

Thompson 2008
David Thompson. *The History of Watches*. New York, 2008.

***Time: The Greatest Innovator* 1986**
Time: The Greatest Innovator. Timekeeping and Time Consciousness in Early Modern Europe. Exh. cat. edited by Rachel Doggett, with Susan Jaskot and Robert Rand. Folger Shakespeare Library. Washington, D.C., 1986.

***Timepieces for Royalty* 2005**
Timepieces for Royalty, 1850–1910, by Patek Philippe. Exh. cat. Patek Philippe Museum. Geneva, 2005.

***Treasures of the Kremlin* 1997**
Treasures of the Kremlin: Masterpieces of Horology / Sokrovishcha Kremlia: Khudozhestvennye chasy. Catalogue of an exhibition organized by the Ministry of Culture of the Russian Federation and held at Antiquorum, Geneva, in 1994. Geneva, [1997].

***Treasures of Vacheron Constantin* 2011**
Treasures of Vacheron Constantin: A Legacy of Watchmaking since 1755. Exh. cat. National Museum of Singapore. Paris, 2011.

***Triumph of Maximilian I* 1964**
The Triumph of Maximilian I: 137 Woodcuts by Hans Burgkmair and Others. Translated and edited by Stanley Appelbaum. New York, 1964.

Turner 1984a
Anthony J. Turner. "L'Angleterre, la France et la navigation: Le contexte historique de l'oeuvre chronométrique de Ferdinand Berthoud." In *Ferdinand Berthoud 1984*, pp. 143–63.

Turner 1984b
Anthony J. Turner. *The Time Museum: Catalogue of the Collection*. Vol. 1, *Time Measuring Instruments*, pt. 3, *Water-Clocks, Sand-Glasses, Fire-Clocks*. Rockford, Ill., 1984.

Turner 1985
Anthony J. Turner. *The Time Museum: Catalogue of the Collection*. Vol. 1, *Time Measuring Instruments*, pt. 1, *Astrolabes, Astrolabe Related Instruments*. Rockford, Ill., 1985.

Turner 2002
Anthony J. Turner. "Donald Hill and Arabic Water-Clocks." *Antiquarian Horology* 27, no. 2 (Dec. 2002), pp. 206–13.

Uhlirz 1897
Karl Uhlirz, ed. "Urkunden und Regesten aus dem Archive der K. K. Reichshaupt- und Residenzstadt Wien." *Jahrbuch der Kunsthistorischen Sammlungen des Allerhöchsten Kaiserhauses* 18 (1897), pp. I–CC.

Uhrenmuseum Beyer Zürich 1996
Uhrenmuseum Beyer Zürich. *Antike Uhren: Neuerwerbungen*. Munich, 1996.

Vehmeyer 2004
H. M. Vehmeyer. *Clocks: Their Origin and Development, 1320–1880*. Translated by Felix Smart. 2 vols. Ghent, 2004.

Vever 1906–8
Henri Vever. *La bijouterie française au XIXe siècle (1800–1900)*. 3 vols. Paris, 1906–8.

Vignon 2003
Charlotte Vignon. "Deverberie & Cie: Drawings, Models, and Works in Bronze." *Cleveland Studies in the History of Art* 8 (2003), pp. 170–87.

Vincent 1972
Clare Vincent. *Northern European Clocks in New York Collections*. Exh. cat. The Metropolitan Museum of Art. New York, 1972.

Vincent 1983
Clare Vincent. "Paulet London: The Signature of a Huguenot Émigré Clockmaker?" In *Studien zum europaïschen Kunsthandwerk: Festschrift Yvonne Hackenbroch*, edited by Jörg Rasmussen, pp. 217–27. Munich, 1983.

Vincent 2002
Clare Vincent. "Some Seventeenth-Century French Painted Enamel Watchcases." *Metropolitan Museum Journal* 37 (2002), pp. 89–106.

Vincent 2007
Clare Vincent. "Some Seventeenth-Century Limoges Painted Enamel Watch-Cases and Their Movements." *Antiquarian Horology* 30, no. 3 (Sept. 2007), pp. 317–46.

Vincent 2012
Clare Vincent. "Painted Enamels." In Wolfram Koeppe et al., *The Robert Lehman Collection*, vol. 15, *Decorative Arts*, pp. 7–93. New York, 2012.

Vincent and Chandler 1969
Clare Vincent and Bruce Chandler. "Nighttime and Easter Time: The Rotations of the Sun, the Moon, and the Little Bear in Renaissance Time Reckoning." *The Metropolitan Museum of Art Bulletin*, n.s., 27, no. 8 (Apr. 1969), pp. 372–84.

Vincent and Chandler 1989–90
Clare Vincent and Bruce Chandler. "A Case Study of Dependency: The Mathematical Competence of a Renaissance Clockmaker." *Jahrbuch der Kunsthistorischen Sammlungen in Wien* 85–86 (1989–90), pp. 163–81.

Vincent and Chandler 2011–12
Clare Vincent and Bruce Chandler. "Rudolf II's Celestial Globe on the Wings of Pegasus." *Jahrbuch des Kunsthistorischen Museums Wien* 13–14 (2011–12), pp. 105–17.

Vincent and Leopold 2008
Clare Vincent and J. H. Leopold. "James Cox (ca. 1723–1800): Goldsmith and Entrepreneur." In The Metropolitan Museum of Art, *Heilbrunn Timeline of Art History*. New York, 2000–. www.metmuseum .org/toah/hd/jcox/hd_jcox.htm (Nov. 2008).

Vincent and Leopold 2009
Clare Vincent and J. H. Leopold. "Seventeenth-Century European Watches." In The Metropolitan Museum of Art, *Heilbrunn Timeline of Art History*. New York, 2000–. www.metmuseum.org/toah/hd /watc/hd_watc.htm (Mar. 2009).

***Viollet-le-Duc* 1980**
Viollet-le-Duc. With contributions by Bruno Foucart et al. Exh. cat. Galeries Nationales du Grand Palais. Paris, 1980.

Virginia Museum of Fine Arts 1937
Virginia Museum of Fine Arts. *Catalogue: The Henry P. Strause Collection of Clocks*. Richmond, 1937.

Voet 1993
Leon Voet. "Antwerp, the Metropolis and Its History." In *Antwerp: Story of a Metropolis, 16th–17th Century*, edited by Jan Van der Stock, pp. 13–17. Exh. cat. Hessenhuis, Antwerp. Ghent, 1993.

Wainwright 1989
Clive Wainwright. *The Romantic Interior: The British Collector at Home, 1750–1850*. New Haven, 1989.

Ward-Jackson 1958
Peter Ward-Jackson. *English Furniture Designs of the Eighteenth Century*. Victoria and Albert Museum. London, 1958.

Wardropper 2011
Ian Wardropper. *European Sculpture, 1400–1900, in The Metropolitan Museum of Art*. New York, 2011.

Warncke 1979
Carsten-Peter Warncke. *Die ornamentale Groteske in Deutschland, 1500–1650*. 2 vols. Quellen und Schriften zur bildenden Kunst 6. Berlin, 1979.

"Watches Bought by J. P. Morgan" 1910
"Famous Watches Bought by J. P. Morgan. The Marfels Collection, Worth $360,000, Comprises Some of the Rarest Known Timepieces." *New York Times*, Apr. 24, 1910, p. 12 (magazine sec.).

Waters 1958
David W. Waters. *The Art of Navigation in England in Elizabethan and Early Stuart Times*. New Haven, 1958.

Watson 1956
F. J. B. Watson. *Furniture: Text with Historical Notes and Illustrations*. Wallace Collection. London, 1956.

Watson 1960
F. J. B. Watson. *Louis XVI Furniture*. New York, 1960.

R. Webster and M. Webster 1998
Roderick Webster and Marjorie Webster. *Western Astrolabes*. Historic Scientific Instruments of the Adler Planetarium & Astronomy Museum 1. Chicago, 1998.

Weinhold 2000
Ulrike Weinhold. *Emailmalerei an Augsburger Goldschmiedearbeiten von 1650 bis 1750*. Munich, 2000.

Weiss 1982
Leonard Weiss. *Watch-Making in England, 1760–1820*. London, 1982.

***Wenzel Jamnitzer* 1985**
Wenzel Jamnitzer und die Nürnberger Goldschmiedekunst, 1500–1700. Goldschmiedearbeiten: Entwürfe, Modelle, Medaillen, Ornamentstiche, Schmuck, Porträts. Exh. cat. Germanisches Nationalmuseum Nürnberg. Munich, 1985.

White 2012
Ian White. *English Clocks for the Eastern Markets: English Clockmakers Trading in China & the Ottoman Empire, 1580–1815*. Sussex, 2012.

Whitestone 2012
Sebastian Whitestone. "The Chimerical English Pre-Huygens Pendulum Clock." *Antiquarian Horology* 33, no. 3 (Mar. 2012), pp. 347–58.

Wilbourn and Ellis 2001
A. S. H. Wilbourn and R. Ellis. *Lincolnshire Clock, Watch and Barometer Makers*. Lincoln, 2001.

Williamson 1910
George C. Williamson. *Catalogue of the Collection of Jewels and Precious Works of Art, the Property of J. Pierpont Morgan*. London, 1910.

Williamson 1912
George C. Williamson. *Catalogue of the Collection of Watches, the Property of J. Pierpont Morgan*. London, 1912.

Willscheid 2012
Bernd Willscheid. "Abraham and David Roentgen: Moravian Artisan and Merchant-Diplomat." In Koeppe 2012, pp. 17–23, 240.

Wilson et al. 1996
Gillian Wilson, David Harris Cohen, Jean-Nérée Ronfort, Jean-Dominique Augarde, and Peter Friess. *European Clocks in the J. Paul Getty Museum*. Los Angeles, 1996.

Wypyski 2000
Mark T. Wypyski. "Technical Appendix: Compositions of Enamels on the George Watch." *Metropolitan Museum Journal* 35 (2000), pp. 150–52.

Yates 1984
Frances A. Yates. "Imperial Mysteries." In *Collected Essays*, vol. 3, *Ideas and Ideals in the North European Renaissance*, pp. 214–20. London, 1984. [Review of J. R. W. Evans, *Rudolf II and His World: A Study in Intellectual History, 1576–1612*. Oxford, 1973. Originally published in *New Statesman*, May 18, 1973.]

Zeeman 1996
J. Zeeman. *De Nederlandse staande klok*. Zwolle, 1996.

Zek and R. Smith 2005
Yuna Zek and Roger Smith. "The Hermitage Peacock: How an Eighteenth Century Automaton Reached St. Petersburg." With "A Brief Description of the Mechanism" by Mikhail Guryev. *Antiquarian Horology* 28, no. 6 (June 2005), pp. 699–715.

Zinner 1956
Ernst Zinner. *Deutsche und niederländische astronomische Instrumente des 11.–18. Jahrhunderts*. Munich, 1956.

Zinner 1968
Ernst Zinner. *Leben und Wirken des Joh. Müller von Königsberg genannt Regiomontanus*. 2nd edition. Osnabrück, 1968.

Zorn 1820
Johann Zorn the Elder. *Sammlung der merkwürdigsten Ereignisse in der ehemaligen Reichsstadt Kempten*. Kempten, 1820.

Index

Page numbers in *italics* refer to illustrations and captions.

Entries in **boldface** are the titles of the principal works.